3rd International Conference on Computers and Management (ICCM 2017)

Kota, India
28-29 December 2017

Editors:

C. P. Gupta
R. K. Banyal
Sh. Dinesh Soni
Seema Sharma

ISBN: 978-1-5108-5316-4

Printed from e-media with permission by:

Curran Associates, Inc.
57 Morehouse Lane
Red Hook, NY 12571

Some format issues inherent in the e-media version may also appear in this print version.

Printed by Curran Associates, Inc. (2017)

International Association of Academicians Connecting Scholars, Scientists and Engineers (IAASSE)

www.iaasse.org
info@iaasse.org

Additional copies of this publication are available from:

Curran Associates, Inc.
57 Morehouse Lane
Red Hook, NY 12571 USA
Phone: 845-758-0400
Fax: 845-758-2633
Email: curran@proceedings.com
Web: www.proceedings.com

TABLE OF CONTENTS

Design and Implementation of Energy-Aware Hierarchical Clustering Technique of WSN for Improving Network Life 1
Meenakshi Yadav, Anoop Bhola, Chandra Kumar Jha

Fusion of K-means Algorithm with Dunn's Index for Improved Clustering .... N/A
Amit Bhadana, Manoj Singh

Modeling for VM Allocation Using Particle Swarm Optimization 12
Taskeen Zaidi, Ram Pratap

Impact of Method Noise on SAR Image Despeckling 19
Prabhishek Singh, Raj Shree

Transition in Step Network Through Simulation Tool 23
Taskeen Zaidi, Nitya Nand Dwivedi

Pair-Wise Selection Approach for Test Case Prioritization in Regression Testing 29
Shilpi Singh, Raj Shree

Privacy Policies: Preserving Confidentiality of Big Data 36
Kanika, Alka Agrawal, R.A. Khan

A Review: Study and Analysis of Images in Different Color Models 45
Neetish Kumar, Deepa Raj

Software Defects Prediction Using AI Technique: A Review 52
Sunil Kumar Singh, Raj Shree

Avert Traffic Violations by Automatic License Plate Detection Using Deep Learning Technique 58
S. Preethi, Kumar P Madhan, S Pradeep, Rosaline R Anto Arockia

The Survey of Machine Learning Algorithm for Component Based Software Data Exchange 65
Amit Verma, Gurpreet Singh Kamboj, Iqbaldeep Kaur

IOT Based Interactive Smart Refrigerator 72
N. G. Murali, S. Aarthi, M. Ethiraj, S. Baghavathi Priya

Prevention of Bike Accidents Using an Intelligent Helmet 79
P. N. Vignesh, Rosaline R. Anto Arockia, M. Barath, K. A. Athar Zafeer

Code Smell Detection Text Mining Tool Analysis for Source Code Improvization 86
Amit Verma, Ashish Kumar, Iqbaldeep Kaur

ARIS: A Machine Learning Algorithm to Test Games 93
S. C. Shivani, S. Santhankalakshmi, S. Baghavathi Priya

A Road Map to Big Data and Machine Learning 103
S. Sbha, S. Bafhavathipriya

Smart-EVM Using Multi-modal Biometrics with Embedded Security 110
R. Pavithra, Kumar N. Sharath, P. Siddhartha, G. Anitha

Smart Applications in Smart City and Improved Traffic Management System Using Collaborative Approach Among Nano Robots 116
Mamata Rath, Bibudhendu Pati, Binod Kumar Pattanayak

A Robust Fall Detection System Using Deep Learning Algorithms 124
K. Durga Devi, G. Anitha, S. Baghavathi Priya

Visitor Counter in Indian Railways 129
S. Vasanthakumar, N. Sangamithra, K. Vijay, K. Sai Yashwanth, M. Mehfooza

Performance Evaluation of Nonlinear Filters for Impulse Noise Removal 133
Kaushal Sishor, Prabhishek Singh

Manifold Surveillance Issues in Wireless Network and the Secured Protocol 139
Mamata Rath, Bibudhendu Pati, Binod Kumar Pattanayak

Improving DV-Hop Based Localization Algorithms in Wireless Sensor Networks by Considering Only Closest Anchors 148
AManpreet Kaur, Padam Kumar, Govind P. Gupta

3D Facial Model for Analysing the Facial Paralysis 160
Banita, Poonam Tanwar

An Intuitionistic Fuzzy AHP Based Multi Criteria Recommender System for Life Insurance Products 170
Akshay Hinduja, Manju Pandey

Agile Sink Based Data Gathering Protocol Employing Genetic Algorithm Utilizing Binary String (MSDGP-GAB) for Prolonged Network Lifetime in Wireless Sensor Networks 180
Amiya Bhusan Bagjadab, Sushrree Bibhuprada B. Priyadarshini, Dinesh Dash

Bug Model based Intelligent Recommender System with Exclusive Curriculum Sequencing for Learner-Centric Tutoring ... 187
Ninni Singh, Neelu Jyothi Ahuja, Amit Kumar

Collaborative Model for Security in Cloud ... 195
Brijesh Pandey, Abhineet Anand

Data Characterization of ISBSG R12 Using Data Analytics: An Exploratory Study ... 199
Ghazi Alkhatib, Khalid Al-Sarayrah

Data Security Issues and their Solutions in Cloud Computing ... 207
Anubhav Raj Singh, Abhineet Anand

Cloud Computing in Banking Sector ... 211
Shashwat Singh, Abhineet Anand

Security and Compliance Management in Cloud Computing ... 214
Ahtisham Hashmi, Aarushi Ranjan, Abhineet Anand

Brand Positioning Strategy in Marketing Management ... 221
D. Prabha

A Comparative Study of Job Stress Level of Software Professionals: A Case Study of Private Sector in India ... 233
Geeta Kumari, Ashfaue Alam, Gaurav Joshi

An Efficient Technique to Sort Large Datasets Using Merge of Multiple Streaming Files ... 240
Tanu Chaturvedi, Manoj Singh

A Study of the Impact of Data Warehousing and Data Mining Implementation on Marketing Effort ... 244
Kanika Chaudhry, Sanjay Dhingra

3D Facial Model for Analysing the Facial Paralysis ... 251
Banita, Poonam Tanwar

An Institutionistic Fuzzy AHP Based Multi Criteria Recommender System for Life Insurance Products ... 261
Akshay Hinduja, Manju Pandey

Ontology Development Utilizing Social Network Data Attributed to Drugs ... 270
Puja Munjal, Priyank Kumar, Akshay S. Nair

Author Index

Design and Implementation of Energy-Aware Hierarchical clustering technique of WSN for Improving network life

Meenakshi Yadav
Research Scholar
Aim & Act, Banasthali University
Banasthali Rajasthan, India
yadavmeenakshi@gmail.com

Anoop Bhola
Assistance Professor
Aim & Act, Banasthali University
Banasthali, Rajasthan, India
anupbhola@gmail.com

Chandra Kumar Jha
HOD, CSE
Aim & Act, Banasthali University
Banasthali, Rajasthan, India
ckha1@gmail.com

***Abstract*— Sensors are used to monitor the environmental conditions. Group of those autonomous sensors are called wireless sensor networks. These networks are self configured and infrastructure less. Each sensor node contains electrical and mechanical devices. Wireless sensor network has many issues related to design like, data aggregation, lifetime, address of node, mobility, deployment etc. With respect to these design issues many work has been introduced, LEACH is one of them. LEACH has increases the network life by distributing the load among the nodes. In this paper we introduced a new algorithm to improve the network life. We use grid method and maximum energy set of sensor node to increase network life. Grid method divides the network into subparts called clusters. Division of network is based on number of sensor nodes. Maximum energy set consider only those nodes have maximum energy. Maximum energy has been identified by calculating desired energy for communication of cluster head. Cluster head has been selected only from maximum energy set. Simulations results show that LEACH protocol nodes being to die earlier than LEACH-Emax. By round 100 LEACH losses 80 % nodes but LEACH-Emax lost only 40 % nodes. So LEACH- Emax performs better than LEACH and network life has been increased.**

***Index Terms*— LEACH ; LEACH-Emax ; Cluster Head ; Wireless sensor network ; clustering ; Virtual Gird**

I. Introduction

Now a day's wireless Sensor Network plays very important role in human life. Wireless Sensor Network Applications that are used in our life includes Healthcare, Environment and agriculture, public safety and military systems, industry, transportation systems. Now it is desirable to run WSN applications for long period of time and for this energy of sensor nodes is very important factor.

It is desirable to run wireless sensor network for long period of time and for this energy of sensor node is important factor. Major factor of energy drain is optimization of Radio, reduction of data; sleep/awake schemes, Energy-efficient routing, and repletion of Battery. Wireless sensor networks drain their energy due to routing procedure. Routing procedure of wireless sensor network is one of the main reasons of energy depletion. Nodes which are closer to sink deplete their energy very quickly because they have lots of operation to do.

Now there is some energy saving mechanisms available for routing techniques. These are cluster architecture, energy as routing metric, multipath routing, relay node placement and sink mobility. Author [10] provides a relationship between energy-efficient mechanism and application requirements explained in Table 1. In [11] author gives a classification of energy-efficient mechanism explained in fig 1.

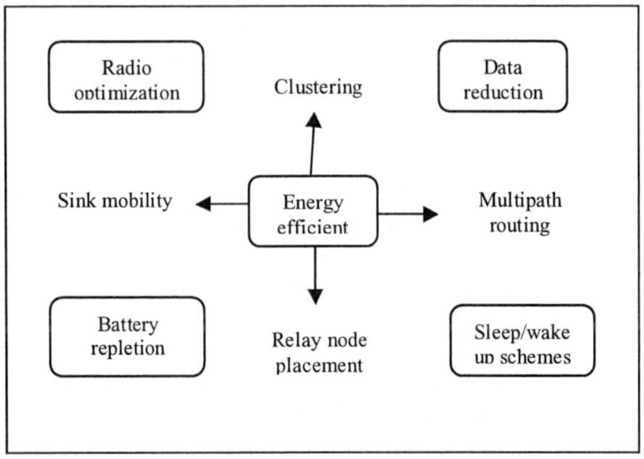

Fig 1. Energy efficient mechanism classification.

Clusters are used to divide the network and these clusters are managed by sensor nodes called cluster heads. This technique is called cluster architecture is one of the way to manage energy efficiency. Clustering technique is manages energy efficiency because i. Less communication range requires less transmission power, ii. CH's role reduces the number of transmission iii. Coordination and aggregation operations also reduced, iv. Using CH rotation technique energy consumption has balanced.

There are major proposed approaches to handle the consumption of energy problem of wireless sensor network nodes. Literature review gives the various energy efficient protocols proposed for energy saving.

Table 1. Relationship between energy efficient mechanism & application requirement

S. No.	Relationship between energy-efficient mechanism & application requirement	
	Energy-Efficient mechanism	Requirements
1.	Data Reduction	Delay, Qos, Scalability
2.	Sleep/wakeup schemes	Robustness, coverage, delay, Qos
3.	Radio optimization	Coverage, robustness
4.	Energy-efficient routing	Scalability, robustness, coverage, mobility, scalability

II LITERATURE SURVEY

W. R. Heinzelman et al [1], describe that lots of sensing nodes are available in sensor network. Energy efficient and less in cost is major quality of sensor nodes. Author designed a low-energy adaptive clustering hierarchy technique for reducing dissipation of energy. Clustering setup phase is used for implementing clustering technique.

Most clustering algorithm selects cluster heads and this CH simultaneously works as a relay node to transfer the data to sink node or other node. Now this is inefficient with respect of energy efficiency. Mehdi Tarhani et al [2], proposed a new distributed algorithm called scalable energy efficient clustering hierarchy (SEECH). In this algorithm CHs and relays selects separately between sensor nodes. This is based on the condition of nodes. High nodes are selected as CHs and low energy nodes are selected as relay nodes. Simulation results shows that SEECH is best suitable for large scale network and have better CH distribution.

Reliability and connectivity in WSNs has to be ensured by clustering protocol. Transmission of messages, data control packets are the main reason of energy consumption. Three main adjustment parameters for cluster heads election are energy consumption adjustment degree and exact distance that each data traverses to reach the BS. Sensor nodes having three main components, sensing subsystem for data acquisition, processing subsystem for local data processing and wireless communication subsystem for transmitting necessary data. Maryam Sabet et al [3], has proposed an energy efficient hierarchical cluster based routing algorithm for WSN. The Main idea of this protocol is selection of CH that is based on local information at the time of construction of routing tree. In selection of CH residual energy of node and its distance to base station is considered. Author use routing and clustering scheme number of control packets would be reduced and power of nodes is saved. Imbalanced load distribution between CHs is the main reason of random deployment. To solve this problem proposed protocol opt next node by considering residual energy in an area where density is very low.

Dejing Zhang et al [4], proposed an algorithm that is based on the idea of structure compose of edge nodes. Random structure transformed into virtual circle. Greedy forwarding is used for transmission and overhead is also reduced. The virtual circle is used to reduce length of routing path and transmission delay. Proposed protocol gives high delivery ratio, short path length, less control packet overhead and energy consumption.

Geographic routing does not require global topology so it is good approach in large scale WSNs. Sensor node take routing decisions according to geographic locations. If a sensor do not have neighbor close to sink than geographic routing cannot calculate hop count. It is called local minimum problem. Hari Prabhat Gupta et al [5], proposed a clustering technique named energy-efficient homogeneous clustering that selects cluster heads according to residual energy. Author also consider the obstacles in cluster and proposed a technique to optimize the routing path. For this author use Dijkstra's shortest path algorithm.

Failure of base station is a big problem in wireless sensor network. Multiple base stations could be a solution but it increases battery consumption and requires more energy devices. Runwei Zhang et al [6], proposed a scheme in which multiple BS has been deployed but at a time only one BS is in active mode, rest BS act as normal sensor nodes. This algorithm is asymptotically optimal in some conditions. For selecting active BS a HEF (highest energy first) algorithm also proposed.

Clustering is an energy saving technique for WSN. Tarachand Amgoth et al [7], gave solution of following issues i. Network is not well distributed ii. Improper selection of CH

A new energy-aware routing algorithm ERA is the solution of above mentioned problems. Proposed algorithm each sensor node selects its CH independently so that there is no need to pass any control message. Each sensor node checks both residual energy and distance for joining CH.

Maryam Sabet [8], proposed a clustering approach called MLRC (Multi-Level Route aware Clustering). In MLRC, nodes can have desired information of possible route to the destination. This approach also clears extra generation of routing control packets by implementing cluster formation and routing tree construction.

Ado Adamou [9],proposed a routing algorithm called ABC-SD using artificial Bee Colony approach and designed a multi-objective fitness function for cluster head selection. The authors have used the cost based function to solve the routing problem.

Jennifer Yick [10], focuses on recent literature and gives the issues related to individual and group sensor nodes in wireless sensor network. Author has covered the issues like localization; coverage of various wireless sensor network.

Finally, author provides the summary of current sensors technologies.
TiffennRault [11], gives a top-down survey of designing wireless sensor network in terms of application requirement and lifetime extension. The author has provided the categories of applications and their specific requirements. Also ,classification of energy saving schemes and their specific requirements has been discussed. Main requirements identified by the author are scalability, coverage, latency, QoS, Security, mobility and robustness. Finally author provides a classification of energy-efficient mechanisms.
Shipla Mahajan [12], has used graph theory concept to find the minimum distance from source to destination. BFS technique has been used to divide the network into sub regions and calculate the energy at each phase.
SamanSiavashi [13], introduced a new clustering protocol for load balancing. In the protocol network is divided into virtual circle having variable radiuses. This radiuses and cluster size will increase with respect to distance to the base station. Leader nodes are used for collecting and compressing the data load balancing and balanced distribution of energy. Consumption around the network is also achieved by this protocol.

III. NETWORK MODEL

Binary Disc communication model:-In binary disc communication model sensor is denoted by s. These sensors have the ability to communicate with other sensor nodes within the radius of disc called cluster. So

$$||A(s,r)|| = \pi r^2 \quad (1)$$

Where r is the communication range of s. Now suppose we have two sensor nodes i and j . They can communicate with each other directly and are known as neighbor if and only if Euclidean distance between them is not more than r. Euclidean distance is used to measuring the distance in the plane. Suppose we have two points with coordinated (x,y) and (a,b). Now the distance between them is

$$dist((x,y),(a,b)) = \sqrt{(x-a)^2+(y-b)^2} \quad (2)$$

We have used same radio model that has been used in previous work [1]. To run the transmitter radio electronic and power amplifier we use transmitter which dissipated energy for radio hardware. For running radio electronics, receiver dissipated energy.

IV. ENERGY CONSUMPTION MODEL

We use a simplified model for calculating consumption of energy in communication. Free space model is used when d_0 is greater than d and energy dissipation is d^2. If d is greater than d_0 multipath fading channel model is used, where energy dissipation is d^4. The energy consumption is computed for distance d and k-bit packet is as follows.

Equation 3 is used for calculating threshold distance d_0

$$d0 = \sqrt{\varepsilon_{fs}/\varepsilon_{mp}}$$

For receiving k-bit packet a node consumption energy has been calculated using equation (5)

$$E_{Rx} = k * E_{elec} \quad (5)$$

Cluster head has aggregate the data of sensor nodes. Now equation (6) is used to calculate the energy required for aggregation of data.

$$E_{agg} = E_{DA} * k * n \quad (6)$$

where n = number of message and E_{DA} = required energy to aggregate a bit

The consumption of energy for transmitting a k bits message over distance d is shown in equation

$$E_{trans} = \begin{cases} k * E_{elec} + k * \varepsilon_{mp} d^2 & d < d0 \\ k * E_{elec} + k * \varepsilon_{mp} d^4 & d >= d0 \end{cases} \quad (7)$$

The energy consumption for receiving a message of k bits is shown in equation

$$E_{receive} = k * E_{elec} \quad (8)$$

V. PROPOSED ALGORITHM

Proposed algorithm is divided into five parts. These are Zonal, cluster head selection, Energy calculation, CH Emax selection and communication algorithm. In Zonal algorithm formation of sensor network has been placed using virtual gird formation technique [14] . Network is divided into parts using equation (9). This equation depends on number of sensor nodes. Suppose we have 100 sensor nodes than our network will have 4 zones according to equation (9). Each zone has their sensor nodes and one cluster head to transmit data to Base station. Now cluster head selection algorithm will work for selecting cluster head for every zone. Before selecting Cluster head we need to calculate the energy of sensor nodes. For this we will use energy set algorithm. In energy set algorithm we make two empty nodes set maximum energy node and minimum energy node set. Initially first round all sensor nodes will take place into Emax set. For Emax set CH selection algorithm will call. In CH selection algorithm calculate the threshold value with respect to Emax set. If random number is less than T(s) value set that node as a CH. Initial phase is same as LEACH protocol. After initial phase nodes which have more energy than Edesired energy will fight for CH node. After selecting CH nodes, node sends an advertisement message and tells other nodes that I am cluster head and also tell their coordinates. After receiving advertisement message each node send their coordinates to CH.

Algorithm 1: Energy Set algorithm

1: Calculate do=sqrt(Efs/Emp)

2: Edesired=0.0358

3: **For** i to N

4: Calculate the distance to BS

5: Calculate the distance to CH

6: Call communication algorithm

7: **If** node is CH then

8: **If** distancetoBS< do then

9: calculate energy dissipated in the CH node during a round

sensornodes(i).E_{CH}=(n/k-1)*L*E_{elec}+N/K*L*E_{DA}+L*E_{elec}+L*ε_{fs}*d^2_{BS}

10: Sensornodes(i).E=sensornodes(i).E-sensornodes(i).E_{CH}

11: **Else if** distancetoBS>do

12: sensornodes(i).E_{CH}=(n/k-1)*L*E_{elec}+N/K*L*E_{DA}+L*E_{elec}+L*Emp*d^4_{BS} **else**

13: Calculate energy dissipation for non CH nodes

14: **If** distancetoBS>=distancetoCH

15: **If** distancetoBS<do

16: sensornodes(i).$E_{non\text{-}CH}$= L*E_{elec}+L*E_{elec}+L* ε_{fs}*d^2_{BS}

17: sensornodes(i).E=sensornodes(i).E-sensornodes(i).$E_{non\text{-}CH}$ **else**

18: sensornodes(i).E_{nonCH}=L*E_{elec}+L*E_{elec}+L*E_{mp}*d^4_{BS}

19: sensornodes(i).E=sensornodes(i).E-sensornodes(i).$E_{non\text{-}CH}$ **else**

20: **if** distancetoCH<do

21: sensornodes(i).$E_{non\text{-}CH}$= L*E_{elec}+L*E_{elec}+L* ε_{fs}*d^2_{CH}

22: sensornodes(i).E=sensornodes(i).E-sensornodes(i).$E_{non\text{-}CH}$ **else**

23: sensornodes(i).E_{nonCH}=L*E_{elec}+L*E_{elec}+L*E_{mp}*d^4_{BS}

24: sensornodes(i).E=sensornodes(i).E-sensornodes(i).$E_{non\text{-}CH}$

25: end

26: **if** sensornodes(i).E>Edesired then

27: put into Emax /* set of maximum energy sensor nodes */ **else**

28: put into Emin /* set of minimum energy nodes */

29: Sort Emax in descending order

30: **For** i=1 to N

31: **If** sensornodes(i).E=0

32: Node is dead

33: Dead=dead+1

34: End

35: Dead= total number of node is dead after one round

36: Round one is over

37: For next round

38: **If** CH==1

39: Call CH Emax algorithm for next round CH selection

else

40: Call CH selection algorithm

VI. Simulation and Result Analysis

LEACH-Emax shows effective network life difference when Maximum energy node consider only for CH. The simulation of proposed algorithm shows that LEACH-Emax 's first node died by round 64 and last node died by round 100 is 32. Initial energy of each node was 0.1 joule and figure 2 shows average energy of nodes by round 100. Figure 4 and 5 shows the dead and alive node after completing 100 rounds. Figure 6 represents energy spends by cluster heads during rounds. Non cluster member spend energy shown in figure 7. Simulation parameters are shown in Table 3.

Figure 3 shows the dead nodes comparison between LEACH and LEACH-Emax by round 100. LEACH first node has been dying by round 30 and LEACH-Emax first node die by 48 rounds. After 100 rounds LEACH has lost 38 nodes and LEACH-Emax lost 32 nodes. That means network life has improve by using LEACH-Emax because node begin to die late and less node die after certain round.

Table 3: Simulation Parameters

Parameters	Value
Area	100X100
No. of Nodes	100
Packet Size	2000bit
Initial Energy	0.5J
Sink	(50,50)
ETx	50nJ/bit
ERx	50nJ/bit
Efs	10pJ/bit/m3
Emp	13pJ/bit
EDA	5pJ/bit

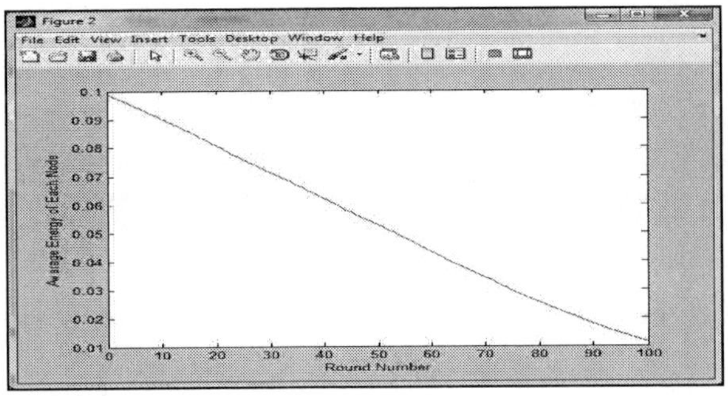

Fig 2: Energy Usages in 100 round

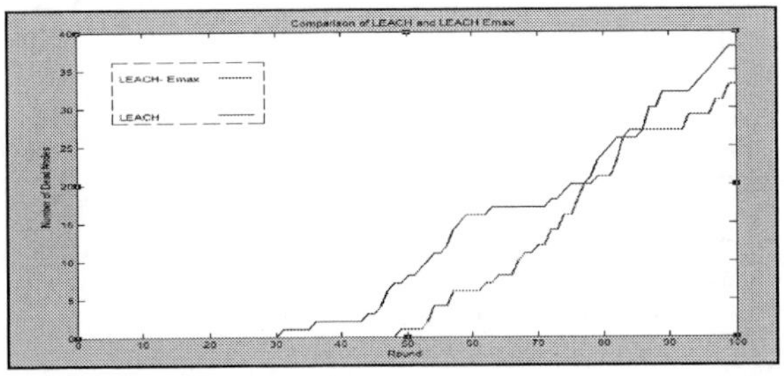

Fig 3: Comparison between LEACH vs LEACH-Emax

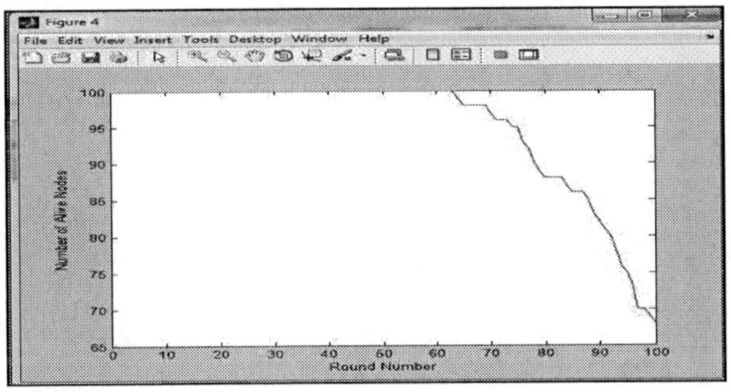

Fig 4: Number of alive nodes vs round

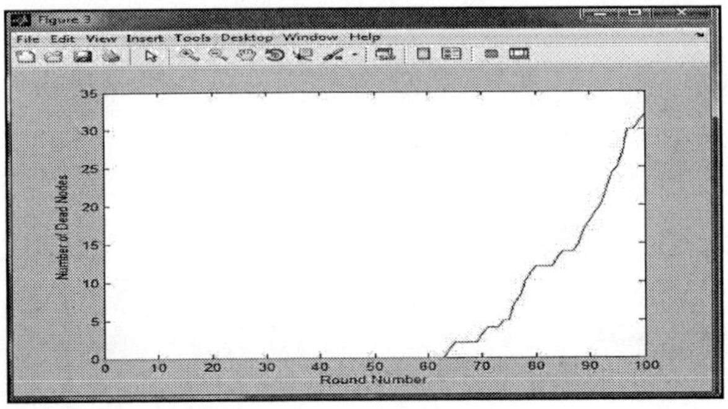

Fig: 5: number of dead nodes vs round

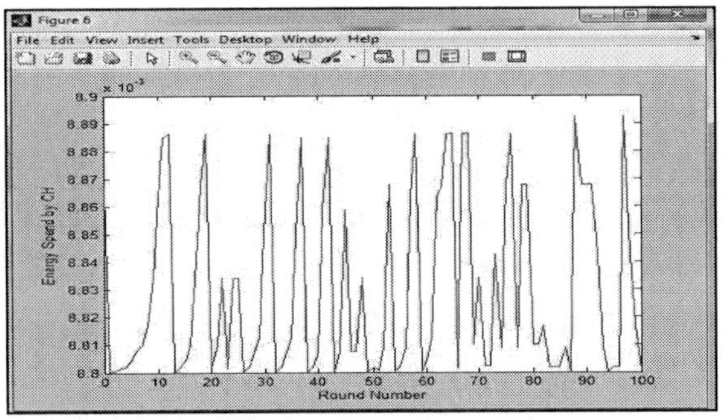

Fig 6: Energy usages by CH vs round

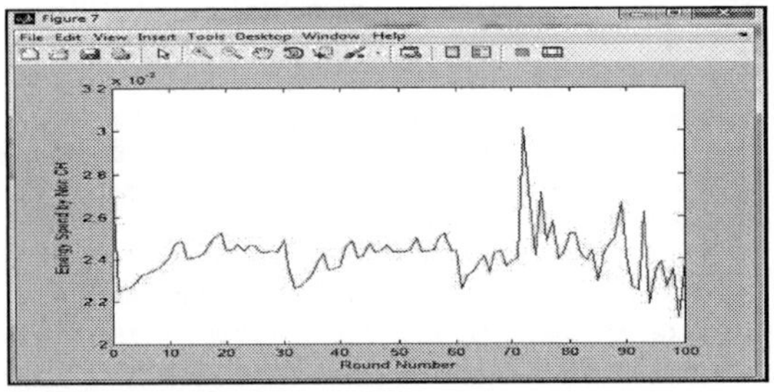

Fig 7: Energy usages by Non CH vs round

VII. Conclusion & Future Scope

In the last decade, we have seen lots of energy efficient protocols for increasing network life of wireless sensor network. Those all protocols are based on Energy Efficient routing techniques. In this paper, we proposed a new protocol based on energy efficient routing techniques. Our algorithm used virtual gird method and node energy for achieving our main target that is network life. The result shows that in our algorithm is able to increase the network life.

Future work of our algorithm is to cover the all area of cluster. According to the position of the cluster head life of network will change. So our next target is to develop the new criteria for cluster head selection, when nodes are far away from sink node.

References

[1] Wendi Rabiner Heinzeleman, Anantha Chandrakasan and Hari Balakrishnan:Enegry Efficient communication protocol for wireless microsensor networks: proceeding of the IEEE 33rd international conference on System Sciences 2000.

[2] Mehdi Tarhani, Yousef S Kavian, Saman Siavoshi: SEECH: Scalable Energy Efficient Clustering Hierarchy Protocol in wireless sensor network: IEEE sensors journal, Vol. 14, no. 11, November 2014.

[3] Maryam Sabet, Hamid Reza Naji: A decentralized energy efficient hierarchical cluster-based routing algorithm for wireless sensor networks: International journal of Electronic and communications, pp. 790-799, Elsevier 2015.

[4] Dejing Zhang , Enqing Dong: A Virtual coordinator-Based Bypassing void routing for wireless sensor networks: IEEE sensors journal, Vol. 15, no. 7, July 2015.

[5] Hari Prabhat Gupta, S.V. Rao, Amit kumar Yadav, Tanima Das: Geographic Routing in clustering wireless sensor networks among obstacles: IEEE sensor journal, Vol. 15, no. 5, May 2015.

[6] Runwei Zhang, Francois Ingelrest, Guillermo Barrenetxea, Patrick Thiran, Martin Vetterli: The Beauty of the Commons: Optimal Load Sharing by Base Station Hopping in Wireless Sensor Networks: IEEE journal on selected areas in communication, Vol. 33, no.8, August 2015.

[7] Tarachand Amgoth, Prasanta K. Jana: Energy-aware routing algorithm for wireless sensor networks: Computers and Electrical Engineering Elsevier 2015.

[8] Maryam Sabet, Hamidreza Naji: An energy efficient multi-level route-aware clustering algorithm for wireless sensor networks: Computer Science and Electrical Engineering ELSEVIER 000(2016) 1-19, August 2016.

[9] Ado Adamou Abba Ari, Blaise Omer Yenke, Nabila Labraoui, Irepran Damakoa, Abdelhak Gueroui: "A power efficient cluster-based routing algorithm for wireless sensor networks: Honeybees swarm intelligence based approach":Network and Computer Applications ELSEVIER 69(2016 77-97, April 2016.

[10] Jennifer Yick, Biswananth Mukherjee, Dipak Ghosal: Wireless sensor network survey: computer networks ELSEVIER 52(2008)2292-2330, April 2008.

[11] Tifenn Rault, Abdelmadjid Bouabdallah, Yacine Challal: Energy efficiency in wireless sensor networks: A top-down survey: Computer Networks ELSEVIER 67(2014) 104-122, April 2014.

[12] Shipla Mahajan, Jyoteesh Malhotra, Sandeep Sharma: Energy balanced optimum path determination based on graph theory for wireless sensor network: IET wireless sensor systems 2015, vol. 5, ISS. 6,pp 290-298, August 2015.

[13] Saman Siavoshi, Yousef S. Kavian, Hamid Sharif: Load Balanced energy efficient clustering protocol for wireless sensor networks: IET wireless sensor systems 2016, vol. 6 , ISS. 3, pp. 67-73.

[14] Abdul Waheed Khan, Abdul Hanan Abdullah: VGDRA: A Virtual Grid-Based Dynamic Routes Adjustment Scheme for Mobile Sink-Based Wireless Sensor Networks: IEEE Sensor Journal vol 15. No. 1 January 2015. DOI 10.1109/JSEM.2014.2347137.

[15] A.Manjeshwar,D.P.Agarwal:TEEN:A routing protocol for enhanced efficiency in wireless sensor networks: in Proc. 15th int. Parallel Distrib. Process. Symp. (IPDPS), vol. 1 Apr 2000,pp. 2009-2015.

[16] A Manjeshwar,D.P.Agarwal: APTEEN: A hybrid protocol for efficient routing and comprehensive information retrieval in wireless , in Proc. 16th Int. Parallel. Distrib. Process. Symp/, 2002, p.48.

Gap in pagination due to unavailable paper.

Pages 7-11

Modeling for VM Allocation using Particle Swarm Optimization

Taskeen Zaidi, Ram Pratap

Faculty of Computer Science & Engineering, Shri Ramswaroop Memorial University, Deva Road, Lucknow, India

ABSTRACT:

Cloud computing is a general term used in the era of information technology. There are various services provided by the cloud providers for the users as per the demand. There are various key issues for cloud providers to provide the services to their users without any fault. Fault in the cloud scenario can be handled either reactively or proactively. Load balancing, reducing energy consumption and optimization of scheduling of tasks can reduce fault. There are various optimization techniques such as Ant colony Optimization(ACO), Particle Swarm Optimization(PSO) and genetic algorithms. Particle swarm optimization (PSO) is a biological population based method for optimizing a real problem to improve a candidate solution with regard to a given measure of quality. PSO was firstly used for the simulation of social behavior of bird or fish as they move in the sky or water respectively in a stylish manner. Selection of the path depends on the fitter members of the swarm and particles flying in the environment following the selected path and generally biasing their movement toward historically good areas of their environment. This algorithm is used to exchange information to share previous data about the carried out search and to find a place with enough food.

KEYWORDS: Particle Swarm Optimization(PSO), Fault Tolerance, Cloudsim, UML.

1. INTRODUCTION AND RELATED WORK:

The recent trend in information technology is cloud computing, it is observed that the cloud services have become an integral part of information technology either it is in the form of different type of services provided by the cloud providers or management of those services.

Cloud computing is a new paradigm in information technology and its popularity has increased for connecting networked enterprises. It enables the internet evolution into a global market of collaborating services. The basic principles of cloud computing is to make the computing be assigned in a great number of distributed computers, rather than local computer or remote server. It is a new kind of computing model that is to say the manufacturer provides relevant hardware, software and services according to the need of client.

The reliability of cloud applications becomes one of the major concerns of cloud service providers and users. Reliability in various types of services is a key concern in today's scenario. As unreliable services may lead to loss of data and revenue [10]. Reliability can be achieved by making the system fault tolerance. i.e. if any fault occurs at the time of running the services it can be removed either proactively or reactively. There are various techniques for handling the fault such as process migration, task scheduling, task resubmission, check pointing etc.

The existing fault tolerance technique in cloud computing considers various parameters such as throughput, response-time, scalability, performance, availability, usability, reliability, associated overhead and security.

We can increase the response time by proper scheduling of cloudlets. Through PSO(Particle swarm optimization), one can distribute the workload across multiple nodes in a distributed environment is known as load balancing.

The proposed problems consist of the two parts one is the modeling and other is the computation of extensive results for load balancing of resources to achieve fault tolerance. Object-oriented modeling approach was invented by the Greedy Booch[1], various diagrams are proposed by Booch et al.[2] and versions of UML are released by an active Object Management Group(OMG) [3-4]. The different tools are available for the designs which are based on the concepts given by the Greedy Booch, et al. The names of tools are Rational Rose, Smart Draw, E-Draw, Ms-Visio, etc. In the proposed research work, any one said tool shall be used for modeling of problems.

In 2002, Pllana and Fahringer [5-6] used the UML for obtaining the performance of the parallel and distributed architecture problems. Saxena and Arora [7] also used the UML for finding the performance of the object-oriented programming languages. Pooley and King[8] have used the object-oriented programming language for

solution of engineering problems. Gooma[9] described concurrent, distributed and real time systems by the use of Unified Modeling Language.
The fault tolerance in cloud computing can be achieved by proper load balancing of resources using efficient scheduling algorithm. Task scheduling can be done by various scheduling strategies of operating systems such as FCFS, SJF, SRTF, RR, RR with SJF and FCFS with SJF scheduling. Comparison of these scheduling algorithms is done by Gibet et al.[11]. Jhawar et al.[12] proposed an innovative, system-level, modular perspective on creating and managing fault tolerance in Clouds. They propose a dedicated service layer approach to hide the details of the fault tolerance techniques to users at the time of implementation. By using this approach, the service layer allows the user to specify and apply the desired level of fault tolerance, and knowledge is not required about the fault tolerance techniques that are available in the cloud and their implementations.
Agraj[13] has proposed an algorithm for load balancing of cloud by considering response time of every request and on the basis of response time next allocation is done, this approach reduces the extra computation loss on server.
Dynamic Time Slice Calculation for round robin process scheduling using fine tuning time slicing of processes which didn't completed in allotted timeslot was well explained through a new method proposed in [14]. Experiments on cloudsim toolkit has been demonstrated by Gibet and Amrani[15], as well as two new scheduling strategies has been proposed that depicts the strength and weakness of scheduling algorithms. Kun L. et al.[16] propose a cloud task scheduling based on load balancing by using ant colony optimization.
Minimization of total cost in task scheduling in cloud can be achieved by optimal resource allocation or task scheduling and it should decide optimal number of systems required in the cloud. Genetic algorithm based scheduling is proposed in [18,23,24]. Optimization of the energy consumption used in task scheduling is done by the genetic algorithm. There are various parameters like performance, scalability, throughput, resource utilization, migration time for task scheduling such that fault can be minimized. As task scheduling is a NP-Complete problem, for scheduling workflows genetic Algorithm has been used [20]. However, genetic algorithm may not be the best approach. Sometimes experiments shows that the performance of PSO algorithm is faster than genetic algorithm in solving static task assignment problem for homogeneous distributed computing systems [21]. Lei et al. [22] have shown that for better scheduling PSO algorithm can be used in place of genetic algorithm.
In this paper, particle swarm optimization based scheduling technique is presented for allocation of incoming jobs to VMs to available resources optimally, minimize the resource consumption and achieve a highly fault tolerance system.
Our main focus in this paper is as follows:

- We develop a model for task-allocation of cloud to minimize the overall cost of execution.
- We design a approach that uses PSO to allocate VM to the tasks to increase computing cost.

2. PARTICLE SWARM OPTIMIZATION STEPS:

PSO is used for searching the best path in the search space(swarm). A single solution is called particle. Each particle has a fitness/cost value that is evaluated by the function to be minimized, and each particle has a velocity that directs the "flying" of the particles.
The algorithm steps are as follows:
1.Initialize particle with pso parameters(random velocity and random position)
2.Calculate pBest.
3.Find gBest by choosing particle with lower cost.
4.Update velocity and position of each particle with fitness function.
5.Repeat 2-4 step until termination criteria met.

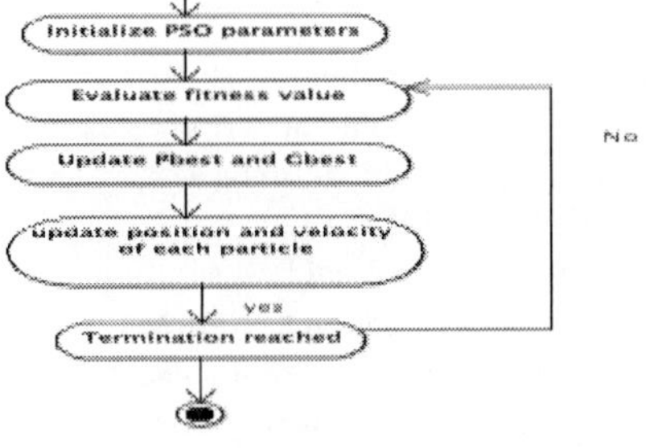

Figure:1 UML Activity diagram illustrating the particle swarm optimization algorithm.

UML activity diagram is depicted in figure 1 which represents the steps of PSO. As activity diagram represents the actions and activities occur during the representation of a problem and here PSO parameters are initialized and after evaluation of fitness value the pBest and gBest value will be updated and velocity and position of each particle will also be updated and if search criteria is fulfilled the activity will be terminated but if search is incomplete, again repeat the activities to achieve termination condition.

3. PSO ALGORITHM:

Fault Tolerance is one of the basic issue in the field of cloud computing research. For achieving fault tolerance we should focus on the scheduling of tasks. Given a set of jobs, a set of VMs, a set of constraints and an objective function, how should jobs be allocated to resources? Task scheduling based PSO algorithm will be proposed to solve this question. Decreasing the makespan of tasks is the basic goal (objective function) from the proposed method. To model task scheduling, PSO is instantiated with particles, each maintaining one potential solution to the entire scheduling problem(pB). The position of a particle is being placed in a search space. Furthermore, the global best(gB) position will indicate the best possible scheduling solution. The PSO algorithm tracks the overall best solution found by any of the particles in the PSO and the best solution here is associated with the makespan length. The pseudo code of the proposed PSO procedure is shown in Algorithm.

Algorithm 2: Pseudo code of the proposed PSO procedure

```
Input: List of Cloudlet (Tasks) and List of VMs
Output: The best solution for fault tolerance on VMs

Steps: 1. Initialize parameters such as particles, tm and set t=1.
Set gB=null and produce solution randomly for each particle
    2. For each particle calculate fit value
       If the fit value is better than pB
       Set pB = current fit value
       If pB is better than gB
       Set gB = pB
    3. Arrange particles by their pB scores, best to worst
    4. For each particle calculate pV
       Use pV to update particle Data
    5. Increment t by one.
    6. If (t < tm)
              Goto step 2
              Else
              Print gB .
              End If
    7. Return
```

Each Pv is updated using this equation:

$$v_n(t+1)=zv_n(t)+c1r1[\hat{}\ x_n(t)-x_n(t)]+c2r2[g(t)-x_n(t)]$$

- n shows particle index
- z shows inertia coefficient
- c1,c2 implies acceleration coefficients.
- r1,r2 implies random values regenerated every velocity update
- $v_n(t)$ shows the particle's velocity at time t
- $x_n(t)$ shows the particle's position at time t
- $\hat{}\ x_n(t)$ shows the particle's individual best solution as of time t
- g(t) shows the swarm's best solution as of time t
- Inertia coefficient usually lies between 0.8 and 1.2
- Coefficient limits the size of the step the particle takes toward its individual best$\hat{}\ x_n$ causes the particle to move to the best regions the swarm has found so far

Equation For updating the position of the particle : $x_n(t+1)=x_n(t)+v_n(t+1)$

4. CLOUDSIM:

CloudSim works as a library for the simulation of cloud scenarios. It provides essential classes for describing data centres, computational resources, virtual machines, applications, users and policies for the management of various parts of the system such as scheduling and provisioning.

CloudSim provides a generalized and extensible simulation framework that enables seamless modeling and simulation of app performance. By using CloudSim, developers can focus on specific systems design issues that they want to investigate, without getting concerned about details related to cloud-based infrastructures and services.

5. RESULTS & DISCUSSION:

Various users connect to cloud at different time span to execute PSE and request for virtual machine. Users connected through distributed network and VMs required by users will be greater than physical host, so that physical resources will be used efficiently. The allocation of resources in this work is represented in FCFS manner. In the presented algorithm group of hosts are considered as swarm and each host in cloud is considered as particle in the swarm. Users request for the VM for execution of tasks and it is initialized by the random best and each host has position according to its load(host ID). Load is defined in terms of resource utilization and calculated as VM total MIPS/host total MIPS. The neighbouring nodes are identified by hostID and neighbour size and selected randomly. At each iteration particle move to its neighbour for searching of an underloaded host and velocity of particle is the load difference between the host and neighbouring host. If the neighbouring host has lesser load than the original one then the particle forwarded towards it with greater velocity and task execution finished. The total number of tasks executed are 300 and the total data transferred is 20000MIPS.Table 1 shows the parameters values for PSO and Table 2 shows allocation of virtual machines to the tasks and it is analyzed that 100 tasks cost is 4000 MIPS , 200 tasks cost 10000 MIPS and 300 tasks cost 20000MIPS as shown in figure 3.The overall results depicted maximum number of tasks are executed through PSO scheduling and task failure is also less.

Table 1. Parameter values for PSO

Type	Parameters	Values
Datacenter	Number of Datacenter	1
	Number of PE per Datacenter	1
Processing Element(PE)	Speed of PE	1000-100000MIPS
	Power Consumption	0.28-3.45kW
Task	Total Number of Tasks	300
	Length of Tasks	2000-200000 Million Instruction

Number of cloudlet 300 Cached 0 Data transferred 200000

Table 2. Allocation of Virtual Machines

Number of Tasks	100	200	300
VM0	28	30	34
VM3	9	8	9
VM5	32	23	30
Sum	69	61	73

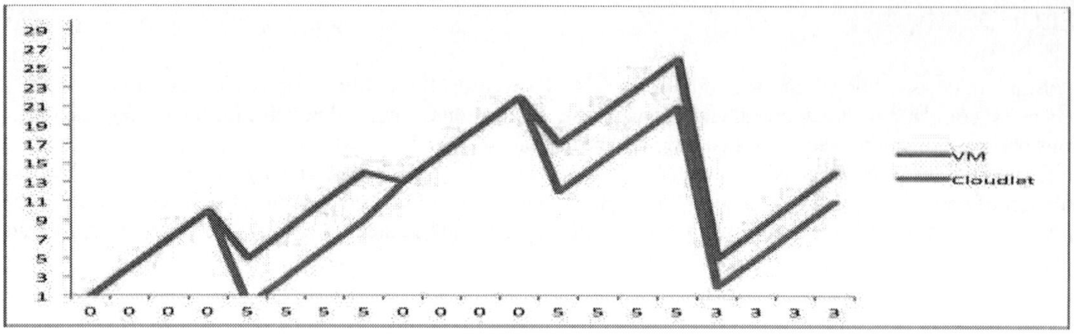

Figure:2 Allocation of virtual machines to tasks

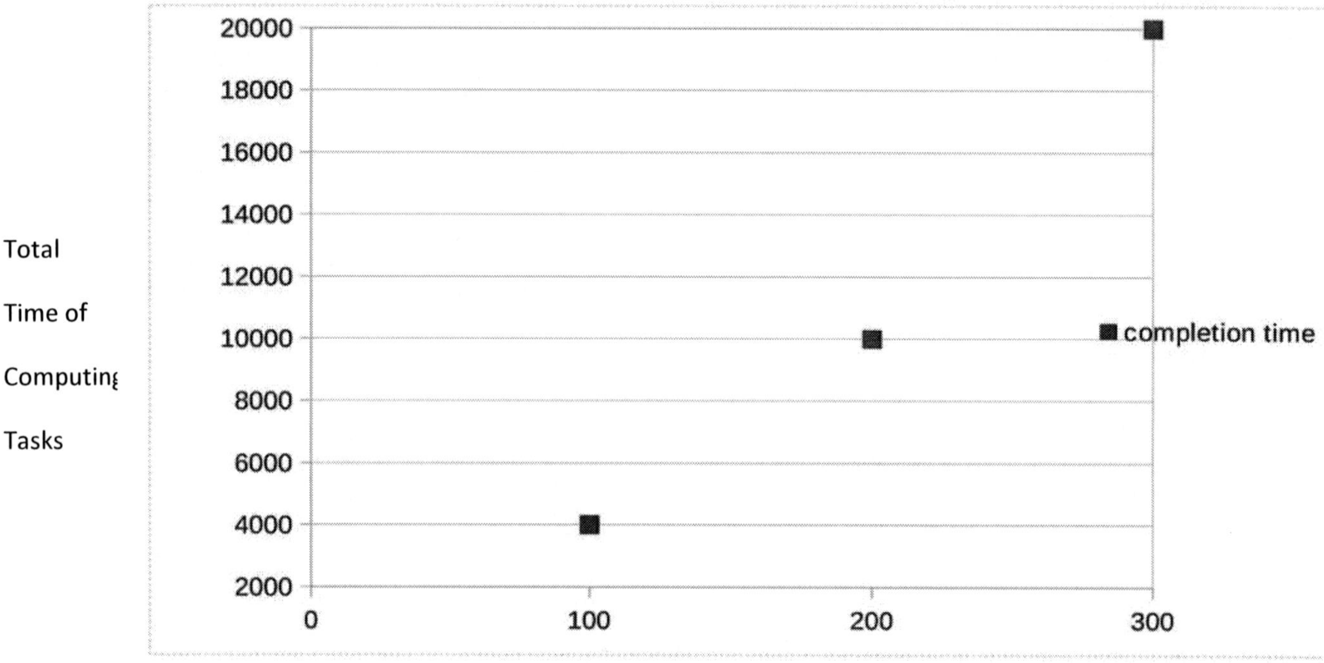

Figure:3 Completion time of algorithm

CONCLUSION:

Particle swarm scheduling workflow is used to schedule interrelated tasks and simulation results shows that PSO not only decrease the total amount to complete task but also maximum number of tasks are executed on the basis of computing power of virtual machines provided by datacenters. As well as in PSO virtual machines are allocated randomly and tasks are executed with minimal overheads.

FUTURE WORK:

The future work can be extended by observing no relationship or relationship among the tasks. This type of scheduling does not exists in online environment where multiple users are connected to perform computation tasks so this scheduling workflow may be implemented to transform physical resources to virtual machines so that small and mid size organizations will collaborate with the cloud environment.

REFERENCES:

[1] Booch, G.(1994), Object-Oriented Analysis and Design with Applications, *Addison Wesley*.

[2] Booch, G., Rambaugh, J. and Jacobson, J.(1999), The Unified Modeling Language, *Addison Wesley*.

[3] OMG (2001), Unified Modeling Language Specification, *http://www.omg.org*.

[4] OMG (2002), XML Metadata Interchange (XML) Specification, *http://www.omg.org*.

[5] Pllana, S. and Fahringer, T.(2002), On Customizing the UML for Modeling Performance Oriented Applications, *Springer-Verleg*.

[6] Pllana, S. and Fahringer, T.(2002), UML Based Modeling of Performance Oriented Parallel and Distributed Applications, *Winter Simulation Conference*.

[7] Saxena, V. and Arora, D.(2009), Performance Evaluation for Object-Oriented Software Systems, *ACM-SIGSOFT*, 34(2).

[8] Pooley, R. and King, P. (1999), The Unified Modeling and Performance Engineering, *IEEE Software*, 146(1).

[9] Gooma, H. (2001), Designing Concurrent, Distributed and Real Time Applications with UML, *IEEE 23rd International Conference on Software Engineering*.

[10] Object Management Group. March 2002, UML Profile for Schedulability, Performance & Time Specification, OMG Adopted Specification pt/02-03-02, Object Management Group.

[11] Gibet Tani Hicham, EI Amrani Chaker (2016), "Cloud computing CPU allocation and Scheduling Algorithms Using Cloudsim Simulator" International Journal of Electrical and Computer Engineering(IJECE), vol.6, no.4, pp. 1866-1879, ISSN:-2088-8708.

[12] Jhawar, Ravi, Vincenzo Piuri & Marco Santambrogio(2013), "Fault tolerance management in cloud computing". A system level perspective" Systems Journal. IEEE 7.2: 288-297. Journal of Computer Sciences And Applications.

[13] Agraj Sharma & Sateesh k. Peddoju(2014), "Response time based load balancing in cloud computing" International Conference on Control, Instrumentation, Communication and Computational Technologies (ICCICCT), INSPEC Accession Number: 14825170, DOI: 10.1109/ICCICCT.2014.6993159

[14] G. S. N. Rao, *et al.*(2015), "Dynamic Time Slice Calculation for Round Robin Process Scheduling Using NOC," *International Journal of Electrical and Computer Engineering,* vol/issue: 5(6), pp. 1480~1485.

[15] Gibet Tani Hicham and El Amrani Chaker (2016) "Cloud Computing CPU Allocation and Scheduling Algorithms Using CloudSim Simulator" *International Journal of Electrical and Computer Engineering,* Vol. 6, No. 4, pp. 1866~1879

[16] Kun L., Gaochao X., Guangyu Z., Yushuang D. and Dan W.(2011), "Cloud Task scheduling based on Load Balancing Ant Colony Optimization", Chinagrid Conference (ChinaGrid), pp. 3–9.

[17] Medhat A.T., Ashraf B.E., Arabi E.K. and Fawzy A.T.(2013), "Cloud Task Scheduling Based on Ant Colony Optimization", on the 8th International Conference on Computer Engineering & Systems ICCES, pp. 64-68.

[18] Zhao C., Zhang S., Liu Q., Xie J., and Hu J.(2009), "Independent Tasks Scheduling Based on Genetic Algorithm in Cloud Computing," in Proceedings of the IEEE International Conference on Wireless Communications, Networking and Mobile Computing, China, pp. 1-4.

[19] Pandey S., Wu L., Guru S. and Buyya R.(2010), "A particle swarm optimization-based heuristic for scheduling workflow applications in cloud computing environments", In: International conference on advanced information networking and applications. IEEE Computer Society, pp. 400-407.

[20] J. Yu, R. Buyya, and K. Ramamohanarao(2008). Workflow Scheduling Algorithms for Grid Computing, Springer Heidelberg, volume 146, pages 173–214.

[21] A.Salman.(2002), Particle swarm optimization for task assignment problem, Microprocessors and Microsystems, 26(8):363– 371.

[22] L. Zhang, Y. Chen, R. Sun, S. Jing, and B. Yang(2008). A task scheduling algorithm based on pso for grid computing. International Journal of Computational Intelligence Research, 4(1).

[23] Chenhong Z., Shanshan Z., Qingfeng L., Jian X. and Jicheng H.(2009), "Independent Tasks Scheduling Based on Genetic Algorithm in Cloud Computing", IEEE International Conference on Wireless Communications, Networking and Mobile Computing, PP. 1 – 4.

[24] Kai Z., Huaguang S., Lijing L., Jinzhu G. and Guojian C.(2011), "Hybrid Genetic Algorithm for Cloud Computing Applications", IEEE International Conference on Asia-Pacific Services Computing Conference (APSCC), PP. 182 – 187.

[25] Buyya, R., Ranjan, R. and Calheiros, R.N.(2009), "Modeling and simulation of scalable cloud computing environments and the cloudSim toolkit: challenges and opportunities ", in Proceedings of the 7th High Performance Computing and Simulation Conference, Leipzig, Germany.

[26] X. Kong, J. Huang, C. Lin, P.D. Ungsunan(2009), “Performance, fault tolerance and scalability analysis of virtual infrastructure management system”, 2009 IEEE international symposium on parallel and distributed processing with applications, Chengdu, China, Aug 9-12.

[27] P.Kahkipuro(1999), UML Based Performance Modeling Framework for Computer-Based Distributed Systems. In: R. Dumko (Ed.), Proceedings of 2nd International Conference on Unified Modeling Language (UML'99), pp.167-184. Springer (LNCS vol.2047).

[28] Pandey S., Wu L., Guru S. and Buyya R.(2010), "A particle swarm optimization-based heuristic for scheduling workflow applications in cloud computing environments", In: International conference on advanced information networking and applications. IEEE Computer Society, pp. 400-407.

[29] Dhepthie P., Sivanandam U.R. and Mathiyalagan S.N.(2010), "Grid scheduling using enhanced pso algorithm", international Journal on Computer Science and Engineering, vol. 2, no. 2, pp. 145150.

[30] Kang Q. and He H.(2011), "A novel discrete particle swarm optimization algorithm for meta-task assignment in heterogeneous computing systems", Microprocess Microsyst, vol. 35, no. 1, pp. 10-17.

[31] Gibet Tani Hicham and El Amrani Chaker(2016),“Cloud Computing CPU Allocation and Scheduling Algorithms Using CloudSim Simulator” *International Journal of Electrical and Computer Engineering,* Vol. 6, No. 4, pp. 1866~1879.

[32] CloudSim: A Toolkit for Modeling and Simulation of Cloud Computing Environments and Evaluation of Resource Provisioning Algorithms Rodrigo N. Calheiros, Rajiv Ranjan, Anton Beloglazov, César A. F. De Rose, and Rajkumar Buyya , Cloud Computing and Distributed Systems (CLOUDS) Laboratory Department of Computer Science and Software Engineering The University of Melbourne, Australia

[33] Fahimeh Ramezani, Jie Lu, Farookh Khadeer Hussain(2014), Task-Based System Load Balancing in Cloud Computing Using Particle Swarm Optimization, International Journal of Parallel Programming, Volume 42, Issue 5, pp 739–754.

[34] Shaobin Zhan, Hongying Huo(2012), Improved PSO-based Task Scheduling Algorithm in Cloud Computing ,Journal of Information & Computational Science 9: 13, 3821–3829.

[35] Zhulin Li1,Cuirong Wang3,Haiyan and Tongyu(2016), Application of PSO Algorithm Based on Improved Accelerating Convergence in Task Scheduling of Cloud Computing Environment, International Journal of Grid and Distributed Computing Vol. 9, No. 9 , pp.269-280 http://dx.doi.org/10.14257/ijgdc.2016.9.9.23.

[36] Chen, Wei-neng; Zhang, Jun (2010). "A novel set-based particle swarm optimization method for discrete optimization problem". IEEE Transactions on Evolutionary Computation.14(2):278–300. doi:10.1109/tevc.2009.2030331

[37] Parsopoulos, K.; Vrahatis, M. (2002). "Particle swarm optimization method in multiobjective problems". Proceedings of the ACM Symposium on Applied Computing (SAC). pp. 603–607.

[38] Bonyadi, Mohammad reza.; Michalewicz, Z. (2014). "An analysis of the velocity updating rule of the particle swarm optimization algorithm". Journal of Heuristics.20(4): 417–452. doi:10.1007/s10732-014-9245-2

[39] Kennedy, J.; Eberhart, R. (1995). "Particle Swarm Optimization". Proceedings of IEEE International Conference on Neural Networks. pp. 1942–1948.doi:10.1109/ICNN.1995.488968

[40] Anqi Xu, Yang Yang, Zhenqiang Mi, Zenggang Xiong(2015), "Task Scheduling Algorithm Based on PSO in Cloud Environment", 2015 IEEE 12th Intl Conf on Ubiquitous Intelligence and Computing and 2015 IEEE 12th Intl Conf on Autonomic and Trusted Computing and 2015IEEE 15th Intl Conf on Scalable Computing and Communications and Its Associated Workshops (UIC-ATC-ScalCom), vol. 00, no. , pp. 1055-1061, doi:10.1109/UIC-ATC-ScalCom-CBDCom-IoP.2015.196.

[41] Shekhar Singh, Mala Kalra(2014), "Scheduling of Independent Tasks in Cloud Computing Using Modified Genetic Algorithm", 2014 International Conference on Computational Intelligence and Communication Networks (CICN), vol. 00, no. , pp. 565-569,2014, doi: 10.1109/CICN.2014.128

[42] ElinaPacini, CristianMateos, CristianMateos(2014),”Dynamic Scheduling based on Particle Swarm Optimization for Cloud-based Scientific Experiments”, CLEI ELECTRONIC JOURNAL, VOLUME 14, NUMBER 1, PAPER 2, APRIL 2014.

[43] Buyya, R., Ranjan, R. and Calheiros, R.N.(2009), "Modeling and simulation of scalable cloud computing environments and the cloudSim toolkit: challenges and opportunities ", in Proceedings of the 7th High Performance Computing and Simulation Conference, Leipzig, Germany.

[44] E.Pacini, C.Mateos, and C.Garc´ıa Garino(2014), “Distributed job scheduling based on Swarm Intelligence: A survey,” Computers & Electrical Engineering, vol. 40, no. 1, pp. 252-269.

[45] Frederic Nzanywayingoma and Prof. Yang Yang(2017), “Analysis of Particle Swarm Optimization and Genetic Algorithm based on Task Scheduling in Cloud Computing Environment”, (IJACSA) International Journal of Advanced Computer Science and Applications, Vol. 8, No. 1.

Impact of Method Noise on SAR Image Despeckling

Prabhishek Singh/ Research Scholar
Department of Information Technology
BBAU, Lucknow, India
prabhisheksingh88@gmail.com

Raj Shree/ Assistant Professor
Department of Information Technology
BBAU, Lucknow, India
rajshree.bbau2008@gmail.com

***Abstract*— This paper introduces the concept, use and implementation of method noise in the field of Synthetic Aperture Radar (SAR) image despeckling. Method noise has the capability to enhance the efficiency and performance of any despeckling algorithm. It is easy, efficient and enhanced way of improving the results. The difference between speckled image and despeckled image contains some residual image information which is due to inefficiency of the denoising algorithm. This article will compare the results of some standard methods with and without use of method noise and prove its efficiency and validity. It also shows its best use in different ways of denoising. The results will be compared on the basis of performance metrics like PSNR and SSIM. The concept of method noise is not restricted to only SAR images. It has vast usage and application. It can be used in any denoising procedure such as medical images, optical image etc. but this paper shows the experimental results only on the SAR images. This paper is purely focused on method noise, so other methods and filters mentioned in the paper will not be discussed.**

Keywords—method noise;speckle noise ;SAR image; wavelet thresholding.

I. INTRODUCTION

Image despeckling is an emerging arena of image processing which handles the speckled image by improving it and recovering it to its original SAR image form. SAR is the form of Radar that is fixed on the satellites and aircraft that takes images of high resolution of the broad areas of the earth surface. While capturing such images it has to deal with various weather conditions, day and night, so a special treatment is needed to handle such images because in such case chance of noise intrusion is higher. This granular pattern kind of noise that attacks in such scenario is called as the Speckle noise. SAR images are different from optical images. Since SAR images interact with the ground features in ways different from optical radiation so special treatment is required while interpreting the SAR images. While capturing the broad areas of terrain, SAR has to handle the weather condition, day and night. Unlike optical images, SAR images are formed by the coherent interaction of the transmitted microwave with targets (terrain). This coherent interaction causes random constructive and destructive interference resulting in salt and pepper noise throughout the image.

In the last twenty years, there have been many despeckling techniques established that remove the multiplicative speckle noise and by preserving and enhancing the important details of the image. In satellite imagery, many standard filter are in use with satisfactory outcomes including frost filter [1], kuan filter [2], kuwahara filter [3], [4], lee filter [5],[6], mean filter [7], and median filter [8], but the problem with these conventional methods is that they lose major details during smoothening process. There are other methods projected which are based on the wavelet to diminish the speckle noise in the SAR images [9]-[17]. Wavelet delivers the finest way to isolating the noisy part from the original image as the noise persist in the small coefficients and important information exists in the large coefficients and when wavelet thresholding is applied then it eliminate all the small coefficient part.

It is believed that complete denoising is not possible as any operation; not only denoising, degrades the image up to some extent. Therefore it is needed to perform some sort of preprocessing or post processing to achieve as visually good image as possible. A concept of method noise is introduced in last few years which act as post processing step for enhancing the quality of the image. This method has the advantage of being used in any filtering technique, but mostly used in the case of the inefficient filtering methods. The concept of method noise can be used in any type of image denoising application such as medical image, optical image etc and working of it is also same as discussed here. There are very less but sufficient literature available of method noise usage and implementation. Antoni Buades, Bartomeu Coll and Jean Michel Morel in 2004 [18] presented a paper on image denoising methods where they discussed about the mathematical analysis of the method noise. In 2012, Hua Zhong, Member, Chen Yang, and Xiaohua Zhang [19], introduced a new weight for nonlocal means denoising using method noise. In 2013, B. K. Shreyamsha Kumar [20, 21] used method noise in two different work one one Image denoising based on gaussian/bilateral filter and its method noise thresholding and another on Image denoising based on non-local means filter and its method noise thresholding. In 2016, Manoj kumar and Manoj Diwakar [22], presented a new locally adaptive patch variation based CT image denoising using method noise. In 2017, Prabhishek Singh [23], proposed a homomorphic method using anisotropic diffusion as pre-processing step. Median and wiener filters are used on the approximate part of the image to remove blurring. Method noise thresholding is used to restore the unfiltered part of the despeckled image.

The rest article is divided into three sections: Section II describes the concept and use of method noise, Section III presents the numerical experiments with test results and discussion. Last section concludes the article.

II. Method Noise

A. Concept

All despeckling approaches depend on the filtering constraint 'v'. This constraint measures the degree of filtering applied to the image. For maximum methods, the parameter v depends on an approximation of the noise variance σ^2. Method noise is a kind of a post processing step. It is used after the filtering is applied. It enhances the result and improves the quality of the image. Method noise is simple to understand and implement.

The difference between the noisy image and denoised image shows the residual image information which arises due to the inefficient denoising algorithm, which is called as method noise. Let say, D is the noisy image and after denoising it we get E as the final denoised image. Now mathematically E1 is evaluated by below equation,

$$E1 = D - E \quad (1)$$

Now E1 contains the residual image information, so further any denoising scheme can be applied to E1 like thresholding or any filtering scheme. After denoising E1, let say E2 is achieved. Then below equation is performed to get the resultant denoised image, E3 which contains the lowest noise. The Fig 1 and 2 describes the step by step procedure of using method noise.

$$E3 = E2 + E \quad (2)$$

B. Use

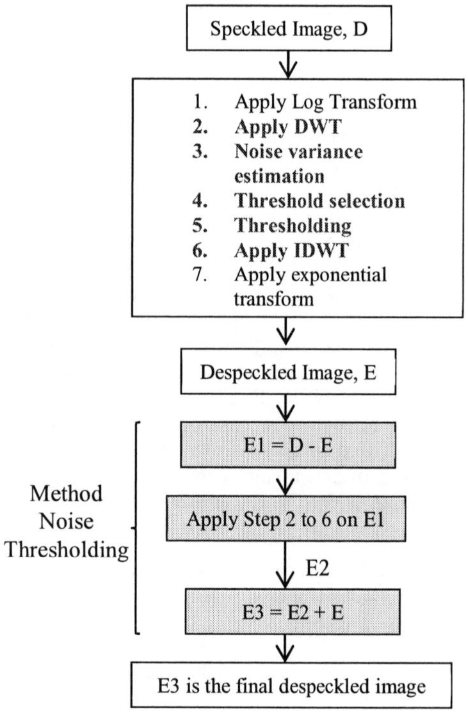

Fig 1. Wavelet based despeckling using method noise thresholding

Method noise can either use thresholding or directly uses any denoising filter. Method noise is a highly adaptive way to improving a degraded image. It is a 100% working method. Any standard or custom filter can be used directly in method noise or even thresholding can be performed on method noise, but it is experimentally observed that use of thresholding on method noise is more efficient than any other denoising method.

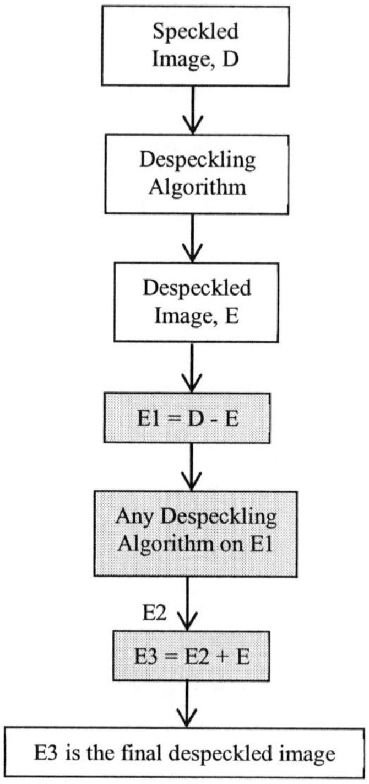

Fig 2. General model of method noise filtering.

III. Numerical Experiments with Results and Discussion

The experimental results are performed in both the cases; with and without method noise and the validity and efficiency of despeckling algorithm using method noise is shown on some real SAR images. The real SAR image is shown in Fig 3(a) and Fig 3(b) shows speckled SAR image at $\sigma = 20$. The SAR image is taken from open public database, i.e., Sandia National Laboratories, Airborne ISR, available at: http://www.sandia.gov/RADAR/imagery/. SAR image is the Ka-band image of a variety of military vehicles in the desert near Albuquerque, NM.

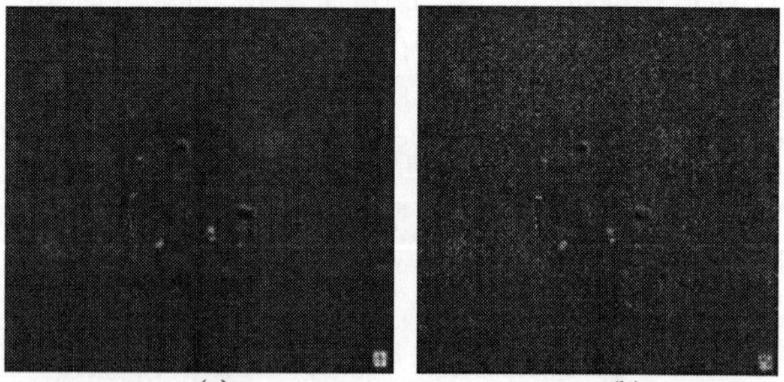

(a) (b)

Fig 3. SAR images. (a) Original SAR image (b) Speckled SAR image

The proposed method resizes the SAR images to 512×512 images for the faster execution of below algorithm. It uses db2 type wavelet basis in dwt2 function of MATLAB. The implementation of the method noise is experimentally performed using almost all the standard methods and filters. Here the resultant SAR images are shown using the db2-DWT thresholding using Bayesian shrinkage rule with and without method noise in the Fig 4(a) and 4(b).

The performance metrics used to analyze the quality of the image are PSNR and SSIM. The mathematical aspects of these measures are available in [17]. Higher the value of PSNR better is the image quality and in SSIM, the value near to 1 indicates the good quality and near to 0 indicates bad quality. These results are shown in Table 1, using various despeckling filters and methods. The comparison is made using methods; frost, homomorphic frost, kuan, homomorphic kuan, lee, homomorphic lee, mean, median, hard and soft thresholding, universal threshold, visu threshold.

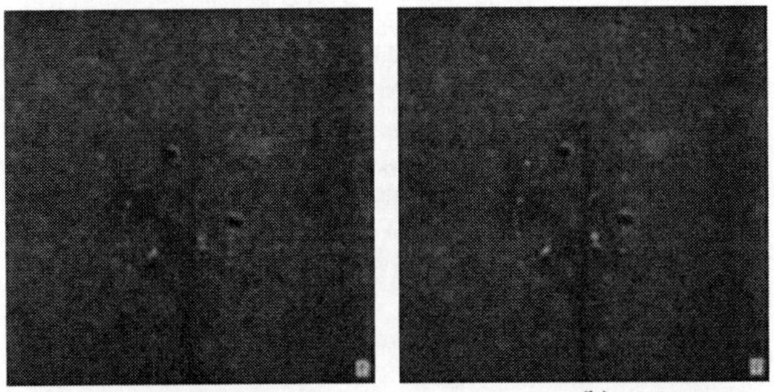

(a) (b)

Fig 4. Despeckled Images (a) without method noise (b) with method noise

The effectiveness of use of method noise can be judged by analyzing the Fig 4 and In Fig 4, it can be seen that Fig b is much clear and smoothen than Fig a. Speckle noise is removed and even edges are well preserved.

Table 1. Performance evaluation of despeckling techniques with and without method noise using PSNR and SSIM

	S. no	Techniques	PSNR w/o method noise	PSNR with method noise	SSIM w/o method noise	SSIM with method noise
Speckled SAR Image Fig 3(b). σ = 20	1	Frost	18.5679	19.0001	0.7006	0.8025
	2	Homomorphic Frost	18.5031	19.5238	0.7309	0.7993
	3	Kuan	18.9513	20.8937	0.7892	0.8002
	4	Homomorphic Kuan	18.1243	18.9937	0.7911	0.8258
	5	Lee	18.4526	19.0023	0.7872	0.8235
	6	Homomorphic Lee	18.8039	18.9790	0.7095	0.7925
	7	Kuwahara	19.6609	20.9008	0.8974	0.9002
	8	Mean	16.0001	16.9909	0.7931	0.8632
	9	Median	16.9278	18.2973	0.8002	0.8403
	10	Soft Thresholding	19.7049	20.7395	0.8901	0.9567
	11	Hard Thresholding	18.8419	19.5637	0.8193	0.8881
	12	Universal Threshold	17.4019	18.6792	0.8991	0.9006
	13	Visu Threshold	16.0002	16.9835	0.8031	0.8563
	14	Bayesian Threshold	19.9509	21.2386	0.9181	0.9500

Fig 5 and 6 shows the plot of PSNR and SSIM of all mentioned despeckling techniques with and without use method noise. In both figures it can be observed that PSNR and SSIM values of the techniques using method noise are higher than techniques without method noise. This shows the validity and effectiveness of method noise.

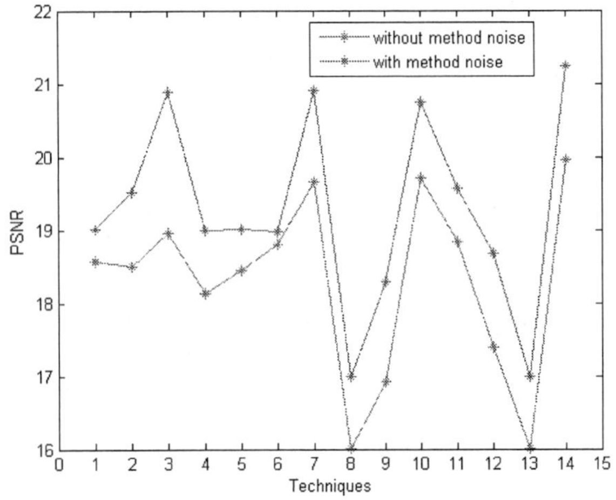

Fig 5. Plotting PSNR of all despeckling techniques with and without method noise.

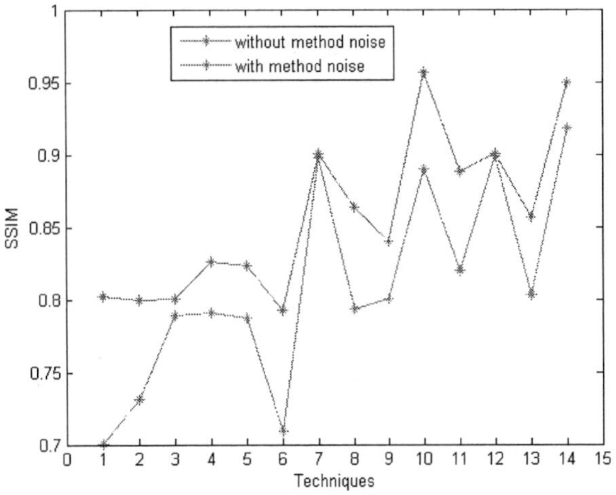

Fig 6. Plotting SSIM of all despeckling techniques with and without method noise.

IV. CONCLUSION AND FUTURE WORK

This paper reviews the concept, use and practical implementation of the method noise. It proves that the use of method noise in any despeckling or denoising algorithm enhances the visual appearance of the restored image and preserves the important details. This paper gives the qualitative and quantitative analysis of the method noise. The tests are performed over the real SAR dataset available at open public databases. The results are shown in images and by using performance metrics like PSNR and SSIM.

There is no limitation of scope of use of method noise either in spatial domain or in transform domain. In transform there the possibility of best use of method noise is higher and much efficient. In DWT, SWT the concept of method noise can be used at approximate and detailed component of the image and even at the last after the algorithm ends. There are many other smart ways of using method noise in transform domain.

REFERENCES

[1] V.S.Frost et al, "A model for radar images and its application to adaptive digital filtering of multiplicative noise", IEEE Trans. Pattern Anal. AndMachine Intell.,vol. PAMI-4, pp.157-166. 1982.

[2] D.T.Kuan et al., "Adaptive restoration of images with speckle", IEEE Trans. Acc. Speech and signal Proc. Vol. 35, no.3 pp.373-383, March 1987.

[3] M. Kuwahara. K. Hachimura, S. Eiho, and M. Kinoshita, "Processing of RI-angiocardiographic images, in Digital Processing of Biomedical Images", K. Preston Jr. and M. Onoe, Editors. New York: Plenum, 1976. pp. 187202.

[4] J. E. Kyprianidis, H. Kang, J. and Dllner ,2009, "Image and Video Abstraction by Anisotropic Kuwahara Filtering". Computer Graphics Forum, 28: 19551963.

[5] J.S.Lee, "Digital image enhancement and noise filtering by use of local statistics", IEEE Trans. On Pattern Analysis and Matching Intelligence, vol. PAMI-2, pp.165- 168, 1980.

[6] J.-S. Lee, "Refined filtering of image noise using local statistics", Comput. Graph. Image Process., vol. 15, no. 2, pp. 380389, Apr. 1981.

[7] Tinku Acharya and Ajoy K. Ray, "Image Processing Principles and Applications", 2005 edition A John Wiley Sons, Mc., Publication.

[8] Anil K.Jain, "Fundamentals of Digital Image Processing", first wdition, 1989, Prentice Hall, Inc.

[9] D. L. Donoho, "De-noising by soft-thresholding," IEEE Trans. Inform. Theor., vol. 41, no. 3, pp. 613–627, May 1995.

[10] L. Gagnon and A. Jouan, "Speckle filtering of SAR images: A comparative study between complex-wavelet-based and standard filters," in Proc. SPIE, Wavelet Applications in Signal and Image processing V, 1997, vol. 3169, pp. 80–91.

[11] E. Hervet, R. Fjørtoft, P. Marthon, and A. Lopès, "Comparison of wavelet-based and statistical speckle filters," in Proc. SPIE SAR Image Analysis, Modelling, and Techniques III, F. Posa, Ed., 1998, vol. 3497, pp. 43–54

[12] M. Simard, G. DeGrandi, K. P. B. Thomson, and G. B. Bénié, "Analysis of speckle noise contribution on wavelet decomposition of SAR images," IEEE Trans. Geosci. Remote Sensing, vol. 36, no. 6, pp. 1953–1962, Nov. 1998.

[13] H. Guo, J. E. Odegard, M. Lang, R. A. Gopinath, I. W. Selesnick, and C. S. Burrus, "Wavelet-based speckle reduction with application to SAR based ATD/R," in Proc. IEEE Int. Conf. Image Processing (ICIP), 1994, vol. 1, pp. 75–79.

[14] J. R. Sveinsson and J. A. Benediktsson, "Almost translation invariant wavelet transformations for speckle reduction of SAR images," IEEE Trans. Geosci. Remote Sensing, vol. 41, no. 510, pp. 2404–2408, Oct. 2003.

[15] Prabhishek Singh, Dr. Raj Shree, "Statistical Modelling of Log Transformed Speckled Image", published online in Vol. 14 No. 8 AUGUST 2016 International Journal of Computer Science and Information Security, (pp. 426-431).

[16] Prabhishek Singh, Raj Shree, "Analysis and effects of speckle noise in SAR images", published in 2nd International Conference on Advances in Computing, Communication, & Automation (ICACCA) (Fall) Year: 2016, Pages: 1 - 5, IEEE Conference Publications.

[17] Prabhishek Singh, Raj Shree, "A New Computationally Improved Homomorphic Despeckling Technique of SAR Images", IJARCS, Volume 8, No. 3, March-April 2017.

[18] Antoni Buades, Bartomeu Coll, Jean Michel Morel, "On image denoising methods", Available: www.ece.lsu.edu/gunturk/EE7700/OnImageDenoisingMethods.pdf

[19] Hua Zhong, Member, IEEE, Chen Yang, and Xiaohua Zhang, Member, IEEE, "A New Weight for Nonlocal Means Denoising Using Method Noise", IEEE SIGNAL PROCESSING LETTERS, VOL. 19, NO. 8, AUGUST 2012.

[20] B. K. Shreyamsha Kumar, "Image denoising based on gaussian/bilateral filter and its method noise thresholding", SIViP (2013) 7:1159–1172 DOI 10.1007/s11760-012-0372-7.

[21] B. K. Shreyamsha Kumar, "Image denoising based on non-local means filter and its method noise thresholding", SIViP DOI 10.1007/s11760-012-0389-y.

[22] Manoj Kumar, Manoj Diwakar,"A New Locally Adaptive Patch Variation Based CT Image Denoising", International Journal of Image, Graphics and Signal Processing(IJIGSP), Vol.8, No.1, pp.43-50, 2016.DOI: 10.5815/ijigsp.2016.01.05.

[23] Singh, P., Shree, R. A new homomorphic and method noise thresholding based despeckling of SAR image using anisotropic diffusion. Journal of King Saud University – Computer and Information Sciences (2017), http://dx.doi.org/10.1016/j.jksuci.2017.06.006

Transition in Step Network Through Simulation Tool

Taskeen Zaidi, Nitya Nand Dwivedi

***Abstract*— IPV6 is next generation protocol developed by Internet Engineering Task Force(IETF) for the replacement of existing IPV4 due to address depletion and security issues. Transition mechanisms drafted by IETF Next Generation Transition Working Group(NGtrans) to replace IPV4 with IPV6.Transition mechanism include dual stack ,header translation and tunneling. The current work is based on IPv4 to IPv6 transition mechanisms through tunneling on static step network. This paper describes the design and simulation scenario between devices of a network configured with IPv6 protocol, employing tunneling as transition mechanisms all that on the network simulator tool GNS3 and live traffic flow analysis through wireshark.

Index Terms*— *IPv6-IPv4, tunneling, RIP,GNS3,wireshark

I. Introduction

Host and routers connected in dual stack method may use tunneling to route IPV6 packets by IPV4 region. The tunneling can be done in different ways through connectivity between router-router, host-router, host-host ,router-host. In router to router and host-router mechanism IPV6 packet is tunneled through a router and there is no relation between router source address and final destination address so tunnel is configured manually. In host-host and router to host IPV6/IPV4 packets tunnel from a host or a router to destination and the tunnel endpoint address and final destination host address is same so tunnel is configured automatically.

IPV4 and IPV6 addresses and header format are well explained in [1].IPV4 to IPV6 transition was performed on a campus Network to reduce cost by Dai[2]. Internet service providers (ISPs), home networking equipment manufacturers, and web companies around the world united to redefine the global Internet and permanently use IPv6 for their products and services[3] to provide large range of IP addresses and services. Author[4] explained the necessity of IPV6 use and deployed transition strategies like dual stack, IPv6 and NAT IPv4 for customers and combinations of IPv6, IPv4 and NAT to translate IPV4 data to IPV6. Shortcoming of IPV4 addresses and need for migration to IPV6 is well explained as well as the article analyzed the impact of IPV6 on real time communication during transition[5]. Authors[6] have analyzed the performance of running multimedia applications on IPv4 and the compared with IPv6 and it is observed that IPV6 with dual stack infrastructure performed better than IPV4 during real time communication. The IPV4 to IPV6 transition strategies are implemented by the authors[7] through simulation tool with testing and verifications . On 8 June 2011, IPV4 came in existence as a successor to IPV4 to solve address depletion problem as a next generation protocol [8]. Configuring IPV4 network with transition mechanism to IPV6 is well explained [9]. TCP/IP operations, network applications, network maintenance and network utilization through TCP/IP suite is well explained in[10]. A survey[11] has been conducted on IPV4 to IPV6 transition mechanism in which IPV4 address depletion problem ,need of IPV6 addresses were surveyed and transition mechanisms were also studied. The research paper [12] focused on the most concepts of the IPv6 transition mechanism i.e. addressing, address allocation, routing with the RIPng protocol, the dual stack and tunneling mechanism is implemented on packet tracer and performance of network was monitored through GNS3. The structural optimization has been done in [13] to minimize the function and to satisfy set of constraints. A new kind of static step topology proposed by Zaidi and Saxena[14] for interconnections of devices in distributed environment. Zaidi and Saxena [15] have validated the execution of task in distributed manner on step network using a state transition model. Authors [16,17] have estimated the performance of step network on OPNET modeler tool by routing different types of packets through queuing mechanism and analyzed delay, traffic sent and received etc. in network.

In the present paper Router-router tunnel has been created on step network through which IPV6/IPV4 routers are interconnected by IPV4 region and IPV6 packets encapsulated between them. A manual tunnel has been created through GNS3 and performance is estimated on wireshark.

II. Background

A. Step Topology

A new kind of topology called as step topology as shown in figure 1 proposed by Zaidi and Saxena[15]for interconnection of handheld devices in step manner which may be desktop computer systems, laptops, mobile, etc. This topology is modification of bus topology and ladder topology by varying the steps that interconnect N numbers of computer systems. This topology works well if the link between two computers connected through bus topology fails. In this topology if individual node is busy then tasks can be executed on next node by using message passing technique and the devices can be connected through wired as well as through wireless network.

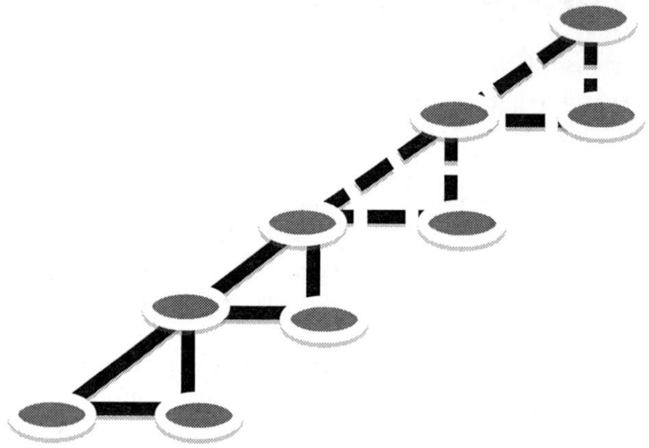

Figure 1:Step Topology

This Internet Protocol Version 4 having unique 32 bit numeric identifier. Each client can be recognized over internet for this version. Its address scheme having 2^32 addresses means it can manage 4 billion addresses over an internet. Each address of this version represented in the form of decimal notation and binary notation. In decimal notation representation is through 4 octets in decimal numbers separated by periods.

B. IPv6

IPV4 protocol has some demerits like address depletion problem, not suitable for real time communications as well as with less security parameters like encryption and authentication. So IPV6 was proposed by to overcome the demerits of IPV4 which was modified to provide better format and length of IP addresses as well as protocols like ICMP is

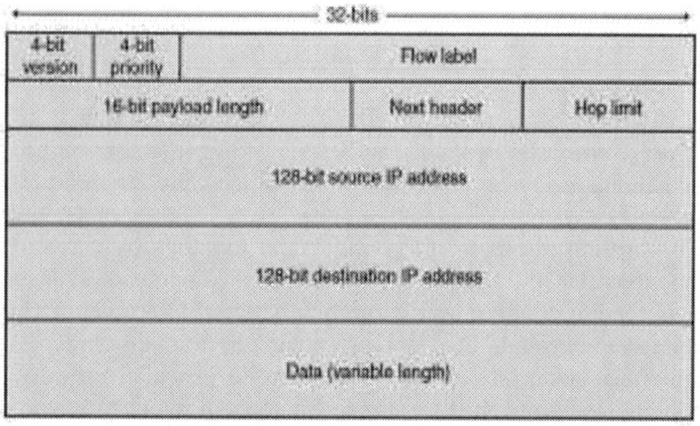

also modified and protocols of network layer like ARP, RARP and IGMP are deleted or included with ICMPv6 protocol.
Due to the faster growth of internet and its service like mobile IP, VoIP, videoconferencing the IPv4 will be soon replaced with IPv6.The IPv6 provides larger address space ,better header format, new options ,larger extension, resource allocation and more security than IPv4 protocol.

Figure 2:IPv6 header format[1]

IPv6 Address Format

IPv6 address is 128 bits long specified in hexadecimal notation and 128 bits is divided into 8 section. The leading zeros in IPv6 address can be omitted but trailing zeros couldn't. The IPv6 provides 2^{128} addresses and it may be categorized into unicast, multicast, allycast, reserved and local address.

III.GNS3

GNS3 is a open source software Simulation tool that is useful for graphical representation of virtual and real devices in a complex network. In GNS3 cisco IOS are emulated using Dynamips.GNS3 has GUI part and this GUI provides interface to the users that allows them to build complex networks using a variety of supported Cisco routers.

The large organization used GNS3 like NASA, Walmart, AT&T and so on.

IV.WIRESHARK

Wireshark is a network protocol analyzer tool formally called as Ethereal and which capture and analyzed performance of the network in real time communication and display data in human readable format. This tool captures the packets through color coding and filters inspect the packet belonging to data link layer, network layer, transport layer and application layer. The bottom pane shows raw frame having hexadecimal values on left and ASCII values on right.

IV.ROUTING

In IPv6 can routing may follow two methods either static routing or dynamic routing.

1- Static routes are manual routes defined by the administrator so the router learns about a source and destination in a remote network, and are usually used when the routing is processed from a network to a single connection network accessible by only one route.
2- dynamic routes are automatically configured , IPv6 uses updated versions of the same routing protocols available for IPv4 like RIPng, EIGRP for IPv6, IS-IS for IPv6, MPBGP4 (Multi-Protocol BGP) and OSPFv3.

V.TRANSITION

Transition from IPv4 to IPv6 is not instant process but require several years, the migration from IPv4 protocol to IPv6 protocol are implemented through some transition mechanisms like tunneling, dual stack and header translation.
Dual stack: In this method IPv4 & IPv6 protocols are implemented on each node in the network;, each node have two addresses, one is used for IPv4 and other assigned for IPv6. It is easy to implement and is widely accepted; but it has the drawback that the network topology requires two tables and two routing processes.

Tunneling: In tunneling, IPv6 traffic is encapsulated inside IPv4 packets. IPv4 source is the own local router, and the destination will be the router connected at the end of the tunnel. In this mechanism when the destination router receives the IPv4 packet, it encapsulates and sends forwards the IPv6 traffic that was encapsulated. The step network connectivity is shown in figure 2.

IV. EXPERIMENTAL STUDY

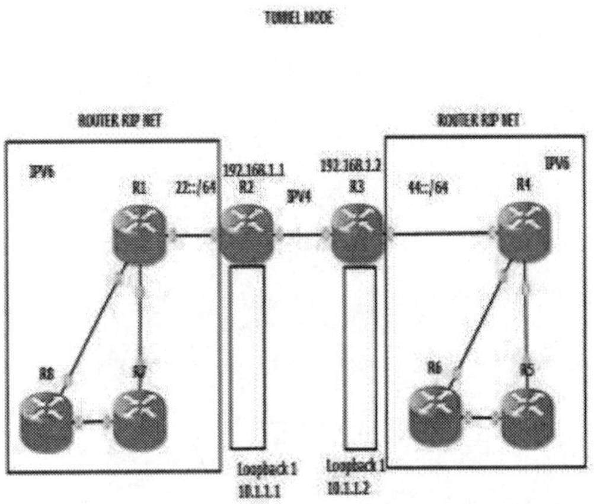

Figure: 3. Tunneling in Step Network

1). Set Address of ipv6 and ipv4 Router:

First step is to set address of ipv6 and ipv4 router (R1 & R4), for this process we are following some steps ,given below in figure 3;

R1#conf t
Enter configuration commands, one per line. End with CNTL/Z.

R1(config)#int f 1/0

R1(config-if)#ipv6 address 22::1/64

R1(config-if)#no shutdown

R1(config-if)#exit

R1(config)#int lo1

R1(config-if)#ipv6 address 11::1/64

R1(config)#int lo2

R1(config-if)#ipv6 address AA::1/64

R1(config-if)#exit

R1(config)#exit

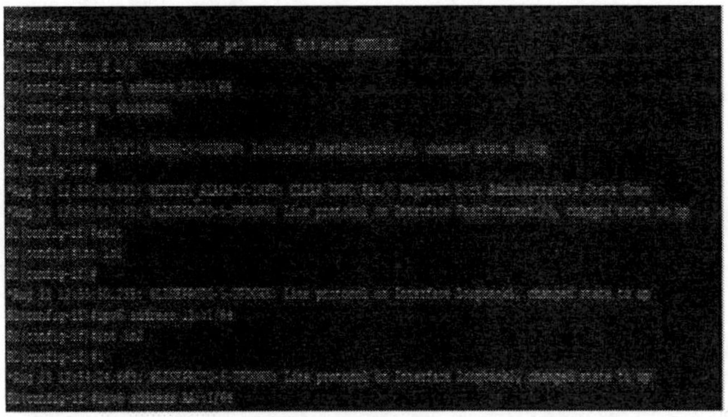

Figure: 4.:IPV6 and IPV4 address configuration

After addressing we show all connection by this given manner in figure 4:

R1#sh ipv6 int b

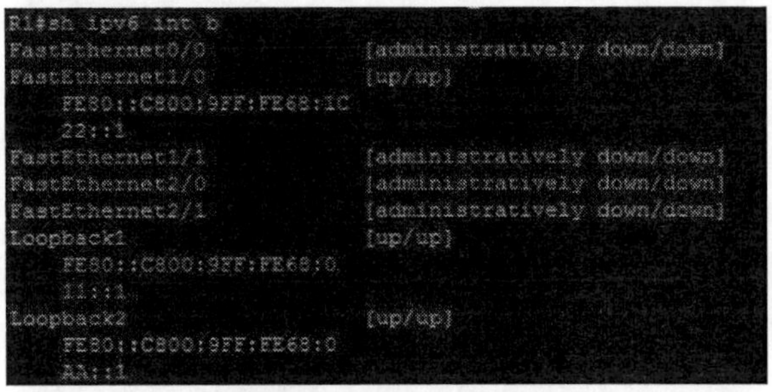

Figure: 5.IPV6 interface

2). Tunnel Creation:

For transition from IPV4 –IPV6 a tunnel is created and encapsulates IPV6 traffic inside IPV4 at the same time. IPV4 source router is local and destination router will be at the tunnel end. Destination router receives the IPV4 packet, encapsulate it and forward to IPV6.

Tunnel creation step is given below:
R3#config t
R3 (config)#int tunnel 23
R3 (config-if)#

Figure: 6 Tunnel creation

3). Router RIPng:

Routing Information Protocol Next Generation (RIPng) used for IPv6 which is updated versions of the routing protocols available for IPv4 (RIP);. the routing steps are given below in figure 5;
R3#config t
R3 (config)#ipv6
R3 (config-if)#ipv6 router rip net

R3 (config-rtr)#exit
R3 (config)int f 1/0
R3 (config-if)#ipv6 rip net enable

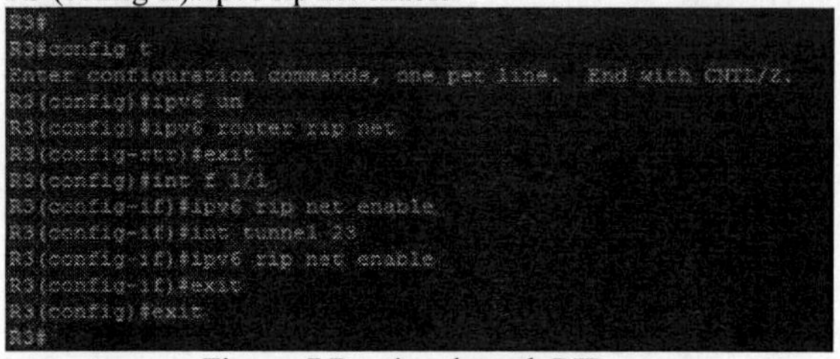

Figure: 7 Routing through RIPng

4). Testing:

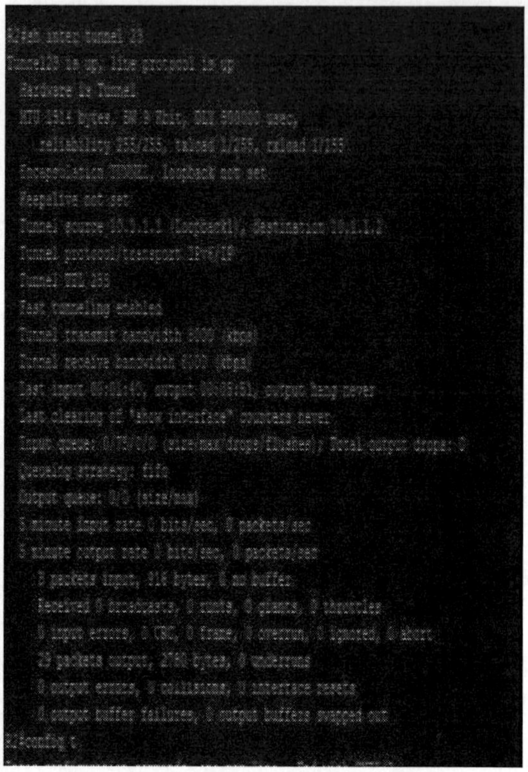

Figure 8(a) Tunnel testing

Router 1 and Router 4 Connection Testing:

Figure 8(b) Tunnel testing

R1 & R4 Connection

Router 2 and Router 3 Packet Testing :

R2 & R3 Connection

Figure 8(c) Tunnel testing

Figure 8: Performance results on Wireshark

VI. CONCLUDING REMARKS

IPV6 networks overcome the limitations of IPV4 with a better header format, new functionalities and wide range of addresses. Transition mechanisms are used to run IPV4 and IPV6 addresses in same infrastructure according to organization needs. In the current work a manual tunnel is created which is a secure mechanism for ISPs, datacenters to transfer packets. The manual tunnel provides better QoS network and experimental results show that tunneling mechanism solves the problem of internet growth and live report of traffic has been analyzed through wireshark simulation tool.In future work we will analyzed the causes of broken IPV6.

REFERENCES

[1]. Forouzan, B. A., 2006.Data Communications and Networks, Tata McGraw Hill.

[2]Kuobin Dai.; "IPv4 to IPv6 Transition Research Based on the Campus Network", 2nd International Symposium on Intelligence Information Processing and Trusted Computing, 2011.

[3] IPv6 users' site: http://www.ipv6.org, accessed on 14/9/2017.

[4]Philip Smith.; "IPv6 Transition Strategies", APRICOT Singapore, 19th Feb – 1st March 2013.

[5]http://www.polycom.com/global/documents/whitepapers/ipv4-to-ipv6-migration-whietpaper.pdf

[6] Ummi Suraya Shaharuddin, Ruhani Ab Rahman, Murizah Kassim, Mat Ikram Yusof, "Performance comparison of multimedia applications over IPv4 and IPv6 Dual stack technology", *Frontiers of Information Technology (FIT) 2016 International Conference on*, pp. 1-6, 2016.

[7] Trúchly Peter, Helebrandt Pavol, Danielovič Lukáš, "Implementation and evaluation of IPv6 to IPv4 transition mechanisms in network simulator 3", *Systems Signals and Image Processing (IWSSIP) 2016 International Conference on*, pp. 1-4, 2016, ISSN 2157-8702.

[8] http://www.worldipv6launch.org/

[9]http://www.networkworld.com/community/blog/configuringipv6- routing-through-ipv4-micros.

[10] W. Richard Stevens, TCP/IP Illustrated, Volume 1: The Protocols, First Edition December 15, 1993

[11] Peng Wu, Yong Cui, Jianping Wu, Jiangchuan Liu, Chrisetz, Transition from IPv4 to IPv6: A State-of-the-Art Survey, IEEE COMMUNICATIONS SURVEYS & TUTORIALS.

[12] Lefty Valle-Rosado, Lizzie Narváez-Díaz, Cinhtia González-Segura, Victor Chi-Pech , "Design and Simulation of an IPv6 Network Using Two Transition Mechanisms", International Journal of Computer Science Issues (IJCSI); Vol. 9 Issue 6, Nov.2012.

[13] J. E. Akin and J. Arjona-Baez. Enhancing structural topology optimization, *Engineering Computations* 18(3-4): pp. *663- 675.* 2001.

[14] Zaidi T. and Saxena, V., "Step Topology for Static Interconnection of Computer Systems under Distributed Environment", 3rd World Conference on Information Technology organized by University of Bercelona, Nov. 14-17, 2012.

[15] Zaidi, T. and Saxena, V., "Modeling and Validation of Execution of Tasks on High Speed Network under Distributed Environment",ACM SIGSOFT (ISSN No.: 0163-5948),USA, Vol. 38(3), PP. 1-6, May (2013), http://dl.acm.org/citation.cfm?id=2464540&dl=ACM&coll=DL&CFID=365362445&CFTOKEN=46914 359.

[16] Zaidi, T.and Saxena, V., "Performance Estimation of Static StepTopology Across Distributed Network Environment",ACM SIGSOFT (ISSN No.: 0163-5948),USA, Vol. 39(6), (2014, Nov.),doi:10.1145/2674632.2674644.

[17] Zaidi. T and Nityanand"Performance of Step Network Using Simulation Tool" International Journal of Computer Science and Information Security, Vol. 14 No.10. October 2017.

Pair-Wise Selection Approach for Test Case Prioritization in Regression Testing

Shilpi Singh
Department of Information Technology
Babasaheb Bhimrao Ambedkar University
Lucknow, 226025, India
shilpi.singh.it@gmail.com

Raj Shree
Department of Information Technology
Babasaheb Bhimrao Ambedkar University
Lucknow, 226025, India
rajshree.bbau2009@gmail.com

***Abstract*—Software regression testing is one of the essential phases of software development lifecycle used by developers to validate software before the next release. Executing all test cases may be impractical in regression testing under limited time and resources. History reveals that coverage based test case prioritization techniques do not always give satisfactory results. In this context, we propose a pair-wise similarity based test case prioritization approach. The approach reorganizes the execution order of test cases based on the similarity value of test case pairs computed in three levels. Each level represents the integration of selected coverage criteria. We designed and conducted empirical studies on a standard case study to validate the effectiveness of our proposed techniques. The result shows that by incorporating similarity-based approach with multiple coverage criteria; prioritization can be more effective than any other proposed coverage based approach in terms of APFD.**

Keywords—regression testing; test cases; test case prioritization; similarity-based; APFD

I. Introduction

Regression testing is a very complex activity in perspective of time and cost. More than 50% of the cost is used in software maintenance phase [4]. With the continuous advancement in software systems, test suites often grow very large and it is impractical to re-execute all test cases within limited time and resources. Various optimization techniques have been proposed to solve the above problem, where, the test case prioritization is one of them that reorders test cases according to some selected specific criteria, such that the test cases with higher coverage are executed earlier [1, 5]. The aim of any prioritization technique is to increase the possibility of meeting certain criteria by the resultant test suite with earlier fault detection ability. Utilizing code coverage information as selection criteria, coverage-based test case prioritization reorders the test cases to maximize code coverage as early as possible [1]. However, previous studies show that in some cases, code coverage as selection criteria is not sufficient to guarantee a high fault detection rate [6].

In recent years, similarity-based test case prioritization techniques, combining clustering approach [7], ART-approach [8] and other similarity-based prioritization [9], have gained more attention. Similarity-based test case prioritization techniques primarily concentrated on test case diversity that helps to detect more faults [10, 11]. But, most of the techniques use single criteria to measure the diversity between test case pairs that are not sufficient to get an optimal result. However, the optimal test suite is best generated by multiple coverage criteria [12, 13].

In this paper, we describe several similarity-based prioritization techniques based on pair-wise selection strategy. Pair wise comparison of test cases is a fundamental strategy to inspect test cases and choose an association between them in a finite test set. Our technique evaluates the similarity degree for each test case pair in three levels and accordingly assigns the execution order to the test cases in a test suite. We also empirically evaluate their improvement in fault detection rate that let developers initiate debugging and amending faults before the release of any software product. The results show that some of the proposed techniques can attain higher fault detection rate, in terms of APFD, in comparison with the other considered techniques and random ordering.

The rest of the paper is organized as follows. Section II illustrates the background of the proposed work. After that, we presented our proposed test case prioritization techniques in Section III, followed by an experimental evaluation in Section IV. Finally, we conclude this paper in Section V.

II. Background

A. Test Case Prioritization

Test case prioritization represents one of the regression testing techniques with the aim of improving the rate of fault detection of a test suite. The technique encourages software quality assurance by improving the chance of earlier execution of the essential test cases. That results in earlier detection of faults as well as earlier initiation of debugging process. The test case prioritization problem is framed as follows [1]:

Given: a test suite TS; the set of permutations PT of TS; and, a function f from PT to the set of all real numbers.

Problem: To find $TS' \in PT$ such that, $\forall TS'' \in PT \Rightarrow f(TS') \geq f(TS'')$.

B. Coverage Similarity

The test case pair is said to be similar, if they are identical in terms of some selected criteria, where, the criteria may be coverage also. Coverage might be a branch, statement, def-use, control-flow, MC/DC, function, path, and data flow etc.

We can apply more than one criterion to measure the similarity value, which represents how much the test case pair is identical to each other [12, 15]. With the help of coverage similarity, any prioritization technique can improve the ordering of test cases which may also increase the fault detection rate.

III. Proposed Approach

In this section, we present our proposed test case prioritization techniques, mainly includes four steps:

Instrumentation: Collect coverage information (statement, MC/DC, and branch coverage) for test suite by executing the test cases over software system.

Distance calculation: Calculate the distance between test case pair for each criterion.

Calculate integrated similarity values for each test case pair: integrate the similarity values of test case pairs for each criterion.

Apply prioritization techniques and calculate APFD: Apply techniques to order the test cases and then evaluate fault detection effectiveness of prioritized test suite.

A. Test Case Similarity

The objective of the similarity based test suite prioritization strategy is to order the test cases based on the similarity values among them. The similarity degree between each pair of test cases is calculated by certain distance measure. The resultant ordered test suite must satisfy the coverage requirements as the original one. Hence, the goal is to achieve maximum requirement coverage and higher fault detection rate by the ordered test cases.

Cartaxo et al. [14] define a distance measure that calculates the similarity degree between a pair of test cases stated as paths.

$$Similarity\ function[i,j] = nit/Avg(|i|, |j|) \tag{1}$$

Where nit represents the number of identical transition and (|i|, |j|) represents the average transition between path lengths. With the help of the calculated similarity degree of each pair of test cases the $n \times n$ square similarity matrix is created, where n is the number of paths and each path represented as i $(1 \leq i \geq n)$ is called a test case.

Definition 1: Coverage - Set; a Coverage-Set of any test case T is a set of coverage triples$\{\langle s_1, m_1, b_1\rangle, \langle s_2, m_2, b_2\rangle, \ldots, \langle s_n, m_n, b_n\rangle\}$, where a triple $\langle s_i, m_i, b_i\rangle$ signifies a statement coverage specification s_i, modified decision/condition coverage (MC/DC) m_i, and a branch specification b_i. Let $(T) = \{s_1, s_2, \ldots, s_n\}$, $M(T) = \{m_1, m_2, \ldots, m_n\}$, and $B(T) = \{b_1, b_2, \ldots, b_n\}$, represent the set of statement coverage specifications, the set of MC/DC specification, and the set of branch specification, exercised in the execution of test case t to validate the software to be tested, respectively. Here coverage set may be of more than three coverage criteria which absolutely depend on user's choice. We further explain the coverage similarity in Definition 2.

Definition 2: Coverage Similarity; we represent three steps of evaluating similarity degree between two test cases T_i and T_j i.e. (i) Statement similarity specification (CS-I), (ii) MC/DC similarity specification and statement similarity specification (CS-II), and (iii) Branch, statement, and MC/DC similarity specification (CS-III).

Let the Coverage Set of any test case pair T_i and T_j be $\langle S_i, M_i, B_i\rangle$and $\langle S_j, M_j, B_j\rangle$ respectively. Let the distance between statement, MC/DC and branch coverage of the test case pair T_i and T_j be $\pi(S_i, S_j), \pi(M_i, M_j)$ and $\pi(B_i, B_j)$. Where, the distance is calculated by applying Eq.1. The proposed techniques use the 'Geometric Mean' to evaluate the integrated similarity degree between each pair of test cases T_i and T_j, which is calculated in three steps:

Step 1: $$CS - I = \pi(S_i, S_j) \tag{2}$$

Step 2: $$CS - II = \sqrt[2]{\pi(S_i, S_j) \times \pi(M_i, M_j)} \tag{3}$$

Step 3: $$CS - II = \sqrt[3]{\pi(S_i, S_j) \times \pi(M_i, M_j) \times \pi(B_i, B_j)} \tag{4}$$

However, we demonstrate our techniques using three criteria, but it is also flexible to simplify the above equations to function on more than three criteria.

B. Test Case Prioritization

Our proposed technique uses similarity degree between each pair of test cases to rank the test cases.

Suppose we have a test suite 'TS' of 'm' number of test cases. Select all possible pairs of different test cases and divide them into K different groups. Each group comprising test case pairs with the same similarity value and it is designated by G_k $(1 \leq k \leq K)$, where k represents the group index. A smaller k specifies all test case pairs of that group having maximum similarity value.

The proposed similarity based prioritization techniques are illustrated as follows:

a) PS1 (Total CS-i similarity prioritization): The technique generates K different groups of test case pairs using their similarity values CS-i. At first, a test case pair of maximum similarity value is selected and chooses any one test case T from that pair randomly. Continuously all the pairs containing T were selected from the same group. In case of a tie, the technique arbitrarily picks one pair to break this. Repetitively, the above process is executed initially for the group, and once every test cases have been selected from that group, then the other remaining groups are processed in the ascending order until every single test case has been selected.

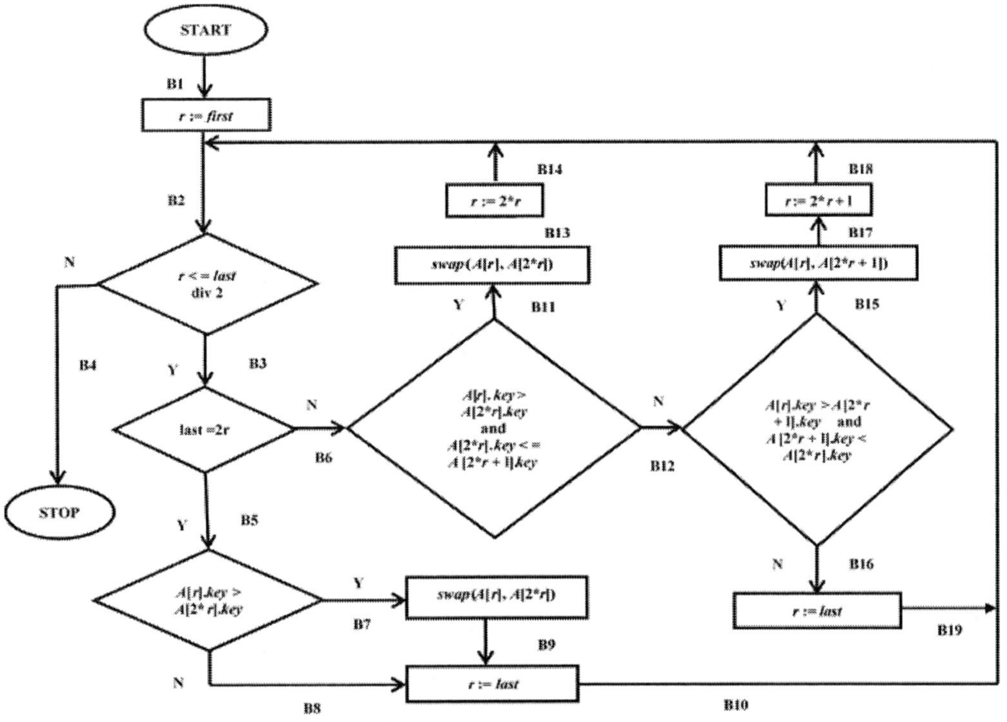

Fig. 1. Control flow diagram of pushdown procedure

b) PS2 (Total CS-i dissimilarity prioritization): The technique is similar to PS1, apart from the selection process for test case pair having minimum similarity values, and the above process is executed in ascending order of the index for remaining groups.

c) PS3 (Iterative CS-i dissimilarity prioritization): In descending order ($G_m to\ G_1$) of the group index, the technique selects one test case pair from each group. Excluding the selected pairs, the above selection process repeats on the remaining groups until every test cases have been included for prioritization purpose.

d) PS4 (Iterative CS-i similarity prioritization): This technique is equivalent to the above technique i.e. PS3, apart from the test pair selection process from each group is in ascending order of the group index ($G_1 to\ G_m$) instead of in descending order.

e) PS5 (Advanced iterative CS-i dissimilarity prioritization): The technique select one test case pair (T_a, T_b) from group G_m and then the further test case pairs are selected containing T_a or T_b, if available, from each group in descending order of the remaining groups ($G_{m-1} to\ G_1$). Afterwards, the selected test case pair from the group is to be removed. For each remaining groups, this technique reiterates the above discussed selection process until all the test cases have been included for prioritization purpose.

f) PS6 (Advanced Iterative CS-i similarity prioritization): This technique is similar to the above technique i.e. PS3, apart from that the selection process of test case pair from each group is executed in ascending order of the group index ($G_1 to\ G_m$), instead of in descending order.

IV. Experimental Result And Discussion

This section presents the experimentation and evaluation of the proposed prioritization techniques. The experimentation compares the relative performance and effectiveness of the proposed techniques with some standard state-of-the-art prioritization techniques [1].

A. Subject Program

Fig. 1 presents a control flow diagram of the standard pushdown procedure [3], a case study on which the proposed techniques have been performed to evaluate the performance. This work also uses hand-seeded faults [2] for the subject program. We have inserted different types of errors in the faulty version of the subject program which is represented by fault matrix (see Table I). In the proposed work, three different coverage criteria i.e. statement, MC/DC, and branch coverage are used to evaluate the distance between the pair of test cases. Based on the calculated distance (similarity degree) values, further prioritization will be processed. To collect the coverage information of test cases for each selected criterion, the subject program and the source code were instrumented.

B. Effectiveness Measure

The performance metric "average percentage of faults detected" (APFD) introduced by Elbaum et al. [1] has been widely used to evaluate any prioritization techniques. A Higher value of APFD concludes improved fault detection rates.

Let TS be a test suite of n test cases, F represents a set of k faults exposed by test suite, and TF_i signifies that the fault i reveals by the first test case of the prioritized test suite TS'. The equation to calculate APFD value for test suite TS' is as follows:

$$APFD = 1 - \frac{TF_1 + TF_2 + \cdots + TF_m}{nm} + \frac{1}{2n} \quad (5)$$

TABLE I. FAULT MATRIX FOR PUSHDOWN PROCEDURE

Test Cases	F1	F2	F3	F4	F5	F6	F7
T1		×	×				
T2	×	×		×			
T3	×	×		×	×	×	
T4	×					×	
T5		×	×				
T6							
T7		×	×				
T8	×			×			
T9	×					×	
T10	×	×		×	×		
T11		×	×				
T12	×	×				×	×
× designate fault is revealed and blank cell indicates fault is not revealed							

C. Experimental Evaluation and Comparison

Before applying any prioritization techniques, the distance between each pair of test cases must be calculated by using Eq. 1. Table II displays the computed similarity values of test case pairs for each selected criterion. We evaluate the similarity values of every possible test case pairs in three levels using Eq-2, Eq-3, and Eq-4 in Tables III. We observe from Tables III that, the similarity values between test case pair are relatively different at each level. These values illustrate that use of more than one criterion in similarity-based approach gives the optimal result as compare to conventional prioritization techniques.

With the help of these coverage similarity values, further prioritization techniques are applied to get ordered test cases. We use Table IV to show the results of different pair-wise test case prioritization techniques (PS1 to PS6) using CS-I similarity values. By considering those similarity values, the different test case pairs of T1 to T12 are categorized into different groups (see leftmost columns of Table IV). By implementing each technique from PS1 – PS6, the possible ordering of test case pairs is shown in the rightmost columns of Table IV. Similarly, all the mentioned prioritization techniques are also applied to CS-II and C-III similarity values.

We also analyze the results of proposed as well as conventional techniques on the subject program in Table V. For each technique, we deliver a valid ordering of test cases in Table V. For single test case prioritization techniques i.e. S2, S3, and S4, we use three coverage metrics (i.e., Statement, MC/DC, and Branch) to order the test cases. And, for similar test pair prioritization techniques i.e. from PS1 to PS6, we use the coverage similarity metrics i.e. CS-I, CS-II, and CS-III to order the test cases.

To validate the results, we measure the APFD value of the prioritized test suite by each technique using Eq. 5. For example, the resulting APFD's for the three test case orders (for Random, Total-St Coverage, and Advanced Iterative CS-i Dissimilarity Prioritization) are 62.56%, 38.62%, and 72.0%, respectively. The test order by PS-5 is, in fact, an optimal ordering of the test suite in comparison to the test order by S-1 (random) and S-2, ensuring the earliest discovery of the maximum faults. The APFD percentage illustrates that the similarity based prioritization techniques give a better result as compared to the other conventional techniques. The analysis of different prioritization techniques is illustrated in Table V.

TABLE II. SIMILARITY VALUES OF TEST CASE PAIRS FOR EACH CRITERION

Test Cases		T1	T2	T3	T4	T5	T6	T7	T8	T9	T10	T11	T12
T1	Stmt.		0.55	0.25	0.27	0.83	0.33	1.00	0.27	0.50	0.67	0.83	0.60
	MC/DC		0.37	0.20	0.22	0.60	0.33	1.00	0.25	0.33	0.57	0.60	0.50
	Branch		0.46	0.25	0.26	0.66	0.33	1.00	0.26	0.42	0.66	0.66	0.61
T2	Stmt.			0.55	0.33	0.62	0.40	0.55	0.60	0.54	0.88	0.62	0.50
	MC/DC			0.50	0.27	0.57	0.37	0.37	0.62	0.50	0.75	0.57	0.36
	Branch			0.53	0.29	0.54	0.41	0.46	0.57	0.53	0.76	0.63	0.41
T3	Stmt.				0.70	0.27	0.50	0.25	0.70	0.63	0.50	0.27	0.58
	MC/DC				0.66	0.20	0.33	0.20	0.55	0.60	0.50	0.20	0.60
	Branch				0.64	0.26	0.42	0.25	0.64	0.60	0.50	0.26	0.56
T4	Stmt.					0.30	0.75	0.27	0.60	0.70	0.30	0.30	0.63
	MC/DC					0.22	0.57	0.22	0.44	0.66	0.27	0.22	0.66
	Branch					0.28	0.72	0.26	0.57	0.64	0.27	0.28	0.60
T5	Stmt.						0.37	0.83	0.30	0.55	0.55	1.00	0.50
	MC/DC						0.33	0.60	0.25	0.50	0.37	1.00	0.33

	Branch						0.36	0.66	0.28	0.58	0.46	1.00	0.42
T6	**Stmt.**							0.33	0.75	0.50	0.36	0.37	0.45
	MC/DC							0.33	0.66	0.33	0.37	0.33	0.33
	Branch							0.33	0.72	0.42	0.33	0.36	0.40
T7	**Stmt.**								0.27	0.50	0.66	0.83	0.60
	MC/DC								0.25	0.33	0.57	0.60	0.50
	Branch								0.26	0.42	0.66	0.66	0.61
T8	**Stmt.**									0.41	0.54	0.30	0.38
	MC/DC									0.27	0.62	0.25	0.27
	Branch									0.35	0.53	0.28	0.33
T9	**Stmt.**										0.50	0.55	0.90
	MC/DC										0.36	0.50	0.77
	Branch										0.41	0.63	0.78
T10	**Stmt.**											0.55	0.58
	MC/DC											0.37	0.50
	Branch											0.46	0.56
T11	**Stmt.**												0.40
	MC/DC												0.33
	Branch												0.42

TABLE III. TEST CASE SIMILARITY VALUES FOR TEST CASE PAIR USING E-2, E-3, AND E-4.

Test Cases	Levels	T1	T2	T3	T4	T5	T6	T7	T8	T9	T10	T11	T12
T1	CS-I		0.55	0.25	0.27	0.83	0.33	1.00	0.27	0.50	0.67	0.83	0.60
	CS-II		0.45	0.22	0.24	0.70	0.33	1.00	0.25	0.40	0.61	0.70	0.54
	CS-III		0.45	0.23	0.24	0.69	0.33	1.00	0.25	0.41	0.63	0.69	0.56
T2	CS-I			0.55	0.33	0.62	0.40	0.55	0.60	0.54	0.88	0.62	0.50
	CS-II			0.52	0.29	0.59	0.38	0.45	0.60	0.51	0.81	0.59	0.42
	CS-III			0.52	0.29	0.57	0.39	0.45	0.59	0.52	0.79	0.60	0.41
T3	CS-I				0.70	0.27	0.50	0.25	0.70	0.63	0.50	0.27	0.58
	CS-II				0.67	0.23	0.40	0.22	0.62	0.61	0.5	0.23	0.58
	CS-III				0.66	0.24	0.41	0.23	0.62	0.60	0.5	0.24	0.57
T4	CS-I					0.30	0.75	0.27	0.60	0.70	0.30	0.30	0.63
	CS-II					0.25	0.65	0.24	0.51	0.67	0.28	0.25	0.64
	CS-III					0.26	0.67	0.24	0.53	0.66	0.27	0.26	0.62
T5	CS-I						0.37	0.83	0.30	0.55	0.55	1.00	0.50
	CS-II						0.34	0.70	0.27	0.52	0.45	1.00	0.40
	CS-III						0.35	0.69	0.27	0.54	0.45	1.00	0.41
T6	CS-I							0.33	0.75	0.50	0.36	0.37	0.45
	CS-II							0.33	0.70	0.40	0.36	0.34	0.38
	CS-III							0.33	0.70	0.41	0.35	0.35	0.39
T7	CS-I								0.27	0.50	0.66	0.83	0.60
	CS-II								0.25	0.40	0.61	0.70	0.54
	CS-III								0.25	0.41	0.62	0.69	0.56
T8	CS-I									0.41	0.54	0.30	0.38
	CS-II									0.33	0.57	0.27	0.32
	CS-III									0.33	0.56	0.27	0.32
T9	CS-I										0.50	0.55	0.90
	CS-II										0.42	0.52	0.83
	CS-III										0.41	0.55	0.81
T10	CS-I											0.55	0.58
	CS-II											0.45	0.53
	CS-III											0.45	0.54
T11	CS-I												0.40
	CS-II												0.36
	CS-III												0.38

TABLE IV. ORDERING OF TEST CASES USING COVERAGE SIMILARITIES (CS-I)

Similarity Value	Group		Selected test pairs in order						
	Index	**Test Case Pairs**	**Seq. No.**	**PS1**	**PS2**	**PS3**	**PS4**	**PS5**	**PS6**
1.00	G1	(T1, T7) (T5, T11)	1	(**T1**, **T7**)	(**T1**, **T3**)	(**T1**, **T3**)	(**T1**, **T7**)	(**T1**, **T3**)	(**T1**, **T7**)
0.90	G2	(T9, T12)	2	(**T5**, **T11**)	(T3, **T7**)	(T1, **T4**)	(**T9**, **T12**)	(T1, **T4**)	(T1, **T5**)
0.88	G3	(T2, T10)	3	(**T9**, **T12**)	(T1, **T4**)	(**T8**, **T11**)	(**T2**, **T10**)	(T1, **T6**)	(T1, **T10**)
0.83	G4	(T1, T5) (T1, T11) (T5, T7) (T7, T11)	4	(**T2**, **T10**)	(T1, **T8**)	(**T6**, **T7**)	(T1, **T5**)	(T1, **T9**)	(T7, T10)
0.75	G5	(T4, T6) (T6, T8)	5	(T1, T5)	(T3, **T5**)	(T6, **T10**)	(**T4**, **T6**)	(T1, **T2**)	(T1, **T12**)
0.70	G6	(T3, T4) (T3, T8) (T4, T9)	6	(T1, T11)	(T3, **T11**)	(**T5**, T6)	(**T3**, T4)	(T3, **T12**)	(**T2**, T7)
0.67	G7	(T1, T10)	7	(T5, T7)	(T4, T7)	(T8, **T12**)	(T1, T10)	(T1, T12)	(T1, **T9**)
0.66	G8	(T7, T10)	8	(T7, T11)	(T7, T8)	(**T2**, T6)	(T7, T10)	(T3, T9)	(T1, **T6**)
0.63	G9	(T3, T9) (T4, T12)	9	(**T4**, **T6**)	(T4, T5)	(T8, **T9**)	(T4, T12)	(T1, **T10**)	(T1, **T4**)
0.62	G10	(T2, T5) (T2, T11)	10	(T6, **T8**)	(T4, **T10**)		(T2, **T11**)	(T3, **T8**)	(T1, **T3**)
0.60	G11	(T1, T12) (T2, T8) (T4, T8) (T7, T12)	11	(**T3**, T4)	(T4, T11)		(T2, **T8**)	(T1, **T5**)	(T5, **T11**)
0.58	G12	(T3, T12)	12		(T5, T8)			(T1, **T7**)	(T1, T11)
0.55	G13	(T1, T2) (T2, T3) (T2, T7) (T5, T9) (T5, T10) (T9, T11) (T10, T11)	13		(T8, T11)			(T3, T7)	(T2, T5)
0.54	G14	(T2, T9) (T8, T10)	14		(T1, **T6**)			(T3, **T11**)	(T5, T9)
0.50	G15	(T1, T9) (T2, T12) (T3, T6) (T3, T10) (T5, T12) (T6, T9) (T7, T9) (T9, T10)	15		(**T2**, T4)				(T5, T12)
0.45	G16	(T6, T12)	16		(T6, T7)				(T11, T12)
0.41	G17	(T8, T9)	17		(T6, T10)				(T5, T6)
0.40	G18	(T2, T6) (T11, T12)	18		(T5, T6)				(T5, **T8**)
0.38	G19	(T8, T12)	19		(T6, T11)				- - -
- - -		- - -	- - -		- - -				- - -

TABLE V. ANALYSIS OF DIFFERENT PRIORITIZATION TECHNIQUES

Category	Name	Index	Order of Test Cases											
			T1	***T2***	***T3***	***T4***	***T5***	***T6***	***T7***	***T8***	***T9***	***T10***	***T11***	***T12***
Single Test Case Prioritization Strategy	***Random***	S1	2	4	1	11	8	10	5	3	7	9	12	6
	Total-St Coverage	S2	8	4	1	5	11	9	10	6	2	3	12	7
	Total-MC/DC Coverage	S3	11	5	2	4	9	8	12	7	1	6	10	3
	Total-Br Coverage	S4	9	6	2	5	11	8	10	7	1	4	12	3
Similar Test Pair Prioritization Strategy	***Total C-i similarity prioritization (PS1)***	CS-I	1	7	12	9	3	10	2	11	5	8	4	6
	Total C-i dissimilarity prioritization (PS2)	CS-I	1	10	2	4	6	9	3	5	12	8	7	11
	Iterative C-i dissimilarity prioritization (PS3)	CS-I	1	11	2	3	9	6	7	4	12	8	5	10
	Iterative C-i similarity prioritization (PS4)	CS-I	1	5	10	8	7	9	2	12	3	6	11	4
	Advanced iterative C-i dissimilarity prioritization (PS5)	CS-I	1	6	2	3	10	4	11	9	5	8	12	7
	Advanced Iterative C-i similarity prioritization (PS6)	CS-I	1	6	10	9	3	8	2	12	7	4	11	5
	Total C-i similarity prioritization (PS1)	CS-II	1	7	9	10	3	11	2	12	5	8	4	6
	Total C-i dissimilarity prioritization (PS2)	CS-II	1	12	2	6	4	10	3	7	11	8	5	9
	Iterative C-i dissimilarity prioritization (PS3)	CS-II	1	12	2	4	3	11	5	6	10	8	7	9
	Iterative C-i similarity prioritization (PS4)	CS-II	1	5	8	9	7	10	2	11	3	6	12	4
	Advanced iterative C-i dissimilarity prioritization (PS5)	CS-II	1	8	2	4	3	6	12	5	7	9	11	10

	Advanced Iterative C-i similarity prioritization (PS6)	CS-II	1	6	11	10	3	8	2	9	7	4	12	5
	Total C-i similarity prioritization (PS1)	CS-III	1	7	12	11	3	9	2	10	5	8	4	6
	Total C-i dissimilarity prioritization (PS2)	CS-III	1	9	2	4	5	11	3	7	12	8	6	10
	Iterative C-i dissimilarity prioritization (PS3)	CS-III	1	8	2	3	6	10	4	5	12	7	11	9
	Iterative C-i similarity prioritization (PS4)	CS-III	1	5	11	10	9	7	2	8	3	6	12	4
	Advanced iterative C-i dissimilarity prioritization (PS5)	CS-III	1	7	2	3	10	5	11	4	6	8	12	9
	Advanced Iterative C-i similarity prioritization (PS6)	CS-III	1	6	11	10	3	8	2	9	7	4	12	5

V. CONCLUSION

Pair wise selection of test case is a fundamental strategy to compare and prioritize them by measuring their associations between them. Using the idea of similarity approach with multiple criteria is quite attractive to arrange the test cases in some specific order. In this paper, we have proposed test case prioritization techniques based on this strategy for the regression testing. Our techniques consider three coverage criteria i.e. statement, MC/DC, and branch coverage associated with each pair of test cases to calculate the similarity value between them. Based on such quantification, we have developed a family of new prioritization techniques to rearrange test cases. We have empirically verified that our techniques are achievable, and some of them are more effective than existing techniques or random ordering in terms of APFD.

In future, we will try to combine more criterions to analyze the prioritization results more effectively. We are also trying to implement those techniques on different case studies with larger data set.

References

[1] Elbaum, S., Malishevsky, A.G., Rothermel, G. (2002). Test case prioritization: A family of empirical studies. IEEE Transactions on Software Engineering (IEEE TSE), 28(2): 159-182.

[2] Andrews, J.H., Briand, L.C., Labiche, Y. and Namin, A.S.:'Using mutation analysis for assessing and comparing testing coverage criteria', IEEE Transactions on Software Engineering, 2006, 32(8), pp.608-624.

[3] Chen, T.Y. and Lau, M.F.: 'A new heuristic for test suite reduction', Information and Software Technology, 1998, 40(5-6), pp.347-354.

[4] M. J. Harrold and A. Orso. Retesting software during development and maintenance. In FOSM'08, pp. 99-108, 2008.

[5] Rothermel, G., Untch, R., Chu, C., & Harrold, M. (2001). Prioritizing test cases for regression testing. IEEE Transactions on Software Engineering, 27(10), 929–948.

[6] Marick, B. (1994). The craft of software testing: Subsystem testing including object-based and objectoriented testing. Champaign: Prentice-Hall.

[7] S. Yoo, M. Harman, P. Tonella, and A. Susi. Clustering test cases to achieve effective and scalable prioritisation incorporating expert knowledge. In ISSTA'09, pp. 201-212, 2009.

[8] B. Jiang, Z. Y. Zhang, W. K. Chan, and T. H. Tse. Adaptive random test case prioritization. In ASE'09, pp. 233-244, 2009.

[9] Y. Ledru, A. Petrenko, and S. Borody. Prioritizing test cases with string distances. Automat. Softw. Eng., 19(1):65-95, 2012.

[10] H. Hemmati and L. Briand. An industrial investigation of similarity measures for model-based test case selection. In ISSRE'10, pp. 141150, 2010.

[11] H. Hemmati, A. Arcuri, and L. Briand. Achieving scalable model-based testing through test case diversity. ACM Trans. Softw. Eng. Methodol., 22(1):1-42, 2013.

[12] Singh S, Shree R. A combined approach to optimize the test suite size in regression testing. CSI transactions on ICT. 2016 Dec 1;4 (2-4):73-8.

[13] Sharma, C., and Singh, S., "Mechanism for identification of duplicate test cases," In Recent Advances and Innovations in Engineering (ICRAIE), (pp. 1-5). IEEE (2014).

[14] Cartaxo, E.G., Machado, P.D. and Neto, F.G.O., 2011. On the use of a similarity function for test case selection in the context of model- based testing. Software Testing, Verification and Reliability, 21(2), pp.75-100.

[15] Singh S, Shree R. A Multi Criteria based Test Suite Optimization Framework. International Journal of Software Engineering and Its Applications (SERSC). 2017 , 11 (1), pp. 77-86 .

Privacy Policies: Preserving Confidentiality of Big Data

Kanika, Research Scholar
Department of Information Technology,
Babasaheb Bhimrao Ambedkar University
Lucknow, UP, India
sharma.kanika247@gmail.com

Alka Agrawal, Assistant Professor,
Department of Information Technology,
Babasaheb Bhimrao Ambedkar, University
Lucknow, UP, India,
alka_csjmu@yahoo.co.in

R.A. Khan, Professor
Department of Information Technology
Babasaheb Bhimrao Ambedkar University
Lucknow, UP, India,
khanraees@yahoo.com

Abstract— Information security has become a buzzword today. As individual's data is fragmented everywhere in the cyberspace, it has increased the risk of privacy breach of user's information. In involvement of multiple parties with the scattered environment of big data provide a rich ground for unauthorized parties to misuse the data including information theft, unauthorized access, privacy attacks etc. Exponential growth in misuse of individual's information has imposed the researcher and practitioners to create privacy policies regarding the same. Privacy preservation is a way to share anonymous information to ensure protection against identity disclosure of a user. In this paper, the authors have proposed privacy-preserving policies to address privacy and security issues along with the suggestions of user's data. The proposed policies have been implemented with Hadoop and with the help of an example; usefulness of the proposed policies has been demonstrated. It is claimed that a significant improvement over user's privacy can be achieved compared to the existing scenario.

Keywords—Big Data; Big Data Security; Privacy Policy.

I. INTRODUCTION

In the modern age, technology is all around. The user can do anything with a single click such as a book the ticket, shopping, taking an appointment, looking medical reports, etc. With the smartphones ownership climbing to 75% from 35% in 2011, the technology has become so accessible for each. In America, 74% of American adults have reported that they always connected to the Internet via mobile devices such as cell phones, tabs, etc. [3]. It is such a technological age where modern technology provides strong accessibility and connectivity. This is the bright side of the technology but there is a flip side. The technology is also creeping into user's privacy and confidentiality. People are living in the internet era, where user's identity can be revealed just in a click. Whatever they do on the internet can be very easily tracked and utilized by the organization seeking user's data for their purpose. These organizations may very easily sell users' data to the third party according to their requirement without users 'permission.

Today Information sharing poses a threat to a person's privacy or organizational secrecy. The dilemma of information use and privacy protection becomes more and acuter in these days. According to the study, there is a huge amount of private data available to be collected and analyzed. The use and access of the collection of personal information are necessary for providing high-quality service [20]. Organizations are a prosperous source of user's personal information and represent additional chances for economically motivated cybercriminals. As an example, when a user applies for rental properties, then applicants are usually necessary to provide photocopied documents containing such as personal identity information legal name, date of birth, and passport etc, financial information – proof of income and customer details and other information like contact details such as email addresses, and mobile, applicant's address, and other references [21].

On the other hand, many surveys recommend that individuals are extremely concerned about privacy during dealings with multi-type of information services. For example, in 2005 P&AB showed that 67% of respondents to choose not to register at a website or shop on the web just because of the concerned about the use of individual's information. To handle the dilemma between privacy safety and information utilization, the research on privacy-preserving mining on data has turned out to be essential in current years [2].

In real medical data, from the voter registration list, around 87% of the people were uniquely recognized by matching some attributes which were publicly available by basic mapping operation. The revelation of person's sickness may have outrageous social results and exposure of a person's income data raises stress about the security of individual [5]. Present marketers can aggregate different data sources to shape profiles of individual about customers that can be utilized to barely target people through different types of the advertisement [3]. Increasing use and demands of big data, organizations are facing privacy issues. User's privacy is still a major problem and providing security has become very crucial.
This paper as organized as section II describes the literature survey, in section III of this paper briefly describes Big Data Security and Hadoop framework. In the section, IV proposed the privacy policy for information sharing. In section V, statistical analysis and results have been explained and finally, the paper concluded in Section VI.

II. LITERATURE SURVEY

Ashwin Machanavajjhala et.al [9] has discussed the confidentiality of data misuse which may cause harm data Provider. They have described that distribution of such microdata encourage progress in public & science approach, assist citizens to find out about their social orders, & allow students to expand the data analysis skills. Mikko Siponen et.al [10] have discussed the importance security in research. They have proposed five guidelines to build the realistic applicability of field study utilizing employee's purposeful Internet Service Provider infringement. Richard Baskerville et.al [11] has defined the security framework which is focused on the organization the appropriate balance between obstacle and response paradigms. They have conducted a comparative investigation with a European organization. This investigation analyzed & exactly verifies why and how organizations adjust between their counteractive action and reaction policy. Waldo Rocha Flores et.al [12] have presented experimental study that on which behavioral factors of data security administration drive the foundation of sharing the data security facts in organizations. The investigation followed research design method. The result showed the major influenced on the establishment of sharing security information in the organization.
Lei Xu [13] et.al have discussed the privacy-preserving data mining techniques. They have explained various data mining techniques to reduce the privacy risk and unwanted exposure of personal data. In this paper, they have identified four unique roles of the user of data mining applications. S. Sicari et.al [14] has discussed that traditional security techniques cannot be directly applied to the heterogeneous environment. They have emphasized the need for flexible infrastructure to deal with the security threats. In this paper, they have presented some research challenges, identifying open issues, and suggesting some hints for future research. Joseph L [15] they have discussed the threats to the use of telehealth. They explained that the use of telehealth solutions without proper security and privacy policies provider will lack trust.

III. BIG DATA SECURITY AND HADOOP FRAMEWORK

A. Importance of Big Data Security

Information is continuously expanding and it is going to be bigger with time. In this paper, authors have discussed some incidents to show the flip side of technology in a heterogeneous system. The main purpose is to discuss ICT infrastructure vulnerability and to show how criminal steal sensitive data of users. How our ICT infrastructure is so vulnerable [1]. Here authors described some latest cyber case studies of identity fraud cases in table 1. The most important security challenge with the heterogeneous system is that the owner of the data (data creator) might not have control on where the data is located [16]. Data creator may create both sensitive and nonsensitive data. As far as the data is not sensitive, there is no concern for data security. But the problems start with the sensitive data. Once the data is released from the data creator, the organization gathering or collecting the data may sell the data to the third party according to their need. Thus, awareness about maintaining the confidentiality of massive amounts data is must [3].

Year		Description	Reason	URL
2016 Cases	I	According to FACC, in a cyber fraud, 50 million Euros was stolen by an attacker by posing an email.	Email-Id	**Austria's FACC, hit by cyber fraud, fires CEO,** Available at: https://www.reuters.com/article/us-face-ceo-idUSKCN0YG0ZF
	II	In Balajinagar a 49-year old man, in a tele-phishing attack has turned out to be the victim by losing Rs. 24978. he was reportedly been duped by the anonymous attacker.	Mobile No	**46-year-old man dupedby tele-phishers in Aurangabad,** Available at: http://timesofindia.indiatimes.com/city/aurangabad/46-year-old-man-duped-by-tele-phishers-in-aurangabad/articleshow/56972419.cms
	III	A 61-year-old man retired from government organizations has been duped by an anonymous attacker. He has duped by Rs 3.35 lakh while he was trying to purchase flight tickets.	Mobile No	**61-year-old retired government employee becomes victim of tele phishing,** Available at: http://timesofindia.indiatimes.com/city/aurangabad/61-year-old-retired-government-employee-becomes-victim- of-tele-phishing/articleshow/55303909.cms
	IV	Cybercrime sleuths busted a 'Nigerian fraud' gang and from Delhi 3 people were arrested. The gang was acting like raw material suppliers and sent a fake e-mail. they duped Rs 13 lakh from a firm selling poly vinyl chloride garments in Gowliguda	Email-Id	**Nigerian gang dupes city firm of Rs 13L, 3 held, Available at** http://timesofindia.indiatimes.com/city/hyderabad/Nigeria n-gang-dupes-city-firm-of-Rs-13L-3-held/articleshow/55021965.cms
	V	A businessman from Raipur, Tushar Mohanty was trapped by false call and website like the government's one. According to Mahendra Limaye IT expert and lawyer, on June 25, 2014, in Nagpur, a similar complaint was lodged, by Bodhiratna Full. The amount was transferred to the account of same accused — SK Ibrahim, but in different Axis Bank branch in Balasore, Odisha.	Mobile No	**Chhattisgarh IT department asks PNB to payback Rs 22.36L to phishing victim, Available at:** http://timesofindia.indiatimes.com/city/nagpur/Chhattisga rh-IT-department-asks-PNB-to-payback-Rs-22-36L-to- phishing-victim/articleshow/52423336.cms
	VI	A banker Srinivas Reddy received a mail from the 'Rio Olympic Committee' offering a whopping 40% discount on air tickets to watch the Rio de Janeiro games which are going to be held in August.	Emaii-id	**Watch out for Rio phishing scam!, Available at:** http://timesofindia.indiatimes.com/city/hyderabad/Watch- out-for-Rio-phishing-scam/articleshow/52333371.cms
	VII	On 11 October 2016, a 45-year-old man has been duped by unknown tele-phishers to the amount of Rs 36,480. He received a call on his mobile from an unknown number. The caller claimed to be an agent of the nationalized bank on which the victim has a savings account.	Mobile No	**Aurangabad Zilla Parishad clerk duped of Rs 36,480 via tele-phishing,** Available at: http://timesofindia.indiatimes.com/city/aurangabad/zp- clerk-duped-of-rs-36480-via-tele-phishing/articleshow/56408706.cms

B. Hadoop Framework

Hadoop [17] is an open source framework which is used to handle, store, manage and analyze a large amount of data. This large and scattered data cannot be handled by the conventional database techniques. The massively parallel architecture of Hadoop, help to support for managing hardware failure. Hadoop has two main core components; HDFS and MapReduce. *Hadoop Distributed File System* is used for storage of data; divides data into smaller chunks and stores it across the cluster of machines. HDFS has a master-slave framework which is made by data nodes that can store blocks of data, fetch the data on request, and report to the name node and *MapReduce* is a data processing engine. It is a Java programming model, with two main functions: map and reducer. The map takes raw data as input and organizes it as a pair of key-value. Reducer handles the intermediate key-value pairs provided by the Mapper [18].

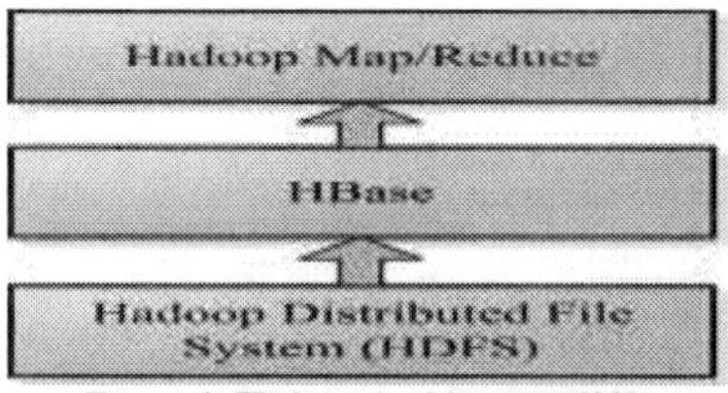

Figure 1: Hadoop Architecture [22]

C. Hbase

Hbase is the distributed database, based over HDFS. HBase's every table is stored with columns and rows as a multi-dimensional sparse map, and each cell having a time stamp. Row and column's cell value is exceptionally known by Value. HBase has own Java client API, and in HBase tables can be utilized input and output source for MapReduce jobs with TableInput-TableOutputFormat [19].

IV. Proposed Privacy Policy for information sharing

The growing numbers of individuals, sensors, and devices, which are linked by a digital system, have transformed the capacity to produce, exchange, spread, and fetch the data. A user's digital identity encompasses a wide choice of traceable attributes such as name, email-id, mobile no, DOB, passwords, pin, and behaviors etc. These attributes may be able to recognize any individual uniquely. The collection of huge data sets and the use of analytics on the data sets clearly implicate privacy concerns. Now a day's digital user is no longer completely unidentified as virtually all form of communication and activities by the user generate information which can be gathered, combined and examined. It is possible that information assembled for one reason can be retrieved for another without user consent [3]. Data security is the process of protecting and maintain the confidentiality, integrity, and availability of data whether in storage, processing or in transmission. The tasks are becoming harder of ensuring data security and preserving privacy as information is combined and multiplied or shared more broadly all over the world. Information about person's area, 'health, and online activity etc are exposed to analysis, raising worry about losing control over data, confidentiality, integrity, and availability [4].

The problem of disclosure or publishing of the data gathered from creator by the collector such that individuals personal sensitive information is preserved as well as the published data is highly useful are highly recommended [8].In this scenario where individuals data is fragmented everywhere in the cyberspace, there is need to impose big data privacy policies to avoid misuse of individuals information. The privacy policies should be adhered by information creators and information collector both in order to avoid loss of privacy. Keeping in view the need for the hour the authors have proposed privacy policies for big data. These policies when implemented may ensure privacy to the individual as well as the organization. It is expected that these policies will secure and aware individuals for their security.

A. Proposed Privacy policy (PP)

1) PP1: This policy states that while providing services, organizations must provide with use the choice to share their information or not. Here share is a variable which can have two values {0, 1} such that share=0 shows not permitted to share and share=1 shows permission to share.

$share \in \{0, 1\}$
(I) If share= 1 then
Organization is authorized to share creators' data
(II) If share= 0 then
Organization is not authorized to share creators' data

---

2) **PP2**: the organizations must present users with all their security strategies. Here R stands for rules.

R1: Privacy Policy must clearly define organization's security strategies.
R2: There should be no hidden policies.
R3: Protection of information should be under the control of the organization.

The users should be aware of the use of their information. So the organization should make clear and unbiased policies. There should be no hidden policies which affect the user's privacy. User's wish must strictly be followed.

In order to implement privacy policy PP1 using hadoop a step by step process is shown in table 2.

Table 2: step by step Process of privacy policies

```
1. Create configuration for Hbase
2. Create connection from cluster
3. Create Scan object to scan the Htable
4. Create ResultScanner
5. while (resultset==empty)
6. Get the Scanner object from the Htable using scan object which contains
the content of HBase table.
8. for(each row obtained) do
    (a) for (each cell<- rs (Result object)) do.
      (b) Get the value of 'share' column from HBase table 'user'
  and column family 'PersonalData' into 'flag'
    (c) if (flag==yes) then
    (d) Print the data of the user (referred to as sharing of data)
    (f) else if (flag== 0) then
    (g) print "Organization is not authorized to share"
    endif
    endif
9. close the scanner
end for
end for
end while
```

V. Design of Experiment

The proposed privacy policies have been implemented in Hadoop 2.5.2 (pre-built 32-bit i386-Linux native and java version SDK Oracle Java 1.8.0 25 (8u25) with the system specifications CPU Intel i3 M370 2.40 GHz, RAM 6 GB 1600 MHz.

A. Dataset used

A dataset of student performance of UCI machine learning repository has been used for the experimental evaluation of proposed policy. The data obtained from [23] was prepared according to the requirement avoiding unnecessary details. Attributes of dataset are shown in table 3. The data set has 2000 students' records. On the basis of results, accuracy of proposed policy has been checked.

Table 3: Attributes of Dataset

Attribute	Description
Name	Student's name
Contact no	Student's contact number (numeric)
Email_id	Email id of student
Sex	Student's Gender (binary: Female or male)
Age	Student's age (numeric: from 15 to 22)
School	School name ()
Address	Student's address (binary: urban or rural)
Fam_size	Number of family members (binary: ≤ 3 *or* > 3)
Guardians	student's guardian (nominal: mother, father or other)
Share	Share to agree own data (binary: yes or no)

B. Result Analysis and discussion

To evaluate the usefulness of proposed privacy policy (PP1) authors have uploaded the data set in hdfs and using the package hbaseorg.apache.hadoop.hbase.mapreduce.ImportTsv – Dimporttsv data has been imported from hdfs to hbase. It has been stored in hbase in the form of column and column-family. Then the hbase has been activated using hbase shell command start-hbase.sh and the connection has been established with java code using HBaseConfiguration.create function. After executing the code the record of only those users was obtained who were agreeing to share their information as shown in Figure 2.

```
Organization Name: A2ZTech
Family : PersonalData Qualifier : ContactNo : Value : 9965423265
Family : PersonalData Qualifier : EmailId : Value : abc@gmail.com
Family : PersonalData Qualifier : Fjob : Value : teacher
Family : PersonalData Qualifier : Mjob : Value : at_home
Family : PersonalData Qualifier : Name : Value : Ajay
Family : PersonalData Qualifier : absences : Value : 6
Family : PersonalData Qualifier : address : Value : U
Family : PersonalData Qualifier : age : Value : 18
Family : PersonalData Qualifier : famrel : Value : 4
Family : PersonalData Qualifier : famsize : Value : GT3
Family : PersonalData Qualifier : guardian : Value : mother
Family : PersonalData Qualifier : health : Value : 3
Family : PersonalData Qualifier : internet : Value : no
Family : PersonalData Qualifier : reason : Value : course
Family : PersonalData Qualifier : romantic : Value : no
Family : PersonalData Qualifier : school : Value : GP
Family : PersonalData Qualifier : [illegible]
Family : PersonalData Qualifier : share : Value : yes
Family : PersonalData Qualifier : [illegible]
```

Figure 2: records of creators who agreed to share thier data

To measure the usefulness of the proposed privacy policy, probability theory has been used to compare the loss of privacy in existing scenario and the proposed approach. In the existing flow of information, the probability of privacy loss is 1 (complete privacy loss) because for the users, as they are not provided with the customized policies. But through proposed privacy policies privacy loss can be reduced and hence privacy can be preserved.

A database consisting of the data of n users {u1......un}, where $n \in R$(Real numbers) is concluded. For example, let there are five users u1......u5 with their associated share variable 0,1,1,0,0 respectively such that $share \in \{0,1\}$. Then

Users	Share
u1	0
u2	1
u3	1
u4	0
u5	0

$$Probability\ of\ Privacy\ Loss = \frac{\text{Number of favourable outcomes}}{\text{Total number of outcomes}}$$

Where favourable outcomes represent number of users who agreed to share their data and total number represent total number of users.

$$\text{Probability of Privacy loss P(L)}=\frac{2}{5}$$

$$\text{P(L)}=0.4$$

Privacy loss of existing scenario is 1 because existing policies doesn't offer the customize option but privacy loss in proposed scenario is 0.4. Hence it can be easily concluded that with the help of proposed privacy policies the risk of privacy loss can be reduce. Those users who deny sharing his/her data, there is no risk of privacy loss because organization is not authorized to share data.

C. Comparison

In a heterogeneous environment, user generates their own data with a little concern about security and privacy of their information. Generally, services industries provide a platform to access their services with one click. Unfortunately, they ask for the personal information in exchange. Now the user is left with only two choices; reject the offered terms and conditions or accept them. Rejection will deprive them of the services and acceptance will compromise their privacy. Where organizations impose their own policy on the user and user has to accept the policy in order to avail the service. The existing scenario of information flow is shown in fig 3 (a). In contrast, user's privacy and security can easily be maintained with a slight modification in the organizational policy while providing its services. The idea is to ask the user's choice that whether they want to disclose their information to the third party or not. With a little vigilance user's privacy can be maintained. If a user wants to access services of any organization then they should provide an option to customize the policies according to their requirement as shown in fig 3(b). Hence with these policies, the risk of privacy loss can be reducing. Users will be aware of the sharing of their data. Those users who deny sharing their data there is no risk of privacy loss. Dennis Broeders [7] et.al clearly explained that in organization policies there is no interference by user's side. Hence in this paper authors has shown the graphical representation of existing scenario and also proposed the creator's policy.

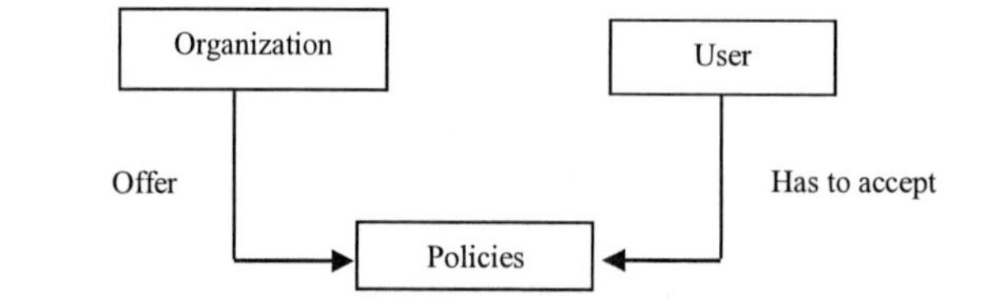

Figure 3(a): Existing Organization Policy

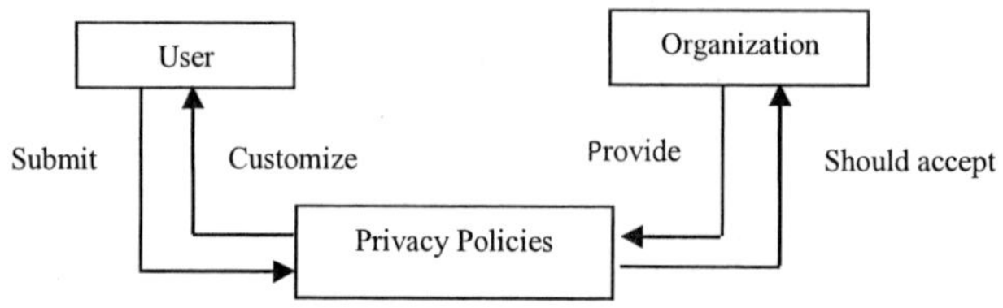

3 (b) Proposed Creator policies

VI. CONCLUSION

Big data is a new word which has come into picture since past few years. It is the collection of different formats of data. Several issues arise in big data due to its structure and unstructured formats of data such as privacy, storage, analysis, sharing etc. Due to its nature, traditional tools are not able to handle these issues of big data. The major challenge raised by big data is how to classify sensitive information which is stored in an unstructured format. With big data, protection of user‘s privacy has become one of the main issues. In this interrelated infrastructure, there is no such type of privacy policy exists that can preserve the privacy of an individual or prevent from unauthorized access to information. Organizations sell data to the third party and from where data goes which place no one is aware of it. Hence, it is the demand of time to finalize and impose big data privacy policies to avoid unauthorized access and misuse of individual‘s information. So here authors developed such policies that prevent the unauthorized access of user‘s information. These policies are implemented in Hadoop, an appropriate tool to handle all the issues in big data.

REFERENCES

1. Callanan, Cormac & Jerman, Borka & Jerman Blažič, Andrej. (2015). User Awareness and Tolerance of Privacy Abuse on Mobile Internet: an Exploratory Study. Telematics and Informatics. 33.10.1016/j.tele.2015.04.009.
2. Li, J., Yang, J. J., Zhao, Y., & Liu, B. "A top-down approach for approximate data anonymisation." Enterprise Information Systems 7.3 (2013): 272-302.
3. Eastin, M. S., Brinson, N. H., Doorey, A., & Wilcox, G. "Living in a big data world: Predicting mobile commerce activity through privacy concerns." Computers in Human Behaviour 58 (2016): 214-220.
4. Tene, Omer, and Jules Polonetsky. "Privacy in the age of big data: a time for big decisions." Stanford Law Review Online 64 (2012): 63.
5. Purushothama, B. R., and B. B. Amberker. "Duplication with Trapdoor Sensitive Attribute Values: A New Approach for Privacy Preserving Data Publishing." *Procedia Technology* 6 (2012): 970-977.
6. Clifton, C., Kantarcioğlu, M., Doan, A., Schadow, G., Vaidya, J., Elmagarmid, A., & Suciu, D... "Privacy-preserving data integration and sharing." *Proceedings of the 9th ACM SIGMOD workshop on Research issues in data mining and knowledge discovery*. ACM, 2004.
7. Broeders, D., Schrijvers, E., van der Sloot, B., van Brakel, R., de Hoog, J., & Ballin, E. H. (2017). Big Data and security policies: Towards a framework for regulating the phases of analytics and use of Big Data. Computer Law & Security Review, 33(3), 309-323.
8. Mani, Deepa, Kim-Kwang Raymond Choo, and Sameera Mubarak. "Information security in the South Australian real estate industry: A study of 40 real estate organizations." *Information Management & Computer Security* 22.1 (2014): 24-41.
9. Machanavajjhala, Ashwin, and Jerome P. Reiter. "Big privacy: protecting confidentiality in big data." XRDS: Crossroads, the ACM Magazine for Students 19.1 (2012): 20-23.
10. Siponen, Mikko, and Anthony Vance. "Guidelines for improving the contextual relevance of field surveys: the case of information security policy violations." European Journal of Information Systems 23.3 (2014): 289-305.
11. Baskerville, Richard, Paolo Spagnoletti, and Jongwoo Kim. "Incident-centered information security: Managing a strategic balance between prevention and response." *Information & management* 51.1 (2014): 138- 151.
12. Flores, Waldo Rocha, EgilAntonsen, and Mathias Ekstedt. "Information security knowledge sharing in organizations: Investigating the effect of behavioral information security governance and national culture." *Computers & Security* 43 (2014): 90-110
13. Xu, L., Jiang, C., Wang, J., Yuan, J., & Ren, Y. Information security in big data: privacy and data mining'. *IEEE Access*, *2*, (2014), 1149- 1176.
14. Sicari, Sabrina, et al. "Security, privacy and trust in the Internet of Things: The road ahead." *Computer Networks* 76 (2015): 146-164.
15. Hall, Joseph L., and Deven McGraw. "For telehealth to succeed, privacy and security risks must be identified and addressed." *Health Affairs* 33.2 (2014): 216-221.
16. Reddy, C. Kishor Kumar, et al. "Third-party data protection applied to cloud and XACML implementation in the Hadoop environment with sparql." *IOSR Journal of Computer Engineering (IOSRJCE) ISSN* (2012): 2278- 0661.
17. Chen, Ting, and Kenjiro Taura. "A Comparative Study of Data Processing Approaches for Text Processing Workflows." *High-Performance Computing, Networking, Storage and Analysis (SCC), 2012 SC Companion:* IEEE, 2012.
18. Landset, S., Khoshgoftaar, T. M., Richter, A. N., & Hasanin, T. A survey of open source tools for machine learning with big data in the Hadoop ecosystem. *Journal of Big Data*, 2015, *2*(1), 24.
19. Taylor, R. C. An overview of the Hadoop/MapReduce/HBase framework and its current applications in bioinformatics. *BMC Bioinformatics*,2010, *11*(12), S1.
20. Chen, T., Chaabane, A., Tournoux, P. U., Kaafar, M. A., & Boreli, R. How much is too much? Leveraging ads audience estimation to evaluate public profile uniqueness. In *International Symposium on Privacy Enhancing Technologies Symposium* . Springer, Berlin, Heidelberg, 2013, pp. 225-244.
21. Mani, Deepa, Kim-Kwang Raymond Choo, and Sameera Mubarak. "Information security in the South Australian real estate industry: A study of 40 real estate organizations." *Information Management & Computer Security* 22.1 (2014): 24-4.
22. Chen C.P., & Zhang, C.Y., "Data-intensive applications, challenges, techniques and technologies: A survey on Big Data", Information Sciences, 275, 314-347.

A Review: Study and Analysis of Images in Different Color Models

Neetish Kumar Dr. Deepa Raj
DCS, BBAU Lucknow

Abstract: ***Apart from having lots of methods for compression of color images, the importance of lossless color image is irreplaceable in many important situations. Today is the world of electronic gadgets which generates voluminous data that includes the various forms of multimedia data. In these data collections, images need more space to store the content and need more bandwidth to transmit through a network. By using Image compression the size of the image can be reduced which helps in less utilization of memory and transmitted across a network with less bandwidth. Due to the efficient compression techniques the execution time for transmission drastically dicreases and throughput of machine attains at a satisfactory level. This leads to the wider acceptance of the compression performance in much wider domaim.***

Keywords: Compression, Enhancement, Transmission

Introduction:

In the current scenario, in our daily life not a single field id untouched with the digital technology. Advancement in the digital technology has also changed the way of communication. Due to this change visual appearance are more preferred over the text. It leads to the motivation of reduction of the size of multimedia data. Compression techniques are widely explored in two categories e.g. lossy and lossless. According to their name, in lossy compression same extent of inappropriate information is discarded while in case of lossless compression the original image can be perfectly reformed without loss of data. The motivation behind the color image processing deals with various factors one thing may be the more sensitivity of human visual systems towards the color images. Another factor assures that color is a powerful deceptor that often simplifies object identification and extraction from a scene. Second, humans can discern thousands of color shades and intensities, compared to about only two dozen shades of gray.

The resolution if an image is hihgly related to the picture element, commonly known as pixel. The more the no of pixels of a particular image have, the more and more clarity it get. Each pixel stores the color information of an image in terms of bits.

Color image processing comprises of two major areas namely full color and pseudo color processing. In full-color processing, the images in question typically are acquired with a full-color sensor, such as color tv camera or color scanner. In the second category, the problem is one of assigning a color to a particular monochrome intensity or range of intensities.

Literature survey:

Seyun kim et. al [4] presented a lossless color image compression called the hierarchical prediction and context-adaptive arithmetic coding. In this approach, YC_uC_v color space of the image is generated from an RGB image. Later this method is compared with VSBHP (variable size block hierarchical prediction and the performance somehow was increased.

Zhang, Zhou et al [1,2,3] developed algorithms for lossy as well as lossless compression of images, among those the most widely used are lossless CALIC, JPEG, JPEG-LS, LOCO-I, JPEG2000 (lossless). Among these the development of LOCO-I and CALIC are in the process of state of art standardization JPEG, most of the useful ideas in LOCO-I are accepted for JPEG-LS, however, at the cost of more computations, CALIC can achieve better compression performance.

WDR based approach is also used for compression by C.Wang [10]. In this scheme, an original RGB image is transformed into YCbCr color space, due to this transformation, the correlation among RGB planes is reduced. By empirical evaluation, it can be observed most of the image information lies in illuminance i.e. Y plane that helps in achieving high compression performance in chrominance color components. While Cb and Cr components have much less information than that of Y.

In some other wavelet-based approach, a wavelet-based simultaneous fusion, encryption and compression technique is used by C. Wang et al [9, 13]. The sparse representation of source images using DWT has helped in keeping properties of source images in the reconstructed fused image. The low and high frequency are fused using different rules and both frequency coefficients are simultaneously encrypted and compressed with the help of pseudo random number and pseudorandom permutation.

S.Sathappan and P.suresh babu [14] used Image compression by Reversible Color Transform (RCT) method. The size of the image can be reduced which helps in less utilization of memory and transmitted across a network with less bandwidth. The Modified Hierarchical Prediction (MHP) encodes C_u and C_v of chrominance channel, then they are decomposed into sub-images to predict the vertical, horizontal and diagonal pixels for effective image compression. After that luminance image Y is encoded using a technique called Variable Sized Blocks Hierarchical Prediction (VSBHP) coding scheme. This gives much better result than the previous existing approach.

3. Different Color Model

The goal of the color model is to expedite the blueprint in some standard and mostly in a generalized way.

3.1 RGB Color Model

In RGB color model each color appears in its primary components of red, green, and blue. This model is based on a Cartesian coordinate system in which at the origin of the cube the color is black, the farthest point from the origin the color is white and the line joining between the two represent grayscale. The different corners depict different colors of the cube. The effect of using RGB color model is that it expresses very close to the form we grasp colors using alpha and gamma receptors in our retinal. It is the basic and crucial color model used in any other medium that projects the color or television. And widely used for Web graphics, but it cannot be used for print production.

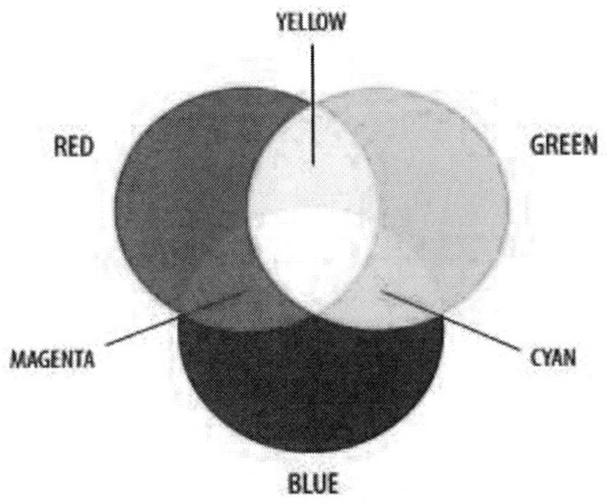

Fig.1 RGB color model

3.2 CMYK Color Model

It is the model representing the image in secondary color namely Cyan, Magenta, and yellow. When a surface coated with cyan pigment is illuminated with white light, no red is reflected from the surface. The RGB to CMY conversion is performed with a simple operation.

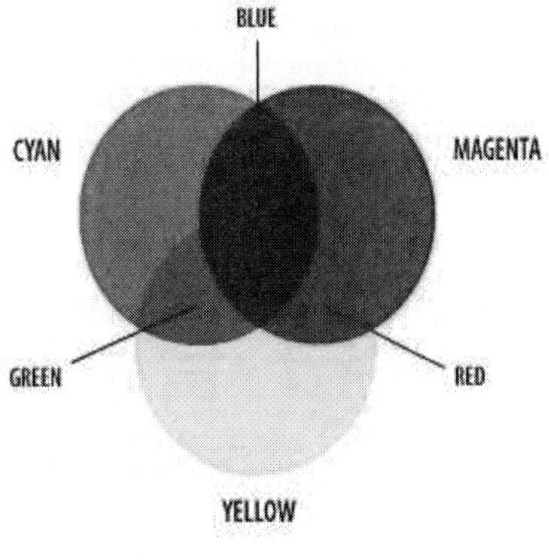

Fig.2 CMYK color model

3.3 HSI Color Model

The RGB and CMY color model systems are best suited for the hardware implementation. Unfortunately both the color model not suits for describing colors for human interpretation. When human view a color object, it can be described by its Hue, Saturation, and intensity. The HSI model also has the advantage that it decouples the color and gray scale information in an image, making it suitable for many of the gray scale techniques developed yet.

4. Compression Strategy

The data compression refers to the process of reducing the amount of data required to represent a given quantity of information. The two types of compression strategy are as follows.

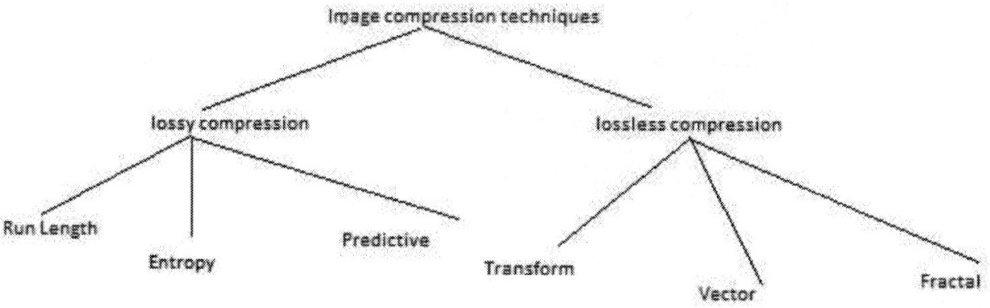

4.1 Lossy vs Lossless

The lossless technique is meant for restoring the data files similar to the original one. In certain cases it becomes very necessary viz. processing for word file, executable processing codes, tabular formats records, etc. [12]. In such cases, loss of a single bit of information can utter the intent of the original contents. The same doesn't apply to the file could be stored and transmitted without having entire detail intact. Mostly, real-world data contains noise and removing them hardly impact the data and information contained. The technique which brings alteration to the original content during compression is termed as lossy. Lossy compression is distinct from lossless compression in terms of effectiveness, the former brings more efficient. High compression ratio is a clear indication of added noise to the data.

Lossless	Lossy
run-length	CS&Q
Huffman	JPEG
delta	MPEG
LZW	

a. Lossless or Lossy

Method	Group size: input	output
CS&Q	fixed	fixed
Huffman	fixed	variable
Arithmetic	variable	variable
run-length, LZW	variable	fixed

b. Fixed or variable group size

Fig.3 Compression techniques[15]

5. Redundancy in the Data

There are mainly three types of redundancies that can be identified while dealing with the two-dimensional intensity arrays namely Coding redundancy, Spatial and temporal redundancy and irrelevant information. Through the different compression techniques, the above redundancies are either eliminated or reduced. There are two algorithm which deals with coding redundancy

5.1 Huffman Coding

It is the quite good and most prominent technique to eliminate coding redundancy [5]. The smallest possible number of code symbols is produced by this method per source symbol. There is a no of steps followed for the reduction symbols to achieve the smallest code. In the first step of this approach, a series of source reductions are created by ordering the probabilities of the symbols. Further combining the lowest probability symbol into a single symbol takes place that replaces them in the next source reduction. In the second step to code each reduced source, starting with the smallest source and working back to the original source. This procedure generates the optimal code for a set of symbols and probabilities subject to the constraint the symbols be coded one at a time.

5.2 L Z W Coding

It is a dictionary-based approach that follows these steps.

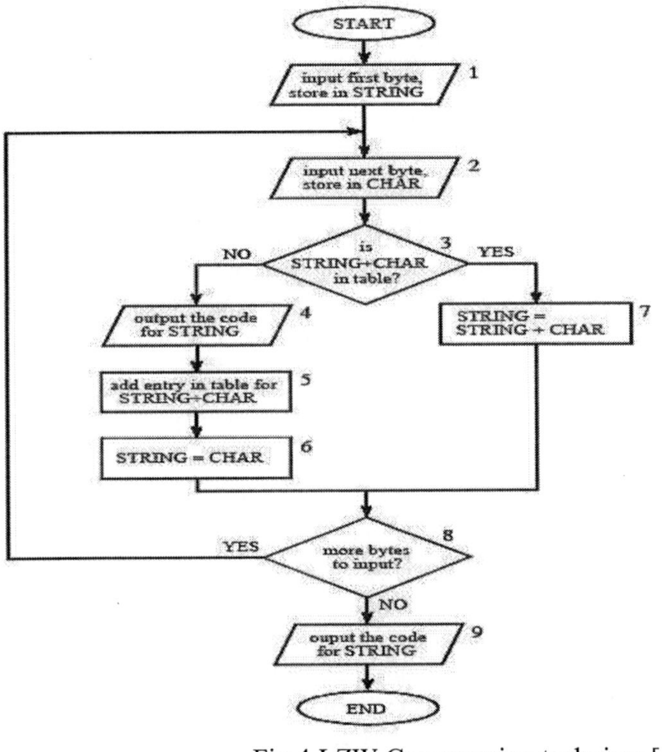

Fig.4 LZW Compression technique[15]

6. Image Enhancement

Image Enhancement is the process of improving the image quality for a specific application. The process of enhancement is divided into two broad categories, namely spatial domain method and frequency domain method. Spatial domain method works directly on pixels whereas in frequency domain the image is first converted into Fourier transform. There and techniques of enhancement through which we get a more enhanced image respective of previous one like histogram processing, histogram equalization, histogram matching, bit plane slicing, contrast stretching etc [6][7]. Another most important tool for image enhancement is filtering.

6.1 Filtering: A filter is a device or a material that is used for suppressing or minimizing waves or oscillations of certain frequencies. It is used to remove different types of noises [8]. Through Convolution and Correlation, we perform filtering operation. For filtering, we have to generate a mask and use convolution or correlation to find the sum of product at each point. There are various types of filters e.g. low pass filter or high pass filter and they are further subdivided as the Gaussian filter, Laplacian filter, Butterworth filter etc.

7. Issues and Challenges

Challenges related to compression: Now a day, we are dealing with a voluminous amount of storage that needed to occupy less bandwidth during efficient transmission. Data warehousing cost are drastically reduced by compressing the files because more files can be stored in available storage space when they are compressed. Transmission time also reduces as compared to previous. There is a lot of algorithms for image compression; still, there is a need for such compression techniques that cause less degradation of an image during compression. In terms of transmission time, error rate and many other concerns there is a vast scope of compression and needed to look into it.

8. Conclusion

This paper gives a brief review of the different color models. In terms of efficient data transmission, it is highly desirable to occupy less bandwidth during transmission so some types of compression strategies also discussed that are generally used for effective transmission of data. Usage of lossy and lossless methods is briefly analyzed. The paper tells about the enhancement of images at some instant.

References

[1] Y. Zhang, L.Y. Zhang, J. Zhou, L. Liu, F. Chen, X. He, "A review of compressive sensing in information security field", IEEE Access. 4 (2016) 2507–2519.

[2] N. Zhou, A. Zhang, F. Zheng, L. Gong, "Novel image compression–encryption hybrid algorithm based on key-controlled measurement matrix in compressive sensing", Opt. Laser Technol. 62 (2014) 152–160.

[3] N. Zhou, A. Zhang, J. Wu, D. Pei, Y. Yang, "Novel hybrid image compression— encryption algorithm based on compressive sensing", Optik 125 (2014) 5075–5080.

[4] Kim, Seyun, and Nam Ik Cho. "Hierarchical prediction and context adaptive coding for lossless color image compression", *IEEE Transactions on image processing* 23.1 (2014): 445-449.

[5] R. Huang, K.H. Rhee, S. Uchida, "A parallel image encryption method based on compressive sensing", Multimedia. Tools Appl. 72 (1) (2012) 71–93.

[6] N. Zhou, H. Li, D. Wang, S. Pan, Z. Zhou, "Image compression and encryption scheme based on 2D compressive sensing and fractional", Mellin transform, Opt. Commun. 343 (2015) 10–21.

[7] Alfalou, C. Brosseau, "Optical image compression and encryption methods", Adv. Opt. Photonics 1 (3) (2009) 589.

[8] Alfalou, A. Mansour, M. Elbouz, C. Brosseau, "Optical Compression scheme to multiplex and simultaneously encode images", in: Optical and Digital Image Processing Fundamentals and Applications, Wiley, New York, 2011, p. 463.

[9] N. Zhou, S. Pan, S. Cheng, Z. Zhou, "Image compression–encryption scheme based on hyper-chaotic system and 2D compressive sensing", Opt. Laser Tech- nol. 82 (2016) 121–133.

[10] C. Wang, J. Ni, Q. Huang, "A new encryption-then-compression algorithm using the rate-distortion optimization", Signal Process., Image Commun. 39 (2014) 141–150

[11] Pearlman, William A., et al. "Efficient, low-complexity image coding with a set-partitioning embedded block coder", *IEEE transactions on circuits and systems for video technology* 14.11 (2004): 1219-1235..

[12] Ahumada Jr, Albert J and Peterson, Heidi A. "Luminance-model-based DCT quantization for color image compression'', SPIE/IS\&T 1992 Symposium on Electronic Imaging: Science and Technology, 365—374,1992

[13] Nadenau, Marcus J and Reichel, Julien and Kunt, Murat,"Wavelet-based color image compression: exploiting the contrast sensitivity function", IEEE Transactions on Image Processing, 58—70, 2003

[14] Sathappan, S., and P. Suresh Babu. "Block-based prediction with Modified Hierarchical Prediction image coding scheme for Lossless color image compression", *Wireless Communications, Signal Processing and Networking (WiSPNET), International Conference on*. IEEE, 2016.

[15] Rafeal C. Gonzalez, Richard E. Woods "Digital Image Processing"

Software Defects Prediction using AI Technique- A Review

Sunil Kumar Singh *Rajshree*
Department of Information Tecnology
Babasaheb Bhimrao Ambedkar, University

Abstract--This paper provides a literature review of the use of various strategies for artificial intelligence techniques inside the area of software program disorder prediction. This literature evaluation may be very useful, since it brings a higher expertise of the field of observe, and that is an essential contribution of this paper. This literature overview could be very beneficial, since it brings a better expertise of the sphere of study, and that is an vital contribution of this paper. From the literature review this situation draws a extremely good deal of hobby with the aid of researchers and a notable algorithms are present associated with software defect prediction based totally coding in the place of Software Engineering. Faults in software program structures continue to be a main hassle. A software fault is a illness that causes software program failure in an executable product. Knowing the reasons of feasible defects as well as figuring out popular software program technique areas which could want interest from the initialization of a undertaking should store money, time and paintings. The possibility of early estimating the potential faultiness of software program may want to help on making plans, controlling and executing software program development sports. This paper surveys literature review of articles for the beyond many years with the intention to explore how numerous prediction methodologies had been advanced throughout this era with the intention to contend with the troubles associated with software program illness.
Keywords: Software defect, Artificial intelligence, Neural Network, Fuzzy logic, Data prediction

1. Introduction:

These days, severa programming improvement businesses have their own precise development save, which broadly speaking consists of a rendition control framework and a bug following framework. This has maximum likely validated treasured for programming deformities expectation. The forecast of the imperfection inclination of a product framework decrease the mission disappointments and decrease the combination rate amid the advancement and support stages. As the span of programming tasks gets to be larger, software defect forecast methods will assume a vital component to strengthen engineers and in addition to boost up time to promote it with greater reliable programming objects. Defect prediction strategies are proposed either to group the product modules as blemished or non-imperfect or hypothesis the quantity of imperfections inside the product lessons or modules. Imperfection expectation due to defects will give one extra possibility to the development group to retest the modules or records for which the inadequacy probability is excessive.

Machine mastering calculations are related properly in problem areas with changing features and regularities. Programming satisfactory assessment is a decent pattern of the above rationalization. The product metric records of modules or programming joined with disorder facts frames the structure of the device studying calculations. These calculations execute a probability conveyance and check out mistakes. The methods prominently applied for programming imperfection forecast troubles are selection trees, neural gadget and Bayesian conviction machine.

Software defect prediction manner has been taken into consideration to be too complicated, steeply-priced and time-consuming, as well as there were lack of answers for wrapping required tools into one, well-known, illness prediction framework which might be used for one-of-a-kind software tasks. To fill this hole, Madeyski and Majchrzak proposed a brand new, extensible (plugin-primarily based) framework called DePress. DePress (Defect Prediction for Software Systems) builds upon the KNIME framework and lets in development of graphical work and makes use of an intuitive, consumer-pleasant interface. Being intuitive and highly customizable, the DePress makes itself an ideal tool which can be conveniently applied (thanks to its consumer-pleasant interface and a huge range of plugins) in extraordinary industrial software program development tasks for software defect prediction. Detailed description of DePress framework and its competencies may be located on DePress internet site or inside the article by Madeyski and Majchrzak.

There are diverse residences or metric attributes located and utilized for programming defects prediction as part of the writing. Rather than coping with such a ramification of belongings, it would be beneficial and simple inside the event that we could decide the association of metrics which might be most vital and make use of them more to foresee the defects. In this paper we have carried out evaluate of numerous strategies like ANN, Fuzzy good judgment, Fuzzy Art map and so on. To decide the compelling connections the various software metric attributes and defect prediction. In software program defect prediction there are many supervised system mastering strategies like (neural community, guide vector system, Naïve Bayes etc.) exist which can lessen the time span and fee of the venture. For Predicting the defect in Software there's also one new supervised gadget studying technique i.e. Fuzzy ARTMAP. The metric attributes are utilized within the taken into consideration evaluate papers normally has used software program datasets which made openly available with a specific give up aim to empower repeatable, obvious, refutable, and/or improvable prescient fashions of software program engineering. In maximum of the cases there is NASA MDP dataset which are on hand to anticipate the imperfections within the software program merchandise. The point of proposed examine is to research whether or not metric based assessment inside the early lifecycle (i.e. Necessity measurements), metric based assessment within the past due lifecycle (i.e. Code measurements) and metric based assessment inside the early lifecycle (i.e. Necessity measurements) joined with metric primarily based assessment in the late lifecycle (i.e. Code measurements) can be utilized to recognize defectiveness issue inclined modules making use of exceptional supervised and unsupervised prediction and estimation strategies.

2. Related Work:

In this section we have got given a summarized evaluate of numerous studies which can be accomplished in the field of software disorder prediction in final couple of many years. We have defined approximately numerous techniques their blessings and the concluding results that have contributed loads within the development of especially dependable degree of software illness prediction mechanism.

Software defect prediction is a promising, new technique to increase each, software program nice and development pace. Unfortunately, the fee effectiveness of software program illness prediction in business settings isn't eagerly shared by using the pioneering corporations. In specific, the value effectiveness of the usage of the DePress open supply software measurement framework, developed through Wroclaw University of Science and Technology, and Capgemini software program improvement business enterprise, for defect prediction in industrial software development initiatives have now not been formerly investigated. Thus, on this work, Jaroslaw Hryszko et. Al. (2017), [16] explore whether disorder prediction can undoubtedly effect an industrial software improvement task through producing profits. To meet this goal, we carried out a disorder prediction and simulated potential best assurance charges based on the fine prediction result, in addition to the proposed Quality Assurance (QA) approach. Results of our investigation were positive: we estimated that fine warranty charges may be reduced by nearly 30% when proposed method could be used, at the same time as envisioned DePress device usage Return on Investment (ROI) is absolutely 73 (7300%), and Benefits Cost Ratio (BCR) is 74. Such promising outcomes have triggered the recognition of continued utilization of the DePress-based totally software defect prediction for real industrial tasks run by means of Volvo Group.

Software defection prediction isn't always best important for improving software program satisfactory, but also useful for software take a look at effort estimation. As is widely recognized,80%of the fault takes place in20%of the modules. Therefore, Xiaotao Rong et. Al. (2016) [17], want to discover the maximum error susceptible modules correctly and accurate them in time to store time, money, and strength. Support vector machine (SVM) is a complicated type method that fits the defection class. However, research show that, the value of parameters of SVM version has a extremely good have an impact on on its type accuracy and the choice method lacks concept guidance that makes the SVM version uncertainty and low efficiency. In this paper, a CBA-SVM software program illness prediction version is proposed, which take gain of the non-linear computing ability of SVM version and optimisation capacity of bat algorithm with centroid strategy (CBA). Through the experimental evaluation with other models, CBA-SVM is proved to have a higher accuracy.

Fenton and Neil (1991) contend that notwithstanding the truth that there are such a massive variety of research in the writing, software program defect forecast issue is a long way for purchasing perfect results. There are a few wrong presumptions approximately how defects are characterised or watched and this has brought on misdirecting consequences. Their case can be visible higher while we see that some papers signify defects as watched inadequacies while a few others symbolize them as ultimate ones. They can gauge the software program attributes by using looking ahead to the size and multifaceted nature, testing, system pleasant statistics, multivariate technique and so forth [1]. R. Chidamber and Kemerer (1994) paper supplied new businesses of software metrics that is to be followed for the item orientated design. By assessing those metrics they found that those metrics tend to numerous residences and advocate a few strategies wherein item oriented technique would possibly fluctuate from conventional technique. They execute six-diverse units of metrics called WMC, RFC, NOC, DIT, CBO, and LOCM [2]. Venkata U.B. Challagulla (2005) proposed a specific device studying models for spotting fallacious actual-time software program modules using various set of NASA dataset like KC1,PC1,CM1,JM1 is to be taken to anticipate the s/w product defects. When we ascertain the suggest absolute blunders of various to be had software predictions it's miles to be observed that KC1 dataset is excellent to anticipate the illness [3]. A.Gunes koru (2005) takes a few machines gaining knowledge of algorithms to foresee programming defects in software program module in five NASA datasets i.E. CM1, JM1, KC1, KC2, and PC1. They finished illness prediction utilizing magnificence-stage data for KC1 as opposed to approach level data. For this example, the utilization of sophistication-stage information brought about enhanced forecast execution in opposition to the making use of approach level records [4]. Anuradha Chug et al. (2010) suggest distinctive grouping and bunching techniques with a goal to assume programming imperfection. The execution of three information mining classifier calculations named J48, Random Forest, and Naive Bayesian Classifier (NBC) are assessed in view of various criteria including ROC, Precision, MAE, RAE and so on. Grouping method is then linked at the information set making use of okay-implies, Hierarchical Clustering and Make Density Based Clustering calculation [5]. Shanthini et al.(2012) covered the paintings with the number one objective to break down the execution of various classifiers on disorder expectation based totally on open region NASA statistics set KC1; they broke down the execution of the classifiers making use of standard measures, as an instance, exactness, review and F-degree. This have a look at affirms that development of the SVM models is appropriate, versatile to OO frameworks, and treasured in looking forward to shortcoming inclined lessons for extra extended quantity of measurements (class) [6]. C. Akalya Devi et al. (2012) proposed a hybrid thing willpower technique which offers a superior illness estimation than the traditional routines. NASA's open dataset KC1 available at promise software facts storage is utilized. To examine the execution overall performance of the product defects forecast fashions accuracy, imply absolute mistakes (MAE), Root mean squared mistakes (RMSE) qualities measurements are applied [7]. Ahmet Okutan et.Al. (2012) proposed a unique system making use of Bayesian structures to research the connections among programming measurements and imperfection inclination. They utilize nine information sets from Promise software program dataset and show that RFC, LOC, and LOCQ are greater feasible on defect prediction expectation [8]. Martin Shepperd et.Al.(2012), investigates the diploma to which dispensed examinations considering the NASA software program defect datasets units are giant and moreover prescribed that the provenance of the statistics units they utilize .This document additionally describes that pre-processing of dataset in adequate factor of interest is beneficial to empower critical replication and it additionally positioned exertion in comprehension the records dataset previous to use in making use of in system getting to know [9]. V.Jayaraj et.Al. (2013) proposed the exactness of the disorder prediction of Boosting techniques for s/w defects expectation deliberating the KC1 dataset is tested. They applied 21 gadget degree metrics to anticipate the defects within the data records via using three gadget mastering calculation of boosting approach [10]. Malkit Singh (2013) labored on a neural device strategy and Levenberg Marquardt (LM) mechanism is created and the exactness of proposed framework is better that polynomial relation based totally neural gadget functions. In this paper Levenberg-Marquardt (LM) calculation based neural device studying method is utilized for the illness estimation because of programming imperfections at an early section of the product advancement lifestyles cycle [11].

Martin Shepperd (2014) disorder forecast analysts targeted on the direct use of blind analysis it beautify reporting conventions and lead more intergroup research retaining in mind the quit aim to found easier understanding problems. Ultimately, studies is required to parent out if this inclination is not unusual in exclusive programs place. In this paper they take a huge variety of Dataset for imperfection forecast where the exactness of Nasa MDP is advanced to some thing other dataset [12]. Pushpavathi T.P et al. (2014) reports an research for awaiting illness prediction in s/w modules making use of coordinated method of genetic set of rules based fuzzy c-method clustering with random woodland calculation. This technique was produced making use of Genetic Algorithm based Fuzzy C-implies bunching with Random Forest grouping related on specific records set and research turned into done. At long last outcomes were authorized with the usage of 5 NASA open space software illness facts sets [13]. Sunida Ratanothayanon et al. (2012)has been proposed two classifier for the software program defect prediction i.e. Back Propagation Neural Network and Radial Basis Functions with Gaussian kernels as classifiers and bring effects on NASA dataset are validated and investigated on the idea of suggest rectangular blunders and percent of accuracy [14].

3 Methodology Involved in S/W disorder prediction:

We have reviewed numerous articles to examine the distinct strategies which are worried in this decade for best software illness prediction. It has been located that synthetic intelligence strategies are extensively used for estimating the abnormalities in software by utilising the various sorts of software metrics.

Table 1. Summarized Description of Technology used in s/w Defect Prediction in Year Wise Manner.

S. No.	Authors Name	Technique	Result
1.	Venkata U.B. Challagulla, Farokh B. Bastani, I-Ling Yen, Raymond A. Paul, [3]	Support Vector Logic Regression	--
		NN for Discrete goal field	--
		Logistic Regression	--
		Naïve Bayes	--
		Instance Based Learning	--
		J48 Tree	--
		1-Rule	--
2.	Shanthini. A, Chandrasekaran.RM, [6]	Naïve Bayes	68.27%
		Support Vector Machine	80%
3.	C. Akalya Devi, K. E. Kannammal and B. Surendiran, [7]	Neural network	76.27%
		Radial Basis Function	69.52%
4.	V.Jayaraj, N.Saravana Raman [10]	Boosting with decision Stump	86.94%
		Boosting with REP tree	86.52%
		Boosting with M5	87.37%
5.	Malkit Singh, Dalwinder Singh Salaria [11]	Linear function based Neural Network	80.3%
		Quadratic Function Based Neural Network	78.8%
		Levenberg-Marquardt (LM) algorithm based neural network	88.1%
6.	Martin Shepperd, David Bowes, and Tracy Hall [12]	Density based Clustering Approach	58.63%

4. Conclusion

This paper presents a literature review of using diverse techniques for artificial intelligence techniques inside the discipline of software program disorder prediction. This literature overview could be very beneficial, since it brings a better expertise of the sphere of study, and that is an vital contribution of this paper. From the literature review it can be concluded that this situation draws a extremely good deal of hobby with the aid of researchers and a notable algorithms are present associated with software defect prediction based totally coding in the place of Software Engineering. We have reviewed numerous articles to analyze the specific strategies which can be worried in this decade for perfect software illness prediction. So we finish that we in destiny paintings there are superb scope of the application of Fuzzy good judgment and neural network primarily based strategies for software defect prediction.

It has been determined that however numerous techniques like Support Vector Logic Regression, neural network, Boosting and so forth. Techniques are analyzed for disorder prediction but none of them gives the accuracy higher than 88 percent. Hence there is a large scope inside the discipline of defect prediction. We can in future don't forget advanced hybrid mechanism like Fuzzy Artmap in acting extra dependable disorder prediction algorithm improvement.

References:

[1]. Norman Fenton, N.E. and Neil, M. (1999), "A Critique of Software Defect Prediction Models", IEEE Transactions on Software Engineering, vol.25, no. 5, pp. 675-689.

[2]. R.Chidamer and Kemerer, "A Metrics Suit for Object Oriented Design" IEEE Transaction Software Engineering, vol.20, no.6, June 1994.

[3]. Venkata U.B. Challagulla, Farokh B. Bastani, I-Ling Yen, Raymond A. Paul, "Empirical Assessment of Machine Learning based Software Defect Prediction Techniques", IEEE, 2005.

[4]. A.Gunes Koru, "An Investigation of the Effect of Module Size on Defect Prediction Using Static Measures" ACM SIGSOFT Software Engineering Notes, 2005.

[5]. Anuradha Chug, Shafali Dhall "Software Defect Prediction Using Supervised Learning Algorithm and Unsupervised Learning Algorithm", International Journal of computer science and engineering Vol.27, no.5 2010.

[6]. Shanthini. A, Chandrasekaran.RM, "Applying Machine Learning for Fault Prediction Using Software Metrics", International Journal of Advanced Research in Computer Science and Software Engineering, Volume 2, Issue 6, June 2012.

[7]. C. Akalya Devi, K. E. Kannammal and B. Surendiran, "A Hybrid Feature Selection Model for Software Fault Prediction", International Journal on Computational Sciences & Applications (IJCSA) Vo2, No.2, April 2012.

[8]. Ahmet Okutan Olcay Taner Yıldız, "Software defect prediction using Bayesian networks", Empirical Software Eng (2014) 19:154–181 © Springer Science+Business Media, LLC, 2012.

[9]. Martin Shepperd, Qinbao Song Zhongbin Sun Carolyn Mair "Data Quality: Some Comments on the NASA Software Defect Data Sets" IEEE Transaction on Software Engineering, Vol. 28, Oct 2012.

[10]. V.Jayaraj, N.Saravana Raman "Software Defect Prediction using Boosting Techniques", International Journal of Computer Applications (0975 – 8887) Volume 65– No.13, March 2013.

[11]. Malkit Singh, Dalwinder Singh Salaria, "Software Defect Prediction Tool based on Neural Network", International Journal of Computer Applications vol.70-N0.22, May 2013.

[12]. Martin Shepperd, David Bowes, and Tracy Hall "The Use of Machine Learning in Software Defect Prediction", IEEE Transactions On Software Engineering, Vol. 40, NO. 6, June 2014.

[13]. Pushpavathi T.P, Suma V, Ramaswamy V, "Defect Prediction in Software Projects-Using Genetic Algorithm based Fuzzy C-Means Clustering and Random Forest Classifier", International Journal of Scientific & Engineering Research, Volume 5, Issue 9, September-2014.

[14]. Sunida Ratanothayanon, Chouvanee Srivisal, Sirirut Vanichayobonand, and Ladda Preechaveerakul, "Comparative Classifiers for Software Quality Assessment", IACSIT International Journal of Engineering and Technology, Vol. 4, No. 4, August 2012.

[15]. Supreet Kaur, and Dinesh Kumar, "Software Fault Prediction in Object Oriented Software Systems Using Density Based Clustering Approach", International Journal of Research in

Engineering and Technology (IJRET) Vol. 1 No. 2 March, 2012.
[16] Jaroslaw Hryszko et. al. "Assessment of the Software Defect Prediction Cost Effectiveness in an Industrial Project" vol. 504 of Advances in Intelligent Systems and Computing, pp. 77{90, Springer, 2017.
[17] Xiaotao Rong"A model for software defect prediction using support vector machine based on CBA" Int. J. Intelligent Systems Technologies and Applications, Vol. 15, No. 1, 2016

AVERT TRAFFIC VIOLATIONS BY AUTOMATIC LICENSE PLATE DETECTION USING DEEP LEARNING TECHNIQUE

Preethi S[1], Madhan Kumar P[1], Pradeep S[1], Anto Arockia Rosaline R[1]

[1]Rajalakshmi Engineering College, 602105 Thandalam, Chennai, Tamil Nadu

{preethi.s.2014.it, madhankumar.p.2014.it, pradeep.s.2014.it, antoarockiarosaline.r}@rajalakshmi.edu.in

Abstract

Over the past few years, the number of traffic accidents and congestion has been increasing enormously due to the violation of the traffic rules. Traffic congestion is becoming one of the major issues in metropolitan cities. Current traffic system is of fixed time concept in which huge traffic cannot be given more time for the vehicle passing, so they tend to violate the traffic rules. Realizations have produced results which depicted road accidents have been one of the leading issues currently in every city. Such issues will lead to so many disruptions to the entire system as well as exhausts our precious time. One such problem is driving the wrong way on a one-way and no entry signs. So, in order to address this issue and improvise the traffic disciplines, many solutions to the current technologies have been proposed. The proposed system will detect moving vehicles in the one way and no entry roads through a camera sensor (water resistant), which will capture the images of the vehicles and process it through deep learning technology. This technology is widely used nowadays and there are a lot of interesting applications in computer vision. The system makes use of deep learning technique along with image recognition that will capture the number plate from the vehicle, extracts the vehicle registration number portion of the plate, segment it and then is transformed into alphanumeric characters which are used for recognition. These alphanumeric characters are compared with one or more databases in order to track the person who owns the vehicle. Once tracking is completed successfully owner's personal details such as his/her name, address, mobile number etc would be grabbed. After grabbing their personal details, an alert message will be sent to their mobile stating about the violation caused as well as the penalty amount to be paid. Though the number of the vehicles has been increasing tremendously, the infrastructure of the road has not yet been better. This proposed system will help in reducing manual works, bringing discipline on roads as well as reduces traffic-related problems which bring disruptions to the entire system.

Keywords: One-way, License Plate, Detection, Deep Learning, Traffic, Violation.

1. Introduction

The records from many of the countries revealed that higher percentage of serious road accidents have occurred at the road junction due to disobeying or violating the traffic rules. There are number of different technologies that are helpful in capturing the traffic congestions and as well as to make an efficient congestion management [1]. Even though there are advantages, it also has drawbacks such as complexity, cost, and installation problems etc. as discovered by Aditi *et al.* [1]. There are number of technological related solutions that have been proposed in order to minimize the issues that are associated to the traffic related behavior. For the past few years, there has been substantial focus on number plate detection and recognition techniques. One such technique has been implemented through smart phones where image processing is also used which was proposed by Priyamvadha [17] and also vehicle localizations are done using Vertical Edge Map and Hough Transform Based technique discovered by Satadal *et al.* [20]. The proposed system has made use of deep learning technique with image recognition technique to capture and extract the alphanumeric characters [3] from the number plate that will reduce the manual work.

Unlike traditional methods, deep learning techniques automatically picks out features and it is one of the game changing technology in the area of computer vision, automatic recognition tasks and natural language processing shown by Naga *et al.* [13]. Few applications of Deep Learning are Computer Vision, Speech Recognition, Translation, Chat Bots, IoT, Image Recognition, Medical etc [26].

The system has chosen the image recognition technique using deep network just because it has achieved remarkable progress in the recent years [6]. Recognition of an on-road vehicle's number plate plays an important role in many of the real-time application scenarios.

Automatic Number Plate Recognition (ANPR) a mass surveillance system which will capture the image of the vehicles and once captured it recognizes their license number. ANPR can be used in the detection of stolen vehicles as well. The detection of the stolen vehicles is completed by making use of the ANPR systems that are located in the highways. The vehicle plate image is captured by the digital cameras and the image is being processed to get the number plate information. A rear image of a vehicle is firstly captured and then processed using algorithms. And then the number plate area is localized using a novel which is a feature-based number plate localization technique which consists of various algorithms.

Deep learning is based on learning about data representations which can either be supervised or unsupervised learning explored by Naga *et al.* [13].

Deep learning has best in class performance on problems that will perform other solutions in the multiple domains. One such solution is that, when consistent images are challenging due to environmental conditions, deep learning can detect more defects. It is an architecture that can be adapted to new problems very easily such as time series, language, vision etc. This methodology can recognize patterns and classify them easily.

The main advantage is to reduce the need for feature engineering. These are the reasons to choose deep learning as the processing technique.

The detected number plate is then processed using image recognition technique in order to remove the noise. Once noise is completely removed, then the result produced will be moved to the segmentation phase where the character segmentation happens individually, that will be extracted from the captured number plate.

Hence, the characters that have been segmented are now normalized. After the normalization of characters have been completed it is been sent to the algorithm. Finally, these characters are converted to encoded digits. From this information, it is possible to track the owner details through the databases and then an alert message will be sent to the vehicles owner's mobile which will incur a penalty amount.

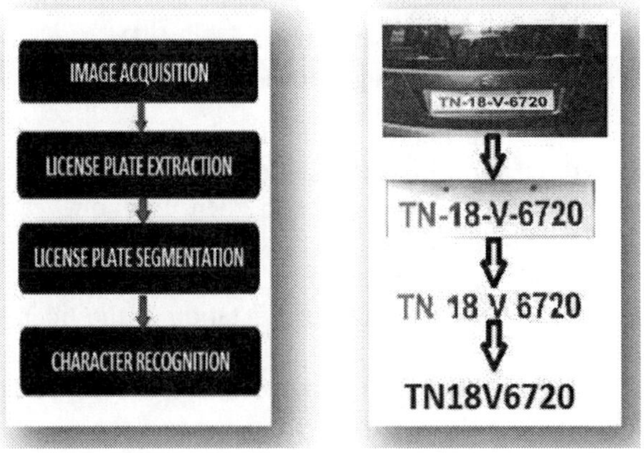

Figure 1 Four stages of automatic license plate recognition

There are four categories of automatic license plate recognition [29] as shown in Figure 1, which was depicted by Shan Du *et al.* [18], [10], [19], and [22]. They are as follows:

a. Image Acquisition
b. Extraction of License Plate
c. Segmentation of License Plate
d. Recognition of Characters

2. Literature Survey

Some of the present technologies are as follows:

2.1 License Plate Detection:

License plate Detection looks into an input image and outputs probable license plate bounding boxes. Although many of plate detection algorithms have been proposed in the past few years, it is still a challenging issue to detect the license plate accurately. The existing algorithms are classified into four categories as mentioned by Hui Li *et al.* [11]: Edge-based, Color-based, Texture-based, and Character-based.

Edge-based methods try to explore the regions with higher edge densities than in the image as license plates [11]. Color-based approaches are based on the examination that license plates color is generally different from that of the car body [11].

Texture-based approaches try to detect the license plates based on the unconventional pixel intensity spreading in plate regions [11], [25]. Character-based approaches consider the license plate as a string of characters and detect it by observing the presence of characters in the image [11].

2.2 License Plate Recognition:

Past work on license plate recognition generally needs to perform the character segmentation phase in the number plate initially and then find out each segmented character using the optical character recognition (OCR) techniques [11], [4], [21], [24]. Present algorithms on the segmentation of the license plate can be categorized into two categories as follows: Projection-based and connected component (CC) - based [30].

Projection-based approaches make use of the histograms of vertical as well as horizontal pixel projections for the character segmentation [2], [25]. The binary image of license plate is projected horizontally to find out the top and bottom boundaries of the characters [8]. The binary license plate is actually labeled into the component based on the 4 or 8 neighborhood connections in CC-based methods.

2.3 Radio Frequency Identification (RFID):

The RFID technology has been made use in the intention of identification of those number plates as well as tracking that is done by the radio waves. Many of the tags of RFID consist of at least two parts. The first one is an integrated circuit which is actually used for storing and processing the target's information, and then it also performs modulation and demodulation of a radio frequency (RF) signal as well as few other functions as well. Secondly it is an antenna which is used for the transmission and reception for the signal that is captured during the entire process. Two categories of the RFID devices are: A RFID that is called an active RFID device which can transmit signals autonomously along with a battery and the other one called passive RFID device that has no battery which requires an external source to produce signal transmission [1].

2.4 License Plate Localization:

In the license plate localization technique, the license plate is located from the image which is captured by the camera. Vehicle speed, heavy traffic and the lightning conditions are the major issues in detection. Nowadays, security is the major concern. Mostly, the license plates are characterized by its high contrast between its characters and background. Technology improvements like infrared imaging and high-resolution cameras, and the utilization of high reflective backgrounds in license plate manufacturing have refined the accuracy of ANPR systems. And the hardware used connects to the accuracy of the system [14].

2.5 Video Data Analysis:

Video data analysis contains digital image processing technique for automatically analyzing the scene of interest and extracts the information for managing the traffic system [7]. The CCTV cameras are used to capture the images and then load the image into disk for testing [5]. Each image that has been captured from the camera are then stored as separate entity, similar to a digital camera at home [12].

Observing the scene constantly which is under the inspection is a computational task that might also produce the inconsistent results. So, image acquisition happens through sensors that are specialized which can be either infrared or ultrasound sensors.

The cameras contain the videos that are actually maintained during the process of analysis [9]. The software that is present inside that camera would crop the needed information from that captured video initially. Information such as (Volume of the vehicle, average velocity of the vehicle etc.) is then given as input to the fuzzy system to get processed. Thus, after processing, it outputs the level of traffic congestion [9].

3. Proposed Architecture

The architecture diagram of the proposed system is diagrammatically represented in the Figure 2.

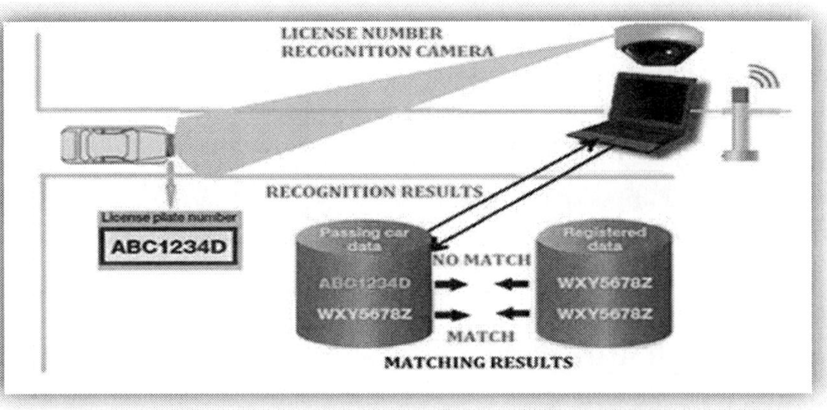

Figure 2 Architecture Diagram

The proposed system makes use of deep learning technique along with image recognition that will capture the number plate using the camera and extracts the vehicle registration number portion of the plate using segmentation and then is transformed into alphanumeric characters which are useful for recognition. Then with the help of the trained data sets the registration number will be tested against them and if it matches it will be considered as the output which is the registration number of the vehicle. Deep Learning can easily identify the defects that are difficult to detect and train [28]. More number of hidden layers has been used here to have more number of combinations to check and the accuracy is enhanced in this system.

4. Result and Analysis

Only few particular methods for building as well as training the neural networks have been covered in Deep Learning technique [6], [23]. It wipes of the manual step of finding out the features in the input data that is raw. Instead, it will depend on the training process to identify the most useful patterns among the inputs that are processed [27].

In the proposed system, the training has been made using 60000 samples and 10000 samples have been validated from it. From these samples 28*28 images were flattened to a 784 vector for each image.

The digits recognized from the loaded data set are shown in Figure.3:

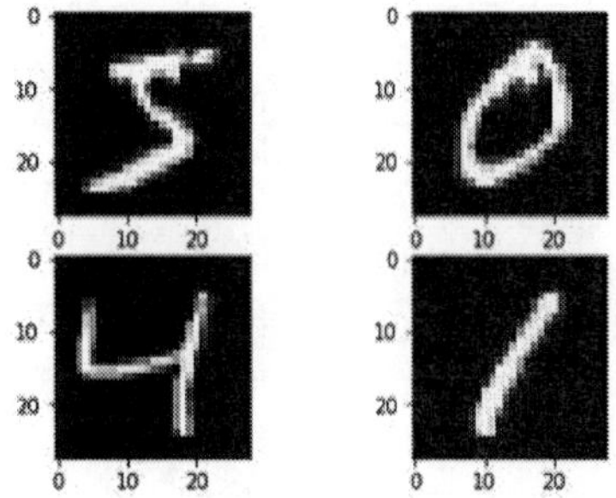

Figure 3 Output

The following Table. 1 displays the value loss (val_loss) and value accuracy (val_acc) of the 10000 samples in 10 Epochs:

Table 1. Loss and Accuracy

EPOCH	LOSS	ACCURACY	VAL_LOSS	VAL_ACC
1	0.2811	0.9200	0.1404	0.9571
2	0.1115	0.9676	0.0955	0.9724
3	0.0724	0.9794	0.0703	0.9762
4	0.0505	0.9852	0.0702	0.9776
5	0.0357	0.9901	0.0636	0.9799
6	0.0276	0.9928	0.0686	0.9792
7	0.0204	0.9952	0.0556	0.9823
8	0.0144	0.9968	0.0580	0.9829
9	0.0103	0.9981	0.0608	0.9816
10	0.0077	0.9987	0.0591	0.9821

Epoch is nothing but a division of time that is the beginning of a period.

On the basis of the Table 1. The proposed system thereby reduces the loss and increases the accuracy over the 10000 validated images. The Baseline Error is predicted as 1.79%.

Layer type and the output shape are shown in the Table.2 as follows:

Table 2. Finding out number of Params

LAYER (TYPE)	OUTPUT SHAPE	PARAM #
Conv2d_6 (Conv2D)	(None, 32, 24, 24)	832
max_pooling2d_6 (MaxPooling2)	(None ,32, 12, 12)	0
dropout_4 (Dropout)	(None, 32, 12, 12)	0
flatten_4 (Flatten)	(None, 4608)	0
dense_13 (Dense)	(None, 128)	589952
dense_14 (Dense)	(None, 10)	1290
Total params: 592,074.0 Trainable params: 592,074.0 Non-trainable params: 0.0		

The graphical representation of the evaluated accuracy and loss are as follows:

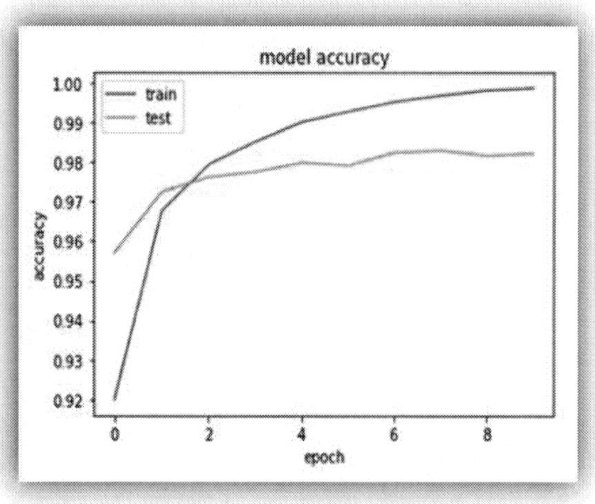

Figure 4 Model Accuracy

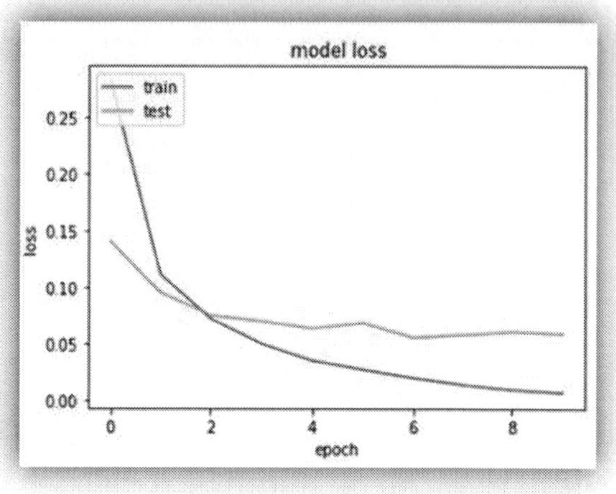

Figure 5 Model Loss

As the epoch (period marked by distinctive character) increases the accuracy of the trained and the test data is also increased which is shown in the Figure 4.

Increase in epoch results in drastic decrease in loss of the model accordingly which is shown in the Figure 5.

5. Conclusion

This proposed system has used deep learning techniques in the field of automatic license plate detection system. It includes segmentation of the image and recognition of the character using the trained data sets. Another important aspect in this system is the neural networks in which more number of hidden layers is used to find more combinations and thereby to increase the overall accuracy from 95% to 98%. The reason for implementing the deep learning is that the time required will be reduced and the accuracy is enhanced with better results. This system is useful for the following:

1. The data that can be used to train the neural networks are the real time data and those data are the images fetched from the cameras in one-way, no entry, signals, parking lots, etc.

2. Any kind of rule violation can be caught and the enforcement can be preceded instantly.

The details of the vehicle and the respective owner information can be tracked.

6. Future Scope

This proposed system may not be successful during rainy seasons because of the poor visibility, fog etc. Enhancement should be made even during bad weather conditions with a better-quality camera.

Number plates that are of regional languages like Tamil, Telugu, Malayalam etc can also be automatically detected in the future enhancements.

References

1. Aditi Dambe, Upasana Gandhe, Varsha Bendre, "Automatic Penalty Charging for Violation of Traffic Rules", International Journal of Advanced Research in Electrical, Electronics and Instrumentation Engineering Volume 2, Issue 2, February 2013.

2. Alekhya Nalla, Sri Vidya.S, "Vertical Edge based Car License Plate Detection Method", Chaitanya Institute of Science and Technology.

3. Amr Badr, Mohamed M, Abdelwahab, Ahmed M. Thabet and Ahmed M. Abdelsadak," Automatic Number Plate Recognition System ", Annals of the University of Craivoa, Mathematics and Computer Science Series Volume 38(1), Pages 62-71 ISSN: 1223-6934.

4. Atul Kumar, Sunila Godara, "A Review on Number Plate Recognition ", International Journal of Science and Research (IJSR) ISSN (Online): 2319-7064 Volume 4 Issue 5, May 2015.

5. Bailey D.G, Irecki. D, Lim B.K, Yang.L," Test Bed for Number Plate Recognition Applications".

6. Bharath P Hedge, Mahalakahmi. S," Automatic License Plate Detection Using Deep Learning Techniques ", Information Science Engineering Bangalore Vol.5(1):107-103, May 2017.

7. Chang J.k, Seungteak Ryoo, Heuiseok Lim J," Real-time Vehicle tracking Mechanism with license Plate Recognition from Road Images ", Supercomputer (2013) 65:353-364 DOI 10.1007/s11227-011-0580-x.

8. Chao Gou, Kunfeng Wang, Yanjie Yao and Zhengxi Li, "Vehicle License Plate Recognition Based on External Regions and Restricted Boltzman Machines", IEEE transactions on intelligent transportation systems, Volume 17 No 4, April 2014.

9. Emmanuel Di Nardo, Lucia Maddalena and Alfredo Petrosino," Video-Based Access Control by Automatic License Plate Recognition ".

10. Fajas F, Farhan Yousuf, Remya P. R, Adarsh P. Pavanan, Sajan Ambadiyil, Varsha Swaminathan, "Automatic Number Plate Recognition for Indian Standard Number Plates", First Workshop on Emerging Technologies and Devices in Signal Processing 2012.

11. Hui Li, Chunhua Shen," Reading Car License Plates Using Deep Convolutional Neural Networks and LSTMs".

12. Lakshmi. K, Deepa. R, Gayathri.S, Rajaram.N. R, Vimal Kumar. S.M," Smart Traffic Management System ", International Journal of Advanced Research Methodology in Engineering & Technology, ISSN 2456-6446 Volume 1, Issue 3, May 2017.

13. Naga, Surya, Sandeep, Angara," Automatic License Plate Recognition Using Deep Learning Techniques (2015).

14. Neha Rana, Pawan Kumar Dahiya, "License Plate Localization Method Based on Vertical Edge Detection", International Journals of Advanced Research in Computer Science and Software Engineering, June 2017.

15. Nupur, Alisha," A Review Paper on License Plate Recognition System", International Journal for Research in Applied Science & Engineering Technology Voprel 5 Issue 4, April 2017.

16. Paras Goyal, Iqbal Singh C-Dac, Mohali, "Security System for Vehicle using Number Plate Detection and RFID", International Journal of Computer Applications (0975 – 8887) Volume 97– No.8, July 2014.

17. Priyamvadha Krishna Kumar," Automatic Number Plate Recognition(ANPR) through Smart Phones using Image Processing Techniques", IOSR

Journal of VLSI and Signal Processing (IOSR-JVSP) Volume 4, Issue 4, Version 3 (Jul-Aug 2014).

18. Shan Du, Mohamed Ibrahim, Mohamed Shehata and Wael Badway," Automatic License Plate Recognition (ALPR): A State-of-the-Art Review ", IEEE transactions on circuits and systems for video technology, vol.23 February 2013.

19. Sai Krishna. P, "Automatic Number Plate Recognition by Using MATLAB", International Journal of Innovative Research in Electronics and Communications (IJIREC) Volume 2, Issue 4, June 2015, PP 1-7 ISSN 2349-4042 (Print) & ISSN 2349-4050.

20. Satadal Saha. "License Plate Localization Using Vertical Edge Map and Hough Transform Based Technique", Advances in Intelligent and Soft Computing, 2012.

21. Shah. A.N, Gaikwad. A.S, "A Review- Recognition of License Number Plate using Character Segmentation and OCR with Template Matching", International Journal of Advanced Research in Computer and Communication Engineering Vol. 5, Issue 2, February 2016.

22. Siva Vinayaka Pavana Hiranya. P, Venkata Suresh, Sabhanayagam. T, "Car License Plate Detection using Structured Component Analysis", 2014 IJEDR | Conference Proceeding (NCETSE-2014) | ISSN: 2321-9939.

23. Syed Zain Masood Guang Shu Afshin Dehghan Enrique G. Ortiz fzainmasood, Guangshu, Afshindehghan, "License Plate Detection and Recognition Using Deeply Learned Convolutional Neural Networks", September 2016.

24. Teik Koon Cheang, Yong Shean Chong, Yong Haur Tay, "Segmentation-free Vehicle License Plate Recognition using ConvNet-RNN ".

25. Wenzhe Shi1, Jose Caballero1, Ferenc Husz´ar1, Johannes Totz1, Andrew P. Aitken1, Rob Bishop1, Daniel Rueckert1, Zehan Wang1, ". Real-Time Single Image and Video Super-Resolution Using an Efficient Sub-Pixel Convolutional Neural Network", September 2016.

26. http://caffe2.ai/docs/applications-of-deep-learning.html

27. www.oreilly.com/ideas/what-is-deep-learning

28. acquireautomation.com/news/2017/02/15/3-huge-advantages-to-deep-learning/

29. www.i-scholar.in

30. dl.dropboxusercontent.com

31. research.ijcaonline.org

The Survey of Machine Learning Algorithm For Component Based Software Data Exchange

Amit Verma
CGC Landran, Mohali, INDIA
Email ID: dramitverma.cu@gmail.com

Gurpreet Singh Kamboj
CGC Landran,Mohali, INDIA
Email ID: kambojgurpreetsingh@gmail.com

Iqbaldeep Kaur
CGC Landran, Mohali, INDIA
Email ID: iqbaldeepkaur.cu@gmail.com

***Abstract*—Software engineering is growing area in which the software system contains specifically the design,data flow and operations. Machine learning is provided the better classification and more accuracy in design and retrieve the components from the storage manager.Reusability plays the vital in component development which minimizes the software cost in the modules and as well as in product sometimes.Component modules must design and verified accurately to take the decision for component reusability.This technique helps to time-saving,less cost and optimization purposes.But it is hard to implement and it needs the technical knowledge of design,reverse engineering because sometimes it happens that a developer needs to modify the current module for better customer satisfaction.The hybrid approach can also get implemented for more efficiency of development.Optimization with Genetic algorithm takes the raw data and facts and rule are applied to processed data and priorities are made.The component ranked on the basis of quality,issues and other factor.Component-based software reuse is used in development with the advancement of the internet makes the great scale of component possessions from. In this survey paper, here explained the machine learning algorithm, i.e. supports vector machine, fuzzy interference system, etc., Semantic- based models, types of Software reusability and principles.**

Keywords—Component-Based Software Reuse; Quality-Based Software Reuse, Principles And machine learning techniques

I. Introduction

In software productivity is slowing progressions and maximum requirement defines that most software developers increasingly search themselves in the end of the software emergency that inhibits their ability to produce high quality and cost effective software [1].

Software re-use is seen as the individual solution to optimizing time to market and enhancing and productivity and quality of development. Currently,important features of software reusability will be covered [2].Reusable software assumes the functional domains and saves the important time of the real word and it also increases productivity.Functional domain helps the software to enhance the product and update the software structure,quality in the existing software component[3].It simplifies the concept of software engineering and deeply using the powerful techniques in modules for cost saving,reliability,and for better productivity.Operation time needed to make the product with the already existing module has been very less and hence the powerful way to decrease the quantity of work.It is easy to say in theory, but harder to get implemented in real time.Finally, decreasing the threat of schemes that are independent and dependent on source data [4]. Component-based system development takes care of customer requirement concern by developing the proper system with using the component reuse.It deals with the key factor like quality of software, operation cost, and throughput of the software system. The data exchange model is used by CBSE for development of the application.It also includesthe storage structure and model of the object. To access the reusable objects by taking one or more component into concern the object model is used [5].The component models are:

- Microsoft Component-Object Model, Dispersed Component-Object Model.
- Component Object Application Broker Design.
- Enterprise Java Beans (EJB).

Component based model tells standard,specify the catalyst between application software and component and used to build the application by using models[6].The various phases of component development are Requirements analysis, design, development and testing. It has the capacity for easy management,effective development time ,better productivity and less cost.The most challenging task is to have unsatisfied requirements being faced in component-based software approach.

Table 1. Differentiate the types of component based retrieval

COM: Model for Component Units	Enterprise Java Beans	Common Object Application Broker Architecture
ODIBTW C&C	• Used for MCoRS	• MA&I uses IIOP PTI
Allows PL having PTF to be used as SC.	• RC built to IO all JP	• Offers R,I,PFS

C is made of objects with I&S.	• TB (S), OB(E) and TB(MD)	R,CDP,E
COM C like exe files or DLL	S is maintained till the time CC is alive.	C&S to DS

ODI BTW C&C-Outlines Direct Interaction Between Components and Clients, Macros-Modular Construction of Robust Systems, MA&I-Middleware Architecture And Infrastructure, PTI-Protocol To Interoperate, PL-Programming Language, PTF-Pointer To Function, SC-Source Code, RC-Reusable Component ,IO- inter-operate , JP- Java Platforms-Reusable, I-Interoperable, PFS-Portable Features Specification, C-Component, I&S-Identity and States, TB-Time Based, S-Session, OB-Object Based, E-Entity, TB-Token Based, Message Driven, R-Reliable, CDP- Consistent Distributed Programming , E- Environment, CC-Calling Client, C&S-Conformance and Standardization, DS-Developing System.
In component based software engineering using the machine learning approaches. We classify the huge amount of the component, in the database. In machine learning divide the data into two phases:
-Training State
-Testing State

II. COMPONENT BASED SOFTWARE ENGINEERING TECHNIQUES

There are three perspectives of component retrieval methods currently available and are shown in Figure 1.

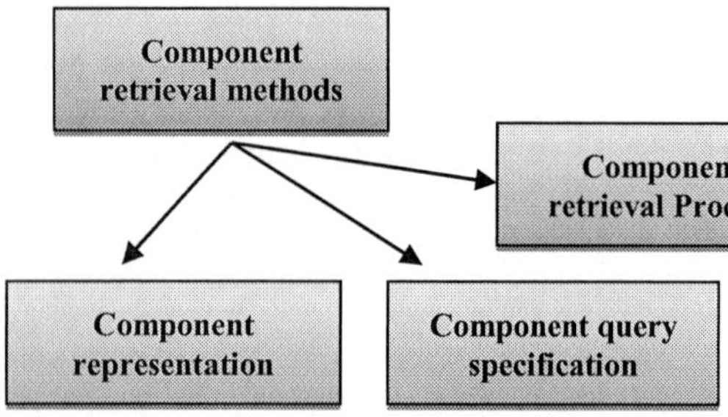

Fig 1 Retrieval Methods

Three perspectives are:Component representation, component query specification and retrieval component. It selects component from the reusable component repository and data mining method used to implement the mining method efficiently. Component representation helps to get the proper detail of the component and its characteristics.Thus, it plays the very key role in the selective component from a large number of components.Component query specification helps on user perspective.The user plays the key role in this type of component perspective. Component retrieval process contains the methodology and systematic process to get the knowledgeable components.

Table 2.Experimental results of Software component retrieval

The Method of Retrieval	Components in Repository	Component Retrieved	Relevant Component Retrieved Relevant	Components in the index	Precision (%)	Recall (%)
Tfr	400	380	320	350	84	91
MDLF	400	372	323	348	86	92
MRBR	400	375	340	344	90	97
Mdr	400	392	375	380	96	98

Tfr -Traditional faceted retrieval, MDLF - MDL File based retrieval, MRBR -Metadata repository based retrieval, Mdr - Metadata repository

III. PRINCIPLES OF SOFTWARE REUSABILITY

Problems are always made to solve them again and again.The main principle of reuse is to not solve the problem that has been already solved.Many of the software systems and application are based on previously developed component that is being used by customers and various companies.Systematic development of product mainly helps to attain the best goal and reusability is also the key goal [7]. The range of software reuse is from 15% to85%, depending on the area in which application is being developed.
There is the lot of progress in the reuse[8],so better model for component reuse must be used.It does not mean that the work is getting easier.The extra work is needed to do for component reuse.Software requirement must be integrated for easy understanding and adapt into the new system.It has to proper design, implemented and documented for the future purpose.

IV. TYPES OF REUSE

The various types of re-use are :
(i) Horizontal
(ii) Vertical
(iii) Component-based Software reuse and
(iv) Quality-Based software reuse.

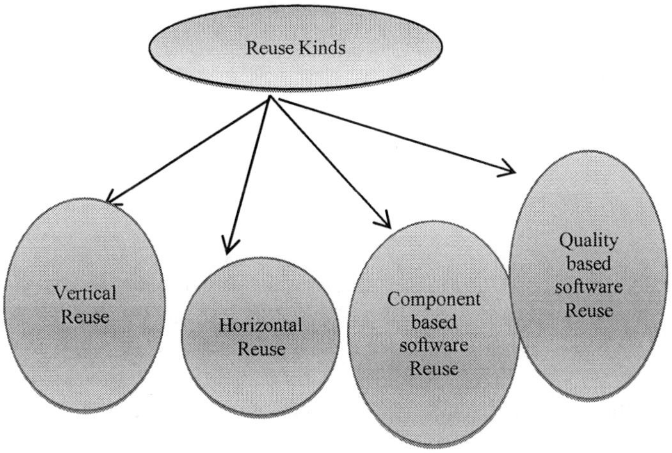

Fig 2. Types of Software Reuse

A. Horizontal reuse- The software component in horizontal reuse uses the extensive difference of applications[8].It contains the library of component like to connect list class, string operation, graphical user interface purposes if code resource is being used.It can be used in commercial and application with the superior system such as email and word processing system.A lot of software and resources of code are available at several positions on the internet.

B. Vertical reuse (Semantic Behavior) –Vertical reuse is very useful expressively untapped by the software community for current & future software development efforts.The structure with comparable functionality is the basic idea behind reuse of software. The different engineering impression is usedby an application and study. Domain engineering is a self iterative procedure of the lifecycle that takes the effects of strategic business objects. It effect the efficiency of application and associated procedures.Application engineering is the development which helps to produce the better customer requirements. Engineering has the impact to have better leverage knowledge, high-quality production and understanding the requirements of client[9].

C Component Based Software Reuse-In the Component-based Reuse the software isthe lifecycle consumes the key factor, it depends on the size & complexity of software.The productivity,enhances through using valid model and hence the profit is made in reuse.By attempting software reuse the scalability enhances as per the good demand for developing software from component-based software reuse manner [10].

D Quality based Software Reuseeffort It takes the attention on reuses objects[11].It has the ability to design artifacts by the desired functionalityview. Researchers always argue that from a non-functional (quality) perspective, it is always better to proceed under some assumptions.The main role is to get unite and use the reuse idea for goal-oriented programming.Quality-based reusability is allowed by goal driven procedures.The Software reuse is the main aim of software engineering study, which improves the progress cost,efforts,team size and most valuable time.

V. BENEFITS OF SOFTWARE REUSE

It is always said that it is extra effort to the systems which needs to be maintained But the different stories were made to the growth of this area.It includes quality,liability,reliability,reduction in time.Quality products are being produced by planning and repeating the cycle day by day and have the software advantage to perform well.Development time is less hence it is always better and time is a powerful asset to any organization development [12]. It is always the practice of company to take the less development effort and time under the deadline project work.

VI. CHALLENGES OF SOFTWARE REUSE

A very strong structural impact must occur in the area of engineering.The specific market section using the massive reuse is challenging task to adapt it [13].

The various challenges of software reuse are[14]:

a)Customer requirements are significant for preserving the creation line and must adapt to the good client.Better two-way communication must be there.

b)Defining a procedure for the employee for the creation line and preserve the standard.

c)Training package for management,design, application and test-all stages are also the important key concern.

VII. PREVIOUS WORK

Mälardalen et al. [15]presents impression on component based system reusability in workshop. The goal of the workshop was to unite the entire researcher together and command the arguments and research results together and compare the results.

Moiz et al. [16]presented a formal of the art of the extreme change in component skill from component engineering to area engineering

Sajad Shirali et al. [17] discussed, particularly of the works done in the field of recovery of the components from the libraries through the help of formal methods have been surveyed and reviewed.

Dutta et al. [18]described the reusable component storage and recovery as per the demand. It means the storage, retrieval of the component and their working feature was the main concern.

Gupta et al. [19] presented the model which classifies the storage and retrieval of the component which consider information based ontology. The interrelated components are stored together or cluster is made so that in future it will easy to identify a component.

Penix et al. [20]planned an approach that ships the on top of the formal psychological feature from the recovery to the organization stage of employing. Software system elements square measure categorized by linguistics structure measure derived from their official demand.

Wang et al. [21] bestowed a background and therefore the progressive of component-based software system engineering, (CBSE hereafter),a rising software system machinery aiming at developing high-quality software system with the lower value. A variety of analyses to image around CBSE square measure mentioned that match well into a superior software system engineering sequence as the student comes at tiny faculties.

Crnkovicl et al. [22] delineate that The aim of the workshop was to assemble researchers and practitioners from system engineering, software system construction and since component-based software system engineering teams so as to exchange involvements and analysis results from these domains.

Basha et al. [23] development of domain specific mechanisms and its impact on the effort in terms of value and time remains a difficult drawback. The half primarily based technology has reborn over an amount of your time from a straightforward module to the domain specific elements. It defines a state-of-art of the forceful modification in element technology from element engineering to domain engineering.

CAI et al. [24]presents the survey, describes the drawbacks and address the problemthat were coming day by day.The main stress was to design, development, and for maintenance activities.

Grundy et al.[25] described the explanation for a component-based approach to emerging, such simulation tools, the design and support tools, research worker has recycled, some resultant tools and gear services research worker have developed, and summaries attainable future analysis directions during this space.

Table 3.Comparative Analysis Techniques for Component Reuse

Methodology	Author	Purpose/issue
SBA for R of RBC	Fanchao et al. [26]	• Study the M of BCR
SBRM of RSC	Nedhal et al. [27]	• Define the MP that is related to CBD
SBR of SC through FI	Ioana Şoraet al.[28]	• Define the Principles Used in the SOC
ACR &R and A using FS	Penix et al. [29]	• I&R of C pertinent to a problem
CA of CBM	Kaur et al.[30]	• Model to provide PD, based on W ,WNT and LICBA
UGA to IIRS	Radwan et al.[31]	• Define FF for the app(IR)
A strategy to IC and CA	Basha et al.[32]	• Identification of BC
Rof Most RRCUGA	Bhatia et al. [33]	• Enhances the chance of RC from the repository
ESA for the RTS using MGA	Amuthakkannan et.[34]	• effective solution for CA in CBSE
CC & Reusing DMT	Hassel bring et al.[35]	• Provides an OB B/WP&R

SBA-Specification Based Approach, R-Retrieval, RBC-Reusable Business Component, M-Method, BCR-Business Component Retrieval, SBRM-Semantic-Based Retrieving Model, RSC- Reuse Software Component, MP-Major Problem, Specification-based Retrieval, SC- Software Components, FI- Fuzzy Inference, SOC-Specification of Components, Retrieval and Adaptation, FS-Formal specifications, I&R-Edification And Retrieval, C-Component, CA-Characterization and Architecture, CBM-Component Based Models, PD-Platform Dependent, W-Window, LICBA-Language Independent Component Based Applications, UGAIIRS-Using Genetic Algorithm to Improve Information Retrieval Systems, FF-Fitness Function, IR-Information Retrieval, ICCA-identify components using clustering approach, BC-Business Component , RRCUGA-Relevant Reusable Component Using Genetic Algorithms, RC-retrieving component,RTS-Real time systems, MGA-Multi-level Genetic Algorithm, CA-Component Assembly, CC & R-Component Classification and Retrieval DMT-Data Mining Techniques, OB-Optimal Balance, B/W-Between, P&R-Precision and Recall

VIII. Machine Learning Algorithms

It is the subfield of engineering science that bounces computers the power to check while not being expressly programmed. Machine learning based on the learning and have guessed or prediction over the set of inputs. It unites the strategies and mathematical optimized procedure.

In this section described that the machine learning algorithm used in component based software engineering. In component based science engineering is used to SVM , NN, FIS and ANN algorithm. In those algorithms used for classification purpose. It means a huge amount of component data set identify the component classify based on training and testing phase. We create a knowledge based on a classification approach to classify the component in the large amount of Datasets.

Various styles of machine learning are

(i) Neural Network (ANN)
(ii) Fuzzy Interference system
(iii) Support Vector Machine

(i) Neural Network (ANN):

The Neural network sets of interconnected nodes and has a weight on the nodes and the threshold function is used to train the network. Training is done over the network and specific output is taken that is required. The network is being trained until the required result made. It is the cluster of biological neurons to solve the real life problems. One neuron is connected to another neuron by axons. And the threshold value is the value helps to train the network[36].

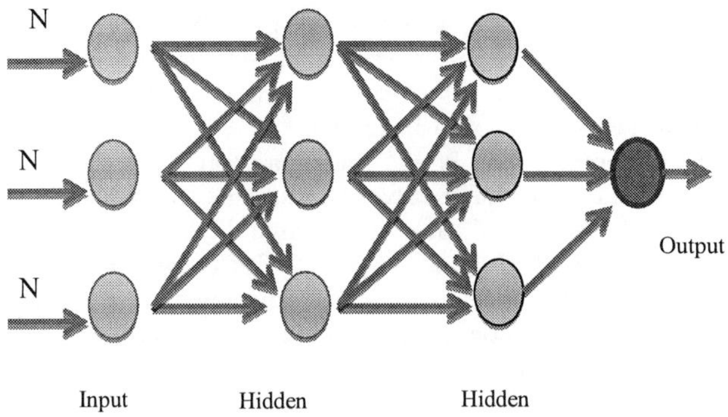

Fig 3 Neural Networks

It has set of layers.The Input layer takes the inputs and gives it for processing to the hidden layer.There can be more than one hidden layer.The output is taken from the output layer's neurons.

Fuzzy Logic:The standard system that will perceives and takes precise input and produces a particular output supported the input applied. A fuzzy illusion system could be a theme that uses fuzzy set thought to map inputs which may say extracted options to urge optimize output. The method includes all the items that's scientifically have mentioned within the previous section: membership functions, mathematical logic staff, and if-then rules. Fuzzy illusion schemes are absolutely applied in fields resembling involuntary management information classification, call analysis, professional resembling involuntar y management, information classification call analysis, professional, system& laptop vision [37].

Input o/p

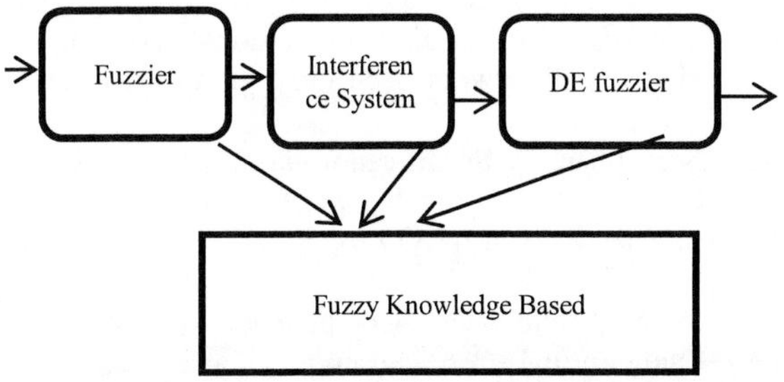

Fig 4. Fuzzy Interference System

Support Vector Machine:It is analgorithm in which learning takes place.It is used for regression and classification purposes.The main goal is to use for the problem which contains classification categories. Data items are plotted on the space with the help of the algorithm on the basis of coordinate [38].

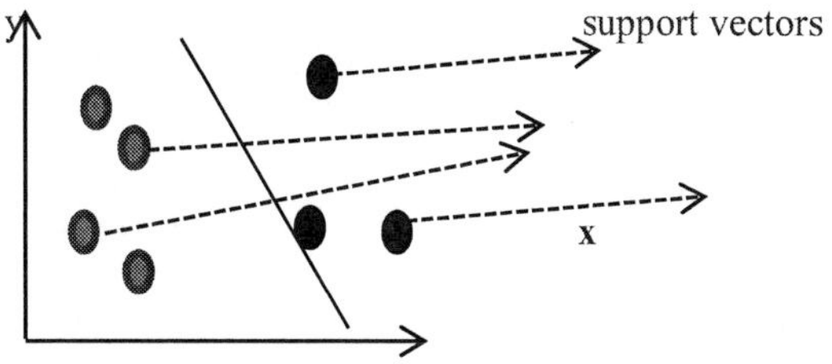

Fig 5. Support Vector Machine

IX. Semantic Data Model

It is an abstract record model during which linguistics data is enclosed. This suggests the instances which are described by the model[39].Linguistics knowledge models change that the cases, specific facts that embrace their sense.The second quite linguistics knowledge models square measure sometimes meant to createlinguistics databases.

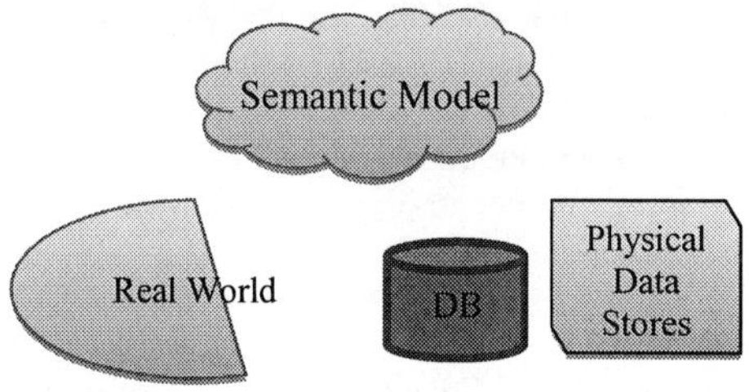

Fig 6. Semantic-based model

The different kind of database management system like network based,relational, and object-oriented are not reliable for the requirement.The model must relate to each other on processing based system and decisive action to be taken [40].

X. Conclusion

The benefits are using the reusability of the component,it needs the phases and proper dedication to start reusability. Repositories of code assets should be created and maintained in a good way. Reusable resources should be designed for better understanding and for decreasing the development efforts. Individuals should be skilled for code recycling and for proper programming.Forcreating quality necessities a distinguished dimension in code recycles is to be made.Machine learning algorithm gives a final output with best results to component retrieval and data exchange .It is always important to enhance the quality and development efforts for the betterment of reuse. The model which enhances the reusability of the component must get fitted into constraints that are available with better results.

References

[1] Software Productivity Consortium Services Corporation. Reuse-Driven Software Process Guidebook Product Description, SPC-93146-N, version 01.00.04, Herndon, VA, 1995.

[2] Baragry, Jason. Summary of the ICSE 16 Panel on Software Reuse, Sorrento, Italy, 1994.

[3] Brownsword, Lisa and Paul Clements. A Case Study in Successful Product Line Development, Software Engineering Institute Technical Report, CMU/SEI-96-TR-016, October, 1996.

[4] Allied Signal. Reuse Key Process Areas, August, 1996.

[5] Software Engineering Institute. Software Reuse Key Process Areas, Level 3: Defined, August, 1996.

[6] Villalba, Jose Manuel. ISORUS: Implementation and Evaluation of a Software Reuse Methodology, ESSI Application Experiment 10936 Version 2, December, 1995.

[7] Krueger, Charles W. "Software reuse." ACM Computing Surveys (CSUR) 24, no. 2 (1992): 131-183.

[8] Frakes, William, and Carol Terry. "Software reuse: metrics and models." ACM Computing Surveys (CSUR) 28, no. 2 (1996): 415-435.

[9] Chapin, Ned, Joanne E. Hale, KhaledMd Khan, Juan F. Ramil, and Wui-Gee Tan. "Types of software evolution and software maintenance." Journal of software maintenance and evolution: Research and Practice 13, no. 1 (2001): 3-30.

[10] Shaw, Mary. "Architectural issues in software reuse: It's not just the functionality, it's the packaging." In ACM SIGSOFT Software Engineering Notes, vol. 20, no. SI, pp. 3-6. ACM, 1995.

[11] Kim, Yongbeom, and Edward A. Stohr. "Software reuse: survey and research directions." Journal of Management Information Systems 14, no. 4 (1998): 113-147.

[12] Devi, T. Rajani, and B. Rama. "BENEFITS OF SOFTWARE REUSE." Futuristic Trends in Engineering, Science, Humanities, and Technology FTESHT-16 (2016): 10.

[13] Crnkovic, Ivica. "Component-based software engineering—new challenges in software development." Software Focus 2, no. 4 (2001): 127-133.

[14] Crnković, Ivica. "Component-based software engineering-new challenges in software development." CIT. Journal of computing and information technology 11, no. 3 (2003): 151-161.

[15] Crnkovic, Ivica, Stig Larsson, and Judith Stafford. "Component-based software engineering: building systems from components at 9th IEEE conference and workshops onengineering of computer-based systems."ACM SIGSOFT Software Engineering Notes 27.3 (2002): 47-50.

[16] Basha, N. MdJubair, and Salman Abdul Moiz. "Component based software development: A state of art." Advances in Engineering, Science and Management (ICAESM), 2012 International Conference on.IEEE,2012.

[17] Shirali-Shahreza, Sajad, and Mohammad Shirali-Shahreza. "Using Formal Methods in Component Based Software Development." Innovations and Advances in Computer Sciences and Engineering. Springer Netherlands, 2010.429-432.

[18] Dutta, Stobak, and SabnamSengupta. "Retrieval of software component version from a software version database: A graph based approach."Computer Engineering and Applications (ICACEA), 2015 International Conference on Advances in.IEEE, 2015.

[19] Gupta, S., and Ashok Kumar. "Reusable Software Component Retrieval System." International Journal of Application or Innovation in Engineering and Management 2.1 (2013): 187-194.

[20] Penix, John, Phillip Baraona, and Perry Alexander. "Classification and retrieval of reusable components using semantic features." Knowledge-Based Software Engineering Conference, 1995.Proceedings, 10th. IEEE, 1995.

[21] Wang, Ju An. "Towards component-based software engineering." Journal of Computing Sciences in Colleges.Vol. 16.No. 1.Consortium for Computing Sciences in Colleges, 2000.

[22] Crnkovic, Ivica, Stig Larsson, and Judith Stafford. "Component-based software engineering: building systems from components at 9th IEEE conference and workshops on engineering of computer-based systems." ACM SIGSOFT Software Engineering Notes 27.3 (2002): 47-50.

[23] Basha, N. MdJubair, and Salman Abdul Moiz. "Component based software development: A state of art." Advances in Engineering, Science and Management (ICAESM), 2012 International Conference in.IEEE, 2012.

[24] Cai, Xia, et al. "Component-based software engineering: technologies, development frameworks, and quality assurance schemes." Software Engineering Conference, 2000.APSEC 2000.Proceedings.Seventh Asia-Pacific.IEEE, 2000.

[25] Grundy, John, Warwick Mugridge, and John Hosking. "Constructing component-based software engineering environments: issues and experiences." Information and Software Technology 42.2 (2000): 103-114.

[26]MengFanchaoet al. ,"A Specification-Based Approach for Retrieval of Reusable Business Component for Software Reuse", in World Academy of Science, Engineering and Technology 15 2008, pp. 936-943.

[27] Dr.Nedhal A. Al Saiyd, Dr. Intisar A. Al Said, Ahmed H. Al Takrori,"Semantic-Based Retrieving Model of Reuse Software Component", IJCSNS International Journal of Computer Science and Network Security, Vol. 10, No. 7, July 2010, pp.154-161.

[28] IoanaŞoraet al. ,"Specification-based Retrieval of Software Components through Fuzzy Inference", in ActaPolytechnicaHungarica of Vol. 3, No. 3, 2006, pp. 121-135.

[29] John Penix,"Automated Component Retrieval and Adaptation Using Formal specifications".

[30] Er. IqbaldeepKaur et al. "Characterization and Architecture of Component Based Models", in (IJACSA)

International Journal of Advanced Computer Science and Applications, Vol. 1, No. 6, December 2010, pp. 66-71.
[31] Ahmed A. A. Radiant al. "Using Genetic Algorithm to Improve Information Retrieval Systems", in World Academy of Science, Engineering and Technology 17 2008, pp. 1021-1027.
[32] N MdJubair Basha1 et al. ,"A strategy to identify components using clustering approach for component reusability", in ACSIT, CS & IT 06, pp. 397–406, 2012.
[33] Rajesh Bhatia et al. ,"Retrieval of Most Relevant Reusable Component Using Genetic Algorithms".
[34] R. Amuthakkannan et al. "Effective Software Assembly for the Real time systems using Multi-level Genetic Algorithm", International Journal of Engineering Science and Technology (IJEST), Vol. 3 No. 8 August 2011 6190, pp. 6187-6201.
[35]Sharma, Achala, and Daman Deep Kaur. "Component Classification and Retrieval Using Data Mining Techniques." In *Proceedings of National Conference on Challenges & Opportunities in Information Technology (COIT-2007), RIMT-IET, Mandi Gobindgarth. March 23 2007*, pp. 58-62. 2007.
[36] Grundy, John, Warwick Mugridge, and John Hosking. "Constructing component-based software engineering environments: issues and experiences." *Information and Software Technology* 42, no. 2 (2000): 103-114.
[37] Jang, J-SR. "ANFIS: adaptive-network-based fuzzy inference system." IEEE transactions onsystems, man, and cybernetics 23, no. 3 (1993): 665-685.
[38] Joachims, Thorsten. Making large-scale SVM learning practical. No. 1998, 28. Technical Report, SFB 475: Komplexitätsreduktion in Multivariaten Datenstrukturen, Universidad Dortmund, 1998.
[39]Heidenreich, Florian, Christian Wende, and Birgit Demuth. "A framework for generating query language code from OCL invariants." *Electronic Communications of the EASST* 9 (2007).
[40] Jang, J-SR. "ANFIS: adaptive-network-based fuzzy inference system." IEEE transactions on systems, man, and cybernetics 23, no. 3 (1993): 665-685.

IOT BASED INTERACTIVE SMART REFRIGERATOR

Murali.N.G[1], Aarthi.S[1], Ethiraj.M[1], Baghavathi Priya.S[1]

[1]Rajalakshmi Engineering College, 602105 Thandalam, Chennai, TamilNadu

{murali.ng.2014.it, aarthi.s.2014.it, ethiraj.m.2014.it, baghavathipriya.s}@rajalakshmi.edu.in

Abstract

Rapid improvement in technology tend to use smarter devices in day to day life, one such device is refrigerator. In the modular kitchen and shops refrigerator plays a major role in preserving food items. There is a need for more efficient way to monitor the amount of food materials left for the forth coming days and in case of shop it is necessary to avail the required quantity to improve the business. The proposed Internet of Things(IoT) system detects the shortage of food items, by transmitting the quantity of available food items to the users through mobile application. It gives an alert to the users to place an order if the weight falls below the threshold value. Classification and Regression (Prediction Algorithms) are used in the proposed system to prefer seasonal fruits and vegetables to users.

Keywords: IoT, Mobile Application, Predictive Analysis, Refrigerator.

1. Introduction

With tremendous improvement in technology, all devices are connected to the internet which forms the internet of things. The sensors are used to collect the data and send them to a host where it is intended to be processed over the internet. Improvement in the technologies, made our day-to-day life simpler. The technologies implemented using IoT in electrical appliances at homes made it smarter [1]. One of those technologies is smart refrigerator which is used to store the food items. Refrigerators are used to prevent the spoilage of food and keep it fresh. It reduces illness and make our lifestyle healthier in the modern world [2]. The proposed IOT based system uses Raspberry pi as the central server to make the fridge smarter [1].

Load cell is used to find the weight of the available food in analog form which is then fed into HX711 (an A to D converter) to obtain the weight in digital form. Intelligent home automation system uses the mobile devices like tablet and smart phones to control the functioning of home appliances anywhere from the world through internet [1]. Smart fridge is connected to the network via a protocol through which it can communicate with the user and make it interactive. Mobile application has been developed to monitor the quantity of things in the refrigerator [2]. When the weight of the contents measured by the load cell falls below the threshold value then a message will be sent to the user through mobile application notifying that there is an urge to place an order [14]. The order can be placed just by accepting or rejecting the suggestion in the notification itself, which automatically places an order [3]. Our focus is to develop a weight monitoring system and a mobile application to monitor and manage the smart fridge which makes the work done by the humans simpler.

2. Survey

Nikhil Kakade, Prof. (Dr.) S. D. Lokhande [1], has proposed a system," IoT based Intelligent home using Smart Devices" that sense the daily needs of particular items in the refrigerator and automatically places an order to the grocery shop.

Deepti Singh, Preet Jain [2], has proposed the system "Smart Refrigerator" which can sense the weight of the food items placed in the refrigerator and sends a notification to the user's mobile through an application when the weight falls below the threshold value.

Emily Moin [3], has proposed the system "Smart Refrigerator for Grocery Management" which identifies the weight and expiry dates of the food items in the refrigerator and sends customized notification to the user. The proposed system finds the weight and expiry dates of the food items and notifies the user through application which helps to place the order when the contents fall below the threshold value.

Poonam B. Patil, Roopali R. Patil, Swati V. Patil has proposed a system "Home Automation System using Android and Arduino Board" which implements the methodology of using mobile application to control the home appliances remotely [4]. It uses GSM modem to transmit the data to mobile.

Folasade Osisanwo, Shade Kuyoro, and Oludele Awodele has proposed a system, "Internet Refrigerator-a typical IoT "[5]. This system makes use of RFID. The refrigerator is Wi-Fi enabled to transmit data.

Surinder Kaur, Rashmi Singh, Neha Khairwal and Pratyk Jain has proposed the system "HOME AUTOMATION AND SECURITY SYSTEM", this paper focused to reduce the human effort by automating electrical devices [6]. It sends messages to users. It is also focused to save electricity.

Shama Mubeena, N. Swati has proposed a system," The Design and Implementation of a Wi-Fi Based User-Machine -Interacted Refrigerator" [7], which uses Wi-Fi for wireless communication. It demonstrates monitoring of fridge and notify user through mail id.

B. Ramesh, J. Lingaiah has proposed the system," Raspberry Pi Based Interactive Home Automation System through E-Mail" [8]. This system uses Email rather than Bluetooth to send notification to user as it is not efficient. It also uses LEDs to indicate switching action.

Nishchol Mishra, Dr. Sanjay Silakari has proposed a model in "Predictive Analytics: A Survey, Trends, Applications, Opportunities & Challenges" they have mentioned the classification and regression as the two main objectives of predictive analytics [9]. Where the classification, classifies the things according to the predefined class and uses numeric variables for data attributes. And Regression is used to study the relationship between the variables.

Jessica Tran et al, has proposed a system, "Automated Demand Response Refrigerator Project" in which they gave a dashboard to view the sensor data and control the refrigerator remotely [10].

Soundhar Ganesh S, et al, in their paper," Raspberry Pi Based Interactive Home Automation System through Internet of Things" used Raspberry pi to interface the internet with embedded systems [11].

Carson Kai-Sang Leung et al, in "A Machine Learning Approach for Stock Price Prediction", has proposed a deep learning approach for structural support vector machines (SSVMs) to perform classification on complex inputs [12].

M.P. Sathish et al, in "Home Automation through E-Mail using Raspberry Pi" has used the e-mail to instruct the Raspberry pi, the operations to be performed [13]. Where the pi reads the content and performs the operations accordingly and acknowledges accordingly.

Prapulla S B et al, in "SMART REFRIGERATOR USING INTERNET OF THINGS" has used the sensors for sensing and monitoring the contents [14]. This smart fridge notifies the remote user using SMS or email services.

Rajendra Banjade, Suraj Maharjan, in" Product recommendations using linear predictive modeling" has proposed linear regression to improve the functioning of the system [15].

Seema L Vandure, Manjula Ramannavar and Nandini S Sidnal has proposed "Trend Projection using Predictive Analytics" [16]. In which they have used Linear Regression and SVM for the prediction of market sales.

Xiaoxiao Guo, Chang Liu, Wei Xu, Hui Yuan and Mingming Wang has proposed "A Prediction-Based Inventory Optimization Using Data Mining Models", the demand prediction for inventory optimization [17]. They used the classification and prediction based on Back propagation to get the sample data and then on the basis of output obtained they have applied the formulations.

Kavya et al, has proposed "A Review On Predictive Analytics in Data Mining", that provides a predictive score for each individual product, to determine or influence the organizational processes across high number of individuals [18].

A. Alheraish proposed a system "Design and implementation of home automation system" [19]. Which represents the use of remote control system using GSM. It tests PC-environment.

Sarthak Jain, Anant Vaibhav propose a system "Raspberry Pi based Interactive Home Automation System through E-mail" [20]. This paper designs the system in which communication is through e-mail. It uses the efficient algorithm for this in python environment. LED switches are used here.

Khusvinder Gill, Shuang-Hua yang proposed a system namely "Home Automation System –Secure Remote Access" [21]. This paper aims at protecting personal data that go round the network. It uses various algorithm for protecting the data generated by the automated device.

Sharon Panth, Mahesh Jivani has proposed a system called "Home Automation System (HAS) using Android for Mobile Phone" [22]. This paper helps to reduce the human efforts by using mobile phones. It uses Android platforms. The HAS is interfaced with microcontroller. This device is accessed through mobile application.

Ravi Kishore Kodali, Vishal Jain, has proposed "IoT based smart security and home automation system", conceptualizes the idea of connecting to real world objects using internet [23].

Ming Wang et al, has proposed a system, "An IoT based appliance control system for smart homes", in which they used the smart controller wireless sensor and actuator network (WSAN) [24].

Mukesh P et al, has proposed a system," Smart Refrigerator using IoT" [25]. In which they provided the communication with outsiders.

Hasin-Han Wu, has proposed a system, "Low-Cost Smart Refrigerator", it describes the overall design of a low-cost Smart Refrigerator built with Raspberry Pi [26]. Next, it has two sensors controlling each camera, which are hooked up to our Raspberry Pi board.

3. Proposed Work

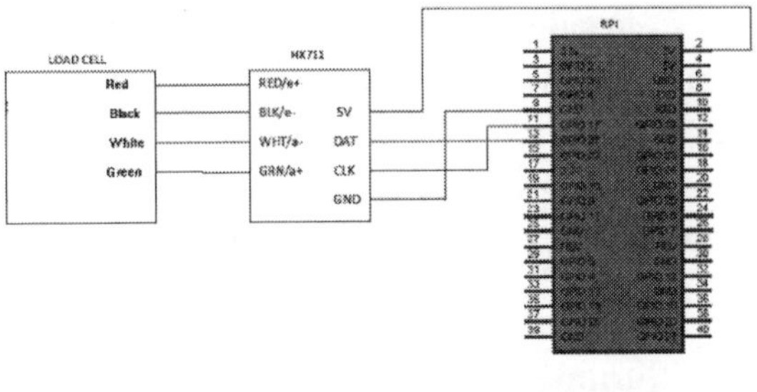

Fig1: Block diagram of a proposed system

Fig1 shows the block of a Proposed System which consists of Load Cell, HX711 & Raspberry Pi 3. The Load Cell shown in Fig4, measures the weight of the food items which is placed inside the refrigerator in analog form. HX711 shown in Fig3, converts the value form analog into digital form which in turn passed to the Raspberry Pi. Fig2 shows the pin configuration of Raspberry Pi. When the value falls below the threshold value, the notification will be sent to the user through mobile application.

3.1 Raspberry Pi

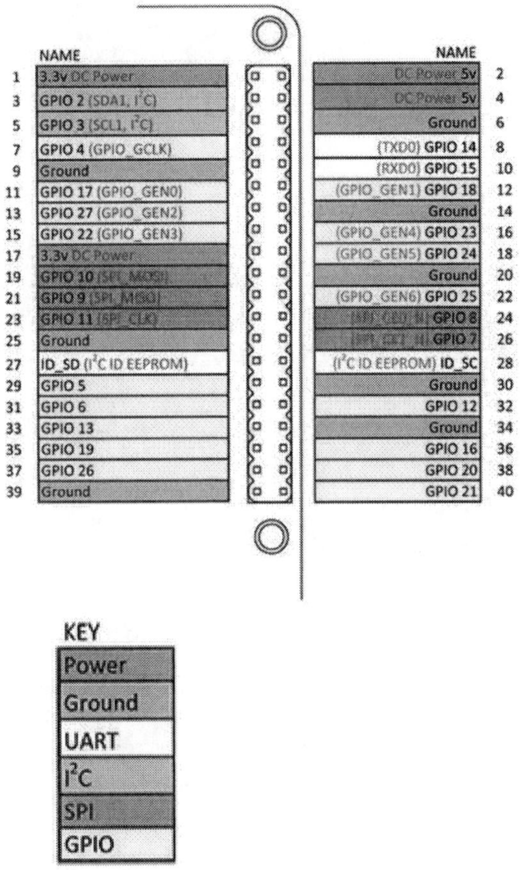

Fig2: Pin diagram of Raspberry Pi 3

3.2 HX711

HX7ll Amplifier has five input wires such as RED, BLACK, WHITE, GREEN and YELLOW. Here Yellow wire is an optional ground wire and other are come from the load cell. Sometimes yellow is replaced by a larger black wire, foil or loose wires.

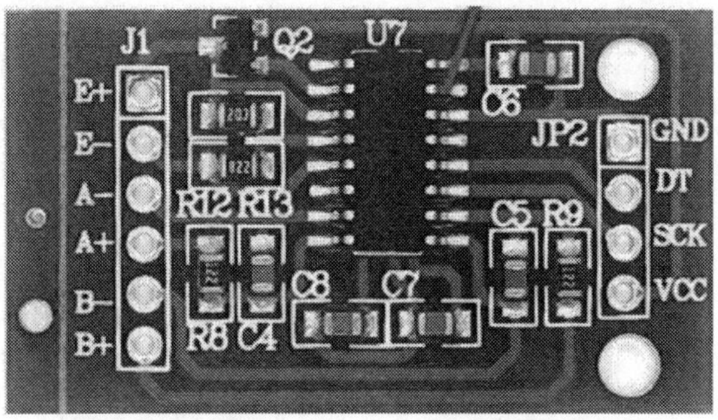

Fig3: HX711 Board

3.3 Load Cell

A Load cell measures and weight of the thing which is resting on it. It produces the output as analog signals which intern passed into the HX711 Board.

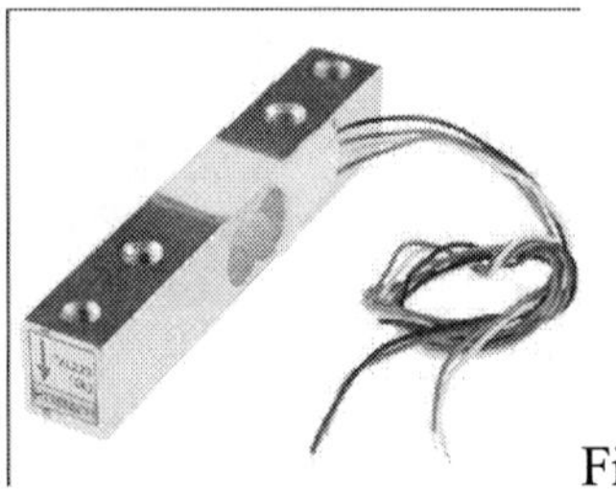

Fig4: Load Cell

4. Conclusion & Future Works

A Smart Refrigerator system has been proposed for sensing the weight of a food item which is placed in the refrigerator and places an order to grocery shop with the user permission. Thus, this system saves manual effort and time in predicting the future needs.

In future this system may be expanded to detect the freshness of the food items and also suggest the dishes that can be made from the available food items in the fridge considering the freshness of that item. This system may also be made to display the content inside the fridge from a remote place.

References

[1] Nikhil Kakade, Prof. (Dr.) S. D. Lokhande," IoT based Intelligent home using Smart Devices", International Journal of Innovative Research in Computer and Communication Engineering, vol. 4, Issue 6, June 2016.

[2] Deepti Singh, Preet Jain, "IoT Based Smart Refrigerator System", International Journal of Advanced Research in Electronics and Communication Engineering (IJARECE), Volume 5, Issue 7, July 2016.

[3] Emily Moin," "Smart Refrigerator for Grocery Management", Technical Disclosure Commons, Defensive Publication Series, May 05,2015.

[4] Poonam B. Patil, Roopali R. Patil, Swati V. Patil," Home Automation System using Android and Arduino Board", International Journal of Innovative Research in Science and Engineering Technology, Vol.5, Issue 4, April 2016.

[5] Folasade Osisanwo, Shade Kuyoro, and Oludele Awodele," Internet Refrigerator", 3rd International Conference on Advances in Engineering Sciences & Applied Mathematics (ICAESAM'2015) March 23-24, 2015.

[6] Surinder Kaur, Rashmi Singh, Neha Khairwal and Pratyk Jain," HOME AUTOMATION AND SECURITY SYSTEM", Advanced Computational Intelligence: An International Journal (ACII), Vol.3, No.3, July 2016.

[7] Shama Mubeena, N. Swati," The Design and Implementation of a Wi-Fi Based User-Machine -Interacted Refrigerator", ISSN 2319-8885, Vol.06, Issue.14, April-2017.

[8] B. Ramesh, J. Lingaiah," Raspberry Pi Based Interactive Home Automation System through E-Mail", International journal of Innovative Technologies ISSN 2321-8665, Vol.04, Issue.15, October-2016.

[9] Nishchol Mishra, Dr. Sanjay Silakari, "Predictive Analytics: A Survey, Trends, Applications, Oppurtunities & Challenges", (IJCSIT) International Journal of Computer Science and Information Technologies, Vol. 3 (3), 2012, 4434- 4438.

[10] Jessica Tran, Jordan Gilles, Ryan Mann, and Vishnu Murthy, "Automated Demand Response Refrigerator Project", CE 186, OCTOBER 2015.

[11] Soundhar Ganesh S, Venkatash S, Vidhyasagar P, Maragatharaj S, "Raspberry Pi Based Interactive Home Automation System through Internet of Things", International Journal for Research in Applied Science & Engineering Technology (IJRASET), Volume 3 Issue III, March 2015.

[12] Carson Kai-Sang Leung, Richard Kyle MacKinnon and Yang Wang, "A Machine Learning Approach for Stock Price Prediction", University of Manitoba, Winnipeg, MB, Canada.

[13] M.P. Sathish, Dr. S.A.K. Jilani, Mr. D. Girish kumar, "Home Automation through E-Mail using Raspberry Pi", International Journal of Advanced Research in Electronics and Communication Engineering (IJARECE) Volume 4, Issue 9, September 2015.

[14] Prapulla S B, Dr. Shobha G and Dr. Thanuja T C, "SMART REFRIGERATOR USING INTERNET OF THINGS" Journal of Multidisciplinary Engineering Science and Technology (JMEST) ISSN: 3159-0040 Vol. 2 Issue 7, July – 2015.

[15] Rajendra Banjade, Suraj Maharjan," Product recommendations using linear predictive modeling", Internet (AH-ICI), 2011 Second Asian Himalayas International Conference, 4-6 Nov. 2011.

[16] Seema L Vandure, Manjula Ramannavar and Nandini S Sidnal, "Trend Projection using Predictive Analytics", International Journal of Computer Applications,2014, Volume 97 - Number 19.

[17] Xiaoxiao Guo, Chang Liu, Wei Xu, Hui Yuan and Mingming Wang, "A Prediction-Based Inventory Optimization Using Data Mining Models", Computational Sciences and Optimization (CSO), 2014 Seventh International Joint Conference on 4-6 July 2014.

[18] Kavya V, Arumugam S, "A Review On Predictive Analytics in Data Mining", International Journal of Chaos, Control, Modelling and Simulation (IJCCMS) Vol. 5, No. 1/2/3, September 2016.

[19] A. Alheraish, "Design and implementation of home automation system", IEEE Trans. Consumer Electronics, vol. 50, no. 4. Pp.1087–1092, 2004.

[20] Sarthak Jain, Anant Vaibhav, Lovely Goyal Student member, IEEE, "Raspberry Pi based Interactive Home Automation System through E-mail", International Conference on Reliability, Optimization and Information Technology -ICROIT 2014.

[21] Khusvinder Gill, Shuang-Hua yang," Home Automation System –Secure Remote Access" Sage Journal, Vol 41, issue 10,2008.

[22] Sharon Panth, Mahesh Jivani "Home Automation System (HAS) using Android for Mobile Phone", International Journal of Electronics and Computer Science Engineering, ISSN- 2277-1956.

[23] Ravi Kishore Kodali, Vishal Jain, "Iot based smart security and home automaion system", Computing, Communication and Automation (ICCCA), 2016 International Conference on.

[24] Ming Wang, Guiqing Zhang, Jianbin Zhang, Chengdong Li," An IoT based appliance control system for smart homes", Intelligent Control and Information Processing(ICICIP),2013 Fourth International Conference on 9-11 june 2013.

[25] Mukesh P Mahajan, Rohit R Nikam, Vivek P Patil, Rahul D Dond, "Smart Refrigerator using IoT", International Journal of Latest Engineering Research and Application (IJLERA) ISSN:2455-7137, Volume-02, Issue-03, March-2017, PP-86-91

[26] Hsin-Han Wu, Yung-Ting Chuang, "Low-Cost Refrigerator", Edge Computing (EDGE), 2017 IEEE International Conference on.

PREVENTION OF BIKE ACCIDENTS USING AN INTELLIGENT HELMET

Vignesh P.N[1], Anto Arockia Rosaline R[1], Barath M[2], Athar Zafeer K A[2]

[1]Rajalakshmi Engineering College, 602105 Thandalam, Chennai, Tamil Nadu

[2]R.M.K College of Engineering and Technology, 601206 Thiruvallur, Tamil Nadu

Abstract

Bike accidents have been a serious issue especially in many cities. Even though government has framed a law that by-passers can help the injured victim without any legal enquires, people still think that they might be called for any concerns. Existing models have proposed way to prevent alcohol-less driving or only a methodology to notify the occurrence of an accident to nearby police stations. These models eliminate the problem of wearing the helmet but failed to notify the occurrence of an accident. It implements Microcontroller 8051 as their processor and Force sensing resistors to detect the accident and notify using a text message presenting the coordinates separately. The proposed system uses an intelligent helmet that fits into the helmet, which alerts the government aided emergency services and also sends a message to them and close relatives using GSM and GPS modules. This system has overcome the problem of inconvenient way of viewing the location by integrating google maps through the text. It has used Arduino as its processor. Infrared sensor and alcohol detector will be embedded inside the helmet. The device will be integrated with the bike via a wireless transmitter. Once the device evaluates the input of both sensors, the ignition system will be available for the user to start the bike. When an accident takes place the vibration sensor which is embedded inside the helmet will be triggered and the input signal will be sent to the receiver in the bike. Now the receiver which has a GSM and GPS module attached to it identifies the location and sends the location information of the victim to government aided emergency services initially and then to close relatives in the form of a text message.

Keywords: Arduino, GSM, GPS, RF transceiver, government aided services, location, and accident prevention.

1. Introduction

In Asia, the largest motorcycle markets namely: Indonesia, India, China, and Vietnam. In India with an estimation of 37 million motorcycles/mopeds produced in a year, was home to the largest number of motorized two wheelers in the world. China came a close second with 34 million motorcycles/mopeds in 2002. With this much motorcycle traffic in India alone, the fatalities per year due to the motorcycle is about 130.1/1,00,000 motorcycles. And there are new motorcycles added of the current amount of motorcycle that is present in India, every year.

So, after a benevolent thought, the proposed system was made to reduce the death toll by at least to a small percentage. The solution to this problem was to use the traditional safety device that government has sanctioned to do something more than the device is doing right now in the streets. This proposition makes it smart. Data gathered on the ways to reduce the accidents suggested the cause of this predicament. It was found out that most of the fatalities were because of carelessness of the people. The system was introduced to make it not easier but rather necessary. The first thought of the process was that the rider must wear a helmet. As per Section129 of Motor Vehicles Act 1988[10] makes it required for every single person riding a two-wheeler must wear protective headgear following to standards of the BIS (Bureau of Indian Standards). But, most of the time people ignore the law and ride allegedly. So, to make sure that the rider wears the helmet all the time, a microcontroller within the helmet is introduced. This will make the ignition system of the motorcycle to be in ON state only if the rider wears a helmet. And it will also check at regular intervals whether the helmet is still worn by the rider or not. Thus, the safety is ensured at every step of the journey. This solved the first cause.

Now, second most cause of accidents is drunk and driving. In India, drunken drive case is a criminal offense by The Motor Vehicle act 1939[10] which states that the bike rider will get punished upon violating the rule. So, a sensor is placed, that would sense the alcohol content from the breath of the rider and stop the ignition. Now, this solves the second predicament.

Final most cause of an accident that can occur whilst riding bikes. The following was found rather crucial. Most of the times, victims die because of delayed health and healing. To prevent this, the Arduino in the bike was programmed to send a signal to the ambulance and few of the relatives or friends who has been defined by the rider to be called upon emergency situations. The program not only sends a signal but also it sends the location of the accident to the receivers. Moreover, it is in the format of google maps link so that a receiver can instantaneously access the location of the accident and navigate to that place. This is all interfaced by a reliable, bug free program and hardware.

2. Literature Survey

2.1 Intelligent Helmet

The model proposed here is that driver can start the bike only if did not consume any alcohol and wear the helmet. If an accident occurs it can be reported to the nearest police stations and relatives. This model is achieved by implementing the idea using a microcontroller 8051. The location and SMS will be sent through the GSM [6][1] and GPS module. An abort switch [4] is added to this model only if the accident is minor.

An IR sensor is used for checking the condition whether the driver has worn the helmet or not. Wireless communication is achieved through RF transceivers. Alcohol Sensor will validate whether the driver is drunk [19] or not. Accelerometer is used to validate the occurrence of an accident to the driver

The main drawback in this model is that IR sensor doesn't absorb black light so the output will not be a valid one if the user wears the helmet as the inside surrounding will contain black light. The methodology followed in this model can be improved by sending the coordinates to a centralized hospital rather than sending to a police station [4]. And another drawback in this method is that the output location message cannot be read as it is displayed.

2.2 Smart-Tec Helmet

Prudhivi Raj *et all.* [7] has proposed a model, unless the driver had worn the helmet he is not allowed to start the bike. An ADXL3[7] sensor along with GPS (Global Positioning System) is used to measure the impact of an accident and triangulate the coordinates of the accident and send the location to a pre-set number assigned in the GSM [7] [17] module present. The working of this proposed model is that the helmet worn is identified by the LM355D [6] temperature sensor and in case of an accident the location will be calculated and sent while the temperature inside the helmet will be regulated to control the blood clotting process which takes place at the time of the accident.

The main drawback in the model is that artificial regulation of temperature can be achieved inside the helmet as that of a temperature between some human scalps. When an accident occurs, theoretically the temperature conditions inside the helmet can be achieved and thus can even result into a fatal situation. The output which contains location message cannot be read as it is displayed.

2.3 Smart Helmet

Saravana Kumar K *et all.*[8] has proposed model is to force the driver to wear the helmet throughout the journey and a voice intake module [8] is placed for verifying if the valid user is wearing the helmet. And it takes the values from the ultrasonic sensor, if the conditions are satisfied then the ignition is made available for the user. The working of the model is when the rider wears the helmet, the ultrasonic sensor calculates the distance [13] between the user and helmet and then microphone which is placed will intake the password which makes this the helmet to be an independent device for the user.

The main drawback of using the voice synthesizer [8] is that convenient usage of helmet cannot be achieved and only the particular user can start the bike. And another drawback of this model is when the particular driver is drunk and operates the vehicle, the rider's location cannot be found.

2.4 Intelligent Helmet

Chitte P.P *et all.* [2] has designed a helmet taking into consideration of the bike riders safety. The main features which are included in the model is the alcohol sensor (MQ3) [2] for detection of drivers who has consumed alcohol. GSM for locating the driver's current location and the CLCD display is used in displaying the current status of the rider whether the helmet is worn or not. The RF module helps in communication [15] with bike and the helmet section. The process starts by user wearing the helmet which then proceeds to alcohol test. Once all the tests has been completed the user is allowed to start the bike and if an accident occurs, the GSM [17] module along with GPRS will triangulate the position and send to the pre-set numbers.

The main drawback of this methodology of finding the location is that only if the internet connection is available for the GSM sim which is inserted, it can triangulate the position. Usage of CLCD [2] is quite not user-friendly and space management can be improved

2.5 Solar Powered Smart Helmet

Dileep Kumar P *et all.* [3] proposed a model suggests a way where attending calls during traffic jams causes accidents and as the previous models excluding the alcohol sensor. This method implements wholly on the method of Bluetooth [3] communication. If the user meets with any accident the GPS and GSM [17] will triangulate the position and send it to the Close relatives. An additional feature added in this model is the Bluetooth calling feature from the helmet. RF transceivers [15] make the wireless communication easier and cheap than the Bluetooth.

Due to Bluetooth calls made by the users, Accident levels might increase based on the carelessness of the riders. And another flaw in this model is that anyone can access the helmet without any constraint and very much ease of access is possible.

2.6 Smart Helmet for Accident Prevention

Mohd Khairul Afiq Mohd Rasli *et all.* [5] proposed a model which consists of LED, BLDC and FSR [5]. The system's main idea of is to indicate, when the driver is exceeding above 100KPH and continuous travelling at that speed might end up in fatal as well. The working of this model is, speed sensor is used to measure the vehicle's speed and a comparator IC LM311 is used when the user drives at a maximum speed of 100KPh. And whenever the user exceeds the threshold speed, the LED which is integrated with the bike will glow only when the helmet is worn and the speed is controlled. By achieving this accident impact and damage can be reduced.

The main disadvantage of the model is that there is no indication whether the driver is wearing the helmet or not. And in-case of any accident, the system does not notify the occurrence which may lead to fatality of the victim.

3. Proposed System

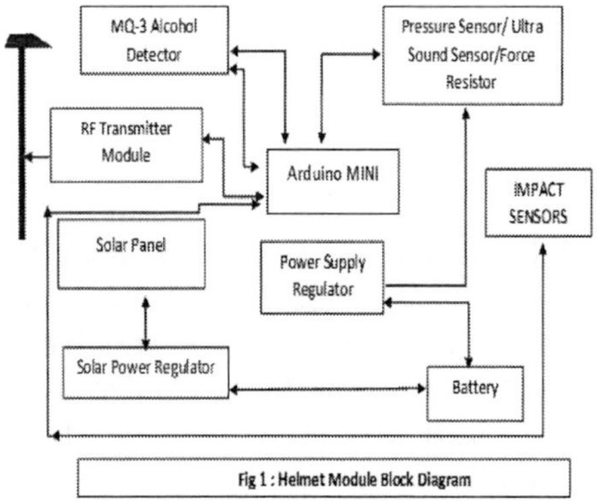

Fig 1. Helmet Circuit

In Figure 1, Arduino processes the incoming signals and controls the flow. At first Ultrasound sensor detects the presence of closure and next the MQ-3 alcohol sensor validates the state of the driver and sends a HIGH signal to the bike section through the RF transmitter. Power supply to the circuit is given by a 9v battery. Any change in state of the driver will disrupt the ignition system of the bike. On occurrence of an accident the impact sensors will send a HIGH signal to the bike section, triggering the GSM and GPS modules to triangulate the position of the driver.

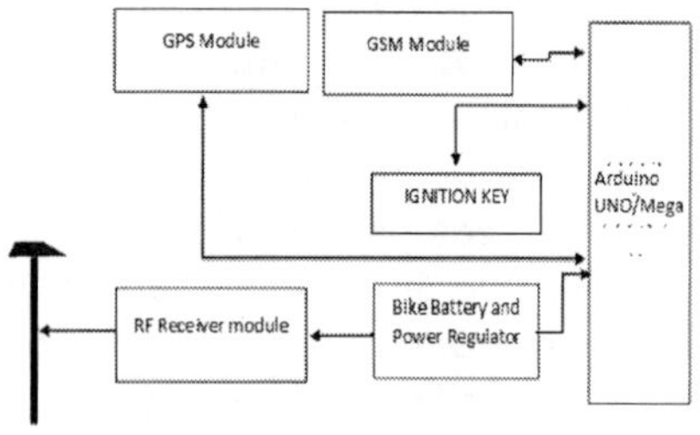

Fig 2 : Bike Circuit Module Block Diagram

Fig 2. Bike Circuit

In Figure 2, the ignition system is made available once a HIGH signal is received by the receiver and power supply for the circuit is given through the bike's power supply. Once an accident has occurred, a HIGH signal will be received by the receiver and GSM along with GPS modules will be triggered to triangulate the position and send the coordinates to the respective services and members.

3.1 Components

3.1.1 Arduino UNO

Arduino is a multifeatured [11] open source board and uses variety of microprocessors and controllers respectively. The board is equipped with multiple Analog and digital ports for interfacing the modules. It features serial port communication and USB communication on some models. One of the main reason Arduino overcomes Microcontroller is that the board uses C/C++ programming instead of assembly level language which becomes user-friendly and easy to code.

3.1.2 Ultrasonic Sensor

Ultrasonic sensors generally called as transducers [13] which work similarly to radar. It measure the distance of the object through trig and echo mechanism. They generate sound waves above 18000Hz by converting electrical energy to sound waves and vice versa, which can be measured and displayed. The distance travelled [14] can be calculated using the equation

$$\mathbf{I = I_0 e^{-ax}}$$

3.1.3 SIM900A GSM Module

SIM900A module is a compact and reliable [17] wireless module and is a complete Dual-band 900/1800 MHz which can be used in many customer applications. GSM module is capable of features which consist of voice calls, text messages and these features can be achieved through built-in AT commands. Low power consumption is the major advantage of SIM900A module.

3.1.4 NEO-6M GPS Module

The NEO-6M module is a standalone high performance [18] position receiver. The compact architecture and power consumption makes it compatible to be used in battery operated mobile devices. Position of the user is calculated within 1 second. Architecture of this module suppresses the jamming and multi path effects which makes it perform under challenging environments.

3.1.5 RF Transceivers

The RF module is a cost-effective component which can be used for wireless communication [15]. The module communicates using radio frequency and have a range up to 500 feet. RF modules operates at a specific frequency of 433 MHz for communication. When the logic 1 signal is applied to transmitter it sends out a 5v supply [16] to the receiver. By increasing the transmitter's power, the range of communication is increased along with excess drain of electrical energy.

3.1.6 Vibration Sensor

Vibration Sensors are used to display and measure the linear velocity [12] or acceleration. Vibrations are very subtle and humans do not notice every one of them, but vibration is the key for a machine's health and abnormal vibrations in a machine leads to failure of the device. It works on the principle of piezo-electric effect by sensing force and converting those signals into electrical energy.

3.1.7 Alcohol Sensor

Alcohol Sensor or Gas sensor detects the presence of alcohol and produces the output in an analog format [19]. It has a sensing range of 0.04 mg//L to 4mg/L and is cost-efficient along with high performance to detect alcohol.

3.2 Implementation

The proposed system has two major divisions. One is the helmet circuit and the other is the bike circuit.

3.2.1 Helmet Circuit:

The helmet circuit consists of an Arduino board which controls the Ultrasonic sensor [14], vibration sensor [12], and the alcohol sensor [19]. The power supply to the board and the other modules is given through a 9v battery supply.

3.2.2 Bike Circuit:

The bike circuit consists of another Arduino which controls the GSM [17] and GPS [18] modules. Both the helmet and the bike are connected through the RF transceiver circuit or a WI-FI module.

3.2.3 Working:

The working starts from the helmet part. The helmet part and bike circuit acts as a switch to the bike's ignition system. Once the biker wears the helmet, the Ultrasonic sensor goes high and if he is not drunk, the alcohol sensor remains low. Supposing that both the conditions are true, the signal is wirelessly transmitted to the bike's Arduino from the helmet Arduino. Now the ignition system of the bike is turned ON. In case of an accident occurs, the vibration sensor embedded with the helmet reads an Analog value. If the obtained Analog value is greater than the threshold value set, the signal is transmitted to the bike's Arduino. This Arduino then activates the GPS module and tracks the location of the area. Now this location is sent as a text message by the GSM module attached with a sim card to the government aided emergency services and any five emergency contact numbers.

3.2.4 Proposed System Implementation

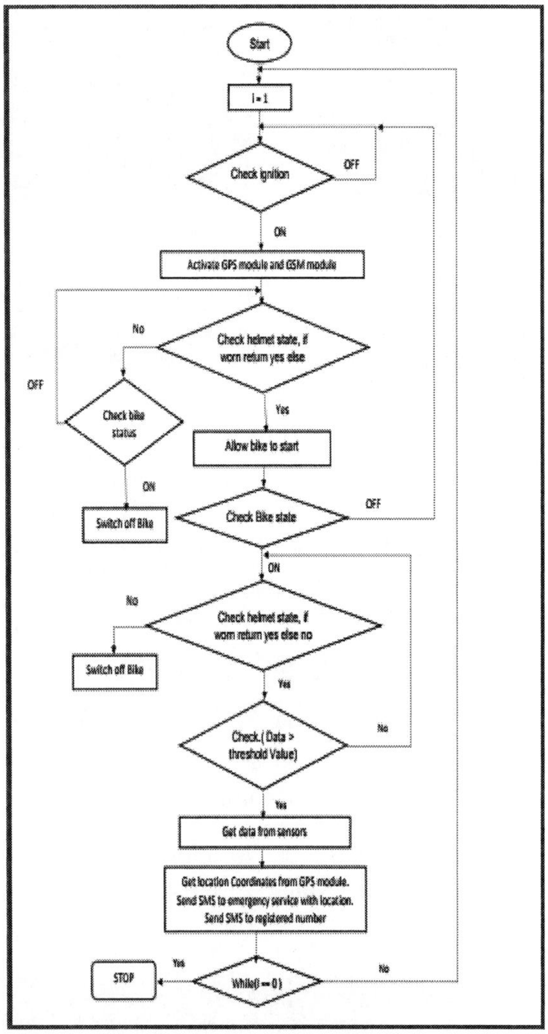

Fig 1: Implementation

The proposed model system's implementation is shown in Fig 1.

4. Result and Analysis

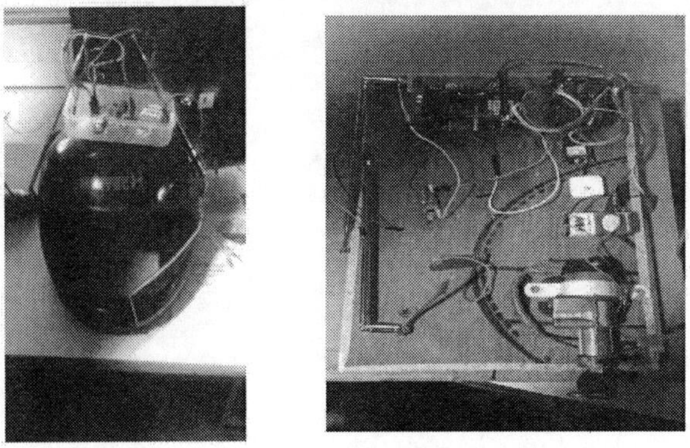

Fig 2: Helmet and bike Circuits

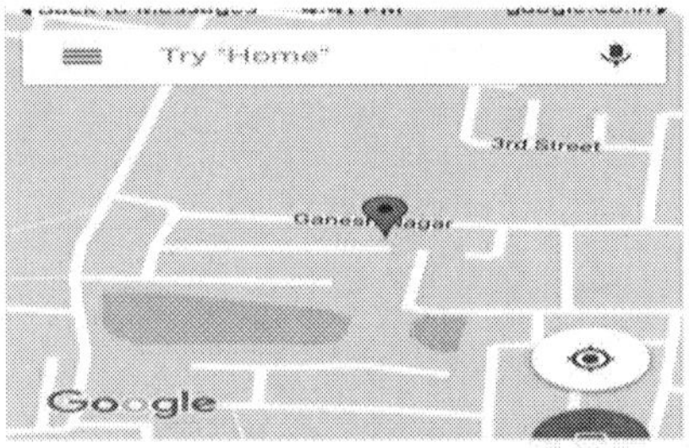

Fig 3: Google Maps location

Figure 2 displays the location of the accident in Google Maps, which is integrated with the text message.

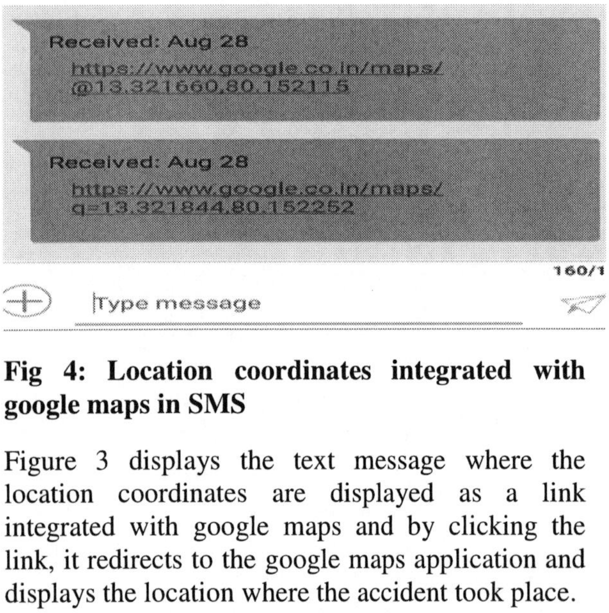

Fig 4: Location coordinates integrated with google maps in SMS

Figure 3 displays the text message where the location coordinates are displayed as a link integrated with google maps and by clicking the link, it redirects to the google maps application and displays the location where the accident took place.

5. Conclusion

The proposed system paves a way into next step for safety and security of bike riders. The results of the implemented model above prove the following, as shown in Fig 2. Ignition system will be available only if the rider wears the helmet throughout the journey., if the rider consumes any alcohol the ignition will be turned off. As shown in Fig 3&Fig 4, in-case of an emergency or accident the location of the rider will be sent to government aided services in the form of latitude and longitude co-ordinates., the proposed system will create an awareness amongst the people about the importance of wearing a helmet and value for life.

6.Future Scope

The main challenge faced in this scenario is unavailability of GSM signal in complex environment which can be overcome by using mock GPS signal technique and another feature to be implemented in the system is, whenever the alert of an accident is sent, the location data will be sent to the cloud and data will be analysed. Once analysed overall report will be forwarded to the government and respective actions will be taken in the accident-prone areas for more safety measures.

7. References

[1] Ayush Garg, Swati Gupta, Harpeet Kaur. "Smart Helmet". International Journal of Computer Applications National Symposium on "Modern Information & Communication Technologies for Digital India (MICTDI).e-ISSN: 0975 – 8887

[2] Chitte P.P, Salunke Akshay S , Thorat Aniruddha N, Bhosale Nilesh T. "Smart Helmet & Intelligent Bike System" . International Research Journal of Engineering and Technology (IRJET) e-ISSN: 2395 -0056.

[3] Dileep Kumar P, Kodanda Ramaiah G.N, Subramanyam A, Mrs. Dharani M. "A Solar Powered Smart Helmet with Multifeatures". International Journal of Engineering Inventions e-ISSN: 2278-7461.

[4] Jennifer William, Kaustubh Padwal, Nexon Samuel, Akshay Bawkar, SmitaRukhande. "Intelligent Hemet". International Journal of Scientific & Engineering Research, Volume 7, Issue 3, March-2016 e-ISSN 2229-5518

[5] Mohd Khairul Afiq Mohd Rasli, Nina Korlina Madzhi. "Smart Helmet with Sensors for Accident Prevention". 2013 International Conference on Electrical, Electronics and System Engineering e-ISBN 978-1-4799-3178-1

[6] Nitin Agarwal, Anshul Kumar Singh, Pushpendra Pratap Singh, Rajesh Sahani. "Smart Helmet". International Research Journal of Engineering and Technology (IRJET) e-ISSN: 2395 -0056

[7] Prudhvi Raj R, Sri Krishna Kanth Ch, Bhargav Adityaand A, Bharath K. "Smart-tec Helmet" . Research India Publications, Advance in Electronic and Electric Engineering. Volume 4, Number 5 (2014), ISSN 2231-1297

[8] Saravana Kumar K, Anjana B.S , Litto.Thomas, Rahul K.V. "Smart Helmet" . International Journal of Science, Engineering and Technology Research (IJSETR), Volume 5, Issue 3, March 2016. ISSN: 2278 – 7798

[9] https://en.wikipedia.org/wiki/List of countries by motor vehicle production

[10] https://en.wikipedia.org/wiki/Motor Vehicle Act ,1988

[11] https://en.wikipedia.org/wiki/Arduino

[12]http://www.globalspec.com/learnmore/sensors_transducers_detectors/acceleration_vibration_sensing/vibration_sensors

[13] http://sensorwiki.org/doku.php/sensors/ultrasound

[14]http://education.rec.ri.cmu.edu/content/electronics/boe/ultrasonic sensor/1.html

[15] https://en.wikipedia.org/wiki/RF_module

[16] http://www.edgefxkits.com/blog/rf-transceiver-module-with-block-diagram-explanation/

[17] http://www.circuitstoday.com/interface-gsm-module-with-arduino

[18] https://wiki.eprolabs.com/index.php?title=GPS_Module_NEO6MV2

[19] https://www.elprocus.com/mq-135-alcohol-sensor-circuit-and-working/

Code Smell Detection Text Mining Tool Analysis For Source Code Improvization

Amit Verma
CGC Landran, Mohali, INDIA
Email ID: dramitverma.cu@gmail.com

Ashish Kumar
CGC Landran,Mohali, INDIA
Email ID: ashishk887@gmail.com

Iqbaldeep Kaur
CGC Landran, Mohali, INDIA
Email ID: iqbaldeepkaur.cu@gmail.com

***Abstract*— Code smells area unit connected with poor writing that commits error or bugs with the issues that need to refactor by using some techniques. Tools used to refactor and help to detect efficiently the code smell ie the bugs must get detected. During this paper, the main focus is on code smells and on tools that can detect and refactor the bad smell efficiently. This paper shows the study of varied categories and issues that area unit baby-faced by the research worker. This study investigates however skilled package developers and code smell. Code smells indicates the code or style which follows some patterns and rules that the developers and testing team must follow while doing their work.The maintenance and cost factor becomes less if the proper code smell technique is used by companies people.**

Keywords— Code smell, information Clumps, Blob Class, Code Duplication (internal/external), Check vogue, JDeodorant, PMD

I. INTRODUCTION

Code Smell contains package systems that bear changes which will result in package economic condition. Code smells area unit usually thought of as vital to the quality of the package system[1]. They have an effect on altered code units, comparable to categories and ways.So, if the necessary tools and technology must get used to stopping the package degradation. The maintenance effort gets an increase if necessary care is not taken.Code smell must get removed as soon as possible so quality and effort to software system will be low with less hurdle. In the real world, new engineering developers get to know about the smell in the code as before long as they begin learning programming or motor in a very package theme [2]. If novice developers area unit has to be compelled to practical approach then efficiency becomes the main concern and become the good approach to work on. Code smells isn't an unimportant process to newbie developers those working in good environment[3].This process need special care and proper analysis from SDE ie Senior Develepor Engineer, that can help better for the feasibility of code smell solutions [4]. The Code Smell is possible to detect and refactor[5], but it is not necessary every developer do get know about code smell of product developed by another software developer so the code documentation becomes necessary from all the way[6].The product of software must get divide into submodule so the other developer gets to know which modules contain error or code smell which has to be removed.

Code smells square measure usually thought-about as the key factor of package demotion.It is classified in two classes per the existence of scope [7]: intra-class and inter-class.

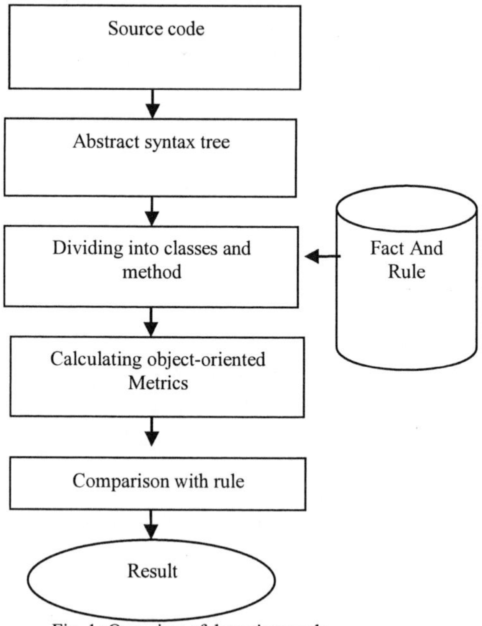

Fig. 1: Overview of detection mode

These two classes have features.Intra-class smells square measure abnormal pattern that square measure placed inside a specific category and, thus their definitions check with inner parts of a specific category.The example of this smells is the Long methodology and help to attain the objective in well manner.

It is always said that intra-class code smell proved whenever a task of the methodology is long and to a fault advanced.

And to opposite side, inter-class smells are the square measure of people where there is an effect of more than two categories.Thus it is said that more than two categories are there to check the part scattered. Feature Envy is the best example of this code smell.It is always advised to the software developer to do comprise the study of classes and its sub function in order to get the best result.

Table one below contains Class,Smell Type, and its methodology as told by the Fowler.It contains Inter class as well as Intra class features those helps in gaining outline of code smell representation.

Table 1 – Classification of Code Smells

Class	Smell Type	Methodology
Intraclass	LM	L,C
	UF	VCBNU
	DC	CS>1
Interclass	DCL	Classes that have only fields
	FE	Technique interested in systems of another than in its own class
	LC	NETWP

LM-Long technique , L-Long, C-Complex ,VCBNU-Variable Created however ne'er Used, CS-Code Structure UF-Unused Field, DC-Duplicated Code, DCL-Data category, FE-Feature Envy ,LC-Lazy category, NETWP-Not Enough to figure Properly.

Tablel shows the classification of Code Smells.Its major classes from Intra-Class and inhume category square measure delineated in higher than the table.

The classification of code smells is vital as a result of while not this step it's insufferable to understand wherever refactoring actions square measure required.Refactoring present actions needed for software system longevity[8]. sadly, many recent studies involving business software system comes have reportable however laborious the method of characteristic code smells is thanks to numerous factors. First, their square measure many styles of code smells listed[9]. Therefore, the developers must be ready to determine occurrences of every kind of code smell.

II. CODING STANDARDS

It is necessary to check source code quality factor of software system development is conformity to writing standard code. Writing standard code make sure that everybody within the software team will perceive which will helpfull in raising their company software quality. It becomes tougher for a giant team of programmers to do developing, integrating, testing and maintaining software product if one team not writing the standard good quality code. It becomes a lot of necessary in Associate in Nursing setting wherever developers square measure the coding standard[10].All developers concerned within the project need to understand and appreciate the rules decent to create software system in keeping with them.If developers don't see a selected rule, or even simply don't believe that this rule is helpful then it is always a good to code in his/her way.In alternative cases, the pointers are also there so that it's simple to overlook a number of them throughout development. once the project comes underneath time constraints, these items square measure becomes stronger. Code quality is improved by guaranteeing that the code is up to the writing standards.

III. BACKGROUND

This section provides procedural background to software system maintenance process; Cs and software system metrics, the threshold for software system metrics and risk assessment.

A. Maintenance of software system

The alteration in software system created when delivery therefore on correct mistakes, to change presentation or alternative aspects is understood as software system maintenance. The elaborated study on however an inspiration functions before it will modification it's the preliminary task. it's often connected with tough and laborious to know systems. Maintenance method is littered with software engineer experience, occurrence, system documentation and also the nature of the system itself. the value of software system maintenance accounts to eightieth of the estimation code charge and enhancements account for seventieth to eighty-fifth of the upkeep effort. numerous kind of software system maintenance square measure curative maintenance production with bugs corrections, reconciling maintenance regarding system varies as desires and setting Amendment and perfective maintenance attempting to recover the standard of a system. Maintenance method is littered with programming skills, system documentation, expertise and also the behavior of the system itself.

B. Code Smell (CS)

CSs square measure commonly not errors, they're not specifically wrong and don't presently avoid the program from functioning. this might be thought of as software system softness is the structure that will be growing the chance of errors or faults in future. Here it's involved with the succeeding code smells[11].

•Long Method: it's outlined as, a operate that has developed to massive lines of code.The long technique, demanding it becomes to scan, to alternate, to keep up etc.

•Long Parameter List: Whenever developer produces techniques with parameters, he ought to understand that the larger the parameter list, the tougher it becomes to keep up this method. The Cs is well-defined as numerous parameters passed into a method, this is often totally different object orientating programming, Associate in Nursing long parameter list technique will shift by passing an object during this place of the parameters as a result of a long parameter isn't easier to scan, change.

•Empty Catch: If software engineer users the attempt to catch blocks typically they left the catch half empty with no code classified it. Either code will grip the exception, then the catch clause mustn't be empty, or the code can't handle the exception, then there mustn't be try/catch block in the slightest degree.

C. Software system Metrics

Software Metrics square measure an estimable extent of the software system. during this paper, they're the center of attention solely on basis of metrics as mentioned to within the subsequent Fig. 2.

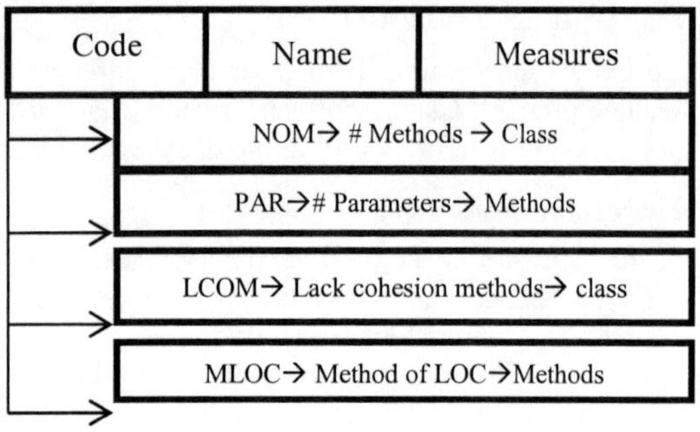

Fig 2: Object-oriented software metric

IV. PREVIOUS WORK

Krishna et al.[12] To assess the probability that a code rearrangement to address terrible code scents will yield the change in the imperfection inclination of the code. Strategy: Researcher present XTREE, a system that dissects a verifiable log of deformities seen beforehand in the code and creates an arrangement of valuable code changes. Any awful stench that requires changes outside of that set can be deprioritized (since there is no authentic confirmation that the awful stench brings about any issues).

Hermans et al.[13] investigate the code smells similitude with regards to piece based programming dialect Scratch. They lead a controlled try different things with 61 fledgling Scratch software engineers, in which researcher isolated the amateurs into three gatherings. 33% get a non-rotten program, while alternate gatherings get a program experiencing the Duplication or the Long Method smell individually. All subjects at that point play out a similar cognizance errands on their program, after which researcher measure their time and rightness. The aftereffects of the trial demonstrate that code smell,in fact, impacts execution: subjects taking a shot at the program displaying code smells perform fundamentally more awful.

Kumar et al.[14] this paper looks at the current perspectives of the apparatuses for program code smells identification. It portrays look into request about the consistency of their answers, their capacity to speak to the districts of code most influenced auxiliary rot, and the result of their reactions with reference to prospect-programming advancement.It offers to react to them by breaking down the generation of four attributes code notice indicators connected to six changed renditions of-Gantt extend, an open premise framework written in Java.

Abdelmoez et al.[15] in this paper, portrayed to utilize hazard origination in assessing code smells distinguished in the code. As an impenetrable of the idea, they built up a programmed chance based code smells location instrument. They utilize the apparatus to perceive challenges in a C# contextual analysis. Code smells, for example,

(i) Long Method
(ii) Long Parameter list
(iii) Message Chain and
(iv) Empty Catch has been distinguished for the situation ponder.

Rani et al.[16] portrayed as refactoring is an execution for enhancing programming structure without fluctuating its conduct which can be utilized to expel awful stenches and developments programming practicality.Code smells are a mechanical component of programming that may indicate a code or plan troublesome that makes programming hard to advance and safeguard and may trigger refactoring of code. There are numerous reflex location instruments to help people, in conclusion, smells yet these devices are stage subordinate. For e.g. in covering researcher can execute the main java code. Automation recognition instruments are restricted for recognizing some terrible stenches. So to see the quantity of awful stenches, they need to chip away at numerous location instruments so the window based GUI application is progressed in the visual studio device which distinguishes all the more awful stenches giving to their Object-Oriented Metrics.

Hecht et al.[17] describe the associate empirical study that combines performance impacts of three automation performance code smells Internal Getter/Setter, Ignoring methodology, and Hash Map.To perform this study, the author has given four versions.The author tried to correct each bad smells.

Reis et al.[18] gift conducted a quasi-experiment by hundred eighteen Java applications, classified into 6six application domains, and as well as seven kinds of code smells to check the developed hypotheses, it's been terribly very important to use the Kruskal-Wallis and analysis of variance tests.

Fowler et al.[19] gave definitions for twenty-two totally code smells and given method known as refactoring. Refactoring is set of the procedure by which the code is adjusted into the accurate format.The new techniques and models are applied into the refactoring.

Emden et al.[20] present the approach for automatic code smell detection.The new model jCOSMO developed, It is written in java and it takes input as ASCII file.The feedback is given by this tool and then the correction is made.It has increased the possibilities to encourage the researcher to put efforts into this.

Mantyla et al.[21] presents the categories that are Bloaters, Object-oriented abusers, modification preventers, unnecessary Encapsulation, Couplers. The theories were made to get insight into code smell testing.

Mantyla[22] Analyses have been done on the basis of behaviour of defected patterns and useful to build the tool support.

Khomh et al.[23] given a theorem based approach whether the specific category of the program contains bad smells or not. There exist several approaches in theorem to specify and sight into effected code smells. Most of the approaches were based on unit manual or supported rules. Manually smells is the time overwhelming method and depends on developers programming expertise.

Moha et al.[24] argued that the metric-based strategies area unit cant exactly determines unhealthy bad smell.

Zhang et al.[25] present the design approach of bad smell and it approaches the pattern of ASCII text file, in order that unhealthy smells are often known through examining these patterns in ASCII text file.

Kaur et al.[26] presents codes smell predictors for the machine learning examples.But there was unbalanced in the strategies and categories did not get fit into the system easily.

Shizhe et al.[27] describe code unhealthy smells have the organic process property, and therefore propose a unique methodology to sight three code unhealthy smells by mining code organic process data: duplicated code, small-arm surgery, and divergent modification. It exploits association rules strip-mined from modification history of code structures, upon that they outline heuristic algorithms to sight the three unhealthy smells.

Fu et al.[28] present the idea of code smell belonging from 3 systems to the developer of companies according to the tested projects.Auther tells the style of drawback into the code smell on the basis of tested projects.

Kessentini et al.[29] presents code-smells detection as a distributed fashion.It takes the parallel approach with the optimization method to detect the code smell. they used Parallel organic process algorithms P-EA .

V. SORTS OF CODE SMELL CATEGORIES

"Refactoring: up the planning of Existing Code"[30].This paper recognized twenty-two code smells as indicators of probable style flaws which will cause maintainability problems. During this section it's been given simply many of the additional necessary smells that are here:

a)Data category: information|the info|the information class represent a category with the appropriate interface that distributes data components. Allowing alternative categories to get its internal information, information categories subsidize to a style that's fragile and laborious to keep up.

b)Blob category: The Blob is associated overly giant sophisticated category, that has minimum one Blob Operation. The category is less cohesive and too powerfully coupled to the system.

c)Code Duplication (internal/external): Code Duplication is an exact code is being used in the system more than once.It increases the code maintenance, efforts. It is divided into 2 parts: (i) internal duplication - consist strategies that are part of the class and (ii) external duplication –no relation to the operation.

d)Feature Envy: Feature Envy refer method that accesses the data of other objects than to its own data.It helps for better code organization and helps for less code duplication.

e)God category: The God Class is an associate overly complicated category that gathers an excessive amount of practicality and manipulates information from alternative categories.

Table 2: Various CS Classes and Modules

Code Smell	**Definition**	**Variable used**	**Results**
LM	WDMWR	CC,LOC,#M	LOC >50 then no variable used; CC > 50
LPL	MCS	#P, $\sum$n POM, AP	NOP > 7; $\sum$n POM = 148; M in C = 88; AP = 3; #P > AP
LC	NETH	LOC, IV, DOI	LOC > 300; LM > 5; DIP> 3; coupling >10
DC	DNRC	UBoD	UBoD =24
LaC	LaC should PR	#T, LOC	SoM ==0; LOC<=300; #M <=2
LCB	DECB	#UCB	TUCB = 5
DuC	DuC exists if CMWO	#DCB	T#DCB =19

LM- Long Method, WDM- Well-Defined Methods With Refactoring , CC- Cyclomatic Complexity, LOC-Lines of Code, #M-Number of Methods, LPL-Long Parameter List, MCS- Many Constraints Passed, #P-Number of Parameter, POM-Parameter of Method, AP-Average Parameter, LC-Large Class, NETH-Not Enough To Handle, IV-Instance Variable, DOI- Depth of Inheritance, UBoD-Unused Block of Data, DC-Dead Code, DNRC-Delete Not Required Code, LaC-Lazy Class , PR- Predominantly Request, #T-Number of Technique, SoM-Several of Method, WMC-Weighted Method Count, #UCB-Number of Unused Catch Block, TUCB-Total number of Unused Catch Block, LCB-Lazy Catch Block, DECB- Discover Empty Catch Block, DuC-Duplicate Code, CMWO- Code Match With Other, #DCB-Number of Duplicate Code Block, T#DCB- Total Number of Duplicate Code Block.

Table 2 above shows the various detection classes and modules. These have different features.These have to get optimized to have the good quality of code and efficiency.

Table two higher than shows the varied detection categories and modules. These have completely different options.These have got to get optimized to own smart quality of code and potency.

VI. TOOLS FOR AUTOMATED DETECTION OF SMELL

It tells the various tools and technology used for Automated detection of smell.Some tools had developed to progress code quality throughout software system growth, alternative tools to support re-engineering and maintenance activities.

Table 3 –Detection of Code smell by tools

Tool	Version	Type	Language analysed	Refactoring	Link to code
Checkstyle	5.4.1 2011	EP,SA	J	N	Y
Decor	1.0 2009	SA	J	N	N
IPlasma	6.1 2009	SA	C++, J	N	N
INFusion	7.2.11 2010	SA	C, C++, J	N	N
JDeodorant	4.0.4 2010	EP	J	Y	Y
PMD	4.2.5 2009	EP,SA	J	N	Y

EP-Eclipse, SA-Stand-Alone, J-Java

Table 3 shows the assorted code smell detection tools.

Tools which are developed mostly are not able to refactor well on code smell.Jdeodorant is the one which provides the refactoring.

Different tools use the various languages and its kind additionally varies[31], the tools contains the reliable characteristics Following are the tools have different characteristics:

a)Checkstyle : Checkstyle2 is developed for developers to use the Java code efficiently by applying rules. it's capable to sighting the massive category, Duplicate code, Long technique, and Long Parameter List.

b)DÉCOR Moha[32] outlined associate degree method that contains proper detection and style smell which occurs in programs.Hence programming is efficiently being used to code.

c) Patterns: Code smells associated with some pattern are identified and use the algorithm to use the parameter like accuracy and recall.The particular signature or pattern helps to find the bugs in the system.

d) INFusion :INFusion4 is the evolution of the current business evolution of IPlasma. INFusion is ready to sight quite twenty style flaws and code smells, like Duplicated Code, information category, God category, strategies and categories those are heavily coupled.

e) iPlasma : This tool is an associate degree that contains support to the study phases from model abstraction to the high-level metrics.iPlasma contains the disharmonies such as Duplicate code, God class, Refused parent heritage and Feature envy.This tool is specific to collaboration and detection of smells[33].

f) JDeodorant : JDeodorant is a Java language-based tool.It uses the plugin on to the browser and detects code smells in java programs. The issues evolved which can be transformed into refactoring.It also ranks the issues on priority basis.

f) PMD : PMD takes inputs as ASCII text file and it is written in Java .The bugs and issues are detected by this tools and helpful for almost every kind of code smell.

VII. Drawbacks of Code Smell

Code smells are based on the result of erroneous coding and standard that becomes dangerous if rapid action is not taken[34]. Code smell life cycle plays vital role and has various major parts like development, maintenance, and evolution.Evolution contains the suitability to customers and their feedback.The value of the projects is the main goal then only the customer can get satisfied. Maintenance cost is also high if poor code style is used. Code smells will help the developer code troublesome to know, alter and enhance and this is the hurdle to some programmers.

VIII. Simulation and Result

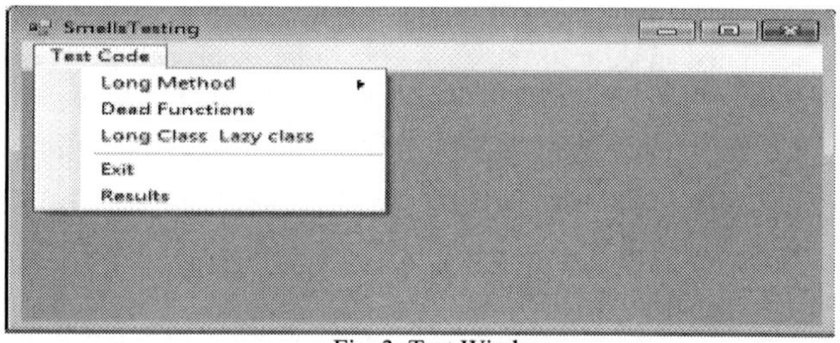

Fig. 3: Test Window

Test window is also working as the linker between test modules and other parameters calculations. These are performing and transfer their calculation results on this window.

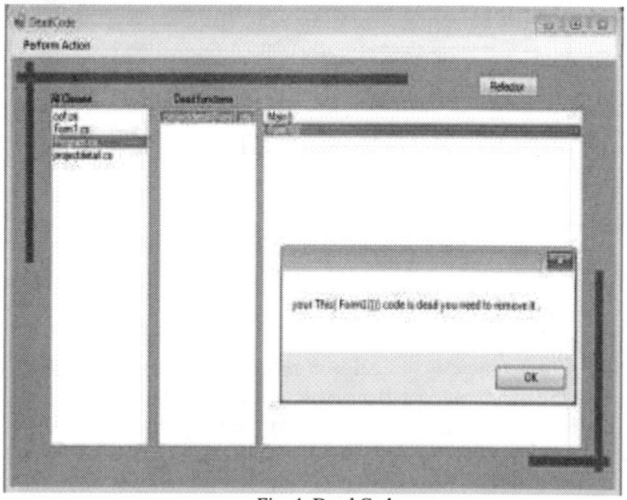

Fig. 4: Dead Code

Dead code means, delete code that isn't being used. That's why it contains source control systems. The approach is detecting the dead code from a large code module very efficiently

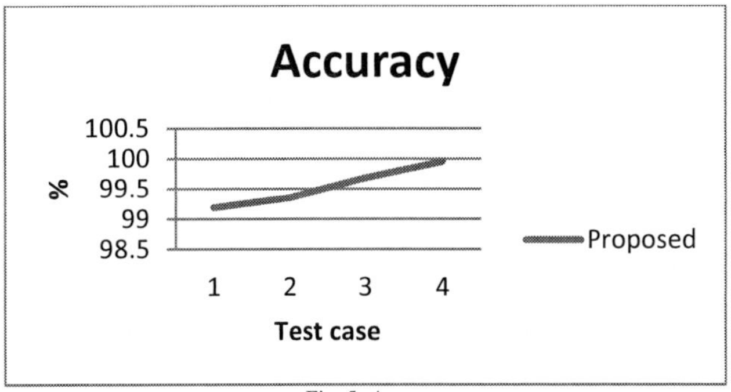

Fig. 5: Accuracy

The performance accuracy approach is maximum in the proposed graph as calculated from the various test modules.

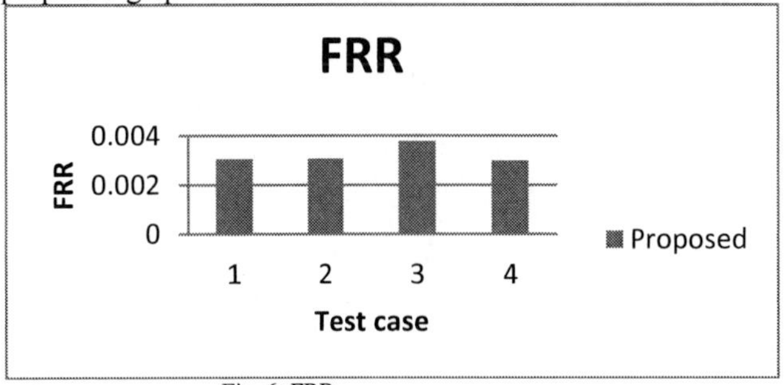

Fig. 6: FRR

As in the proposed parameters, the FRR is stable on 0.003 so it can show accuracy more than 98 as in the accuracy graph

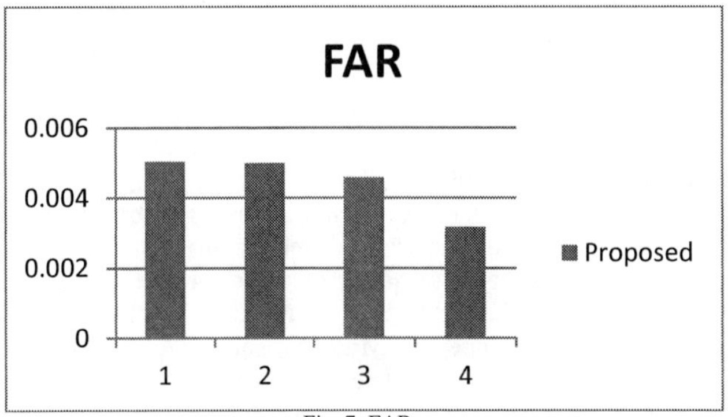

Fig. 7: FAR

Here in the graph, the value of FAR is stable or below 0.005. As in the result, the accuracy goes higher in overall results.

IX. CONCLUSION

Code smells are pattern based characteristics that indicate a code to have error or bug and these do not fit into the standard.It's important to research the strength of tools, varied ways, and categories. With the assistance of facts and rules, the code smells will be simply corrected in less time.Due to the variation within the syntax, the tools are completely different for the various language. Approach working with three different languages and detect the long method,dead code,lazy class and long class bad smells from the code. These are refactoring for c++ and java programming languages along with detection of .net projects. The hybrid approach detect bad smells as long method, lazy class, dead code, long class from uploaded projects and refactor some of them. Proposed algorithm performs both detection and optimization for all the cases to enhance the output of the parameters. Overall output of proposed approach better than other existing approaches and also perform detection on more than an existing tool in terms of programming languages. Some improvement techniques or optimization are helpful for better path finding.It optimizes the performance of code inside less value and time.

REFERENCES

[1]Fowler, Martin, and Kent Beck. *Refactoring: improving the design of existing code*. Addison-Wesley Professional, 1999.

[2] Estácio, Bernardo, Roberto Oliveira, Sabrina Marczak, Marcos Kalinowski, Alessandro Garcia, Rafael Prikladnicki, and Carlos Lucena. "Evaluating collaborative practices in acquiring programming skills: Findings of a controlled experiment." In *Software Engineering (SBES), 2015 29th Brazilian Symposium on*, pp. 150-159. IEEE, 2015.

[3] Hermans, Felienne, and Efthimia Aivaloglou. "Do code smells hamper novice programming? A controlled experiment on Scratch programs." In *Program Comprehension (ICPC), 2016 IEEE 24th International Conference on*, pp. 1-10. IEEE, 2016.

[4] Braught, Grant, John MacCormick, and Tim Wahls. "The benefits of pairing by ability." In *Proceedings of the 41st ACM technical symposium on Computer science education*, pp. 249-253. ACM, 2010.

[5] Bryton, Sérgio, Fernando Brito e Abreu, and Miguel Monteiro. "Reducing subjectivity in code smells detection: experimenting with the long method." In *Quality of Information and Communications Technology (QUATIC), 2010 Seventh International Conference on the*, pp. 337-342. IEEE, 2010.

[6] Murphy-Hill, Emerson, and Andrew P. Black. "Seven habits of a highly effective smell detector." In *Proceedings of the 2008 international workshop on Recommendation systems for software engineering*, pp. 36-40. ACM, 2008.

[7] Fowler, Martin, and Kent Beck. *Refactoring: improving the design of existing code*. Addison-Wesley Professional, 1999.

[8] Opdyke, William F. "Refactoring object-oriented frameworks." (1992): 361-396.

[9] Mantyla, Mika V., Jari Vanhanen, and Casper Lassenius. "Bad smells-humans as code critics." In *Software Maintenance, 2004. Proceedings. 20th IEEE International Conference on*, pp. 399-408. IEEE, 2004.

[10] Van Emden, Eva, and Leon Moonen. "Java quality assurance by detecting code smells." In *Reverse Engineering, 2002. Proceedings. Ninth Working Conference on*, pp. 97-106. IEEE, 2002.

[11] Schumacher, Jan, Nico Zazworka, Forrest Shull, Carolyn Seaman, and Michele Shaw. "Building empirical support for automated code smell detection." In *Proceedings of the 2010 ACM-IEEE International Symposium on Empirical Software Engineering and Measurement*, p. 8. ACM, 2010.

[12] Krishna, Rahul, Tim Menzies, and Lucas Layman. "Less is more: Minimizing code reorganization using XTREE." *Information and Software Technology* 88 (2017): 53-66.

[13] Hermans, Felienne, and Efthimia Aivaloglou. "Do Code Smells Hamper Novice Programming?." *Report TUD-SERG-2016-06* (2016).

[14] Kumar, Rohit, Jaspreet Singh, and AmandeepKaur. "An Empirical Study of Bad Smell in Code on Maintenance Effort." International Journal of Computer Science Engineering (IJCSE),2015 .

[15] Abdelmoez, Walid, EssamKosba, and Ali FalahIesa. "Risk-based code smells detection tool." In The International Conference on Computing Technology and Information Management (ICCTIM), p. 148. Society of Digital Information and Wireless Communication, 2014.

[16] Rani, Anshu, and HarpreetKaur. "Detection of bad smells in source code according to their object oriented metrics." International Journal for Technological Research in Engineering 1, no. 10 (2014): 1211-14.

[17] Hecht, Geoffrey, Naouel Moha, and Romain Rouvoy. "An empirical study of the performance impacts of android code smells." In *Proceedings of the International Workshop on Mobile Software Engineering and Systems*, pp. 59-69. ACM, 2016.

[18] dos Reis, José Pereira, Fernando Brito e Abreu, and Glauco de F. Carneiro. "Code smells incidence: does it depend on the application domain?." In *Quality of Information and Communications Technology (QUATIC), 2016 10th International Conference on the*, pp. 172-177. IEEE, 2016.

[19] Fowler, Martin, and Kent Beck. *Refactoring: improving the design of existing code*. Addison-Wesley Professional, 1999.

[20] Van Emden, Eva, and Leon Moonen. "Java quality assurance by detecting code smells." In *Reverse Engineering, 2002. Proceedings. Ninth Working Conference on*, pp. 97-106. IEEE, 2002.

[21] Mantyla, Mika, Jari Vanhanen, and Casper Lassenius. "A taxonomy and an initial empirical study of bad smells in code." In *Software Maintenance, 2003. ICSM 2003. Proceedings. International Conference on*, pp. 381-384. IEEE, 2003..

[22] Mäntylä, Mika. "An experiment on subjective evolvability evaluation of object-oriented software: explaining factors and interrater agreement." In *ISESE*, pp. 287-296. 2005.

[23] Khomh, Foutse, Stéphane Vaucher, Yann-Gaël Guéhéneuc, and Houari Sahraoui. "A bayesian approach for the detection of code and design smells." In *Quality Software, 2009. QSIC'09. 9th International Conference on*, pp. 305-314. IEEE, 2009.

[24] Moha, Naouel, Yann-Gael Gueheneuc, Laurence Duchien, and Anne-Francoise Le Meur. "DECOR: A method for the specification and detection of code and design smells." *IEEE Transactions on Software Engineering* 36, no. 1 (2010): 20-36.

[25] Zhang, Min, Tracy Hall, and Nathan Baddoo. "Code bad smells: a review of current knowledge." *Journal of Software: Evolution and Process* 23, no. 3 (2011): 179-202.

[26] Kaur, Arvinder, Kamaldeep Kaur, and Shilpi Jain. "Predicting software change-proneness with code smells and class imbalance learning." In *Advances in Computing, Communications and Informatics (ICACCI), 2016 International Conference on*, pp. 746-754. IEEE, 2016.

[27] Fu, Shizhe, and Beijun Shen. "Code Bad Smell Detection through Evolutionary Data Mining." In *Empirical Software Engineering and Measurement (ESEM), 2015 ACM/IEEE International Symposium on*, pp. 1-9. IEEE, 2015..

[28] Fu, Beijun Shen. "Code Bad Smell Detection through Evolutionary Data Mining." In *Empirical Software Engineering and Measurement (ESEM), 2015 ACM/IEEE International Symposium on*, pp. 1-9. IEEE, 2015.

[29] Kessentini, Wael, Marouane Kessentini, Houari Sahraoui, Slim Bechikh, and Ali Ouni. "A cooperative parallel search-based software engineering approach for code-smells detection." *IEEE Transactions on Software Engineering* 40, no. 9 (2014): 841-861.

[30] Fowler, M. (1999). Refactoring: improving the design of existing code. Pearson Education India

[31] Emerson Murphy-Hill and Andrew P. Black. An interactive ambient visualization for code smells. In Proceedings of the 5th international symposium on Software visualization, SOFTVIS '10, pages 5–14, Salt Lake City, Utah, USA, 2010. ACM. doi:10.1145/1879211.1879216.

[32] NaouelMoha, Yann-GaëlGuéhéneuc, Anne-Françoise Le Meur, Laurence Duchien, and Alban Tiberghie.From a domain analysis to the specification and detection of code and design smells. Formal Aspects of Computing, 22:345–361, 2010. doi:10.1007/s00165-009-0115-x.

[33] Cristina Marinescu, RaduMarinescu, PetruMihancea, Daniel Ratiu, and Richard Wettel.iPlasma: An integrated platform for quality assessment of object-oriented design. In Proceedings of the 21st IEEE International Conference on Software Maintenance (ICSM 2005), pages 77–80, Budapest, Hungary, September 2005. IEEE Computer Society.(Industrial and Tool Proceedings), Tool Demonstration Track.

[34] Mantyla, Mika V., Jari Vanhanen, and Casper Lassenius. "Bad smells-humans as code critics." In *Software Maintenance, 2004. Proceedings. 20th IEEE International Conference on*, pp. 399-408. IEEE, 2004..

ARIS: A MACHINE LEARNING ALGORITHM TO TEST GAMES

[Advanced Rating Intelligent System]

Shivani.S.C , Santhanalakshmi.S, Baghavathi Priya.S ,

[1]Rajalakshmi Engineering College, 602105 Thandalam, Chennai, TamilNadu

{shivani.s.c,santhanalakshmi.s, baghavathipriya.s }@rajalakshmi.edu.in

ABSTRACT

The world is being simulated with entertainment for the human races in form of video, game, music, sports and so on. There is a mixture of good and bad entertainment in society and unfortunately young minds couldn't find the difference between them and become the victims of the bad entertainment. Thus growing influence of games among younger generation cause major damage in their lifestyle. Games are permitted by Entertainment Software Board Rating (ESBR) by various categories, but humans aren't always conscious about everything, but whereas computers are! By giving knowledge of humans to select a safe and secure game this Artificial Intelligence project is used. Computer is allowed to play the game instead of humans by using Machine learning algorithm which gives the ability to learn without being programmed explicitly and it will give a report of what will be the impact of human brain if they play that particular game.Thus, there will be no sneak peak games to take life of humans. The main advantage of this project is that it will not allow any dangerous game that will change the human mind to stress or kill themselves. It is also very simple that the machine can take intelligent decisions.

1.INTRODUCTION

Artificial Intelligence is a technology used to develop intelligent machines. By Intelligence, they mean the ability to think, imagine, create, understand and recognize patterns. It also learns how to make choices by learning from past experiences. It is a search system to map intelligence and the underlying hardware and incorporate the ability of formalizing thoughts into the system[2]. It comes to a conclusion by using predictive logic to relate various real world events. Turing test is an Intelligent behavior which makes the system to fool a human by performing various tasks and decisions .ability to achieve human-level performance[3]. Evolutionary AI is designed modifies itself based on the system. The AI will improve its performance by testing a new version against an old version. It identifies the best of them and uses that form then on. In real world, computers show that they can even replace human beings. Emotional Intelligence(EQ)[26]-unlike humans,[27] who aren't always particularly good at reading others and are prone to missing emotional signals or being fooled by lies[24]. Machine learning is the ability of the machine to learn without being explicitly programmed. Especially, machine learning in gaming industry are used widely in order to gain the player's ability by shifting policy and approach, to a certain extent than by civilizing the ability of opponents. Main concept in learning, is the adjustment of behaviors[5] with the goal of improving the performance. This concept can be used for various safety purposes. One of the most important things is that all type of games including malicious games can also take place either in online and in play store which will even take human life. For example, in recent 2017 there has been a popular game called blue whale which took so many people lives. This game brainwashes children by throwing them challenges, which include self mutilation, waking up at unearthly hours and watching scary videos and listening to haunting music sent by the curator. The catch of the sport is that after you transfer it, you won't be ready to uninstall it because the app additionally hacks your phone .Apparently ,once you conform to be a part of the sport, you're not allowed to back out. If you do, the creators threaten you as they have all of your personal information. Every games which are taking place in the online and play store are certified by a board called Entertainment Software Rating Board(ESRB)[25].Those ratings are given by humans who work there. Humans are not perfect all the time whereas computers never make mistake, good at repetitive tasks, very intelligent and they are predictable. Arise is the machine learning algorithm which will make the computer to learn how to play a game and to feel the same way as human brain do. When the machine is allowed to play the game they will produce a report of what will the impact of human being by playing a particular game. This will help the human race to stay safe without harming ourselves for the sake of entertainment. As we consider entertainment is the biggest relaxation in human life. Those things have to be much secured, for that computers are the best choice in order to predict and rate the games.[13]

2. EXISTING SYSTEM

Interactive knowledge acquisition systems aim at having interactions with a human expert to create analyze, modify, or expand an expert system. Two approaches exist. First approach was proposed by Bennett's ROGE (Bennett, 1985) explains how to design interactive knowledge systems. The system asks questions such that it learns about the basic structure of the task. It results in a prototype expert system which accepts additional knowledge. Second approach helps the expert by allowing them to add knowledge or alter the on hand knowledge to progress the system's performance. Davis (Davis, 1982) proposed this approach [1].

Interactive knowledge based consultants[2] openly incorporates new knowledge by learning and analyzing the methods used by their users to solve a problem by normal use of the system. A useful research by Tom Mitchell thought lectures at IJCAI-83[1]. They acquire knowledge on their own without human interaction. There are two types: inductive learning systems and deductive learning systems. *Inductive learning systems*:[1] Valiant has extended on learn ability concept in a less time

efficiency. His frame work determines when an AR system has fully learned all the concepts. Segan proposed a bias, which is based on Kolgomerov complexity to determine the gap between correct and incorrect values in a noisy learning system. *Deductive learning systems*:[1]. In learning by macro-operators can slow down the system performance because it saves the macro and compares with all the available ones. To avoid this problem, Minton suggested an approach which saves the macro only under two situations- "S-MACRO" when an operator is used twice And "T-MACROS" when the operators overcome a local maximum. In 1947, Arthur L. Samuel, built a checker's program, simpler than a chess game. The two focal papers relating his research (Samuel 1959; Samuel 1967)[2]
became milestone papers in Artificial Intelligence. He invented a variety of learning techniques like alpha-beta cut-off's and quiescent search to improve the efficiency of the program. He considered this program as a base to machine learning and now many of the successful algorithms can be traced back to Samuel's work. Machine learning algorithms require careful modification of model parameter. The tuning requires expert experience and brute force search. Ryan P. Adams form Harvard university[3] proposed a framework that uses automatic optimization of performance of any learning algorithm using Gaussian Process(GP)[5].Most of the comparison functions take into account an algorithm and asses its performance with a selected algorithm which is available. In such cases it doesn't give the real performances. Lars Kotthoff, Ian P. Gent and Ian Miguel[4] proposed an approach which compares all the algorithm and ensures always a best algorithm is selected. The methods used are case-based reasoning, classification, regression and statistical relational learning[7].Analyzing of these algorithms requires maintaining data privacy and integrity. Nathan Dowlin et al proposed an approach called *cryptonets*[8]. It converts neural networks into cryptonets which is also a neural network that can be applied to encrypted data[9].Deep neural networks[10] are a recent trend in artificial intelligence to model numerical and statistical models. In order to generate multiple response maps which have different range of values in magnitude, the existing neural networks which employs ReLU have to make use redundant filters to improve its performance. ReLU(Rectified Linear Unit) separates noise and signal. Yangli et al proposed a Multi-bias non-linear activation layer which is placed after the convolution layer which is used to discover the hidden information in magnitude of responses. The machine learning algorithms mainly focus on minimizing errors over a unclassified datasets, estimating complexity of algorithms, establishing bounds of errors(Vapnik 1996). Some algorithms account for variable selection and handling missing values while others require additional pre-processing tasks. Brett Wujek et al proposed certain best practices to guide the practitioner through data preparation, modelling and deployment[11].Uri Shaham et al proposed how deep learning is used in the background of crowd sourcing and unsupervised ensemble learning[12]. They proved that the David and Skene model. This model assumes that all the classifiers are provisionally independent is equivalent to the Restricted Boltzmann Machine(RBM), which has only one hidden node. In this model, a posterior probability can be estimated using a trained RBM. When the classifiers violate the conditional independence, they applied the RBM based Deep Neural Net (DNN)[13].VR-PCA algorithm by Shamir[14] is used for the fastly computing the leading singular

vectors. Block version of the algorithm is proven by him along with how the iteration improves the analysis and also about the properties like convexity and non-convexity of an optimization problem[15].Maria Florina Balcan And Vitaly Feldman had proposed a model for designing a system which uses active learning algorithms[16] which is not modified by the classification noises. The algorithms are statistical because they depend on estimating the expectation functions of segregated examples. A statistical query framework of Kearns was built by them. They show how a statistical algorithm is converted into an active learning algorithm[17].

3. PROPOSED SYSTEM

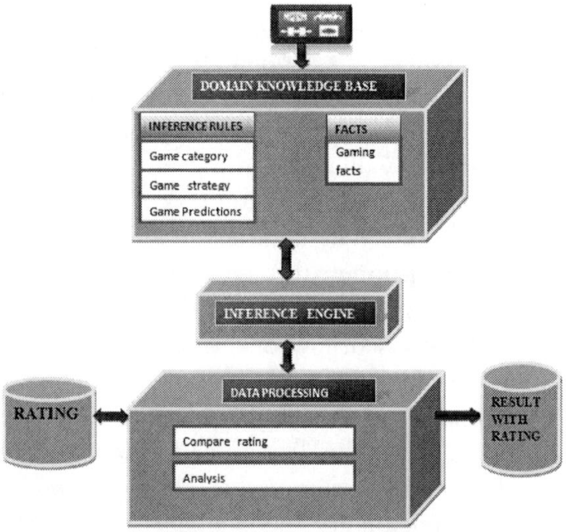

3.2.Domain knowledge base

Domain knowledge is a knowledge which is used to refer the area of human expertise, to predict the correct actions with respect to the gaming events. The events may be an autonomous computer action, or an area of special authority. A knowledge base is an organised collection of facts about the system's domain. Domain knowledge describes about the environment in which our system operates. It has two components- Inference rule and facts.

3.3.Inference rule

An inference rule consists of a function which accepts the input, analyzes it, gains some knowledge and makes progress towards the conclusion. It has the following processes- game strategy, game category and game prediction.

3.3.1.Game strategy: Game strategy is an algorithm which describes how to play a game. It tells the player what to do at a particular situation.

3.3.2.Game category: Game category describes the type of a game. Examples of game categories are Massive Multiplayer Online (MMO) games, puzzle, action, simulation.

3.3.3Game prediction: game predictions are guesses about future results. For example in cricket game, the final score is predicted based on run rates.

3.3.Facts

3.3.1.Gaming facts: Facts are information about games which is proved as true. It is a part of report or evidence. It is verified by statistical or mathematical concepts and relations. They are stored in the knowledge base to save our purpose of reasoning. For example, a cricket team consist of 5 bowlers, 5 fielders and 1 wicket keeper. This is an accepted fact and proven to be true and correct.

3.4.Inference engine:

Inference engine is a component which applies inference rules to the knowledge base and derives some conclusions. The knowledge represented by the inference engine is in the form of IF<condition> THEN <expression> format. For example, If the score of two teams are equal, and if a team has minimum wickets than other team, then it is the winning team. The output of inference engine is the reduced knowledge, here in our case it is the expert knowledge about the games, which can be then used for data processing.

3.5.Rating database:

A database is an entity which stores some information that is used for future reference purposed. This database stores rating information. It has certain strategies to give rating. When it satisfies all the strategies, a game can be rated good and when it satisfies only some of it, it can be rated accordingly. This is used by the data processing module to give appropriate results.

3.6.Data processing:

The knowledge from the inference engine is processed along with the information stored in the rating database to produce the reports, which contains the result of two modules- compare rating and analysis.

- ***Compare rating:*** This module compares the information and gives correct rating for the game input.
- ***Analysis:*** This module analyses the rating produced by the previous module to find its correctness.

3.7.Result database:

This database stores the result along with rating as a report. This report is displayed to the game tester. They can use this information to decide whether a game is good or bad and appropriate to the specified age group.

4. DISCUSSIONS

Games are generally classified into perfect and imperfect information. The classification is shown in Figure 2 and the perfect information is shown in Table 1 and imperfect information is shown in Table 2.

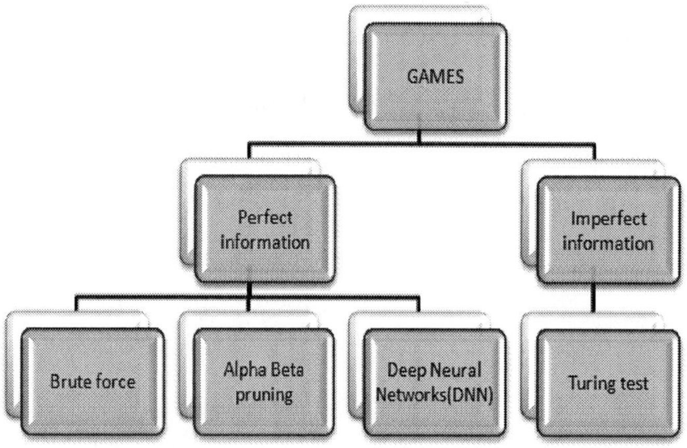

4.1.PERFECT INFORMATION:

ALGORITHM	ADVANTAGES	DISADVANTAGES
Brute force algorithm: **This algorithm selects a node at random and tests if it is a goal. It returns a solution and the path through which it has attained the solution.**	• Useful for simple games. • Cost effective.	• Inefficient for large and complex games. • Time consuming to explore all the choices.
Alpha-beta pruning: **This algorithm stops evaluating a path when it finds at least one proof that this path is worse than the**	• It is suitable for two-player games like chess, tic-tac-toe. • Efficient time and space	• Small error in evaluation of a node can lead to a huge problem. • One could choose a poor move if the evaluation function is not

previous one. So it prunes away the branches.	complexity.	that good. • It is not feasible to search the entire game tree.
Deep neural networks: **Deep neural networks are distinguished from the normal neural network by their depth ,ie. The no. of nodes through which the data passes**	• It combines features of the output of previous layer. • It can compactly represent large set of functions than a normal one layer neural network	• .Availability of labeled data for supervised data is very low. Hence training is difficult. • Training a deep network has the problem of bad local optima. • When using backpropagation, the magnitude of derivatives decreases as the depth of levels increases.

4.2.IMPERFECT INFORMATION

TEST	ADVANTAGE	DISADVANTAGE
Turing test: **It is a method of describing Whether a computer has the thinking capability like a human. According to this test, a computer is assumed to have intelligence if it is able to imitate human response under some important situations. In Turing's test, if the human who is conducting the test is unable to identify the answer which is given by a computer or by another human being to be correct, then the computer have "passed" the test.**	• It can be directly used to compare which of the two machines is intelligent. • Avoids internal discussions about consciousness. • Eliminate partiality between living organisms.	• It introduces mistakes in arithmetic problems to confuse the interrogator. • It produces result as a binary value - it doesn't specify a level of intelligence.

4.3. EMOTIONAL INTELLIGENCE

• Machines appear as if they need emotional feelings, however currently they also are programmed to find out the way to show feelings which alters the machine to appear sympathetic.

- Machines are currently given the ability to identify and acknowledge human expressions importantly their feelings like happiness, stress, interest. This kind of communication is essential for incorporating an additional behaviour into the system.
- Emotional intelligence computers measure or predict human emotions by victimization of their intelligence. We can make a machine to play a game and to provide reports concerning the impact of human brain once subjected to play specific game.

5. CONCLUSION

Artificial Intelligence and its technology always remain an interest in human lives and gives us new topics, ideas and results. It may give the machines an ability to think and perceive human actions using various concepts and techniques. Artificial intelligence have made tremendous contributions in many areas. Artificial Intelligence plays an important role in the various fields. This paper, based on the concept of artificial intelligence to give us the safest entertainment. ARIS, this project is especially used to predict the game strategy and rate the game whether it is safer or not. Machine is allowed to play the game by using machine learning algorithm and it will provide the report and rating of the game. Thus by using this project the people will identify the safer game

REFERENCE

1. Thomas G. Dietterrich, Nicholas S. Flann, David C. Wilkins, "A Summary of Machine Learning Papers From IJCAI-85".
2. Davis, R. and Lenat, D., "Knowledge-based systems in artificial intelligence", McGraw-Hill, 1982.
3. Johannes F¨urnkranz, " Machine Learning in Games: A Survey", Technical Report OEFAI-TR-2000-31.
4. Ryan P. Adams, Jasper Snoek, Hugo Larochelle," Practical Bayesian Optimization of Machine Learning Algorithms
5. Lars Kotthoff , Ian P. Gent and Ian Miguel," An Evaluation of Machine Learning in Algorithm Selection for Search Problems", AI Communication ISSN 0921-7126.
6. Jonas Mockus, Vytautas Tiesis, and Antanas Zilinskas. The application of Bayesian methods for seeking the extremum. Towards Global Optimization, 2:117–129, 1978.
7. Lars Kotthoff, Ian Miguel, and Peter Nightingale. Ensemble classification for constraint solver configuration. In *CP*, pages 321–329, September 2010.
8. Nathan Dowlin, Ran Gilad-Bachrach, Kim Laine, Kristin Lauter, Michael Naehrig, John Wernsing," CryptoNets: Applying Neural Networks to Encrypted Data with High Throughput and Accuracy", Proceedings of the 33 rd International Conference on Machine Learning", New York, NY, USA, 2016. JMLR: W&CP volume 48.

9. Aslett, Louis JM, Esperanc,a, Pedro M, and Holmes,Chris C. "A review of homomorphic encryption and software tools for encrypted statistical machine learning". arXiv preprint arXiv:1508.06574, 2015b.

10. Hongyang Li,Wanli Ouyang, XiaogangWang," Multi-Bias Non-linear Activation in Deep Neural Networks", Proceedings of the 33 rd International Conference on Machine Learning, New York, NY, USA, 2016. JMLR: W&CP volume 48.

11. Brett Wujek, Patrick Hall, and Funda Güneş," Best Practices for Machine Learning Applications", Paper SAS2360-2016, SAS Institute Inc.

12. Uri Shaham, Xiuyuan Cheng, Omer Dror, Ariel Jaffe, Boaz Nadler, Joseph Chang ,Yuval Kluger, "A Deep Learning Approach to Unsupervised Ensemble Learning", Proceedings of the 33 rd International Conference on Machine Learning, New York, NY, USA, 2016. JMLR: W&CP volume 48,2014

13. LeCun, Yann, Bengio, Yoshua, and Hinton, Geoffrey. "Deep learning. Nature", 521(7553):436–444, 2015.

14. Ohad Shamir, "Fast Stochastic Algorithms for SVD and PCA:Convergence Properties and Convexity", Proceedings of the 33 rd International Conference on Machine Learning, New York, NY, USA, 2016. JMLR: W&CP volume 48.

15. Johnson, R. and Zhang, T. Accelerating stochastic gradient descent using predictive variance reduction. In NIPS, 2013.

16. Maria Florina Balcan," Statistical Active Learning Algorithms", Volume 12, 2015.

17. V. Feldman, "A complete characterization of statistical query learning with applications to evolvability". Journal of Computer System Sciences, 78(5):1444–1459, 2012.

18. Joonatan Mänttäri, Jonas Larsson, "Applications of Artificial Neural Networks in Games; An Overview", 2014.

19. Huang, K.Y., Chang, W.L., "A neural network method for prediction of 2006 World Cup Football Game". The 2010 International Joint Conference on Neural Networks (IJCNN), 18-23 July 2010.

20. Agostinelli, Forest, Hoffman, Matthew, Sadowski, Peter, and Baldi, Pierre, "Learning activation functions to improve deep neural networks", In ICLR workshop, 2015.

21. T. Mitchell. *Machine Learning*. Boston: McGraw-Hill, 1997.

22. Rohit Arora, Suman, " Comparative Analysis of Classification Algorithms on Different Datasets using WEKA" International Journal of Computer Applications (0975 – 8887) Volume 54– No.13, September 2012.

23. Poonam Mahana, Gurbhej Singh, " Comparative Analysis of Machine Learning Algorithms for Audio Signals Classification", IJCSNS International Journal of Computer Science and

Network Security, VOL.15 No.6, June 2015.

24. Rosalind W. Picard, MIT Media Laboratory, "Toward Machines with Emotional Intelligence",2015.
25. https://www.genosinternational.com/emotional-intelligence.
26. David Bruce Fogel, " Evolving artificial intelligence",University of California at San Diego La Jolla, CA, USA ©1992.
27. Dr.Pranav Patil,"Artificial Intelligence education:Emotional Computation",International journal of research in computer application and robotics,Vol.4,February 2016.
28. Huma shah and Kevin Warwick(2016)"Imitating gender as a measure of Artificial Intelligence:Is it necessary?",in proceedings of the 8th International Conference on Agents and Artificial Intelligence(ICAART2016).
29. Dr.Pranav Patil,"Emotional Artificial Intelligence and its life research to facing troubles ",International journal of research in computer application and robotics,Vol.4,April 2016.

A ROAD MAP TO BIG DATA AND MACHINE LEARNING

S. Subha[1], S. Baghavathipriya[2]

[1]Rajalakshmi Institute of Technology, 600124 Kuthambakkam, Chennai, TamilNadu

[2] Rajalakshmi Engineering College, 602105 Thandalam, Chennai, TamilNadu

{subha.s@ritchennai.edu.in, baghavathipriya.s@rajalakshmi.edu.in}

Abstract

Big Data is a buzzword amongst businessmen and computer professionals nowadays. Large amount of data is blowing up at an extra ordinary rate due to enormous developments in the fields of social media, web technologies, health care and mobile devices. A small piece of information may be unimportant or irrelevant to people but millions and millions of data points can enlighten them to do a task. Machine learning(ML) plays a vital role in the field of data analytics. ML is mainly based on statistics. In modern machine learning problems, thousands of dimensions of data are taken and predictions are based on some hundreds of coefficients. In the domain of E-learning, hundreds of dimensions can be taken and predictions can be made based on the browsing history of the users. The problem can be narrowed down using deep learning and the challenges in e-learning field can be minimized. E-learning provides a quality educational experience. This paper aims at providing a brief overview on Machine learning along with Big data and its challenging factors in the field of e-learning platform.

Keywords: Machine learning, Big Data, E-learning, deep learning.

1. Introduction

The big data arena has erupted over the last year with unbelievable technological advancements. **Big data** is "high-volume, -velocity and -variety information assets that demand cost-effective, innovative forms of information processing for enhanced insight and decision making". This definition is given by Gartner. It makes use of large amounts of data to enable knowledge discovery and better decision making. According to a survey, more than 90% of world's data today has been created in the last two years alone. Every day 2.5 Quintillion bytes of data are created. Data stored grows 4xFaster than world economy. As data grows big every second, there comes an important strategy to provide solutions for the predictive analytics. It is none other than the deep learning[2]. Solutions are given with increased processing power and some enhancements in graphic processors. Among 22% of the useful data, only less than 5% of data was actually analyzed in

2013. By 2020, more than 30% of data could be made useful for data analytics[11].

2. Existing System

"Machine learning" is a buzz word in the field of data analytics in recent years. It educates the systems to automatically learn and progress from experience without being explicitly programmed. It is an application of artificial intelligence (AI).

Nowadays, web-based learning becomes an alternate to face to face education and E-learning becomes an effective tool in the learning process which is followed in many colleges and universities world wide[7]. For example, University of Maryland, Baltimore County(UMBC) use a learning analytics tool which is integrated into their institutions' LMS[12]. It helps them to track progress of the student. Handling data in a vast amount becomes a challenging issue in e-learning platforms. Also research steps are taken to process the data before uploading in an e-learning platform. Since late 1990s, many worldwide organizations are developing standards and specifications for e-learning technologies. Better learning can be obtained by better and efficient content [18]. It is used to enhance knowledge and performance.

2.1 E-learning platforms

E-learning is another popular field in which big data plays a very vital role. Creation of individual e-learning materials gives an efficient interaction between the learners and the content in e-Learning systems[17].

Various themes of e-learning platforms based on recent trends and innovations are represented in Figure 1. Out of these themes, Big data gives the analysis of the frequently visited e-learning modules of the users. The irrelevant learning modules can be separated from the users' modules list.

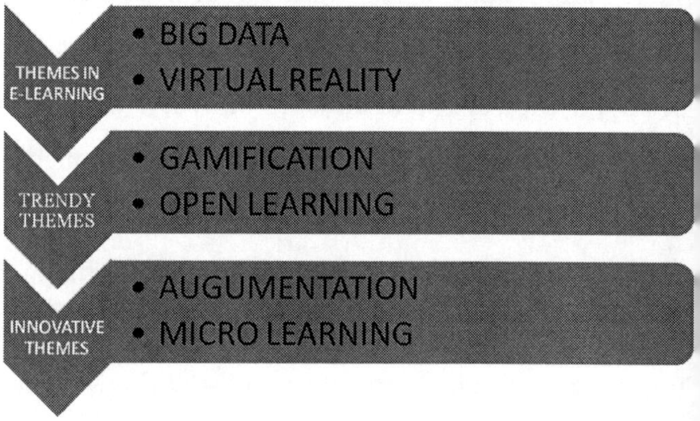

Fig.1 Themes of e-learning

2.2 Survey on Big Data

Machine learning aims at developing computer programs that can access data and can be used by themselves. There are many research challenges in implementing machine learning techniques in big data. One of the important challenges is the sheer size of the data[9]. Human- and machine-generated data has an overall 10x faster growth than traditional business data. E-learning growth rates in various countries are depicted in Fig.2. Data can be easily documented. Also there are many challenging fields in handling big data such as financial services, health care, transport, biology, online advertising etc. But better predictions and smarter decisions can be taken using big data[24]. Measuring and managing the data can be done more precisely than the earlier era. Various stages of data mining such as data cleaning, data integration and data processing must be done effectively in an e-learning platform to make it popular among the learning community.

Inaccurate or incomplete data can be determined using data cleaning. Merging of new information with the existing information can be achieved by data integration, an important stage of data mining. Meaningful information is produced from the data collection using data processing.

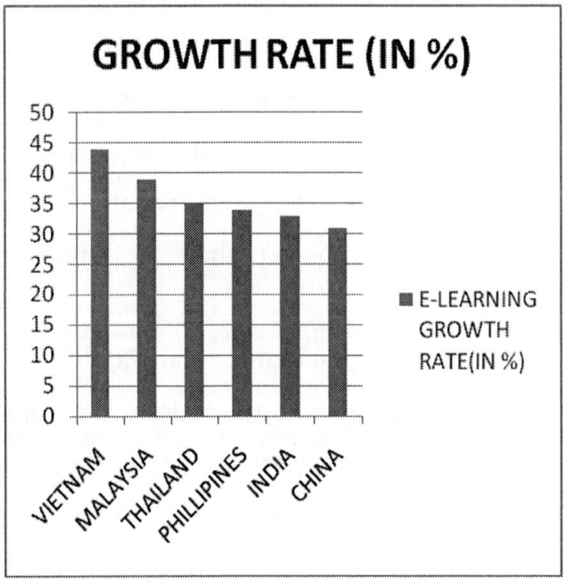

Fig.2 Comparison of E-learning growth rates.

2.3 About Machine Learning

According to the survey of the Mckinsey Global Institute, Machine learning is considered as one of the main drivers of Big Data revolution[1]. The two main categories of learning tasks are the Supervised and Unsupervised learning. It is depicted in Fig.3

In supervised learning, users infer a function from labeled training data. New examples can be mapped using the inferred function. The output datasets are given which are used to train the machine and get the desired outputs. Classification and Regression are examples of supervised learning. Classification assigns items in a large collection to target classes whereas regression predicts a number. In unsupervised learning, users must try to find hidden structure in unlabeled data. Here data is clustered into different classes and the datasets are not given. Clustering is an example of unsupervised learning. In clustering, the intra cluster similarity is high whereas the inter cluster similarity is low.

Another sub-domain of machine learning is **Reinforcement learning** which is purely based on the external environment. Feedbacks are collected from the external environment through many interactions. It learns from those feedbacks[4].

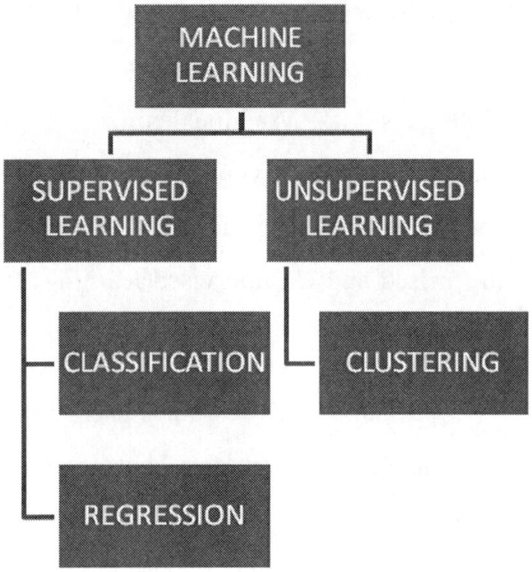

Fig.3 Categories of Machine learning

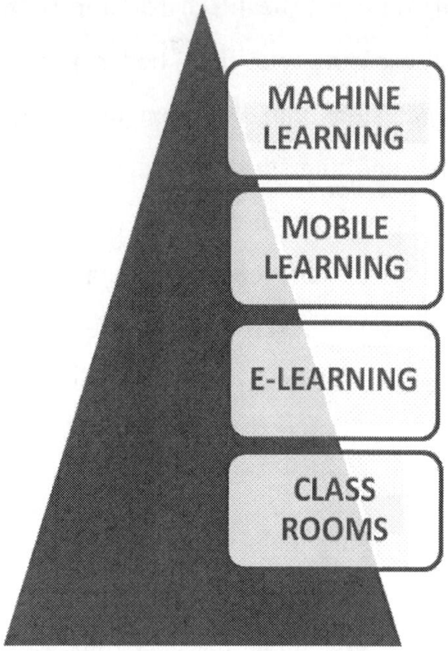

Fig. 4 Levels of teaching methodologies

2.4 Branches of Machine Learning

Deep learning and Online learning are the branches of machine learning. They are the key efforts to overcome the challenges of Machine learning with Big data. As they are widely used in the field of education, there is a drastic growth in the usage of teaching methodologies. It is depicted in Fig.4.

As the data grows bigger day by day, **deep learning** plays a key role in providing big data predictive analytics solutions. Deep learning denotes a collection of machine learning techniques that learn multiple levels of representations in deep architectures. Also it portrait the human behavior analysis.

Online machine learning is a method of machine learning in which data becomes available in a sequential order. It is used to update our best predictor for future data at each step. It is just a contradiction to batch learning techniques which generate the best predictor by learning on the entire training data set.

Extreme Learning Machines(ELM) is considered as an important emerging machine learning techniques[15].Though ELM is a regression model, it can be easily adapted for classification. Also web analytics is one of the Business Intelligence(BI) technologies which gives a vivid idea of how people to a company or industry's website interact with the pages[23]. A unifying learning framework can be constructed by considering the adaptive application of deep learning methods.

3. Discussions

Big data analytics often involve integrating diverse data from several sources. Data may vary in terms of data type, format, data model and semantics. The two major categories of data heterogeneity are the syntactic and semantic heterogeneity. Both these types attracted renewed attention with the emergence of big data.

Syntactic heterogeneity deals with the diversity in data types, file formats, data model and data encoding whereas Semantic heterogeneity deals with the differences in meanings and interpretations[1]. If there is a need for data analytics with integrated data sets, these syntactic variations must be reconciled.

The crux in Big Data learning is that it is unable to solve both imbalanced and large-volume data learning problems[14]. As data comes from various sources, these data can have different formats. Also the data to be processed may be of different types. For example, the categorical data may be combined with numerical data or the data with images may be added with categorical data. Before data processing, data pre-processing and data cleaning are done to configure data to fit within a given model. Works of Wei Ding et al.[10] features the challenging issues in the data-driven model. Lot more revolution happens in the big data domain. As e-learning becomes the most renowned technology in the field of education, inclusion of data analytics is treated as an important subject. Many methods are evolving to process the data before uploading in an e-learning environment.

4. Conclusion

Many challenges arise for Machine Learning algorithms as various data types are represented one at a time. They are not designed in such a way to handle various types of data representation. Our future work will create an efficient unified generalization for handling any kind of data. Also consideration of data handling in e-learning platform will be done in an efficient way. A learning technique called transfer learning has emerged as a new technique for improved learning result of tasks performed.

5. Future Scope

As big data aims at forecasting the trends in online education nowadays, there is a great demand for data scientists in the field of education. The future work of this paper aims at addressing the issues related to data processing in e-learning environment. Big data emerges as a biggest tool for online educators, by providing a vivid picture on the future of e-learning. User-generated data can be processed to give better understanding of the domain.

References

1. Alexandra L'Heureux, Katarina Grolinger and Miriam A. M. Capretz, "Machine Learning With Big Data:Challenges and Approaches", IEEE Access, June 2017.

2. Xue-Wen Chen and Xiaotong Lin, "Big Data Deep Learning: Challenges and Perspectives", IEEE Access, May 2014.

3. Donald C. Wunsch et al., "Efficient and Rapid Machine Learning Algorithms for Big Data and Dynamic Varying Systems", IEEE Transactions on Systems, Man and Cybernetics: Systems.

4. Zeeshan Ahmad Lodhia and Akhtar Rasool, and Aurav Hajela, " A survey on machine learning and outlier detection techniques ", IJCSNS International Journal of Computer Science and Network Security, vol.17 No.5, May 2017.

5. Jiquan Ngiam,Aditya Khosla,Mingyu Kim,Juhan Nam,Honglak Lee,Andrew Y. Ng, "Multimodal Deep Learning", Proceedings of the 28th International Conference on Machine Learning, ICML 2011,pg.no.689-696.

6. Tom M. Mitchell, "The Discipline of Machine Learning", July 2006 CMU-ML-06-108.

7. M. Samir Abou El-Seoud, Islam A.T.F. Taj-Eddin, Naglaa Seddiek, Mahmoud M. El-Khouly, Ann Nosseir, "E-Learning and Students' Motivation: A Research Study on the Effect of E-Learning on Higher Education".

8. Mazen Ismaeel Ghareb ,Saman Ali Mohammed, " The Role Of E-Learning In Producing Independent Students With Critical Thinking" , International Journal Of Engineering And Computer Science ISSN:2319-7242 Volume – 4 Issue - 12 December, 2015 Page No. 15287-15297.

9. H.V. Jagadish et al., " Big Data and Its Technical Challenges", Communications of the ACM, vol 57,no.7, pp 86-94,2014.

10. Wei Ding et al., "Data Mining with Big Data", IEEE Transactions on knowledge and Data Engineering,vol 26, Issue 1, P.no.97-107,January 2014.

11. Venkat N. Gudivada, Ricardo Baeza-Yates, Vijay V. Raghavan, "Big Data: Promises and Problems", IEEE Computer Society,vol 48, Issue no.3,March 2015.

12. Beth Dietz-Uhler & Janet E. Hurn, "Using Learning Analytics to Predict (and Improve) Student Success: A Faculty Perspective", Journal of Interactive Online learning, Volume 12, Number 1, Spring 2013 ISSN: 1541-4914.

13. Mingxing Duan et al., "A Parallel Multiclassification Algorithm for Big Data Using an Extreme Learning Machine", IEEE Transactions on neural networks and learning systems.

14. Yudong Yao et al., "Distributed and Weighted Extreme Learning Machine for Imbalanced Big Data Learning", Tsinghua Science and Technology, ISSN

1007-0214 04/09 pp160–173 Volume 22, Number 2, April 2017.

15. Anton Akusok et al., "High-Performance Extreme Learning Machines: A Complete Toolbox for Big Data Applications", Digital Object Identifier 10.1109/Access.2015.2450498, June 2015.

16. Dominic Breuker, "Towards Model-Driven Engineering for Big Data Analytics – An Exploratory Analysis of Domain-Specific Languages for Machine Learning", 47th Hawaii International Conference on System Science,2014.

17. Tavangarian et al., "Is e-Learning the Solution for Individual Learning?", Electronic Journal of e-Learning, v2 n2 p273-280 2004.

18. Norm Friesen, "Three Objections to learning objects and e-learning standards", April 2003.

19. John Bourne, Dale Harris,Frank Mayadas, "Online Engineering Education: Learning Anywhere, Anytime", JEE The research journal for engineering education, January 2005.

20. N. Jones, "Computer science: The learning machines", Nature, vol.505,no.7482, pp. 146-148,2014.

21. L.P. Chen and C.Y. Zhang, "Data-intensive applications, challenges, techniques and technologies: A survey on big data", Inf. Sci., vol.275, pp. 314-347, August 2014.

22. L.Yang et al., "Transfer learning over big data", in Proc. 10th Int. Conf. Digit. Inf. Manage.(ICDIM), Oct.2015, pp.63-68.

23. S. Chaudhuri, U. Dayal, and V. Narasayya, "An overview of business intelligence technology," Communications of the ACM, vol. 54, no. 8, pp. 88–98, 2011.

24. A. McAfee and E. Brynjolfsson, "Big Data: The Management Revolution," Harvard Business Review, October, 2012.

25. Y. Zhai, Y.-S. Ong, and I.W. Tsang, "`The emerging 'big dimensionality'",IEEE Comput. Intell. Mag., vol. 9, no. 3, pp. 14_26, Aug. 2014.

Smart-EVM using Multi-model Biometrics with embedded security

Pavithra R [1], Sharath kumar N [1],Siddhartha P [1], Anitha G[1]

[1]Rajalakshmi Engineering College, 602105 Thandalam, Chennai, TamilNadu

{pavithra.r.2015.it,sharathkumar.n.2015.it,siddhartha.p.2015.it, anitha.g}@rajalakshmi.edu.in

Abstract:The present EVM faces voter authentication issues. TheSmart-EVM's are proposed to overcome this problem. The Smart-EVM uses Multimodal Biometric Validation to identify the voter distinctively along with storing of votes in thedatabase. The validation is done by scanning Aadhar card along with Biometric(fingerprint). For the cases in which the biometric validation is not possible a Smart Card is provided to that particular voter through which the voter is identified distinctively. Once the voter has casted the vote a message will be sent for the acknowledgment and a reminder message for the voters who didn't cast their votes. This will eliminate the Multiple Frauds in voting.

Keywords - Electronic Voting Machine (EVM),Smart-EVM, e-voting, Multimodal Biometric, Authentication, Security.

1. INTRODUCTION

Voting is the procedure of electing the right person by the people to form the constituency. In many countries it is made compulsory for the people to vote. Several frauds occur in India due to lack of proper authentication and manual validation of people records.

Today's technology has improved for better casting of votes. But tampering of e-voting machines and multiple voting problems are increasing day-by-day, In Peter Wolf et.al. In order to prevent these problems multi-modal biometrics for authentication of voters along with encrypting database containing votes casted by voters are implemented in Smart EVM. India's Aadhar database contains the largest biometric values in the world. The first step of verification is by using the Aadhar card of the voter andthe second step is multimodal biometrics verification. The biometric valuestaken from the voter at the time of voting are compared with the values of Aadhar of the particular voter. Thus the Smart-EVM provides more secured voting.

2. RELATED WORKS

In today's World Electronic Voting Machine is used in different countries and they adopt different technologies for authenticating people uniquely.

2.1. Via Internet

The California E-voting suggest a strategy towards completing the objective to provide the voters with the possibility to vote their ballot at anytime from anywhere via Internet, In Prashanth P et.al. A analysis of e-voting technology has been provided in "e-voting security study". The paper identifies various threats and possible attacks in such voting systems.

2.2. Integrated keyboard and screen

In Brazil all the votes are currently registered by e-voting machines. The Brazilian Supreme Court adopts the usage of Electronic voting methodology in 1996. In the year 2000, Brazil government had totally transformed to electronic voting and established over 400,000 machines in election, Referred Article. The voting machine has integrated screen and keyboard. In order to vote for a parties (or) candidate, voter has to press on the keyboard number designed for particular candidate. The selected candidate image is also displayed in the screen. Voter can ensure, modify, confirm or reject and choose the candidate. The voting machine will produce the result once the voting finished in both digital and printed details of number of votes for each parties.

2.3.EVM using Control unit and Ballot unit

In India first election using e-voting was held from April 20 to May 10, 2004.The legal approval in the year 1989 to allow the use of e-voting, but were never used for entire general election before this. Electronic voting machine has two units: control unit and Ballot unit, In Abu-Shanab et.al(2010).one unit is under the control of the polling officer and the other unit is for the use of voters to cast their vote. The Ballot unit requires the citizen to cast their vote by pressing the button corresponding to the candidate's name and symbol, and then the control unit registered the vote,Referred Article. A light next to the button will glow and a beep sound is used for an indication, that the voter has casted their vote successfully. The electronic voting machine is portable and can operate on a battery power source in remote areas.

2.4.Replacement of Ballot paper with Machine:

In Belgium e-voting was approved by law in 1994, and they are widely used in 1999 and 2000 general and municipal elections. In the general elections, 3.1 million Belgian citizens were able to cast vote electronically, Referred Article. Belgium applies similar approach as Ireland, as it does not modify the voting process, but rather replaces ballot paper with a machine at the polling station and uses electronic counting system to count the overall result. Some difficulties faced by Belgium election is that, delays occurred in voting process in some localities causing some polling stations to remain open after closure time. Voters therefore have to wait for a long to cast their vote, but most did wait, due to compulsory voting system and fines for declining.

2.5. Hare-Clark System:

The Australian Capital Territory (ACT) is one of eight states and territories. In Australia representative of the parliamentary assembly are elected using electoral system known as the Hare-Clark system, In Prashanth P et.al. Hare-Clark is an opposite of single transfer vote system used in Ireland. An applicant needs to collect a allotment of votes, to be elected. Each voter has a single vote, and can be transferred from one candidate to another on the basis to the preference shown until all the vacancies are filled. In ACT, the Hare-Clark system is used to elect 17 candidates from 3 multi-member constituencies, Referred Article. One major problem is that, when two candidates were separated by only two or four votes, after recounting they had 100 mistakes.

2.6. EVM validation using Identity:

In Argentina the system is basically based on the machine already used in country Brazil. The e-voting parallel ATMs. During the election each voter has to provide their identity proof at the booth and the officer enters the identity number on the keyboard with a display, In Prashanth P et.al. If it matches, then the `voters are allowed to cast their vote. The screen displays the active parties with a number, In David Friedman et.al. The voter has to choose preference by pressing key with the selected party number. If the voter wants to change the preference, then they can press the red key, Referred Article. Once the preference has been made the voter presses White key and then the Red key to authenticate.

2.7. Touch Screen Voting Machine:

In UK, they tested technological improvement to cast their vote using touch-screen voting machine, Referred Article. Some administrations allow voters to cast their vote using electronic methods like interactive voice response (IVR), pc-based system and handheld mobile devices. Some administrations allow voters to cast their vote in public places such as shopping centers.

2.8. SMS Remote Voting:

Spain has examined with various forms of e-voting. These include diverse technologies in addition to strictly Irish-style e-voting systems such as Internet and SMS remote voting, In Prashanth P et.al. On November, 2003, three e-voting tests were successfully conducted. This includes remote voting via the internet for voters living abroad, and touch-screen voting integrated with electronic counting system, In Mr. Sanjay Kumar et.al.

2.9.Problems in the present:

The countries which have implemented Biometrics face some problems while validating the finger-print value, Referred Article. This problem is due to fingerprint fading that occurs by accidents, ageing and chemotherapy, In RashmiNade et.al (2015),Sonja Hof et.al.To overcome the problems faced by each country shown in Table 1 Smart-EVM is implemented.

TABLE1. Problems faced in each country.

COUNTRY	ELECTION TYPE	PROBLEMS
India	State	Authentication is not dependable and falsification.
Belgium	General and municipal	Voter has to wait for a long time to cast their vote.
Australia	ACT federal	Manual counting
UK	Local government	Mobile e-voting and also the use of Interactive Voice Response(IVR)
Spain	Municipal	Voting via Internet (risk of hacking)
Canada	Municipal	poor management of voting systems (especially lack of security measures)

3. METHODOLOGY

The traditional EVM's do not validate voters identity. It is used only for storing the votes which are casted by the voters, Referred Article. This is the loop hole found in e-voting in India. The solution for this is the Smart-EVM that not only keep count on the votes polled but also does the validation of the voter. The Validation is done by using biometrics. The biometric techniques used are fingerprint recognition, Iris recognition and face recognition. The values of this biometrics are present in the Aadhar database. It is not necessary to have a voter id. Aadhar database contains enough details about the voter so that Aadhar card acts as a Voter ID card. The Voter has to verify the Aadhar number and provide his biometrics (fingerprint, Iris, Face recognition) to continue to vote, In Peter Wolf andMR.C.G.Raghvendhraet.al (2011). The persons who are unable to validate through biometrics can undergo manual validation. This manual validation is done by using Smart card. The voters who are not recognized by the Biometrics can apply for the Smart card. This gives a unique identification for the voter. These specific voters should validate themselves by using the provided Smart card and Aadhar card. From Figure2. The use of Multimodal biometrics rather than using single modal biometrics is that the multimodal biometrics provides a better authentication and the failure rate for the multimodal biometrics is less compared to the single modal biometrics, In Vidyasree.P et.al(2016). The Multimodal biometrics can also meet failure conditions. The cases like fingerprint fading of a person by age and Iris recognition failure due to cataract and astigmatism. These are the only cases which results in the failure of the new EVM have and are thus rectified by using Manual Validation.

The Aadhar database consists of details like Residential Address, Date of birth, Fingerprint, Face recognition values of the voters. The details of the citizens who are valid for voting i.e. the citizens whose age is above 18 is stored in a centralized database. Another database consists of the details of the voters who are going to access the voting booth in particular ward.

A voting booth may contain more than one Voting machine. These voting machines are connected through a LAN and the Database which contains the details of the voters of that particular ward is common to all the Voting Machines. The Voters who has casted their votes are marked in the ward database.

The Smart-EVM consists of a separate database to store the votes polled. The database in every EVM has a unique encryption which protects the data tampering and a password is used to access the information during the counting of votes. This architecture is depicted in Figure 1.The confirmation message will be sent to the Voter. Also a reminder message will be sent to the voters who have not casted their votes yet.

Figure 1 – System Architecture

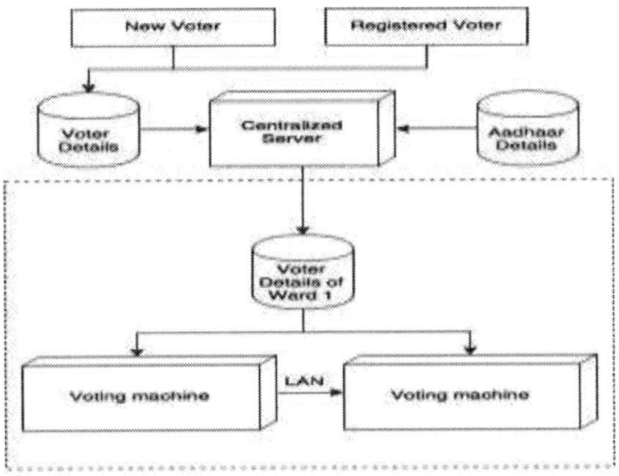

Figure 2- System Flow

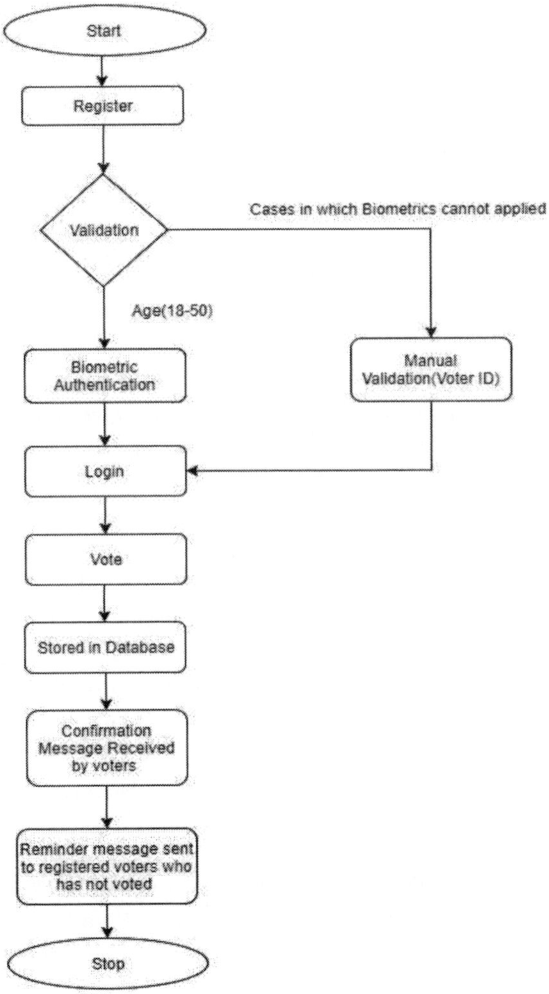

4.IMPLEMENTATION

The samples obtained from the smart e-voting machine are obtained and saved as per the UIDAI-Biometric-Specifications shown in Table 2. Then the samples will be compared to the Biometric values which are obtained from the Aadhar card database.

Table 2 – UIDAI Specifications

Parameters	Specification
Extractor Quality	At least 12 minutiae points generated during extraction
Resolution	500 DPI
Image type	8bits, 256 levels
Extractor Template	ISO 19794-2

The voter gets authenticated by Biometrics feature matching. This approach has three procedures fingerprint alignment, minutiae matching and similarity level computation.

4.1.Fingerprint alignment:

Fingerprint alignment is done by obtaining two minutiae from fingerprint A and two minutiae from fingerprint B under certain strategy. Then coordinate transform on fingerprint B are performed according to four minutiae.

4.2.Minutiae matching:

Let A and B be the template and input fingerprint trying to be matched. A and B may not have the same feature point. Let p and q be the number of points for A and B, In XI-FENG TONG et.al(2012), Philippe Parra et.al.

$$\mathbf{T = \{p_1, p_2, ... p_p\}, \text{ with } p_i = \{x_i , y_i , \theta_i\} \; i = 1...p}$$

$$\mathbf{I = \{p'_1 , p'_2 , ...p'_q\}, \text{ with } p'_j = \{x'_j , y'_j , \theta'_j \} \; j = 1..q}$$

Two minutiae points p_i and p'_j are considered to match , if their position and orientation are nearby. This can be represented using Spatial Distance (sd) and Direction Difference (dd), In Vidyasree.P et.al (2016).

$$sd(p_i, p'_j) = sqrt((x_i - x'_j)^2 + (y_i - y'_j)^2) < R_0$$

$$dd(p_i, p'_j) = min(|\theta'_j - \theta_i|, 360 - |\theta'_j - \theta_i|) < \theta_0$$

R_0 and θ_0 are tolerance parameter that can be adjustable.

4.3.Similarity Level Computation:

Similarity level of each matched minutiae pair is computed and then by accumulating the similarity level of each matched minutiae pair, similarity level between the two fingerprints is obtained, In XI-FENG TONG et.al(2012), LukaszWIĘCŁAW et.al(2009).

The comparison is done by using minutiae matching method and the results set obtained are

Table 3 – values of FAR,FRR and Accuracy in % from Unimodal traits

Minutiae matching	FAR	FRR	Accuracy Level
Fingerprint	10.16	8.54	91.4
Iris	9.34	11.56	87.65

Table 4 – values of FAR,FRR and Accuracy in % from Multimodal traits

Minutiae matching	FAR	FRR	Accuracy Level
Fingerprint + Iris (Score level)	3.87	5.36	93.87
Fingerprint + Iris (Feature level)	3.32	2.54	96.23

5. CONCLUSION

Smart-EVM overcomes the problem of falsification (or) multiple voting which are the major drawbacks of the previous voting methods like paper-based methods, machine voting, online voting, postal voting, open ballot methodand provides more secured way of voting.

The accuracy of voter identification is increased by using fingerprint, face and iris recognition. No two voters can have same biometric values hence the rate of fraud or mistake is highly reduced. The messaging function included in Smart-EVM will help in increase the vote count. Thus Smart-EVM voting is effective method to verify the voter and also to store the votes casted by the voters. As the previous voting methods like paper-based methods, machine voting, online voting, postal voting, open ballot methods have some problems which can be cracked by frauds

6. FUTURE WORK

The implemented techniques and algorithms can be enhanced in the future. Face recognition technique can also be included with this Biometrics. By including this technique the accuracy rate is further increased and FRR rate is reduced. Audio guided output can also be implemented for the convenience of visually impaired Voters.

7. REFERENCES

1.Vidyasree.P, Dr. S. Viswanadha Raju and, Dr. G.Madhavi "Desisting the Fraud in India's Voting process through Multimodal Biometrics", 2016 IEEE 6th International Conference on Advanced Computing.

2.RashmiNade,MonaliRout, Punam Agawane, Jayshree Shinde,"Online Voting System Using Three Factor Authentication", International Journal of Innovative Research in Computer and Communication Engineering (An ISO 3297: 2007 Certified Organization) Vol. 3, Issue 3, March 2015.

3. XI-FENG TONG, PENG-FEI LI, YU-XIANG HAN," An Algorithm For Fingerprint Basic Minutiae Feature Matching", Proceedings of the 2012 International Conference on Machine Learning and Cybernetics, Xian, 15-17 July, 2012.

4.Abu-Shanab E., Knight M. and Refai H,"E-voting System: A Tool For E-democracy", Management and Research Practice .Vol. 2 Issue 3 (2010) pp.: 264-274".

5."Analysis of Electronic Voting System Implemented in Various Countries".

6. Prashanth P, Bungale and Swaroop Sridhar," Electronic Voting - A Survey", the Johns Hopkins University.

7. David Friedman, Charles Wright, Dan Kalowsky

and John Daniel,"Electronic Voting Literature Review Computer".
8.Mr. Sanjay Kumar and Dr. Ekta Walia (Professor & Head),"Analysis of Electronic Voting System In various Countries".
9.Philippe Parra," Fingerprint minutiae extraction and matching for identification procedure",University of California.
10.Łukasz WIĘCŁAW,"A Minutiae-based Matching Algorithms In Fingerprint Recognition System",JOURNAL OF MEDICAL INFORMATICS & TECHNOLOGIES Vol. 13/2009, ISSN 1642-6037.
11.Peter Wolf, "Introducing Biometric Technology in Election".
12.Sonja Hof,"E-voting and biometric System?", university of Linz, Austria.
13.MR.C.G.Raghvendhra,"Biometric Voting Machine",Autonomous Institute , Affiliated to VTU,May 2011
14.http://bio-metrica.com/biometrics-performance-determination.
15.https://www.edgefx.in/fingerprint-recognition-based-biometric-voting-machine/.

Smart Applications in Smart City and Improved Traffic Management System Using Collaborative Approach among Nano Robots

[1]Mamata Rath, [2]Bibudhendu Pati, [3]Binod Kumar Pattanayak
[1]Dept. of IT, C.V.Raman College of Engineering, Bhubaneswar, India,mamata.rath200@gmail.com
[2]Department of Computer Science and Engineering, C. V. Raman College of Engineering, Bhubaneswar, India, patibibudhendu @gmail.com
[3]Department of Computer Science and Engineering, Siksha 'O' Anusandhan University, Bhubaneswar,India, binodpattanayak@soauniversity.ac.in

Abstract-

To implement automatic communication in vehicular ad-hoc network (VANET) for various applications, it is highly essential to deal with various challenges of wireless network scenario. Efficient Traffic management with right light indicators and congestion control are issues to be handled successfully in wireless network using advanced technology. To avoid such problems many smart cities are currently implementing network based traffic control systems that works on the principle of traffic automation with solution of the above mentioned issues. The basic challenge lies in usage of real time data communication and analytics performed with on-line traffic information and correctly applying it to some the traffic flow. In this context, a brief study on various smart applications in wireless network and VANET has been done in this article and an improved network traffic management system has been proposed that performs intelligent data communication using very flexible robotic technology with swarm intelligence of soft computing.

Keywords: Wireless Network, Vehicular Ad-hoc Network , Smart City, Traffic Management, Video Monitoring, Signal System, Robotics

1.INTRODUCTION

Basic characteristics of designing an improved traffic control system includes connecting traffic signals and traffic control centres with GIS enabled digital road map of the town using intelligent computational power of data analytics as a key module. In this context, the basic challenge lies in usage of real time analytics on on-line traffic information and correctly applying it to some basic traffic flow. Data analytics tools takes data from the Traffic Management System and using GIS mapping under real time support they provide useful information to the drivers in the vehicles and help reducing the traffic congestion. Additionally, basic tourist information such as visiting places, parking area and distance are also projected in real time basis on large digital screens installed at city centres entrance points to guide the drivers towards their destination. This helps to save fuel and finally to save a lot of time spent in searching various visiting places. The smart living style in metro cities is also fulfilled as the environment becomes pollution free and more hygienic.

In the current technology, Vehicular Ad-hoc Networks (VANETs) are becoming more popular applications in road traffic management and control systems. The problem faced by smart cities in terms of traffic congestion issues are better soluble by the use of VANETs as there is a network connectivity between the vehicle and the network infrastructure. Therefore, predictable information regarding road condition ahead and route information can be directed to the smart vehicles in transit and intelligent decisions can be taken sufficient time before any problem occurs. In other ways VANET in smart cities helps to reduce the problems of congestion, accidents, crime, parking problems and population overhead. Due to the overall development of the wireless technology, their applications are immense on vehicles and vehicles have been converted to smart vehicles to be accessed under smart traffic applications. The traditional driving systems and drivers have also converted to smart drivers with more technical knowledge of receiving smart signals from traffic controllers, understanding them and act accordingly. VANETs support flexible communication between vehicles and traffic controlling systems in both infrastructure based and andin wireless medium without fixed infrastructure. The proposed traffic congestion solution in smart city uses an improved technical explanation to the problem with powerful data analytics made by mobile agent dynamically under VANET scenario in a smart city.

Swarm intelligence provides an intelligent approach to optimization problems in distributed manner. Its logic is embedded in nano robots to collaboratively perform distributed tasks intelligently. The umbrella term swarm intelligence refers to the effort taken to design algorithm inspired by cooperative behavior of social insect colonies and other animals. Swarm intelligence helps us to find solution of distributed optimization problems in such a way that centralized control of global model is not required. In Vehicular Ad-hoc Networks challenge lies in application areas such as determining an alternate suitable route availability during congestion in the network. There are some appropriate algorithms which show that biologically inspired concepts provide a significant performance over traditional approaches. In the context of smart traffic control in the proposed approach, large number of nano robots are coordinated in decentralized and distributed manner at the junction points where an intelligent logic has to be applied regarding any critical decision in traffic points. Such controlling points include estimation of total number of vehicles, checking congestion status, arrival of new vehicles, decision to be taken for re-routing the vehicle in other direction or to continue in the same route, what should be the best strategy to decide how many stop points should be there in congested traffic, to control information regarding other traffic points etc. The idea used here is that multiple number of simple nano robots which act as micro-controllers at various points can do complex decision making logic in a collaborative and distributed way in a group. In swarm intelligence, the collaborative behaviour of social insects, such as the honey-bee's dance, the wasp's building of nest, the construction of termite mound or the ants making a path with a colony are measured as strange aspect of biology. Many scientific researches have proved that individuals need not require any specific skill or knowledge to exhibit such complex behaviours. The individual members in social insects colony are not informed before time regarding their local status or global objective. There is also no controller that guides them about their responsibility. The swarm intelligence is evenly distributed throughout all the agents who are basically members to achieve their respective goals, but the individual agents can not accomplish their mission without cooperation from rest of the agents.Social insects exchange information and communicate the location of a food source or the existence of any danger to their mates. This type of communication between the individuals is based upon the concept of locality, where there is no idea about the global situation. The implicit changes that takes place in the surroundings for communication is the key factor to be considered during design of intelligence based algorithm in any soft computing based strategy. Insects modify their activities because of the earlier changes made by their mates in the location. Another example of swarm intelligence is the construction of termites where the worker insects modify their behaviour as a result of which the nest is formed. Similarly business organisations also are formed by collaboration, interaction and communication between individual workers. There interactions are communicated throughout the colony and therefore the colony can find solution of the problems, where as the individuals cannot solve the problems. These collective behaviors are termed as self-organising behaviours. These theories can be used to demonstrate how social insects demonstrate complex collaborative behaviour that comes out from communications from individuals behaviour.

2. LITERATURE SURVEY

Mobile Cloud Computing supports technical development in smart cities. An Improving Healthcare application using mobile cloud computing and big data analytics has been proposed [1] where a cloudlet-based mobile cloud-computing infrastructure has been developed. Comparative study and analysis has been done with a benchmark evaluation of Hama's graph package and Apache Giraph using PageRank algorithm[2]. Comparative studies and empirical evaluations have been performed in big data applications in this article. For dynamic usage of electricity in smart city , a novel approach for clustering of electricity consumption behavior has been applied [3] and Markov model is applied to model the dynamic electricity consumption and a clustering technique has been developed by fast search and find of density peaks (CFSFDP) which is primarily carried out to obtain the typical dynamics of consumption behavior.A scheduling algorithm, which is called multi clouds partial critical paths with pretreatment (MCPCPP), for big data workflows in multi clouds is presented [4]. This algorithm incorporates the concept of partial critical paths, and aims to minimize the execution cost of workflow while satisfying the defined deadline constraint.A hierarchical distributed Fog Computing architecture to support the integration of massive number of infrastructure components and services in future smart cities has been carried out [5] and a smart pipeline monitoring system based on fibre optic sensors and sequential learning algorithms to detect events threatening pipeline safety has been developed.An Ant Colony Optimization (ACO) based joint VM migration model for a heterogeneous, MCC based Smart Healthcare system in Smart City environment [6] has been proposed where the user's mobility and provisioned VM resources in the cloud address solves the VM migration problem.Smart transportation system is very much in smart city context. Therefore, to analyze how big data analytics can be used to build a smart transportation system has been proposed in [7] and it imposes that Smartphones should be linked to smart traffic signals to achieve the objective of smart transportation system.It is essential to provide better service by deploying traffic indicators to update the traffic details instantly [8]. A mobile application is developed as user interface to explore the density of traffic at various places and provides an alternative way for managing the traffic.Currently big data analytic techniques are extensively used in smart city applications [15] and application based architectures are proposed [16] for internet of cities.A brief literature survey has been carried out using spatio-temporal parallel database approach for smart transport system in [17].CityPulse as a data analytic framework has been elaborated for smart cities in [18]. Due to air pollution in smart cities the average health condition of people are greatly affected. The linkage of data analytics in health sector in urban area has been illustrated in [19] in smart city context.A multi-tenant cloud based approach for self sustained smart buildings in smart cities has been proposed in [20]. Mobile Robot Sensor Networks supports mission critical applications where there is communication between sensor nodes play vital role during the real time applications[21]. In [22] soft computing based Particle Swarm Optimization (PSO) strategy is used to evaluate the social behaviors of the insects and to apply them during the design of multi robot system. The observed collective behavior of insects are then applied for the development of controlling system in smart vehicles of traffic system. It explains the analogy of sensory motor system that allows navigation and natural fly in insects which supports collaborative control of robots. This research article also investigates fundamental concept of collaboration among biologically inspired robots that emulates insect foraging and look for behavior.

3. STUDY AND ANALYSIS

A detailed study and analysis about mechanism used to handle the smart city challenges and their solutions has been carried out in this section which are incorporated by eminent researchers in the direction of implementing smart systems and smarter devices for better performance of the smart city. The analysis describes how the core area of emerging challenging problems is addressed such as emerging transportation complexity and its related information. Secondly, how technologies and applications have been integrated with existing systems in the context of city to deal with transportation and traffic challenges. There are some innovative methods on how advanced data and intelligent transportation systems (ITS) technologies and applications can be used to reduce congestion, to keep travelers safe, protect the environment, respond to climate change, connect underserved communities, and support economic vitality. Table 1. Shows the basic contributions in this area with type of application considered in the respective literatures.

Table .1. Smart Applications in smart city with implementation details

Sl no	Literature	Year	Details of Designed Application
1	L. A. Tawalbeh, *et al.* [1]	2016	Improving Healthcare application using mobile cloud computing and big data analytics.
2	K. Siddique, *et al.* [2]	2016	a benchmark evaluation of Hama's graph package and Apache Giraph using PageRank algorithm
3	Y. Wang, *et al.* [3]	2016	a novel approach for clustering of electricity consumption behavior dynamics.
4	B. Lin, *et al.* [4]	2016	a scheduling algorithm, which is called multiclouds partial critical paths with pretreatment (MCPCPP), for big data workflows in multiclouds is presented
5	B. Tang, *et al.* [5]	2017	a hierarchical distributed Fog Computing architecture to support the integration of massive number of infrastructure components and services in future smart cities
6	M. M. Islam, *et al.* [6]	2017	Ant Colony Optimization (ACO) based joint VM migration model for a heterogeneous, MCC based Smart Healthcare system in Smart City environment.
7	S. Shukla, *et al.* [7]	2016	how big data analytics can be used to build a smart transportation system
8	P. Rizwan, *et al.* [8]	2016	to provide better service by deploying traffic indicators to update the traffic details instantly
9	D. Singh, *et al.* [9]	2016	visual big data analytics which involves processing and analyzing large scale visual data such as images or videos to find semantic patterns that are useful for interpretation.
10	R. A. Alshawish, *et al.* [10]	2016	Reviews on the potentials where Big Data technology can drive a city to be smart.
11	N. Ianuale, *et al.* [11]	**2016**	The integration of lot of generated data from the heterogeneity and diversity of smart city data sources.
12	Y. Sun, *et al.* [12]	**2016**	Building Smart and connected communities SCC for a community to live in the present, plan for the future, and remember the past.
13	W. Yuan *et al.* [13]	**2015**	To develop a smart work performance measurement system.
14	Z. Lv *et al.* [14]	**2016**	A 3-D global browser is employed to load multiple types of demand data from the city, such as 3-D building model data, residents' information, and real-time and historical traffic data.

Fig1. Shows the advanced technologies that are used in smart city for automation of various applications. Connected vehicles is One of the finest feature of smart traffic management which is the connected vehicle

concept and it has high advantages like preventing motor vehicle crash rate which leads to prevention of death rate in the society.Out of various safety features the basic feature should be to avoid the crash before it takes place.

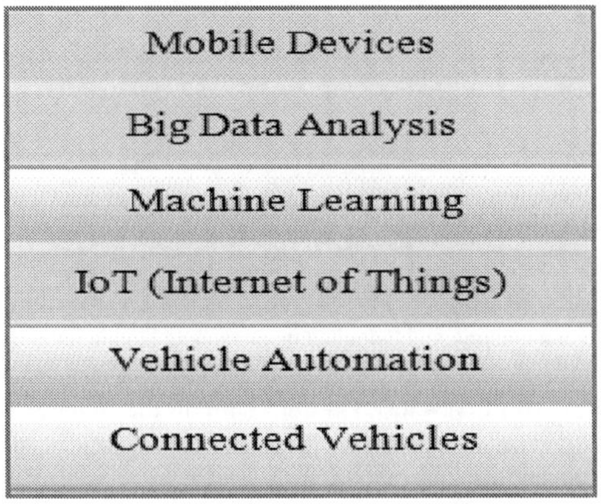

Fig.1 Advanced Technologies used in smart city scenario

Advantage in V2V (Vehicle to vehicle) communication. which supports nearby vehicles to exchanged data on their position is that they use these data to warn drivers of potential collisions. Vehicle-to-Vehicle (V2V) Communications allows nearby vehicles to exchange data on their position and use these data to warn drivers of potential collisions. This v2v technology are capable of warning drivers of potential collisions that are not visible to sensors, such as a stopped vehicle blocked from view, or a moving vehicle at a blind intersection. Unprecedented and transformative technology are extendable to other vehicle types, road users, and infrastructure .On-board Sensors are used in v2v technology perform a lot of intelligent tasks which have been implemented in many cases such as warning systems in star rating program, announcement by automakers to make automatic braking standard equipment announcements to include automatic braking in star program. Self-Driving

4. THE PROPOSED APPROACH

An Intelligent Traffic Management Framework has been proposed here as depicted in fig.2. The proposed framework deals with traffic controlling system as the core module and it has the sub-modules such as video control system, Traffic Control System,, Supervisory computer control system and smart peripheral devices.The Traffic Control System manages and controls the heavy traffic during pre-defined rush period on the road. It uses the video monitoring system to identify excess traffic through video camera and when the amount of vehicles in particular path increases a pre-calculated threshold value, it informs the traffic control in-charge with an alarm indicating "traffic limit reached" and prevents any further vehicle to enter in that path. This is done by stopping that path with automated gates and with proper information written. So the next vehicles would be diverted towards another selected path, hence controlling the traffic. The signal system incorporates efficient transmission and uninterrupted communication by sending and receiving correct signal in proper time events. The smart devices module handles the correct configuration of sensors to capture and detect the events and send required information to control points. Similarly deployment of CCTV Camera at noticeable traffic points which covers maximum range of scenario is also important activity of this module.

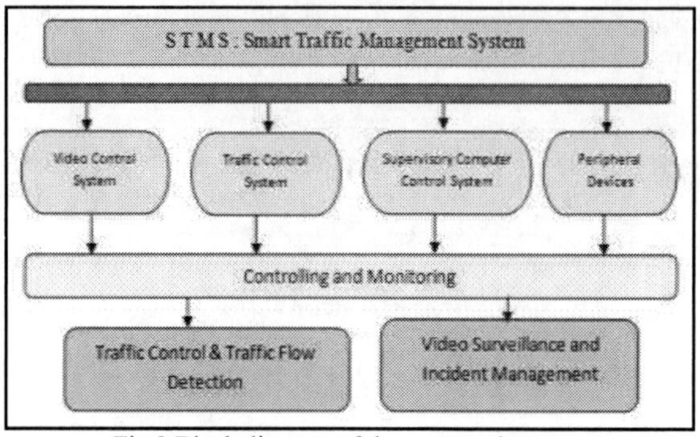

Fig.2.Block diagram of the proposed system

Fig.2 shows the basic block diagram of the proposed system with all the functional components and controlling system. The proposed traffic management system includes the controlling of signal communication between different traffic towers of the city, sending and receiving the appropriate control frames, transmission of traffic status and congestion related information to supervisory computer system. Nano robots are deployed at various control points in the said approach for better communication and collaboration among different modules using swarm intelligence logic embedded within them. A distributed approach remains functional among various nano robots which perform communication, collaboration, association and message passing among each other to achieve the centralized objective of smart traffic control. Traffic control and Traffic flow Detection and Video Surveillance and Incident Management are the two basic controlling modules in the designed system that communicates all the functional components to ensure proper automated traffic control in smart city scenario.

4.1 Functional Mechanism of STMS

The Main Controlling System of proposed STMS works in centralized and de-centralized mode. In centralized mode it is controlled by the hardware and software controlling units and in decentralized mode it is controlled by a regional controller of the area specific roadways network system. In local networks also it can be operated by a traffic light controlling system. Basic function of different components of the system are discussed in the current section. The video control system generates system information database and distributes the corresponding sub set information to required control technology based equipments. The traffic light controller as shown in fig. 5 controls and monitors the traffic lights based on the signals generated from the signal control system using associated control algorithms embedded in smart devices.

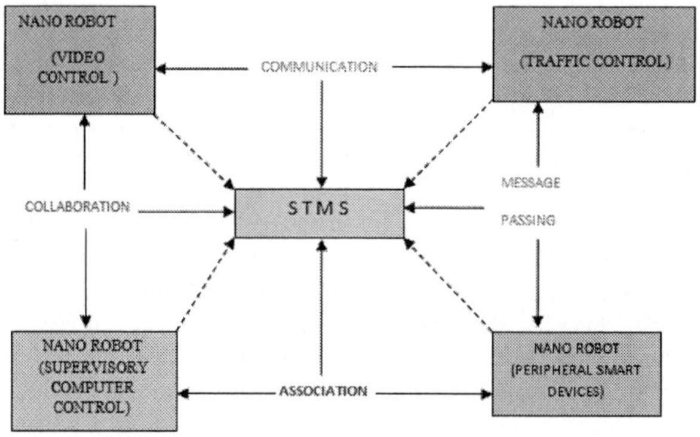

Fig.3 Collaborative approach of Nano robots in the proposed system

As shown in fig.3 a circulated approach is applied among various modules of the STMS. Nano robots deployed at specific functional devices perform communication, collaboration, association and message passing among each other to achieve the centralized management of smart traffic control. Supervisory computer control system controls the overall controllable parameters of the system, different modes of operation during traffic signal transmission and installation, regularly monitors technical conditions of the equipments, checks the continuous activated operation of the traffic flow during congested traffic. The peripheral devices such as video and voice capturing devices, LAN switch, video servers, database servers, plasma monitors attached to the STMS continuously generate statistical information using which the supervisory computer control system generates system performance report and regular traffic situation report. Traffic control and Traffic flow Detection and Video Surveillance and Incident Management are the two basic controlling modules in the designed system that communicates all the functional components to ensure proper automated traffic control in smart city scenario.

4.2 Safety and Security in STMS

The proposed system preserves safety of the vehicles as well as the lives of the passengers as other connected vehicles always remain in contact with each other. Therefore, the vehicle can run safely with higher mobility with road congestion information and weather up-to-date information. In the proposed system, the vehicles are connected with other vehicles through network and they have smart board equipped with them which operate based on sensor information. Data from connected vehicles makes travel easier and also help to handle the bus and other vehicles less polluting and makes it easier for drivers to foresee hazardous weather environment . The sensors fixed at the smart boards have multiple features such as generating warning alarm at any dangerous events. Sensors also keep track of each and every moment of the drive specifically it is important when any single traveler travels . The sensor stores the body postures of the human body in its memory and can detect any abnormal event such as accident, heart-attach, any external attack or even can sense any unusual activity in the vehicle and can alert other connected vehicles during accident for help. The traffic control and traffic flow detection system also includes traffic rule violation detection, e-challan generation, traffic analytics and simulation modelling os unforeseen situations. Any exceptional incidence taking place on the road such as theft, robbery, murder can be easily detected by the video surveillance and incident management module resulting prevention of such activities.

4.3 Pre-requisites for proposed system

This section provides an average assessment of basic pre requisites before implementing the proposed model in a metropolitan city. Fundamental requirement for the proposed traffic control framework includes one urban traffic control centre, centralization of 200 intersection points in the city, approximately 4,700 vehicle loop detectors, 60 video detection cameras, fifty signalisation devices for blind persons , replacement of approx. 1,400 signal points, Continuous service maintenance applications .Co-ordination among all the major systems in a smart city such as all critical city systems like transportation, energy, public services, public safety, health care, telecommunications are capable of communicating with each other to allow coordination and improve efficiency. They are capable of generating, transmitting and processing data about a wide variety of related activities within the city. The proposed applications focus on how emerging transportation data, technologies, and applications can be integrated with existing systems across a city, helping both cities, citizens, and businesses achieve goals for safety, mobility, sustainability, and economic vitality in an increasingly complex, interdependent and multimodal world.

5. SIMULATION SET UP

The proposed traffic model has been simulated using ns2 simulation tool. The nodes in a VANET can sense moving information around them which helps in monitoring the traffic, controlling the speed of the vehicles and many other traffic congestion parameters. In a VANET, the vehicles which act as mobile stations move within the VANET network range. Mobile stations are configured with various communication parameters. Two types of communication are possible using the VANET nodes, vehicle to vehicle communication and vehicle to infrastructure(V2I). In this simulation work, we have used the V2I approach in which vehicles interact and response with the road side sensor units through network routing devices at the road side. To simulate a realistic VANET scenario, ns2 has been integrated with SUMO and MOVE tool .

Table 1. Network parameters used in Simulation

Parameter	**Value**
Channel Type	Wireless Channel
Propagation	Radio-propagation model
Network Interface	Wireless Phy
MAC Type	MAC/802_11
Interface Queue Type	Drop Tail
Antenna Model	Antenna/OmniAntenna
Max Packet Size in ifq	100
Simulation Tool	Ns2

Table 1. depicts the network parameters used during simulation in Ns2 . There are two basic elements in MOVE such as the map editor and the vehicle movement screen. To crate the road topology, the map editor is used and to create the vehicle movements, the vehicle movement editor is used. This editor also helps the users to specify vehicle route information such as total number of vehicles to be included in the simulation scenario in a particular route, the vehicle departure time, origin and destination of vehicle, transit period of the vehicle, speed etc which are configured during simulation. We have specified the vehicle configuration here as explained in section 3.3.The RSU (Road Side Unit) nodes and general vehicle nodes are configured with various network parameters. IEEE 802.11p protocol designed for VANET is also in-built in ns2. The output of the MOVE goes to a trace file containing simulation results which can be visualized in NAM and further be analysed using awk, tcl or any other scripting language in order to get various analytical output. This section shows the comparative analysis of the proposed model with traditional traffic system.

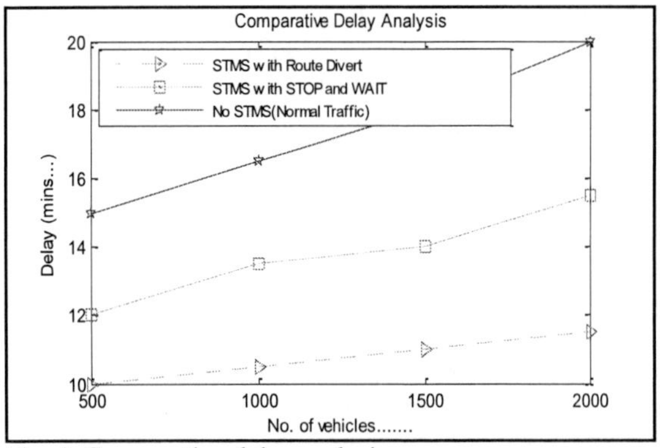

Fig. 4 Comparative delay analysis

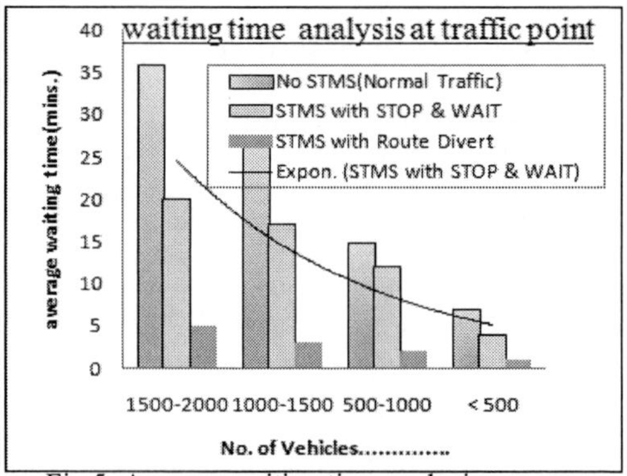

Fig.5 Average waiting time analysis

The simulation has been carried out under three traffic scenario with variable number of vehicles and the results are obtained by extracting output values from trace file created after simulation. The data has been cultutured as required using the awk scripts. Traffic Scenario 1 is No STMS which refers to the normal traffic position with no automated software used. Scenario 2 refers to STMS with Route Divert. As depicted in section 3.5 this scenario includes the result when the vehicle driver has selected to divert to alternate route at signal point SP1.1. Scenario 3 refers to STMS with STOP and WAIT which shows the result of simulation when the vehicle driver selected to stop for some time and wait till the congestion is released. Fig. 4 shows the comparative delay analysis of our proposed traffic model with three scenario. In STMS with route divert option the delay is minimum as there is no time spent for wait and the minor delay occurred is due to the time for deciding the option to be selected at signal point SP1.1 and re-route the vehicle direction in alternate way.Fig.5 shows the analysis of waiting time in the said three scenario. The x-axis indicates the range of vehicles and y-axis indicates the average waiting time by vehicles. It can be seen that as the traffic congestion increases, the average waiting time also increases.

6.CONCLUSION

In network wireless systems, it is very challenging to design successful traffic control strategy due to unpredictability of wireless medium. In the age of current technology, metro cities are facing various critical issues due to increasing volume of population, increasing traffic problems and almost all service oriented application areas.A modern traffic control system using connected vehicle technology has been proposed in this research article with an integrated approach of solving general traffic related issues in a high volume traffic gateway. For the overall benefit of the transport system, various modules like video monitoring, smart traffic control system, signal system and smart devices are included in the presented approach with detailed structure of their smart functionality. It has a high rate of success after implementation due to the usage and intelligent interpretation of programming logic into smart devices.

References

[1] L. A. Tawalbeh, R. Mehmood, E. Benkhlifa and H. Song, "Mobile Cloud Computing Model and Big Data Analysis for Healthcare Applications," in *IEEE Access*, vol. 4, no. , pp. 6171-6180, 2016.

[2] K. Siddique, Z. Akhtar, E. J. Yoon, Y. S. Jeong, D. Dasgupta and Y. Kim, "Apache Hama: An Emerging Bulk Synchronous Parallel Computing Framework for Big Data Applications," in *IEEE Access*, vol. 4, no. , pp. 8879-8887, 2016.

[3] Y. Wang, Q. Chen, C. Kang and Q. Xia, "Clustering of Electricity Consumption Behavior Dynamics Toward Big Data Applications," in *IEEE Transactions on Smart Grid*, vol. 7, no. 5, pp. 2437-2447, Sept. 2016.

[4] B. Lin, W. Guo, N. Xiong, G. Chen, A. V. Vasilakos and H. Zhang, "A Pretreatment Workflow Scheduling Approach for Big Data Applications in Multicloud Environments," in *IEEE Transactions on Network and Service Management*, vol. 13, no. 3, pp. 581-594, Sept. 2016.

[5] B. Tang; Z. Chen; G. Hefferman; S. Pei; W. Tao; H. He; Q. Yang, "Incorporating Intelligence in Fog Computing for Big Data Analysis in Smart Cities," in *IEEE Transactions on Industrial Informatics* , vol.PP, no.99, pp.1-1.

[6] M. M. Islam; M. A. Razzaque; M. M. Hassan; W. Nagy; B. Song, "Mobile Cloud-Based Big Healthcare Data Processing in Smart Cities," in *IEEE Access* , vol.PP, no.99, pp.1-1.

[7] S. Shukla, Balachandran K and Sumitha V S, "A framework for smart transportation using Big Data," *2016 International Conference on ICT in Business Industry & Government (ICTBIG)*, Indore, 2016, pp. 1-3.

[8] P. Rizwan, K. Suresh and M. R. Babu, "Real-time smart traffic management system for smart cities by using Internet of Things and big data," *2016 International Conference on Emerging Technological Trends (ICETT)*, Kollam, 2016, pp. 1-7.

[9] D. Singh, C. Vishnu and C. K. Mohan, "Visual Big Data Analytics for Traffic Monitoring in Smart City," *2016 15th IEEE International Conference on Machine Learning and Applications (ICMLA)*, Anaheim, CA, 2016, pp. 886-891.

[10] R. A. Alshawish, S. A. M. Alfagih and M. S. Musbah, "Big data applications in smart cities," *2016 International Conference on Engineering & MIS (ICEMIS)*, Agadir, 2016, pp. 1-7.

[11] N. Ianuale, D. Schiavon and E. Capobianco, "Smart Cities, Big Data, and Communities: Reasoning From the Viewpoint of Attractors," in *IEEE Access*, vol. 4, no. , pp. 41-47, 2016.

[12] Y. Sun, H. Song, A. J. Jara and R. Bie, "Internet of Things and Big Data Analytics for Smart and Connected Communities," in *IEEE Access*, vol. 4, no. , pp. 766-773, 2016.

[13] W. Yuan *et al.*, "A Smart Work Performance Measurement System for Police Officers," in *IEEE Access*, vol. 3, no. , pp. 1755-1764, 2015.

[14] Z. Lv *et al.*, "Managing Big City Information Based on WebVRGIS," in *IEEE Access*, vol. 4, no. , pp. 407-415, 2016.

[15] M. V. Moreno *et al.*, "Applicability of Big Data Techniques to Smart Cities Deployments," in *IEEE Transactions on Industrial Informatics*, vol. 13, no. 2, pp. 800-809, April 2017.

[16] J. M. Schleicher, M. Vögler, S. Dustdar and C. Inzinger, "Application Architecture for the Internet of Cities: Blueprints for Future Smart City Applications," in *IEEE Internet Computing*, vol. 20, no. 6, pp. 68-75, Nov.-Dec. 2016.

[17] Z. Ding, B. Yang, Y. Chi and L. Guo, "Enabling Smart Transportation Systems: A Parallel Spatio-Temporal Database Approach," in *IEEE Transactions on Computers*, vol. 65, no. 5, pp. 1377-1391, May 1 2016.

[18] D. Puiu *et al.*, "CityPulse: Large Scale Data Analytics Framework for Smart Cities," in *IEEE Access*, vol. 4, no. , pp. 1086-1108, 2016.

[19] E. Fotopoulou *et al.*, "Linked Data Analytics in Interdisciplinary Studies: The Health Impact of Air Pollution in Urban Areas," in *IEEE Access*, vol. 4, no. , pp. 149-164, 2016.

[20] N. Kumar, A. V. Vasilakos and J. J. P. C. Rodrigues, "A Multi-Tenant Cloud-Based DC Nano Grid for Self-Sustained Smart Buildings in Smart Cities," in *IEEE Communications Magazine*, vol. 55, no. 3, pp. 14-21, March 2017.

[21]Z. Mi, Y. Yang and J. Y. Yang, "Restoring Connectivity of Mobile Robotic Sensor Networks While Avoiding Obstacles," in *IEEE Sensors Journal*, vol. 15, no. 8, pp. 4640-4650, Aug. 2015.

[22] S. C. Nair, E. M. Coronado, M. T. Frye and Y. Qin, "Swarm intelligence for the control of a group of robots,"*10th System of Systems Engineering Conference (IEEE SoSE)*, San Antonio, TX, 2015, pp. 205-207,2015.

A Robust Fall Detection System Using Deep Learning Algorithms

Durga Devi K[1], Anitha G[1], Baghavathi Priya S[1]

[1]Rajalakshmi Engineering College, 602105, Thandalam, Chennai, Tamil Nadu

[1]{durgadevi.k.2015.it, anitha.g, baghavathipriya.s}@rajalakshmi.edu.in

Abstract: Due to the increase in aging society, there is a need for computer vision based system to monitor the elder people's day to day activities. Aging may limit their activities and cause falls. Recent fall detection systems are lack in accuracy. The goal of this research work is to construct a vision based monitoring system for elderly people which will detect falls using deep learning algorithms. Fall detection systems are extensively used for monitoring the elderly who live alone. Non – invasive assistive technology is the finest way for monitoring. In this research work a single camera is used to capture the daily activities of elderly. To classify the abnormal and normal activities the Deep Learning algorithms Deep belief network and Restricted Boltzmann classifiers are used. The proposed system produces better accuracy 86% and fewer false alarms.

Key words: Deep Learning, DBN, fall detection, Computer vision.

1. Introduction

An article in times of India said that there is a tremendous growth in aging population in the last few years in all over the world. They don't want to spend more money on hospital environments and caretakers. They want to live independently and at the same time safely. The older adults are facing lots of challenges in daily life. The challenges may be due to chronic diseases, increase in health care costs, and the shortage of caregivers, dependencies, or larger impact on society. Due to chronic diseases, elderly may experience some emergency situations like tremor, chest pain, faint, forward fall, and backward fall. During that time they cannot get up or call the assistance by themselves. Unnoticed such events cause severe problems including death. So the development of assistive technology to monitoring the human activities, in both normal and abnormal situations, is important for the intension of event detection and also to improve their quality of life. Special interest is paid in the detection of the rigorousness of the case that can signify the injury level and assistance request type. So it is so important to monitor elderly people when they live alone at home. Hend Alkittawi(2017) stated that deep neural networks will increase the fall detection accuracy and decrease the false alarms in his thesis.

2. Related Work

Many sensing technologies have been used in home monitoring application. Various researchers like nambu et al, and Ogava et al.(2000) have analysed the use of sensors, motion detectors to obtain information about the use of ADL in the home. Various projects have been developed using sensors for home monitoring. For example, Gloucester Smart Home project developed by Adlam et al.(2001) in Bath Institute of Medical Engineering used sensing devices to monitor water level and water temperature in the bath and issues a automated remainder to the elder to turn off the taps. Switches also used to help people in doing ADL activities. For example, switches and motion sensors were used by Mihailidis et al. to monitor whether the taps were on or off during hand washing activity performed by dementia people. Schiele et al.(2001) stated that switches and Motion detectors provide a location of the user but it is not sufficient to get the context of the user. For example, if a person is in kitchen, a sensor cannot provide information like who is in the kitchen, where he is, whether he is sitting or standing or lying. These types of additional information are also very important in the detection of fall and other accidents. A number of sensors are required to detect additional information like this which often result in an obtrusive environment. So a new set of hardware and tools are needed.

Some sensors are wearable sensors that provide better results than the previous type of embedded sensors. Telephone-based personal emergency response system (PERS) uses these types of sensors and hardware. The PERS contains button and it can be worn as a necklace or a wristband and it is connected to a residential phone line. Some researchers like Miskelly et al.(2000) have investigated remote health monitoring devices that measure and track pulse, temperature, pulse rate and blood pressure. But they require the elderly to wear the devices at all the time and the elderly people supposed to take the necessary measurements manually and feed the data to the system, which then automatically sends to an evaluation and critical station. These systems are not appropriate for more serious emergency situations (e.g. stoke). The major problem with wearable sensors is that the older people may fail to remember to wear the device or lost it and also they may feel inconvenience to wear the devices whole day. The application of Radio Frequency Identification Devices has increased (RFID) now a day. Wilson et al.(2003) stated that RFID is also used to identify the person and track their actions. Sloman and Murray found that RFID tags also are used in identifying the person, storing the past medical data, and routine drug delivery. It also has the same limitations as other wearable devices like the person must wear it throughout the day and often required more number of sensors to be placed all through the user environment. Recently many researchers are developing solutions based on computer vision for elderly home care.

The video camera has potential advantages over sensors. In technical a single camera can replace many numbers of sensors to monitor the activities performed in a room by older people. The last few years have shown a large interest in video-based solutions. The major reason for this interest is the cost of the cameras. Good quality videos are now available at very low cost. With a rising elderly population in India, increasing burden of never-ending diseases and rising demand for post-surgery care, healthcare providers have started using technology to provide home-based care. It includes the visiting doctors, care givers, monitoring services. These services provide a hospital like environment. Some of the high-end providers have even started providing ventilators and such critical hospital equipment. The services even include storage of medical records and

prescriptions. They offer only hospital-like environment at homes. The abnormal activities cannot be detected. Engineering students of Amrita Vishwa Vidyapeetham University, in Kerala, India, developed a Home monitoring system for elderly called HOPE, the system monitors persons heart rate, movement and body temperature by fixing sensors on the human body. When the reading falls out of range then the data is send to a caregiver through a smart phone application. In the existing systems, a number of sensors have been involved. People have to wear such sensors in their body throughout a day. They may feel the discomfort of wearing many sensors in their body. Old age people may forget to wear sensors due to dementia. Anitha et al.(2015) recommended a non-invasive system has to be developed to monitor the daily activities of elderly. A number of innovative research projects in the area of intelligent environment, particularly within the framework of healthcare for grown up adults, are recently developing video surveillance based monitoring agents.

3. Human Action Recognition using Deep Learning

The most extensively used algorithms are Deep learning algorithms. They have been used to various complex problems in different context. Deep Learning models have multiple layers to represent different levels of abstraction. These models have increased the accuracy of results in various domains such as speech recognition, visual object identification, drug discovery and genomics. Image classification, object detection, and scene recognition are the applications of convolutional neural networks.. Recurrent neural networks are suitable for sequential data such as text and speech for machine translation and also applied to image classification. Due to these features deep learning algorithms have greater impact on action recognition applications. Now a day's action recognition using deep learning is used in videos also. Large video sets can be processed with deep learning techniques and also produces promising results with greater accuracy. Deep learning systems learn the best features and recognize actions in videos. Convolution nets are used in videos. Artificial neural networks, (ANNs), and Feed forward neural networks are power full techniques to solve complex problems using Deep Learning. Fig.1 shows the general structure of a Deep Belief Network.

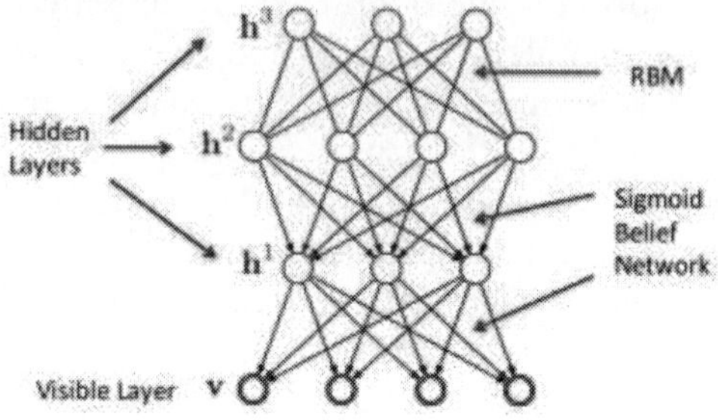

Fig.1. General Structure of Deep Belief Network.

4. System Components

The fall detection system contains the following components. Video sensor, background subtraction, feature extraction, classification, and decision. Fig.2. shows the system components.

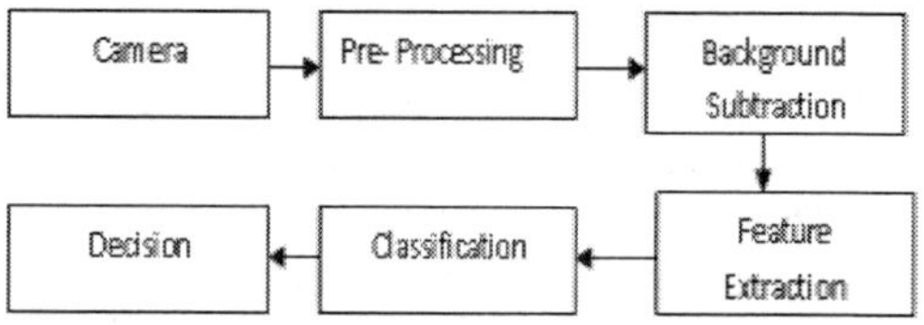

Fig.2. System Components

4.1. Background Subtraction

After completing all the pre processing steps, the object or human silhouette is extracted from each frame. In this paper code book method is used to perform the background subtraction process. let ζ = c1,c2,...c L represent the codebook for the pixel consisting of L code words, for each codeword ci and a six-tuple vector.

4.2. Classification

In this research work, deep belief networks (DBNs) and restricted Boltzmann machines(RBMs) are used to analyse the features and classify the inputs into one of the four classes. Hierarchical learning methods of the deep learning algorithms help to learning the natural progression from low level to high level structure as seen in natural complexity, therefore it helps to monitor what is being learnt and to direct the machine to better subspaces. For example, when an image is given as input, the first layer represents the edges of the features, the second layer represents the object parts of the features and the third layer represents the objects in the features. The restricted Boltzmann machine (RBM) is a generative stochastic neural network that can learn a probability distribution over its set of inputs, which has a hidden layer and a visible layer, the structure of which is shown in Fig. 3

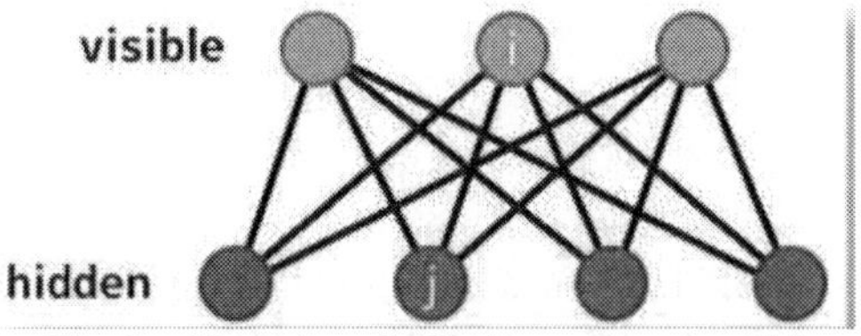

Fig.3. Restricted Boltzmann machine

RBM is trained to maximize the product of probabilities assigned to some training set V, the algorithm used mostly to train the RBMs is to optimize the weight vector W. The DBN is both generative and discriminative model. It has two training phases. In the generative phase it assign weights and in the discriminative phase it fine tune the classification task.

Initially, unsupervised method is followed in the network to train the weight layer as RBM. The RBM is constructed between an input layer and a hidden layer. Then, we stack another hidden layer on top of the RBM to form a new RBM. It continues to stack layers on top of the network until all hidden layers have been initialized. After this learning step, the DBNs can be further trained in a supervised way to perform classification.

5. Evaluation Results

Here, we discuss the efficiency of our fall detection system. Totally 15 elder people were involved to create the dataset. They performed different postures and activities and 2094 postures which includes 726 stands, 726 sits, 726 bends and 726 lies. They are used to train the classification system and 294 postures which include 73 stands, 73 sits, 73 bends and 75 lies are used to test the system.

5.1. Background Subtraction Results

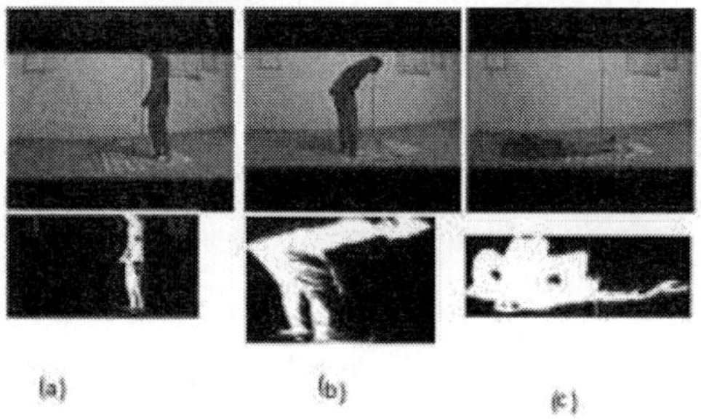

Fig.4. Background subtraction
a) standing b) bending c) lying activities.

In Fig.4 the first row depicts the original frames of the video clippings and second row depicts the background subtraction results of various activities.

5.2. Classification Results

The RBM gives 86% of results which is shown in Table 1. DBN produces good accuracy for different number of hidden layers.

Hidden Layers Number	100	200	500	1000
Classification rate	75.7%	80.8%	85%	82%
False Detection rate	5.0%	7.5%	3.7%	5.5%

Table 1: Classification Result from DBN for Different number of hidden layers.

6. Conclusion

A robust video surveillance based fall detection system using deep learning methods is used in this work. This system produces good results compared to traditional machine learning algorithms. The false alarm rate is also reduced. More number of training samples would be needed for better accuracy. In future work more training samples could be used to improve the accuracy.

References

1. M. Nambu, K. Nakajima, A. Kawarada, and T. Tamura, "A System

to monitor elderly people remotely, using the power line network," Presented at the world congress on Medical Physics and Biomedical Engineering, Chicago, IL, 2000.

2. M.Ogava, S. Ochiai, K. Shoji, M. Nishihara, and T. Togawa, "An attempt of monitoring daily activities at home," presented at the World Congress on Medical Physics and Biomedical Engineering, Chicago, IL, 2000.
3. D. Adlam, C. Gibbs, and R. Orpwood, "The Gloucester smart house bath monitor for people with dementia," in *Physica Medica, Eur. Congress of medical physics and Clinical Engineering*, vol. 17,2001, p. 189.
4. A. Mihailidis and G. Fernie, W. L. Cleghorn, "The development of a computerized cueing device to help people with dementia to be more independent, *Technol. & Disability*, vol. 13, pp. 23-40, 2000
5. B. Schiele and S. Antifakos, "Beyond position awareness," presented at the 3rd Int. Conf. Ubiquitous Computing, Atlanta, GA, 2001.
6. *The study of Emergency Response System for the Elderly*, Maclaren-plan search, Canada Mortgage and Housing Corporation, Ottawa, 1988.
7. F. G. Miskelly, "Assistive technology in elderly care," Age and Aging, vol. 3, no. 6, pp. 455-458, 2001.
8. H. Asada, P. Shaltis, A. Raisner, S.Rhee, and R. Hutchinson, " Mobile monitoring with wearable photoplethysmographic biosensors," IEEE Eng. Med. Biol. Mag., vol. 22, pp. 28-40, Mar. 2003.
9. K. Doughty, R. Lewis, and A. McIntosh, "The design of a practical and reliable fall detector for a community and institutional applications," presented at the Telemed '99 Conf., London, U.K., 1999.
10. D. Wilson and C. Atkeson, *The Narrator: A Daily Activity Summarizer Using Simple Sensors in an Instrumental Environment.* Pittsburgh, PA: Carnegie Mellon Univ., 2003.
11. M. Sloman, "Ubiquitous Computing for Healthcare in the Community," Ubicare, 2003.
12. C. J. Murray, "Implantable chips make first run at Personal ID," Embedded.com, 2003.
13. http://timesofindia.indiatimes.com/india/Indias-elderly-now-at-home-with-healthcare/articleshow/47423515.cms
14. Megalingam, Rajeshkannan, "Automated voice based home navigation system for the elderly and the physically challenged", IEEE 13th International Conference on Advanced Communication Technology(ICACT), 2011.
15. G Anitha. S. Chandrakala, " Vision-Based Healthcare Monitoring for Elderly", International Journal of Applied Engineering Research(IJAER) Special Issue, Volume 10, No.9,2015.
16. Pengming Feng, Miao Yu, Syed Mohsen Naqvi, Jonathon A. Chambers, "Deep Learning in Fall Detection", Proceedings of the 19th International Conference on Digital Signal Processing, Aug, 2014.
17. Hend Alkittawi," A Deep-Learning-Based Fall-Detection System To Support Aging-In-Place", thesis, 2017.

VISITOR COUNTER IN INDIAN RAILWAYS

Vasanthakumar S [1] , Sangamithra N [1] , Vijay K [1] , Sai Yashwanth K[1] , Mehfooza M [1]

[1]Rajalakshmi Engineering College, 602105 Thandalam, Chennai, Tamil Nadu

{vasanthakumar.s.2015.it,sangamithra.n.2015.it,vijay.k.2015.it,saiyashwanth.k.2015.it,mehfooza.m}@rajalakshmi.edu.in

Abstract:Every country wants to ensure a safe, fast and reliable rail services for all its passengers. Many countries are changing its rail infrastructure due to operational inefficiency, safety and security issues. This work is concentrated on predicting the number of passengers in every compartment of a sub-urban train. The main motive of this system is to equalize the number of passengers in each compartment. This helps to avoid accidents due to overcrowd. Travellers leaning out of local trains due to overcrowding and poor ventilation inside the train are at a risk of being hit by electric poles that are all along the tracks leads to a lot of accidents during the crowded hours. These accidents can be avoided by designing a system that counts the number of passengers in each compartment by placing few IR sensors at the entrance of each compartment and transmitting the count to next station. Passenger, looking at the count displayed in their station can board the desired compartment before arrival of train rather than checking all the compartments after arrival of train and at last boarding in running train in a crowded compartment.

Keywords: IR sensor, Arduino, sub-urban train

1. INTRODUCTION

Indian Railways (IR) is operated by government of India. It is the fourth largest railway network in the world after the United States, Russia, and China. IR comprises 119,630 kilometers (74,330 mi) of total track over a route of 66,687 km (41,437 mi) with 7,216 stations at the end of 2015-16. In 2015-16, IR carried 1.101 billion tons of freight annually and 8.107 billion passengers annually or more than 22 million passengers a day.[1] IR operates both long distance and suburban rail systems and ran on average 13,313 passenger trains daily in 2015-16.[2]Still the IR struggles to meet the increasing demand for passenger transportation due high population and inefficient use of rail assets. Most common reasons behind railway deaths were 30% had fallen from running train due to overcrowding and 48% hit by train while crossing railway track .[3]Young people take more risk as compared to others. They will try to board in running train, hanging on doors or bars, travelling on the roof in overcrowded trains. Accidental deaths (98%) outnumbers the suicidal deaths (2%).[3] This might be due to the overcrowding of locals at peak hour, hanging on doors, hit by train while crossing the track in hurry and travelling on the roof. This system focuses on equalizing passengers in each compartment to avoid over-crowding. The cost of system is low.

2. HARDWARE PLATFORM

Arduino Uno

Arduino Uno is a microcontroller board based on Atmega328. It has 14 input/output pins of which, 6 are analog inputs, 6 can be used as PWM outputs, a 16Mhz quartz crystal, a USB jack connection, a power jack, an ICSP header and a reset button. An important aspect of the Arduino is its standard connectors, which let users connect the CPU board to a variety of interchangeable add-on modules termed shields. This board has a 5 volt linear regulator and a 16 MHz crystal oscillator.

Infrared Sensor Module

An Infra-Red(IR) sensor is an electronic device which can measure the heat of an object as well as detects the motion. An IR sensor consists of emitter, detector, and associated circuitry. The emitter is an IR LED(Light Emitting Diode) and detector is an IR photodiode The principle of IR sensor working is when IR light falls on photodiode its resistance and output voltage change in proportion to the magnitude of IR light received.

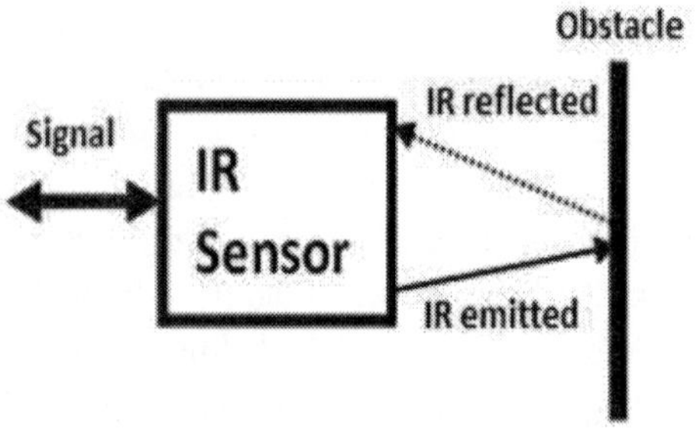

Bluetooth Module

A Bluetooth module is a small wireless system that uses CSR Blue core 04-External single chip Bluetooth system with AFH(Adaptive Frequency Hopping Feature) and CMOS technology. Modules are typically small PCB's that include a Bluetooth processor, as well as all other hardware needed to run the device. This often includes an antenna connector or antenna matching circuit, and (if not integrated into the Bluetooth processor) the Bal-un, PA, and LNA or Any crystals, or crystal oscillators that are needed to run the radio or any power components needed. This can include decoupling capacitors, inductors/chokes, and in some cases DC/DC converters or non-volatile memory. This is needed for Bluetooth processors from some manufacturers, as the processor was designed to include little/no memory at all, or only includes one-time programmable memory.

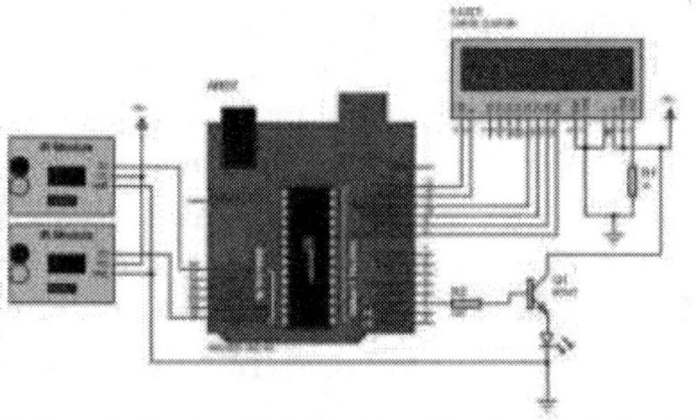

The circuit consists of Arduino Uno and Infra-Red (IR) sensors.

3.WORKING

The IR sensor module uses Infra Red signal to detect the people entering through the door or entrance. This was done by sending a pulse from IR signal and detecting the reflected signal using photodiode. The IR signal will be detected only when a person going through the path. Two IR sensors are used. One to count the number of people entering the train and the other sensor to count the number of person leaving the train. These sensors are placed at the entrance of each compartment. If sensor 1 senses a person, it informs the Arduino that a person has entered the train so that it increments the count. At the same time, it gives a delay of

1sec so that the person can cross the second sensor and the count is maintained correctly.[5] When the person exits the train the sensor 2 decrement the count. It also provides a delay of 1sec to maintain count correctly. If there is at least 1 person on the train the LED will glow otherwise it is off. The count is displayed on the LCD screen. The vacant and occupied seats are displayed as green and red respectively and the total number of passengers is stored in the database. When the train leaves the current station the details from the database is sent to the next station, so the passengers are aware of the available seats. The details can also be displayed to the passengers in mobile phone via Bluetooth or Wi-Fi.

Indicates all seats in the compartment are vacant.

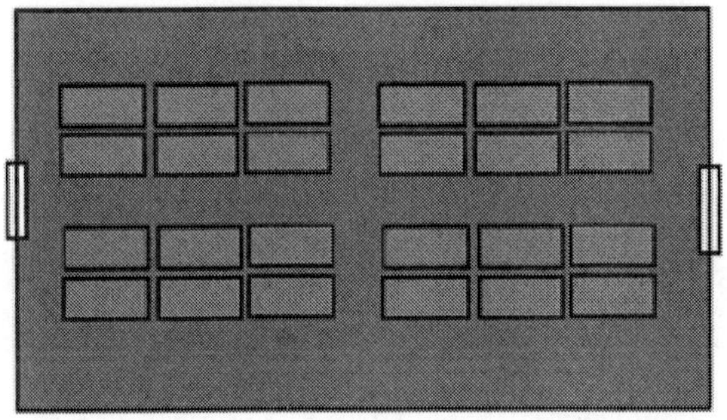

Indicates 5 seats are occupied.

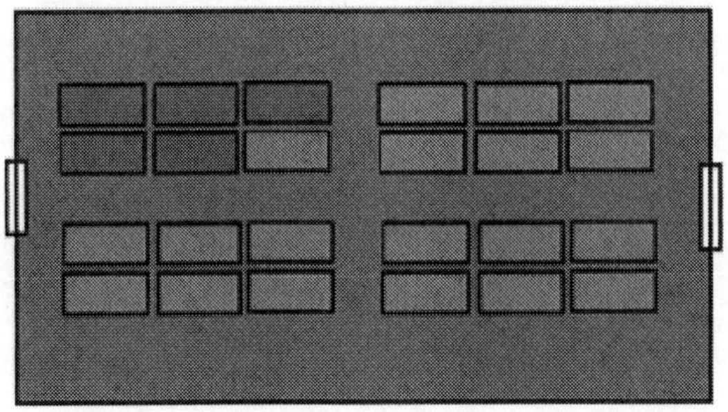

Work flow of the system

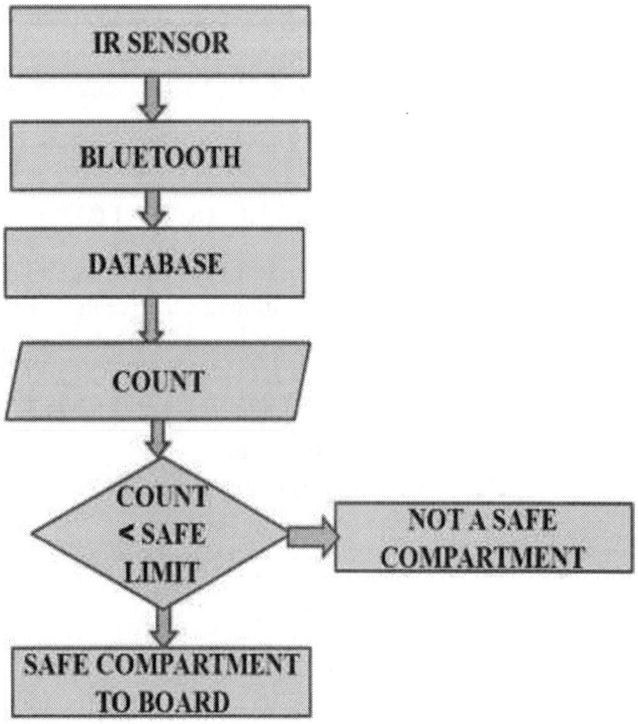

4.ADVANTAGES:

- Low cost and easy to implement.
- Since simple components are used it can be replaced easily.
- To avoid overcrowding and passengers can travel safely and comfortably.
- Can work 24X7 without any problem.
- It helps the passengers to know whether or not seats available before boarding the train.
- With the number of tickets sold and number of passengers in

the train, the railway department can find the number of people travelling without the tickets.

5. LIMITATIONS:

It is used when one person cut the rays of the sensor and hence cannot be used when two or more persons enter the door simultaneously since IR sensor cannot detect if lot of people are entering at the same time.

6. FUTURE IMPLEMENTATIONS:

- Voice alarm system can be added to indicate that seats are filled and persons cannot enter inside.
- Metal detector can be added for security reasons.
- Ultrasonic sensors can be used to replace IR sensor.

7. CONCLUSION:

Nowadays accidents are increasing day by day. Of these major accidents occur due to overcrowding and also due to human faults. This project is designed to avoid overcrowding by knowing the seats available using IR sensor. The system helps the passengers to travel safely and comfortably. This system also helps the government to shift trains based on number of persons travelling on the train in particular season or time.

8. REFERENCES:

[1]Indian Railways – Lifeline of the nation (A White Paper).

[2]Indian Railway vision 020.Government of India, Ministry of Railway, (Railway Board) December 2009.

[3]N. Sambamurthy and Sk. Hasane Ahammad “Prevention of Train Accidents Using Wireless Sensor Networks”.

[4]Parag Chatterjee and Asoke Nath “ Smart Computing Applications in Railway Systems -A case study in Indian Railways Passenger Reservation System” in International journal of Advanced trends in computer science and engineering.

[5]Subhankar Chattoraj and Aditya Chakraborty “Bidirectional Visitor Counter with Automatic Room Light Controller and Arduino as the master controller” in International Journal of Scientific and Research publication.

Performance Evaluation of Nonlinear Filters for Impulse Noise Removal

Kaushal Kishor/ Assistant Professor
Naraina College of Engineering & Technology, Kanpur, Uttar Pradesh, India
kaushalsriv@gmail.com

Prabhishek Singh/ Research Scholar
Department of Information Technology
BBAU, Lucknow, India
prabhisheksingh88@gmail.com

Abstract- In this paper, various impulse noises filters are studied. These are median filter; center weighted median filter, pixel-wise MAD (mean of the absolute deviations from the median) filter and new adaptive median filtering technique. Here a novel, effective and simple impulse noise detector switching median filter is proposed. The proposed method compares the difference value of the current pixel with the brightest and the darkest pixels in its working window and uses the difference value to determine whether the current pixel is corrupted by impulse noise. To avoid the false alarm generated in this first stage, the candidate pixels are passed through a second stage using local statistics. Extensive simulation results show that proposed method substantially outperforms all another existing method, in terms of suppressing impulse noise while preserving image details. Since proposed method is algorithmically simple and requires low computational complexity, it is suitable to be implemented by hardware and applied to many real-time applications.

Keywords
Mean Square Error (MSE); Peak Signal to Noise Ratio (PSNR); Probability Density Function (PDF); Median Filtering (MF); New Adaptive Median Filtering Techniques (NAMFT).

I. INTRODUCTION

In image processing, various linear and nonlinear filtering methods have been proposed. Linear filtering techniques used for noise reduction in images are characterized by mathematical simplicity and can effectively reduce noise with spectral components that do not overlap with those of an image. However, linear filters cannot effectively reduce impulse noise and have a tendency to blur the edges of an image. In such situations, median filters, which are nonlinear filters, provide an effective solution. Median filters have good edge preserving ability, can eliminate impulse noise, and have moderate noise attenuation ability in the flat regions of an image.

The operations of a median filter involve the application of a window to move over an image and to replace the value at the center pixel with the median of all the pixel values within the window. In so doing, a pixel with a distinct intensity (in the case of an impulse) as compared to those of its predefined, neighbors will be eliminated. The implementation of a standard median filter is simple and the filter can process an image in a fast manner. The performance of a median filter is average for filtering impulse noise in highly corrupted images. This difficulty can be overcome with success up to some extent by another nonlinear filtering technique using center weighted median (CWM) filters [2].

Center-weighted median filter, which a weighted median filter is giving more weight only to the central value of each window. This filter can preserve image details while suppressing impulse noise, statistical properties show that CWM filter can outperform the median filter. The traditional median filters process all the pixels of the image, without taking account of whether or not a pixel is corrupted by impulse noise. To avoid this disadvantage, it is important to detect whether the current pixel is corrupted [1, 3]. These approaches involve a preliminary identification of corrupted pixels in an effort to prevent alteration of true pixels; among those is Pixel-wise (MAD) filter [1].

The pixel-wise median of absolute deviation from median (PWMAD) filter does not require optimizing parameters or previous training. Still, it removes impulse noise very efficiently, while preserving image details. Since both of its steps, detection and estimation are based on the same median structure, only a simple median filter is required for practical realization. This filter successfully removes all types of impulse noise with arbitrary probabilities [12, 13].

In this paper, an efficient impulse noise filter has been proposed. In the first stage of detection, both global and local characteristics of the noisy image are used. Use of global characteristics lowers the computational complexity. The second stage is fashioned in a different way for better performance. The proposed method can handle image corruption even up to 90% impulse noise density. As noise is of the limited range within two boundaries, the uncorrupted pixels can be intelligently filtered out and could be used to estimate the corrupted pixels [14, 15].

II. IMPULSE NOISE MODEL

Impulsive noise can be classified as salt-and-pepper noise (SPN) and random-valued impulse noise (RVIN) [5, 6, and 10]. An image containing impulsive noise can be described as follows:

$$x(i,j)=\begin{cases}\eta(i,j) & \text{with probability } p\\ y(i,j) & \text{with probability } 1-p\end{cases} \quad (3.1)$$

Where $x(i,j)$ denotes a noisy image pixel, $y(i,j)$ denotes a noise-free image pixel and $\eta(i,j)$ denotes a noisy impulse at the location (i,j). In salt-and-pepper noise, noisy pixels take either minimal or maximal value i.e. $\eta(i,j)\in\{L_{\min},L_{\max}\}$, and for random-valued impulse noise, noisy pixels take any value within the range minimal to maximal value i.e. $y(i,j)\in[L_{\min},L_{\max}]$. where $L_{\min},L_{\max}$ denote the lowest and the highest pixel luminance values within the dynamic range respectively. So that it is a little bit difficult to remove random-valued impulse noise rather than salt and pepper noise [3]. The main difficulties, which have to face for attenuation of noise, is the preservation of image details. Figure 1 may best describe the difference between SPN and RVIN. In the case of SPN, the pixel substitute in the form of noise may be either $L_{\min}=0$ or $L_{\max}=255$. Whereas in RVIN situation it may range from $L_{\min}$ to $L_{\max}$. Cleaning such noise is far more difficult than cleaning fixed-valued impulse noise since, for the latter, the differences in gray levels between a noisy pixel and its noise-free neighbors are significant most of the times. In this thesis, we focus only on *random-valued impulse noise* (RVIN) and schemes are proposed to suppress RVIN.

III. PERFORMANCE MEASURES

The metrics used for performance comparison of the different type of filters are defined below:

1. Mean Squared Error (MSE)

In statistics, the mean squared error or MSE of an estimator is one of many ways to quantify the amount by which an estimator differs from the true value of the quantity being estimated. Here it is just used to calculate the difference between an original image with a restored image. Given that original image Y of size $(M\times N)$ pixels and as a reconstructed image $\hat{Y}$, the MSE(dB) is defined as:

$$MSE(dB)=\frac{1}{M\times N}\sum_{i=0}^{M-1}\sum_{j=0}^{N-1}\left(Y_{i,j}-\hat{Y}_{i,j}\right)^2 \quad 4.1$$

2. Peak Signal to Noise Ratio (PSNR)

PSNR analysis uses a standard mathematical model to measure an objective difference between two images. It estimates the quality of a reconstructed image with respect to an original image. The basic idea is to compute a single number that reflects the quality of the reconstructed image. Reconstructed images with higher PSNR are judged better.

Given that original image Y of size $(M\times N)$ pixels and as reconstructed image $\hat{Y}$, the PSNR (dB) is defined as

$$PSNR(dB)=10\log_{10}\left(\frac{255^2}{\frac{1}{M\times N}\sum_{j=1}^{N}\left(Y_{i,j}-\hat{Y}_{i,j}\right)^2}\right) \quad (4.2)$$

3. Subjective or Qualitative measure

Along with the above performance measure, subjective assessment is also required to measure the image quality. In subjective assessment measures, characteristics of human perception become paramount, and image quality is correlated with the preference of an observer or the performance of an operator for some specific task. However perceptual quality evaluation is not a deterministic process.

IV. EXISTING MEDIAN FILTERING TECHNIQUES

Salt and pepper (Impulse) noise can successfully remove by Median Filtering Technique (MFT) from the distorted image but in this case, the filtered image suffers the blurring effect. In the case of median filtering techniques, each pixel is taken to calculate the median values and also each pixel is replaced by that calculated median values. Since all those pixels including affected and unaffected are considered to calculate the median and unaffected pixels are also replaced by this calculated median which distorts the image. This undesirable feature prevents the median filtering techniques from providing higher PSNR or better quality image [5, 6, 9].

To overcome this problem, some preventive measures must be ensured so that the affected pixels are not considered while calculating the median, and the unaffected pixels are not replaced at all. In the proposed approach these two features have been considered. These two features ensure that the affected pixels are not considered during the calculation of median and the unaffected pixels are not changed.

V. PROPOSED TECHNIQUE

The impulse noise, particularly, the salt and pepper noise is considered as the extreme case among all types of noises. To recover the images affected by this noise, a new technique is proposed. For Salt and Pepper noise, the pixel value of the noisy image is converted to 0 and 255. When we use Median Filtering Technique we take 3 × 3 or 5×5windows and find out the Median value and replaced center pixel by the median value and then move pixel to pixel and cover all pixel. To avoid the problems that are present in the existing median filtering techniques, we have developed an algorithm, which is a modification of Median filtering.

The detection of impulse noise i.e. salt and pepper noise is done in two stages with the assumptions that a noise pixel takes a gray value which is substantially different from the neighboring pixels in the filtering window. However, the grey levels of the pixel in the noise-free region vary smoothly, separated by edges. The first detection stage creates a noise map to get the position of the corrupted pixel. The second stage confirms the false detection during the first stage. [9].

The proposed algorithm is given below:

VI. PROPOSED ALGORITHM

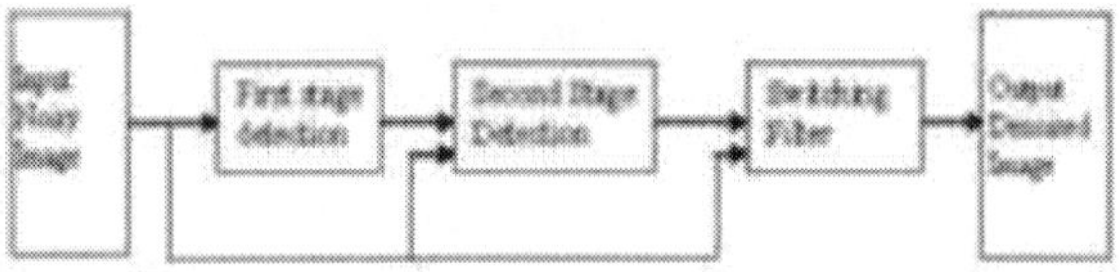

Figure1. Proposed filter

First stage detection (uses global characteristics of the image)

S_{max} – overall max value of noise image
S_{min} – overall min value of the noise image

If 'nimg 'is the noisy image then Temporary noise map (temp) can be calculated as

$$Temp(i, j) = \begin{cases} 1, & \text{if } (S_{max} - nimg(i, j)) < T_1 \,\|\, (nimg(i, j) - S_{max}) < T_2 \\ 0, & \text{otherwise} \end{cases}$$

T1=T2 for fixed noise impulse value i.e. 255 & 0.

T1&T2 may vary if noise distributes over a range of pixels i.e.
Pepper = $[0, m_1]$, Salt = $[255- m_2, 255]$, m_1 & m_2 can be equal.
Thus this first stage noise map covers various variant of noise model

Second stage of detection (uses local characteristics of the image & adaptive window size)

Step 1: For a window of size W
Find out the number of corrupted pixels in window W through temporary noise map. If a number of corrupted pixels are less than half of total pixels then go to step 2 otherwise go to step 3.

Step 2: Find out the S_{max} & S_{min} (local max or min in window) for a particular pixel location
If (S_{max} – nimg (i, j)) < T_1 & (nimg (i, j) - S_{max}) >T_2, replace the corresponding value to 0 (that pixel is corrupted)
else leave that pixel & go to step 1 for next noisy pixel.

Step 3: Increase the window size W= W+2 & go to Step 1.
Modified noise map obtained from the second stage is the final noise map having value 0 & 1.
1 represents the corresponding pixel in noise image is noise or corrupted.

0 represents the corresponding pixel in the noisy image is uncorrupted.

Filtering Stage (switching filter at noisy pixel location)

Replace the noisy pixel with the median of the uncorrupted pixel under the window consideration. Here Window size should be same as used in second stage detection for the same pixel location.

VII. SIMULATION AND RESULT

Now, we will discuss the performance analysis, and result between Median Filtering and our proposed New Adaptive Median Filtering Techniques (NAMFT). In our paper, we have considered PSNR, SNR and visual perception as the criteria of comparison. If SNR and PSNR increase, the noise will be reduced. If the noise level increases, the PSNR value decreases. So the filtering technique, which provides greater PSNR reduces more noise from the corrupted image.

Median Filtering Technique is considered as a very good method to remove Salt and Pepper noise from the noisy images. It works better up to 90% level of noise. This technique outperforms the existing median filtering techniques. PSNR value at different noise level is shown in table 1.
The PSNR Vs. Noise (Salt and Pepper Noise) Level by a median, CWM, PWMAD, NAMFT, and for the proposed technique is given in figure 3. This filter gives the best result at the window size of 3x3 and it can be changed to 5x5 with negligible effects. The restoration of lenna.jpg image (256 × 256) by proposed technique at different noise level are shown in figure 2

(a) Original lenna Image

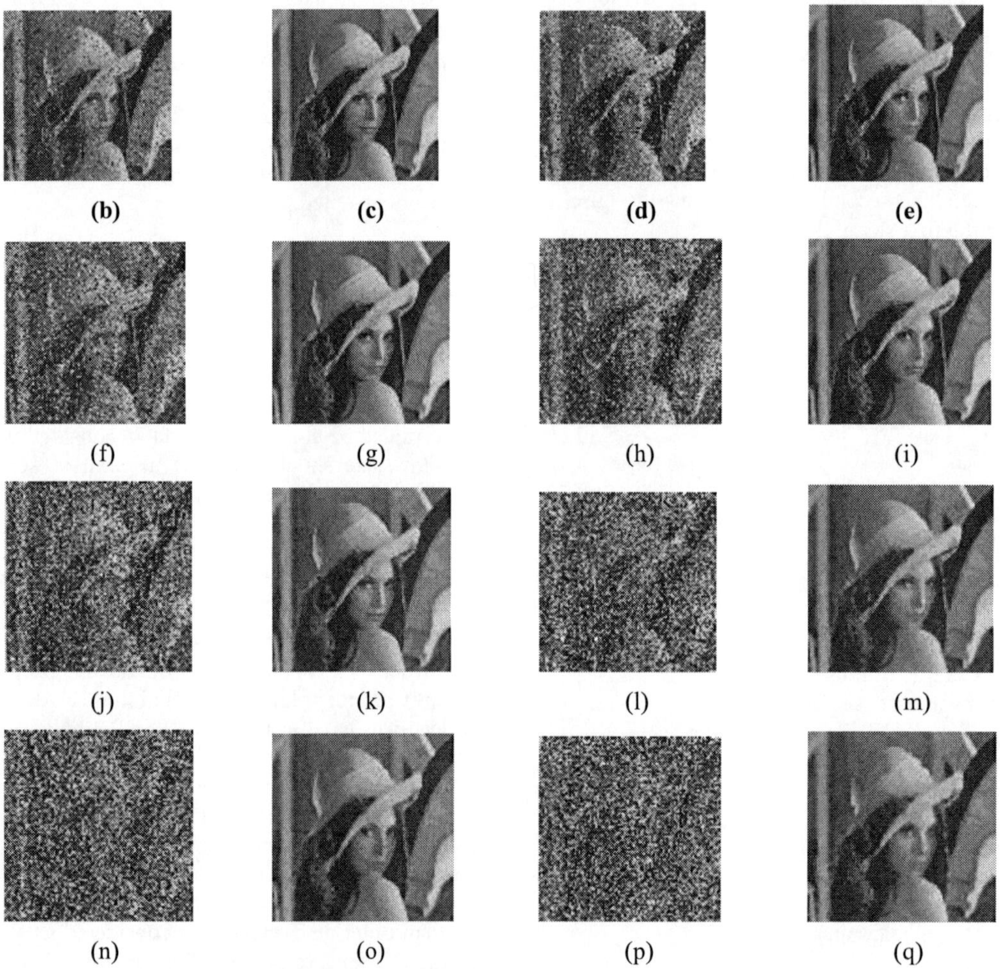

Figure2. Simulation result of proposed filter for gray scale lenna image of size (256x256) at different noise levels.
(b) noise level 10%, (c) recovered from (b), (d) noise level 20%, (e) recovered from (d)
(f) noise level 30%, (g) recovered from (f), (h) noise level 40%, (i) recovered from (h)
(j) noise level 50%, (k) recovered from (j), (l) noise level 60%, (m) recovered from (l)
(n) noise level 10%, (o) recovered from (n), (p) noise level 20%, (q) recovered from (q)

Filter	Noise Density							
	10%	20%	30%	40%	50%	60%	70%	80%
Median	31.22	27.49	22.79	18.78	15.11	12.14	10.06	8.13
CWM	32.13	28.39	24.38	19.63	16.32	13.23	10.56	8.57
PWMAD	30.22	28.77	27.03	24.87	21.56	18.54	14.72	11.24
NAMFT	34.618	33.463	31.745	30.441	28.727	26.892	24.524	22.221
Proposed algorithm	40.60	36.30	33.49	31.16	28.65	27.04	25.33	24.36

Table 1: PSNR values of the different considered and proposed filter at different noise densities.

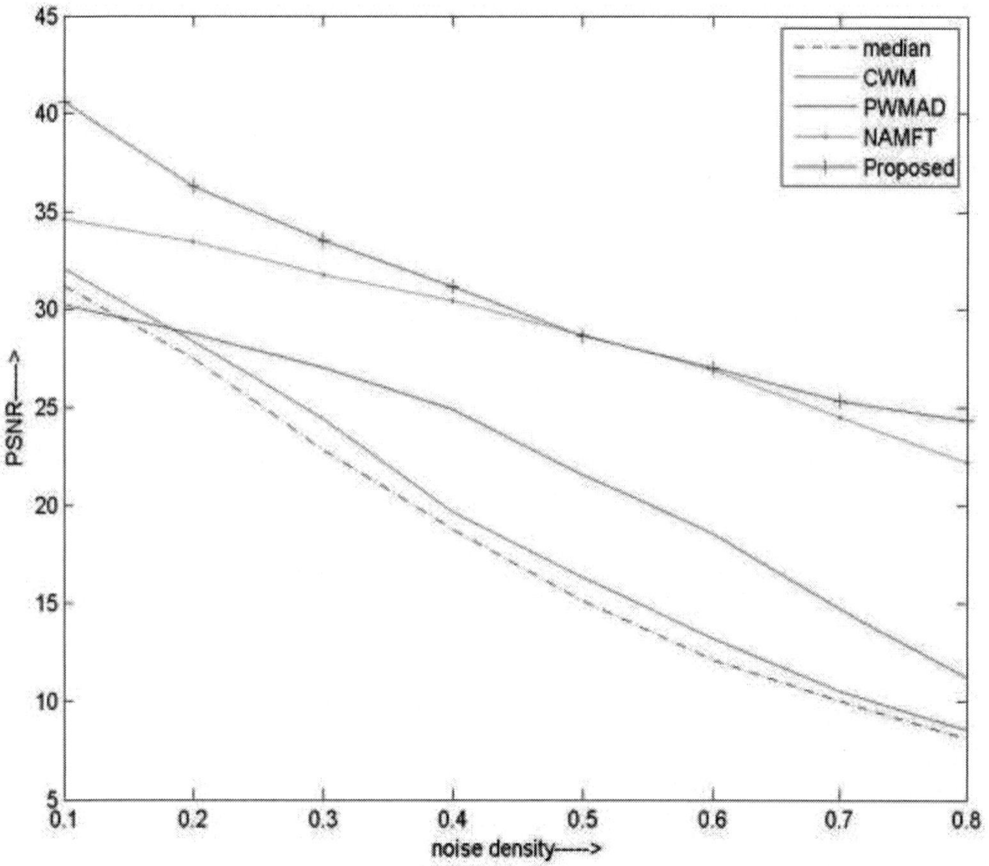

Figure 3: PSNR of the filtered image vs. noise level for different considered filters and the proposed filter.

VIII. CONCLUSION AND FUTURE SCOPE

In this paper, a new filtering technique is developed, which is better than the existing Median Filtering Technique for Salt and Pepper noise. Here, it is introduced that a new two-stage detection technique to remove the false alarm. The PSNR and the quality of the image increase. This technique gives the best result at a low level of noise and as the noise increases the PSNR curve decreases slowly. Finally, we can say that our proposed technique can achieve the filtering operation of an image corrupted with impulse noise up to 90%. It performs better than that of the traditional median filtering techniques and we hope that our effort will help to improve the future experiments over image processing and performance analysis. In future this approach can be implemented to other noise models to improve the quality of the image and new techniques can be utilized to in two-stage detection to enhance the blurring effect at high level of noise densities.

IX. REFERENCES

[1] Chen T. and Wu H.R., "Space variant Median Filters for restoration of Impulse Noise Corrupted images", *IEEE Trans. on Circuits and Systems – II, Analog and Digital Signal Processing*, vol. 48, no. 8, pp. 784-789, Aug. 2001.

[2] Chen T. and Wu H.R., "Adaptive impulse detection using center-weighted median filters," *IEEE Signal Process Letter*, vol. 8, no.1, pp.1–3, January 2001.

[3] R. Yang, L. Yin, M. Gabbouj, J. Astola, and Y. Neuvo, "Optimal weighted median filters under structural constraints," IEEE Trans. Signal Processing, vol. 43, pp. 591–604, Mar. 1995.

[4] R. Coifman and D. Donoho, "Translation invariant de-noising," in Lecture Notes in Statistics: Wavelets and Statistics, vol. New York: Springer-Verlag, pp. 125-150, 1995.

[5] A.K.Jain, "Fundamentals of digital image processing", Prentice-Hall of India,1989

[6] Gonzalea R.C, Woods R.E., "Digital Image Processing", 3rd edition, Pearson Education, 2009.

[7] Rajoo Pandey," An Improved Switching Median filter for Uniformly Distributed Impulse Noise Removal", Proceedings Of World Academy Of Science, Engineering And Technology, Volume 28, April 2008.

[8] Fei Duan, Yu-Jin Zhang," A Highly Effective Impulse Noise Detection Algorithm for Switching Median Filters", IEEE Signal Processing Letters, Vol. 17, , NO. 7, July 2010.

[9] Rong-Oing Jai, Hanqing Zhao, Weijhao," Convergence Analysis of the Bregman method for the variational model of image denoising ", Applied and Computational Harmonic Analysis, No. 27, Pp. 367-379, 2009..

[10] Patel P., Tripathi A., Majhi B., Tripathi C.R., "A New Adaptive Median Filtering Technique for Removal of Impulse Noise from Images ", *ICCCS'11*, Feb,2011.

[11] Tripathi A.K., Ghanekar U., Mukhopadhyay S. "Switching median filter: advanced boundary discriminative noise detection algorithm", *IET Image Process.*, Vol. 5, Iss. 7, pp. 598–610, June, 2010.

[12] Singh, P., Shree, R. A new homomorphic and method noise thresholding based despeckling of SAR image using anisotropic diffusion. Journal of King Saud University – Computer and Information Sciences (2017), http://dx.doi.org/10.1016/j.jksuci.2017.06.006

[13] Prabhishek Singh, Dr. Raj Shree, "Statistical Modelling of Log Transformed Speckled Image", published online in Vol. 14 No. 8 AUGUST 2016 International Journal of Computer Science and Information Security, (pp. 426-431).

[14] Prabhishek Singh, Raj Shree, "Analysis and effects of speckle noise in SAR images", published in 2nd International Conference on Advances in Computing, Communication, & Automation (ICACCA) (Fall) Year: 2016, Pages: 1 - 5, IEEE Conference Publications.

[15] Prabhishek Singh, Raj Shree, "A New Computationally Improved Homomorphic Despeckling Technique of SAR Images", IJARCS, Volume 8, No. 3, March-April 2017.

Manifold Surveillance Issues in Wireless Network and the Secured Protocol

[1]Mamata Rath, [2]Bibudhendu Pati, [3]Binod Kumar Pattanayak
[1]Dept. of IT, C.V.Raman College of Engineering, Bhubaneswar, India,mamata.rath200@gmail.com
[2]Department of Computer Science and Engineering, C. V. Raman College of Engineering, Bhubaneswar, India, patibibudhendu @gmail.com
[3]Department of Computer Science and Engineering, Siksha 'O' Anusandhan University, Bhubaneswar,India, binodpattanayak@soauniversity.ac.in

ABSTRACT

With fast increase of web users, more individuals approach worldwide data and correspondence innovation, as a result of which the issues of using web as a worldwide platform and empowering the smart objects and machines to co-ordinate, discuss, register and figure gradually emerges. Information transmission through a wireless network involves the radio signals, the arrangement of information packets and the network topology. As each segment is correlated to each other, it is very essential to employ security mechanism in these components and real security control must be connected on them. Thus, security plays a critical factor in wireless network. This article highlights security issues in current wireless networks such as Mobile Ad-hoc network and IoT supported networks and it also proposes a security based S-RAID protocol design for security control in cluster based wireless networks. Simulation results show proficiency and better transmission rate of our proposal when it was compared with other similar approaches.

1.INTRODUCTION

As wireless network is a centre innovation developed in new age, the essential security challenges incorporate consistent communication with unwavering quality in the network. In a wireless network with no foundation where there is no base station and access point, the possibility of defenselessness is more. The cell phones are allowed to move toward any path as yet keeping up network with other portable hubs. Because of this exceptional nature of wireless network , outline of wireless network convention with high security includes in particularly basic. Again , because of dynamic change in topology, the network change happens powerfully thus the network is decentralized and more defenseless than wired based network in numerous angles.

In a special wireless networks like WSN and Mobile Ad-hoc Network (MANET), electronic devices and gadgets such as tablets, PCs, mobile phones, machines with specially appointed correspondence capacity are connected together to make a system. MANET is a self-organizing structure of flexible switches related hosts associated by secluded connections. The routers move randomly and compose themselves accordingly; along these lines, the systems remote topology may change quickly and capriciously. In these type of network each node acts as router and because of dynamic changing topology the accessibility of hubs is not generally ensured. It likewise does not ensure that the way between any two hubs would be free of pernicious hubs. The remote connection between hubs is exceptionally vulnerable to connection assaults such as passive eavesdropping, active interfering, etc.Due to inflexibility in the infrastructure of it affects the security feature whenever any kind of extreme computation is done to perform encryption. So due to this problem it is important to build a secured connection which can provide high security solution to provide secured services like authentication, confidentiality, integrity, non-repudiation and availability. So here security is provided in each and every layer

Wireless networks have all around refreshing as of late because of its incredible highlights, for example, self configurable work stations called hubs and they themselves can do their own upkeep . There are many open security issues in wireless network, for example, its open design of network, its common medium, the issue of asset limitations, and alterable network topology. In the network layer of the network different attacks happens amid directing of the data packets from one station to other. There are some special attack types in which routing tables are changed, however, most of the attacks takes place on smart devices because there is very few security policy employed to protect them.Wireless networks have got well appreciated in recent years due to its fantastic features such as self configurable work stations called nodes and they themselves can do their own maintenance . There are many open security issues in wireless network such as its open architecture of network, its shared medium, the problem of resource constraints, and changeable network topology and real time applications[26].In the network layer of the network model various attacks takes place during routing of the packets from one mobile device to other. There are some forwarding attacks which leave the routing tables alone, but changes the delivery of packets. Due to any weakness of the design of the underlying protocol, many attacks happen as a result of which there is denial of service to authenticated devices and many other type of problems take place.

2. RELATED WORK

A detailed study and review has been conducted at this part of the article to understand various contributions made by eminent researchers in this field. Transmission of audio data with secured mechanism has been discussed in [1] where the authors have provided dual safety measures by encrypting and decrypting the audio at each node in the route using stream ciphering method. Security threats and their possible solutions have been discussed in [2] and it also focuses on how modification of data is done using optimization technique for security. The author [3] discusses about the various security problems and how to prevent them which are adopted in the network layer. Spoofing attack and their prevention techniques has been discussed in [4]. The author proposed a model i.e. PBM (Policy Based Management) that deals with 4 entities in [9] such as QoS, network resources, configuration and security. It has discussed about the vulnerability, challenges and security attacks on ad-hoc routing protocols. A bargained hub may disregard the secrecy rule of security and uncover vital data like private and open keys, status of hub, passwords, ideal course to approved hubs, geographic area of hubs and other control information in parcel headers to unapproved hubs introduce in the system [10].A secured on-demand routing protocol has been proposed in [11] that prevents various attacks in MANET and another regression based trust model for MANET has been implemented in [12] that ensures guaranteed packet delivery in wireless medium. Authors in [13] proposed a light weight trust based routing protocol that prevents any external attacks in MANET and a mobile agent based secured platform has been designed in [19] that ensures improved network life time with better throughput when compared with other similar approaches.

3. SECURITY THREATS IN WIRELESS NETWORK

In the information interface layer, most of the attacks takes place because of any lacuna in Wireless Encryption Protocol. So also another sort of attack called Denial of Service (DoS) happens in wireless network which the attacker keeps the communication between the network and a specific hub part by separating it from the gathering.. There are numerous novel commitments to create secured conventions to avert such attack in the network. The essential goal of security execution in wireless networks is to keep maintainable availability over multi-jump wireless channels to give interface level security arrangements and furthermore security instrument arrangement at network level . Typically in a wireless network , two methodologies are utilized for information transmission amongst source and destination, proactive and receptive. While planning security answer for wireless network , care ought to be produced to check the results of network execution with expanding overhead because of complex rationale utilized as a part of security arrangement .There must be an adjust level according to reproduction result and after that lone last usage ought to be completed. There are some steering attacks in the network layer by gatecrashers which take information from the directing tables of the hubs remotely. In sending attack, the interloper or the attacker changes the goal address of the packets with the goal that data from the communication channels are occupied towards the programmer computer rather than the goal. The Specific attack component and their fuse completely relies upon the hidden convention configuration In message authentication method to secure the communication, one way hash work in light of shared key is utilized. To accomplish greater security, the information must be sent alongside the MAC address of the framework. The MAC address of the sender must be checked by the recipient before accepting and sending affirmation by the collector as it were. In such case there will be less overhead on the network as there is no compelling reason to do rehash transmission because of attack .Based on the necessity of directing conventions either source based steering or separation vector directing happens or connection state steering is utilized.

Here some network using IoT devices and technology are reported that uses security features for prevention of attack. Traditional Internet security methods cannot be applied in wireless network context in terms of not having clear line of defence. In this section a comparative analysis has also been carried out with different secured routing protocols with their security factor as the basic criteria. It is a very challenging task to manage security at the IoT environment as here many heterogeneous devices are networked together. Current research shows that the networks due to IoT are prone to many attacks such as malware, botnets, DoS (Denial of Service) attack , Web based malware, android malware and spam. Therefore there is need of developing a standard secured frame work for communication in IoT [15]. Table 1 shows details of some important IoT based security approaches with their detailed functionality.

Table.1. Details of IoT based and smart Security Approaches

S.No	Literature	Description	Security Issues
1.	S.L. Keoh *et.al.*[14]	Here the standard security protocol i.e. CoAP an application protocol is designed	A standardized security protocol is indispensable for the success of IoT.
2.	D. Airehrour *et.al.*[15]	It manages the security at the IoT environment as there are many heterogeneous devices linked together.	Many attacks such as malware, botnets, DoS (Denial of Service) attack , Web based malware, android malware and spam are analysed .
3.	H.Kumarage *et.al.*[16]	Security and privacy is very important in IoT when it is integrated with Cloud Computing.	Security in Cloud based IoT devices has been analysed.
4.	J.Zhou *et.al.*[17]	The challenging issue here is how to securely forward the packets.	The query privacy for cloud-based IoT users should be well protected.
5.	K.Zhang *et.al.*[18]	There is privacy and security concern while designing smart city applications and architecture.	The ever growing volume of data and devices in smart city poses open problems for intelligent services and privacy.

4. SECURITY PREVENTION USING MOBILE AGENTS

In the current motorized advancement, mobile agent are every now and again utilized as a part of remote system based applications since utilization of these product agents spares time and data transfer capacity. A new estimate has been proposed in [21] to improvement and evaluate the course dependability of the Mobile Agent based System which is composed by the required Quality of Service (QoS) parameters. In the proposed work the Mobile Agent based System contains some agent bunches as indicated by classes of QoS prerequisites. Each gathering handles a specific sort of utilization for which those mobile agents are produced. Distinctive agent bunch have particular QoS errand to be satisfied so they organize themselves specifically network designs utilizing which they can play out their activities. As the edge work of the proposed framework is excessively intricate, its execution has been re-enacted utilizing Monte Carlo Simulation. Checking agents are utilized as a part of [22] to gather the connection data and to evaluate dependability of the connections utilizing different time parameters, for example, interface expiry time, interface bundle blunder rate, got flag's quality. Other than these, vitality effectiveness has been accomplished by utilizing leftover battery control lastly ascertaining the Route choice likelihood with the utilization of fluffy rationale. An enhanced bundle conveyance proportion and decrease in vitality utilization have been discovered subsequent to reproducing the proposed framework. A Mobile Agent in a multi-jump condition receives coordinated dissemination (DD) in agent based paradigm. With proposer design of parameters an expanded simulation demonstrates the proposed mobile agent-based coordinated dispersion (MADD) better system execution in wording enhanced bundle conveyance apportion and lessened end to end conveyance inactivity.

A trust-construct framework situated in light of Mobile Agent strategy with improved security has been proposed in to permit preparing of mobile agent usefulness in the system and dynamic connection among agent and the host. Amid data accumulation a domain key is utilized which gives the mobile agent to ascertain the trust a chance to level of the host station and as needs be the mobile agent gathers its operational history and implement Quality of administration component on it. Finding an ideal course for the mobile agents which bit by bit intertwine information amid their versatility starting with one station then onto the next is a principal issue amid the examination of Quality of Service assessment of multi agent based disseminated framework. In the proposed Mobile Agent based framework the structure has been displayed as a non-cyclic and coordinated diagram that indicates the hubs as hosts and the edges are spoken to as connections. Each edge is given a weight that signifies QoS (Quality of Service) parameter esteem, for example, interface deferral and dependability.

5. THE PROPOSED SECURITY PROTOCOL S-RAID

Our designed protocol works as a utility support for security service to the mobile applications executed by mobile devices and mobile stations in wireless network. The proposed security protocol S-RAID (Secured Reliable with Authentication and Intrusion Detection) efficiently handles the security requirements of mobile devices in wireless networks such as WSN, MANET, VANET and IoT enabled networks. The basic module of the protocol called the S-RAID Security Engine initially performs the registration and grouping of mobile stations. It is done as per the service type preferences of the mobile stations and mobile devices. As depicted in the flow diagram, the security engine RAID first configures the group. Number of mobile stations in a group is determined by the network administrator as per the given quality of service criteria. The security engine checks the service type requirement of the node either reliable data transmission, availability and authenticity, intrusion detection and defence against attack. A client may select one or more than one type of service. Depending upon the type, the corresponding methods are invoked by the engine in order to provide the correct service.

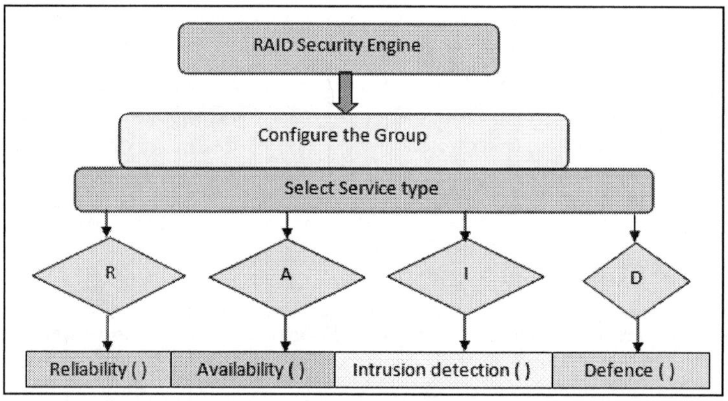

Fig.1. Basic block diagram of the proposed protocol

In the proposed approach, an extensive security technique has been implemented by extending the design of PDO AODV [25] protocol with extended security service. It uses an energy efficient strategy [24] for optimization of routing.The RAID is a security provision service offered by a group of mobile agents in which each agent offers the specific service for which it has been intended. The proposed RAID security protocol uses four mobile agents for providing security service to group of mobile stations.

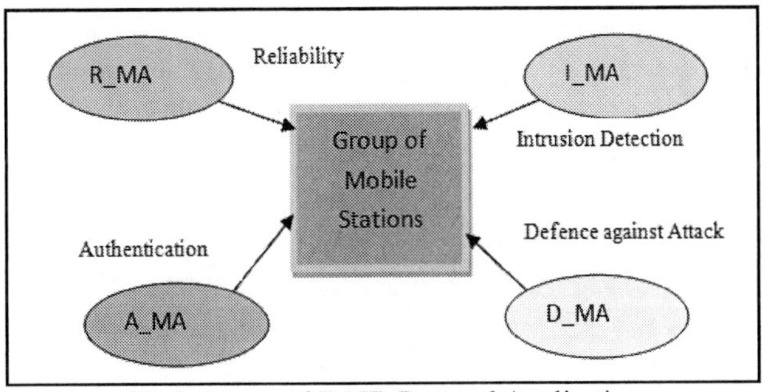

Fig,2. Proposed RAID Protocol Application

This service utility gets activated for those clients which are registered for this service by the protocol. R_MA mobile agent checks the reliability of the transmission by continuous monitoring of the packets during their transmission from source to destination. A_MA mobile agent authenticates each sender from which a route request query comes to any of the registered member station. It validates the ip-address of the sender with the stored address in the destination mobile station routing table and sending a second authentication code to the original sender from A_MA. If both the response address and the ip-address matches then it allows the destination station to communicate further with the sender otherwise not. This prevents the network from DoS attack on the receiver station. Next the D_MA mobile agent is meant for defence against attack. Function of this agent is to detect any type of attack in the surrounding network and to notify the firewall regarding this so that the access can be blocked at the level of routers. The I_MA agent has been configured to handle the intruders,those who cause harm due to replay attack and Man-in-the Middle attack. It uses an improved and secured Intrusion Detection System (IDS) framework that has been proposed in our previous work [23].

6. COMPARATIVE ANALYSIS AND SIMULATION

This section describes comparative analysis among different protocols based on their performance. Those factors have been considered for comparison which affect the security issues to a greater extent such as link failure, end-to-end delay, packet drop ratio etc. Four representative protocols have been considered for simulation from each leading category of protocols in MANET such as DSR, AODV,OLSR and a game theory based improved secured protocol. Mechanism of the said protocols has been explained in this section with technical background. The S-DSR (Secure- Dynamic Source Routing) protocol [5] is proposed by the author where the author secures the traffic against potential attacks without decreasing network performance. A game theoretic scheme [6] that uses LCTF (Least Total Cost Factor) is used to transfer data packets from source to destination have been proposed by the author. A protocol [7] SD-RAC (Secure and Distributed Robust Address Configuration) has been proposed by the author low overhead identity based distributed dynamic address configuration scheme for secure allocation of IP address to authorized nodes of a managed MANET.S-AODV protocol [8] that analyzes the adaptive strategy and delays the verification of digital signatures has been proposed by the author.

Table 2. Simulation Parameters

Simulation parameters	Data/Value
Channel Type	Wireless Channel
MAC Protocol	802.11
Simulation area	2000 x 2000 m
Protocols	S-RAID.S-AODV,SD-RAC,LCTF,S-DSR
Model for Node Movement	Random way point
Data rate	10 mbps
Simulator	Ns2.35

The simulation tool Ns 2.35 has been used in this research work to simulate the performance of the above discussed protocols to report their performance during comparison. Table 2 shows the network simulation parameters considered during the simulation process for simulating the protocols considered for evaluation of energy efficiency and security based protocols.

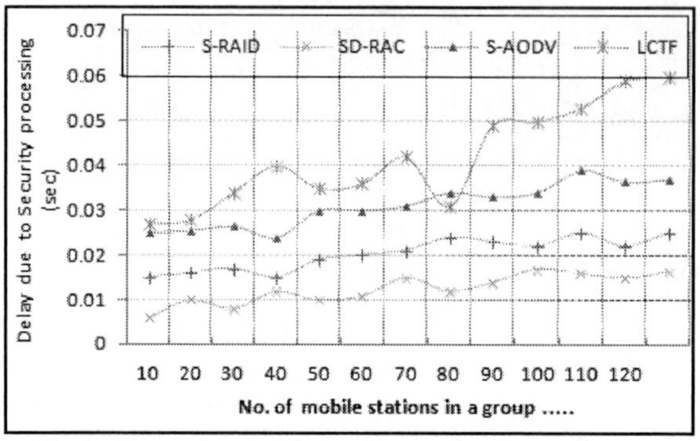

Fig.3. Comparison of Delay due to security processing

Fig.3. shows the comparison of our proposed protocol S-RAID with other security based protocols based on delay due to security processing. During simulation we have recorded the starting time of the security function execution and the end time from the trace file which is generated after simulation of the network scenario in ns2. . Hence we could achieve the time taken by the system for security processing. Here we have presented the simulated value for all the discussed methods with their approaches and also recorded their execution time. In fig.1 we have shown the delay which is caused during transmission of packet from source to destination during the security process implementation.

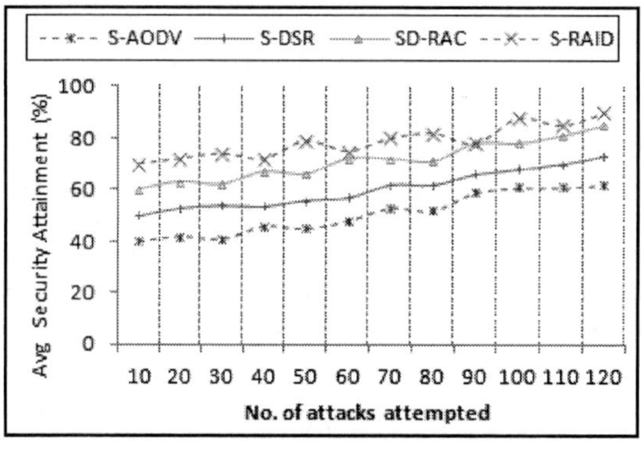

Fig.4 Comparison of average security attainment

Fig.4. shows the comparison of our proposed protocol S-RAID with other security based protocols in wireless network. Here average security attainment refers to number of transmissions successfully carried out with security provision attained by the group of mobile stations. We can see from th simulation that in an average our protocol attains about 70% which is a better result in comparison to others.

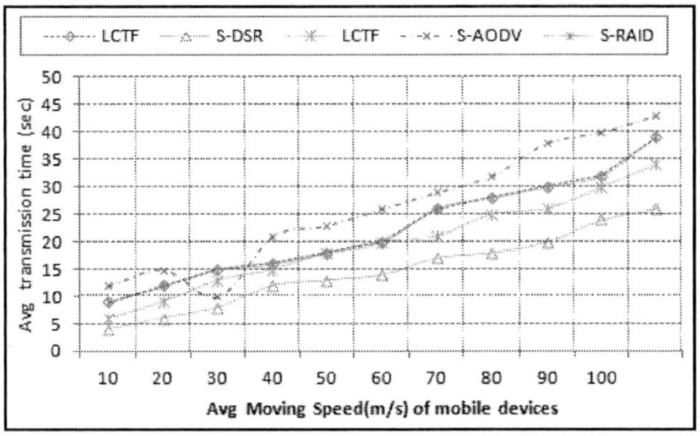

Fig.5 Comparison of average transmission time

Fig.5. shows the comparison of our proposed protocol S-RAID with other security based protocols in wireless network. It can be observed that the average transmission time with speedily moving mobile devices increase due to the fact that there are many issues due to high mobility such as link failure and repair routes, re-routing the packets. Re-authenticating the newly assigned next hop nodes by the mobile agents. In our simulation, it can be seen that the time ranges from 7 sec to 40 sec in average with increase of speed of mobile devices from 10 to 100 respectively.

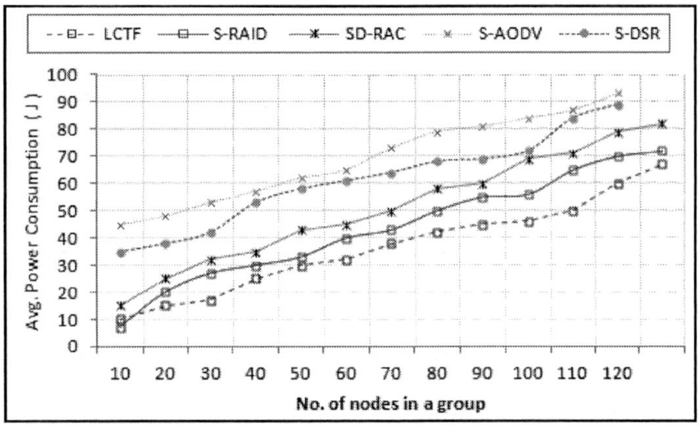

Fig.6 Comparison of average power consumption

Fig.6. shows the comparison of our proposed protocol S-RAID with other security based protocols in wireless network. It can be observed that when number of nodes (mobile stations) in a group is less then it consumes less power and as the number of mobile nodes increases, the power consumption increases proportionally. As the proposed approach uses a very efficient security strategy of registration with the mobile agents, so it consumes more power. But it can be observed that under the same network parameters, other approach consumes more power in comparison to our strategy.

7. CONCLUSION AND FUTURE SCOPE

The level of security and reliability in network can be attained by employing the security mechanism in a protocol and as per the complexity level, the delay and data drop and other network performance will be affected. But minor difference in these factors can be tolerated in a network when there is minor loss in terms of more retransmission attempts in comparison to prevention of the heavy loss due to attack in the network. Future scope of this research article is that it can act as a base platform to impose some advanced security technique during design of a secured routing protocol for wireless network.

REFERENCES

[1] M. S. Athulya and V. S. Sheeba, "Security in Mobile Ad-Hoc Networks", *Computing Communication & Networking Technologies (ICCCNT), 2012 Third International Conference on*, Coimbatore, 2012, pp. 1-5.

[2] Jan Von Mulert, Ian Weich and Winston K.G. Seah, "*Security threats and solutions in MANETs: A case study using AODV and SAODV*", Journal of Network and Computer Applications, Elsevier,Vol. 35,pp.1249-1259,2012.

[3] Praveen Joshi," *Security Issues in Routing protocols in MANETs at network layer*", Procedia Computer Science, Elsevier,Vol.3,pp. 954-960,2011.

[4] Yuseok, K. Tae-Hyung, K. Yuna, and K. Jong, "*LTOLSR: Attack-tolerant OLSR against link spoofing*, " 7th Conference on in Local Computer Networks (LCN), pp. 216-219, 2012.

[5] A. Echchaachoui, A. Kobbane and M. Elkoutbi, "*A new trust model to secure routing protocols against DoS attacks in MANETs*", 2015 10th International Conference on Intelligent Systems: Theories and Applications (SITA), Rabat, 2015, pp. 1-6.

[6] Debjit Das, Koushik Majumdar and Anurag Dasgupta, " *Selfish Node Detection and Low Cost Data Transmission in MANET using Game Theory*",11th International Multi-Conference on Information Processing (IMCIP-2015),Science Direct,pp.92-101, 2015.

[7] Uttam Ghosh and Raja Datta, " *A Secure Addressing Scheme for Large-Scale Managed MANETs*",2015 IEEE Transactions on Network and Service Management,Vol.12,No.3,pp.483-495, 2015.

[8]D. Cerri and A. Ghioni, "Securing AODV: the A-SAODV secure routing prototype," in *IEEE Communications Magazine*, vol. 46, no. 2, pp. 120-125, February 2008.

[9] Slavica V.Bostjancic Rakas,Valentina V.Timecenko, "*Quality of Service and Security Issues in MANETenvironment*",22nd Telecommunications Forum (TELFOR),Serbia,Belgrade,IEEE, Nov. 2014.

[10] P.Dhivya, Dr. S. Karthik and Dr. T. Kalai Kumaran, " *SOA Based Secure Data Transmission over CMEA Protocol in MANET*", 2015 Procedia Computer Science, Science Direct,pp.434-440, 2015.

[11] Z. Wan, K. Ren and M. Gu, "USOR: An Unobservable Secure On-Demand Routing Protocol for Mobile Ad Hoc Networks," in *IEEE Transactions on Wireless Communications*, vol. 11, no. 5, pp. 1922-1932, May 2012.

[12] R. Venkataraman, M. Pushpalatha and T. R. Rao, "Regression-based trust model for mobile ad hoc networks," in *IET Information Security*, vol. 6, no. 3, pp. 131-140, Sept. 2012.

[13] N. Marchang and R. Datta, "Light-weight trust-based routing protocol for mobile ad hoc networks," in *IET Information Security*, vol. 6, no. 2, pp. 77-83, June 2012.

[14] S. L. Keoh, S. S. Kumar and H. Tschofenig, "Securing the Internet of Things: A Standardization Perspective," in *IEEE Internet of Things Journal*, vol. 1, no. 3, pp. 265-275, June 2014.

[15] David Airehrour, Jairo A. Gutierrez, "An analysis of secure MANET routing features to maintain confidentiality and integrity in IoT Routing", .http://www. researchgate. net/ publication /277078202, Last accessed on - August 2016.

[16]H. Kumarage, I. Khalil, A. Alabdulatif, Z. Tari and X. Yi, "Secure Data Analytics for Cloud-Integrated Internet of Things Applications," in *IEEE Cloud Computing*, vol. 3, no. 2, pp. 46-56, Mar.-Apr. 2016.

[17]J. Zhou, Z. Cao, X. Dong and A. V. Vasilakos, "Security and Privacy for Cloud-Based IoT: Challenges," in *IEEE Communications Magazine*, vol. 55, no. 1, pp. 26-33, January 2017.

[18]K. Zhang, J. Ni, K. Yang, X. Liang, J. Ren and X. S. Shen, "Security and Privacy in Smart City Applications: Challenges and Solutions," in *IEEE Communications Magazine*, vol. 55, no. 1, pp. 122-129, January 2017.

[19] Rath M, B.K.Pattanayak: "MAQ: A Mobile Agent Based Quality of Service Platform for MANETs", , International Journal of Business Data Communications and Networking, 13(1), January ,2017.

[20] Rath M. U.P.Rout"Congestion Control Mechanism for Real Time Traffic in Mobile Adhoc Networks." *Computer Communication, Networking and Internet Security, Lecture Notes in Networks and Systems,* vol 5.pp.149-156, **Springer**,2017.

[21]Chowdhury C., Neogy S. "Reliability Estimation of Delay Tolerant QoS Mobile Agent System in MANET". Computer Information Systems – Analysis and Technologies. Communications in Computer and Information Science, vol 245. Springer, 2011.

[22]Palaniappan, S. and Chellan, K. (2015) Energy-Efficient Stable Routing Using QoS Monitoring Agents in MANET. EURSIP Journal on Wireless Communications and Networking,Springer, 2015.

[23] B.Pattanayak ,Rath M., (2014) "A Mobile Agent Based Intrusion Detection System Architecture For Mobile Ad Hoc Networks", Journal of Computer Science,Vol. 10,pp 970-975.

[23] M.Rath, B.K. Pattanayak, B.Pati, "Energy Efficient MANET Protocol Using Cross Layer Design for Military Applications", Defense Science Journal Vol. 66, No. 2,pages.146-150, 2016.

[25] M.Rath, B.K. Pattanayak, B.Pati, "Load Balanced Routing Scheme for MANET with Power Optimization", International Journal of Communication Networks and Distributed Systems (IJCNDS), Inderscience Publishers,Vol 19, No. 4 , pg 394-405. , 2017.

[26] Mamata Rath, Binod Kumar Pattanayak, " Energy Competent Routing Protocol Design in MANET with Real time Application Provision", International Journal of Business Data Communications and Networking, 11(1), 50-60, January-March 2015.

Improving DV-Hop Based Localization Algorithms in Wireless Sensor Networks by considering only closest anchors

Amanpreet Kaur[a] **Padam Kumar**[b] **Govind P Gupta**[c]
[a,b]Department of Computer Science & Engineering
Jaypee Institute of Information Technology, Noida, India
[c]Department of Information Technology
National Institute of Technology, Raipur, India
[a]amanpreet.kaur1410@gmail.com

Abstract-Localization problem has gained a significant attention in the field of wireless sensor networks in order to support location-based services or information such as supporting geographic routing protocols, tracking events, targets, and providing security protection techniques. A number of variants of DV-Hop based localization algorithms have been proposed and their performance is measured in terms of localization error. In all these algorithms, while determining the location of a non-anchor node, all the anchor nodes are taken into consideration. However, if only the anchors close to the node are considered, it will be possible to reduce the localization error significantly. This paper explores the effect of the close anchors in the performance of the DV-Hop based localization algorithms and an improvement is proposed by considering only the closest anchors. The simulation results show that considering closest anchors for estimation of the location reduces localization error significantly as compared to considering all the anchors.

Keywords- wireless sensor networks, localization, DV-Hop, anchor, accuracy

I. Introduction

Wireless sensor network (WSN) is a wireless network that consists of low-priced, less energy tiny nodes called sensors along with a central server called base station. The sensor nodes examine the event and send the event information to the Base station via multi-hop communication [1]. In location-based applications, location information of sensor node that has detected the event is also significant along with event information. Thus, Localization, a way to find the location of a sensor node, is a very important problem.

With respect to the hardware required for computing the coordinates of the node, the localization algorithms can be divided into two categories: range-based and range-free [2]. Range-based need expensive equipments to find distance estimates or angle estimates between nodes [3]. Range-free algorithms derive location information using approximate distance estimates between nodes [4]. The concept used in the range-free algorithm is that location can be estimated if the approximate distance of the node from some nodes that know their location, is known. Such nodes are called anchor nodes. Due to hardware limitations, range-free algorithms like DV-Hop [5] achieve cost effectiveness but have low localization accuracy. The anchor nodes play an important role in deciding the location of non-anchor nodes in range-free algorithms. In these range-free algorithms, normally all the anchors in the network are required to determine the location of the non-anchor node. But rather than considering all anchor nodes, if only a few near anchors are considered then it is easier to locate a node with better precision. Thus it is more significant to study the influence of near anchors on DV-Hop based algorithms to improve their localization accuracy.

In this paper, most of the known DV-Hop based algorithms are surveyed and the effect of the closest anchors is explored. Improvement gained by considering only a few near anchors instead of all the anchors for finding the location of non-anchor nodes in their last phase has been evaluated. These improved algorithms have been compared with original algorithms to analyze the impact of the closest anchors on the localization error. It is observed that the closest anchors have a significant impact in reducing localization error of all these algorithms.

II. Related Work

1. Original DV-Hop Algorithm

The Algorithm [5] was first proposed by Dragos Niculescu and Badri Nath in 2001. It is a distributed localization algorithm where each node tries to determine its location by knowing its number of hops from each anchor node. The algorithm works as: Given the network with n anchors, in the initial step, the anchor nodes broadcast their location information and hop value (initially equal to 0) to all other nodes in the network. Receiving non-anchor node increments the hop value by one and saves location information along with hop for every anchor in its hop count table. Thus, each non-anchor node j gets location information and the smallest number of hops (hop_{ij}) from every anchor i in the network in the first step. The second step enables all the non-anchor nodes to get approximate distance from every anchor node by multiplying hop_{ij} from each anchor i with the average distance per hop (Ahd_i) computed by each anchor. Equation (1) is used by anchor i to compute Ahd_i in this step.

$$Ahd_i = \frac{\sum_{j=1\, j\neq i}^{n} \sqrt{(x_i - x_j)^2 + (y_i - y_j)^2}}{\sum_{j=1\, j\neq i}^{n} hop_{ij}} \quad (1)$$

Equation (2) is used by node j to find its distance from anchor i.

$$d_{ij} = Ahd_k \times hop_{ij} \quad (2)$$

where Ahd_k is the average hop distance of nearest anchor k from node j.

The last step enables all the non-anchor nodes to find their location by using least square method [5]. The explanation of least square method is as follows:

If the x-coordinates and y- coordinates of a node UN and anchor A_i are (x_{un}, y_{un}) and (x_i, y_i). Then, we get the following system of equations by Euclidean Distance formula:

$$\left.\begin{array}{c} (x_{un} - x_1)^2 + (y_{un} - y_1)^2 = d_{1un}{}^2 \\ (x_{un} - x_2)^2 + (y_{un} - y_2)^2 = d_{2un}{}^2 \\ \vdots \\ (x_{un} - x_n)^2 + (y_{un} - y_n)^2 = d_{nun}{}^2 \end{array}\right\} \quad (3)$$

Equation (4) can be derived in the form of matrix from Equation (3) as follows:

$$AX_{un}=B \quad (4)$$

$$\text{where } A = 2 \times \begin{bmatrix} x_1 - x_n & y_1 - y_n \\ x_2 - x_n & y_2 - y_n \\ \vdots & \vdots \\ x_{n-1} - x_n & y_{n-1} - y_n \end{bmatrix}, X_u = \begin{bmatrix} x_{un} \\ y_{un} \end{bmatrix},$$

$$\text{and } B = \begin{bmatrix} x_1^2 - x_n^2 + y_1^2 - y_n^2 - d_{1n}^2 - d_{unn}^2 \\ x_2^2 - x_n^2 + y_2^2 - y_n^2 - d_{2n}^2 - d_{unn}^2 \\ \vdots \\ x_{n-1}^2 - x_n^2 + y_{n-1}^2 - y_n^2 - d_{n(n-1)}^2 - d_{unn}^2 \end{bmatrix}$$

Equation (4) can be converted to Equation (5) as follows:

$$X_{un} = (A^T A)^{-1} A^T B \quad (5)$$

Equation (5) uses Least square method [5] to get coordinates of node UN. Thus all anchor nodes play a role in determining the location of the node. But, if we try to consider only a few anchors that are close to a given non-anchor node, then there are more chances to locate the node with higher precision.

2. Weighted Centroid Localization(WCL)

WCL algorithm [6] was proposed by Bingjiao Zhang et al. in 2012. Like DV-Hop, It uses the influence of all anchor nodes, but attaches more weight to near anchors. This is the simplest weighted scheme. The algorithm involves two steps. The first step is similar to that used in original DV-Hop Algorithm. The second step uses weighted centroid Equation (6) to estimate the coordinates of a node j as coordinates (x_j, y_j) .

$$x_j = \frac{\sum_{i=1}^{n} w_i x_i}{n} \ , \ y_j = \frac{\sum_{i=1}^{n} w_i y_i}{n} \qquad (6)$$

where $(x_i, y_i), 1 \leq i \leq n$, are coordinates of ith anchors and w_i is the weight assigned to it which is set to $\frac{1}{hop_{ij}}$.

3. Improved Weighted Centroid Method

In [6], Bingjiao Zhang, Minning Ji and Lianhai Shan in 2012 proposed another improved weighted centroid algorithm (IWCL) which further improves localization accuracy of the algorithm by changing weight value to $w_i = \left(\frac{1}{hop_{ij}}\right)^{\frac{1}{s}}$ where s is the ratio of average hop distance (Ahd_i) and communication radius. The algorithm works in three steps. The first and second steps are similar. In the third step, every non-anchor node tries to determine its location using Equation (6), where the value of weight takes into account the communication radius.

4. Hyperbolic Algorithm

In [7], Guozhi Song and Dayuan Tam proposed a Hyperbolic Algorithm to further reduce the localization error in DV-Hop Algorithm. The first step is same as that of original DV-Hop Algorithm. The second step uses an average of average hop distances (AHD) computed by all anchor nodes using Equation (7) instead of average hop distance of each anchor node.

$$AHD = \frac{\sum_{i=1}^{n} Ahd_i}{n} \qquad (7)$$

Thus the non-anchor nodes compute their distances from each anchor node by multiplying AHD with the number of hops. In the third step, hyperbolic method [7] is used instead of least square method to get the coordinates of every non-anchor node.

5. Improved Weighted Centroid DV-Hop Algorithm

This was developed by Guozhi Song and Dayuan Tam in [7]. It is similar to weighted algorithms discussed above, but with the difference that weight value is calculated as $\frac{\sum_{i=1}^{n} hop_{ij}}{n \times hop_{ij}}$.

In all above related works, it is observed that in their last step, all the anchor nodes in the wireless sensor network play a role in determining the location of a node. Thus, even if a particular anchor node is very far from given non-anchor node, its coordinates are used to find location. For example, in Fig. 1, for node N1, if we only use near anchors A1, A2 and A3, then it is expected to localize the node with higher precision. There is no importance of taking into account far nodes like A6 and A7 to localize node N1. These far nodes will shift the coordinates more towards them. In previous approaches, all the anchor nodes determine the location of the node. We propose that only near anchors be considered.

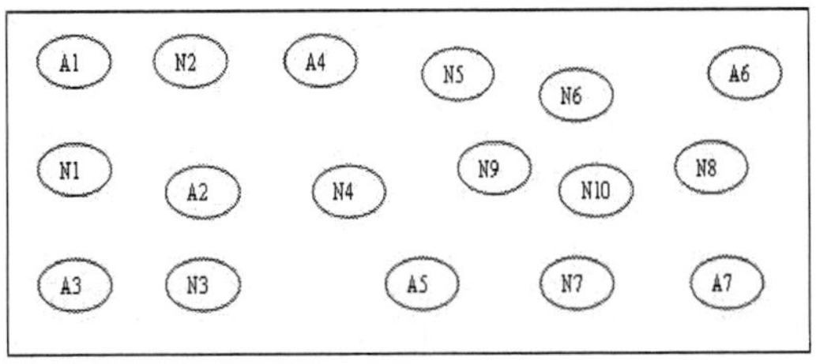

Fig. 1. WSN Network

III. Improved DV-Hop Algorithm and its Improved Variants

In this section, we present an improvement in the last step of all the algorithms discussed in Section 2, by restricting the consideration of anchor nodes to only a few closest anchors, in determining the location of non-anchor nodes. The idea of using near anchors is that localization accuracy gets improved if only neighbor anchors that are close to non-anchor node are used.

1. Improved DV-Hop Algorithm

The improved version of the original DV-Hop [5] Algorithm works in following three steps:

Step 1: Similar to the first step of original DV-Hop [5] Algorithm.

Step 2: All the anchors find their average hop distance and send this to all other nodes in the network. Other nodes compute their distances from each anchor by multiplying number of hops with average hop distance.

Step 3: Find few (say *t)* near anchor nodes of each node. From the simulation results, it is proved that the optimum value of *t* is 5. Unlike, DV-Hop Algorithm, apply least square method by using coordinates of only this t near nodes instead of taking all anchor nodes coordinates. In Equation (4), the only *t* near anchors is used instead of n anchors. Thus Equation (4) is transformed into following Equation (8).

$$AX_{un}=B \qquad (8)$$

$$where\ A = 2 \times \begin{bmatrix} x_1 - x_t & y_1 - y_t \\ x_2 - x_t & y_2 - y_t \\ \vdots & \vdots \\ x_{t-1} - x_t & y_{t-1} - y_t \end{bmatrix}, \mathrm{X_u} = \begin{bmatrix} \mathrm{x_{un}} \\ \mathrm{y_{un}} \end{bmatrix},$$

$$\text{and } B = \begin{bmatrix} x_1^2 - x_t^2 + y_1^2 - y_t^2 - d_{1t}^2 - d_{unt}^2 \\ x_2^2 - x_t^2 + y_2^2 - y_t^2 - d_{2t}^2 - d_{unt}^2 \\ \vdots \\ x_{t-1}^2 - x_t^2 + y_{t-1}^2 - y_t^2 - d_{t(t-1)}^2 - d_{unt}^2 \end{bmatrix}$$

2. An Example of Improved DV-Hop Algorithm

Consider a following WSN area of 50 $\times$ 50 m^2 containing 50 nodes randomly deployed in it. Let there be 10 anchor nodes.

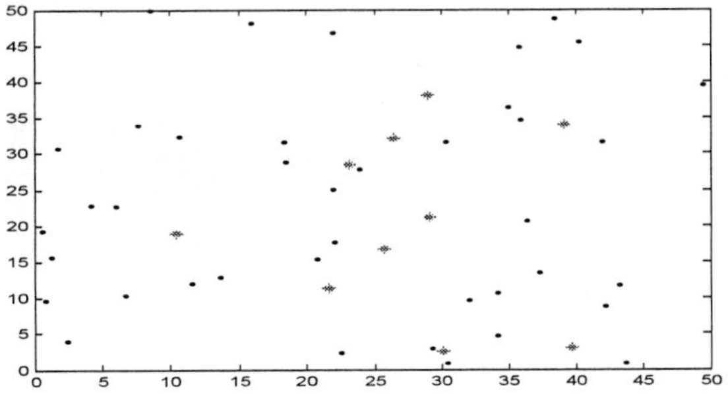

Fig. 2. WSN Area

Let us suppose we want to find the location of particular node N whose actual coordinates are <26.24,27.812> present in this area. The steps followed in Original and Improved DV-hop are:

Step 1: The first step is same for both the algorithms. The anchor nodes send their location information to all nodes. Let the *x* and *y* coordinates of 10 anchor nodes be as shown in Table 1.

Table 1. Coordinates of anchors

Anchor id	x	y
1	29.14	21.175
2	25.776	16.698
3	21.645	11.297
4	28.99	38.018
5	26.491	32.026
6	10.453	18.991
7	39.166	34.042
8	23.055	28.391
9	39.711	2.9591
10	30.143	2.5134

Table 2 show the outcome of step 1 for a particular node N.

Table 2. Minimum number of hops of node N from every anchor

Anchor id	Minimum hops
1	1
2	1
3	1
4	1
5	1
6	1
7	1
8	1
9	2
10	2

Step 2: In the second step, all the anchor nodes compute their average hop distances (Ahd_i) using Equation (1). Table 3 shows the average hop distances computed by every anchor in the network.

Table 3. Average distance per hop computed by all anchors

Anchor id	(Ahd_i)
1	14.481
2	14.792
3	17.751

4	21.51
5	17.163
6	22.477
7	22.675
8	16.104
9	25.95
10	22.877

The node N after getting average hop distances from each anchor computes its distance from every anchor *i*. Table 4 shows the distance of node N from each anchor *i*.

Table 4. Distance of node N from each anchor i

Anchor i	d_{uni}
1	21.51
2	21.51
3	21.51
4	21.51
5	21.51
6	21.51
7	21.51
8	21.51
9	43.021
10	43.021

Step 3: Least square method is used to find the location of node N. Unlike Original DV-Hop Algorithm, Improved Algorithm uses only *t* (let it be 5) near anchors to determine location of node N. Thus the Equation (8) becomes

$$AX_{un}=B \qquad (8)$$

$$\text{where } A = 2 \times \begin{bmatrix} x_1 - x_5 & y_1 - y_5 \\ x_2 - x_5 & y_2 - y_5 \\ \vdots & \vdots \\ x_4 - x_5 & y_4 - y_5 \end{bmatrix}, X_u = \begin{bmatrix} x_{un} \\ y_{un} \end{bmatrix},$$

$$\text{and } B = \begin{bmatrix} x_1^2 - x_5^2 + y_1^2 - y_5^2 - d_{15}^2 - d_{un5}^2 \\ x_2^2 - x_5^2 + y_2^2 - y_5^2 - d_{25}^2 - d_{un5}^2 \\ \vdots \\ x_4^2 - x_5^2 + y_4^2 - y_5^2 - d_{45}^2 - d_{un5}^2 \end{bmatrix}$$

Solving Equation (8) by least square method, we get coordinates of Node UN as <31.38, 17.144>. In Original DV-Hop algorithm, the Equation (4) results into coordinates of node N as <14.06,42.895>. Thus Node UN coordinates obtained from Improved Algorithm are closer than obtained from original DV-hop Algorithm. Thus proposed Algorithm is better than Original DV- Hop Algorithm.

3. Improved Hyperbolic Algorithm

In the Hyperbolic algorithm, we offer modification in the Step 2 and Step 3 phase of the localization. The proposed improved Hyperbolic algorithm has following three steps:

Step 1: Similar to the first step of original DV-Hop Algorithm.

Step 2: The anchors find their average hop distance and send it to all other nodes in the network. The non-anchor node finds the t anchors close to it and finds the average of average hop distances of this t near anchors. The non-anchor node computes distances from each anchor by multiplying average hop distance with hop values.

Step 3: Apply hyperbolic method by considering only t near anchor nodes to determine coordinates of every node.

Similarly, WCL, IWCL, and IW-DV-Hop Algorithms can be improved by refining their last step. In their improved variants, the location of the node is determined by using following Equation (9).

$$x_u = \frac{\sum_{i=1}^{t} w_i x_i}{t}, \quad y_u = \frac{\sum_{i=1}^{t} w_i y_i}{t} \qquad (9)$$

where (x_i, y_i) are coordinates of t near anchors and w_i is the weight assigned to each anchor.

IV. Simulation Results and Discussions

We have simulated the algorithms using MatLab2007. We compare all original DV- Hop Algorithms with the proposed modifications one by one using a parameter localization error. The localization error is defined by following equation (6):

$$Localization\ error = \frac{1}{m \times r} \sum_{i=1}^{m} \sqrt{(x_a - x_u)^2 + (y_a - y_u)^2} \quad (6)$$

where m is the total number of non-anchor nodes, $<x_a, y_a>$ are the actual coordinates and $<x_u, y_u>$ are the estimated coordinates of non-anchor node and r is the communication radius of sensors.

The simulation setup considers a square area of 500×500 m^2 in all experiments. The other experimental parameters taken are shown in Table 5.

Table 5: Simulation parameters

Simulation Parameters	**Value**
WSN Area	500×500
Total Nodes	Vary from 300 to 550
Anchor Nodes	Vary from 50 to 175
Total iterations	50
r	100
t	5

For simulation, we have selected t to be equal to 5. We performed the simulation for $t=3$ and $t=4$, but it was observed that with these values of t, the proposed algorithms are not able to localize many non-anchor nodes, especially nodes at the boundary as most of the near anchor nodes coordinates form the collinear points, resulting in high localization error. To determine coordinates, the reference points should be non-collinear. Thus, we have taken the next smallest value of t as 5. The comparison is done in terms of localization errors of the original algorithms and proposed modification under varying parameters such as total number of nodes and total anchor nodes. We have taken 50 iterations (different topology for each iteration) for each simulation and average results have been plotted.

1. Value of *t* for the proposed algorithms

To determine the value of t, I have considered two experiments and found that the optimum value of t is 5. For the first experiment, 100 anchors are deployed in WSN Area. From Fig 3, it is observed, that if small number of near anchor nodes are considered, then accuracy is improved. After the value of t becomes 5, the localization error becomes almost constant, thus, the minimum value of anchors nodes to be considered is 5. For second experiment, 50 anchors are deployed in WSN Area. Again, it is observed that t=5 near anchors give least localization error.

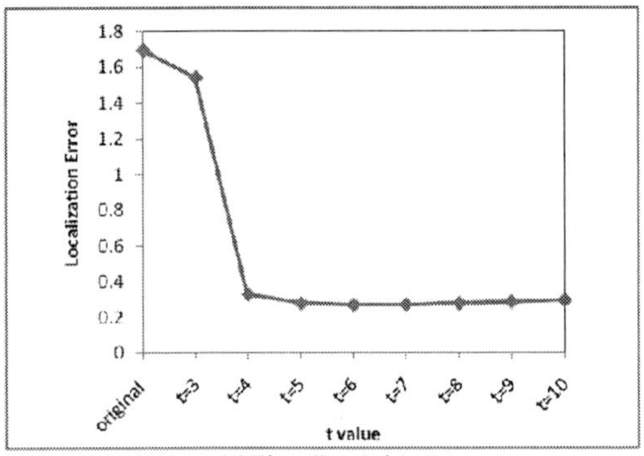

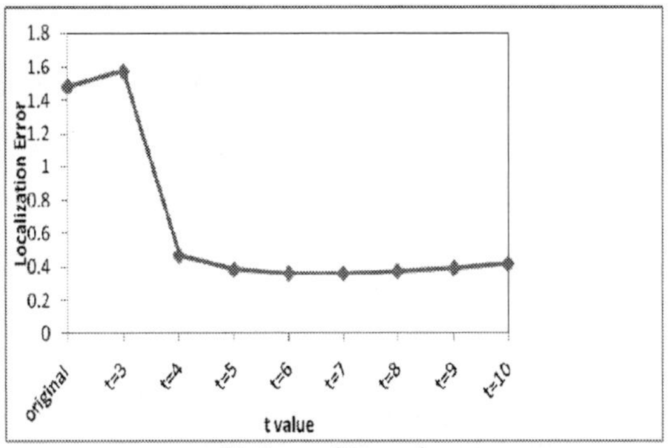

(a)First Experiment (b) Second Experiment

Fig. 3. Comparison of Original and Improved DV-Hop by varying t value

Thus, the conclusion is that the best value of t is 5.

2. Comparative results for algorithms and their improved versions

In this simulation, original algorithms are compared with proposed modifications in terms of localization error by increasing anchor nodes and the total number of nodes.

A. By varying anchor nodes

Figs 4 (a)-(e) shows the relationship of localization error and a different number of anchor nodes for original algorithms and improved ones. With the increase in the number of anchor nodes, the localization error of improved algorithms becomes significantly less than the original algorithms.

Fig 4 (a) proves that the Improved Algorithm reduces the localization error by 60%.

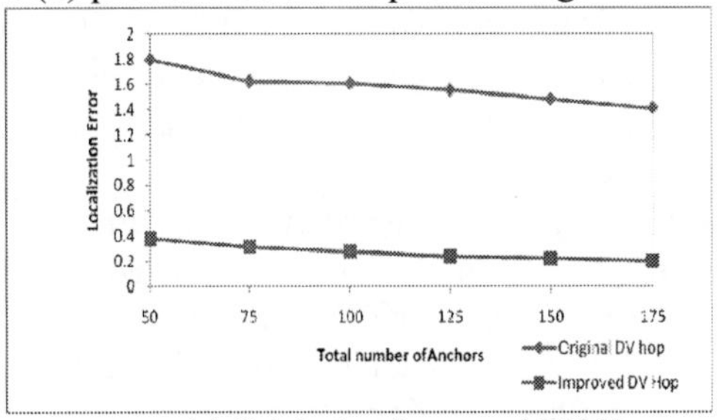

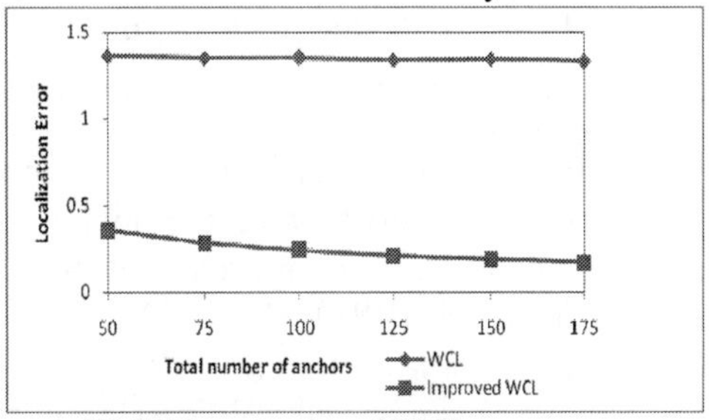

(a) Original vs Improved DV-Hop (b) WCL vs Improved WCL

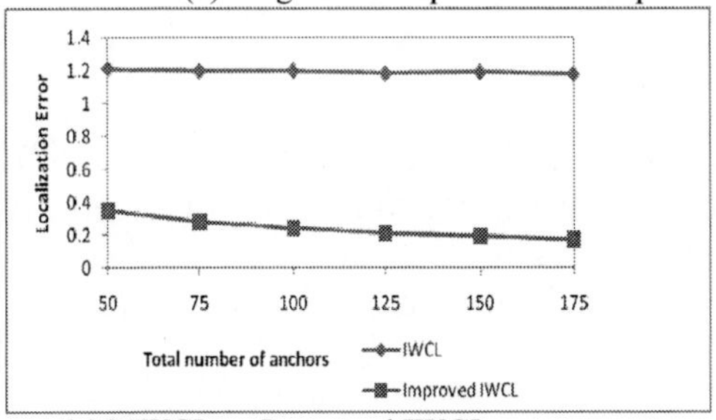

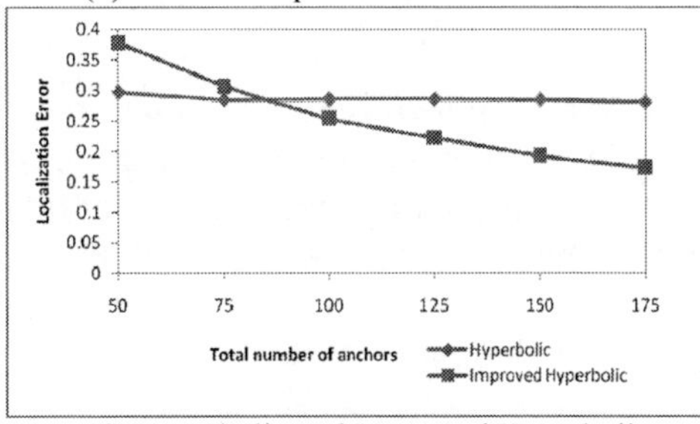

(c)) IWCL vs Improved IWCL (d) Hyperbolic and Improved Hyperbolic

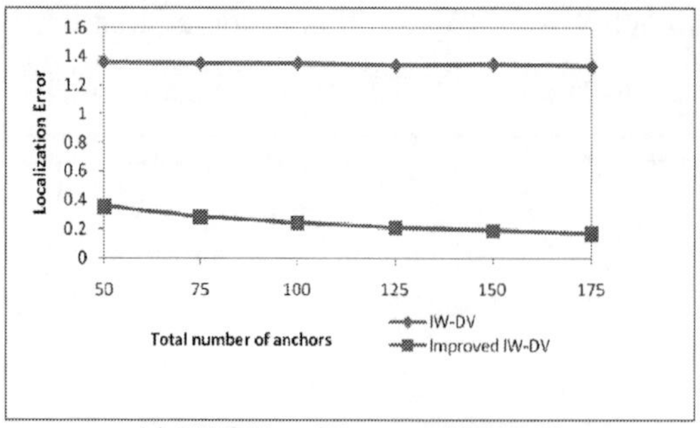

(e) IW-DV and Improved IW-DV
Fig.4. Comparison of by varying total number of anchors

In the results shown in Fig 4(b), it is shown that Improved WCL reduces localization error to large extent when compared with WCL. If the anchor nodes are increased, then Improved WCL reduces localization error to large extent as compared to WCL where there is a slight change in the value of localization error.

From Fig 4(c) , it is clear that Improved IWCL algorithm has higher localization accuracy as compared with IWCL algorithm. When the number of anchor nodes is varied from 50 to 175, for IWCL, the localization error slowly decreases from 1.21 to 1.18, while for Improved IWCL algorithm, error decreases very fast from 0.35 to 0.17.

In Fig 4(d), simulation results for Hyperbolic and improved hyperbolic algorithm are presented by varying number of anchors, while keeping communication radius and the number of nodes constant. In this simulation experiment, the proposed algorithm outperform hyperbolic DV- Hop algorithm in terms of error if the anchor ratio is more than 20 %. If the anchor count is 50, Hyperbolic Algorithm has lower localization error as compared to Improved Hyperbolic, but as the anchor nodes are increased, the Improved hyperbolic algorithm behaves better than Hyperbolic algorithm. As shown in Fig 8, Improved Hyperbolic has localization error of 0.25, while Hyperbolic Algorithm has localization error of 0.28 when anchor nodes are 100. The error of Improved Hyperbolic decreases drastically from 0.25 to 0.17 when anchor nodes are increased from 100 to 175.

As depicted in Fig 4(e), when the anchor count is increased, the localization error of both algorithms decreases and Improved IW-DV Hop Algorithm has lowest localization error when compared with IW-DV Hop Algorithm in this paper. For example, when the anchor count is 50, the localization error of IW-DV Hop is 1.36 while for Improved IW-DV Hop is 0.35. On average, Improved IW-DV Hop has very low localization error as compared to IW-DV Hop Algorithm.

B. By varying total number of nodes

In Figs 5(a)-(e), the relation of localization error with an increase in the total number of nodes is shown for original and improved Algorithms by keeping the total count of anchors as 50. From Fig 5 (a), it is observed that both these algorithms have little effect on localization error when increasing total number of nodes and proposed algorithm gives better results than original DV- Hop Algorithm.

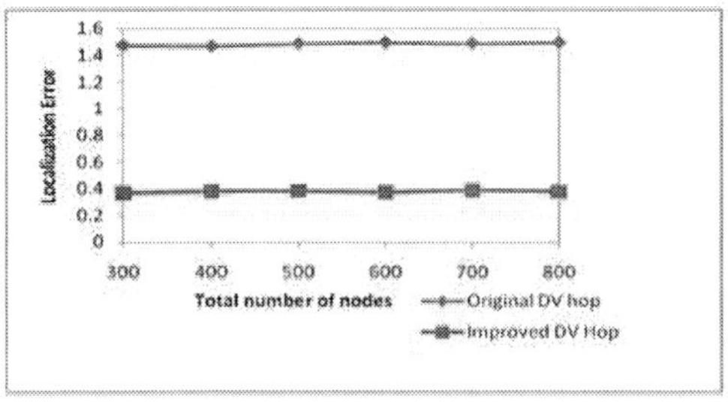

(a) Original vs Improved DV-Hop

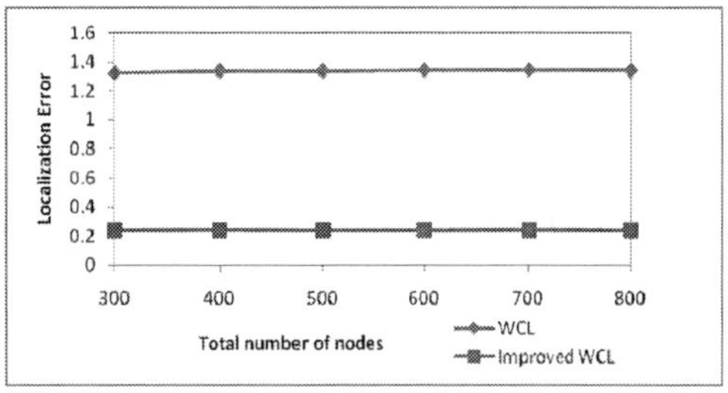

(b) WCL vs Improved WCL

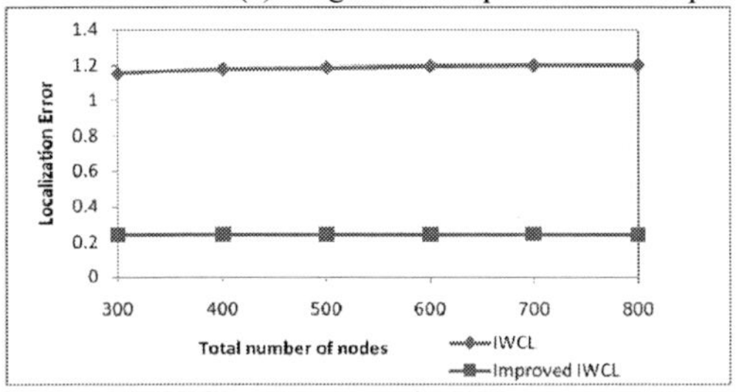

(c)) IWCL vs Improved IWCL

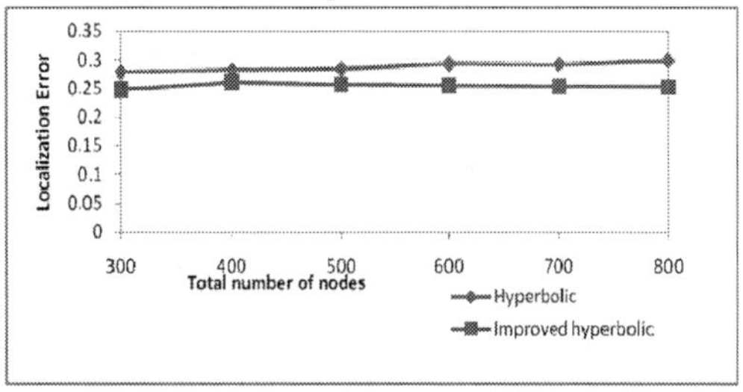

(d) Hyperbolic and Improved Hyperbolic

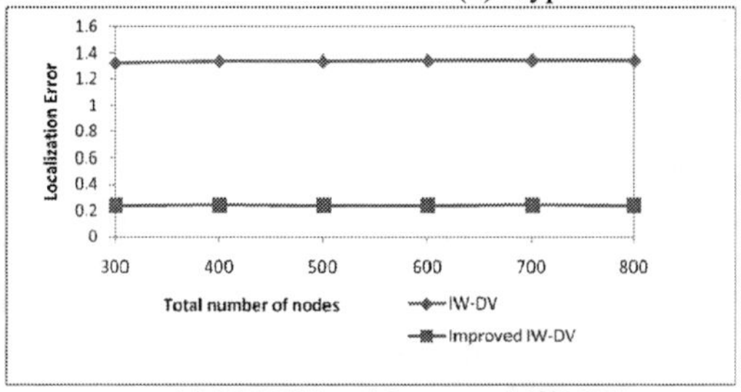

(e) IW-DV and Improved IW-DV

Fig. 5. Comparison by varying total number of nodes

Simulation results for IWCL and Improved IWCL algorithm where the total count of nodes is varied are shown in Fig 5 (c). It can be again observed that Improved IWCL has lower localization error as compared to IWCL as IWCL has localization error that is in between 1.15 to 1.2, whereas Improved IWCL has an error that lies in between 0.23 to 0.24. Also Improved IWCL is more stable algorithm as localization error is almost same when the total number of nodes is varied.

As depicted in Fig 5 (d), with the increase of the total number of nodes, the localization error of improved hyperbolic is lower than hyperbolic algorithm while keeping total anchor nodes and communication radius constant.

Fig 5 (e) illustrates results for IW-DV Hop and Improved IW-DV Hop when the total count of nodes is varied keeping anchor nodes constant. Proposed algorithm achieves higher localization accuracy compared to IW-DV Hop. Average localization error of IW-DV Hop and Improved IW-DV Hop is 1.33 and 0.24, respectively.

Figs 4 and 5 prove that the proposed algorithms outperform original algorithms when compared in terms of localization error when varying parameters: total anchor nodes and total nodes. Thus, the idea of taking only near anchors improves localization accuracy of DV- Hop algorithms. I have applied this idea on few DV-Hop algorithms. In general, it can be applied to all DV-Hop algorithms.

V. Conclusions and Future Scope

In wireless sensor networks, where cost is one of the important factors, range-free localization algorithms are more popular due to their cost effective nature. Among these range-free localization algorithms, DV-Hop algorithm is preferred because of its significance to localize any kind of node having even less than three neighboring nodes. Due to its popularity, many DV-Hop based algorithms have been proposed. These algorithms use all the anchor nodes to localize a given node, which affects its localization accuracy. To improve localization accuracy, an improvement has been made by considering only a few near anchor nodes for finding location of node as near anchors are the best option to localize a given node with the minimum number of hop counts. In order to prove this, the improved algorithms have been implemented and simulated. The simulation results show that the near anchors have an important role in localization accuracy. The accuracy gets better by nearly 1R meter when we use few near anchors to localize a node.

In future, we will try to reduce energy for all these algorithms which is also the limitation of all these DV-Hop based algorithms. Also, anchor mobility needs to be considered in all these algorithms.

References

[1] Liu, H., Nayak, A., & Stojmenovic, I. (2010). Applications, models, problems, and solution strategies. *Wireless Sensor and Actuator Networks: Algorithms and Protocols for Scalable Coordination and Data Communication*, 1-32.

[2] He, T., Huang, C., Blum, B. M., Stankovic, J. A., & Abdelzaher, T. (2003, September). Range-free localization schemes for large scale sensor networks. In *Proceedings of the 9th annual international conference on Mobile computing and networking* (pp. 81-95). ACM.

[3] Kunz, T., & Tatham, B. (2012). Localization in wireless sensor networks and anchor placement. *Journal of Sensor and Actuator Networks*, *1*(1), 36-58.

[4] Panwar, A., & Kumar, S. A. (2012, January). Localization schemes in wireless sensor networks. In *Advanced Computing & Communication Technologies (ACCT), 2012 Second International Conference on* (pp. 443-449). IEEE.

[5] Niculescu, D., & Nath, B. (2003). DV based positioning in ad hoc networks. *Telecommunication Systems*, *22*(1), 267-280.

[6] Zhang, B., Ji, M., & Shan, L. (2012, September). A weighted centroid localization algorithm based on DV-hop for wireless sensor network. In *Wireless Communications, Networking and Mobile Computing (WiCOM), 2012 8th International Conference on* (pp. 1-5). IEEE.

[7] Song, G., & Tam, D. (2015). Two novel DV-Hop localization algorithms for randomly deployed wireless sensor networks. *International Journal of Distributed Sensor Networks, 2015.*

[8] Alrajeh, N. A., Bashir, M., & Shams, B. (2013). Localization techniques in wireless sensor networks. *International Journal of Distributed Sensor Networks*, *9*(6), 304628.

[9] Nagpal, R., Shrobe, H., & Bachrach, J. (2003). Organizing a global coordinate system from local information on an ad hoc sensor network. In *Information processing in sensor networks* (pp. 553-553). Springer Berlin/Heidelberg.

[10] Bahl, P., & Padmanabhan, V. N. (2000). RADAR: An in-building RF-based user location and tracking system. In *INFOCOM 2000. Nineteenth Annual Joint Conference of the IEEE Computer and Communications Societies. Proceedings. IEEE* (Vol. 2, pp. 775-784). Ieee.

[11] Tomic, S., & Mezei, I. (2016). Improvements of DV-Hop localization algorithm for wireless sensor networks. *Telecommunication Systems*, *61*(1), 93-106.

[12] Peng, B., & Li, L. (2015). An improved localization algorithm based on genetic algorithm in wireless sensor networks. *Cognitive neurodynamics*, *9*(2), 249-256.

[13] Akyildiz, I. F., Su, W., Sankarasubramaniam, Y., & Cayirci, E. (2002). A survey on sensor networks. *IEEE Communications magazine*, *40*(8), 102-114.

[14] Shang, Y., & Ruml, W. (2004, March). Improved MDS-based localization. In *INFOCOM 2004. Twenty-third AnnualJoint Conference of the IEEE Computer and Communications Societies* (Vol. 4, pp. 2640-2651). IEEE.

[15] Hou, S., Zhou, X., & Liu, X. (2010, July). A novel DV-hop localization algorithm for asymmetry distributed wireless sensor networks. In *Computer Science and Information Technology (ICCSIT), 2010 3rd IEEE International Conference on* (Vol. 4, pp. 243-248). IEEE.

[16] Han, G., Chao, J., Zhang, C., Shu, L., & Li, Q. (2014). The impacts of mobility models on DV-hop based localization in mobile wireless sensor networks. *Journal of Network and Computer Applications*, *42*, 70-79.

[17] Wang, X., Fu, M., & Zhang, H. (2012). Target tracking in wireless sensor networks based on the combination of KF and MLE using distance measurements. *IEEE Transactions on Mobile Computing*, *11*(4), 567-576.

[18] Safa, H. (2014). A novel localization algorithm for large scale wireless sensor networks. *Computer communications*, *45*, 32-46.

[19] Venkatesh, S., & Buehrer, R. M. (2006, April). A linear programming approach to NLOS error mitigation in sensor networks. In *Proceedings of the 5th international conference on Information processing in sensor networks* (pp. 301-308). ACM.

[20] Kaur, A., Kumar, P., & Gupta, G. P. (2016). Localization in Wireless Sensor Networks: A survey. *International Journal of Innovations & Advancement in Computer Science IJIACS ISSN*, 2347-8616.

[21] Kaur, A., Gupta, G. P., & Kumar, P. (2017). A Survey of Recent Developments in DV-Hop Localization Techniques for Wireless Sensor Network. *Journal of Telecommunication, Electronic and Computer Engineering (JTEC)*, *9*(2), 61-71.

[22] Kaur, A., Kumar, P., & Gupta, G. P. (2017). A weighted centroid localization algorithm for randomly deployed wireless sensor networks. *Journal of King Saud University-Computer and Information Sciences*.

[23] A.Kaur, P.Kumar, G.P.Gupta," A novel DV-Hop algorithm based on Gauss-Newton method", In IEEE International Conference on Parallel, Distributed and Grid Computing,pp. 625-629, 2016.

[24] Ahmad, T., Li, X. J., & Seet, B. C. (2016, June). A self-calibrated centroid localization algorithm for indoor ZigBee WSNs. In *Communication Software and Networks (ICCSN), 2016 8th IEEE International Conference on* (pp. 455-461). IEEE.

[25] Ahmad, T., Li, X. J., & Seet, B. C. (2017). Parametric Loop Division for 3D Localization in Wireless Sensor Networks. *Sensors*, *17*(7), 1697.

3D FACIAL MODEL FOR ANALYSING THE FACIAL PARALYSIS

Banita
PhD Research Scholar
School of Computer Science
Lingaya's University
Faridabad, Haryana
banita861023@yahoo.com

Dr. PoonamTanwar
Associate Professor
School of Computer Science
Manav Rachna International University
Faridabad , Haryana
poonam.tanwar@rediffmail.com

ABSTRACT:

Facial expressions play a vital role in facial recognition and also help to evaluate the level of facial paralysis. The dimensions of facial expressions can also be represented by movement of facial muscles which is directly proportional to the ageing factors. As the facial muscles weakens, it changes the facial expressions of both the sides of the face which can be evaluated by use of image processing. Image processing introduced a new platform for various methodologies to evaluate the level of facial paralysis. Image processing techniques are helpful for facial recognition, facial expression and to identify the degree of paralysis. Number of technologies has been introduced by the researchers in terms of 2Dimensional (2D) and 3Dimensional (3D). 3D imaging like Multiboosting and Support Vector Machine (SVM) Classifiers, KD Tree portrait rendering process, Vertex Tent Coordinate (VTC) and Automatic Land Marking (ALM). The common image databases used for face recognition in 2D and in 3D are FRET, UMB-DB, UMB- DB and FRGC. This Paper introduces the high accuracy of facial expressions in 3 Dimensional as compared to 2 Dimensional facial images.

Keywords: facial expressions, face recognition, image processing, 3DUltrasonography, Classification

I. INTRODUCTION:

Facial expressions plays a vital role in face recognition, evaluating dimensions of facial muscles, analysis of facial movement and also evaluating the level of facial paralysis. There are 6 universal facial expressions which are Happiness, Anger, Fear, Disgust, Sadness, and Surprised which are evaluated by the use of facial landmarks [1]. For facial landmarks one of the most common and easy techniques is Salient Point Detection method which can be static or dynamic but the accuracy may vary with change in the mode i.e. static or dynamic [1]. When the landmarks have been marked manually then it is the dynamic mode whereas when landmarks have been fixed and can't be changed then it is termed as static mode. The average recognition rate is 97% has been achieved by using machine learning algorithm which has been used for face recognition as well as for facial expressions [1]. In 3D using Bosphorus Dataset, 24 facial landmarks are used for evaluating the dimensions of face along with different facial regions. In frontal face image 12 landmarks have been used in common for case of 2D [29]. The 3D facial landmarks give large data for face recognition and facial expressions [2]. While in 2D using Bosphorus dataset 18-20 facial landmarks are used for evaluating the dimensions of face along with different facial regions. Facial land marking has been marked on face at rest and face at motion or performing facial expressions in 2D as well as in 3D facial imaging. While comparison between 2D and 3D there is high resolution in 3D and also overcome the pose variation dimensions [27] whereas low resolution in 2D and also there is a problem in pose variation dimensions [4]. 2D imaging of face includes the coordinates along X-axis and Y-axis whereas in 3D imaging of face includes the dimensions along X-axis, Y-axis and Z-axis. Height and width of facial surface is covered in 2D whereas Height, width and depth of facial surface is covered in 3D by use of 3D-MAD (3-Dimensional Mask Attack Database) [26].Tanasai Sucontphunt et.al.[5] presented an interactive 3D facial expressions posing system through 2D portrait manipulation. To remove head motion, Singular Value Decomposition (SVD) has been used [5].

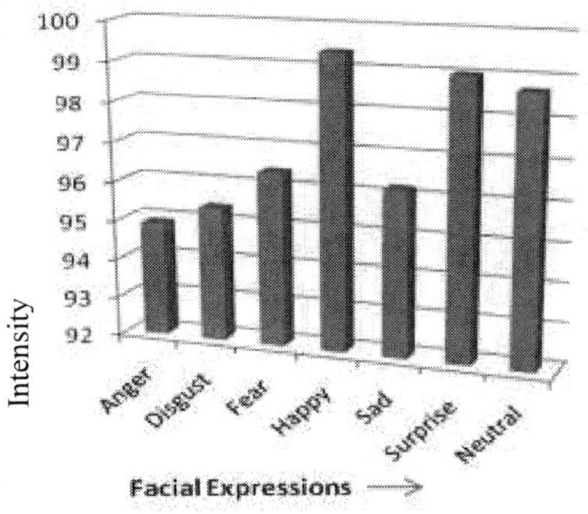

Fig.1. Computer recognition Intensity

The most likely similar expressions were sad-fear and disgust-angry as clearly shown in Fig.1.[7].

II. DATASETS FOR FACE RECOGINITION

For face recognition database which have been widely used are:

1. *BU-3DFE:*BU-3DFE (Binghamton University – 3 D Facial Expressions is one of the commonly used databases of 3D facial expressions [1] [18]. The facial landmarks used in BU-3DFE database have specific deformations evaluation of face with the help of various facial expressions. This dataset includes only facial expressions and its respective facial image at rest. The evaluation is strictly based on the distance calculation between control point and the reference point on facial regions.

2. *UMB-DB:* It is defined as "University Of Milano Bicocca- Face Database". UMB-DB has been used for evaluating facial images in 3D. UMB-DB includes the set of 3 Dimensional as well as 2Dimensional facial images at rest and at motion.

3. *Bosphorus Database:* Bosphorus dataset in commonly used in 2 Dimensional as well as 3 Dimensional facial images [33] [24]. It includes 6 basic emotions with respect to 28 action Units. In 3 Dimensional there are 24 landmarks which have been placed along with different facial regions.

Fig.2 Datasets used for 2 Dimensional Image

4. *FERET:* Face Recognition Technology (FERET) is a dataset which has been used for automatic facial landmarks recoginition. FERET dataset is based on facial images which is further evaluated in terms of facial recognition. FERET is a collection of large database of facial images at rest and facial images at motion. Independent Component Analysis and Neural Networks the two common methods used in 2D face images with the help of FERET database. 200 images in both methods has been recorded and the recognition rate after evaluation, 89 % and 99 % respectively [2] which represents that FERET provides high recognition rate in 2D facial images.

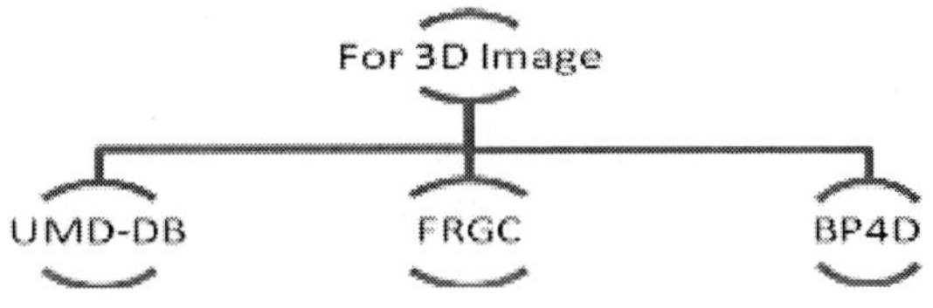

Fig.3 Datasets used for 3 Dimensional Image

5. *BU-4DFE:* It is generally used for evaluation of facial expressions by use of video recording. The facial expressions in videos have been decoded as per the facial landmarks with the help of image processing. In BU-4DFE 6 expressions have been recorded for evaluation but it does not include the facial land marking process.

6. *FRGC:* Face Recognition Grand Challenge FRGC) is the advancement of face recognition technology [22]. There are 3 categories of FRGC:

- FRGC dataset
- FRGC BEE
- Baseline algorithm

FRGC generally record the images on random selection and is further splits in to two sections: First section includes testing process and the second section includes training process [22]. For facial recognition in 3D FRGC v2.0 database is widely used [24]. It represents competitive performance and good generalization ability [24].

III. DATASETS FOR FACIAL EXPRESSIONS:

Dataset for face recognition and facial expression evaluation is used and it also helps in the evaluation of degree of facial paralysis. Facial paralyzed patients suffer from Dysfunctioning of muscles with respect to the facial expressions. Due to which there has been a huge change in the dimensions of face. For calculating the level of facial paralysis, image processing plays a great role. Facial Image can be stored at rest and at motion. By comparing the distance of different facial regions, the level of facial paralysis can be calculated. In facial paralysis left side of face has been compared with the dimensions of right side of face. More the difference in dimensions, severe is the facial paralysis. But facial paralysis can be 100% cured only when the precaution has been followed by the facial paralyzed patients within 72 hours of paralysis and cured within 90 days. There may be any reason for facial paralysis but it can be cured by various drugs like Acyclovir, Corticosteroids. For facial recognition different datasets have been used by researchers.
Similarly for facial paralysis evaluation different datasets have been used to evaluate the degree of facial paralysis and the accuracy of detecting facial paralysis.

1. *FACES:* Facial expression Coding System (FACES) is commonly used in case of video recording of facial expressions. FACES is basically used to analyze the frequency and intensity. FACES is lagging in terms of accuracy as it only includes 4 facial expressions i.e. Happiness, Sadness, Anger, Fear. Kring and Sloan in 2007 introduce FACES to analyze the four expressions in two different types of sections. The first section is totally based on the video recorded in an intended emotion session [15]. Second section includes the facial images which are actually from the corresponding intended emotion session .Facial Images have been stored for evaluation of degree of facial paralysis. Facial image can be in 2 Dimensional or in 3 Dimensions.

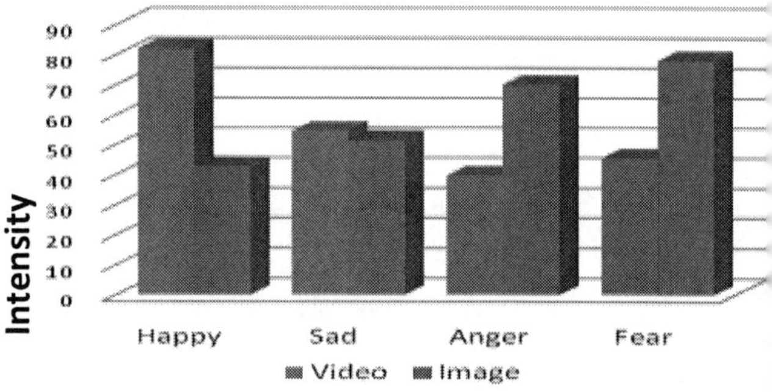

Fig.4 Comparison of Image and Video of emotions in terms of intensity.

The four facial expressions have been recorded with FACES dataset. Each facial expression consists of two different variations in intensity as video and image data have been stored simultaneously. Fig.3 indicates that there is a huge intensity variation during "Happy" facial expression. But on the second facial expression i.e. "Sad" approximate equal intensity have been recorded. FACES conclude that facial image has more accuracy and intensity while comparing with the video of facial expressions. Hence concludes image processing plays a great role in evaluation of intensities at different facial expressions.

2. *BFSC:*Basic Facial Shape Component (BFSC) is used in detecting facial expressions. BFSC basically uses 6universal expressions and at last facial expressions get compared with the face at rest [21][17].

BFSC deals with the shape of face whether smiling, anger. Hence deals with 6 facial expressions as Anger, Disgust, Fear, Happiness, Sad, and Surprised. Cornella Lanz et.al. [20] Proposes a robust method for facial landmarks localization using 2 Dimensional facial expression images. It concludes that a deviation of one pixel corresponds to about 1.5 millimetersbecause the landmark positions has been marked manually which results in slight variation [20].

Boqing Gong et.al.[21] represent a 3 Dimensional face with expression. It is generated by the two categories. First category includes the shape of face, dimensions of face along X,Y and Z-axis. Second category includes Expressional Shape Component (ESC) [21] which includes the deep information of the facial expressions and its respective dimensions.

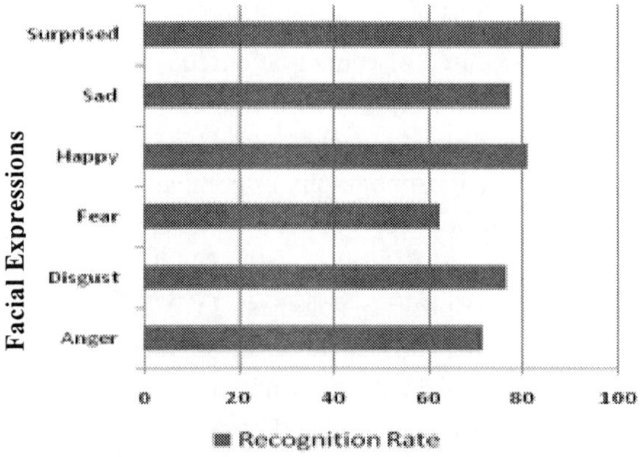

Fig.5 Average Recognition accuracy

The lowest recognition rate is under facial expression "Fear". The highest recognition rate has been achieved in facial expression "Surprised".

3. *FACS:* Facial Action Coding System (FACS) has been used for describing facial movements. FACS includes 9 different Action Units (AU) [3][8]. AU can be termed as facial landmarks while evaluating degree of facial paralysis. Before evaluating the face image this method divide the image into two halves. Upper part of face and lower part of face. Different facial regions indicated by number of different landmarks. AU varies with change in facial expressions. Lei Zhao et.al. [3] concludes that many structural details may be lost when histogram of entire image is evaluated directly.

4. ***VTC:*** Vertex Tent Coordinate is the encoding method which is used for face representation at rest and face at motion. It is represented by "v ".
Local Geometry of face = First Component + Second Component.

Here first component includes matrix which consists of set of vectors. Second Component includes additional matrix which is termed as v_{n+1}[6]. The main advantage of VTC is that the face geometry which is represented in VTC is not based only on triangle basis but it further introduces new mesh technology for evaluation of face dimensions at rest and during expressions. The VTC based deformation transfer is represented as Q.

$$Q = w \mid w^T(ww^T)^{-1} \quad [6]$$

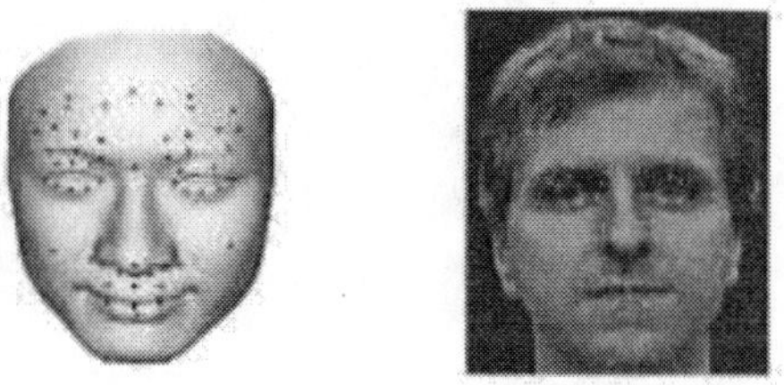

Fig.6 Landmarks on 3D face image and 2D face image. [6]

VTC method has been used to calculate the variation in dimension between face at rest and face during expression. VTC based deformation transfer method has been used to map the source expression on to the target facial expression. [6]

Facial landmarks vary in 2 Dimensional face images and in 3 Dimensional face images as in Fig.5. Facial image at rest and facial image during expressions has been recorded and analyzed by use of VTC analogy.

5. ***3D Ultrasonography:*** 3 Dimensional Ultrasonography has been used in medical science. It is used for detecting the area affected by facial palsy. 3D Ultrasonography is used for analyzing facial muscles.
Ratio = Palsy Side of face / Healthy side of face [14].
Gred Fabian Volk et.al. 2014 proposed 3D Ultrasonography on 7 facial palsy patients. There are 5 facial muscles on which 3D Ultrasonography worked upon:
    - Frontal Muscles
    - Orbicularis Oculi Muscles
    - Depressor AnguliOris Muscles
    - Depressor Labii inf. Muscles
    - Mentalis Muscles

Due to weakness in facial muscles there has been a huge variation in face during facial expressions.

Fig.7 3D Ultrasonography [14]

The perspective of 3D Ultrasonography in medical science is to evaluate the performance of different facial muscles and compare the performance between healthy and affected side of face [14].

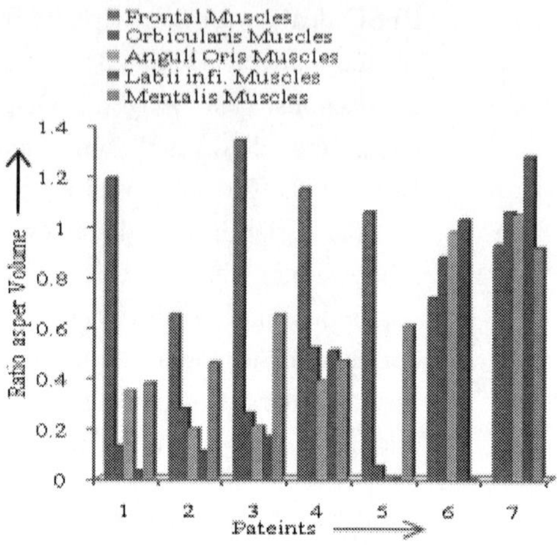

Fig.8.Facial Palsy ratio using Partial Volume (mm^3)

3D Ultrasonography has been used for facial paralyzed patients by evaluating the affected region in facial muscles. By evaluated the variation in facial muscles along with left and right side of face it can be easily detected that whether the facial palsy can be cured or cannot be cured. Large variation in ratio represents the more affected region in facial muscles. The advantage of 3D Ultrasonography as compared to MRI is cost effective, better accessibility and fast potential to quantify facial muscle sand its respective volumes. In MRI technique of medical science facial muscles has been evaluated as symmetrical or asymmetrical whereas in 3D Ultrasonography it detects the actual level of damage in facial muscles i.e. zygomaticus, Orbicularis oris and Oculi, Levatorlabiisuperioris and nasalis muscles [14].

As 3D Ultrasonography has been used in medical science to detect whether the constructive surgery is helpful to the facial paralysis patient [14]. 80% of facial paralyzed patients have defective healing after surgery which indicates that there is change in dimensions of face during expressions and at rest. Also 3D Ultrasonography helps to monitor the time course of muscle gain or muscle loss after therapeutic intervention in the face [14].

IV. Effectiveness in 3D

There are number of findings in 2D and in 3D in case of trailhead maps. It leads to different strength and weaknesses for trailhead maps communication w.r.t. 2D and 3D. In 3D the properties of 2D remains as such but additional to that it contains perspectives that diminishes the scale of distant [9]. Yi Lin et. al [10] in 2016 proposed a novel approach for analyzing Smile expression which has been split in to three categories:

- *Static:* Face image recorded at rest
- *Smile:* Face image recorded during smile expression.
- *Laugh*: Face image recorded during extreme smile i.e. laugh. It is a full-fledged smiling expression at maximum limit.

All the three categories have been analyzed using three dimensional reconstruction and analysis along with dimensions of left side of face and right side of face. Facial Landmarks localization [11] has been applied to evaluate the relationship between smile and laugh. BerkGokberk et.al [11] concludes that 3D face recognition when used with 2D then it results to make face a very strong biometric modality which has been widely acceptable for general public in terms of accuracy [11]. GuodongFeng et.al. [19] in 2014 established and analyze the facial motion by use of reliability test. The study meets the level of clinical and researchers need for detecting the face motion during different expressions. Debbie S. Ma et.al.[23] in 2015 introduced the Chicago face database which includes both physical and subjective norming data to analyze the mean suitability of gender and target race by use of adobe Photoshop software.

V. PARAMETERS IN 3D EVALUATION:

Algorithm is strictly based on 3D image processing which is very helpful to calculate the distance between healthy and affected side of face. It is used to detect the degree of facial paralysis and to detect the damage of facial nerve. Face model in 3D works on four facial nerve branches {out of five branches}. In this study out of five branches of the facial nerve four branches have been taken for study:

a. Temporal branch
b. Zygomatic branch
c. Buccal branch
d. Mandibular branch.
e. Cervical branch {not included in study}

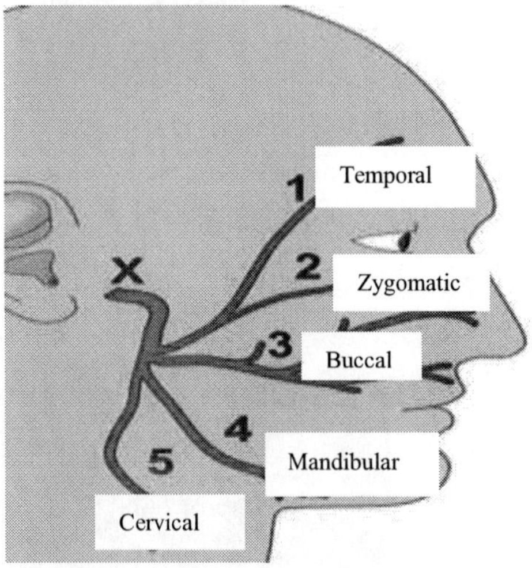

Fig.9 Branches of facial nerve.

Degree of facial palsy= Affected facial region – healthy facial region.

By considering ear to ear coverage i.e. depth, there will be high accuracy in calculating the degree of facial palsy.

RESULT OF PREPROCESSING:

Before preprocessing facial image of facial palsy patient, is stored and preprocessing is done, which helps to analyze the edges of face. The variation in distance evaluation of the facial landmarks shows the level of facial paralysis w.r.t HBGS.

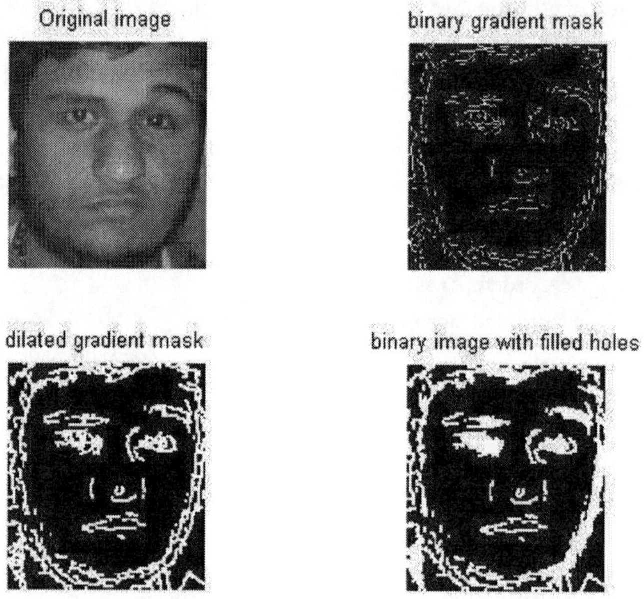

Figure 10. Preprocessing of face model

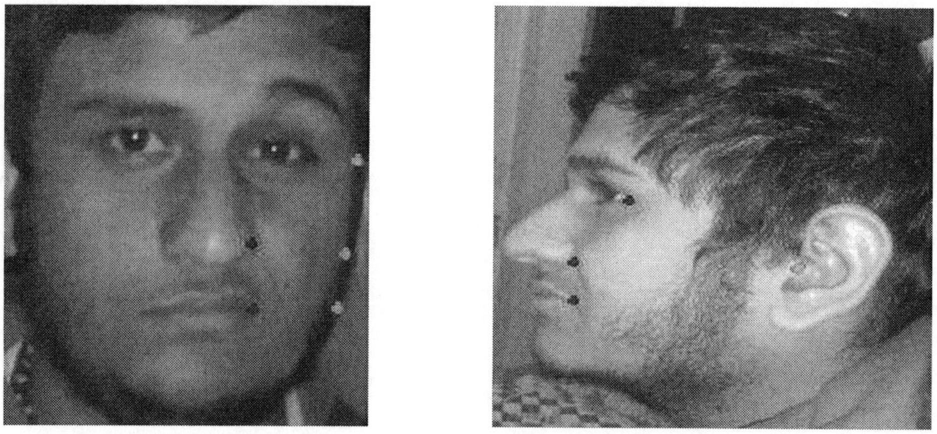

Fig.10 Left side facial landmarks [2D, 3D]

Facial landmarks are indicated in different fiducial points. Red color facial landmarks on facial regions represent the reference points in terms of 2D and green color landmarks represent key points in 2D facial image as in fig.10. Whereas red color facial landmarks on facial regions represent the reference point and green color landmark represent the key point in 3D facial image.

TESTING AND OUTCOMES

In testing phase the best distance evaluation were found in 3D image because it deals with ear to ear coverage of face model of facial paralyzed patients. Algorithm actual works on the facial paralyzed patients in terms of detecting the level of facial paralysis and its prognosis.

Table1. Comparison between various techniques and their outcomes

Work	Methodology	Outcomes
PitchayaSitthi-Amorn et.al. [12]	• Optical coherence Tomography 3D scanner.	• System allows for self-calibration of print heads and 3D scanning.
Kevin W. Bowyer et.al. in 2005 by Elsevier [13]	• Multimodal 2D+3D, 3D sensors.	• Multimodal performance is greater than the performance of 2D alone.
Lijun Yin et.al in 2008 [16]	• HMM based 3D spatial temporal facial descriptor.	• Average correct recognition rate of 90.44% for distinguishing 6 prototypic expressions
Kenneth Alberto Funes Mora et.al. in 2014 [25]	• RGB-D Camera • Gaze estimation algorithm	• Help to advance the development of Gaze estimation technologies under less constrained conditions.
Omkar M. Parkhi et.al. in 2015 [28]	• YouTube Face dataset (YTF) • Labeled faces in the wild dataset (LFW) • Equal error rate (EER)	• Large scale dataset assembled.
Shu Zhang et.al. [30]	• K-means algorithm is used.	• Achieves a high density of 3D face point cloud.
Bouguezzi Adel et.al. in 2014, Vol.2 No. 5-A [31]	• Medical prescriptions are considered.	• Evaluation is done on the basis of medical treatment.
Gary Lekakis et.al.in 2016 [32]	• 3D Imaging	• 3D data used to increase the predictability of surgical results in Rhinoplasty.
Amir Zadeh et.al. in Nov. 2016 [34]	• Deep neural network (DNN)	• DCLM is able to accurately align the 68 facial landmarks.

VI. Conclusion:

This study represents a new concept of dataset used in 3 Dimensional facial images for face recognition as well as for facial expressions. Intensity may vary with change in facial expressions. Surprised facial expression results in highest recognition rate whereas fear facial expression shows lowest recognition rate. Bosphorus dataset with use of landmarks o facial expressions helps to evaluate the level of facial paralysis in 2D as well as in 3D. As per the observation study works for facial paralysis but existing are in facial expressions and face recognition.

It is further concluded that for analyzing facial paralysis and dimensions of face in 3D, Bosphorus dataset and VTC is helpful in great extent. Adding large number of landmarks and considering respective facial regions in 3D is one of the future directions for evaluating the level of facial paralysis.

References:

[1] Ahmed Maalej, Boulbaba Ben Amor, Mohamed Daoudi , AnjuSrivastava, Stefano Berretti "Shape Analysis of Local facial Patches for 3D Facial Expression Recoginition",Vol.44, No.8, January 2012.

[2] J.Bobulski , "Multimodal face recognition method with two dimensional hidden Markov Model", Vol.65, No.1, 2017.

[3] Lei Zhao, Zengcai Wang and Guoxin Zhang "Facial Expression Recognition from Video Sequences Based on Spatial-Temporal Motion Local Binary Pattern and Gabor Multiorientation Fusion Histogram", Vol.2017, Article ID 7206041 .

[4] Michel F.Valstar, Enrique Sanchez-Lozano, Jeffrey F. Cohn, Laszlo A. Jeni, Jeffrey M. Girad, Zheng Zhang, Lijun Yin and MajaPantic"FERA 2017-Addressing Head Pose in the Third Facial Expression Recognition and Analysis Challenge", February 2017.

[5] TanasaiSucontphunt, Zhenyao Mo, Ulrich Neumann and Zhigang Deng ,"Interactive 3d Facial Expression Posing through 2D Portrait Manipulation", May 2008.

[6] Mingli Song and Zhao Dong "A Generic Framework for Efficient 2D and 3D Facial Analogy", IEEE Transactions on Multimedia.

[7] Lijun Yin, Xiaozhou Wei, Yi Sun, Jun Wang and Matthew J. Rosato "A 3D Facial Expression Database For Facial Behaviour Research", Publishes in Automatic Face and Gesture Recognition, 7th International Conference of IEEE, 2006.

[8] T. Fang, X. Zhao, O. Ocegueda, S.K. Shah and I.A. Kakadiaris "3D Facial Expression Recognition : A Prespective on Promises and Challenges", pp-603-610.

[9] David Schobesberger, and Tom Patterson "Evaluating the Effectiveness of 2D vs. 3D Trailhead Maps", January 2008.

[10] Yi Lin, Han Lin, Qiuping Lin, Jinxin Zhang, Ping Zhu, Yao Lu, Zhi Zhao, JiahongLv, Min Kyeong Lee &YueXu , "A novel three dimensional smile analysis based on dynamic evaluation of facial curve contour", Open Access in Scientific Reports, February 2016.

[11] BerkGokberk, Albert Ali Salah, NeseAlyiiz and LaleAkarun, "3D Face Recognition ", Chapter 1 in Handbook of Remote Biometrics in Springer, pp - 217-246.

[12] PitchayaSitthi-Amorn, Javier E. Ramos, Yuwang Wang, Joyce Kwan, Justin Lan, Wenshou Wang and WojciechMatusik, "MultiFab: A Machine Assisted Platform for Multi-material 3D Printing", Published by The Computational Fabrication Group, 2015.

[13] Kevin W. Bowyer, Kyong Chang and Patrick Flynn, "A Survey of approaches and challenges in 3D and multi-modal 3D+2D face recoginition", Published in Computer Vision and Image Understanding by Elsevier, Vol .1, No.15, 2006.

[14] Gerd Fabian Volk, Martin Pohlmann, Mira Finkensieper, Heather J Chalmers and Orlando Guntias-Lichius, "3D-Ultrasonography for evaluation of facial muscles in patients with chronic facial palsy or defective healing: a pilot study", Vol. 14, No.4, Open access in Bio Med Central, 2014.

[15]Peng Wang, Frederick Barrett, Elizabeth Martin, Marina Milonova, Raquel E Gur, Ruben C. Gur, Christian Kohler and RaginiVerma, "Automated video-based facial expression analysis of neuropsychiatric disorders", Journal of Neuroscience Methods 168 (2008) pp. 224-238, 2008.

[16] Lijun Yin, Xiaochen Chen, Yi Sun, Tony Worm and Michael Reale, "A High – Resolution 3D Dynamic Facial Expression Database", 2008.

[17] Lijun Yin, Xiaochen Wei, Peter Longo and AbhineshBhuvanesh, "Analyzing Facial Expressions Using Intensity-Variant 3D Data For Human Computer Interaction", IEEE, 2006.

[18] Asim Jan and HingyingMeng, "Automatic 3D Facial Expression Recognition using Geometric and Textured Featured Fusion".

[19] GuodongFeng, Yang Zhao, XuTian, ZhiqiangGao, "A New 3-Dimensional Dynamic Quantitative Analysis System of Facial Motion: An Establishment and Reliability Test ", Vol.9, Issue 11, November 2014.

[20] Cornelia Lanz, Joachim Denzler and Horst-Michael Gross, "Robust landmark localization for facial therapy applications",.

[21] Boqing Gong, Yueming Wang, JianzhuangLui and Xiaoou Tang, "Automatic Facial Expression Recognition on a Single 3D Face by Exploring Shape Deformation", Beijing, China, pp 569-572, Oct. 2009.

[22] Yinije Lei, Mohammed Bennamoun, Munawar Hayat, YulanGuo, "An efficient 3D face recognition approach using local geometrical signatures", Elsevier Ltd. , 2013.

[23] Debbie S. Ma, Joshua Correll and Bernd Wittenbrink, "The Chicago face database: A free stimulus set of faces and norming data", Vol.47, pp 1122-1135, Springer, January 2015.

[24] Huibin Li, Di Huang, Jean-Marie Morvan, Yunhong Wang and Liming Chen, "Towards 3D Face Recognition in the Real: A Registration-Free Approach Using Fine-Grained Matching of 3D Keypoint Descriptors", Int J Comput Vis, November 2014.

[25] Kenneth Alberto Funes Mora, FlorentMonay and Jean-Marc Odobez, "EYEDIAP: A Database for the Development and Evaluation of Gaze Estimation Algorithms from RGB and RGB-D Cameras", Eye TrackinG Research & Applications, 2014.

[26] NesliErdogmus and Sebastein Marcel, "Spoofing in 2D Face Recognition with 3D Masks and Anti-spoofing with Kinect".

[27] Amin Jourabloo and XiaomingLui, "Pose-Invariant 3D Face Alignment", Open Access Version by Computer Vision Foundation, IEEE, pp 3694-3702

[28] OmkarM.Parkhi, Andrea Vedaldi and Andrew Zisserman, "Deep Face Recoginition", 2015.

[29] Carlos Andres Cardenas Palacio and Francisco Alejandro Munera Galarza, "Cutaneous Sensibility Changes in Bell's Palsy Patients", American Academy of Otolaryngology- Head and Neck Surgery, 2017.

[30] ShuZang, Hui Yu, Junyu Dong, Ting Wang and HonghaiLui, "Automatic Reconstruction of Dense 3D Face Point Cloud with A Single Depth Image".

[31] Bouguezzi Adel, SouidKawthar, Derbel Amine, Ben Youssef Souha and BoughzalaAbdellatif, "Idiopathic Facial Paralysis", International Journal of Dental Science and Research, Vol.2, No.5-A, 2014.

[32] GaryfaliaLekakis, Peter Claes, Grant S. Hamilton and P.W. Hellings, "Three-Dimensional Surface Imaging and the Continuous Evolution of Preoperative and Postoperative Assessment in Rhinoplasty", Thieme Medical Publishers,New York, USA, 2016.

[33] Anke Schwarz, Esther-Sabrina Wacker, Manuel Martin, M. SaquibSarfraz and Rainer Stiefelhagen, "3D Facial Landmark Detection : How to Deal with Head Rotations? ", Springer International Publishing Switzerland , pp 424-434 , 2015.

[34] Amir Zadeh ,TadasBaltrusaitis and Louis-Philippe Morency , "Deep Constrained Local Models for Facial Landmark Detetction".

AN INTUITIONISTIC FUZZY AHP BASED MULTI CRITERIA RECOMMENDER SYSTEM FOR LIFE INSURANCE PRODUCTS

AKSHAY HINDUJA*
Department of Computer Application,
NIT Raipur, Chhattisgarh, INDIA
hinduja.akshay@gmail.com

Dr. MANJU PANDEY
Department of Computer Application,
NIT Raipur, Chhattisgarh, INDIA
manjutiwa@gmail.com

Abstract. Life insurance products play an important role in providing security for the family and support in times of contingencies. Therefore opting for an insurance product is a very crucial decision for a person. Impact of financial liberalization has affected the insurance market of India. In recent years, life insurance demand has experienced a rapid growth in Indian market. The notable increase in the competition among insurance companies has resulted in numerous insurance products being available in the market. The plethora of insurance products often confuses the buyers and that can lead to a wrong insurance product selection. Therefore, a constant requirement of assistance is growing in order to buy insurance products that are most suitable to consumers' personalized requirements. The existing recommender systems functions based on machine learning techniques that are not suitable for the critical products like Insurance. In order to overcome limitations of the existing recommender systems, we develop an original perception based Multi Criteria Recommender System that suggests insurance products based on intuitionistic fuzzy analytic hierarchy process. The proposed system has been tested by distinguishing insurance officials and experts. They have validated the results and found them significantly accurate. We also carried out an empirical study to check the accuracy of the proposed system and found the results 91% accurate.

Keywords: Multi Criteria Recommender System; Intuitionistic Fuzzy AHP; Life Insurance; Multi Criteria Decision Making.

1. Introduction

Life insurance products play an important part in providing security for the family and support in times of contingencies. These products are actually the risk management tool based on actuarial science. Insurance products do not only protect buyer's family from any contingency but also help in financial planning as an investment instrument. Impact of financial liberalization has also affected the insurance market of India. In recent years, life insurance demand has experienced a rapid growth in Indian market. The remarkable increase in competition within the insurance sector of the India has resulted in a number of insurance products being available in the market. The plethora of different insurance product often confuses the buyers and that can lead to a wrong insurance product selection. Therefore, a constant requirement of assistance is growing in order to buy insurance products that are most suitable to consumers' personalized requirements.

High-quality decisions making requires sufficient amount of information. Nevertheless, numerous instances prove that excess of information can also adversely affect the decision as insufficient information. The scenario of this overwhelming information is called the information overload problem (Adomavicius & Kwon, 2007; T L Saaty, 2008). In order to mitigate this problem, the Recommender System (RS) has been devised. It is greatly admired and helpful instrument of the current e-commerce scenario. Basically, it is an information filtering system that shows the only products and services, likely to be most useful to its users.

In this era of the Internet, the RS has been largely used by E-commerce websites to recommend products and services to their users that are likely to be purchased. These products and services often belong to the class of commodity intended to entertain users like movies, books, music, restaurants and online games. Some other applications of RS are Academic Paper Recommendation(Tang & Mccalla, 2009), Ontology-Based Recommendations for Tourists(Grün, Neidhardt, & Werthner, 2017), Personalized B2B E-

Services(Wu, Zhang, & Lu, 2014) and Intelligent Fashion Recommender System(Wang, Zeng, Koehl, & Chen, 2015). However, a product like Insurance that is meant to serve a vital purpose and whose purpose is to support its holder in future contingency requires more careful selection. The inception of liberalization in the economy and the approval of Foreign Direct Investment (FDI) in the insurance market of India have resulted into growing competition among insurance companies. This increasing competition among companies has given the opportunity to customers to choose insurance products that are most suitable for his/her financial future planning. Insurance products have multifaceted terminology and several features; hence the terms and conditions of the insurance are not easily understandable to the customers. Therefore, need for an RS for insurance products has been felt by consumers.

In this paper, we propose an Intuitionistic Fuzzy AHP (IFAHP) based Multi Criteria Recommender System (MCRS) that recommends most suitable insurance products to its users. User's preferences are elicited using IFAHP, which is intuitionistic fuzzy (Atanassov, 1986) extension of AHP (T L Saaty, 1980), a well known Multi Criteria Decision Making (MCDM) method. The proposed MCRS recommends insurance products that are likely to be most suitable to its users and the process is directed by their contextual preference. Proposed MCRS simplifies the procedure of insurance product selection by hiding multifaceted provisions, clauses, and reckonings of the insurance.

The remainder of the paper is organized as follows: In Section 2, we describe the elementary concepts used in our research. Section 3 portrays related works on recommender system and applications of AHP in recommender systems. Section 4 describes the methodology of the proposed system. We present an illustrative example to demonstrate the working of the proposed system in Section 5. In the last section, we made concluding remarks.

2. Preliminary

2.1 Recommender System:

The recommender system is a useful tool for information filtering and has been established as an effective method to solve *the information overload problem.* It has been developed to save consumers' valuable time while seeking for the services & goods of their required. The *'personalized'* and the *'likelihood to buy'* are the characteristics that distinguish the Recommender Systems from Information Retrieval Systems (Adomavicius, Manouselis, & Kwon, 2011). Recommender systems are classified on the basis of recommendation technique they use. Numerous recommendation techniques are proposed in the literature. All recommendation techniques have three basic blocks: background information, user input and the algorithm that combines the background information and the user input data to arrive at suggestions(Burke, 2007). In his paper, Burke(Burke, 2007) classifies the recommender systems as *Content based system (CBS),Collaborative filtering (CF), Demographic RS, Utility based RS, Knowledge based RS and hybrid RS.* The CBS uses metadata to find similarity among products while CF uses prior ratings to find similarity among users. Utility based RS calculates the utility of the items to users while knowledge based RS uses experts' repository. Hybrid RS can be any combination of aforementioned RSs.

2.2 Intuitionistic Fuzzy Analytic Hierarchy Process (IFAHP)

AHP, developed by (Thomas L Saaty, 1988), is a well-known MCDM method, which has been used in numerous real-world applications(Subramanian & Ramanathan, 2012). Despite its simplicity, AHP is regarded as one of the most powerful tools for managerial decision making. We can summarize the process of AHP in three steps: first, Decomposition of the problem in a hierarchical structure encompassing objective, criteria and alternatives; second, pairwise comparisons of the decision elements using a fundamental linguistic scale (see Table 1) developed by saaty and derivation of local priorities from these pairwise comparisons; third, synthesis of local priorities in order to computer overall priorities of the alternatives. The alternative with higher priority is regarded as the best option.

In spite of all the merits of AHP, it is often criticized for its inability to handle the inherent vagueness and uncertainty of the real-world decision problems. In saaty's AHP, the scale used for pair-wise comparison contains all crisp values. Many researchers applied fuzzy set theory(Zadeh, 1965) for capturing decision makers' opinions to overcome this shortcoming of AHP. Some of the prominent fuzzy AHP concepts are (van Laarhoven & Pedrycz, 1983), (Buckley, 1985) and (Chang, 1996). Although fuzzy AHP has enjoyed a great success nonetheless it fails to capture experts' judgments in a holistic manner. Fuzzy sets are defined by "degree of membership" and "degree of non-membership" but in real-world decision problems, there may be a degree of hesitancy in the judgments of experts due to inadequate knowledge, lack of interest or inherent uncertainty in the problem itself. Atanassov(Atanassov, 1986, 1994, 2012) extended the concept of the fuzzy set to intuitionistic fuzzy set (IFS), which is defined by "degree of membership", "degree of non-membership" and "degree of hesitancy". Formally, we can define IFS as:

$$A = \{(x, \mu_A(x), v_A(x)) | x \in X\} \tag{1}$$

Where x is an element of universal set X, function $\mu_A(x)$ represents degree of membership, function $v_A(x)$ represents degree of non-membership and degree of hesitancy is represented by $\pi_A(x) = 1 - \mu_A(x) - v_A(x)$.

Owing to its powerfulness in handling fuzzy information, the IFSs have been incorporated with several MCDM methods. (Xu & Liao, 2013) proposed intuitionistic fuzzy extension of the AHP method. They maintain the core principal of the AHP: decomposition, pairwise comparison, and synthesis; an intuitionistic fuzzy scale is used to gather experts' opinion (Table 1). They also develop a novel approach to check inconsistency and automatically repair it and priority method to derive priorities of the intuitionistic fuzzy pairwise comparison matrices. Due to the space limitation, only the summary of the methodology is given here, for the detailed methodology of IFAHP please refer (Xu & Liao, 2013).

Table 1: Original AHP scale & equivalent IFAHP scale (Xu & Liao, 2013)

Original AHP Scale	Linguistic Terms	IFS
1/9	Extremely Not Preferred	0.1
1/7	Very Strongly Not Preferred	0.2
1/5	Strongly Not Preferred	0.3
1/3	Moderately Not Preferred	0.4
1	Equally Preferred	0.5
3	Moderately Preferred	0.6
5	Strongly Preferred	0.7
7	Very Strongly Preferred	0.8
9	Extremely Preferred	0.9

** Use of intermediate values is allowed in both scales to present compromise.

3. Related Work

3.1 Recommender System

Recommender System has been an active research area for years and has been implemented in various applications(Manouselis & Costopoulou, 2007). In the realm of e-commerce, recommender system has been an inseparable part of various e-commerce websites (amazon.com, cdnow.com, drugstore.com) and proved itself a powerful technique of predicting user's interesting item(Schafer, 2001).

The majority of recommendation techniques are purely based on data mining techniques and co-relation among items and users without considering contextual information and user's need. Preference elicitation is the biggest challenges in the research area. Many researchers have applied different techniques of preference elicitation and user modeling. (Wang et al., 2015) proposed an Intelligent Fashion recommender system that recommends clothes according to body shape. (Nguyen & Ricci, 2017) proposed a chat-based group recommender system for tourists. (Kermany & Alizadeh, 2017) developed a hybrid recommender system for movie recommendations. The proposed RS integrates multi-criteria collaborative filtering and ontology to reach results. (Song & Sakao, 2018) proposed a Product-Service Systems (PSS) recommendation system, which uses rough theory to deal with vague information. Rough DEMALTEL and rough collaborative filtering are incorporated into recommendation framework. The authors also provide a case study on elevator PSS recommender system.

3.2 Application of AHP in Recommender System

Analytic Hierarchy Process (AHP) is a Multi Criteria Decision Making method introduced by T L Saaty in the late 1970s. Since then, the simplicity, robustness and group decision making are the features that led the AHP to its widespread popularity in the area of decision making. The AHP is most useful when groups of people are working on complex problems that need human opinion. AHP has been widely used in numerous multifarious application; some are resource allocation, healthcare, forecasting, benchmarking and quality management.

Marlinda *et al.*(Marlinda, Kreshana, & Sensuse, 2012) proposed a multi-criteria recommender system with AHP and Content-based Filtering to support potential students or high school graduates in selecting a field of study. Quan & Cho(Quan & Cho, 2014) proposed a Hybrid TV program recommender system that exploits Bayesian network and AHP. The recommender system consists of 3 parts: the first one is Group genre preference inference part that uses a hybrid AHP technique and Bayesian network to predict group preference. The second one is Candidate Program Integration, in this part candidate program is selected based on group preferences calculated in previous part and the last part is Program recommendation, in this part candidate program information is integrated with program preference (elicited by watching history). The proposed system also addressed cold start problem and claimed to solve it using Bayesian network. (Yuen, 2017) developed a new approach of recommendation, in which he uses fuzzy cognitive pair-wise comparisons in order to obtain ranks and grade clusters. The recommendations are based these ranks and grade clusters. The author also presented an application of the approach in smartphone recommendations. (AbdelAzim, Ibrahim, & Aboul-Zahab, 2017) proposed an AHP-based multi criteria rating system for energy efficient buildings. The author uses AHP to obtain weights for evaluating criteria.

4. Application of IFAHP to Life Insurance Recommendation

In this section, we explain framework of the proposed system and the results of an empirical study made to validate the methodology. The proposed MCRS handles the recommendation problem as MCDM problem. We can summarize that the proposed MCRS collects user-specific information and his/her preferences and transform the recommendation problem into MCDM problem. Afterward, the best-ranked alternatives are suggested as user recommendations.

4.1 System Framework

The internal architecture of the proposed system is threefold: the first phase is building knowledge repository, also called *Domain Modeling*, that contains information about products & insurance regulations which is required by the MCRS before initialization of the actual recommendation process; the second phase is collecting information from users called *User Modeling*; and the third phase is the recommendation phase, in which the proposed MCRS performs policy filtering and combines background information and user inputs in order to make inferences (Fig.1).

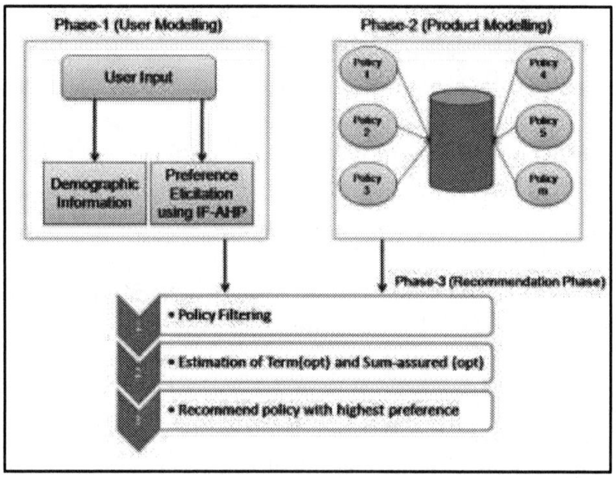

Figure 1 System Framework

4.1.1 Building knowledge repository (Domain Modeling):

In this phase knowledge repository of the MCRS is built that contains information regarding each insurance product exists in policy set and the rules and methods for calculating benefits of the policies. An insurance product contains two subsets: a set of constraints that must be fulfilled and a set of features, which represents the facilities offered by an insurance product to users.

Each insurance product is designed to fulfill specific necessities of different groups of the customer (age group, income group); for instance, children's plan is designed to secure education and future of children, therefore some constraints are associated with every insurance product. We extracted four implicit requirements of an insurance policy from literature survey and interview sessions with domain experts. In order to purchase an insurance product these constraints, particular to the product, must be matched. These constraints are *Entry-Age, Sum-Assured, Term and Maturity-Age.* Entry Age and Maturity-Age define the target age-group, while Sum-Assured defines the "face value" that is payable by the insurance company to the buyer in case of contingency. *Term* is the time period an insurance contract is valid for.

Feature set of an insurance product defines the benefits and facilities, the product offers to its buyer. We identify nine key features of Life Insurance Products through literature reviews and expert interviews. These features are Premium Amount (C1), Payment Flexibility (C2),

Tax benefits (C3), Benefits on death (C4), Benefits on survival (C5), Customer service (C6), Bonus (C7), Special Schemes & Add-ons (C8), Riders plan availability (C9). These features are regarded as evaluating criteria in the proposed system. The proposed MCRS calculates overall priorities of each alternative to a customer by aggregating local priorities of the alternatives over these features.

4.1.2 User modeling:

RS recommend movies, books, songs and other which are likely to be pursued by its user. RSs are expected to make suggestions that match its users' requirements. In order to attain this accuracy, the RS must gain an understanding of users' preferences and their decision procedures(Lakiotaki, Matsatsinis, & Tsoukiàs, 2011). In this phase, the proposed MCRS extracts information related to the users in order to accurately suggest products & services targeted to that user. This phase contains two parts: in the first part, the propose MCRS collects user-specific information from the user and in the second part the MCRS models preferences of the user using the AHP. The proposed MCRS requires *Age* and *Income* mandatorily as this information is required to check the eligibility of customer for buying particular insurance products. Also, age and income attributes are used to estimate the maximum worth of insurance a customer can buy; rules to calculate maximum worth can be found in (Hinduja & Pandey, 2017). The proposed MCRS also collect *Time-period* and expected *Receivable-Amount* on the completion of policy term as optional information. If a user hesitates to provide optional information, the MCRS estimate the optimal Time-period and expected receivable amount for the user

Proposed MCRS employs IF-AHP method for extracting users' preferences for attributes of Insurance Policies. These attributes are considered as assessing criteria for an insurance policy. These preferences exhibit users' personalized requirements and expectations from the policy. The pair-wise comparison is the key tool for preference modeling in the proposed system. All nine features listed in *'features set'* section are compared pair-wise using an HTML form. Users have to choose importance level of one feature over remaining ones and the process is repeated for all features (Fig. 2).

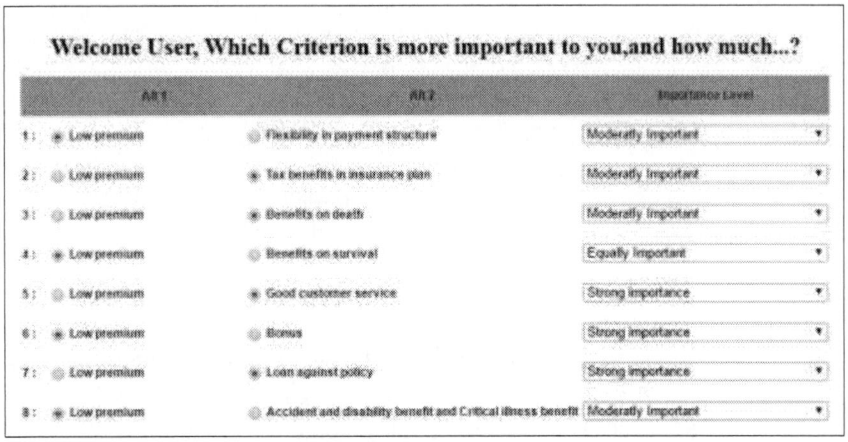

Figure 2: Pair-wise comparison among evaluating criteria of insurance policies

Data collected from the pair-wise comparison is transformed into intuitionistic fuzzy pair-wise judgment matrices. The proposed MCRS derives user preferences for each feature from these matrices using priority method of IF-AHP. 'Consistency check and repair' is also performed for preventing users from providing conflicting preferences.

4.1.3 Recommendation Phase:

In order to arrive at the accurate recommendations, the proposed RS combines the information of the knowledge repository and the information collected from users in this phase. This phase consists of three parts: the policy filtering, selection of optimal term and sum-assured and the recommendation.

The proposed RS performs screening of policies by matching information collected from the user with the constraints of insurance policies. The screening process determines the eligibility of users for each policy existing in product set. This process removes the policies the user is not eligible to buy and also mitigates the computation overhead involved in the overall priority calculation.

After the screening of policies, the proposed MCRS determines the optimal time-period (term) and expected receivable amount (sum-assured) for the user. For this purpose, the proposed system encompasses the complete range of parameters (term & sum-assured) for priority calculation of the policies regarding the users. For a user, the terms and sum-assured are regarded as optimal values for which the policy yields maximum score. In order to calculate the utilities of the policies, the proposed MCRS employs IF-AHP. The user preferences are synthesized with insurance products' partial scores over described nine features. The score of a policy over quantitative criteria is simply estimated by normalizing the quantitative benefits it produces for its customer while the scores for qualitative criteria are obtained by insurance experts and already stored in the knowledge repository.

The previous step results in optimal term and optimal sum-assured of each policy, remaining after screening phase, regarding a particular user of the proposed MCRS. Subsequently, the scores of all the remaining policies are calculated with their optimal values for term and sum-assured. The policy with highest scores is regarded as the most suitable policy to the user and the proposed MCRS recommends it to the user.

4.2 Results of empirical study

An empirical study has been carried out to validate the performance of proposed MCRS. We obtained a list of 230 prospects from an insurance advisor and subsequently collect their demographic information and preferences. From 230 prospects, 195 bought an insurance policy within 6 months of the survey and 178 of them purchased the policy which was recommended by the proposed MCRS. From the results of our empirical study, we can conclude that the accuracy of proposed MCRS is approx 91%. Besides this empirical study, we also validated the proposed MCRS from a panel of 5 domain experts. All of the panel members have more than 10 years experience in the area of life insurance either as insurance advisor or as a development officer. The panel of domain experts also found the results of proposed MCRS fairly accurate.

5. Illustration

In this section, we demonstrate an example for the illustration purpose. In order to simplify the illustration, we have taken only eight insurance products that belong to different categories (e.g. term plans, endowment plan, money-back Plan, children's Plan).

The proposed MCRS first obtains user's demographic information as input (see Table 3). The user's preferences for features of insurance products are elicited through pair-wise comparison subsequently (see Table 4). The IFAHP is used to derive the relative importance of the features to the user. Afterwards, the MCRS matches the user information with the constraints of all policies and eliminates the not-compatible policies. In the illustrative example, four policies are left after policy filtering phase: P1, P2, P4, and P7. Since the desired term period and sum-assured amount is already provided by the user in the example, the recommender system skips the "optimal term & sum-assured selection" phase. The proposed MCRS then evaluates all four policies over each feature for the information provided by the user. The evaluation scores range between 0 and 100 (see Table 5). In order to arrive at the recommendation, the proposed MCRS aggregates the criteria weights and scores of the policies (see Table 6). The system recommends insurance product with the maximum final score to the user, which is P2 in the given example.

Table 2: User Input-- Demographic Information

User Information	Input Values
Age	18
Income	₹ 2,00,000
Term	20
Sum-assured	₹ 15,00,000

Table 6: Policies matched to user profile

Policy	Weights
P1	0.246
P2	**0.271**
P4	0.250
P7	0.232
Total	**1.000**

Table 3: User Input-- User Preference for Criteria

Criteria	Preference
C1	0.1504
C2	0.0672
C3	0.0882
C4	0.1526
C5	0.1526
C6	0.1029
C7	0.1025
C8	0.0920
C9	0.0916
Total	**1.000**

Table 5: User Input-- User Preference for Criteria

Criteria	P1	P2	P4	P7
C1	100	72	92	86
C2	0	100	75	50
C3	60	80	86	70
C4	66	85	86	70
C5	90	88	74	80
C6	75	75	75	100
C7	90	80	90	100
C8	60	80	0	60
C9	100	100	100	0

6. Conclusion

Due to the uncertainty involved in our daily life, buying insurance products is a very crucial decision for contingency management and future financial planning. However, understanding multifaceted provisions of each product is a time-consuming procedure and always manipulated by insurance advisors' biases. The existing recommender systems mainly focus on relations between products and between customers and for this reason they are not competent to cope with the insurance recommendation problem.

In this paper, we develop an original perception based MCRS for insurance products. The core of the proposed MCRS is the users' preferences for insurance features, which represent the users' current requirement for purchasing insurance. In order to gather user preferences, the proposed MCRS uses IFAHP method. The IFAHP appropriately handles the vagueness and imprecision involved in users' cognition while doing pair-wise comparisons. The proposed MCRS's recommendations are guided by users' individualized requirements. The MCRS selects insurance policies that are eligible for users by processing their demographic information, determines their suitability to users and recommends policies with the highest priority. We have tested our proposed MCRS with different parameters (age-group, user preferences) by distinguishing insurance officials and experts. They have validated the results and found them significantly accurate. We also have made an empirical study to validate the proposed system and the accuracy of proposed MCRS assessed in the study is approx 91%.

We will focus on simplifying the process of user modeling in our future research work. Proposed system employs IFAHP for obtaining user preference. AHP is regarded as one of the best MCDM methods when one needs human perception, having said that, it has some limitation also. Pair-wise comparisons take a significant amount of user's effort and time. We hope to improve our system framework so that it requires fewer user interactions but have all the advantages of IFAHP.

REFERENCES:

AbdelAzim, A. I., Ibrahim, A. M., & Aboul-Zahab, E. M. (2017). Development of an energy efficiency rating system for existing buildings using Analytic Hierarchy Process – The case of Egypt. *Renewable and Sustainable Energy Reviews*, *71*(Supplement C), 414–425. http://doi.org/https://doi.org/10.1016/j.rser.2016.12.071

Adomavicius, G., & Kwon, Y. (2007). New recommendation techniques for multicriteria rating systems. *IEEE Intelligent Systems*, *22*(3), 48–55. http://doi.org/10.1109/MIS.2007.58

Adomavicius, G., Manouselis, N., & Kwon, Y. (2011). Multi-criteria recommender systems. *Recommender Systems ...*, (Mcdm), 769–803. http://doi.org/10.1007/978-0-387-85820-3_24

Atanassov, K. T. (1986). Intuitionistic fuzzy sets. *Fuzzy Sets and Systems*, *20*(1), 87–96. http://doi.org/http://dx.doi.org/10.1016/S0165-0114(86)80034-3

Atanassov, K. T. (1994). New operations defined over the intuitionistic fuzzy sets. *Fuzzy Sets and Systems*, *61*(2), 137–142. http://doi.org/http://dx.doi.org/10.1016/0165-0114(94)90229-1

Atanassov, K. T. (2012). *On Intuitionistic Fuzzy Sets Theory* (1st ed.). Springer-Verlag Berlin Heidelberg. http://doi.org/10.1007/978-3-642-29127-2

Buckley, J. J. (1985). Fuzzy hierarchical analysis. *Fuzzy Sets and Systems*, *17*(3), 233–247. http://doi.org/http://dx.doi.org/10.1016/0165-0114(85)90090-9

Burke, R. (2007). Hybrid web recommender systems. *The Adaptive Web*, 377–408. http://doi.org/10.1007/978-3-540-72079-9_12

Chang, D. (1996). Applications of the extent analysis method on fuzzy AHP, *2217*(95).

Grün, C., Neidhardt, J., & Werthner, H. (2017). Ontology-Based Matchmaking to Provide Personalized Recommendations for Tourists. In R. Schegg & B. Stangl (Eds.), *Information and Communication Technologies in Tourism* (pp. 3–16). Springer, Cham. http://doi.org/https://doi.org/10.1007/978-3-319-51168-9_1

Hinduja, A., & Pandey, M. (2017). Multicriteria Recommender System for Life Insurance Plans based on Utility Theory. *Indian Journal of Science and Technology*, *10*(14), 1–8. http://doi.org/10.17485/ijst/2017/v10i14/111376

Kermany, N. R., & Alizadeh, S. H. (2017). A hybrid multi-criteria recommender system using ontology and neuro-fuzzy techniques. *Electronic Commerce Research and Applications*, *21*(Supplement C), 50–64. http://doi.org/https://doi.org/10.1016/j.elerap.2016.12.005

Lakiotaki, K., Matsatsinis, N. F., & Tsoukiàs, A. (2011). Multicriteria user modeling in recommender systems. *IEEE Intelligent Systems*, *26*(2), 64–76. http://doi.org/10.1109/MIS.2011.33

Manouselis, N., & Costopoulou, C. (2007). Analysis and classification of multi-criteria recommender systems. *World Wide Web*, *10*(4), 415–441. http://doi.org/10.1007/s11280-007-0019-8

Marlinda, L., Kreshana, P. E., & Sensuse, D. I. (2012). A Multi- Study Program Recommender System Using Content-Based Filtering and Analytical Hierarchy Process (AHP) Methods, *9*(3), 191–196.

Nguyen, T. N., & Ricci, F. (2017). A Chat-Based Group Recommender System for Tourism. In R. Schegg & B. Stangl (Eds.), *Information and Communication Technologies in Tourism* (pp. 17–30). Springer, Cham. http://doi.org/https://doi.org/10.1007/978-3-319-51168-9_2

Quan, J.-C., & Cho, S.-B. (2014). A Hybrid Recommender System Based on AHP That Awares Contexts with Bayesian Networks for Smart TV. *Hybrid Artificial Intelligence Systems, Hais 2014*, *8480*, 527–536.

Saaty, T. L. (1980). The Analytic Hierarchy Process. *Education*, 1–11. Retrieved from http://www.mendeley.com/research/the-analytic-hierarchy-process/

Saaty, T. L. (1988). What is the Analytic Hierarchy Process? In G. Mitra, H. J. Greenberg, F. A. Lootsma, M. J. Rijkaert, & H. J. Zimmermann (Eds.), *Mathematical Models for Decision Support* (pp. 109–121). Berlin, Heidelberg: Springer Berlin Heidelberg. http://doi.org/10.1007/978-3-642-83555-1_5

Saaty, T. L. (2008). Decision making with the analytic hierarchy process. *International Journal Services Sciences*, *1*(1), 83–98.

Schafer, J. B. E. N. (2001). E-Commerce Recommendation Applications. *Most*, 115–153. http://doi.org/10.1007/978-1-4615-1627-9_6

Song, W., & Sakao, T. (2018). An environmentally conscious PSS recommendation method based on users' vague ratings: A rough multi-criteria approach. *Journal of Cleaner Production*, *172*(Supplement C), 1592–1606. http://doi.org/https://doi.org/10.1016/j.jclepro.2017.10.092

Subramanian, N., & Ramanathan, R. (2012). A review of applications of Analytic Hierarchy Process in operations management. *International Journal of Production Economics*, *138*(2), 215–241. http://doi.org/http://dx.doi.org/10.1016/j.ijpe.2012.03.036

Tang, T. Y., & Mccalla, G. (2009). The pedagogical value of papers: A collaborative-filtering based paper recommender. *Journal of Digital Information*, *10*(2). http://doi.org/10.1109/WKDD.2009.132

van Laarhoven, P. J. M., & Pedrycz, W. (1983). A fuzzy extension of Saaty's priority theory. *Fuzzy Sets and Systems*, *11*(1), 229–241. http://doi.org/http://dx.doi.org/10.1016/S0165-0114(83)80082-7

Wang, L. C., Zeng, X. Y., Koehl, L., & Chen, Y. (2015). Intelligent fashion recommender system: Fuzzy logic in personalized garment design. *IEEE Transactions on Human-Machine Systems*, *45*(1), 95–109. http://doi.org/10.1109/THMS.2014.2364398

Wu, D., Zhang, G., & Lu, J. (2014). A Fuzzy Preference Tree-Based Recommender System for Personalized Business-to-Business E-Services. *IEEE Transactions on Fuzzy Systems*, *PP*(99), 1–1. http://doi.org/10.1109/TFUZZ.2014.2315655

Xu, Z., & Liao, H. (2013). Intuitionistic fuzzy analytic hierarchy process. *Fuzzy Systems, IEEE Transactions on*, *22*(4), 1. http://doi.org/10.1109/TFUZZ.2013.2272585

Yuen, K. K. F. (2017). The fuzzy cognitive pairwise comparisons for ranking and grade clustering to build a recommender system: An application of smartphone recommendation. *Engineering Applications of Artificial Intelligence*, *61*(Supplement C), 136–151. http://doi.org/https://doi.org/10.1016/j.engappai.2017.02.001

Zadeh, L. A. (1965). Fuzzy sets. *Information and Control*, *8*(3), 338–353. http://doi.org/http://dx.doi.org/10.1016/S0019-9958(65)90241-X

Agile Sink based Data Gathering Protocol Employing Genetic Algorithm Utilizing Binary string (MSDGP-GAB) for Prolonged Network Lifetime in Wireless Sensor Networks

[1] Amiya Bhusan Bagjadab, [2]Sushree Bibhuprada B. Priyadarshini, [3]Dinesh Dash
[1] Veer Surendra Sai University of Technology, Burla
[2] C. V. Raman College of Engineering, Bhubaneswar
[3]National Institute of Technology, Patna
[1]amiya7bhusan7@gmail.com,
[2]bimalabibhuprada@gmail.com
[3] dd.dineshdash@gmail.com

Abstract— Out of several challenges encountered in case of wireless-sensor-networks, data collection by the sink is an important issue of consideration. Basically, in static sink based networks (SWSN), the sink node is fixed at a particular position. Further, all the sensors send their sensed data through multi-hop forwarding. However, the loophole of such network is that the nearest neighboring node to the sink expend its energy comparatively faster than rest of the nodes. Thus, if the nearest node to the sink fails, the entire network becomes disconnected. To overcome such situation sometimes a mobile-sink is deployed to collect the sensed-data. In this article, we have devised a mobile-sink based data gathering protocol using genetic algorithm that employs binary string for overcoming the drawback of nearest node failure so as to preserve the connectivity in the entire network. In this proposal, among the sensors some of the sensors are chosen as the cluster heads those are liable to gather the sensed data from own neighbors. Moreover, the deployed mobile sink node moves through the cluster heads so as to collect the overall sensed data. The cluster heads are so chosen that each of the sensor node has at least one neighboring cluster head as well as the length of the cycle formed by the cluster heads is minimized. Results obtained from extensive experimental evaluation and comparative performance analysis justify the superiority of our proffered approach.

Index Terms—**mobile sink, data gathering, binary string**

I. INTRODUCTION

In this modern era of technological progress, the adoration of sensors is predominantly due to their multifold uses in several domains of life. Generally, *Wireless-Sensor-Network*(*WSN*) is comprised of huge no. of sensors having processing, communication as well as measuring capabilities. The sensors are basically used to measure the peripheral states viz. sound, light, pressure, temperature etc and finally communicate their sensed-data to the base-station i.e. the ultimate destination. The location information of sensors needs to be predetermined for sensing the environmental conditions prevailing in the region to be speculated.

The prime goal of the *WSN* is sensing and reporting the data that is sensed to the concerned user. However, the requirement is to prolong the longevity of the corresponding network. Since the devices are deployed with finite amount of battery power, the proper management of energy becomes essential. From various experimental investigations, it is quite known that transmission of data takes bulk amount of energy. Therefore, efficient data gathering along with transmission lowers significant amount of energy expenditure. Various types of energy effective data gathering approaches exist such as *cluster based approach, chain based approach* etc.

A group of nodes are used to form the cluster and one of the nodes out of each and every cluster becomes the cluster-head in case of cluster based method. Further, all the nodes in the cluster communicate the data to the cluster-head. Thereafter, the cluster-head transmits the communicated data to the sink. A different node becomes the cluster head in every round. This results in variable communication distance. The point to be noted is that the sensors expend greater amount of energy in this method. However, in case of chain based method, the nodes send the sensed data to their neighboring nodes and likewise, it frames a chain.

The chain leader further sends the information to the desired base-station. Moreover, the chain-leader is chosen randomly. But the issue is that the communication distance becomes more and variable for sparsely deployed network leading to more amount of energy expenditure. In both the approaches, the sensors send data to the base station through other sensors. Moreover, the communicating distance remains variable such that, the energy expenditure becomes more. This results in rapid dissipation of energy. However, while sending the information to the sink, the nearest neighboring node to the sink that conveys its data to it becomes overloaded with accumulated information from other nodes. Sometimes, it so happens that in case of failure of this node the entire network becomes disconnected as well as the desired data cannot reach the sink node.

To overcome such hurdle, we have developed a novel method called "*Mobile Sink based Data Gathering Protocol Employing Genetic Algorithm using Binary string (MSDGP-GAB)*" that uses genetic algorithm for extending the lifetime of the network while conjointly overcoming the problem of failure of the entire network in case of failure of the nearest neighboring node to the sink due to overloading of larger amount of data.

II. RELATED WORK

In this portion, we have elaborated few of the related works regarding sink based data gathering protocol in case of *Wireless-Sensor-Networks* with static & mobile sinks. As discussed by Khan, Majid I., Gansterer, Wilfried N., Haringb, Guenter. (2013) in [1] *WSN* consists of static sensor-nodes & a static sink positioned in the middle of the observed area of consideration and the nodes monitor several events in the area of interest. Further, a static sink-node is deployed for collecting information in *Wireless-Sensor-Network* through multi-hop forwarding that leads to greater amount of energy expenditure by nearby nodes surrounding the base station.

In real life applications, multi-hop transmission is essential for reporting the information from sources towards the sinks. Therefore, the energy expenditure relies upon the corresponding transmission distance. Again, these static-sinks division the wireless network into still smaller sub-fields while each of them having one static-sink. However, the benefit of multiple static-sinks for energy effectiveness can also be accomplished with a single static-sink by rationally divisioning the respective sensing-field at single level or through hierarchical arrangement.

Such divisioning can either be static or dynamic, as well as it can either be self-organized or predetermined. Further, for averting the expiring of nodes closer to the desired-sink, the divisioning of the field into sub-regions has been done within every cluster, with a determined cluster head to which the local-nodes communicate their data and the cluster-heads tend to attain greater capability than the normal nodes. Again they are liable for forwarding the gathered information to the destined-sink through either single-hops or multiple-hops. Further, the formation or construction of cluster, as well as the cluster-head selection is accomplished so that the amusement of energy during routing will be lowered. This technique also may be increased multilevel hierarchies wherever clusters as well as the structures may either be decisive statically or modified dynamically.

A self-organizing method may be needed to define a cluster, where every sensor node independently chooses if it has to become the cluster-head or not, or whether a rigid normal framework of the clusters is necessary during the starting of the whole-process. In this context, while considering the idea of multilevel hierarchies, the network lifetime may further be improved, employing desired no. of master aggregators. Again, (operation dependent) data aggregation is done at every cluster-head prior to data transmission to the desired sink. In many works as suggested by Wankhade, Suchita R., & Chavhan, Nekita A. (2013) [2], it becomes quite hectic to recharge these sensors or to deploy new nodes to replace the dead nodes. Again, the *WSN* may be needed to provide multiple missions under several conditions and these requirements may not be easily gratified by deploying large number of sensor nodes.

Another method as discussed by Mario Di., Francesco, Anastasi, Das, Sajal k., Giuseppe. (2011) in [3] is that, another method for data gathering of the nodes closer to the desired-sink is the appropriate usage of the mobile-sink. Further, the mobile-sink node is there to gather the information from sensor-nodes as well as to store it to the corresponding base-station. However, because of the failure of this node the whole method fails since just one mobile-sink node is there in use. To run-over the lacuna marked for static-sink, the utilization of a mobile sink has been depicted. Further, a mobile-sink will use many sorts of quality patterns like random mobility, controlled mobility, & fixed path mobility that have consequences with respect to the energy efficiency furthermore as information gathering ways in which.

The random mobility, during this category of the sink uses a random path within the sensor-field. Generally, the sink uses the pull strategy for gathering information from the sensor-nodes. In pull strategy, a node forwards its information only if the corresponding sink sends a invitation for this and in case of push strategy, a node proactively transmits its information to the sink-node. Moreover, single hop information assortment ends up in the strongest lowering of energy expenditure, since no information passing on the sensor-nodes is there. This may lead to incomplete information gathering from *Wireless-Sensor-Network*, like a random mobility pattern there's no such guarantee that either the sink will reach all the nodes within the sensor-field or this would possibly take an excessive amount of time to try and do this. But if the time needed for entire coverage of the field is even lower then the sink is programmed to gather the concerned information from all the nodes that are inside the maximum no. of hops greater than the one. There is a crucial compromise between inclusion time of the *Wireless-Sensor -Network* as well as the dissipation of energy. But, the inclusion time may further be lowered if numbers of mobile-sinks randomly move in the sensor-field in efficient way.

If the information gathering isn't triggered by the concerned sink, however it pursues a push strategy, another main overhead in the case of random sink mobility takes place due to the problem of trailing the recent position of the sink as well as acclimating the routing paths to concerned sink in multi-hop transmissions that leads to enhanced the dissipation of energy.

When, a neighbor node of sink gets such message, & afterward it amends the sink-location in transfered packet. Each node that eavesdrops the packet from neighboring nodes of the sink updates the point coordinates of the sink hence in the course of time all nodes get updated the point coordinates of the sink for geographical routing.

Likewise, He, Liang., Pan, Jianping., Xu, Jingdong. (2011) [4], Rahmaan, K. & Narendran, M. (2012) [5], Donmez, M. Y., Tunca, C., Ersoy, C., Isik, S., (2015) [6], Xu, J., Guo, J., Long, J., Zhou, X., (2010) [7] have proposed and used the framework of multi-agent based mostly information routing as well as mobile-sink pursuiting approach to pick multiple intermediate nodes between a source node as well as the concerned sink, that are regarded as agents. Moreover, these agents (specifically the one nearest to the sink) are the ones which are liable of tracking location of the mobile-sink thereby lowering the route amending cost that eventually diminishes the aloft in tracking the location of the randomly moving sink-node. However, in case of fixed mobility, the sink is programmed to pursue a fixed path in a round robin way.

Further, this fixed path is predetermined. This cannot be influenced by the act of the *Wireless-Sensor-Network* at runtime. The work done in [8] elaborates data aggregation in WSN and [9] discusses the adaptive cluster based data gathering in sensor networks. The work presented in [10] give the theoretical analysis as well as experimental demonstration about a proposed protocol that can make balance between the energy expenditure while enhancing the network life time significantly. L

ikewise, the article [11] presents a delay aware data aggregation protocol. Similarly, the work presented in [12] illustrates that our approach is effective for maximizing the data gathering rate in case of rechargeable WSNs.

In current article, we demonstrate that our algorithm is efficient at maximizing the data collection rate in rechargeable wireless sensor networks. Coverage of the sensor-field is to be assured by an effective approach for selecting the routing-paths for the respective information packets. Moreover, sink mobility is planned so that the entire sensor field can be traversed in lowest feasible time. In case the sink is apt to foresee its future positions this can transmit this data to a node positioned in the proximity of its concerned future position. This node is accountable for gathering the sensed data in its proximity so that actually when sink reaches this position, it would not have to delay for the information and it was considered that the data-rate is alike for all the sensors. In case of differing data-rates across sensors, the energy dissipation can be equalized by the partitioning of the nodes in groups in such a manner that each group has nearly the equal total data rate. An approach which denotes the cluster heads as sub sinks that are used in the concerned sensor field. Each of the sensor node is correlated with one of the sub sinks. Further, the association principle is based on the amount of time the sink gives with each sub sink.

However, if a sub sink has the mobile-sink in its proximity for a longer duration of time, then greater number of sensor-nodes are associated with it and vice-versa, which enhances the throughput of the sensor-field. Controlled mobility means the methods where sink mobility is guided or controlled based on the some parameters of interest, such as residual energy of nodes or predefined objective function or predefined observable events. Similarly, a mobile-sink based method, where the sink attempts to remain away from the nodes with lesser residual energy and attempts to be in the proximity of those nodes that have greater remaining energy. It assists in balancing the dissipation of energy from the corresponding nodes.

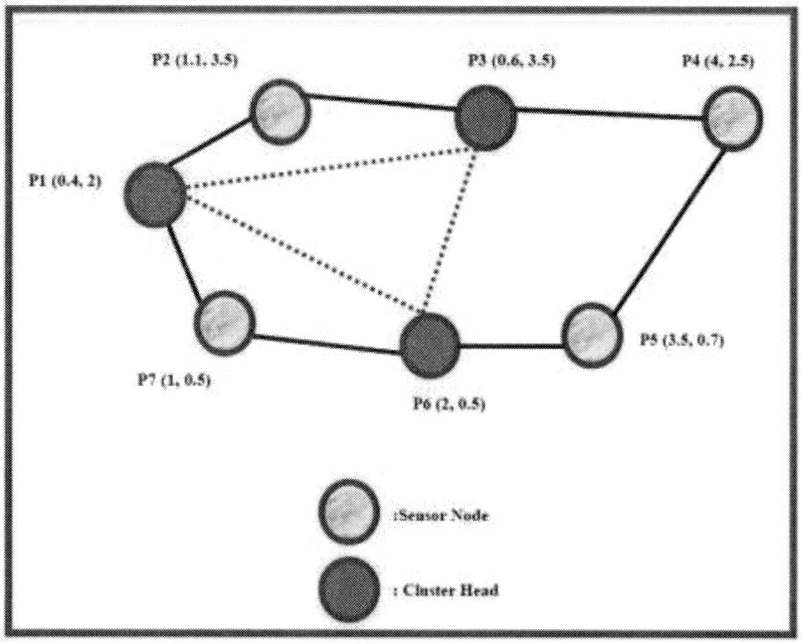

Fig. 1: A scenario of considered problem

III. PROPOSED APPROACH

(A) Motivation

Many researchers have been conducted in *Static Wireless Sensor Networks* (*SWSN*), and so many methods, models as well as algorithms have been developed. Most of the existing studies consider that the sink is static, which works as a gateway between the sensor network and users. Further, all the sensing data from the sensors are relayed to it through multi hop. Therefore, the sensors near to the sink node becomes the bottleneck. As they have to relay the data of other nodes this expends greater amount of energy. Once they die, the sink gets disconnected from the rest of the network where as the rest of sensors are still fully operational having sufficient amount of residual energy. This is regarded as static sink neighborhood problem. To overcome such problem we have proposed a Mobile Sink based Data Gathering Protocol employing Genetic algorithm.

(B) Problem Statement

A set of sensors *P = P1, P2, P3, P4, P5 Pn* with uniform communication range *CR* and locations (*x1 y1*), (*x2 y2*) (*xn yn*) are taken. Two sensors *Pi* and *Pj* are neighbor of each other if *Euclidean distance* between them is lesser than or equal to *CR*. A subset *CH*, known as cluster heads of *P (CH_ P);* is to be selected so that each sensor in *P-CH* has at east one neighbor in *CH* and the whole distance traversed to form a cycle on the nodes in *CH* is the minimal.

A scenario of considered problem is portrayed in Fig. 1. Set of sensos *P = P1, P2, P3, P4, P5, P6, P7;* Cluster heads CH= *P1, P3, P6* . We have given the best cost of the diagram. Further, three cluster heads are given and their coordinates. They are *P1 (0.4, 2), P3 (0.6, 3.5), P6 (2, 0.5)*

Distance from *P1* to *P3* is given as follows:

$$dist1(p_1, p_3) = \sqrt{(x3-x1)^2 + (y3-y1)^2}$$

==

$$= \sqrt{(0.6-0.4)^2 + (3.5-2)^2}$$

$$= 1.51$$

Distance from *P3* to *P6* is given as follows:

$$dist2(p_3, p_6) = \sqrt{(x6-x3)^2 + (y6-y3)^2}$$

$$= \sqrt{(2-0.6)^2 + (0.5-3.5)^2}$$

$$= 3.31$$

Distance from *P6* to *P1* is given as follows:

$$dist2(p_6, p1) = \sqrt{(x6-x1)^2 + (y6-y1)^2}$$

=

$$=\sqrt{(2-0.4)^2+(0.5-2)^2}$$

$$=2.19$$

Cost = dist1(p1, p3) + dist2(p3, p6)+ dist1(p6, p1)
= 1.51+3.31+2.19
= 7.01

Here the best cost is *7.01.*

Constraints:

$CH \subseteq p$

For all $x \in \{p-CH\}$ there exists $y \in CH$ and $\{y,x\} \in E$

Where *E* is the edge of sensor network

(C) Solution:

We have solved the problem using Genetic Algorithm in Data Gathering (chromosome of Binary String where genes are either 0 or 1).

C.1 Genetic Algorithm in Data Gathering (Chromosome of Binary String where Genes are either 0 or 1)

In this scheme, *Genetic Algorithm* (*GA*) is deployed to construct a Mobile Sink Based Data Gathering Protocol in *WSNs*. The major components of *GA* include - *crossover, mutation,* and *fitness function.*

(i) Chromosome: A chromosome is a collection of genes and genes denote the nodes for a particular network. Every chromosome possesses fixed length size decides by the count of nodes. Gene values 1 and 0 represent Cluster nodes and nodes respectively in the network.

***(ii) Population*:** A population is basically a gathering of chromosomes. A novel population is formed in 2 manners namely "*steady-state GA"* and "*generational GA"*. For the case of "steady-state GA", a few chromosomes are displaced in every heredity and the generational GA replaces all the recent chromosomes in every generations. Moreover, a deviation of hereditary *GA* is regarded as *Elitism*, that replicates a certain count of the best chromosomes from the recent generation to the ensuing generation. In addition, a newfangled generation is formed employing "crossover" as well as "mutation operations".

(iii) Fitness function: For the purpose of finding the fitness value we have applied *Euclidean Minimum Spanning Tree (EMST)* as well as *Depth First Search (DFS)*. *EMST* is the minimal spanning tree for a set of *n* points in the concerned plane, where the weight of the edge between every two points is the Euclidean distance between the two points. "Euclidean minimum spanning trees" is employed for getting the links price a hooked amount per unit distance. Afterwards, we have also applied *DFS* for travelling all the nodes in a graph in a specific fashion, while refurbishing as well as verifying their values along the way. We have used to find the *EMST* in a plane is to mark that this is a sub-graph of each
Delaunay triangulation of *n* points, a very diminished set of edges.

a) Enumerate the Delaunay triangulation in O(nlog n) time along with O(n) space. Since Delaunay triangulation behaves as a planar graph, and there exists no greater than three times the number of edges as vertices in any planar graph, which produces merely O(n) edges.

b) Every edge having its span.

c) Scuttle a Minimum Spanning Tree algorithm over this graph to find a Minimum Spanning Tree (MST). As there are O(n) edges, this takes O(n log n) time using any standard MST algorithms.

Further, the anticipated size of the *EMST* for huge count of points has been found out by using the following formula.

The size of the EMST is nearly

$$C(d)n^{((d-1)/d)} \int_{R^d} f(x)^{((d-1)/d)} dx \qquad (1)$$

Where *c(d)* : a constant depending only on the dimension.

Further, two features are minimum spanning trees as well as Delaunay triangulations.

Pseudocode:

Input: A graph *G* as well as vertex *u* of *G*

Output: A classification of the edges in the connected portion of *v* as discovery edges as well as the back edges under consideration.

Function DFS (G, u)
label u is prospected.
for every edge e in G. incident Edges (u) do
Assuming that "edge" e is not yet explored then
w G. adjacent Vertex (u, e)
Assuming that vertex w is unfathomed then
designate e as an exposed edge
call DFS (G,w) recursively
otherwise
designate e as a back edge

(iv) Selection: The determination procedure chooses the chromosomes that can crossover to generate a newfangled chromosome. Further, a chromosome having a higher *fitness value* possess an improved opportunity of determination for the goal of mating. Various determination approaches approaches are there to determine chromosomes for mating like– *"Roulette-Wheel selection", "Rank selection"* and *"Tournament selection"*. We have applied Tournament determination, in the situation where a group of chromosomes is selected arbitrarily from the recent population, where best 2 chromosomes which have maximum fitness values.

(v) Crossover: Crossover is called as the *"genetic operator"* applied on a pair of chromosomes. This generates a new chromosome known as *offspring*. Besides, crossover results depend on the selection process conducted among the population. A crossover operation, whenever the crossover point gets chosen as the best two chromosomes of the group, which has best fitness value as well as the gene cost of individual parents are snapped for forming a pair of child chromosomes.

(vi) Repair function: A repair function is employed to identify as well as repair or prohibit the encompassment of inoperative chromosomes in to the novel generation. For checking validity of the chromosome, we have to find the uncovered sets of the chromosomes.

Uncover sets =
Total nodes or genes of the chromosome-(cluster heads + neighbor of cluster heads)

(vii) Mutation: Mutation performs variation in the ensuing generation. In case of mutation, a node is arbitrarily selected from chromosome and the parent gets changed arbitrarily. Like crossover, the mutation process may generate an "invalid" chromosome, that is also hitched using the repair function.

Description of work done:

In this approach a special node called *mobile sink* moves in the specified zone with minimum cost and gathers data from the concerned sensors.

Following assumptions have been taken:

a. *All sensors are having equal capability.*
b. *The sensors have limited amount of power and they are static in nature.*
c. *The sink is a special node having unlimited power that has mobility power*
d. *Sink will move across cluster heads for trapping data.*

. Our proposed Genetic Algorithm proceeds as follows:

1. ***Generate an arbitrary population.***
2. ***Determine a small subset of the population and make a group.***
3. ***Include the best chromosome in this group.***
4. ***Crossover the best two chromosomes of the group and build two offsprings.***
5. ***Apply Mutation with very low probability.***
6. ***Evaluate the validity of the offspring.***
7. ***If it is found invalid then repair it and make it a valid chromosome.***
8. ***Repeat the above process till convergence criteria gets satisfied.***

IV. Simulations and Performance Assessment

We have conducted comprehensive simulation set up of our profferred protocol using *MATLAB*. In the simulation analysis, we have deployed two hundred sensor nodes arbitrarily in a network zone having communication range 100 meter.

Table 1. Parameters Maintained

parameters	Definition	values
n	No of sensors	200
CR	Communication range	100 m
Length	Length of the region	500
Width	Width of the region	500
Pop_size	Population size	500
Group_size	Group size	10

.

A. Simulation Setup

All the sensors are distributed randomly in a region having Length and Width of 500m each. Every sensor is assumed to report within a fixed unit range. It is considered that the communication range of sensor is 100m. If Euclidean distance between them is $\leq Cr$; then the two sensors Si and Sj are neighbor of each other. One cluster node must be at least one of the neighboring nodes. Further, the cycle is formed using cluster heads for the purpose of covering the entire network area. The mobile sink moves to the cycle for collecting the desired data with minimal distance. Keeping simulation in mind, we have assumed size of group as 10 and size of the population as 500. Moreover, x, y and dist depends on number of sensor nodes.

B. Result Analysis

We have done simulation analysis for analyzing the performance of the proposed protocol. For this, 200 nodes were densely deployed in the sensor field having length of the region and width of the region as 500 metre each. Since the communication range of the sensor node is fixed and in every round of data gathering process, every node will consume a fixed amount of battery power. Further, they are static in nature. Again, the sink is a special node having unlimited power that has capability to move. Mobile Sink moves in the specified region with minimum cost and gathers data from the sensors. Therefore, the mobile sink travels through the cycle on the nodes in cluster heads. The red line as portrayed in Fig. 2 indicates the total distance traversed to make a cycle on the nodes in Cluster Heads; which is found to be the minimal.

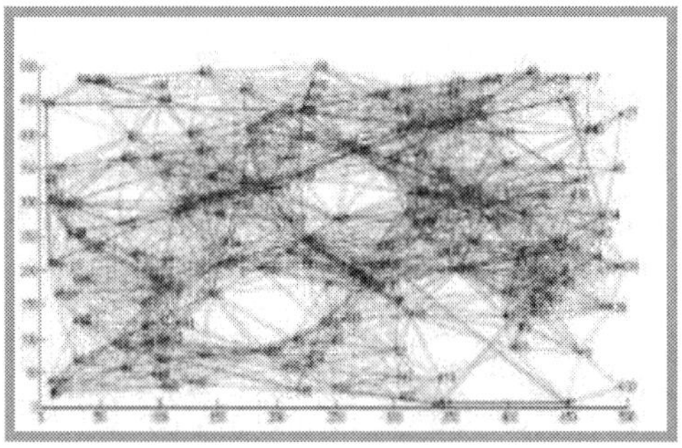

Fig. 2: Proposed graph

V. CONCLUSION

In this article, we have presented a Mobile Sink based Data collefction Protocol in case of Wireless Sensor Networks deploying Genetic algorithm at the same time keeping sensor nodes design as simple as feasible. Further, our proposed protocol enhances the lifetime of the network. Since the sensor nodes exchange information with the "mobile sink" node through cluster nodes, they expend fixed amount of battery power which gives extended lifetime to the desired network. The experimental outcomes clearly demonstrate the entire distance traversed to form a cycle on the nodes in cluster heads is the least. In future, we are planning to measure the performance using various novel algorithms for conducting the comparative performance analysis.

REFERENCES

[1] Majid I. Khan, Wilfried N. Gansterer, Guenter Haringb " Static vs. mobile sink: The in uence of basic parameters on energy e ciency in wireless sensor net-works".Comput Commun, , vol.36, no. 9, pp.965–978, 2013.

[2] Suchita R.Wankhade1 and Nekita A.Chavhan2 "A REVIEW ON DATA COLLEC-TION METHOD WITH SINK NODE IN WIRELESS SENSOR NETWORK", International Journal of Distributed and Parallel Systems (IJDPS), vol. 4, no. 1, pp. 67-74, 2013.

[3] MARIO DI FRANCESCO, SAJAL K. DAS, GIUSEPPE ANASTASI "Data Collec-tion in Wireless Sensor Networks with Mobile Elements: A Survey", *vol.* 8, no. 1, 2011.

[4] Shrikant D. Dhamdhere, Shanthi K.Guru "Robust Data Collection in Wireless Sensor Networks with Mobile Sinks", Journal of Computer Science and Information Technology, vol. 5, no. 4, pp. 4999-5002, 2014.

[5] Neethu M. Nair,A. Felix Arokya Jose "Survey on Data Collection Methods in Wire-less Sensor Networks",International Journal of Engineering Research Technology (IJERT), *vol.* 2, no. 12,pp. 2220-2225, 2013..

[6] Ke Tian, Baoxian Zhang Kui Huangxand Jian Ma "Data Gathering Protocols for Wireless Sensor Networks with Mobile Sinks,, This full text paper was peer reviewed at the direction of IEEE Communications Society subject matter experts for publication in the IEEE Globecom , 2010 proceedings.

[7] Rahmaan K1 and Narendran M2, "Enabling Energy E cient Sensory Data Collection with Mobile Sink,,International Journal of Emerging Trends Technology in Computer Science (IJETTCS), vol. 1, no.2, pp.134-140, 2012.

[8] Nithyakalyani, Dr.S.Suresh Kumar "DATA AGGREGATION IN WIRELESS SEN-SOR NETWORK USING NODE CLUSTERING ALGORITHMS,, Proceedings of 2013 IEEE Conference on Information and Communication Technologies (ICT 2013), , pp. 508-513. 2013.

[9] Khan, Majid I., Gansterer, Wilfried N., Haringb, Guenter. (2013). Static vs. mobile sink: The influence of basic parameters on energy efficiency in wireless sensor networks. *Computer Communications,* 36(9), 965–978

[10] Yu, J., Yingying, Q., Wang, G., Gu, X., "A cluster based Routing Protocol for Wireless Sensor Networks for nonuniform node distribution", AEU- International Journal of Electronics and Communjications", Elsevier, vol. 66, no. 1, pp. 54-61, January 2012.

[11] Hua He ; zhen xu ; Lei Yang, " A Delay-Aware Data Collection Protocol for Low-Duty-Cycle Wireless Sensor Networks", IET Networks, IET Digital Library, 2017. http://digital-library.theiet.org/content/journals/10.1049/iet-net.2017.0090.

[12] Lin, H, B. Di, Gao, D. , Liu, Y., " Maximum Data Collection Rate Routing Protocol based on Topology Control for Rechargable Wireless Sensor Networks", Sensors, vol. 16, no. 8, July, 2016.

Bug Model based Intelligent Recommender System with exclusive curriculum sequencing for Learner-Centric Tutoring

[1]Ninni Singh, [2]Neelu Jyothi Ahuja, [3]Amit Kumar
[1,2,3] # School of Computer Science Engineering, College of Engineering Studies,
[1,2,3] University of Petroleum and Energy Studies, Dehradun, Uttranchal, India, 248001
ninnisingh1991@gmail.com, neelu@ddn.upes.ac.in, amitanit007@gmail.com

Abstract:

Face to face human tutoring in classroom environment amply facilitates, human tutor-learner interaction where in the tutor gets opportunity to exercise his/her cognitive intelligence to understand learner's pre-knowledge level, learning pattern, ability, specific learning difficulties, to be able to offer course content well-aligned as per learner requirement and tutor in a manner that best suits the learner. Reaching upto this level in an ITS is a challenge even today given the advance developments available in field. Till date, ITS systems available, excel well in offering learner-centric content based on learner investigation, provide problem-solving and collaborative support, but lack in one of aspects of empathy, namely design of learner centric curriculum which is of prime importance especially at the onset of tutoring. This paper focuses on ITS, mimicing a human tutor in terms of providing a curriculum sequence exclusive for the learner. Bug model approach has been used for curriculum design and its re-alignment as per requirement, and demonstrated through a prototype tutoring recommender system Seis-Tutor developed for this purpose.

Keywords: Curriculum planner, intelligent tutoring system, adaptive, bug model, learning style, pre-knowledge level, tutoring strategy.

1. Introduction:

Artificial intelligence is an advanced field of research. Its use in the field of education particularly in making teaching and learning more effective, has been significantly exploited in the recent past. This has resulted in development of variety of educational computer artefacts. Further developments have caused origin of the field of intelligent tutoring. This field developed at the intersection of computer science, cognitive psychology and educational research has gained immense popularity in current times particularly due to the development of Intelligent Tutoring systems (Nwana, 1990). These systems termed as cognitive tutors offer tutoring in a manner that best suits the learning preference of the learner. It is a program that not only behaves like a human tutor but also follows the rules and instructions based on the progress and behavior of the learner.

Now-a-days, adaptation and personalization are two important aspects in computer aided instruction systems. On web based education systems, study material resources are available, but with their overloading and accessibility issues. Hence it is difficult for a learner to achieve his/her learning goals in the cyberspace. Reasons, behind the scene, to highlight the importance of adaptivity in their e-learning environment are: First, the systems might be used by learners differing in goals and objectives, pattern of learning, abilities and preferences. Additionally, the learning pattern of two learners may have been same, but the knowledge level of a given learner may escalate and this warrants the need for the system to tutor as per learner's Pre-Knowledge level. Secondly, an adaptive system can help the learner to navigate through a course by providing learner specific learning paths (Gutiérrez. 2007).

Intelligent tutoring systems over the period of time have become increasingly effective, but are difficult and expensive to build authoring tools have originated and have shown limited usage in ITS development in past. Authoring tools are ITS shells along with a user interface that allows non-programmers, to formalize and visualize their knowledge.

Existing Intelligent tutoring system (ITS) authoring systems are broadly classified into two categories: those that are based on traditional curriculum and those that are based on simulating a learning instructional environment. Going by the same philosophy, the current similarly existing authoring tools have been classified into two broad categories: Performance-oriented and Pedagogy-oriented. These render ITS, that fall under the same two categories, pedagogy oriented and performance oriented ITS. Performance-oriented systems, provide rich learning atmosphere in which learner, learns skills by practice and receives related feedback. Pedagogy-oriented systems, teach and sequence canned courseware. These systems pay attention towards representation of their teaching content, tactics and strategies. The performance-based systems provide procedural guidance (step-wise) as and when needed while pedagogy-oriented systems, focus on planning and guidance at a more general level.

Curriculum sequencing is very important in classroom, as well as in ITS, due to its systematic approach, which is congenial to learning. Moreover curriculum sequencing, maps appropriately to a course outline, to be covered. As in classroom teaching, a tutor is expected to provide learning to all learners irrespective of their individual knowledge levels, or learning preferences, hence, a generalized course delivery plan is developed and put into practice. The major drawback of this mechanism is that teacher is not familiar with the pre-knowledge level, thus he or she is able to bring only very limited variation a teaching style. Whereas, in ITS the aim is to overcome this drawback, to a great extent. Till date, the focus in ITS research, has been majorly on tutoring a learner, as per his/her learning preference, but very limited attention, has been paid on curriculum sequencing, which is design of an exclusive learning path for that particular learner. Every learner before being admitting to a course holds some knowledge about the domain. Thus, there is a need to predetermine the knowledge level of the learner and based on that, sequence the learning material for the learner, by choosing items from the pool of courseware. The research shows that if the courses are tutored as per the learner pre-knowledge level and preferences, the overall learning gain and degree of engagement of the learner with ITS ,are enhanced. The present work is focused on providing a learner with exclusive course content sequenced as per learner level and preference. The idea is to develop a system closest in terms of expressing empathy to the learner, with a larger aim of making learning happen.

2. Existing Recommender Systems

Very limited work is reported in learner path sequencing in intelligent tutoring systems. However, a reasonably sizable work on curriculum sequencing is reported in e-learning systems and Learning Management Systems. But the ITS systems have remained unexplored in this context so far. Till now intelligent tutoring system is based on heuristic rules, i.e. during construction of domain, programmer defines rules for all possible situations. This means that they follow same predefined curriculum but recommend remedial actions on each activity of the learner much the same way as the human's do. Most precisely these systems are termed as 'recommender systems'.

Section below presents a brief coverage of different tutoring systems, specifically tutoring recommender systems, with focus on the technique employed for suggesting learning and the mechanism of offering content.

(Chen, 2008) developed intelligent web-based learning system with personalized learning path guidance. Genetic algorithm was used and deducing of correlation between topics and their supporting components was automatic. Noteworthy observation, was that Genetic algorithms do not scale well with complexity. That is, where the number of elements which are exposed to mutation is large there is often an exponential increase in search space size. This makes it extremely difficult to use the technique on problems such as designing and learner path generation. Effectiveness of the course content is compromised and there is increase in overall system complexity.

(Chen, 2011) worked on enhancement of student learning performance using personalized diagnosis and remedial learning system. Their contribution was a Path Finder Algorithm, here the deducing of correlation between topics and their supporting components, was semi-automatic. Here remedial learning path is generated after learner has gone through the course content. This is not productive and provides no benefit to the learner. They start tutoring learner by their default curriculum, after completion of course, they conduct test and based on incorrect responses they suggest learning path. Overall effectiveness of the system is compromised.

(Sengupta, 2012) presented construction of Learning Path using Ant Colony Optimization from a Frequent Pattern Graph. Here again, deducing of correlation between topics and their supporting components was semi-automatic. They presented a predictive model, especially, a keyword based path recommendation model. They are not generating learning path that is exclusive for the learner instead they are creating several hyperlinks, for the unknown terms incorporated in the theory or any text definition.

For example: definition of Protein: Proteins are natural polymer molecules consisting of **amino acids** units. The number of amino acids in proteins may range from two to several thousands. Here amino acids are the hyperlinks. If learner doesn't know what is amino acid then he can avail the facility to click on the hyperlink, for more information about amino acids. The negative side of it is that there is a higher risk for the learner to get lost in this complex hyperspace.

(Hsieh, 2010), presented a mining based approach on discovering courses pattern for constructing suitable learning path. The techniques employed were Apriori Algorithm and Formal Concept Analysis. The process of deducing correlation between topics and their supporting components was semi-automatic. Analysis reveals that this approach is best for the subjects whose course materials are readily available on internet, as against those which are largely tacit knowledge. Further this approach, as per its current implementation is time consuming operation.

(Kardan, 2014), explained on a new personalized learning path generation method : ACO-MAP. The use of Ant Colony Optimization and concept map was reported. The Pre-Knowledge

Level of the learner was considered and deducing of correlation between topics and their supporting components was automatic.

(Haoran, 2017), presented a people-based approach, for discover Learning Path for group users, implementation was using Prototype based aggregation. Pre-Knowledge level was considered. The process of deducing correlation between topics and their supporting components was semi-automatic. In this approach, to determine tutoring strategy temporal boundaries are taken into the consideration.

3. Student Modeling

Continuing further from the concept of various approaches implemented for learner path design, it is being ascertained that student model is a very significant part of the tutoring system, which anchors the whole process of investigating the learner, manages the learner information in real time and utilizes it to direct the learning process for the learner. Section below, highlights some essential information in student model of contemporary systems.

Analyzing a face-to-face human tutoring scenario, three categories of knowledge is usually employed: knowledge of teaching strategy, knowledge of student (style and knowledge grasping level) and knowledge of domain (subject matter). Additionally, one distinctive feature of a good teacher is the ability to identify the learner emotional states and adapt to them during the tutoring session. One of the preliminary aspects of adapting to the learner requirements, involves choosing on appropriate curriculum coverage plan as a function of a response of the Pre-Knowledge level of the learner.

Considering a traditional architecture of an ITS, with a student model and tutoring model, the student model (SM) is frequently updated during the teaching process in accordance with the characteristics of the learner. In coordination with the student model, the tutoring model can predict an appropriate curriculum which is exclusive for that learner. Certain emerging systems of today show inclination towards this approach.

As reported from the existing research there are different levels and types of learner information that is significant in choosing between different curriculum planning and tutoring execution decisions. Some information is stored symbolically, some numerically and some must be kept in the form of detailed history.

Systematic review of past research work reveals that a variety of techniques have been employed to examine learner behavior and suggest curriculum changes to the learner. Some prominent ones are:-

1) **Based upon learner performance:**
   The learner is offered brief assessments periodically, performance in these, is used as an indicator to remedial actions by the system.
2) **Keyword based path recommendation:**
   The learner is offered keywords to further probe on desired topics and gain additional understanding.
3) **Overlay Modeling:**
   The system utilizes artificial intelligence techniques, in which system identifies what the learner does not know, the causes of misconception, and accordingly provides remedial guidance
4) **Bug Libraries:**

A separate catalogue of misconception is created based on the learner responses and necessary guidance is provided.

5) **Dynamic Modeling:**
It is a combination of bug libraries and machine learning techniques. Based on learner behavior, novel errors are modeled by constructing new buggy information dynamically, which is further provides as a remedial action to the learner, by the system.

6) **Tracing Techniques:**
This technique keeps track of all the learner activities performed during tutoring session, and halts whenever the learner deviates from the correct learning path.

In the present case, bug model has been utilized for curriculum and learner-path design.

4. Intelligent Recommender System of Seis-Tutor

Seis-Tutor is a prototype tutoring system developed with implementation of learner-centric curriculum sequencing mechanism with as aim to enable effective learning for the learner.

This section elaborates the intelligent curriculum recommendation by this system with a base philosophy of empathizing with learner and providing guidance by analyzing the learner mistakes. As discussed earlier, the existing recommender systems provide feedback during ongoing tutoring with negligible or no emphasis on providing an appropriate curriculum right at the beginning itself. The present research work is focused on a well-planned systematic start of the tutoring process by a curriculum design suitable to a given learner and presents a navigable learning path.

4.1.1. Exclusive Curriculum Design in Seis-Tutor

Adaptivity is one of the key features of intelligent tutoring systems and research shows that cognizing psychological mind of the learner makes a tutoring system an intelligent tutoring system because it solves learner issues and offers the tutoring content in a manner that learner can grasp easily and effectively. A human tutor in a face-to-face environment, empathizes with the learner, is sensitive towards the learner's behavior and almost seamlessly regulates and adjusts his/her teaching strategy to best suit the learner. Additionally, the human tutor is cautions towards the learner's difficulties and specific weak points and ensures recoverage and repetition, till the time that the learner gains an acceptable understanding and comfort level in the said topic. Reorganizing and re-aligning the course content as per learners comfort, is also an important and indispensable activity. This is an ideal face-to-face classroom teaching learning process environment. The same is being envisioned in teaching learning administered through SeisTutor.

At the inception of learning though SeisTutor, the learner is administered a pretest. The pretest comprises of domain knowledge test as well as a learning style test. As the name suggests, domain knowledge test is targeted at identifying the learner's pre-knowledge level. It aids to scale the performance of the learner on a scale ranging from 'beginner level' to 'expert level' with 'beginner' being at a lowest competency level currently, and 'expert' being at highest level of competency. The learning style test poses questions to the learner, responses to which are directly linked to a particular pattern of learning preference. Thus, this test helps to appropriately bracket the learner into a particular learning style, such as 'visual', 'verbal' etc.

The course content that is to be provided to the learner has been clustered using clustering technique. This result in independent clusters managed and maintained as a pool or a collection. The learner is provided a prerequisite general overview of the course designated as week 0, just before he or she is formally introduced with the course.

The week '0' comprises of content that is very indispensable and fundamental in nature. Then a quiz is offered to the learner. The *course generator* module uses as input the learner pre-knowledge level, learning style and performance in week '0' quiz, to design an exclusive curriculum. An exclusive tutoring strategy which is a combination of pre-knowledge level and learning style is devised for the learner. This curriculum is developed in a manner particularly suitable, for the learning, as per learner behavior and understanding that has been gained by the system about the given learner. Then the tutoring process begins for the learner as per the curriculum identified for the learner. The design of the curriculum is implemented as items of identified from the content pool (termed as learner concept repository course content) , as cluster and linked together to form a sequence, this as executed is 'learner path'. In the present case, tutoring process is being regulated using bug-model. As tutoring process progresses, the incorrect responses of the learner, in the intermitted tests, revamp curriculum sequence in real time.

The section below presents, the implementation of bug model.

As the learner session progresses, the course generator provides the content to the learner. Brief chunks of course content are provided, followed by short quizzes. Each of the questions presented in the quiz are associated with topics and subtopics through a label that serves as an identification keyword for the topic / sub-topic. The response given by the learner for the question is monitored by the *course generator*. The incorrect response of the learner is termed as a 'bug'. Over a given learning session, where a set of topics have been covered and a series of quizzes, have been taken by the learner, the *course generator* is able to populate a list of 'bugs' or 'topics', where the learner may not have been able to provide correct responses, This list is analyzed to be probable catalogue of topic/subtopics that may have not been very clear to the learner or in other words the comfort level of the learner in these topics is much below the acceptable threshold of expected understanding for the given content.

The *course generator* re-aligns the curriculum, comprising of these topics and administers to the learner with an aim to provide additional clarity, repetition and reemphasis on topics that were not understood by the learner.

Each time the course curriculum is available for execution, it is linked with the clustered topics by the *retrieval agent* which causes the content to be displayed to the learner through a learner-friendly interface termed as *learner interface.*

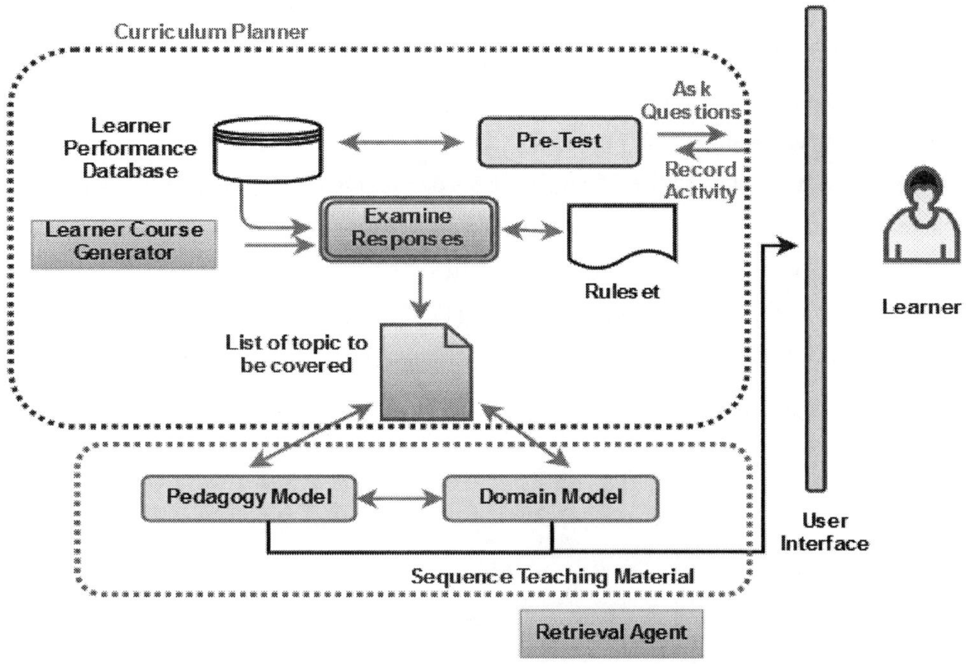

Figure 1 Flow Diagram of Curriculum Planner

5. **Conclusion**

Work flow of curriculum planner module using bug model is elaborated. A human tutor utilizes his/her own cognitive intelligence to identify the learner's emotion, understanding, style, behavior and profile and plans an exclusive curriculum and offers the tutoring contents. The capability of identification and presentation of exclusive curriculum has been built into prototype intelligent recommender, the Seis-Tutor. The ability to provide repetition and reemphasis, on content that was not properly understood by the learner, by analysis of 'bugs' or 'incorrect' responses is developed. This is a contribution towards building empathy in ITS.

6. Acknowledgement

This work is being carried out at University of Petroleum and Energy Studies with the reference number SR/CSI/140/2013. The authors thankfully acknowledge the funding support received from Cognitive Science Research Initiative, Department of Science and Technology for the project. The Authors thank the management of University of Petroleum and Energy Studies, for Supporting the work and granting permission to publish it.

References:

[1] Nwana, H. S. (1990). Intelligent tutoring systems: an overview. *Artificial Intelligence Review*, *4*(4), 251-277.

[2] Gutiérrez, S., & Pardo, B. (2007). Sequencing in web-based education: approaches, standards and future trends. *Evolution of Teaching and Learning Paradigms in Intelligent Environment*, 83-117.

[3] Chen, C. M. (2008). Intelligent web-based learning system with personalized learning path guidance. *Computers & Education*, *51*(2), 787-814.

[4] Chen, L. H. (2011). Enhancement of student learning performance using personalized diagnosis and remedial learning system. *Computers & Education*, *56*(1), 289-299.

[5] Sengupta, S., Sahu, S., & Dasgupta, R. (2012). Construction of learning path using ant colony optimization from a frequent pattern graph. *arXiv preprint arXiv:1201.3976*.

[6] Hsieh, T. C., & Wang, T. I. (2010). A mining-based approach on discovering courses pattern for constructing suitable learning path. *Expert systems with applications*, *37*(6), 4156-4167.

[7] Kardan, A. A., Ebrahim, M. A., & Imani, M. B. (2014). A new personalized learning path generation method: ACO-Map. *Indian Journal of Scientific Research*, *5*(1), 17.

[8] Xie, H., Zou, D., Wang, F. L., Wong, T. L., Rao, Y., & Wang, S. H. (2017). Discover learning path for group users: A profile-based approach. *Neurocomputing*.

Collaborative model for security in cloud

Brijesh Pandey
Student, SCSE, Galgotias University

Abhineet Anand
FACULTY, SCSE, Galgotias University

Cloud Computing is considered as an attractive service model. While there is increasing use of this technology so there are security threats and when it comes to networking aspects, there is a very little support. Cloud Security is a set of technologies or controls which are deployed to secure the data, application and the infrastructure of cloud computing. It is the sub domain of network or information security. Namely the categories of security issues are: Network Security, Interfaces, data security, virtualization, governance, compliance issues and legal issues. Currently the most important problems which are seen in these references are legal issues, compliance and loss of control over data. There is need of advanced technology to secure the cloud in this paper an idea is proposed for data security. Cryptography, Steganography and Hashing are used.This paper deals with data security when the data is stored at the cloud.

INTRODUCTION

Cloud Computing aka **on-demand** service is relatively a new service that allows the user to exchange, access and data storage over the Internet. **Virtualization** plays an important role in the scenario of cloud computing, Infrastructure of cloud is built in which the resources are virtualized and services to clients are provided in form of virtual machines(Abhijeet Singh, 2017).

The explanation of 'cloud computing" from the National Institute of Standards and Technology (NIST)(P.Melland, 2009). is that cloud computing enables ubiquitous, convenient, on-demand network access to a shared pool of configurable computing resources (e.g., networks, servers, storage, applications, and services) that can be rapidly provisioned and released with minimal management effort or service provider interaction.

The three major services in cloud are **IaaS, PaaS and SaaS**(P.Melland, 2009). As cloud is in rapid growth the most important concern is **security**. Every single day we read these news about data leak, data loss and many more.

Security is considered a key requirement for cloud computing consolidation as a robust and feasible multipurpose solution (Avizienis, Laprie, Randell, & Landwehr, 2004).If we want to join more and more people to cloud computing so the security is the most important concern right now. .The trustworthy environment is the basic prerequisite to win confidence of users to adopt such a technology. Latif et al. discussed the assessment of cloud computing risks (Latif & Ali, 2014).The two key factors are **Data storage and Data Protection** however there have been a lot of proposals of data security techniques but this need enhancement (Dumka, Mandoria, Dumka, & Anand, 2015).

Security is the combination of confidentiality, the prevention of the unauthorized disclosure of information, integrity, the prevention of the unauthorized amendment or deletion of information, and availability, the prevention of unauthorized withholding of information (McGregor, Braun, & Brown, 2000).

Service Models

Cloud Computing offers the services according to different models, and per the NIST the most important ones are

- IaaS (Infrastructure as a Service).
- PaaS (Platform as a Service).
- SaaS (Software as a Service).

Software as a Service

Top layer of service model. The service provider develops and host the application as an infrastructure so that the users can use it from different interfaces such as web browsers online e-mail. These can be obtained using different systems like mobile, workstation from anywhere.

Figure 1. Software as a Services

Platform as a Service

This allows the users to build, run and manage their own applications. Basically the service provider offers the hardware and the software tools that are required for the development. The main advantage is that it cuts the coding time as users are using the pre-coded apps to develop their own.

Figure 2. Platform as a Services

Infrastructure as a Service

It is mainly for hosting i.e. it provides the virtualized resources like network, storage and other fundamental requirements so that the user is able to run software like OS.

PROPOSED WORK

Cloud storage is a service of data storage in which the digital data is stored in logical pools, and the data is managed,updated and manipulated by the cloud provider company aka cloud host.

CONCERNS

Major concern are

- Cyber attacks.
- Cryptographic keys

We are proposing a security level system which will be using collaboration of some techniques. The data in cloud storage is classified in terms of more important and less important data.By this we mean that,we will create an extra cloud which will be private and the access to it,will be with us only.So basically we are going to store unimportant i.e. Trash data in it(big data) that will be the amount of data which is

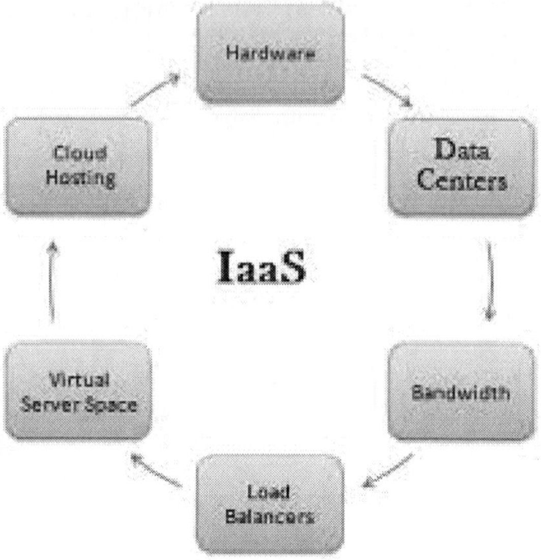

Figure 3. Infrastructure as a Services

not important. The data which is collected through SSL (Secure Sockets Layer) is more secured that is the users data of their cloud. So basically an attacker will attack on the data which is given priority security wise.

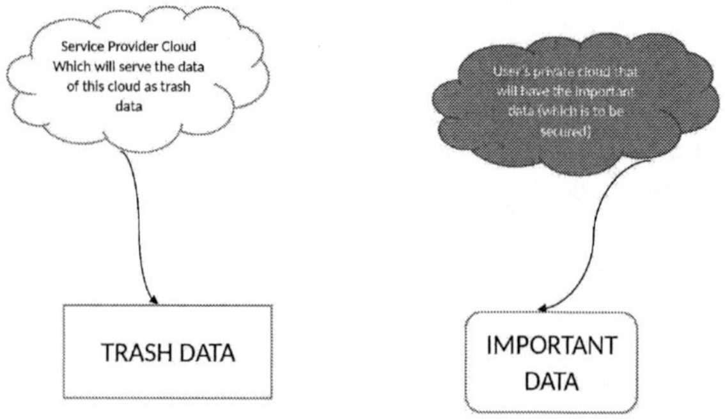

Figure 4. How data is classified for our model

So we are using merging technique here and at last we as the provider will have access to the whole data i.e. users as well as our created cloud. So as per the service provider the data which we have, will be classified on two basis

- Secured data(User data which will be recieved through SSL)
- Trash data(Data of our created cloud)

Idea

Steganography is a technique in which the data is hidden within a document, program, image, protocols or videos. The service provider have the access to secured and trash both the data so the moto is that we collect the programs, images and videos from trash data and hide the users data in them. Basically an attacker will attack on the secured data only so we are manipulating them. After hiding the data inside the pictures and videos. The moto is that no matter if a simple message is encrypted it arouses the interest of people so steganography will be better here. The basic formula of the steganographic procedure can be given by:**Cover media + secret message + stego key = stego-object**. After the files are hidden the image or file which is being used will be divided in the fragments.How we are going to do this? We know that the data is just a combination of bits so in the algorithm we will use a loop which will distribute the bits in equal length which will be able to divide the image in fragments resulting in minimum distortion.

Then comes the second level i.e. encryption. The fragmented segments will be encrypted. What is going to happen is for example Any file (from trash data) is expressed in form of bits. Then we will form a string of bits and it will be encrypted.The **generated key will again be encrypted** so it will deal with the crypto key issue. We know that the longer the key is the better they are so why not to secure the encrypted keys so that hacker really wont be able to decrypt it easily. And to decrypt the key hackers need access to a very powerful machine. And in this idea we are going to use a very high level security that it will take alot of time to understand the hacker that how the data is hidden and secured.And after that the time consumption will be too much.

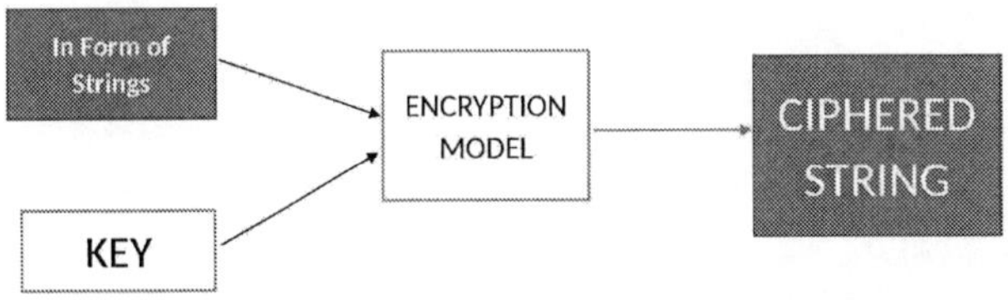

Figure 5. Encryption of fragmented strings

The final layer is including Hashing (It is a technique which transforms a string in a single key or a shorter fixed length value) so we will be using hashing algorithm in the strings which are encrypted before,that is the first time of encryption (after steganography when the bits are grouped) note that the hashing we are using is normal hashing which will not use any kind of password, and these hash values will be distributed among both the clouds. Preference should be given to image files because if to get the message you will want the whole hash values plus every encryption key and at

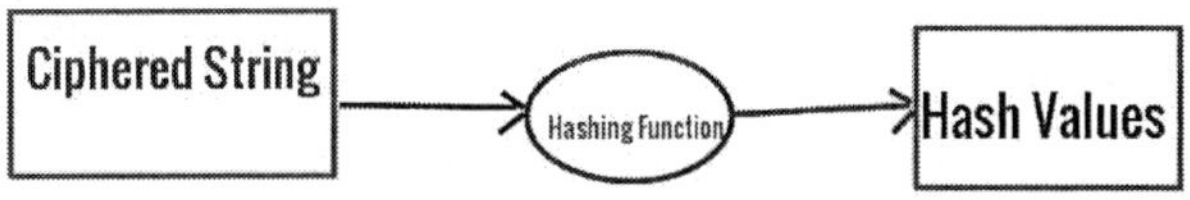

Figure 6. Hashing done at final layer

last you will have to have access to everything then only an attack will be possible.

Here is a figure of the proposed model.The trash data is of our cloud that amount of data is not important and the important data is which is of user.And the figure shows the procedure how our work will be carried out.

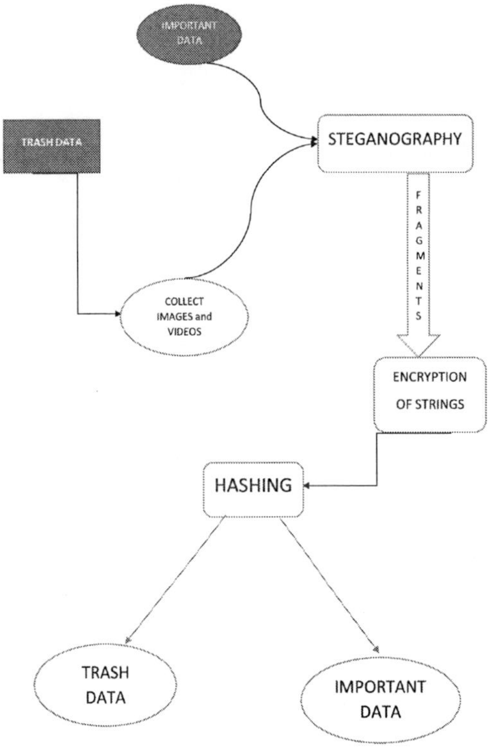

Figure 7. Proposed Model

CONCLUSION and FUTURE WORK

Cloud Computing is the new hot now a days and the major concern is security. People will trust the companies with providing much more security, users are ready to pay huge amount for security. So basically we conclude that user is dependent on data and is dependent on value of data. In this paper we have discussed about cloud computing service model and various issues issues for data breaching. And we propose our own model for better security. The future aspects of the security is quite bright. The data is never fully secured so time to time enhancement is required. Future work of this paper will be including the simulation results of proposal work. The hash values are distributed in both the clouds so as to achieve the security only,think of it in such a way.If a hacker wants to access our data he will have to have access to both the clouds and after that this much breakage that will surely need a lot and it is next to impossible to crack this algorithm. This idea will take the security to a new level. It would be next to impossible to breach the data. Data security will not be compromised any more.

References

Abhijeet Singh, A. A. (2017, April). Data leakage detection using cloud computing. *International Journal Of Engineering And Computer Science, 6(4).* doi: *https* : //*dx*.doi.org/10.18535/ijecs/v6i4.59

Avizienis, A., Laprie, J.-C., Randell, B., & Landwehr, C. (2004, January). Basic concepts and taxonomy of dependable and secure computing. *IEEE Trans. Dependable Secur. Comput.*, *1*(1), 11–33. Retrieved from `http://dx.doi.org/10.1109/TDSC.2004.2` doi: 10.1109/TDSC.2004.2

Dumka, A., Mandoria, H. L., Dumka, K., & Anand, A. (2015, March). Mpls vpn using ipv4 and ipv6 protocol. In *2015 2nd international conference on computing for sustainable global development (indiacom)* (p. 1051-1055).

Latif, A. H. A. S., R., & Ali, Q. (2014). Cloud computing risk assessment: A systematic literature review. future information technology. *Future Information Technology. Lecture Notes in Electrical Engineering*, *276*, 285-295. doi: http://dx.doi.org/10.1007/978-3-642-40861-$8_4$2

McGregor, T., Braun, H. W., & Brown, J. (2000, May). The nlanr network analysis infrastructure. *IEEE Communications Magazine*, *38*(5), 122-128. doi: 10.1109/35.841836

P.Melland, T. (2009). The nist definition of cloud computing. *National Institute of Standards and Technology, 53, 6.*

Data Characterization of ISBSG R12 Using Data Analytics: An Exploratory Study

Ghazi Alkhatib* and Khalid Al-Sarayrah**
The Hashemite University
Zarqa, Jordan

* Correspondence author: g_alkhatib@orange.jo - **KhalidT@hu.edu.jo

Abstract: This paper presents an exploratory study that applies three data analysis techniques: statistical analysis, data clustering, and visualization conducted to the ISBSG R12 data set. Both SPSS and RapidMiner are used to conduct the analysis. While statistical analysis main advantage is the summarization of data, the overall behavior of the data is lost, particularly the view of outlier values. The study applied two techniques in this regard using SPSS: correlation analysis and the general linear model using multiple variables. The statistical analysis showed a high significant level of relationship between and among the selected variables. In the data mining areas, the clustering technique and visualization used both SPSS and RapidMiner (RM). For the selected variables, the number of clusters is determined after several runs, but always coming up with one large cluster and other smaller ones. Finally, visualization technique demonstrates how it could show concentration and trends. In some cases, generated charts from the results of the analysis from the two software packages are juxtaposed and compared. RM charts reveal more information than SPSS. All of these types of techniques were found to be valid with some relevant conclusions. Overall, in order to get an integrated view on a complex data set, such as ISBSG, more than one data analysis techniques are needed to arrive at an adequate understanding of the underlining behavior of the data.

Key words: ISBSG release 12, data analytics, data mining, correlation, clustering, visualization, SPSS, RapidMiner

Research background: review of literature and ISBSG related work

The competitive market of software products demands software companies to deliver reliable and functional products with minimum development costs and time, additionally satisfying customers who have changing needs (Trendowicz & Münch, 2009 1]. The continuous changing markets require the use of an effective software development methodology to be able to enhance and measure both productivity and effort required for each development stage.

Software development methodology is also known as Software Development Life Cycle (SDLC). The Waterfall, spiral, incremental, rational unified process (RUP), rapid application development (RAD), agile software development, and rapid prototyping are examples of different SDLC models (Sommerville, 2015). All of SDLC models have a sequence of phases that must be completed in order to deliver a final software product. In this study, we will consider waterfall and agile software development.

The waterfall model was introduced by Winston W. Royce in 1970 (Royce, 1970), (Sommerville, 2015). It has five consecutive phases that aim to develop large software for delivery to a customer, these phases (in order) are: Analysis, Design, Implementation, Testing, and Maintenance. Each phase has to be fully completed before moving to the next phase. Software manager assigns available resources to each phase. In order to attain the maximum productivity in every stage, [6] proposed a simulation model for Waterfall SDLC to assist project managers to determine the optimal amount of resources required in each phase within the allocated schedule and budget. The successful implementation of waterfall requires that software requirements remain unchanged and fixed in the entire process. Unfortunately, this is not applicable to modern products because customers tend to change their needs frequently.

Recently, lightweight software development methods are needed to respond efficiently to market changes and continuous development. The business meeting of seventeen professional software developers in 2001 had published the Manifesto for Agile Software Development which is based on twelve principles (Beck, et. al, 2001). It is known that most of the agile methods are not new (Cockburn & Highsmith, 2001). Agile development support traditional SDLC in addition to these important values: individuals and interactions, working software, customer collaboration and responding to change.

The use of agile development methods has improved productivity, delivery time as well as customer satisfaction (Lindvall, et. al., 2004). The 2011 CHAOS report from the Standish Group comprised success and failure rates of software projects between waterfall model and agile development. The report cites 12% success rate for waterfall projects and 42% success rates for agile projects. This study was applied from projects conducted from 2002 through 2010 (Cohn, 2011).

Productivity in SDLC: Basically, Productivity in software development is defined as the relationship of an output and its corresponding input. According to (Koch, 2009), productivity considers the relation of output and effort that is measured by using Source Lines of Code (SLOC), Function Points (FP), or further revisions of FP. These measures are usually used when applying classical development methods such as waterfall. Other alternatives are used such as story points for agile development (Wang, 2004). However, these measurements are not applicable for all software engineering tasks (Hernández-López, Colomo Palacios, & García-Crespo, 2013; Bellini, Pereira & Becker, 2008), since few tasks in software development do not produce codes as output.

Productivity in software development processes is influenced by numerous factors. The results of a comprehensive study of 126 publications made by (Trendowicz & Münch, 2009) showed that the main factor in increasing productivity depends upon the capability of developers, followed by tools and methods used within the process. The dependability of human factor makes it difficult to estimate productivity. The results of an empirical study conducted by Rodriguez, Sicilia, Garcia, & Harrison, 2012) analyzed the relationship between productivity and team size showed that there are statistical correlations between team size, effort, productivity and project duration. The study was performed using a preprocessed ISBSG release 10.

The applied SDLC in software projects affects productivity. In agile team projects, productivity is affected by team composition and allocation, external dependencies, and staff turnover. This is the result of a study that analyzed data from two projects (Melo, Cruzes, Kon & Conradi, 2011). Moreover, (Hannay & Benestad, 2010) summarized productivity threats to ten problem areas. They studied factors that compromise productivity in large agile development projects, they conducted repertory grid interviews with 13 project members; each project consists of 11 Scrum teams.

Research methodology

A close scrutiny of the data set led to the use of quality of data rating of A and B only. Vertically, many variables are excluded, while others are considered for the analysis. Some form of theoretical foundation supported such selection, such as the effect of effort on analysis and design on software implementation (Brooks, Jr., 1995), and functional point computation and its relationship to a selection of other variables, such as industry type and development methodology, as specified in the standard of Automated Function Points for transaction processing system (Object Management Group, 2017). Normally, low organizational level transaction processing system dictates different development practices than hardware-based systems, such as telecommunication, and mathematically oriented systems. The inclusion of some variables depicting against time. Horizontally, the data set is visually examined searching for weak data for certain variables which led to the deletion of about 1 percent of the projects. Two software packages are used in the analysis: SPSS and RapidMiner (RM). Statistical analysis included correlation analysis and the general linear model for multiple independent and dependent variables. The clustering techniques using SPSS followed several runs for the number of clusters from 2-10 using K-Means. The objective is to identify a couple of clusters within a group of clusters hoping to isolate outliers. The different cluster runs always revealed one large cluster and other smaller ones. Following the analysis of cluster composition for 2 to 10 using SPSS, the size of 8 came up with three clusters with slight variations and the other 5 with member cases of less than 6. Only the three largest clusters were analyzed. As to visualization charts, the charts were revised to eliminate outliers until an acceptable scatter diagram without many outliers is reached. Also, the research arrives at a new variable representing total efforts. In some cases, effort was not distributed into the different effort related categories, but rather it was reported as a figure under the variable unrecorded. Looking at the figures in this latter column, large figures were included, and for those who distributed effort into the different categories reported a zero figure. Therefore, a new column for the total efforts is created by adding the distributed efforts and considering the unrecorded figure for non-distributed effort as a total effort.

Data analysis

Data analysis of the ISBGS release 12 conducted three types of techniques: traditional statistical analysis, data mining clustering, and visualization.

Statistical Analysis

In this section, two statistical analysis techniques are presented: correlation and general linear model with multi-variables. The next two tables demonstrate correlation between two set of variables, as shown in the two consecutive tables.

Table 1. Correlation analysis among the variables in the analysis.

Correlations						
Variable	Total Defects Delivered	Effort AandD Percent of total	Resourc e Level	Defect Densit y	Speed of Delivery	Manpower Delivery Rate
Total Defects Delivered	1	-.160*	.084	.477**	.036	-.043
Effort AandD Percent of total		1	-.025	-.113	-.106	-.141*
Resource Level			1	-.092	.204**	.204**
Defect Density				1	-.085	-.104
Speed of Delivery					1	.818**
Manpower Delivery Rate						1

Table 2. Correlation analysis among adjusted functional points, total efforts, and defect density.

Correlations Pearson Correlation Sig. (2-tailed)				
	Adjusted Function Points	Total Efforts	Total Defects Delivered	Defect Density
Adjusted Function Points	1	.553**	.190**	-.024
Total Efforts		1	.227**	.015
Total Defects Delivered			1	.459**
Defect Density				1

Note for both tables: *: at alpha of .01. **: at alpha .05 two tailed test.

Shaded areas in both tables indicate significant correlation between the two variables. The above two tables reveal that the selected variables in general are correlated. The strongest correlations are between manpower delivery rate and speed of delivery. A noteworthy observation is the negative relationship between the percentage of analysis and design to total effort from one side, and total defects delivered and manpower delivery rate from the other side.

The next table shows the general linear model using multiple dependent and independent variables sorted from the highest significance to the least and divided into three tiers. In the table below, the top tier list defect density 4 times and overall count of 7 indicating a strong relationship between the dependent and independent variables.

Table 3. General linear analysis using multiple dependent and independent variables -3 tiers

Test in Between Subject Effects			
Source	Dependent Variable	Sig.	Tiers
IndustrySector * DevelopmentType	Defect Density	1.00	1
DataQualityRatingnUM * IndustrySector	Effort AandD Percent of total	0.97	
DataQualityRatingnUM * IndustrySector	Total Efforts	0.94	
DataQualityRatingnUM * IndustrySector	Defect Density	0.93	
DataQualityRatingnUM * DevelopmentType	Effort AandD Percent of total	0.93	
DataQualityRatingnUM * IndustrySector * DevelopmentType	Defect Density	0.92	
DataQualityRatingnUM * IndustrySector	Manpower Delivery Rate	0.91	
DataQualityRatingnUM	Total Efforts	0.88	
DevelopmentType	Defect Density	0.82	
DataQualityRatingnUM * IndustrySector * DevelopmentType	Manpower Delivery Rate	0.69	2
DataQualityRatingnUM * DevelopmentType	Manpower Delivery Rate	0.66	
DataQualityRatingnUM * DevelopmentType	Total Efforts	0.65	
DataQualityRatingnUM	Manpower Delivery Rate	0.62	
DataQualityRatingnUM * IndustrySector * DevelopmentType	Resource Level	0.60	
DataQualityRatingnUM	Effort AandD Percent of total	0.55	
IndustrySector * DevelopmentType	Total Efforts	0.51	
DataQualityRatingnUM * IndustrySector * DevelopmentType	Total Efforts	0.46	
DataQualityRatingnUM	Defect Density	0.43	
DataQualityRatingnUM * DevelopmentType	Defect Density	0.40	
IndustrySector	Defect Density	0.37	3
DataQualityRatingnUM * IndustrySector * DevelopmentType	Effort AandD Percent of total	0.32	
DevelopmentType	Total Efforts	0.28	
DataQualityRatingnUM	Resource Level	0.19	
DevelopmentType	Manpower Delivery Rate	0.19	
IndustrySector * DevelopmentType	Manpower Delivery Rate	0.15	
DataQualityRatingnUM * IndustrySector	Resource Level	0.13	

The top independent variable in the second tier is manpower delivery rate. The results of correlation using F test validates the quality of data assessment. Relationships among other independent and dependent variables show an overall significance except for industry sector, with the highest relationship expressed between and among data quality and industry sector vs. defect density. Overall, this shows the importance of industry section and development type in software development. In the insignificant relationships, industry type leads the list with 6 out of 9 variables. In the dependent variable resource level lead the list with 4 insignificant relationships.

Clustering Using Data Mining Techniques

RapidMiner generation process of two clusters is shown in the following figure. The chart shows the RM cluster members distributed between 2 clusters using the same variables in Table 4. The large cluster members in one cluster dictates portentous stratification to divvy that cluster.

Figure 1. Distribution of cluster members between the two clusters as generated in RapidMiner.

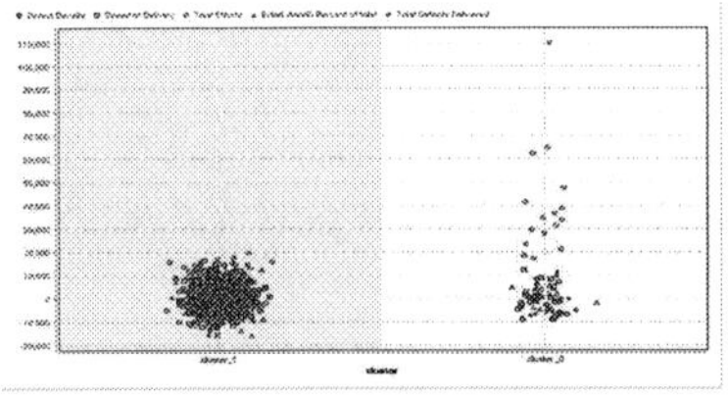

Since cluster of two did not show any variations, several iterations for cluster sizes ranging initially from 2 to 10 were conducted using the variables in the next table, the cluster of 2 showed great skewness with one cluster having 267 cases and the second cluster having only 8 cases. This distribution mimicked the same distribution of cluster 2 above using RM. As the number of clusters increase, the number of cases in each cluster started to distribute, with the decrease of cases in the first cluster. With the analysis of the behavior of cluster membership among the cases, cluster number 8 showed three clusters with acceptable number of cases, and the rest 5 clusters with less than 7 cases each. The largest three clusters of 1, 5, and 4 are analyzed using cluster centers. The variables with increased magnitude of the cluster center values for the largest 3 clusters are: defect density, total defects delivered, normalized work efforts, and total efforts. The other two variables showed inconsistent magnitude of cluster centers are speed of delivery and effort on analysis and design. Overall the analysis identifies three clusters and the fourth one is a summation of clusters 8, 2, 3, 6, and 7 with 17 members. Further clustering analysis could be conducted to identify consistent members of clusters and acceptable cluster centers.

Visualization analysis

This section of the paper presents two types of visualization charts: time dependent and variables dependent.

The following variables are depicted against time: speed of delivery, total defects delivered, a computed variable that represents the percent of total effort of analysis and design to total efforts, and defect density. The chart on time vs. speed of delivery using SPSS reached the highest during the year 2000 when developers were coping with fixing systems to handle the migration from the two-digit year code to the four digit year code. Future estimates may suggest, over a period of five years, slight increase in speed of delivery followed by a decline. The second chart depicting time against total defects delivered shows an approximation of a normal distribution. Future projects may start another cycle of normal distribution in the long run, experience a gradual increase in the total defects delivered.

Figure 2. Depicting speed of delivery (on left) and total defects delivered (on right) over time

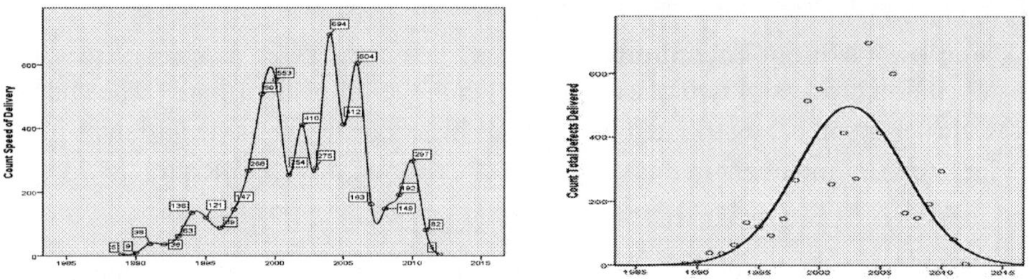

The following two charts depict year of project vs. percent of effort of analysis and design to total effort. Both charts generally have the same distribution, which could be estimated as a normal distribution. Obviously, RM charts are more vivid.

Figure 3. Depicting over time two variables: analysis and design efforts percent of total analysis and design using SPSS (on left) and RM (on right)

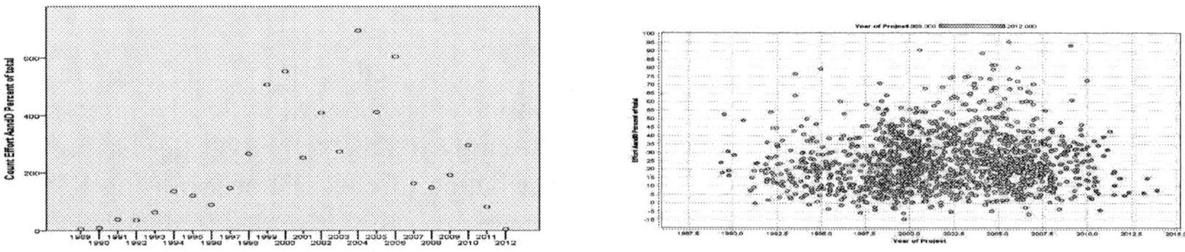

The following SPSS-generated chart shows overall that defect density increases during the latter years. This could be attributed to increased complexity of software projects. Naturally, year 2000 showed increase in defect density.

Figure 4. Depicting defect density over time using SPSS (on left), and total efforts over time using RM. (on right)

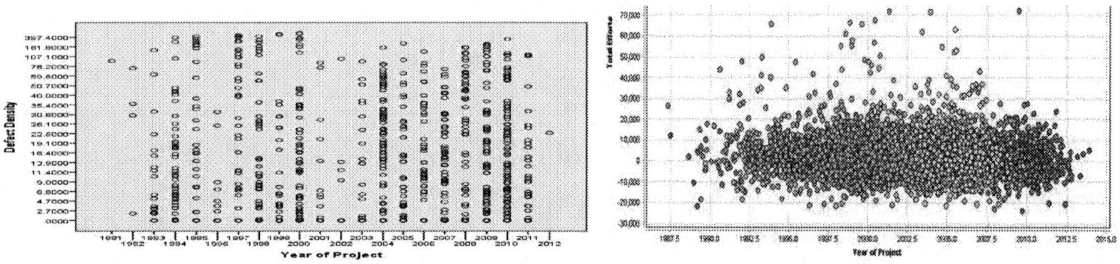

The following chart is generated using RM. The chart shows that the total effort stayed consistent throughout the years, with more outliers appearing in earlier years.

In variables dependent visualization using SPSS, the two charts below reveal an astonishing relationship between total defects delivered vs. percent of analysis and design effort of total efforts, and speed of delivery vs. total defects delivered. The common estimate is the non-linear inverse function: starts with a steep decline, to a curve, then levels off straight.

Figure 5. Depicting percent of analysis and design of total efforts against total defects delivered (on left) and total defect delivered against speed of delivery (on right)

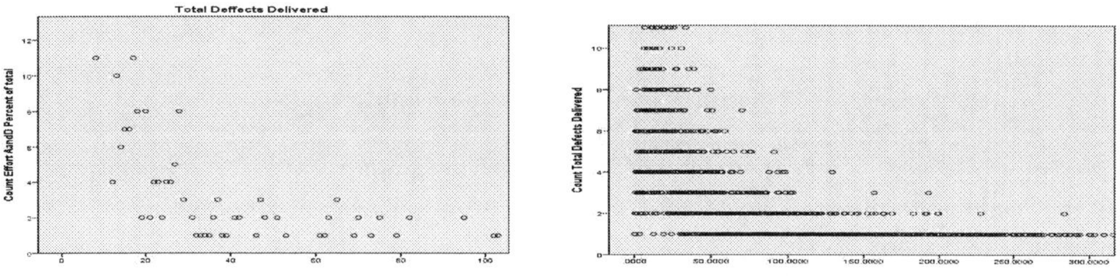

Conclusions and further research

The three type of data analysis showed how three different views can lead to different understanding of the underlining behavior of ISBSG dataset. Below is a list of some of the conclusions of these analysis.

- **Statistical analysis related conclusions:**
    - o A strong relationship between speed of delivery and manpower delivery rate - A relationship between defect density and speed of delivery and manpower delivery rate
    - o Adjusted functional points is related to total efforts and total defects delivered -Total effort is related to total defect delivered.
    - o Overall, the general linear model with multiple dependent and independent variables show significant relationships among the model variables: quality of data, industry sector, and development type as independent variables; and defect density, effort of analysis and design as a total of efforts, total efforts, manpower delivery rate, and resource level as dependent variables.
    - o Effort of analysis and design as a percent of total efforts was negatively related to total defects delivered. This relationship does support the postulate that from-end activities do positively affect subsequent back-end activities.
- **Data mining clustering conclusions:**
    - o Normalized work effort, defect density, total effort, and total defects delivered impacted the formation of the clusters; while speed of delivery, effort on analysis and design had a minor effect in forming the clusters.
- **Visualization related conclusions:**
    - o Year 2000 projects showed a steep upward in speed of delivery, with expected increase in speed of delivery over the next few years - Total defect delivered over time had an approximation of a normal distribution, predicting an upsurge in coming years.
    - o Effort on analysis and design of total effort did not experience any particular behavior over time - Defect density showed an increase towards the latter years - Total efforts over the years stay consistently uniform except for outliers until 2005.
    - o Effort on analysis and design of total efforts vs. total defects delivered and total defect delivered vs. speed of delivery followed a non-linear inverse function.

Lessons learned from these analyses are:

- Need to decide on the criteria for slicing and dicing the data set horizontally and vertically - Attempt to select data with the least minimum missing values as possible.
- Outliers pays major role in the analysis and must be dealt with in the analysis. Also, remove outliers before processing data for analysis - New variables could be recalculated or coded before analysis

References:

Bassil, Y. (2012). "A Simulation model for the Waterfall software development life cycle." International Journal of Engineering & Technology (iJET), Volume 2, Issue 5, pp. 742-749.

Beck, K., et. al. (2001). "Principles behind the Agile Manifesto." http://www.agilemanifesto.org, Retrieved 31 March 2017.

Bellini, C., Pereira, R., & Becker, J. (2008). "Measurement in software engineering: From the roadmap to the crossroads." Int. J. Software Engineering & Knowledge Engineering 18(1), pp. 37-64.

Brooks Jr., F. P. (1995). "The Mythical Man-Month: essays on Software Engineering." Anniversary Edition (2nd Edition), Addison-Wesley Professional; Anniversary edition (August 12, 1995)

Cockburn A. & Highsmith J. (2001). "Agile software development: The business of innovation." IEEE Computer, pp. 120–122.

Cohn, M. (2011). Blog post on 2011 CHAOS report from the Standish Group, http://www.mountaingoatsoftware.com/blog/agile-succeeds-three-times-more-often-than-waterfall. Retrieved 31 March 2017.

Hannay, J. E., & Benestad, H. C. (2010). "Perceived productivity threats in large agile development projects." In Proceedings of the 2010 ACM-IEEE International Symposium on Empirical Software Engineering and Measurement, p. 15.

Hernández-López, A, Colomo Palacios, R., & García-Crespo, Á. (2013). "Software engineering job productivity - a systematic review." International Journal of Software Engineering and Knowledge Engineering, Volume 23, Issue 3, pp. 387- .

Koch, S. (2009). "Exploring the effects of SourceForge.net coordination and communication tools on the efficiency of open source projects using data envelopment analysis." Empirical Software Engineering, Volume 14, Issue 4. Pp. 397-417.

Lindvall, M. et. al. (2004). "Agile software development in large organizations." Computer IEEE, Volume 37, Issue 12, pp. 26-34.

Melo, C., Cruzes, D. S., Kon, F., & Conradi, R. (2011). "Agile team perceptions of productivity factors." In Agile Conference (AGILE), IEEE, pp. 57-66).

Object Management Group, (2017). "Automated Function Points (AFP)." Versions 1.0, OMG Document Number formal/2014-01-03, January 2014. Accessed July 1, 2017 from: http://www.omg.org/spec/AFP/1.0/PDF.

Rodriguez, D., Sicilia, M. A., Garcia, E., & Harrison, R. (2012). "Empirical findings on team size and productivity in software development." Journal of Systems and Software, Volume 85, Issue 3, pp. 562-570.

Royce, W. (1970). "Managing the development of large software systems." Proceedings of IEEE WESCON, 26, pp.1-9.

Sommerville, I. (2015). "Software Engineering." Addison Wesley, 10th ed.

Trendowicz, A. & Münch, J. (2009). "Factors influencing software development productivity - State-of-the-Art and Industrial Experiences." Advances in Computers, 77, pp. 185-241.

Wang, Y. (2004). "On the cognitive informatics foundations of software engineering." In Third IEEE International Conference on Cognitive Informatics, 2004, pp. 22-31.

Data Security Issues and their Solutions in Cloud Computing

Anubhav Raj Singh
Student, SCSE, Galgotias University
anubhavraj.08@gmail.com

Abhineet Anand
Professor, SCSE, Galgotias University
abhineet.mnnit@gmail.com

Cloud Computing is one of the fastest gravitated computing service in IT sector, it has solved the issue of managing and spending time and money on hardware and services. More and more business are storing some or all of their data on the cloud but as the cloud servers are in the remote areas or even in another end of the world, it is possible to modify, hack and erase data. Security breaches are the major issues Cloud Computing is facing which need to be resolved. Data security can be implemented in many ways one of which is data encryption techniques which can be boon for Cloud Computing data security issues. This paper has discussed the various techniques and methods which can be adapted to make this gravitated computing service safer and impenetrable.

I. INTRODUCTION

Cloud Computing is one of the highest rated computing service trending currently in IT sector."A Cloud is a system of interconnected and interdependent physical and virtual computer and computing services which is operated based on negotiations between consumer and cloud service providers"(Buyya, Yeo, Venugopal, Broberg, & Brandic, 2009). Introduction of the cloud has made it easy to mobile our business, infrastructure, and data related to it. By using cloud it is now operable to do computing services from a remote location even if we are sitting in any part of the world. As defined by the US National Institute of Standards and Technology (NIST) 'Cloud computing is a model for enabling ubiquitous, convenient, on-demand network access to a shared pool of configurable computing resources (e.g., networks, servers, storage, applications, and services) that can be rapidly provisioned and released with minimal management effort or service provider interaction'(Mell & Grance, 2011).Cloud Computing has reduced the capital that was being invested in services like infrastructure, software, and others.Cloud Computing provides three major service models.These services are described below (Krishna, Kiran, Murali, & Reddy, 2016):

- Infrastructure as a Service (IaaS) provides basic computing and storage services over the network like servers, processing, data centers, storage, routers on pay as per use basis.
- Platform as a Service (PaaS) provides a cloud based environment for developing other services. PaaS sometimes provide API using which different applications and services can be built.
- Software as a Service (SaaS) provides software services on the cloud where a single occurrence of the software application from a particular organization can be used by multiple user or organization over the cloud.

Cloud Computing has provided us with many benefits but at the same time, we are also putting our privacy at risk.The data stored in the cloud is increasing exponentially.The cloud is servers are in the remote location, it can be in any part of the world and the stored on the cloud can be hacked, manipulated or destroyed. Since now a major section of companies are shifting towards cloud computing, the data security is the more important concern. Although the cloud providers provide us with an assurance that the data stored in the cloud is a 100 per cent safe but it's not hidden from anyone about the different data hacks and data leaks.

Therefore, the data on the cloud must be secured not only from the cloud providers but also from the clients too. Different methods and techniques must be implemented to safeguard the data stored on the cloud. From figure:1 it is clear that data on the cloud is increasing exponentially which should be taken into account in order to secure the data.

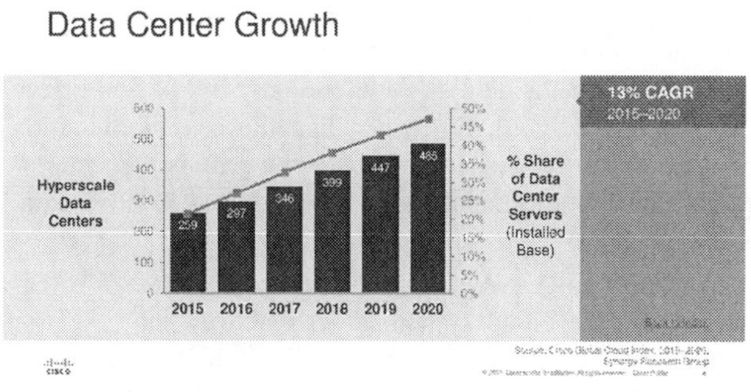

Figure 1. Data Center Growth

II. CLOUD COMPUTING DATA SECURITY

Today small and big all are moving towards cloud data model. Providing data security should be our prime concern. A little carelessness and data can be hacked or leaked which and effect the company or organization in a very harmful way. Data security is considered as the most important factor among the different data challenges in Cloud Computing Fig.2.

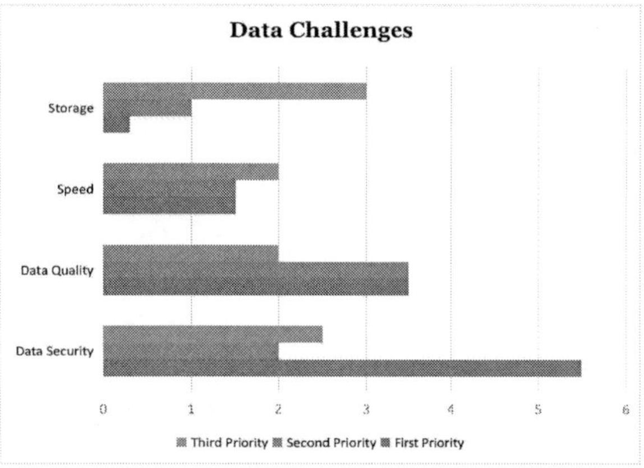

Figure 2. Data Challenges

The security is mainly concerns with CIA i.e, Confidentiality, Integrity, and Availability(Rao & Selvamani, 2015). These the three main areas which should be kept in mind in order to design security especially in Cloud Computing.

1) Confidentiality : As the data stored in the cloud is of different types and many users can access the data available on the cloud, thus confidentiality must be maintained. Confidentiality refers to giving permission or access to particular authorized users only(Sana Belguith, 2015).The data is stored in the remote data servers so to maintain the confidentiality consumer must be aware of its accessibility(Rao & Selvamani, 2015).

2) Integrity : Privacy must be maintained in the cloud, only the people who have authority must be allowed to make changes. Integrity refers to the providing access to modify, edit, delete the data on the cloud only by the authorized people(Sana Belguith, 2015).Any unauthorized modification of the data should be detected. Data integrity is very important in the cloud to maintain the data lost(Rao & Selvamani, 2015).

3) Availability : Availability refers to the process of ensuring that the cloud system is accessible to the end user whenever they want. The extent up to which the data should be available depends on the agreement between the provider and the consumer.

III. LITERATURE REVIEW

Security can be provided to the data in many ways like encryption, hashing, ciphering data, data masking. Today the cloud is not safe, if want to use cloud you have to store the data in the cloud and thus the security and privacy are at risk at every point. Cryptography is the best way to secure data. Data encryption along with hashing can be a possible solution to safeguard the data. Encryption is a method in which data is converted or encrypted in an unreadable form which can be later decrypted when needed using password key.Hashing refers to converting password in a particular set of a string using different hash function algorithm, the benefit of hashing is that we can never go back to the password using hashed string. There is basically two type of cryptography techniques: Symmetric and asymmetric techniques(Sana Belguith, 2015). In Symmetric encryption, the same key is used to encrypt and decrypt the data while in asymmetric encryption two keys are used one is public which is used for encryption while the private key used for decryption of the data. In this paper asymmetric technique is used.

In 2015, R. Velumadhava Rao and K. Selvamani discussed the data security challenges and their solutions in cloud computing(Rao & Selvamani, 2015). In this, they have suggested data encryption as the solution to secure information. RSA signature and identity based on cryptography can also be used to check data integrity.

In 2016, Ishan Sharma, Rajeev Tiwari and Abhineet Anand have described how the analysis of big data is extremely valuable to make decision and increase productivity in bussiness sector.Most of big data is saved on the cloud and as it is extremely valuable it is needed to be secured.(Sharma, Tiwari, & Anand, 2017)

In 2017, Abhijeet Singh and Abhineet Anand have explained how data leakage is big problem in IT firms which is costing them huge loss of capital. Encrypting cloud data is important so that even if data is leaked by any means if would of no use for others.(Abhijeet Singh, 2017)

In 2015, Sana Belguith, Abderrazak Jemai, and Rabah Attia have wonderfully described how using a lightweight cryptographic algorithm can use to solve the problem of security. They have proposed the idea of using a combination of symmetric and asymmetric encryption techniques to provide the safer environment to the cloud data(Sana Belguith, 2015).

In 2015, Selvamani K and Jayanthi S have discussed a little about Public auditing mechanism and use of key and signature generation to secure cloud data in providing security to cloud computing(Selvamani & Jayanthi, 2015).

In 2016, B. Hari Krishna, Dr.S. Kiran, G. Murali and R. Pradeep Kumar Reddy, have also penned down a point to use data encryption as a solution to cloud data security issue(Krishna et al., 2016).

IV. METHODOLOGY

A. Proposed approach to provide data security

In this section, a simple but powerful solution has been provided to secure data on the cloud. Two different methods have been combined to provide the uttermost security to the data. The methods are Data Encryption and password hashing. Data encryption is a conversion of the data into a different form or code which is unreadable until it is reverted back to the same data using a password or decryption key.Encrypting data before uploading is to cloud can be very useful in providing security to the confidential data. We are going to use the asymmetric encryption where the encryption key is public so it can be made available to many people working in the same organization who can encrypt the data before uploading it to cloud. The decryption key in asymmetric encryption method is kept private so it is made available to only to the selected user with whom the organization wants to share the data. The encrypted data which is stored on the cloud is totally secured by the key. But today passwords can be easily broken using different like brute-force attack, dictionary attack, look up tables, reverse look up table or rainbow tables. These all are the simple but powerful method used for hacking. The make our data more secure a method called salted password hashing. Password hashing is a one-way function. It is a fixed length set of strings which contains a random number and letters in some powerful hashing algorithms special character is also used the string acts as a "fingerprint" to authenticate password. If even a bit is changed in the password the hashed string will be completely different. Hashing the asymmetrically encrypted private key will make it a step ahead in security. But to be two steps ahead in security we are going to use the technique called Salted Password Hashing.

B. Powering the new data security algorithm

The data in the cloud is encrypted using an asymmetric approach to data encryption in which encryption key is public but the decryption key private.

1) Private Key Generation : The first step in the proposed model will be the generation of the private key which can only be generated once the data is encrypted using the most secure encryption algorithm like Triple DES, RSA, Blowfish and much more but we should only use the encryption algorithm only provided the experts. After the encryption the data the private key will be generated, which will be further be made more secure.

2) Salted Hashing of the private key : After the generation of the private key, the next thing is to make it more secure and unhackable. We are going to this by salted hashing fig.3.

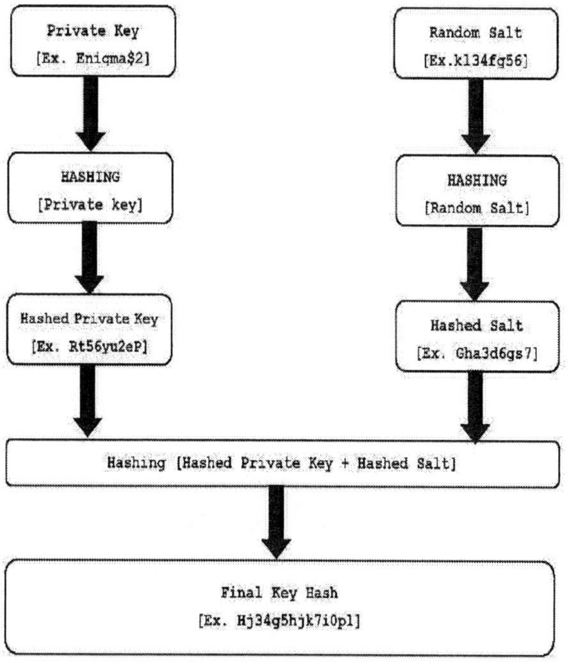

Figure 3. Salted Password Hashing

- First, the private key is hashed using the secure hashing functions like WHIRLPOOL, Ripe MD, SHA512 or SHA256 and the hashed string is stored.
- Next, the salt (a random string) is taken and it is also hashed and stored.
- Now both the hashed private key and hashed salt is combined by appending of prepending the hashed salt with the hashed private key.
- After this, the combination is again hashed and the final key is generated. This is the most secure way to keep the data safe on the cloud. If a hacker tries to crack the private key from the digital signature of the encrypted data, at most efficient way only the private key can be cracked. But as our authentication is based on the final hash the data cannot be decrypted in any condition. The salt will be provided by the cloud provided by the cloud provider and the private key will be safe with the authorized person.

3) Key authentication and data access : The final step will be the access of the data. The user will request the cloud to retrieve the data by entering the private key if the file requested and the private is correct the cloud will select the salt associated with and hash it. It will again hash it with the hashed entered private key if the final key is matches with the decryption key the user is authenticated and the data is provided after decryption.

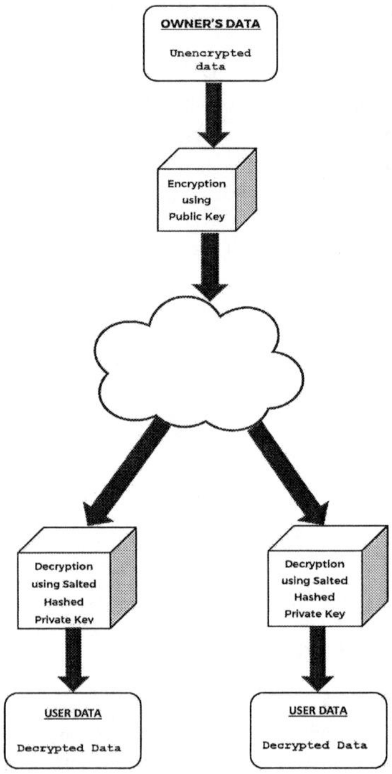

Figure 4. Data access

V. CONCLUSION

Securing cloud data is a very important concern today and to do this use of cryptography techniques is the best way to implement security. In this paper, we have used the combination of two techniques one is asymmetric data encryption and the other is Salted password hashing. Here we first encrypt the data using a public key and then the private key is hashed with a random salt to make the private key secure and encryption unbreakable. The provided technique is fast and the most secure and it can be implemented very easily. This paper just provides an idea how using simple techniques big problems can be solved.Encryption can reduce the global cloud theft and risk of data leak to a great extent. Today most of our personal data including images and videos are on cloud thus providing a secure environment will increase a recognizable shift towards adoptation of cloud computing from small devices like watch to big data centers of MNCs.

VI. FUTURE SCOPE

In near future, more techniques like this can be derived and implemented. Implementation is the only way to test new ideas and find a better solution.In future this proposed idea can be used not only for securing big data centers but can be used in compact and small devices like mobile phones. Implementing this in mobile phones would be a great success as today most of our personal data like sms, emails, images and videos are synced to the cloud provided on it. Hopefully, in future, all the new methodology can be tested by implementing them.Doing this will make cloud computing more secure and a boon to modern IT world.

References

Abhijeet Singh, A. A. (2017). Data leakage detection using cloud computing. *IJECS, 6*. (International Journal Of Engineering And Computer Science (IJECS)) doi: https://dx.doi.org/10.18535/ijecs/v6i4.59

Buyya, R., Yeo, C. S., Venugopal, S., Broberg, J., & Brandic, I. (2009, June). Cloud computing and emerging it platforms: Vision, hype, and reality for delivering computing as the 5th utility. *Future Gener. Comput. Syst., 25*(6), 599–616. Retrieved from `http://dx.doi.org/10.1016/j.future.2008.12.001` doi: 10.1016/j.future.2008.12.001

Krishna, B. H., Kiran, S., Murali, G., & Reddy, R. P. K. (2016). Security issues in service model of cloud computing environment. *Procedia Computer Science, 87*(Supplement C), 246 - 251. (Fourth International Conference on Recent Trends in Computer Science Engineering (ICRTCSE 2016)) doi: https://doi.org/10.1016/j.procs.2016.05.156

Mell, P. M., & Grance, T. (2011). *Sp 800-145. the nist definition of cloud computing* (Tech. Rep.). Gaithersburg, MD, United States.

Rao, R. V., & Selvamani, K. (2015). Data security challenges and its solutions in cloud computing. *Procedia Computer Science, 48*(Supplement C), 204 - 209. (International Conference on Computer, Communication and Convergence (ICCC 2015)) doi: https://doi.org/10.1016/j.procs.2015.04.171

Sana Belguith, R. A., Abderrazak Jemai. (2015). Enhancing data security in cloud computing using a lightweight cryptographic algorithm. , 98 to 103. (ICAS 2015:The Eleventh International Conference on Autonomic and Autonomous Systems)

Selvamani, K., & Jayanthi, S. (2015). A review on cloud data security and its mitigation techniques. *Procedia Computer Science, 48*(Supplement C), 347 - 352. (International Conference on Computer, Communication and Convergence (ICCC 2015)) doi: https://doi.org/10.1016/j.procs.2015.04.192

Sharma, I., Tiwari, R., & Anand, A. (2017). Open source big data analytics technique. In S. C. Satapathy, V. Bhateja, & A. Joshi (Eds.), *Proceedings of the international conference on data engineering and communication technology: Icdect 2016, volume 1* (pp. 593–602). Singapore: Springer Singapore. Retrieved from `https://doi.org/10.1007/978-981-10-1675-2_58` doi: 10.1007/978-981-10-1675-2_58

Cloud Computing In Banking Sector

Shashwat Singh
Student, School of Computer Science and Engineering,
Galgotias University, Greater Noida

Abhineet Anand
Professor, School of Computer Science and Engineering,
Galgotias University, Greater Noida

Abstract-The evolution of Cloud Computing has changed each and every platform which directly or indirectly depends upon the IT Resources. All the IT departments are adopting cloud platforms. The main key point of cloud is "Portability", i.e. data can be accessed from anywhere anytime. As compared to other companies and corporates, banks and other financial institutions have been quite slow in adopting cloud services. The banks which do not adopt cloud services operate completely like software companies. They hire software developers, UI designers, data administrators, security analysts and even software testers. All these things increases the expenditures by which many banks run into loss. The adoption of cloud in banks will allow smaller banks to establish a global brand at a very less cost and many other helpful things will be discussed.
Keywords-cloud computing, cloud data, banking data;

I. INTRODUCTION

A. What is Cloud Computing ??? The exchange of data or IT resources through internet is known as "CLOUD COMPUTING". It is so called , because clouds can shrink and enlarge depending upon the content of water in it, and like that only we needed a platform which can store data like 'clouds storing water', this gave rise to the evolution of cloud platforms . Further computing these data on cloud platforms is termed as cloud computing.

B. TYPES OF CLOUD

Public Cloud - It is a common storage space , from where data can be accessed by anyone without signing or logging in. For example Google.com, anyone can get information about anything on Google .

Private Cloud - It is a storage space , from where one can access data only through signing in by his/her account. Before storing data one has to create an account using secured id and password. For example Google Drive, one can store an access data after signing through Google account.

Community Cloud - It is a storage space , from where a common group of people can access the data. For example a G mail/ group, Google forms etc .

Hybrid Cloud - It is a storage space which is both public-private,Private-community etc. They can be accessed either by one's secured id and password or publicly as well. For example drop box , it can be used as private cloud as well as community cloud be because we can also share data on it.

C. SERVICE/BUSINESS MODEL OF CLOUD COMPUTING

- **INFRASTRUCTURE AS A SERVICE** - When someone buys servers or storage for his business or some other plan, then it is said that the host is lending its infrastructure through internet.
- **SOFTWARE AS A SERVICE** - Users can access software applications hosted by cloud vendors on pay per use basis. The particular software runs on Browser. For example-Facebook introduced the feature of video calling , but we were not using any installed software like Skype, so the video calling was done through the software which was running on the browser through internet.
- **PLATFORM AS A SERVICE** - We can get platforms like Word press,Bloggers.com, you tube etc. , where we can ,make our websites, blogs ,upload our videos on you tube and many other things. All these things we can do through our browser through internet.
- **COMMUNICATION AS A SERVICE** - All the social media is an example of communication as a service, Instagram , Facebook , whats app , Twitter are the examples. We can access our social media account from anywhere in the world. Therefore these are the services provided by cloud computing.

Banking Sector's Growing Needs

The banking industry today is experiencing large scale changes, with the introduction of "Digital India", and more customers are using mobile devices to conduct financial transactions. To survive, banks need to move upstream in order to add more value to their customers and at the same time they also have to maintain the low investment for larger profit, and cloud is what they should hold on. They will get

all the services for their customers for much less investment. All the small banks will get a great chance to expand their brand and to become a large organization.
Temenos is global banking software provider, which provides all the financial soft wares required by the banks. Now it is building a cloud-based version of its core banking application to give customers functionality in the cloud. By developing its new version on the Microsoft Azure platform, Temenos can offer cloud banking capabilities to companies that have traditionally used on-premises solutions, and it can help them meet strict security and compliance requirements. One of the major expenses for banks is IT i.e. in buying soft wares and also extra staff, and with an increasing emphasis on lower margins, they have to look at the cloud as a way of reducing IT costs. Temenos, gives the option to access our banking resources via the cloud rather than buying all the soft wares. Cloud offers a scalable and manageable technology model that reduces IT hardware, maintenance and development costs.[4] This further provides us the agility and flexibility to enlarge the organization, new services and new resources, with consumer needs. It helps in :-
1-Expanding to New Markets
2-Avoiding the Need to Hire More Staff

II. LITERATURE SURVEY

Impact Of Cloud Computing on Banks

Now a days all the companies whether big or small are adopting cloud services in order to grow fast and with less investment . The main reasons for the massive shift towards cloud is the efficiency and economic sense that this technology offers. There is no need of investing in other complex equipment or employing experienced computer programmers to manage the system.[1] In 1994, "Bill Gates" said that in the future, banking would be needed, but banks themselves would not. With every passing year, this statement seems to gain more and more importance.
The banks which have their own IT departments for IT services ,spends a lot of money in their payments and services, which takes them behind as compared to other banks which use cloud services. Further customers have to pay service charges therefore they are not happy ,and thus these type of banks have less number of customers and do not get desired profit.
The banks which adopt cloud services can accelerate themselves fast than others. Customers will have to pay less service charges therefore they will be happy, also the rate of interests in saving bank will be more and for loans will be less because the investment by bank will be less. These banks will earn more profit and will have more customers,because service charge is something which nobody wants to give , and this is the main cause that customers prefer having a bank account in a bank which uses all the soft wares on cloud.
In 2010 Metro Bank in UK became the first bank to adopt cloud services which helped it to keep the technology and service cost low ,increased the scalability and the most important thing was ,all the customers were happy as they don't have to pay service charges. After that it had 40 branches in London which served more than half a million customers. It is a best example of how cloud can change the future of finance.[2]

Percentage of Companies That Use Cloud for Vital Processes in the Financial Sector [2]
46 per - Application development and testing
46 per- Managing customer relationships
43 per- Email
41 per- Storage
41 per- Data Intelligence

III. IDEA PROPOSED

(Single Platform Banking)

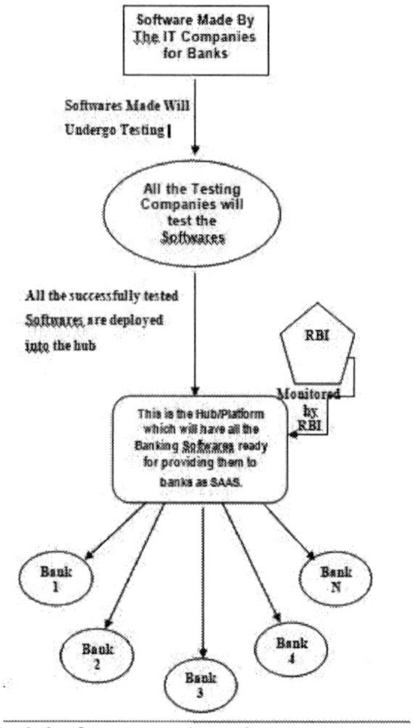

Figure 1. Model of proposed work

A . Explanation:

(Single Platform Banking)

Single Platform Banking is to establish a cloud based powerful platform/organization, which will provide soft wares with high processing speed to all the banks(whether small or large). The banks will get all the required soft wares through Software as a Service on rental base, which will be very less

as compared to the current expenditures of banks on buying their soft wares. All the soft wares which will be made available for banks will be first tested by top IT Software testing companies like CSC , Fortech,Infosys. This organization will be monitored by Reserve Bank Of India(RBI),so it will be now easy to track all the banks.
Since the rental charges will be very low all the banks will rush to adopt this SAAS platform as this will save their lot of capital investment as they don't need to have extra staff for maintenance of the soft wares, because they don't need to actually buy the soft wares. This will also allow small banks to grow and become large ones. As this platform is very cheap, therefore there will be one condition for the banks in order to give something to the common people which is that, all the banks have to decrease their interest on the loans which they offer, a lot of people especially farmers die due to the pressure of, not able to pay the loan.

B. Main Aim and Importance Of Idea

The main point about this idea is that on implementation all the banks will share a common platform or âĂIJSingle PlatformâĂİ . This platform saves the extra expenditures of banks of buying and maintenance of soft wares, whereas now they will get good quality soft wares with high processing speed developed and tested by top IT companies. Major impacts are -:

Farmer Suicide. In India every year many people and thousands of farmers commit suicide because of not being able to pay their loans to bank and in these cases the interest charged by bank is very high because today also a lot of banks are buying costly IT services which increase their investment and expenditure and therefore they increase their interest rate in order to earn good profit. So if these banks adopt this "Single platform banking model" then their investment and expenditure will be very less as compared to earlier, thus the rate of interest for loan will also be less, which will help those poor people and farmers because the pressure of loan will be less and they can concentrate on the solution of the problem instead of committing a suicide.

Monitoring . After the implementation of this "Single level banking" the monitoring of all the banks can be done very easily by RBI because all the banks will be connected o the same platform. All the transaction and account can be easily monitored . However we cannot forget the risk of hacking as well therefore all data will be made safe by this particular organization by good IT engineers and also it will increase the employment. If somehow war has been declared then government can easily control all the banks if required since all the data is at same cloud.

IV. CONCLUSION

From this paper it can be concluded that Cloud Computing has become the backbone of IT. It can take any company from losses into profits. If it is introduced in banking sector then it can change the working of banks completely. This model can help the poor people because the interest rate of banks will be decreased. Therefore the introduction of cloud computing in banking will take the banks Upto next level where both the bank staff and customers will be happy. "This model is good for all the banks as well as for our NATION as well, Cloud can provide sufficient resources by which a small company can become a large company as GOOGLE and FACEBOOK"

V. FUTURE ADVANCEMENT

Artificial IntelligenceâĂŤFrom sci-fi to reality Artificial intelligence (AI) has the potential to transform both front office and back office operations with its self-improving programs, for example, software robots have been deployed in over 200 business process functions, reducing the response time to customers by up to 60 percentage. AI has already proven itself in providing seamless differentiated customer experience on digital channels, and security measures with its integration within the banking infrastructure. Intelligent digital assistants are commonplace, and these self-learning programs keep getting better with every interaction. As 2017 progresses, banks will look to explore more proof of concepts to integrate conversational interfaces into their own strategy. AI can take the banking onto the next level after Cloud Computing where people could inject small and minute robots in their fingers which will have all the data of the persons account and payment can be done very easily with the fingers instead of credit and debit cards. [3]

References

1. https://technofaq.org/posts/2017/08/taking-banking-to-the-next-level-how-saas-revolutionize-the-financial-industry/

2. http://www.theatlantic.com/sponsored/microsoft-2016/how-connectivity-is-moving-banks-forward/927/

3.http://www.huffingtonpost.in/rajashekara-v-maiya/6-technology-trends-that-will-transform-banking-in-2017_a_21645614/

4..https://customers.microsoft.com/en-us/story/core-banking-software-provider-moves-flagship-offering/

Security and Compliance Management in Cloud Computing

Ahtisham Hashmi
Student
School of Computing Science and Engineering
Galgotias University

Aarushi Ranjan
Student
School of Computing Science and Engineering
Galgotias University

Dr. Abhineet Anand
Assistant Professor
School of Computing Science and Engineering
Galgotias University

The businesses are now shifting to the cloud-based services for the enhancement of efficiency, scalability, and flexibility. Small-scale companies are accepting Public Cloud whereas large companies are accepting Private Cloud. The key to Cloud computing is the Virtualization of the resources. An important issue in cloud computing on which attention must be paid is Security and Compliance. The customer has no idea where the data is stored and where the processes are running. The provider must ensure the security of the costumer's data. The public cloud is open, hence it is considered to be less secure. To secure the cloud, it needs planning and resources. Depending upon the types of service the application is providing, it has to comply with the regulations. The compliance is the responsibility of the organizations and the service providers. To understand and then to enforce the regulations is another issue of Cloud computing. This paper focuses mainly on understanding the security issues in cloud computing and cognizes compliance management in Cloud computing, using the "Security as a Service" model of cloud computing. And comparing different SECaaS vendors for different aspects of security and compliance.

Introduction

The Security of data from both the perspective as of customer as well as the vendor is the major issue and concern in cloud computing. Customer shifts the data to the cloud environment without having the idea where the data is going to be stored in the cloud. Cloud is a virtual space provided to the customers with many virtual resources to deploy their applications[1]. This virtual space is provided over the Internet to the customers or developers as an abstract of web-based resources, computers and services to utilize dynamically through which complex web-based systems can be implemented. Cloud provides us many features such as elasticity, scalability, universal access, low entry cost, flexible billing, new service offerings, easy and convenient monitoring.The motivation of the paper came from the drawbacks that existing cloud security system already has. The technologies in cloud computing have their own security solutions but these solutions are provided only from the provider side and this is a drawback for the existing security system in the cloud computing. The customer or Organization does not have any knowledge where its data is stored and also, it does not have access and control to the status of data. Each transaction is controlled by the server (or provider) side. This paper focuses and proposes that the security controls must be ensured from the client (or customer) side through the web browser or the mobile application. The proposed model is Security-as-a-Service model which provides the continuous monitoring of the user's data through the client machine instead of provider side so that the customer can track the status of his data and its transactions[2].

Deployment Models of Cloud

Deployment models in the cloud computing specify how the resources are shared within the cloud. The deployment models distinguish which category of the cloud is to be used by the company on the basis of the size, privacy, access, and proprietorship. It also reduces the cost of expenditure. As most of the companies are moving their businesses to the cloud environment then these companies have to understand which deployment model meets their requirement.[3]

Public Cloud

It exposes the applications, computing resources, storage systems, networks and other services to the customers, businesses or companies over the internet in a virtual environment. These services provided to the customers are either free of cost or pay-as-you-go model is followed at attractive low cost with the subscription mechanism i.e. customer pays either for the use or for the resources that are allocated. It is owned and operated by the third party resources. All the customers share the same infrastructures which are pooled with the limited configuration, availability and security variances. This model is the most recognizable to the customers among all the deployment models. When the application or data is shifted to the cloud then the customers have limited visibility or there is no control and consideration over from where the infrastructure is hosted. This unawareness of the actual location of data can cause security issue in this model[3].

The benefits of public cloud computing are as follows:

Cost Effectiveness : Large level of resources are brought together so that it can benefit from large economies of scale and share the same resources and infrastructure with several customers hence cost is reduced while deploying the applications. Scalability: The services are provided to the customers on demand, a vast pool of resources of public cloud makes available the computing resources. On-demand, these resources can be scaled whenever necessary so the customer does not have to pay for the resources that are not utilized[4].

Utility-Based Costing : pay as per use model is followed, the customer has to pay for those resources such as storage or software which are acquired instead of the actual infrastructure. This avoids the wastage of total capacity of the resource.

Reliability: Physically the data is stored in different data centers and the number of networks and storage are connected together to form the public cloud. If either of the components failed or entire data center goes offline then also the data can be fetched from the multiple data centers and no failure could takes place[4].

The public cloud model also has some disadvantages which are as follows:

Low Security: The data in public cloud model is hosted off-site and hence it is less secure. The resources are shared publicly so the higher level of security cannot be ensured.

Less Customizable: The customization of cloud is less than the private cloud[4].

Private Cloud

The cloud infrastructure which is implemented and provisioned exclusively for the use of single enterprise and is secured by a firewall which is under the governance of IT Department that belongs to the particular corporate is termed as Private Cloud. The single organization owning the Private cloud solution internally or externally may have its customers or its business units to whom services and system are accessible. The organization gives access only to the authorized users which provide greater control over their data. Obstructions with respect to security can be abstained using the private cloud but it is prone to permeability in case of internal data theft and natural disaster. It can be managed and operated by a third party as in Public cloud or by an organization or by the combination of both of them. It delivers similar advantages as a Public cloud but through a proprietary architecture[3].

The benefits of private cloud computing are as follows:

More Security and Privacy: The resources are shared from the segregated pool of resources and the operations are not made available to the general public. Therefore higher security and privacy is ensured.

More Control: Private cloud is accessed by and within a specific organization and hence it has more control over its resources, information, and hardware than public cloud.

The private cloud model comprises of following disadvantages:

Restricted Area: The private cloud is deployed within a campus of a particular organization and it can be only accessed locally. This model cannot be deployed globally.

Limited Scalability: The scalability of resources is not as simple as provided by the Public cloud model because it can be scaled up within the capacity of the internal hosted resources[4].

Hybrid Cloud

An integrated cloud model which is an arrangement of two or more cloud infrastructures such as Public cloud, private cloud or community cloud is called Hybrid Cloud. Here the participating clouds are unique and individual entities but bound to integrate with the technology that enables data and application portability. This model cannot be categorized as a public or private cloud because it follows both and also crosses the boundaries of both these clouds and their providers. The critical or production workloads must be housed internally and no-critical and non-production workloads must be housed in public cloud by a third-party provider.

The benefits of hybrid cloud computing are as follows:

Scalability: Similar to the public cloud and private cloud scalability, the hybrid cloud also provides on-demand scalability either by purchasing new hardware or by renting the hardware.

Cost efficiency: As the public cloud is more cost-effective than private cloud so hybrid cloud also has the same property of saving the cost.

Security: High security of hybrid cloud is ensured due to the high degree of security which is provided by the private cloud.

The hybrid cloud model comprises of following disadvantages:

Networking: Due to the presence of public and private cloud, the networking becomes more complex and the networking issues are generated.

Infrastructural Dependency: Ensuring the redundancy across the data centers is necessary because hybrid cloud model depends upon the internal IT infrastructure.

Cloud Delivery Models

Measuring compliance and achieving compliance are two different things. To make cloud computing secure and compliant, organizations first need to understand the types of cloud computing they might be using to support their objective[5]. For this there are three basic cloud delivery models are:

Software-as-a-Service (SaaS)

SaaS provides a web/internet based access to software applications.The user can use the software on a subscription basis i.e. they can pay for only what they use. The user is offered anywhere access, but this increases the security risk that includes data security, network security, data access, authorization, and authentication.

Platform-as-a-Service (PaaS)

PaaS provides a platform like Red Hat Open Shift, Google App engine as cloud services to its end users to deploy their software applications and develop them.strong authentication is required for the user identification, an audit, and compliance regulation support. For example, Microsoft Windows Azure where despite managing the underlying cloud infrastructure controls the consumer controls the deployed applications.

Infrastructure-as-a-Service (IaaS)

Iaas provides infrastructure components as a service to the end-user on a subscription basis. It allows the provisioning of processing, storage, networks and other fundamental computing resources and deployed applications. For example, Amazon Elastic Compute Cloud(EC2) where the consumer does not manage or control the underlying cloud infrastructure.

Drawbacks of Security at Provider Side

In cloud computing, the security must be ensured at two levels, at customer or user level, and at the cloud service provider level. The end-users and businesses have different visions for cloud computing. For end-user, It means the immediate access to the IT using a web interface and for businesses, it means to reduce the cost. At the provider side, the server must be well secured from the threats and attacks. At user side, the data loss, data tampering, and stealing must not be experienced by other users which are there on the same cloud. Many security issues are faced by the cloud computing because it comprises of several technologies such as virtualization, networks, databases, operating systems, and transaction management etc[4].

Public clouds are major targets for the hackers and continual hacking attempts are made on the public cloud. Large public cloud providers have millions of customers relying on them so, they also have much tight and latest security solutions to provide to the customers. However, there are also chances of the malicious user to penetrate and infect the entire cloud[6].

There are many security concerns and issues that arises when the data is hosted and controlled at the server side i.e provider side such as client i.e is customer or organization which is using the cloud services is not aware of the physical location of data and it is also unable to track the status of the transactions that takes place without contacting to the cloud provider. The cloud customers are not assured whether their data which may be very sensitive will be secure when they shift the data to the cloud without any monitoring in their hand.

Some of the cases are discussed below that are reference for the above discussion about the disadvntage of having the security concerns when the data is controlled from the provider side.

In case, any transaction of the data takes place then it must also to be assured to the cloud customer that the transaction is secure. If an Organisation or a customer shifts its business data to the cloud provider and then that cloud provider became bankrupt or acquired by another business or company. Then it will be the responsibility of the provider to ensure that the data of the organization or any customer which was moved to their cloud enviromnment is as secure as it was before.

The legal governance of data which is shifted to the cloud is another important question that is arised due to the physical location of data and in case, any dispute between the cloud customer and cloud provider arises then judiciary or court system of which country will be responsible for the settlement of the issues.[7]

Compliance

Organizations and consumers have been moving their core business towards cloud but still, there are many challenges to be faced in the cloud and because of that there has been some difficulty in moving a business to cloud. The challenges are-security, privacy, and compliance.

There are a lot of works concerned with security and privacy in the cloud but there are only a few works concerned with compliance aspects respectively. Compliance can be defined in terms of a principle that enforces rules that implement the policies. These policies are nothing but the constituent of regulations.[8]

Regulations are set of rules that manage the use of sensitive data in business. In order to achieve the environmental and public health benefits, a high degree of compliance is required by the regulated community. A wide range of stakeholders and various other non-governmental organizations are informed about the government's interest in assuring compliance. There are different regulations, some are mandatory such as Government and state regulations whereas some are suggestions like industrial suggestions.[9]

Compliance can have different meanings in different fields such as in the field of Healthcare, Compliance means a patient's adherence to a recommended course of treatment. Similarly, Regulatory Compliance means adherence to standards and regulations. Environment Compliance means conforming to environmental laws, regulations, and standards. The cloud customers need to comply with many different industry standards and regulations where we can relate to the 'Cloud Compliance'. An organization takes initiative to comply with regulations in a repeatable process, in order to sustain compliance with the given regulation at a cost less than that of the first deadline.[10]

HIPAA: Health Insurance Portability and Accountability Act (HIPAA)is a set of laws that is supposed to keep the health records and data of the patient secure and intact. It helps in maintaining the standard of electronic health recording systems.

FISMA: Federal Security Management Act. It was endured into the law in 2002.The federal agencies hereby,are required to conduct security programs with full

information reviews.This helps to keep the data at low risk.).

Challenges of Compliance:

Enterprises are looking for specialized compliance software and the consultancies of IT compliance, as the regulations and standards are concerned by corporate management. The ability of an organization to manage both compliance risk and pass compliance audit need to be ensured. The guidelines for compliance target program also varies depending on the industry where the company resides and the data generated and used by them.[11] The Cloud computing comprises of the compliance challenges which are:

Reference Architecture(RA): A generic software architecture that can serve as a reference to indicate where the specific compliance policies should be applied, in the system architecture. Reference Architecture has no platform dependencies, valid for a particular domain. RA is used to guide system design and development. It is a basic challenge for service providers, service brokers, consumers, and auditors. There is no any implementations aspects or vendor specific details in RA.

Patterns: Specific context in which a solution is encapsulated into a surveying problem. It helps improve software equality by promoting re-usability, scalability, and consistency. Patterns can be divided into various categories such as analysis pattern, architecture pattern, security pattern, and design.

Security as a Service model

Security is an important aspect which is to be looked after while shifting to the cloud. The proposed model in this paper for managing the security and mitigate the risks using Security-as-a-Service (SECaaS) model. SECaaS is a business model that allows delivering of the managed security services to the user through the cloud over the internet as other cloud services. It is based on the Software-as-a-Service delivery model of cloud. Security in current cloud services is assumed to be maintained by the cloud providers instead of the user which is using the service[12]. This model provides the monitoring of the data and its related transactions to the side of end-user and decreases the effect of security concerns that arise from the provider side.

The tools of SECaaS as defined by Cloud Service Alliance (CSA), SECaaS includes following tools or services:

Identity and Access Management (IAM): The processes and systems that are responsible for managing the access to resources of an enterprise and assuring that identity if the entity is verified and hence granting the appropriate level of access based on the protected resources, assured identity and other contexts[14].

Data Loss Prevention: Data Loss Prevention must be considered an essential element to achieve an effective security strategy for the protection of data and putting the control on the data to make the data secure when it resides in, moves to or departs from the cloud. It is one of the many layers of the Information protection and control strategy[15].

Web Security: Today the businesses are more user-centric and users are demanding applications and platforms on which they want to work on. And Locations of the devices are no more constant. The web security is embedded with SECaaS and it is known as Web SECaaS which provides dynamic and cloud based services to secure the end-users? devices without the requirement of static security approaches and hardware[16].

Email Security: Email is the most used way of communication between the organizations, businesses and their staff. Data through email is transferred between sender and receiver. But this ubiquitous nature of email makes it the key target to the attacks, scams and malwares. It is to be secured at both ends sender and receiver. SECaaS vendors can analyze the incoming email for malware and can respond to the abnormal activities in mail using a cloud scale and on-demand resources[17].

Security Assessment: The integrity, confidentiality, and availability of data and information ensure that Enterprise achieved their business objectives. The major objective is to ensure the compliance with regulatory and legal requirements for the technologies that are used to support the business processes and decisions. SECaaS solution has been developed to support security assessments through a cloud-hosted environment and stores resulting data after performing the assessments[18].

Business Continuity and disaster recovery: In case of any interruptions of the services, The contingency plans, and measures that are designed and implemented to ensure the operational flexibility came under the Business Continuity and Disaster Recovery. To minimize the cost and maximize the benefits, the cloud-centric BC/DR uses the flexibility of cloud and it is the key benefit of cloud?s resilience. All aspects of the services are mentioned and defined under the Service Level Agreement (SLA)[13].

Intrusion management: In a physical environment, the intrusion management is matured over last decade but in a virtual environment due to massive multi-tenancy, it is difficult to monitor all the interconnecting points between the systems, applications and data sets. The services for intrusion management are delivered via cloud as the questions arise on infrastructure, processes and respond to the intrusion on a cloud environment[19].

Encryption: The primary and most effective technique for data and application protection is Encryption of the data. The keys of encryption must be protected and managed properly. The integrity of the encryption is based on the technology that are providing the cryptographic security solutions[20].

Network Security: Along with the physical network devices, the virtual security devices provide the salient part of the network security in a cloud environment. And it is a crucial responsibility to ensure that there is full visibility of traffic due to the integration with underlying cloud software[21].

Benefits of Security-as-a-Service model are as follows:

Cost: The security services and workloads for maintenance are moved to a cloud platform by the enterprise so that it get ability to increase and decrease the resources instantly and then pay for only those resources and services that it used[9].

Ease of management: The enterprise can monitor all the activities and security using a web interface and can control the tasks that are needed to manage. The SECaaS provider who is delivering the services to the enterprise is responsible to manage the hardware and software.

Scalability: Usage of the information security infrastructure can be rapidly scaled up or down when it meets new demand for workloads

Fast Provisioning: Security applications, devices, and users are provisioned and de-provisioned rapidly, permanently or temporarily depending upon the needs of Enterprise. New users and security services can be provisioned by the Enterprise itself or by requesting new services to the provider.

Expertise: More specialized security than the security which is typically provided to the organizations.

Continuous updates: Continuous updates on Infrastructure and automated security applications are provided by SECaaS which require more resources and effort if performed in-house.

Cost-Effective Compliance: Using SECaaS model, It is ensured for an enterprise that the information security is in alignment with compliance requirements e.g. Health Insurance Portability and Accountability Act (HIPAA) or The Payment Card Industry Data Security Standard (PCI DSS)[11].

Comparative Analysis

This section of the paper is the salient part as it is discussing that which cloud service provider that are providing Security-as-a Service, will give best security to the enterprise according to the requirement of the enterprise. Here, the Comparative analysis takes place between the Cloud Access Security Broker (CASB) of Oracle, Okta Single (Sign-On SSO) which focuses on Identity and Access Management (IAM), Qualys Vulnerability Manager (VM) focuses on the aspect of Network Security, and WhiteHat Sentinel Dynamic which focuses on Website and Application Security..

Oracle CASB

Cloud Access Security Broker (CASB) is a cloud-based service provided by Oracle, that uses an automated security monitoring to protect the entire cloud services by combining the threat detection, visibility, and compliance management. It secures the cloud services against the threats, simplifies the configuration settings and detects the uneven behavior using the user behavior analytics.

Enterprises continuously adopt new cloud services and require more refined security for their entire cloud footprint. Oracle CASB meets modern security requirements of the cloud to protect the enterprise.

Key Features of Oracle CASB are:

- Threat detection using UBA: User behavior Analytics (UBA) in Oracle CASB notices simple incongruences and detects risks if a user is deviating from the baseline. It pulls out the third party threat feeds if Predictive analytics identify the risky user and unusual behaviors like changing permissions, user privileges or altering of configuration settings.

- Complete visibility of cloud environment: Oracle CASB gives a universal view of the cloud environment for all devices and all users. Using this feature an enterprise can identify threats across multiple cloud services and take corrective action to know the source of the problem rather than manually checking for the incidents manually. It also provides the visibility for the applications that are already downloaded from the app stores of the enterprise.

- Integration with existing security solutions: To extend the benefits of the cloud environment, Oracle CASB integrates with existing solutions. If the user already has security solution of an enterprise like Data Loss Prevention (DLP), Next-Generation Firewall (NGF) or Secure Web Gateways (SWG), Oracle CASB builds upon those solutions to maximize the efficiency with minimal investment.

Qualys VM

Qualys Vulnerability Management (VM) is a cloud-based service which provides a global visibility into where IT systems are vulnerable to the latest threat. It continuously identify threats and monitors the unexpected changes in the network. It is most advanced, extensible and scalable solution for continuous vulnerability management and compliance It is well known for its fast deployment and integration with other enterprise systems.

Key Features of Qualys VM are:

- Constant monitoring and alerts: Information Security teams are alerted about the potential threats when VM is integrated with Continuous Monitoring (CM), so that problems can be tackled before they start to violate. Acting as a sentinel for the cloud.
- Agent based detection: To extend the network coverage to the assets that cannot be scanned, VM works with the Qualys Cloud Agents. These self-updating and lightweight agents reside on the assets they monitor and needs no change in firewall, credentials and scan window.
- Comprehensive coverage and visibility: In the mobile and cloud endpoints, the continuous identification of vulnerabilities with Six Sigma (99.99966%) accuracy, and protection of on premise IT assets is done by Qualys VM. Including the automatic security documentation for compliance auditors, Qualys VM also generates custom and role-based reports for multiple stakeholders.

Okta Single Sign-On

The facility of logging in the several applications of an enterprise using the same user credentials is provided by the Single Sign-On (SSO). Okta is a powerful tool for Single Sign-On as it enables the user to access all the applications from a single-access launchpad. IT administrators prefer deploying Okta to reduce the effort and time spent for supporting the organization and it is easy to manage all their applications at a place. It also provides better user-experience to the third-party contractor and employees.

Benefits of Single Sign-On are:

- End to end user audit sessions are performed for the progress of security auditing and reporting.
- Ability to apply the enterprise authentication and authorization policies across the enterprise.
- To understand and implement the identity security in their applications, it removes the application developers.

WhiteHat Sentinel Dynamic

Whitehat Sentinel Dynamic is an dynamic platform which enables deployment of the scalable web security program. It can scale to meet any demand irrespective of how many websites are changed how often. It automatically detects and assesses the code changes to the web applications. It provides the user to remediate the vulnerabilities before it is exploited by an unauthenticated user as it uses the perspective of an adversary to find the weakness. All the vulnerabilities are verified by the WhiteHat's Threat Research Center's security experts.

Key Features of WhiteHat Sentinel Dynamic are:

- Continuous assessment methodology: WhiteHat Sentinel Dynamic constantly scans the websites and offers the automatic detection and continuous assessment of the code changes, as website evolves. It gives alerts for newly found vulnerability and has the ability to retest it without testing from the beginning.
- Open API integration: Sentinel Dynamic can be integrated with Governance Risk and Compliance (GRC), Security Information and Event Management (SIEM), which are much popular bug tracking systems.
- PCI Compliance: By giving the verified vulnerability assessment for internal as well as public websites, services of Sentinel dynamic exceeds the requirements of PCI DSS 3.1. Sentinel integrates with WAF to support the creation of virtual patches that fixes the vulnerabilities and provides the reports needed to pass the auditor inspections.

Conclusion

Cloud computing is an emerging field for sharing and maximal use of the resources. Most of the new businesses choose cloud computing due to its openness, low cost, easy deployment and easy maintenance. As public cloud is open, risks and threats of data loss or theft increases. Many vendors are providing several security solutions to protect the enterprises from the risks. Security-as-a-Service is providing the security solutions to the enterprises that are user-centric instead of provider or vendor-centric, So that user has more visibility to their data and its related security concerns. It is more optimum because user has the control of the security and compliance and visibility of the vulnerabilities, which was not provided by the vendor earlier.

References

1. Kaustubh Rai, Dr. Abhineet Anand, "Deployment of Data Base as a Service and connecting it with the local server",International Journal Of Engineering And Computer Science, ISSN:2319-7242, Volume 6 Issue 5 May 2017, Page No. 21502-21506.

2. Hassan Reza, Madhuri Sonawane,"Enhancing Mobile Cloud Computing Security Using Steganography",Journal of Information Security, July 2016, Page no. 245-259.

3. R.Balasubramanian, M.Aramudhan, "Security Issues: Public vs Private vs Hybrid Cloud Computing", International Journal of Computer Applications (0975 - 8887) Volume 55- No.13, October 2012, Page No. 35-41.

4. Axel Buecker, Koos Lodewijkx, Harold Moss, Kevin Skapinetz, Michael Waidner,"Cloud Security Guidance - IBM Recommendations for the Implementation of Cloud Security".

5. Shalini G., Hamsalatha J, M. Shivakumar," An SOA Model with Security as a Service in Cloud Computing Application-I Banking", International Journal of Engineering trends and Technology, VOl -16, No -6, Oct 2014, ISSN 2231-5381.

6. Prince Jain, "Security Issues and their Solution in Cloud Computing", International Journal of Computing & Business Research ISSN (Online): 2229-6166, Proceedings of 'I-Society 2012' at GKU, Talwandi Sabo Bathinda (Punjab).

7. Sherin Sreedhran, "Security and Privacy Issues of Cloud Computing; Solutions and Secure Framework", IOSR Journal of Computer Engineering, e-ISSN:2278-0061, p-ISSN:2278-8727, Vol. 10, Issue 4 (Mar-Apr 2013), Page No. 33-37.

8. Rabi Prasad Padhy, Manas Ranjan Patra, Suresh Chandra Satapathy, "Cloud Computing: Security Issues and Research Challenges", International Journal of Computer Science and Information Technology & Security, Vol. 1, No. 2, December 2011, ISSN: 2249-9555, Page No. 136-146.

9. Dereje Yimam, Eduardo B. Fernandez, "A survey of compliance issues in cloud computing", Journal of Internet Services and Applications (2016) 7:5, DOI 10.1186/s13174-016-0046-8.

10. Monjur Ahmed and Mohammad Ashraf Hossain, "Cloud Computing And Security Issues In The Cloud", International Journal of Network Security & Its Applications, Vol.6, No.1, January 2014, DOI :10.5121/ijnsa.2014.6103, Page No. 25-36.

11. Mohammed Hussain, Hanady Abdulsalam, "SECaaS: Security as a Service for Cloud-based Applications", ISBN: 978-1-4503-0793-2 DOI:10.1145/2107556.2107564.

12. Deepak H. Sharma, C A Dhote, Manish M. Potey, "Security-as-a-Service from Clouds: A Comprehensive Analysis", International Journal of Computer Applications (0975 - 8887) Volume 67- No.3, April 2013, Page No. 15-18.

13. Abhijeet Singh, Abhineet Anand,"Data Leakage Detection Using Cloud Computing"International Journal Of Engineering And Computer Science (IJECS), https://www.ijecs.in, Volume 6 Issue 4, April 2017, 21141-21144, DOI: 10.18535/ijecs/v6i4.59

14. Cloud Security Alliance, SecaaS Implementation Guidance, Category 1: Identity and Access Management.

15. Cloud Security Alliance, SecaaS Implementation Guidance, Category 2: Data Loss Prevention.

16. Cloud Security Alliance, SecaaS Implementation Guidance, Category 3: Web Security.

17. Cloud Security Alliance, SecaaS Implementation Guidance, Category 4: Email Security

18. Cloud Security Alliance, SecaaS Implementation Guidance, Category 5: Security Assessments

19. Cloud Security Alliance, SecaaS Implementation Guidance, Category 6: Intrusion Management

20. Cloud Security Alliance, SecaaS Implementation Guidance, Category 8: Encryption

21. Cloud Security Alliance, SecaaS Implementation Guidance, Network Security.

BRAND POSITIONING STRATEGY IN MARKETING MANAGEMNT

D. PRABHA

Research Scholar-Vels Institute of Management, Vels University, Pallavaram, Chennai

prabha4131@yahoo.com, Mob no: 7401079484, No: 10, Tulip Flat, Ben Foundation, Padikuppam Road, Anna Nagar West, Chennai

Research Supervisor: **Dr.G. Rajini**, Associatiate professor& Head – MBA (Integrated)

School of Management Studies, Vels University

ABSTRACT

In today's globalizing and continuously developing economies, the competition among enterprises grows quickly, the market share gets narrower; and in order to gain new markets, companies are trying to create superiority over their rivals by positioning new products aimed at consumer behavior and perceptions. In this sense, product positioning strategy in marketing management has emerged and now companies conduct studies on this strategy. Kotler (2010) Brand positioning is the extended version of branding; it is to target consumer' motivation to prefer a brand over others. Brand Positioning plays a vital role in marketing process. Despite the significant role of positioning on developing competitive advantage it has been noticed that, in the recent academic literature few studies highlight the key strategies to positioning product/brand successfully. This study tries to fill in this gap by highlighting the key positioning strategies along with some guidelines for the marketers for formulating effective positioning of their brand in the market. A good number of prior research studies on market positioning of brand/product are reviewed with a view to prepare this study. This literature review integrates the findings of the prior studies and focuses on highlighting key positioning strategies along with some key points that need to remember during positioning and suggests marketing practitioners some guidelines to develop effective positioning Strategies for achieving sustainable competitive advantage.

Key Words: positioning, Strategies, customer, buying decision, marketing practitioners

1. INTRODUCTION

1.1 Introduction and background

AI Ries and Jack Trout (2001) in their book Positioning: The Battle for your mind, introduce the subject by saying "Positioning is not what you do to the product. Positioning is what you do to the mind of the prospect. That is, you position the product in the mind of the prospect. So it's incorrect to call the concept 'Product Positioning'. As if you were doing something to the product itself. Not that positioning doesn't involve change. It does. But changes made in the name, the body of thought that comes to grips with the problems of getting heard in our over communicated society". Alderson (1958) suggested that tasks of marketing are to produce goods from the materials available in nature as per the needs of the households or individuals. Levit (1960) suggested that focus of a firm should be customer oriented. Kotler & Levy (1969) suggested that the functions of marketing are maintaining close relationship (touch) with the customers; identifying needs; developing products as per customers' needs; and to communicate with a view to express firm's objectives. Hooley (2001) suggested that marketing is the process of profitably matching organizational capabilities to the needs and requirements of target customers which is achieved through formulating and manipulating the marketing mix of products, price, promotion, distribution and customer relationships. The firm decides on the products' design characteristics which are likely to appeal to its target buyers to position their products/brands in the marketplace (Cronshaw et al., 1990). Hence positioning forms the core of modern marketing theory and practices (Hooley et al., 2001) and is a necessary condition for a firm to be successful (Cronshaw 1990).

1.2 RATIONAL OF STUDY

In this 21st century, more and more products and services are becoming increasingly similar and competitive in terms of prices, features and capabilities (Marken, 1997) and hence firms need to formulate and implement effective positioning strategy for developing some competitive advantage in order to be successful in the marketplace. Though the importance of positioning is widely accepted by the academic scholars in the literature but it has been noticed that there are not enough literatures on product/brand positioning which were published recently and to the best of my knowledge a limited number of researches/literature reviews were focused on highlighting the all possible ways for positioning of a product/brand in the marketplace. Hence the purpose of this study is to address this gap in the literature and to go for a review of literatures that are relevant with product/brand positioning with a view to highlight the different ways that marketers may consider for positioning their products along with the importance of positioning and some key points to remember during formulating positioning strategies so that marketing practitioners will have a guideline for developing proper understanding in order to formulate and implement right positioning strategies.

1.3 OBJECTIVES

The purpose of the study is to identify and highlight the key strategies for positioning a product or brand in a marketplace along with some key points that need to remember during positioning which might be effective for the practitioners for formulating marketing programs by leveraging the proper understanding of positioning concept in order to find out the way(s) for an organization to compete and to be successful in the changing and chaotic market place. This literature review based on the findings of the published books and articles on positioning is focused on to provide.

1. To study the importance of Brand positioning
2. To study the different steps of Brand positioning
3. To study the positioning Issues and key points to remember while positioning
4. To study the principles of positioning

2 METHODOLOGY AND STRUCTURE OF THE STUDY

As per the objective of the study, with a view to identify and highlight the main positioning strategies and key points that need to remember during positioning a brand/product in the marketplace, prior studies which are relevant with the positioning. In this literature review, first of all introduction and background, rationale of the study, objectives of the study, methodology & structure of the study are discussed which is followed by the main part of this study. This main part (Literature review) is constructed under several sections as per objective of the study. In this literature review, first of all definition of positioning and its importance is discussed then main strategies of positioning have been highlighted with examples from the previous studies. Steps of positioning; key positioning issues and Principles of positioning are explained in brief in the following sections. Finally, discussions & managerial implications, limitations and suggestions for future research are discussed. Full list of references are mentioned at the end.

3 LITERATURE REVIEW

Different scholars defined positioning in different ways. A "position" is a set of buyers at whom the product is primarily aimed (Cronshaw et al., 1990); the place a product occupies in a given market (Ansari et al., 1994); and is the combination of choice of target market and competitive advantage (Hooley et al. , 2001).

Positioning is the act of designing, establishing the company's offer and image and communicating the products' key distinctive benefits in the market so that it occupies a distinct and valued place in the minds of the target customers (e.g. Kotler, 1996; Kotler & Keller, 2009).

Positioning indicates how the business aspires to be perceived by the stakeholders in relation with the competition and the marketplace (Aaker & McLoughlin, 2007).

Cravens & Piercy (2009) mentioned that positioning is deciding the desired perception/ association of an organization/ brand by customers of the target market segment and developing the marketing program with a view to meet (or exceed) the needs and requirements of the customers of that marketplace

The objective of positioning is to locate the brand/product in the consumers' minds so that organization can secure maximize potential benefits (Kotler & Keller, 2009).

Trout & Ries (1972) suggested that the task of positioning is to position the product or brand in the prospects' minds but they pointed out that advertising became ineffective to persuade customer by highlighting product features or customers' benefit due to customers changing habit towards a satisfactory brand instead of best one for any product category in the already mature and complex and hence chaotic marketplace.

Aaker & Shansby (1982) suggested the use of comparative advertising to aid competitor based positioning (e.g. Pontiac against imported cars by comparing mileage and price). They advised to stick with the effective advertising (if any) and to highlight any feature only if it is attributed in the product.

Sujan & Betman (1989) suggested that in order to establish a brand in a niche market, marketer should highlight distinguishing features during communication by a single advertising whereas in case of differentiating a brand they should disperse the features across multiple advertisings.

Ambler & Vakratsas (1999) tried to generalize the effects of advertising but the effectiveness of advertising also depends on other external information sources like word of mouth, magazine articles, PR activities which were not discussed.

Marken (1997) suggested that both advertising and public relations play important role and each publication's presentation should support and reinforce the company's and product's position. He also suggested that firms and their agencies should direct all of their communication efforts to the specific position that they want to achieve and to reinforce it with all promotional tools (e.g. PR, advertising, sales promotion, sales contacts, on-line communications etc.)

Kotler (1996) suggested that firm needs to communicate its positioning effectively to the buyers of the firm's target marketplace. And all members of the firm should have clear understanding about

The brand positioning and need to use it as content with a view to take decision (Kotler & Keller, 2009). Market positioning sets the competitive positioning for the product and creates a detailed marketing mix. The outcome of positioning is the creation of an effective value proposition which is customer-oriented (Kotler & Keller, 2009).

Positioning of a brand/product helps to differentiate it from its competitors on the basis of important attributes to the customers of the target marketplace and develops a distinctive identity for the product/brand in the minds of the customers (Ansari et. al., 1994); creates a unique perception in buyers' minds of the target market segment (Cravens & Piercy, 2009).

An effective positioning is helpful to guide marketing strategy by clarifying the brand's essence, what goals it helps the consumer achieve, and how it does so in a unique way (Kotler & Keller, 2009).

4. IMPORTANCE OF POSITIONING

This study mainly prominence on product features, attributes, benefits, categories, usage, and competitors etc., which play imperative character in product positioning. Therefore product positioning should be well balanced by the company this will build an image of the company's product in the mind to target customers.

Market positioning sets the competitive positioning for the product and creates a detailed marketing mix. The outcome of positioning is the creation of an effective value proposition which is customer-oriented (Kotler & Keller, 2009).

Positioning of a brand/product helps to differentiate it from its competitors on the basis of important attributes to the customers of the target marketplace and develops a distinctive identity for the product/brand in the minds of the customers (Ansari et. al., 1994); creates a unique perception in buyers' minds of the target market segment (Cravens & Piercy, 2009).

An effective positioning is helpful to guide marketing strategy by clarifying the brand's essence, what goals it helps the consumer achieve, and how it does so in a unique way (Kotler & Keller, 2009).

Positioning is an important source of competitive advantage and acts as a support for competitive advantage. (Cronshaw et al., 1990).

Positioning strategy which includes product strategy, distribution strategy, pricing strategy, advertising and sales promotion strategy, sales force strategy, direct marketing strategy, and the Internet strategy points out how (and why) the product mix, line, or brand is to be positioned in the target market segment and hence effective targeting and positioning of the firm's products are core dimensions of market-driven strategy and hence are essential in gaining and sustaining superior performance (Cravens & Piercy, 2009) .

5. STEPS OF POSITIONING

Walker (2003) suggested that there are seven steps of positioning. These are

1. To identify a relevant set of competitive products (at the generic level e.g. new breakfast drink may compete with breakfast cereals and eggs;

2. To identify determinant attributes (e.g. features, benefits, usage, parentage, manufacturing process, ingredients, endorsement, comparison, pro-environment, product class, price/quality, country or geographic area);

3 .To collect data about perception of the customers for products in the competitive set;

4. To analyze the products' current position in the competitive set (to draw perceptual map);

5. To determine customers' most preferred attributes (may be location, price of goods, and service for a retail outlet);

6. To consider fit of possible positions with customer needs and segment attractiveness;

7. To write positioning statement or value proposition to guide development of marketing strategy.

6. Positioning issues/ key points to remember while positioning

There are so many factors that a marketer needs to consider for positioning a product or brand. The key issues or points to be remembered while positioning are briefly mentioned as follows-

- The strategic position should resonate with customer, differentiate the firm from its competitors, and reflect and supported by the culture, strategy and capabilities of the business (Aaker & McLoughlin, 2007)

- While positioning, firm should consider formulating a positioning concept for a particular brand only not for all the competing brands that consists of product category/class and firm should follow that positioning concept over the life of the brand/product (Cravens & Piercy, 2009).

- Corporate/brand name should not be narrow; should reflect the vision of the firm; should not be identical with the name of an established firm and use of initials as name is meaningless and hence not suggested (Trout & Ries, 1972).

• Unnecessary line extension creates confusion and hence decline in market share (Trout & Ries, 1972) but Aaker & McLoughlin (2007, p-237) pointed out that a broad product offering indicates substance, acceptance, leadership, and often the convenience of one-stop shopping.

• Products should be positioned in a particular market segment as products positioned in the wider market to appeal to all were not able to establish in the marketplace (Trout & Ries, 1972). Treacy & Wiersema (1993) supported this as they pointed out that industry leaders are focused in the narrow market segment. But Miles & Slow (1978; cited by Morgan & Strong, 1997) pointed out that 'Prospector' firms are opportunistic and show interest in new and broader markets.

• Management should not forget what made the brand successful and should not create any confusion to the customers/prospects (Trout & Ries, 1972) and multiple concepts may confuse buyers and may weaken the effectiveness of positioning actions (Cravens & Piercy, 2009)

• Management of a new brand should not try to compete on head-to-head against a product leader. Focusing to a niche market or to identify a position where strong competitors have weaknesses is suggested (Trout & Ries, 1972). Aaker & McLoughlin (2007, p-234) also suggested that successful positioning can be done on the basis of a narrow product focus. Hamel & Praha lad (1989) pointed out that one way to creating competitive innovation is to identify loose bricks.

• Positioning should be in a way to adapt in the changing environment and management should be aggressive enough to utilize the opportunity (if any) by taking flexible strategies which are appropriate for the company (Trout & Ries, 1972).

• Trout & Ries (1972) suggested that it is extremely difficult for a company serving in any product category to establish a position in a different product category as evidence from the industries confirmed that transfer of skills to other products or marketing situations was not successful. This view is not always acceptable as existing competitive advantages could be used to build sustainability (Ghemawat, 1986) and competences could be enhanced if they are applied and shared. (Hamel & Praha lad, 1990) establish the position against any opportunity prior to competitors (Trout & Ries, 1972; Cravens & Piercy, 2009). But Aaker & McLoughlin (2007, p-231) pointed out that perception creation is easy if firm's offering is based on product or service innovation.

7. POSITIONING PRINCIPLES

The following Positioning Principles are designed to guide the development of successful product Positioning.

A. The product Positioning Statement is the most basic of all strategic statements concerning a brand.

It is the statement upon which all other strategies and all brand development and executable activities are built.

B. In selecting a Product Positioning we should seek one which is:

1. Believable and consistent with the product's performance;

2. Directly linked to as large a frame of Reference and Market Target where the product can still deliver a meaningful point of Difference;

3. Targeted at delivering the most meaningful benefit/correcting the biggest problem in the Frame of Reference chosen;

4. Unique from Competition;

5. Capable of enduring for the life of the brand;

6. Consistent with Market Target's beliefs/knowledge and behavior/experience.

C. A Product Positioning once established should not be readily abandoned.

Positioning in the minds of consumers is difficult and require time, money, and consistency. Once established, major changes are difficult and often destructive, causing confusion in the minds of consumers.

D. Repositioning a brand is more often unsuccessful than successful .However. when there are major changes in a brand's Frame of Reference (major new competitive entries, technological Innovations,) Market Target (new usage patterns, changed attitudes or lifestyles) or Point of Difference (Product performance changes), then a Positioning change may be required.

E. Effective Positioning is simple in language and straight forward in thought.

8. DISCUSSIONS & CONCLUSION

The purpose of the study was to identify and highlight the major ways for positioning a product or brand in a marketplace along with some key issues that need to remember during positioning. Positioning needs firms to have all relevant information regarding competition and the market to place the brand in the mindsets of the target customers by creating the value offerings with some differentiation from the competitors. Positioning guides marketing strategy; helps to differentiate brands to position in the market; and helps firms to secure financial return from the target market. This study might be helpful for the marketers for planning and developing marketing strategy. The performance of a firm depends on successful positioning of its products or brand in the market place. By developing successful positioning marketers can attract and keep the customers loyal to them and hence can develop long-run relationship with the customers which is very important way to develop sustainable competitive advantage. While positioning analysis marketers need to consider other factors like competitive forces, industry structure, opportunities, threats, resources and competences. As strategists should focus on gazing into the future (Campbell & Alexander, 1997), ignoring other factors might create competitive disadvantage in the long-run

9. LIMITATIONS AND SUGGESTIONS FOR FUTURE RESEARCH.

The positioning concept and suggested guidelines are important for the academics and students for study and would provide scope for further research. Practitioners should be able to get some directions for appropriate positioning of their products. Some of the suggested ways to position a product might not be applicable to all industrial sectors and to all product categories. This study is based on the limited number of articles/books/research studies that I managed to collect or download. List of the articles/books used to do this study are mentioned later. Though I reviewed a good number of articles/books but this is not the exclusive list. There may have some other important studies which were overlooked and hence not reviewed. Hence further review based on more in-depth analysis might develop the findings of this study.

References

Aaker, D. A. and Mcloughlin, D. (2007). *Strategic Market Management*. West Sussex: John Wiley & Sons Ltd., 225-245.

Aaker, D.A. and Shansby, J.G. (1982). Positioning your Product. *Business Horizons*, May/June, 56-62.

Alderson, W. (1958). The Analytical Framework for Marketing. In B. M. Enis, K. Cox & M. P. Mokwa (8th ed.), *Marketing Classics (pp.* 22-32). NJ: Prentice Hall.

Ambler, T. and Vakratsas, D. (1999). How Advertising Works: What Do We Really Know? *Journal of Marketing, 6*3(1), 26-43.

Ansari, A., Economides, N. and Ghosh, A. (1994). Competitive positioning in the market With non-uniform preferences. *Marketing Science.* 13(3/Summer), 248-273.

Cravens, D. W. and Piercy, N. F. (2009). *Strategic Marketing* (9th ed.). Boston: McGraw-Hill Irwin, 193-203.

Cronshaw, M., Cubbin, J. and Davis, E. (1990). The importance of product positioning: Successful entry in the national newspaper market, *Business Strategy Review,* Autumn, 53-73.

Day, G. S. and Montgomery, D. B. (1999). Charting New Directions for Marketing. *Journal of Marketing,* 63 (Special), 3-13.

Ghemawat, P. (1986). Sustainable advantage. *Harvard Business Review*, 64(5, Sep/Oct), 53.

Gronroos, C. (1994). From Marketing Mix to Relationship Marketing: Towards a Paradigm Shift in Marketing. *Management Decision*, 32(2), 4-20.

Hamel, G. (1996). Strategy as revolution. *Harvard Business Review*, 74(1, Jul/Aug), 69.

Hamel, G. and Praha lad, C.K. (1989). Strategic intent. *Harvard Business Review*, 67(3), 63.

Hamel, G. and Praha lad, C.K. (1990). The core competence of the corporation. *Harvard Business Review*, 68(3, May/Jun), 63.

Hooley, G., Greenley, G., Fahy, J. and Cadogan, J. (2001). Market-focused Resources, Competitive Positioning and Firm Performance. *Journal of Marketing Management,* 17, 503-520.

Kotler, P. (1996). *Marketing Management: Analysis, Planning, Implementation, and Control* (8th ed.). New Delhi: Prentice-Hall of India Private Limited, 291-313.

Kotler, P. and Keller, K. L. (2009). *Marketing Management* (13th ed.). New Jersey: Pearson Prentice-Hall, 268-78.

Kotler, P. and Levy, S. J. (1969). Broadening the Concept of Marketing. In B. M. Enis, K. Cox & M. P. Mokwa (8th ed.), *Marketing Classics (pp.* 44-52). NJ: Prentice Hall.

Levitt, T. (1960). Marketing Myopia. In B. M. Enis, K. Cox & M. P. Mokwa (8th ed.), *Marketing Classics (pp.* 3-21). NJ: Prentice Hall.

Marken, G.A.A (1997). What Works in PR? Market Positioning Needs New Look, New Emphasis, *Public Relations Quarterly*, fall, 41-42.

Morgan, R. E. and Strong, C. A. (1998). Market orientation and dimensions of strategic orientation, *European Journal of Marketing*, 329(11/12), 1051-1073.

Porter, M. E. (1996). What is strategy? *Harvard Business Review,* 74(6, Nov/Dec), 61.

Perreault Jr., D. W. and McCarthy, E. J. (2006). *Essentials of Marketing: A Global-Managerial Approach* (10th ed.). Boston: McGraw- Hill Irwin, 72-75.

Schiff man, L. G. and Kanuk, L. L. (2010). *Consumer Behavior* (9th ed.). New Delhi: Pearson Education.

A Comparative Study of Job Stress Level of Software Professionals: A Case Study of Private Sector in India

GeetaKumari[1], Dr. AshfaueAlam[2], Dr. Gaurav Joshi[3]

[1] Jharkhand Rai University, Ranchi, India

Mail id-geekumari@gmail.com

[2] Jharkhand Rai University, Ranchi, India

Mail id-ashfaque.alam@jru.edu.in

[3] LalBahadurShastri Institute of Management, New Delhi, India

Mail id-gauravjoshi12@gmail.com

Abstract: The present study was conducted to a comparative study of job stress level of software professionals in private software industries namely HCL Technologies Limited Noida, IBM India Pvt. Ltd., Gurgaon and Wipro Limited, Greater Noida. Stress is an unpleasant state of emotional and physiological arousal that people experience in various situations and that they perceive as dangerous or threatening to their well-being at their work place now a day's software professionals are facing lots of challenges related to their work. For this study, survey was conducted by using well-designed pretested questionnaire that was administered through e-mail to 360 respondents at HCL Technologies Ltd., Noida, IBM India Pvt.Ltd., Gurgaon and Wipro Limited, Greater Noida. The hypothesis testing has been done by using one sample t-test. Sample size for this study was taken to be 360. Out of these 360 employees, 234 employees were male and 126 were female. The convenience sampling procedure was used for data collection. Findings of this study revealed that the most of the software professionals were stressed due to long working hours and various job stress dimensions namely leave policy, incentive policy, work demand, management support, target, leadership, work isolation, promotion policy, administration, work stagnation, work pressure and working hour in software industries namely HCL Technologies Limited, Noida, IBM India Pvt. Ltd., Gurgaon and Wipro Technologies, Greater Noida.

Keyword: Job stress, leave policy, work demand management support, work pressure etc.

1 Introduction

Stress is an unpleasant state of emotional and physiological arousal that people experience in various situations and that they perceive as dangerous or threatening to their well-being. The word stress means different things to different people, caused by conditions that are based in the corporate culture or personality conflicts. The individual may develop a level of tension that interferes with sleep, making relaxation outside the workplace impossible. Over a time, period of this stress can trigger emotional disorders such as anxiety, depression and in some cases various phobias that further inhibit the ability to enjoy any aspect of living. Now days, there is a standard job stress index that is used in many stress management programs to assess the potential for negative stress to undermine one or more employees. There are also various incarnations of an occupational stress indicator listing that can help individuals determine whether general conditions have the potential to lead to unhealthy stress levels.

2 Review of literature

Job stress has become one of the most serious health issues in the modern world. Lu et al. [1] suggested stress as it occurs in any job and is more pervasive than it was decades ago. The domain of work differs considerably from the working environment that was prevalent 30 years ago: longer hours at work are not unusual, frequent changes in culture and structure are often cited, as well as the loss of lifetime career paths Dale [2] which all leads to greater presence and levels of stress. According to Fotinatos ventouratos [3] defined occupational stress as the mental and physical condition which affects the individual's productivity, effectiveness, personal health and quality of work.

According to Rees [4] Occupational stress, in particular, is the inability to cope with the pressures in a job because of a poor fit between someone's abilities and his/her work requirements and conditions Holmlund-Rytkonen and Strandvik, [5]. It is a mental and physical condition which affects an individual's productivity, effectiveness, personal health and quality of work The main components of the work-stress process are potential sources of stress (stressors), factors of individual differences (moderators/mediators), and consequences of stress (strain) Lu et. al., [6] Stressors (job-related and extra-organizational) are objective events, stress is the subjective experience of the event, and strain is the poor response to stress. Accordingly, the nature and effects of stress might be best understood by saying that some environmental variables (stressors), when interpreted by the individual (cognitive interpretation), may lead to stress. Johnson et.al, [7] worked on the experience of work-related stress across occupations. They have discussed three stress related variables like psychological well-being, physical health and job satisfaction and these variables are compared between 26 different occupations. The occupations like ambulance workers, teachers, social services, customer services - call centres, prison officers and police. The study reveals the high emotional labour associated with the high stress jobs is discussed as a potential causal factor. Kumar [8] suggested that the job stress is the major cause for job dissatisfaction, which creates disturbances in quality of life, so it results unhappiness. Michael R. Frone and Massaran Bamba[9, 10] the relationship of work stressors, those work over load and job insecurity, to employees' alcohol use illicit drug use resulted, support the relation of work stressors to alcohol and illicit drug use before work, during the workday, and after work. Many researchers investigated [11,12,13,14,15,16], the effect of flexible work schedule, factors associated with stress, employee support and training, and telecommuting as potential coping resources to relieve stress. Perceived workload, role ambiguity, work facilitation, and decision latitude are potential stressors of IT professionals. Removing role ambiguity and improving work facilitation reduce work-related stress and allowing employees to have flexible work schedules ease their perceptions of workload.

2.1 Objectives of the study

The main objective of this study is a comparative study of job stress level of software professionals in private software industries namely HCL Technologies Limited Noida, IBM India Pvt. Ltd., Gurgaon and Wipro technologies, Greater Noida.

3 Research Methodology

The population of the study consists of software professionals at software industries in private sector namely HCL Technologies Limited, IBM India Pvt. Ltd., Gurgaon, and Wipro Technologies, Greater Noida. The sample size for this study was taken to be 360. Out of these 360 employees, 234 employees were male and 126 were female. The convenience sampling procedure was used for data collection. The convenience method of sampling was used for data collection. There were the pre-tested questionnaires used as instrument for data collection. The questionnaires were framed on the basis of Likert 5-point scale from strongly agree to disagree, where points are defined as 1, 2, 3, 4, and 5 equals to strongly disagree, disagree, neither agree nor disagree, agree and strongly agree respectively. The hypothesis testing has been done by using one sample t-test.

4 Results and Discussion

As per the analysis of job Stress level, it was analysed on the basis of mean values of the respondents response of various job stress dimensions namely leave policy, incentive policy, work demand, management support, target, leadership, work isolation, promotion policy, administration, work stagnation, work pressure and working hour in software industries namely HCL Technologies Limited, Noida, IBM India Pvt. Ltd., Gurgaon and Wipro Technologies, Greater Noida.

Table 4 A Comparative Analysis of Job Stress Level of Software Professionals Among HCL Technologies, IBM India Pvt. Ltd and Wipro Technologies.

Sl. No.	Variables Job Stress Dimensions	HCL Technologies Limited, Noida Sample Size N=100		IBM India Pvt.Ltd., Gurgaon Sample Size N=160		Wipro TechnologiesLtd.,Greater, Greater Noida, Sample Size N=100	
		Mean(M)	Standard Deviation (S.D.)	Mean(M	Standard Deviation (S.D.)	Mean(M	Standard Deviation (S.D.)
1	Leave policy	3.82	1.313	3.84	1.075	3.79	1.297
2	Incentive policy	2.72	1.429	3.04	1.350	2.47	1.193
3	Work demand	3.20	1.214	2.87	1.209	3.16	1.143
4	Management support	3.25	1.344	3.29	1.362	3.29	1.122
5	Target	3.02	1.333	3.29	1.211	2.95	1.132
6	Leadership	2.84	1.285	2.77	1.250	2.89	1.262
7	Work isolation	3.31	1.337	3.43	1.357	3.27	1.300
8	Promotion policy	3.25	1.359	3.13	1.432	3.29	1.328
9	Administration	2.72	1.429	3.11	1.264	2.64	1.352
10	Work stagnation	3.82	1.313	3.94	1.117	3.81	1.308
11	Work pressure	4.00	1.421	3.78	1.322	3.99	1.418
12	Working hours	4.25	1.140	4.33	.955	4.07	1.148

4.1 Leave Policy

The figure 4.1, illustrates the mean value of the respondent's response of job stress dimension for leave policy in software industries namely HCL Technologies Limited, Noida, IBM India Pvt. Ltd., Gurgaon and Wipro Technologies, Greater Noida. The respondents of IBM India Pvt. Ltd., Gurgaon had been found to have higher mean value of 3.84 as compared to HCL Technologies Limited, Noida Mean value of 3.82 and Wipro Technologies, Greater Noida with mean value of 2.69. From the figure 4.1 IBM India Pvt. Ltd., Gurgaon had more job stress in terms of leave policy as compared to other two companies.

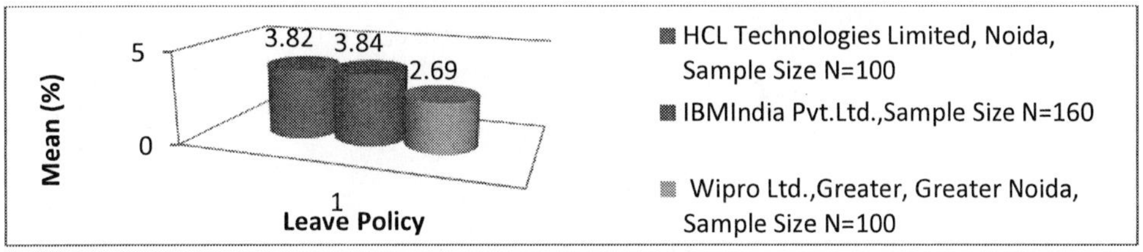

Figure 4.1 Leave Policy

4.2 Incentive Policy

The figure 4.2 illustrates the mean value of the respondent's response of job stress dimension for incentive policy in software industries namely HCL Technologies Limited, Noida, IBM India Pvt. Ltd., Gurgaon and Wipro Technologies, Greater Noida. The respondents of IBM India Pvt. Ltd., Gurgaon had been found to have higher mean value of 3.68 as compared to HCL Technologies Limited, Noida Mean value of 2.9 and Wipro Technologies, Greater Noida with mean value of 3.52. From the figure 4.2 IBM India Pvt. Ltd., Gurgaon had more job stress in terms of incentive policy as compared to other two companies.

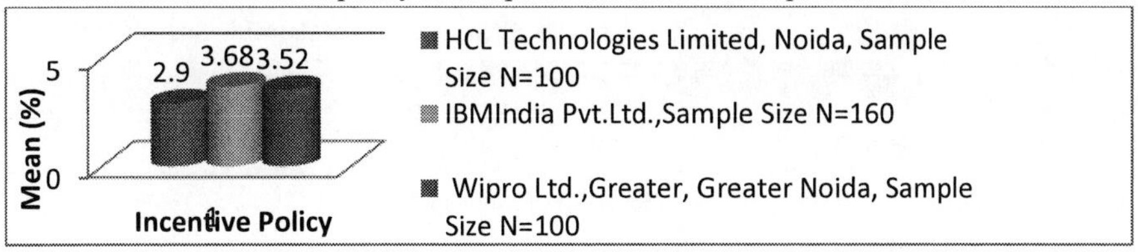

Figure 4.2 Incentive Policy

4.3 Management Support

The figure 4.3 illustrates the mean value of the respondent's response of job stress dimension for management support in software industries namely HCL Technologies Limited, Noida, IBM India Pvt. Ltd., Gurgaon and Wipro Technologies, Greater Noida. In the figure 4.3., the respondents of IBM India Pvt. Ltd., Gurgaon and Wipro Technologies, Greater Noida had been found same mean value of 3.29 and the respondents of HCL Technologies, Noida had been found mean value of 3.25. From the figure 4.3 the respondents of HCL Technologies Limited, Noida had been found less stress in terms of management support as compared to others two companies while the respondents of IBM India Pvt. Ltd., Gurgaon and Wipro Technologies, Greater Noida had been found same stress level.

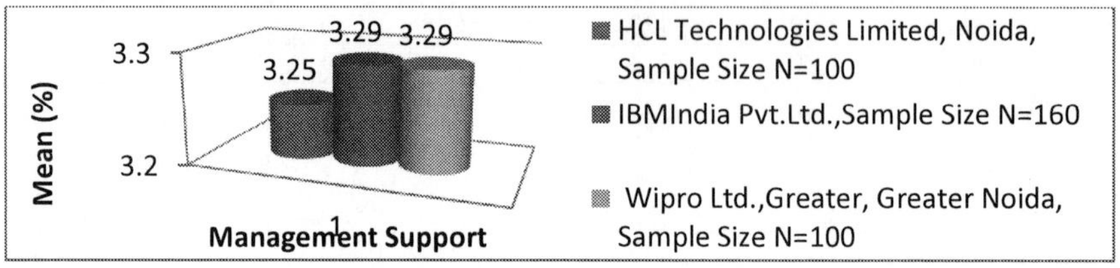

Figure 4.3 Management Support

4.4 Target

The figure 4.4 illustrates the mean value of the respondent's response of job stress dimension for target in software industries namely HCL Technologies Limited, Noida, IBM India Pvt. Ltd., Gurgaon and Wipro Technologies, Greater Noida. The respondents of IBM India Pvt. Ltd., Gurgaon had been observed with higher mean value of 3.29 as compared to HCL Technologies Limited, Noida Mean value of 3.02 and Wipro limited, Greater Noida with mean value of 2.95. From the figure 4.4, IBM India Pvt. Ltd., Gurgaon had more job stress in terms of target as compared to other two companies.

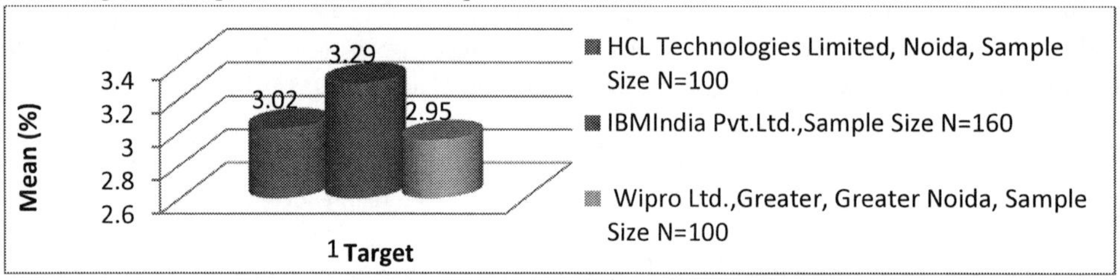

Figure 4.4 Target

4.5 Leadership

Mean value of 2.84 and IBM India Pvt. Ltd., Gurgaon with mean value of 2. 77. From the figure 4.5 the respondents of Wipro Technologies, Greater Noida had more job stress in terms of leadership as compared to other two companies namely HCL Technologies The figure 4.6 illustrates the mean value of the respondent's response of job stress dimension for leadership in software industries namely HCL Technologies Limited, Noida, IBM India Pvt. Ltd., Gurgaon and Wipro Limited, Greater Noida. The respondents of Wipro Technologies, Greater Noida had found higher mean value of 2.89 as compared to HCL Technologies Limited, Noida Limited, Noida and IBM India Pvt. Ltd., Gurgaon.

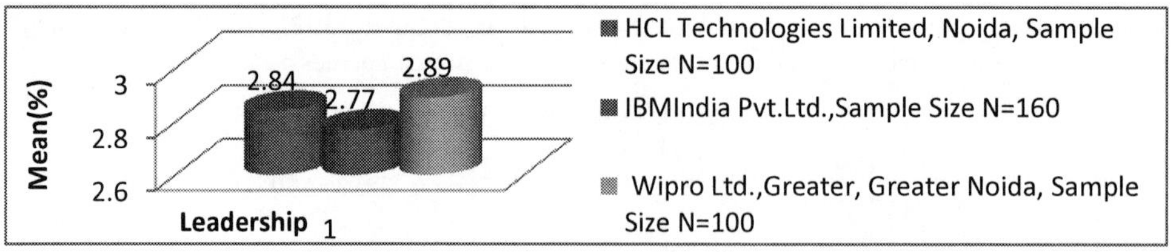

Figure 4.5 Leadership

4.6 Work Isolation

The figure 4.6 illustrates the mean value of the respondent's response of job stress dimension for work isolation in software industries namely HCL Technologies Limited, Noida, IBM India Pvt. Ltd., Gurgaon and Wipro Technologies, Greater Noida. The respondents of IBM India Pvt. Ltd., Gurgaon had found higher mean value of 3.43 as compared to HCL Technologies Limited, Noida Mean value of 3.31 and Wipro Technologies, Greater Noida with mean value of 3.27. From the figure 4.7, IBM India Pvt. Ltd., Gurgaon had more job stress in terms of work isolation as compared to other two companies.

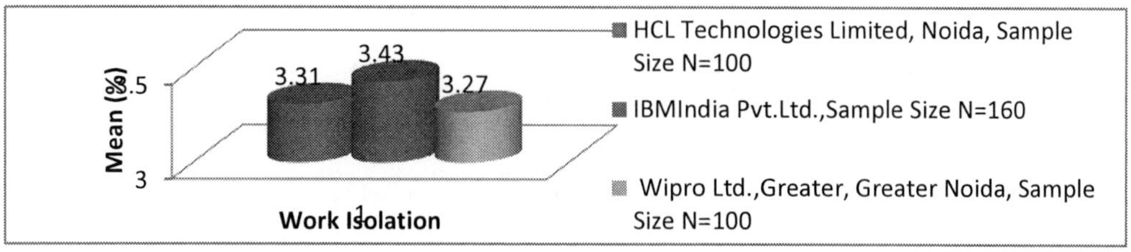

Figure 4.6 Work Isolation

4.7 Promotion Policy

The figure 4.7 illustrates the mean value of the respondent's response of job stress dimension for promotion policy in software industries namely HCL Technologies Limited, Noida, IBM India Pvt. Ltd., Gurgaon and Wipro Limited, Greater Noida. The respondents of Wipro Limited, Greater Noida had found higher mean value of 3.29 as compared to HCL Technologies Limited, Noida Mean value of 3.25 and IBM India Pvt. Ltd., Gurgaon with mean value of 3.13. From the figure 4.8 the respondents of Wipro Technologies, Greater Noida had more job stress in terms of promotion policy as compared to other two companies namely HCL Technologies Limited, Noida and IBM India Pvt. Ltd., Gurgaon.

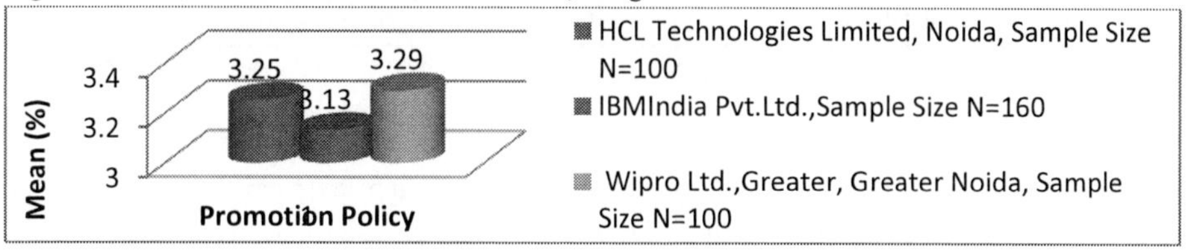

Figure 4.7 Promotion Policy

4.8 Administration

The figure 4.8 illustrates the mean value of the respondent's response of job stress dimension for administration in software industries namely HCL Technologies Limited, Noida, IBM India Pvt. Ltd., Gurgaon and Wipro Technologies, Greater Noida. The respondents of HCL Technologies Limited, Noida had found higher mean value of 3.72 as compared to Wipro Technogies, Greater Noida Mean value of 2.64 and IBM India Pvt. Ltd., Gurgaon with mean value of 3.11. From the figure 4.8 the respondents of HCL Technologies Limited, Noida had more job stress in terms administration as compared to other two companies.

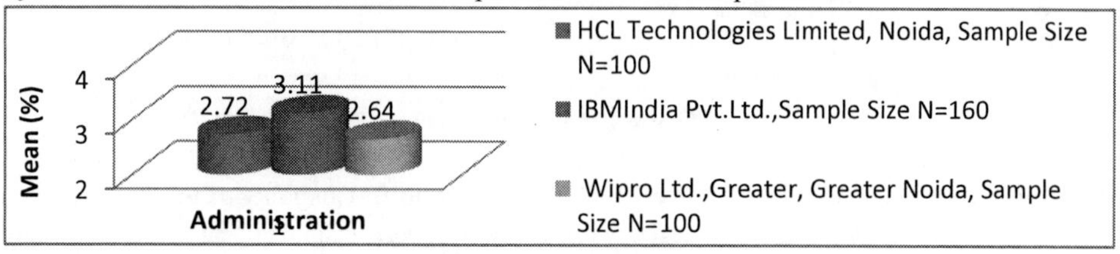

Figure 4.8 Administration

4.9 Work Stagnation

The figure 4.9 illustrates the mean value of the respondent's response of job stress dimension for work stagnation in software industries namely HCL Technologies Limited, Noida, IBM India Pvt. Ltd., Gurgaon and Wipro Technologies, Greater Noida. The respondents of IBM India Pvt. Ltd., Gurgaon had found higher mean value of 3.94 as compared to HCL Technologies Limited, Noida Mean value of 3.82 and Wipro Technologies, Greater Noida with mean value of 3.81. From the figure 4.10 IBM India Pvt. Ltd., Gurgaon had more job stress in terms of work stagnation as compared to other two companies.

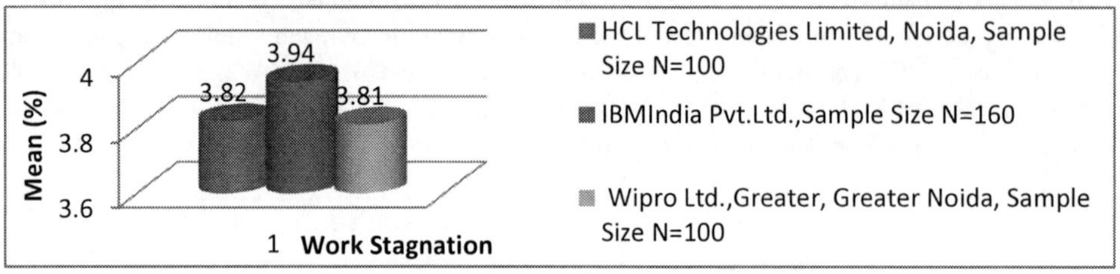

Figure 4.9 Work Stagnation

4.10 Work Pressure

The figure 4.10 illustrates the mean value of the respondent's response of job stress dimension for work pressure in software industries namely HCL Technologies Limited, Noida, IBM India Pvt. Ltd., Gurgaon and Wipro Technologies, Greater Noida. The respondents of HCL Technologies, Limited, Noida had found higher mean value of 4 as compared to Wipro Limited, Greater Noida Mean value of 3.99 and IBM India Pvt. Ltd., Gurgaon with mean value of 3.78. From the figure 4.10 the respondents of HCL Technologies Noida had more job stress in terms work demand as compared to other two companies.

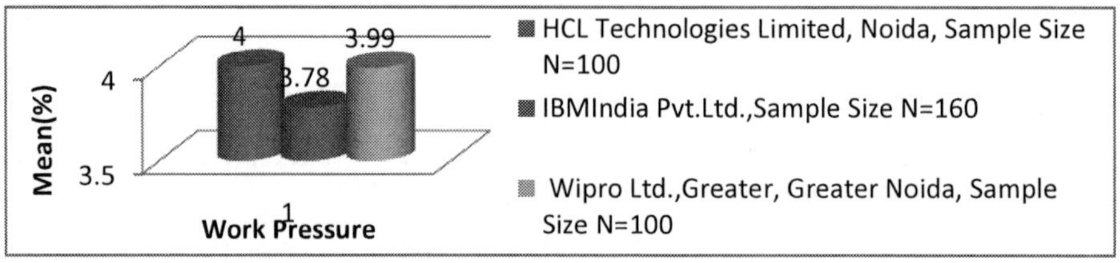

Figure 4.10 Work Pressure

4.11 Working Hours

The figure 4.11 illustrates the mean value of the respondent's response of job stress dimension for administration in software industries namely HCL Technologies Limited, Noida, IBM India Pvt. Ltd., Gurgaon and Wipro Technologies, Greater Noida. The respondents of IBM India Pvt. Ltd., Gurgaon had found higher mean value of 4.33 as compared to Wipro Limited, Greater Noida Mean value of 4.07and HCL Technologies Noida with mean value of 4.25. From the figure 4.11 the respondents of IBM India Pvt. Ltd., Gurgaon had been found more job stress in terms working hours as compared to other two companies.

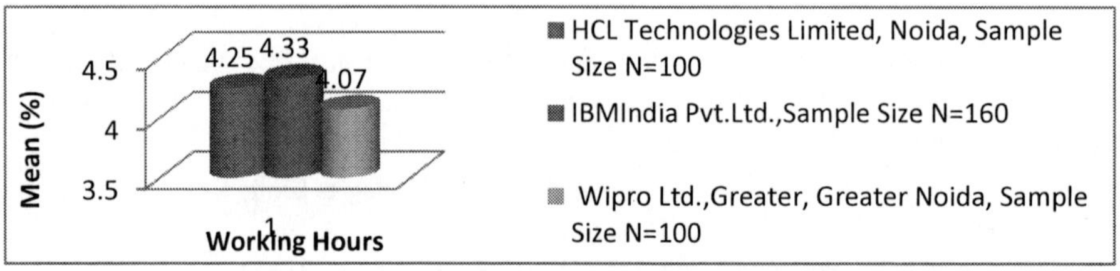

Figure 4.11 Working Hours

From the results, it was concluded that the overall job stress level in IBM India Pvt. Ltd. Limited was more in terms of leave policy, incentive policy, target, work isolation, work stagnation and working hours while respondents of HCL Technologies Limited had been found more in terms of job stress dimensions namely work demand, administration and work pressure. The respondents of Wipro Technologies, Greater Noida had been found more stress in terms of job stress dimension namely leadership, promotion policy, and working hours.

5 Conclusion

Job stress is negatively related to performance. In other words, higher the stress, lower the performance. Workplace stress derives from many sources. Now a day's stress become our part of life. Stress is not bad all the time it has also positive part sometime it is necessary to give better performance. From the findings it is concluded that the overall job stress level in

IBM India Pvt. Ltd., Gurgaon has been found more in terms of various job stress dimensionsnamely leave policy,incentive policy, work demand, management support,target, work isolation,administration and working hours as compared to other two companies while in terms of work pressure HCL Technologies Limited has been found more and in terms of promotion policy WiproTechnologies, Greater Noida has been found more as compare to other two companies.From the one sample test the all variables of job stress dimensions have significant values of (.000). All these values are less than 0.05. So, it is concluded that all the variables of job stress were found statistically significant and it is also concluded that the all variables have great influence on job stress level.

Reference

1. Lu L, Cooper ,C. L, Kao S. F. Y. Zhou ,"Work stress, control beliefs and well-being in Greater China-An exploration of sub-cultural differences between the PRC and Taiwan" Journal of Managerial Psychology, 2003, vol.18 (6),pp.479–510.
2. B.G. Dale, C.L. Cooper, and A. Wilkinson, "Managing Quality and Human Resources: A Guide to Continuous Improvement", Blackwell, Oxford, 1997.
3. R.F. Ventouratos and C. Cooper, "The role of gender and social class in work stress", Journal of Managerial Psychology, 2005, vol. 20,pp. 14-23.
4. W.D. Rees, "Managerial stress – dealing with the causes, not the symptoms", Industrial and Commercial Training, 1997, vol.29 no.2, pp. 35-40.
5. M.H.Rytkomen, and T. Strandvik, "Stress in business relation. Journal of Business and Industries marketing", 2005, vol. 20, no.1, pp.21- 22.
6. Lu L, Cooper ,C. L, Kao S. F. Y. Zhou ,"Work stress, control beliefs and well-being in Greater China-An exploration of sub-cultural differences between the PRC and Taiwan" Journal of Managerial Psychology, 2003, vol.18 ,no.6,pp.479–510.
7. S. Johnson, S. Cartwright, D. Ian, P. Taylor, P , C. Millet, "The experience of work-related stress across occupations", Journal of Managerial Psychology', vol. 20, no.2, 2005, pp. 178-187.
8. K.S. Kumar, "A Study on Job Stress of the Employees with Reference to Banking Sector", International Journal of Management and Transformation, vol. 5,no.1,2011, pp.67-78.
9. R. M. Frone, " Are Work Stressor related to employee substances use?, The Importance of Temporal Context in Assessments of Alcohol and Illicite Drug Use",, Journal of Applied Psychology , vol.93,2008,pp.99-206.
10. MassaranBamba, Stress Management and Job Performance in the Industries Sector of Mali, Journal of Service Science and Management, 2016, 9, 189-194
11. V. V. Raghavan, T. Sakaguchi, R. C. Mahaney, " An Empirical Investigation of Stress Factors in Information Technology Professionals", IGI Global, U.S.A.,2010.
12. R.G.Ratnawat , Dr P.C. Jha, Impact of Job Related Stress on Employee Performance: A Review and Research Agenda, IOSR Journal of Business and Management (IOSR-JBM) e-ISSN: 2278-487X, p-ISSN: 2319-7668. Volume 16, Issue 11.Ver. V (Nov. 2014), PP 01-06.
13. SahukarMadhura, PailoorSubramanya, Pradhan Balaram, Job satisfaction, job stress and psychosomatic health problems in software professionals in India, Indian Journal of Occupational and Environmental Medicine, Year : 2014 | Volume : 18 | Issue : 3 | Page : 153-161.
14. MS Darshan, Rajesh Raman, TS Sathyanarayana Rao, Dushad Ram, BinduAnnigeri, A study on professional stress, depression and alcohol use among Indian IT professionals, Indian journal of psychiatry,Year : 2013 | Volume : 55 | Issue : 1 | Page : 63-69.
15. AnkireddySailaja, Dr.T.Narayana Reddy, Dr.D.Pradeep Kumar, Factors Associated with Job Stress of Software professionals in Bangalore city, IOSR Journal of Business and Management (IOSR-JBM) e-ISSN: 2278-487X, p-ISSN: 2319-7668. Volume 14, Issue 6 (Nov. - Dec. 2013), PP 15-20.
16. AbhaMisra, Globalization and Stress among Computer Professionals, International Journal of Multidisciplinary Research and Development 2015; 2(2): 288-291.

An efficient technique to sort large datasets using merge of multiple streaming files

Tanu Chaturvedi
M. Tech. in Computer Science Engineering
Gurukul Institute of Engineering and Technology
Kota, Rajasthan
Tanu.chaturvedi873@gmail.com

Manoj Singh
HOD of Computer Science Engineering
Gurukul Institute of Engineering and Technology
Kota, Rajasthan
Manojsinghq100@yahoo.com

*Abstract:*This work introduce a improved view and reviewing of algorithm sorting the numbers at large scale in a more accomplished manner and a comparison is done. There are numerous sorting applications are used on abundant amount of data but they are less efficient. In this topic an algorithm is proposed for sorting the numbers at large scale. This algorithm is executed in Microsoft's C# with dot net framework. In this approach input data split to array and rest, and this process continues to the last record of array then merge of multiple input files is executed. To determine that this algorithm is efficient at larger scale there is another algorithm is compared to it with the same datasets.

Index Terms –
Quick Sort algorithm, Binary tree merges, Large datasets.

I. PREFACE

In today's environment Sorting of large amount of different kind of data become challenging part for such data organization who deal with database construction, several data-mining algorithms and search engine indexing specially when there are large sets of data to be sorted in this case maintain the high quality performance is the major challenge. In this work an algorithm is executed based on input data split to array and rest approach, which last to end record of array which gets merged into multiple input file. There are many approaches who deal with the large data sets like Bubble sort and Quick sort but these are traditional approaches and seem less acceptable. The Proposed algorithm is 40% faster than a traditional approach. In this section following algorithm is executed on 1 lakh and 5 lakh records (random number). This proposed algorithm sorts the figures in minimum time and takes less space in the memory and gives the best result from traditional algorithm. In this approach we can sort data with the limit of 1000 MB. This was found far better than the rest algorithms and processed data with the speed almost 30-35 MB per second. The execution time is recorded for each set of data and proposed algorithm and quick sort algorithms are being compared.

Many research teams are strongly working in the area of dealing with large datasets. In the used algorithm we use to sort large datasets in less time. This work has been performed by using a machine which has 6GB of main memory (RAM), 1024 of secondary memory (Hard Disk), and Intel core i5 processor. Clock speed used is 1.64GHz.In this research we have proposed an algorithm which is time and space consuming. The Proposed Approach is executed and demonstrate for different data set. The time is find out by sorting large datasets and its very minimal as compared to other algorithm .The results achieve are comparable with the different algorithms with various datasets.

II. BASE THEORY

The theory on which it works is to sort large data in less time with the use of array. In this work the huge number of datasets has been sorted in very less time and the aftereffects are also set side by side with the traditional algorithm.

III. RECOMMENDED METHOD

The most significant approach that is used here to perform the sorting algorithm is to merges different sets of data by inputting of multiple files. In normal, the priority queue shows low locality of source and gives result very slowly. In this we used to join the various different streams where stream denotes an array and rest .By the rest streams we will create a new array and rest. When we used the streams which exceed the number two, it will builds a binary tree of merges up front and allocated buffer memories and No memory will allocate after that happens .This approach works on integers and any other type of input and supports various options to achieve the input dataset .The most significant approach that is used here to perform the sorting algorithm merges the input data of multiple files. In normal, the priority queue shows low locality of source and gives result very slowly. In this we used to join the various different streams where stream denotes an array and rest. Rest has code to create a new array and rest. When there are more than two streams, builds a binary tree of merges up front and allocated buffer memories and No memory will allocate after that happens .This approach works on integers as well as any other type of input and supports various options to get the input dataset .

IV. RESULTS ANALYSIS

Execution on 1 lakh Records : Here in the first experiment of this dissertation on both Quick Sort and New Approach are applied on 1 lakh random numbers to arrange these numbers in increasing or decreasing order. In this implementation thousands of numbers are generated in text file that is used as input data and output is produced in different text file so it is easy to verify the output is correct or not. After performing different experiments we can easily find out which is better algorithm.

TABLE 1: Execution time for both Quick Sort and Proposed Algorithm

S.No.	Time(in milliseconds)	
	New algorithm	Quick sort
1	146	185
2	148	176
3	154	171
4	146	175

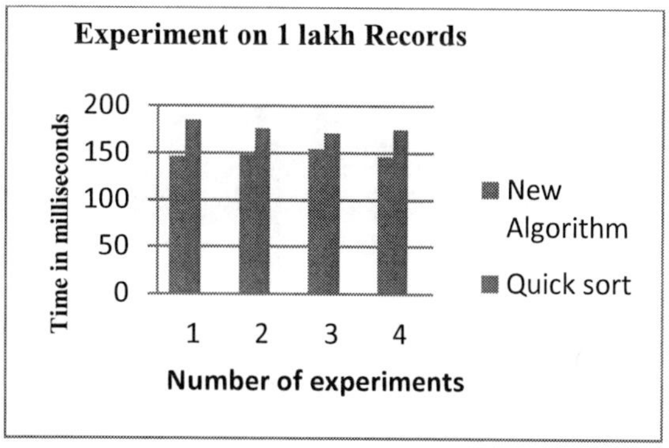

Figure 1: Comparison of Execution Time for 1 Lakhs Records for new algorithm & quick sort algorithm.

From the figure 1 it is showing the execution time for both Quick Sort and New Algorithm .It is clear to say after having these results of both algorithms that New Algorithm is producing output very quickly as compare to Quick Sort Algorithm. Along with the speed accuracy is also maintained perfectly through the Proposed Algorithm. The resulting graph shows the gap between these operations and proves that proposed algorithm is producing efficient and high speed performance.

Execution on 5 lakh Records : Here in this experiment of this paper, both Quick Sort and Proposed Approach are applied on 5 lac random numbers to sort these numbers. In this implementation thousands of numbers are generated in text file that is used as input data and output is produced in different text file so it is easy to verify the output is correct or not .After performing the operation time is examined and speed is maintained we can find out which algorithm is best.

TABLE 2: Execution time for both Quick Sort and Proposed Algorithm

S.No.	Time(in milliseconds)	
	New algorithm	Quick sort
1	378	436
2	372	448
3	369	462
4	362	472

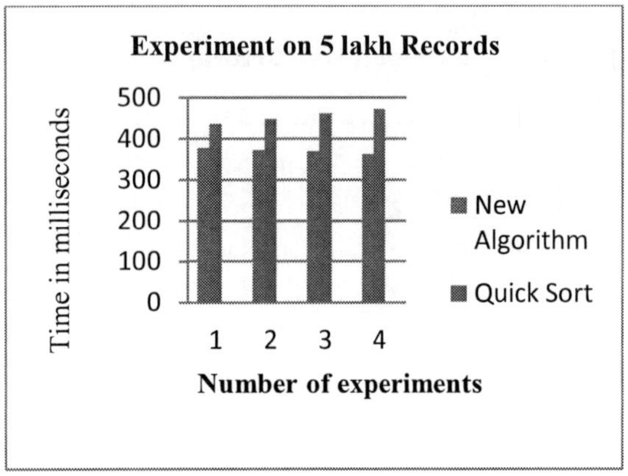

Figure 2: Comparison of Execution Time for 5 Lakh Records for new algorithm & quick sort algorithm.

From the figure 2 it is showing the execution time for both Quick Sort and New Algorithm .It is clear to say after having these results of both algorithms that New Algorithm is producing output very quickly as compare to Quick Sort Algorithm. Along with the speed accuracy is also maintained by the new algorithm.

Average Execution time of all Experiments: These results are calculated from the averages records of the above experiments. Results prove that New Algorithm is producing output very quickly as compare to Quick Sort Algorithm. These are the average cases among all the data we achieve on the both algorithms. The result is given in the table below :

TABLE 3: Average execution time for new algorithm & quick sort algorithm.

Number of Records	Time(in milliseconds)	
	New algorithm	Quick sort
1 lakh	148	176.4
5 lakh	370.6	458.8

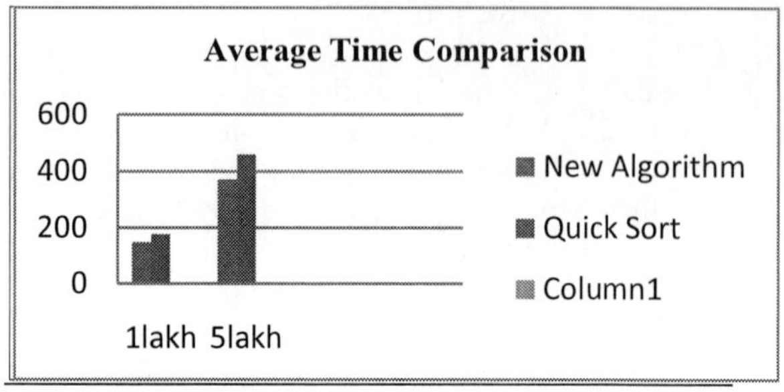

Figure 3: Comparison of Execution Time for new algorithm & quick sort algorithm.

V. CONCLUSION

This work presents the new approach and quick sort working and how the new approach operates the sorting with large numbers of input. It is very clear to see the results which show that New Algorithm is producing output very quickly as compare to Quick Sort Algorithm. Results prove that time and speed accuracy is also maintained perfectly through the Proposed Algorithm. Results show the efficiency and speed of proposed algorithm are above the Quick Sort Algorithm.

VI. FUTURE SCOPE

The today's and future of this area is bright, and full of opportunities and great challenges as it processes high demands. In future we can use it for thel GB of datasets for the high scalable demands and can compare with other algorithms.

REFERENCES

1. Aho I.A., Hopcroft J., Ullman J.: The Design and Analysis of Computer Algorithms. Addison-Wesley, Indianapolis 1974.
2. ZESZYTY NAUKOWE POLITECHNIKI ŚLĄSKIEJ 2014 for bubble sort. On classic bubble sort performance on large datasets SPRINGER 2014.
3. A. Rauh, G.R. Arce, "A Fast Weighted Median Algorithm Based on Quick select", Proceedings of IEEE 17thInternational Conference on Image Processing, HongKong,pp.105–108, 2010
4. L. Rashid, W.M. Hassanein, M.A. Hammad, "Analyzing and Enhancing the Parallel Sort Operation on Multithreaded Architectures", Journal Supercomputer,Springer-Verlag,2009.
5. Mehta M., Agrawal R., Rissanen J. (1996) SLIQ: A fast scalable classifier for data mining. In: Apers P., Bouzeghoub M., Gardarin G. (eds) Advances in Database Technology.

6. P. Tsigas and Y. Zhang, "A simple, fast parallel implementation of quick sort and its performance evaluation on SUN enterprise 10000", Proceedings of 11th Euromicro Workshop on Parallel, Distributed and Network-Based Processing (PDP2003), pp. 372–381, 2003
7. Marcin Wo zniak, Zbigniew Marsza lek, MarcinGabryel, Robert K. Nowicki, "On quick sort algorithm performance for large data sets", Proceedings of KICSS'2013, pp. 647-656, Progress & Business Publishers,2013 First Author Name , IJECS Volume ... Issue ... Month, 2014 Page No.01-02 Page6
8. Omar Khan Durrani, Dr. Khalid Nazim S, "Modified Quick Sort: Worst Case Made Best Sort", International Journal of Emerging Technology and Advanced Engineering, ISSN 2250-2459,Volume5,Issue 8,2015.
9. ThomasH. Cormen, Charles E. Leiserson,Ronald L.Rivest Clifford Stei"Introduction toAlgorithm" Second Edition, Prentice-Hall New Delhi,2004
10. Gina Soileau, Muhammad Younus, Suresh Nandlall, Tamiko Jenkins, Thierry Ngouolali, Tom Rivers, "Sorting Algorithm Analysis",Data Structures and Algorithms (SMT-274304-01-08FA1),2008
11. A. Franco-Arcega, J. Suarez-Cansino, L. G. Flores-Flores, "A parallel algorithm to induce decision trees for large datasets", , vol. 00,no. , pp.1-6,IEEE,2013
12. D. Jimenez, J.J. Navarro, J.L. Larriba-Pey, "An analysis of superscalar sorting algorithms on an R8000 processor", , vol. 00, no. , pp. 125, 1997
13. E.S. de Moura, G. Navarro, N. Ziviani, "Linear time sorting of skewed distributions", String Processing and Information Retrieval Symposium 1999 and International Workshop on Groupware,pp, 135-140,1999
14. Woźniak M., Marszałek Z., Gabryel M., Nowicki R.K. (2016) Preprocessing Large Data Sets by the Use of Quick Sort Algorithm. In: Skulimowski A., Kacprzyk J. (eds) Knowledge, Information and Creativity Support Systems: Recent Trends, Advances and Solutions. Advances in Intelligent Systems and Computing, vol346,Springer, Cham

A Study of the Impact of Data Warehousing and Data Mining Implementation on Marketing Effort

1. Ms. Kanika Chaudhry, Research Scholar, USMS, GGSIP University

2. Dr. Sanjay Dhingra, Associate Professor, USMS, GGSIP University

Abstract

Digitization has steered the growth of data in leap and bound. Business Intelligence technologies have evolved over the years and have become essential tools in analysis of this data. Business Intelligence comprises of technologies including Data warehousing, Data Mining, Business Analytics and Big Data Analytics. Of these Data warehousing and data mining form the base of business intelligence systems implemented across the organisations. This paper discusses the factor responsible for successful implementation of these tools. In this paper a model is proposed which shows that effective implementation of these tools leads to improved information quality and better marketing efforts for an organisation. Thus, paper reviews the previous literature on business Intelligence tools and throws light on the benefits which an organisation realizes through it.

Introduction

The fundamental and foremost thing that encounters the organisations in today's situation is managing of data, extracting the beneficial data and converting the extracted data into worthwhile knowledge for commercial purposes. We can all agree that in the existing economic setting, information and its precision signify an effective goal to any business organisation. A report by the McKinsey Global Institute (Manyika et al. 2011) forecasted that by 2018, the United States single-handedly will have a shortage of 140,000 to 190,000 people with profound analytical skills, as well as a deficit of 1.5 million data- savvy managers with the know-how to examine data to make real choices. In a **1958** article, **IBM researcher Hans Peter Luhn** coined the term **business intelligence**. He defined intelligence as: "the capability to capture the interrelationships of accessible particulars in such a way as to direct action to a preferred objective."

Business Intelligence and Data warehousing & Mining

The notion of **Data Warehousing and Data Mining** is becoming progressively widespread as a business information management tool where it is projected to reveal information structures that can direct decisions in situations of restricted faith.

According to Gartner Group "Data mining and artificial intelligence are at the top five key technology areas that will undoubtedly have a key influence across a varied range of businesses in the next three to five years". This conclusion was arrived at in a 1997 report (Jun Lee & Siau, 2001). Another Gartner group report that came out in 2008 (Godbole & Roy. 2008), says that 80% of information systems data is unstructured and an upsurge of double the size was predicted every three months. Decision support systems had taken up BI in an immense manner. BI's dominance was most noticeable in insurance, retail and banking

Source: Pilot software: An introduction to data mining: discovering hidden value in your data warehouse (1999)

Stage	Business Question	Enabling Technologies	Characteristics
Data Collection (1960s)	What was my average total revenue in the last five years?	Computers, tapes, disks	Retrospective, static data delivery
Data Access (1980s)	What are the unit sales in England in last March?	Relational databases, (RDBMS), Structured Query ,ODBC	Retrospective, dynamic data delivery at record level
Data Navigation (1990s)	What are the unit sales in England in last March? Drill down to Boston	Online analytical processing (OLAP),multidimensional databases,datawarehouses	Retrospective, dynamic data delivery at multiple level
Data Mining (2000)	"What's likely to happen in Boston unit sales next month? Why?	Advanced algorithms, multiprocessor computers, massive databases	Prospective, proactive information delivery

Data-warehouse

With stronger and tougher struggle, organisations are much keener in getting instantaneous and precise information to make improved choices. According to Inmon, (Inmon, 1997) data warehouse technology was described as, ''Gathering data from several distributed sources to shape a central data warehouse. Then operators can use suitable data-analyzing tools for accumulation and investigation on data.'' The main use of data warehouse is to process every aspect of analysis in core data by exploiting data study technology, and it can be a reference of decision-making for enterprises. The various factors for successful implementation of DW are:

S.No.	Author	Critical Success Factor
1.	(Wen, Chou, & Yen, 1997)	Project-related factor (users' choice) technical factors (user interface, hardware selection, data renewal, data loading, etc.)
2.	(Hwang, Ku, Yen, & Chenga, 2004)	Size of the bank ,Champions ,Top management support ,Internal needs, Degree of business competition , Selection of vendor, Skills of project team, Coordination of organizational resources, Participation of end users ,Assistance from information consultants
3.	(Shin, 2003)	Intercept Data quality, Ability to locate data, Access authorization, Ease of use, User training, System throughput, Information utility
4.	(Wixom & Watson , 2001)	Management support, Champion, Resources, User participation, team skills, source systems, Development technology.
5.	(Ramamurthy, Sen, & Sinha, 2008)	Organizational size, organizational commitment, absorptive capacity, organizational scope, organizational data environment
6.	(Xu & Hwang, 2007)	Clearly defined business needs , Top management support ,User involvement/participation , Source data quality , Proper development technology , Adequate IS staff & consultants • Project management (teamwork) , Practical implementation schedule.
7.	(Ang & S.H. Teo, 2000)	Identifying the processes, choosing development options, Adopting incremental change approach, overcoming resistance, choosing project leader, providing formal.

Data Mining

Data mining is applied today in a extensive range of applications, from stalking criminals to brokering information for superstores, from evolving public knowledge for a business to cross-selling, routing warranty claims, holding on to good clients, and weeding out bad clienteles (Berry and Linoff, 1997.A credible definition of data mining is – a process of extracting formerly unknown, hidden, and valuable information from the data found from databases. Data mining has come to become as a acknowledged field of research in the recent past. Business Intelligence (BI) is acquired by using mining. The various factors impacting the successful implementation of Data Mining applications are listed below:

1.	(Chung and Gray,1996)	Relevant prior knowledge, end-user goals, data quality characteristics like, missing values, noise in data.
2.	(Fayyad,piatetsky-shapiro,Simth,1996)	Understanding application domain, data preprocessing, data reduction and projection
3.	(Brachman,et al.1996)	Training,support,data availability, cost-benefit, volume, accessibility, change management expertise
4.	(Cabena,et al,1997)	Project management, sponsor, user group, data management, business analysis
5.	(Sim,2003)	Businessobjectives,application,quality,accessibilty,technique,service,intepretation,using discovered knowledge)
6.	(Barko,Namti,2003)	Data issues, time, scope, resources, people issues, organizational issues
7.	(Lynn,2009)	System Throughput, Data Quality, Ease of Use, Information Utility, Support provided to end-user

Impact on Information Quality and Marketing efforts

To endure in such competitive market settings, retailers have been presenting new marketing models such as "relational marketing", "one-to-one marketing", "enterprise marketing automation", and "database marketing" (D'Aveni, 1994). These marketing conceptions that relate to the significance of filling customer anticipations can hardly be implemented without embracing massive database systems. This conveys the message about the requirement of implementing data warehousing by enterprises. As an outcome, nearly 70 percent of data warehousing projects are related to marketing undertakings. (DeLone & McLean, 1992)
The various factors for measuring marketing performance are:

Enhanced Promotional efforts

Sales promotions are defined as various sale incentives and other approaches so as to escalate short-term sales. Promotional tools comprise of coupons, value-packs, refunds, draws, and others. To increase promotion effectiveness, a constant assessment of the effects of these promotions should be supported and stalked over time.

Enhanced Consumer satisfaction and relationship

To quantify enterprises capability to execute client analysis, the degree of change of knowledge of customer purchasing patterns, identification of current customers, capability to identify client needs and wants, and knack to recognize dependable customers will be included in the study.
The main reason to retain knowledge on clients is to increase customer satisfaction, which in turn creates increased sales and profitability. These efforts come from acknowledgment of the necessity to maintain prevailing customers for a long tenure.

Improved Market segmentation analysis

To measure corporates capability to execute market segmentation, the degree of change in the knowledge of customer demographics, awareness of geographic dimensions of consumer, knowledge of socio-economic dimensions of customer and capability to segment the market will be studied. Retailers are able to look into exhaustive market segments by implementing data warehousing. Data warehousing permits retailers to segment and examine market areas and consumers for successful marketing alternatives.

Improved trend analysis

The performance of the firms implementing data warehousing, in terms of the year-to-year percent change in sales per employee, return on sales, trends in sales, forecasting, cost and profits by product or market can be analyzed. It is discovered that one of the motives for companies to spend in information technology is for supporting organizational growth and understanding the trends. (Brown, Gatian &Hicks, 1995).

Proposed Research Model

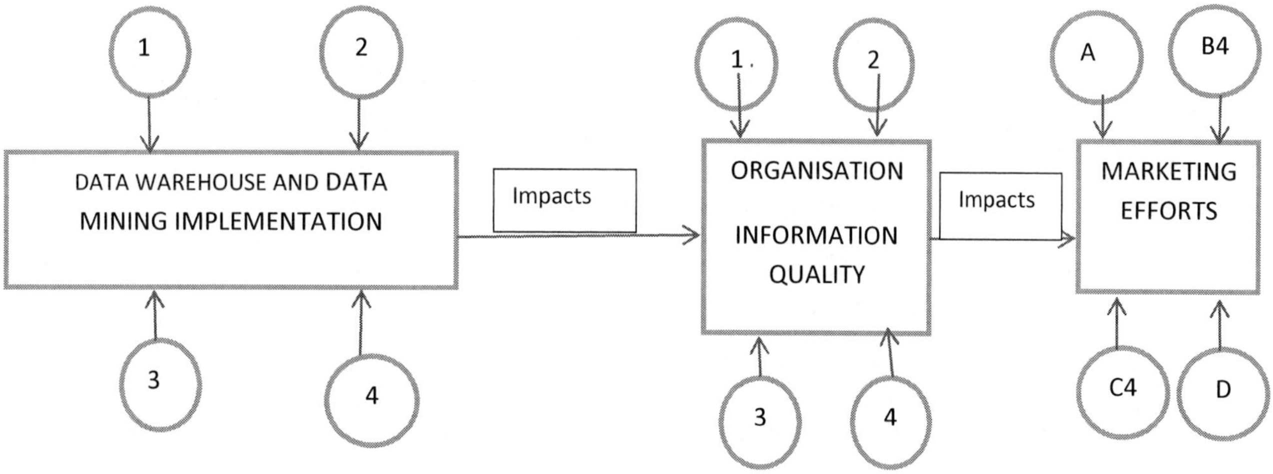

Data Warehouse and Data mining Implementation

Organizational factors (H.R. Nemati, C.D. Barko 2003)

- Management Commitment, (D. Sammon, Finnegan, 2003)
- Champion and sponsorship (Ramamurthy, Sen, & Sinha, 2008)
- Business Objective and Goal Alignment (Ang Eelynn, 2009)

- Business Communication, Monitoring and Feedback (Ang Eelynn, 2009)

Project related factors

- Project drivers/enablers (D. Sammon, Finnegan, 2003),(W. Yeoh, Koronios, A , 2010)
- Resource allocation (B. H. Wixom, Watson, H. J., 2001)
- User participation/consultation (V.Farrokhi, L. Pokorahi,2013)
- Team skills/experience (Wixom and Watson,2001)

Technical factors

- Applications and operating systems (Ang Eelynn, 2009)
- Accessibility, complexity, scalability (Ang Eelynn, 2009)
- Hardware platforms (D. Sammon, Finnegan, 2003)
- Reliable back-end system (V.Farrokhi, L. Pokorahi,2013)
- Technical framework (V.Farrokhi, L. Pokorahi,2013)

Data related factors

- Data quality (Ang Eelynn, 2009)
- Data Integration/storage/Management
- Sources of data (D. Sammon, Finnegan, 2003)
- Data ownership (Nemati & Barko, 2003)

Factors on Information Quality

1. Accuracy (Correctness, clarity, consistency) (Eppler, 2003) (Wand and Wang, 1996)
2. Completeness (comprehensiveness, conciseness) (Eppler, 2003)
3. Format (security, currency, accessibility, convenience) (Eppler, 2003) (Bailey, J.E., and Pearson,1983)
4. Applicability (Timeliness, Traceability, Maintainability) (Eppler, 2003)

Factors/Variables Contributing to Marketing Performance Identified:

A. Improved Promotional efforts (sales promotion, pricing programs, measurement of promotion) (D.Skeels, 1996)

B. Improved Customer profiling (knowledge of purchasing patterns, knowledge of current customers, knowledge of customer needs, knowledge of loyal customers, performing basket analysis, merchandise planning) (Welge,2001) (D.Skeels, 1996)

C. Increased Trend Analysis (Trends in sales, forecasting, cost and profits by product or market) (Welge, 2001)

D. Better Market segmentation analysis (consumer demographics, geographic dimensions, socio-economic dimensions) (Lee, Hong , &Katerattankul, 2004)

Conclusion: With the increasing acceptance of Business Intelligence tools, the scarcity of research in this area has been a growing concern. This research will represent an effort in measuring the impact of Business Intelligence tools on marketing efforts. The framework proposed can be used in evaluating the marketing efforts of across various industries and verticals like telecom, banking, retail, etc. The study will try to explore the link between information quality and marketing performance of organisations. Thus, this study will have policy implications for organisations, i.e., whether data-warehouse and data-mining techniques are able to improve information quality and overall marketing efforts. The organisations will get an understanding as to; whether it is worth investing in data-warehouse and data-mining systems.

References

Ang, J., & S.H. Teo, T. (2000). Management issues in data warehousing: insights from the Housing and Development Board. Decision Support Systems, 11-20.

Barton, D., & Court, D. (2012). Making advanced analytics work for you. Harvard Business Review, 78-83.

Brown, R., Gatian, A. & Hicks. J., (1995), "Strategic information systems and financial performance", Journal of Management Information Systems 11(4), 215–248.

Cervone , H. F. (2016). Organizational considerations initiating a big data and analytics implementation. Digital Library Perspectives, 137 - 141.

Devlin, B.A., Murphy, P.T., (1988), an architecture for a business and information system, IBM Systems Journal, 27 (1), 60–80

DeLone, W. H., and McLean, E. R., (1992) Information systems success: The quest for the dependent variable", Information Systems Research 3, (160–95).

English, L. P. (2005). Business Intelligence Defined, retrieved December 20, 2007, from http://www.b-eye-network.com/view/1119

Elbashir, M., Collier, P., & Davern, M. (2008). Measuring the effects of business intelligence systems:. International Journal of Accounting Information Systems, 135–153.

Ernst & Young LLP, (1998), Retail IT: Ernst & Young's", 17th Annual Survey of Retail Information Technology", Chain Store Age.

Hwang, H.-G., Ku, C.-Y., Yen, D., & Chenga, C.-C. (2004). Critical factors influencing the adoption of datawarehouse technology: a study of the banking industry in Taiwan. Decision Support Systems , 1–21.

Inmon, W.H., (1997), Managing the Data Warehouse, Wiley, New York.

Joshi, K., & Curtis, M. (1999). Issues in building a successful data warehouse. Information Strategy: The Executive's Journal, 28–36.

Lee, S., Hong , S., & Katerattanakul , P. (2004). Impact of Data Warehousing on Organisational Performance of Retailing Firms. International Journal of Information Technology & Decision Making, 61–79.

Manyika, J., Chui, M., Brown, B., Bughin, J., Dobbs, R., Roxburgh, C., and Byers, A. H. (2011). "Big Data: The Next Frontier for Innovation, Competition, and Productivity," McKinsey Global Institute

Nemati, H. R., & Barko, C. D. (2003). Key factors for achieving organisational data-mining success. Industrial Management & Data Systems, 282-292.

Ramamurthy, K., Sen, A., & Sinha, A. (2008). An empirical investigation of the key determinants. Decision Support Systems, 44, 817–841.

Richards, G., Yeoh , W., Chong, A.-L., & Popovič, A. (2014). An Empirical Study of Business Intelligence Impact on Corporate Performance Management. PACIS 2014 Proceedings, (p. 341).

Rudra, A., & Yeo, E. (1999). Key issues in achieving data quality Proc. of the 32nd Hawaii International Conference, 05-08.

Sammon, D., & Finnegan, P. (2000). The Ten Commandments of Data Warehousing. The database for Advances in Information Systems, 31(4).

Shin, B. (2003). An Exploratory Investigation of System Success Factors in Data Warehousing. Journal of the Association for Information Systems, 4, 141-170.

Skeels, D., (July 1996), Retail wars: A data warehouse can be a powerful weapon, Journal of Data Warehousing 1(1) 23–31.

Taub, B. (1999). Data Warehouse Return on Investment: Myths and Mistakes. DM Direct.

Wen, H., Chou, D., & Yen, D. (1997). Building a data warehouse: an overview. Communications of the ICISA, 25–35.

Wixom , B., & Watson , H. (2001). An Empirical Investigation of the Factors Affecting Data Warehousing Success. MIS , 25(1), 17-41.

Xu, H., & Hwang, M. (2007). The Effect of Implementation Factors on Data Warehousing Success: An Exploratory Study. Journal of Information, Information Technology, and Organizations, 2, 77.

3D FACIAL MODEL FOR ANALYSING THE FACIAL PARALYSIS

Banita
PhD Research Scholar
School of Computer Science
Lingaya's University
Faridabad, Haryana
banita861023@yahoo.com

Dr. PoonamTanwar
Associate Professor
School of Computer Science
Manav Rachna International University
Faridabad , Haryana
poonam.tanwar@rediffmail.com

ABSTRACT:

Facial expressions play a vital role in facial recognition and also help to evaluate the level of facial paralysis. The dimensions of facial expressions can also be represented by movement of facial muscles which is directly proportional to the ageing factors. As the facial muscles weakens, it changes the facial expressions of both the sides of the face which can be evaluated by use of image processing. Image processing introduced a new platform for various methodologies to evaluate the level of facial paralysis. Image processing techniques are helpful for facial recognition, facial expression and to identify the degree of paralysis. Number of technologies has been introduced by the researchers in terms of 2Dimensional (2D) and 3Dimensional (3D). 3D imaging like Multiboosting and Support Vector Machine (SVM) Classifiers, KD Tree portrait rendering process, Vertex Tent Coordinate (VTC) and Automatic Land Marking (ALM). The common image databases used for face recognition in 2D and in 3D are FRET, UMB-DB, UMB- DB and FRGC. This Paper introduces the high accuracy of facial expressions in 3 Dimensional as compared to 2 Dimensional facial images.

Keywords: facial expressions, face recognition, image processing, 3DUltrasonography, Classification

I. INTRODUCTION:

Facial expressions plays a vital role in face recognition, evaluating dimensions of facial muscles, analysis of facial movement and also evaluating the level of facial paralysis. There are 6 universal facial expressions which are Happiness, Anger, Fear, Disgust, Sadness, and Surprised which are evaluated by the use of facial landmarks [1]. For facial landmarks one of the most common and easy techniques is Salient Point Detection method which can be static or dynamic but the accuracy may vary with change in the mode i.e. static or dynamic [1]. When the landmarks have been marked manually then it is the dynamic mode whereas when landmarks have been fixed and can't be changed then it is termed as static mode. The average recognition rate is 97% has been achieved by using machine learning algorithm which has been used for face recognition as well as for facial expressions [1]. In 3D using Bosphorus Dataset, 24 facial landmarks are used for evaluating the dimensions of face along with different facial regions. In frontal face image 12 landmarks have been used in common for case of 2D [29]. The 3D facial landmarks give large data for face recognition and facial expressions [2]. While in 2D using Bosphorus dataset 18-20 facial landmarks are used for evaluating the dimensions of face along with different facial regions. Facial land marking has been marked on face at rest and face at motion or performing facial expressions in 2D as well as in 3D facial imaging. While comparison between 2D and 3D there is high resolution in 3D and also overcome the pose variation dimensions [27] whereas low resolution in 2D and also there is a problem in pose variation dimensions [4]. 2D imaging of face includes the coordinates along X-axis and Y-axis whereas in 3D imaging of face includes the dimensions along X-axis, Y-axis and Z-axis. Height and width of facial surface is covered in 2D whereas Height, width and depth of facial surface is covered in 3D by use of 3D-MAD (3-Dimensional Mask Attack Database) [26].Tanasai Sucontphunt et.al.[5] presented an interactive 3D facial expressions posing system through 2D portrait manipulation. To remove head motion, Singular Value Decomposition (SVD) has been used [5].

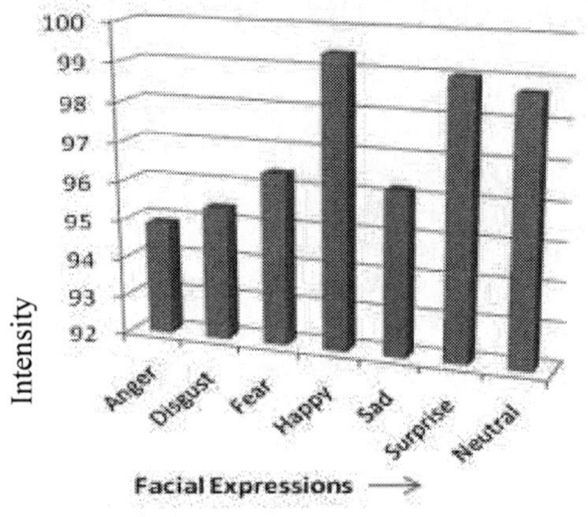

Fig.1. Computer recognition Intensity

The most likely similar expressions were sad-fear and disgust-angry as clearly shown in Fig.1.[7].

II. DATASETS FOR FACE RECOGINITION

For face recognition database which have been widely used are:

1. *BU-3DFE:*BU-3DFE (Binghamton University – 3 D Facial Expressions is one of the commonly used databases of 3D facial expressions [1] [18]. The facial landmarks used in BU-3DFE database have specific deformations evaluation of face with the help of various facial expressions. This dataset includes only facial expressions and its respective facial image at rest. The evaluation is strictly based on the distance calculation between control point and the reference point on facial regions.

2. *UMB-DB:* It is defined as "University Of Milano Bicocca- Face Database". UMB-DB has been used for evaluating facial images in 3D. UMB-DB includes the set of 3 Dimensional as well as 2Dimensional facial images at rest and at motion.

3. *Bosphorus Database:* Bosphorus dataset in commonly used in 2 Dimensional as well as 3 Dimensional facial images [33] [24]. It includes 6 basic emotions with respect to 28 action Units. In 3 Dimensional there are 24 landmarks which have been placed along with different facial regions.

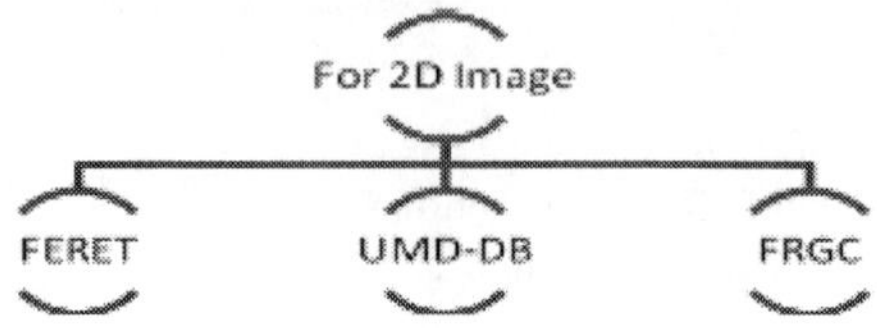

Fig.2 Datasets used for 2 Dimensional Image

4. *FERET:* Face Recognition Technology (FERET) is a dataset which has been used for automatic facial landmarks recoginition. FERET dataset is based on facial images which is further evaluated in terms of facial recognition. FERET is a collection of large database of facial images at rest and facial images at motion. Independent Component Analysis and Neural Networks the two common methods used in 2D face images with the help of FERET database. 200 images in both methods has been recorded and the recognition rate after evaluation, 89 % and 99 % respectively [2] which represents that FERET provides high recognition rate in 2D facial images.

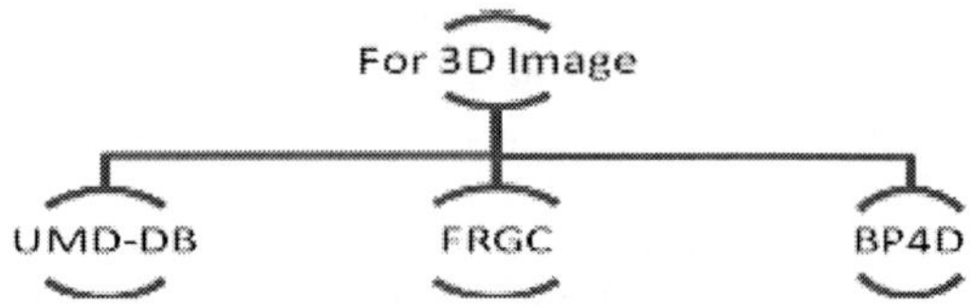

Fig.3 Datasets used for 3 Dimensional Image

5. *BU-4DFE:* It is generally used for evaluation of facial expressions by use of video recording. The facial expressions in videos have been decoded as per the facial landmarks with the help of image processing. In BU-4DFE 6 expressions have been recorded for evaluation but it does not include the facial land marking process.

6. *FRGC:* Face Recognition Grand Challenge FRGC) is the advancement of face recognition technology [22]. There are 3 categories of FRGC:

- FRGC dataset
- FRGC BEE
- Baseline algorithm

FRGC generally record the images on random selection and is further splits in to two sections: First section includes testing process and the second section includes training process [22]. For facial recognition in 3D FRGC v2.0 database is widely used [24]. It represents competitive performance and good generalization ability [24].

III. DATASETS FOR FACIAL EXPRESSIONS:

Dataset for face recognition and facial expression evaluation is used and it also helps in the evaluation of degree of facial paralysis. Facial paralyzed patients suffer from Dysfunctioning of muscles with respect to the facial expressions. Due to which there has been a huge change in the dimensions of face. For calculating the level of facial paralysis, image processing plays a great role. Facial Image can be stored at rest and at motion. By comparing the distance of different facial regions, the level of facial paralysis can be calculated. In facial paralysis left side of face has been compared with the dimensions of right side of face. More the difference in dimensions, severe is the facial paralysis. But facial paralysis can be 100% cured only when the precaution has been followed by the facial paralyzed patients within 72 hours of paralysis and cured within 90 days. There may be any reason for facial paralysis but it can be cured by various drugs like Acyclovir, Corticosteroids. For facial recognition different datasets have been used by researchers.
Similarly for facial paralysis evaluation different datasets have been used to evaluate the degree of facial paralysis and the accuracy of detecting facial paralysis.

1. *FACES:* Facial expression Coding System (FACES) is commonly used in case of video recording of facial expressions. FACES is basically used to analyze the frequency and intensity. FACES is lagging in terms of accuracy as it only includes 4 facial expressions i.e. Happiness, Sadness, Anger, Fear. Kring and Sloan in 2007 introduce FACES to analyze the four expressions in two different types of sections. The first section is totally based on the video recorded in an intended emotion session [15]. Second section includes the facial images which are actually from the corresponding intended emotion session .Facial Images have been stored for evaluation of degree of facial paralysis. Facial image can be in 2 Dimensional or in 3 Dimensions.

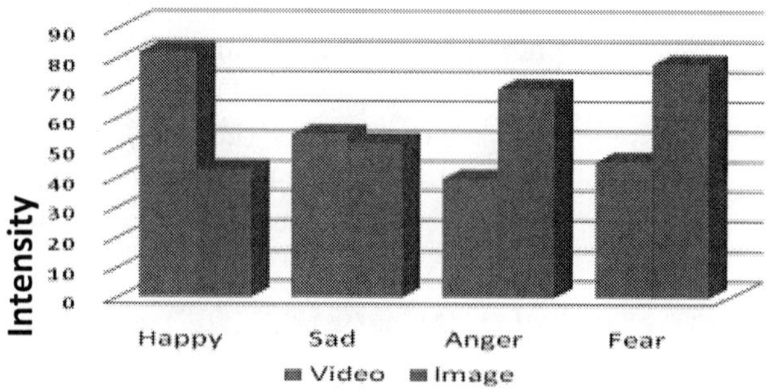

Fig.4 Comparison of Image and Video of emotions in terms of intensity.

The four facial expressions have been recorded with FACES dataset. Each facial expression consists of two different variations in intensity as video and image data have been stored simultaneously. Fig.3 indicates that there is a huge intensity variation during "Happy" facial expression. But on the second facial expression i.e. "Sad" approximate equal intensity have been recorded. FACES conclude that facial image has more accuracy and intensity while comparing with the video of facial expressions. Hence concludes image processing plays a great role in evaluation of intensities at different facial expressions.

2. *BFSC:*Basic Facial Shape Component (BFSC) is used in detecting facial expressions. BFSC basically uses 6universal expressions and at last facial expressions get compared with the face at rest [21][17].

BFSC deals with the shape of face whether smiling, anger. Hence deals with 6 facial expressions as Anger, Disgust, Fear, Happiness, Sad, and Surprised. Cornella Lanz et.al. [20] Proposes a robust method for facial landmarks localization using 2 Dimensional facial expression images. It concludes that a deviation of one pixel corresponds to about 1.5 millimetersbecause the landmark positions has been marked manually which results in slight variation [20].

Boqing Gong et.al.[21] represent a 3 Dimensional face with expression. It is generated by the two categories. First category includes the shape of face, dimensions of face along X,Y and Z-axis. Second category includes Expressional Shape Component (ESC) [21] which includes the deep information of the facial expressions and its respective dimensions.

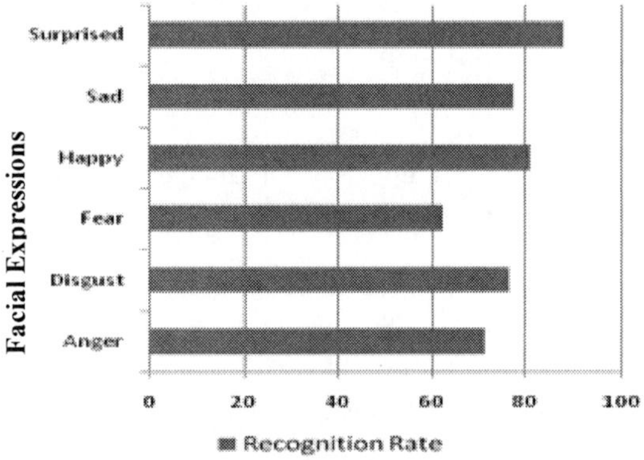

Fig.5 Average Recognition accuracy

The lowest recognition rate is under facial expression "Fear". The highest recognition rate has been achieved in facial expression "Surprised".

3. *FACS:* Facial Action Coding System (FACS) has been used for describing facial movements. FACS includes 9 different Action Units (AU) [3][8]. AU can be termed as facial landmarks while evaluating degree of facial paralysis. Before evaluating the face image this method divide the image into two halves. Upper part of face and lower part of face. Different facial regions indicated by number of different landmarks. AU varies with change in facial expressions. Lei Zhao et.al. [3] concludes that many structural details may be lost when histogram of entire image is evaluated directly.

4. ***VTC:*** Vertex Tent Coordinate is the encoding method which is used for face representation at rest and face at motion. It is represented by "v".
   Local Geometry of face = First Component + Second Component.

   Here first component includes matrix which consists of set of vectors. Second Component includes additional matrix which is termed as v_{n+1}[6]. The main advantage of VTC is that the face geometry which is represented in VTC is not based only on triangle basis but it further introduces new mesh technology for evaluation of face dimensions at rest and during expressions. The VTC based deformation transfer is represented as Q.

$$Q = w^{|} w^{T}(ww^{T})^{-1} \quad [6]$$

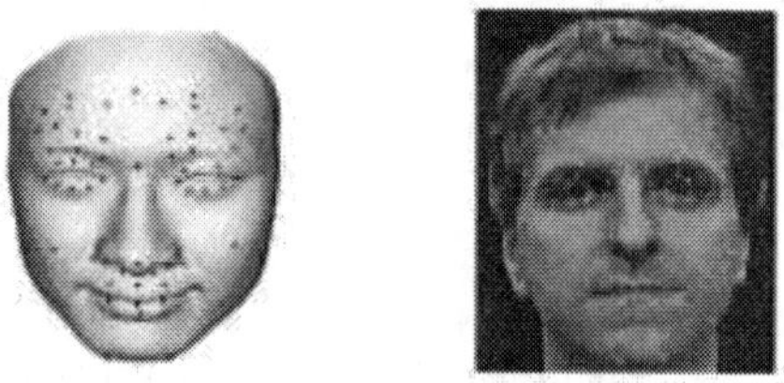

Fig.6 Landmarks on 3D face image and 2D face image. [6]

VTC method has been used to calculate the variation in dimension between face at rest and face during expression. VTC based deformation transfer method has been used to map the source expression on to the target facial expression. [6]

Facial landmarks vary in 2 Dimensional face images and in 3 Dimensional face images as in Fig.5. Facial image at rest and facial image during expressions has been recorded and analyzed by use of VTC analogy.

5. ***3D Ultrasonography:*** 3 Dimensional Ultrasonography has been used in medical science. It is used for detecting the area affected by facial palsy. 3D Ultrasonography is used for analyzing facial muscles.
Ratio = Palsy Side of face / Healthy side of face [14].
Gred Fabian Volk et.al. 2014 proposed 3D Ultrasonography on 7 facial palsy patients. There are 5 facial muscles on which 3D Ultrasonography worked upon:
   - Frontal Muscles
   - Orbicularis Oculi Muscles
   - Depressor AnguliOris Muscles
   - Depressor Labii inf. Muscles
   - Mentalis Muscles

Due to weakness in facial muscles there has been a huge variation in face during facial expressions.

Fig.7 3D Ultrasonography [14]

The perspective of 3D Ultrasonography in medical science is to evaluate the performance of different facial muscles and compare the performance between healthy and affected side of face [14].

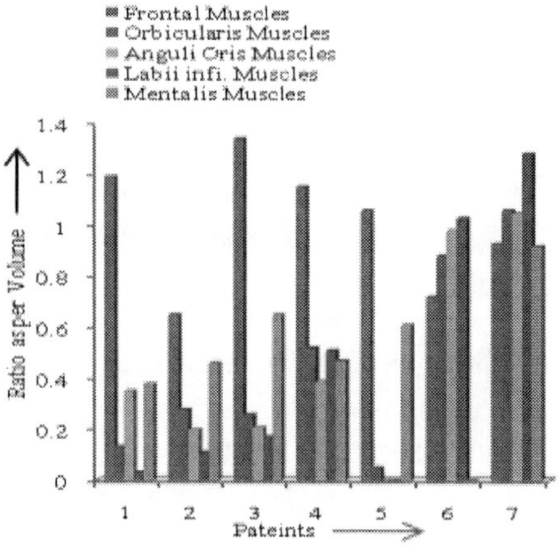

Fig.8.Facial Palsy ratio using Partial Volume (mm^3)

3D Ultrasonography has been used for facial paralyzed patients by evaluating the affected region in facial muscles. By evaluated the variation in facial muscles along with left and right side of face it can be easily detected that whether the facial palsy can be cured or cannot be cured. Large variation in ratio represents the more affected region in facial muscles. The advantage of 3D Ultrasonography as compared to MRI is cost effective, better accessibility and fast potential to quantify facial muscle sand its respective volumes. In MRI technique of medical science facial muscles has been evaluated as symmetrical or asymmetrical whereas in 3D Ultrasonography it detects the actual level of damage in facial muscles i.e. zygomaticus, Orbicularis oris and Oculi, Levatorlabiisuperioris and nasalis muscles [14].

As 3D Ultrasonography has been used in medical science to detect whether the constructive surgery is helpful to the facial paralysis patient [14]. 80% of facial paralyzed patients have defective healing after surgery which indicates that there is change in dimensions of face during expressions and at rest. Also 3D Ultrasonography helps to monitor the time course of muscle gain or muscle loss after therapeutic intervention in the face [14].

IV. Effectiveness in 3D

There are number of findings in 2D and in 3D in case of trailhead maps. It leads to different strength and weaknesses for trailhead maps communication w.r.t. 2D and 3D. In 3D the properties of 2D remains as such but additional to that it contains perspectives that diminishes the scale of distant [9]. Yi Lin et. al [10] in 2016 proposed a novel approach for analyzing Smile expression which has been split in to three categories:

- *Static:* Face image recorded at rest
- *Smile:* Face image recorded during smile expression.
- *Laugh*: Face image recorded during extreme smile i.e. laugh. It is a full-fledged smiling expression at maximum limit.

All the three categories have been analyzed using three dimensional reconstruction and analysis along with dimensions of left side of face and right side of face. Facial Landmarks localization [11] has been applied to evaluate the relationship between smile and laugh. BerkGokberk et.al [11] concludes that 3D face recognition when used with 2D then it results to make face a very strong biometric modality which has been widely acceptable for general public in terms of accuracy [11]. GuodongFeng et.al. [19] in 2014 established and analyze the facial motion by use of reliability test. The study meets the level of clinical and researchers need for detecting the face motion during different expressions. Debbie S. Ma et.al.[23] in 2015 introduced the Chicago face database which includes both physical and subjective norming data to analyze the mean suitability of gender and target race by use of adobe Photoshop software.

V. PARAMETERS IN 3D EVALUATION:

Algorithm is strictly based on 3D image processing which is very helpful to calculate the distance between healthy and affected side of face. It is used to detect the degree of facial paralysis and to detect the damage of facial nerve. Face model in 3D works on four facial nerve branches {out of five branches}. In this study out of five branches of the facial nerve four branches have been taken for study:

a. Temporal branch
b. Zygomatic branch
c. Buccal branch
d. Mandibular branch.
e. Cervical branch {not included in study}

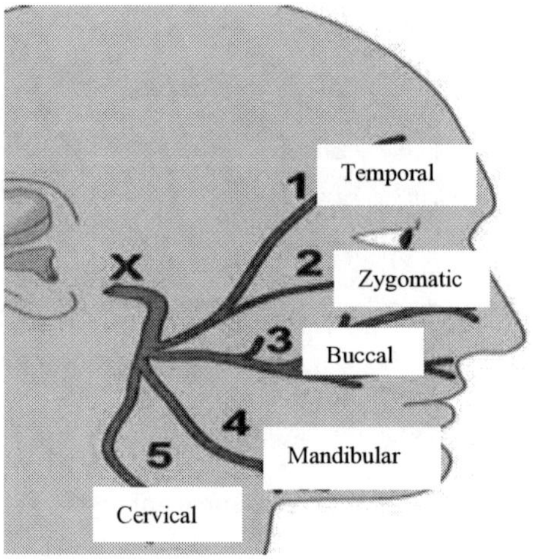

Fig.9 Branches of facial nerve.

Degree of facial palsy= Affected facial region – healthy facial region.

By considering ear to ear coverage i.e. depth, there will be high accuracy in calculating the degree of facial palsy.

RESULT OF PREPROCESSING:

Before preprocessing facial image of facial palsy patient, is stored and preprocessing is done, which helps to analyze the edges of face. The variation in distance evaluation of the facial landmarks shows the level of facial paralysis w.r.t HBGS.

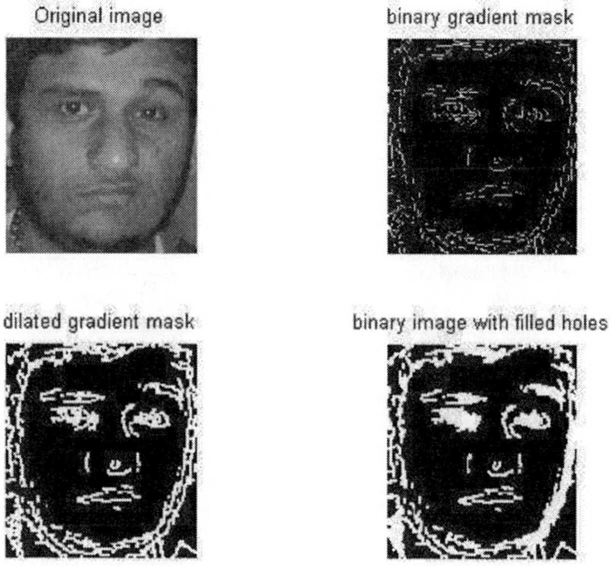

Figure 10. Preprocessing of face model

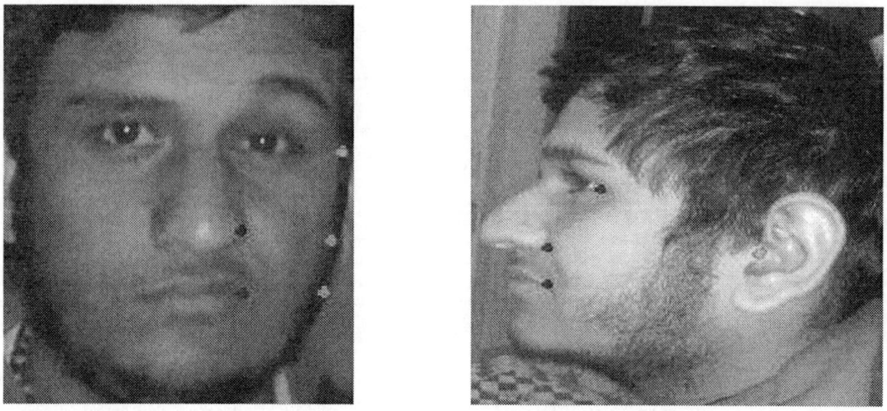

Fig.10 Left side facial landmarks [2D, 3D]

Facial landmarks are indicated in different fiducial points. Red color facial landmarks on facial regions represent the reference points in terms of 2D and green color landmarks represent key points in 2D facial image as in fig.10. Whereas red color facial landmarks on facial regions represent the reference point and green color landmark represent the key point in 3D facial image.

TESTING AND OUTCOMES

In testing phase the best distance evaluation were found in 3D image because it deals with ear to ear coverage of face model of facial paralyzed patients. Algorithm actual works on the facial paralyzed patients in terms of detecting the level of facial paralysis and its prognosis.

Table1. Comparison between various techniques and their outcomes

Work	Methodology	Outcomes
PitchayaSitthi-Amorn et.al. [12]	• Optical coherence Tomography 3D scanner.	• System allows for self-calibration of print heads and 3D scanning.
Kevin W. Bowyer et.al. in 2005 by Elsevier [13]	• Multimodal 2D+3D, 3D sensors.	• Multimodal performance is greater than the performance of 2D alone.
Lijun Yin et.al in 2008 [16]	• HMM based 3D spatial temporal facial descriptor.	• Average correct recognition rate of 90.44% for distinguishing 6 prototypic expressions
Kenneth Alberto Funes Mora et.al. in 2014 [25]	• RGB-D Camera • Gaze estimation algorithm	• Help to advance the development of Gaze estimation technologies under less constrained conditions.
Omkar M. Parkhi et.al. in 2015 [28]	• YouTube Face dataset (YTF) • Labeled faces in the wild dataset (LFW) • Equal error rate (EER)	• Large scale dataset assembled.
Shu Zhang et.al. [30]	• K-means algorithm is used.	• Achieves a high density of 3D face point cloud.
Bouguezzi Adel et.al. in 2014, Vol.2 No. 5-A [31]	• Medical prescriptions are considered.	• Evaluation is done on the basis of medical treatment.
Gary Lekakis et.al.in 2016 [32]	• 3D Imaging	• 3D data used to increase the predictability of surgical results in Rhinoplasty.
Amir Zadeh et.al. in Nov. 2016 [34]	• Deep neural network (DNN)	• DCLM is able to accurately align the 68 facial landmarks.

VI. Conclusion:

This study represents a new concept of dataset used in 3 Dimensional facial images for face recognition as well as for facial expressions. Intensity may vary with change in facial expressions. Surprised facial expression results in highest recognition rate whereas fear facial expression shows lowest recognition rate. Bosphorus dataset with use of landmarks o facial expressions helps to evaluate the level of facial paralysis in 2D as well as in 3D. As per the observation study works for facial paralysis but existing are in facial expressions and face recognition.

It is further concluded that for analyzing facial paralysis and dimensions of face in 3D, Bosphorus dataset and VTC is helpful in great extent. Adding large number of landmarks and considering respective facial regions in 3D is one of the future directions for evaluating the level of facial paralysis.

References:

[1] Ahmed Maalej, Boulbaba Ben Amor, Mohamed Daoudi , AnjuSrivastava, Stefano Berretti "Shape Analysis of Local facial Patches for 3D Facial Expression Recoginition",Vol.44, No.8, January 2012.

[2] J.Bobulski , "Multimodal face recognition method with two dimensional hidden Markov Model", Vol.65, No.1, 2017.

[3] Lei Zhao, Zengcai Wang and Guoxin Zhang "Facial Expression Recognition from Video Sequences Based on Spatial-Temporal Motion Local Binary Pattern and Gabor Multiorientation Fusion Histogram", Vol.2017, Article ID 7206041 .

[4] Michel F.Valstar, Enrique Sanchez-Lozano, Jeffrey F. Cohn, Laszlo A. Jeni, Jeffrey M. Girad, Zheng Zhang, Lijun Yin and MajaPantic"FERA 2017-Addressing Head Pose in the Third Facial Expression Recognition and Analysis Challenge", February 2017.

[5] TanasaiSucontphunt, Zhenyao Mo, Ulrich Neumann and Zhigang Deng ,"Interactive 3d Facial Expression Posing through 2D Portrait Manipulation", May 2008.

[6] Mingli Song and Zhao Dong "A Generic Framework for Efficient 2D and 3D Facial Analogy", IEEE Transactions on Multimedia.

[7] Lijun Yin, Xiaozhou Wei, Yi Sun, Jun Wang and Matthew J. Rosato "A 3D Facial Expression Database For Facial Behaviour Research", Publishes in Automatic Face and Gesture Recognition, 7th International Conference of IEEE, 2006.

[8] T. Fang, X. Zhao, O. Ocegueda, S.K. Shah and I.A. Kakadiaris "3D Facial Expression Recognition : A Prespective on Promises and Challenges", pp-603-610.

[9] David Schobesberger, and Tom Patterson "Evaluating the Effectiveness of 2D vs. 3D Trailhead Maps", January 2008.

[10] Yi Lin, Han Lin, Qiuping Lin, Jinxin Zhang, Ping Zhu, Yao Lu, Zhi Zhao, JiahongLv, Min Kyeong Lee &YueXu , "A novel three dimensional smile analysis based on dynamic evaluation of facial curve contour", Open Access in Scientific Reports, February 2016.

[11] BerkGokberk, Albert Ali Salah, NeseAlyiiz and LaleAkarun, "3D Face Recognition ", Chapter 1 in Handbook of Remote Biometrics in Springer, pp - 217-246.

[12] PitchayaSitthi-Amorn, Javier E. Ramos, Yuwang Wang, Joyce Kwan, Justin Lan, Wenshou Wang and WojciechMatusik, "MultiFab: A Machine Assisted Platform for Multi-material 3D Printing", Published by The Computational Fabrication Group, 2015.

[13] Kevin W. Bowyer, Kyong Chang and Patrick Flynn, "A Survey of approaches and challenges in 3D and multi-modal 3D+2D face recoginition", Published in Computer Vision and Image Understanding by Elsevier, Vol .1, No.15, 2006.

[14] Gerd Fabian Volk, Martin Pohlmann, Mira Finkensieper, Heather J Chalmers and Orlando Guntias-Lichius, "3D-Ultrasonography for evaluation of facial muscles in patients with chronic facial palsy or defective healing: a pilot study", Vol. 14, No.4, Open access in Bio Med Central, 2014.

[15]Peng Wang, Frederick Barrett, Elizabeth Martin, Marina Milonova, Raquel E Gur, Ruben C. Gur, Christian Kohler and RaginiVerma, "Automated video-based facial expression analysis of neuropsychiatric disorders", Journal of Neuroscience Methods 168 (2008) pp. 224-238, 2008.

[16] Lijun Yin, Xiaochen Chen, Yi Sun, Tony Worm and Michael Reale, "A High – Resolution 3D Dynamic Facial Expression Database", 2008.

[17] Lijun Yin, Xiaochen Wei, Peter Longo and AbhineshBhuvanesh, "Analyzing Facial Expressions Using Intensity-Variant 3D Data For Human Computer Interaction", IEEE, 2006.

[18] Asim Jan and HingyingMeng, "Automatic 3D Facial Expression Recognition using Geometric and Textured Featured Fusion".

[19] GuodongFeng, Yang Zhao, XuTian, ZhiqiangGao, "A New 3-Dimensional Dynamic Quantitative Analysis System of Facial Motion: An Establishment and Reliability Test ", Vol.9, Issue 11, November 2014.

[20] Cornelia Lanz, Joachim Denzler and Horst-Michael Gross, "Robust landmark localization for facial therapy applications",.

[21] Boqing Gong, Yueming Wang, JianzhuangLui and Xiaoou Tang, "Automatic Facial Expression Recognition on a Single 3D Face by Exploring Shape Deformation", Beijing, China, pp 569-572, Oct. 2009.

[22] Yinije Lei, Mohammed Bennamoun, Munawar Hayat, YulanGuo, "An efficient 3D face recognition approach using local geometrical signatures", Elsevier Ltd. , 2013.

[23] Debbie S. Ma, Joshua Correll and Bernd Wittenbrink, "The Chicago face database: A free stimulus set of faces and norming data", Vol.47, pp 1122-1135, Springer, January 2015.

[24] Huibin Li, Di Huang, Jean-Marie Morvan, Yunhong Wang and Liming Chen, "Towards 3D Face Recognition in the Real: A Registration-Free Approach Using Fine-Grained Matching of 3D Keypoint Descriptors", Int J Comput Vis, November 2014.

[25] Kenneth Alberto Funes Mora, FlorentMonay and Jean-Marc Odobez, "EYEDIAP: A Database for the Development and Evaluation of Gaze Estimation Algorithms from RGB and RGB-D Cameras", Eye TrackinG Research & Applications, 2014.

[26] NesliErdogmus and Sebastein Marcel, "Spoofing in 2D Face Recognition with 3D Masks and Anti-spoofing with Kinect".

[27] Amin Jourabloo and XiaomingLui, "Pose-Invariant 3D Face Alignment", Open Access Version by Computer Vision Foundation, IEEE, pp 3694-3702

[28] OmkarM.Parkhi, Andrea Vedaldi and Andrew Zisserman, "Deep Face Recoginition", 2015.

[29] Carlos Andres Cardenas Palacio and Francisco Alejandro Munera Galarza, "Cutaneous Sensibility Changes in Bell's Palsy Patients", American Academy of Otolaryngology- Head and Neck Surgery, 2017.

[30] ShuZang, Hui Yu, Junyu Dong, Ting Wang and HonghaiLui, "Automatic Reconstruction of Dense 3D Face Point Cloud with A Single Depth Image".

[31] Bouguezzi Adel, SouidKawthar, Derbel Amine, Ben Youssef Souha and BoughzalaAbdellatif, "Idiopathic Facial Paralysis", International Journal of Dental Science and Research, Vol.2, No.5-A, 2014.

[32] GaryfaliaLekakis, Peter Claes, Grant S. Hamilton and P.W. Hellings, "Three-Dimensional Surface Imaging and the Continuous Evolution of Preoperative and Postoperative Assessment in Rhinoplasty", Thieme Medical Publishers,New York, USA, 2016.

[33] Anke Schwarz, Esther-Sabrina Wacker, Manuel Martin, M. SaquibSarfraz and Rainer Stiefelhagen, "3D Facial Landmark Detection : How to Deal with Head Rotations? ", Springer International Publishing Switzerland , pp 424-434 , 2015.

[34] Amir Zadeh ,TadasBaltrusaitis and Louis-Philippe Morency , "Deep Constrained Local Models for Facial Landmark Detetction".

AN INTUITIONISTIC FUZZY AHP BASED MULTI CRITERIA RECOMMENDER SYSTEM FOR LIFE INSURANCE PRODUCTS

AKSHAY HINDUJA*
Department of Computer Application,
NIT Raipur, Chhattisgarh, INDIA
hinduja.akshay@gmail.com

Dr. MANJU PANDEY
Department of Computer Application,
NIT Raipur, Chhattisgarh, INDIA
manjutiwa@gmail.com

Abstract. Life insurance products play an important role in providing security for the family and support in times of contingencies. Therefore opting for an insurance product is a very crucial decision for a person. Impact of financial liberalization has affected the insurance market of India. In recent years, life insurance demand has experienced a rapid growth in Indian market. The notable increase in the competition among insurance companies has resulted into numerous insurance products being available in the market. The plethora of insurance products often confuses the buyers and that can lead to a wrong insurance product selection. Therefore, a constant requirement of assistance is growing in order to buy insurance products that are most suitable to consumers' personalized requirements. The existing recommender systems functions based on machine learning techniques that are not suitable for the critical products like Insurance. In order to overcome limitations of the existing recommender systems, we develop an original perception based Multi Criteria Recommender System that suggests insurance products based on intuitionistic fuzzy analytic hierarchy process. The proposed system has been tested by distinguish insurance officials and experts. They have validated the results and found them significantly accurate. We also carried out an empirical study to check the accuracy of the proposed system and found the results 91% accurate.

Keywords: Multi Criteria Recommender System; Intuitionistic Fuzzy AHP; Life Insurance; Multi Criteria Decision Making.

1. Introduction

Life insurance products play an important part in providing security for the family and support in times of contingencies. These products are actually the risk management tool based on actuarial science. Insurance products do not only protect buyer's family from any contingency but also help in financial planning as investment instrument. Impact of financial liberalization has also affected the insurance market of India. In recent years, life insurance demand has experienced a rapid growth in Indian market. The remarkable increase in competition within the insurance sector of the India has resulted in a number of insurance products being available in the market. The plethora of different insurance product often confuses the buyers and that can lead to a wrong insurance product selection. Therefore, a constant requirement of assistance is growing in order to buy insurance products that are most suitable to consumers' personalized requirements.

High-quality decisions making requires sufficient amount of information. Nevertheless, numerous instances proves that excess of information can also adversely affect the decision as insufficient information. The scenario of this overwhelming information is called the information overload problem (Adomavicius & Kwon, 2007; T L Saaty, 2008). In order to mitigate this problem, the Recommender System (RS) has been devised. It is greatly admired and helpful instrument of the current e-commerce scenario. Basically, it is an information filtering system that shows the only products and services, likely to be most useful to its users.

In this era of Internet, the RS has been largely used by E-commerce websites to recommend products and services to their users that are likely to be purchased. These products and services often belong to the class of commodity intended to entertain users like movies, books, music, restaurants and online games. Some other applications of RS are Academic Paper Recommendation(Tang & Mccalla, 2009), Critique-Based Mobile Recommendation(Ricci, Nguyen, & Web-based, n.d.), Personalized B2B E-Services(Wu,

Zhang, & Lu, 2014) and Intelligent Fashion Recommender System(Wang, Zeng, Koehl, & Chen, 2015). However, a product like Insurance that is meant to serve a vital purpose and whose purpose is to support its holder in future contingency requires more careful selection. The inception of liberalization in the economy and the approval of Foreign Direct Investment (FDI) in the insurance market of India have resulted into growing competition among insurance companies. This increasing competition among companies has given opportunity to customers to choose insurance products that are most suitable to his/her financial future planning. Insurance products have multifaceted terminology and several features; hence the terms and conditions of the insurance are not easily understandable to the customers. Therefore, need for a RS for insurance products has been felt by consumers.

In this paper, we propose an Intuitionistic Fuzzy AHP (IFAHP) based Multi Criteria Recommender System (MCRS) that recommends most suitable insurance products to its users. User's preferences are elicited using IFAHP, which is intuitionistic fuzzy (Atanassov, 1986) extension of AHP (T L Saaty, 1980), a well known Multi Criteria Decision Making (MCDM) method. The proposed MCRS recommends insurance products that are likely to be most suitable to its users and the process is directed by their contextual preference. Proposed MCRS simplifies the procedure of insurance product selection by hiding multifaceted provisions, clauses and reckonings of the insurance.

The remainder of the paper is organized as follows: In the Section 2, we describe the elementary concepts used in our research. Section 3 portrays related works on recommender system, utility based recommender system, AHP in insurance and decision making in insurance. Section 4 describes the methodology of the proposed system. In Section 5, we made concluding remarks.

2. Preliminary

2.1 Recommender System:

Recommender system is a useful tool for information filtering and has been established as an effective method to solve *the information overload problem*. It has been developed to save consumers' valuable time while seeking for the services & goods of their required. The *'personalized'* and the *'likelihood to buy'* are the characteristics that distinguish the Recommender Systems from Information Retrieval Systems (Adomavicius, Manouselis, & Kwon, 2011). Recommender systems are classified on the basis of recommendation technique they use. Numerous recommendation techniques are proposed in the literature. All recommendation techniques have three basic blocks: background information, user input and the algorithm that combines the background information and the user input data to arrive at suggestions(Burke, 2007). In his paper, Burke(Burke, 2007) classify the recommender systems as: *Content based system (CBS),Collaborative filtering (CF), Demographic RS, Utility based RS, Knowledge based RS and hybrid RS.* The CBS uses metadata to find similarity among products while CF uses prior ratings to find similarity among users. Utility based RS calculates the utility of the items to users while knowledge based RS uses experts' repository. Hybrid RS can be any combination of aforementioned RSs.

2.2 Intuitionistic Fuzzy Analytic Hierarchy Process (IFAHP)

AHP, developed by (Thomas L Saaty, 1988), is a well-known MCDM method, which has been used in numerous real-world applications(Subramanian & Ramanathan, 2012). Despite its simplicity, AHP is regarded as one of the most powerful tool for managerial decision making. We can summarize the process of AHP in three steps: first, Decomposition of the problem in a hierarchical structure encompassing objective, criteria and alternatives; second, pairwise comparisons of the decision elements using a fundamental linguistic scale (see Table

1) developed by saaty and derivation of local priorities from these pairwise comparisons; third, synthesis of local priorities in order to computer overall priorities of the alternatives. The alternative with higher priority is regarded as the best option.

In spite of all the merits of AHP, it is often criticized for its inability to handle the inherent vagueness and uncertainty of the real-world decision problems. In saaty's AHP, the scale used for pair-wise comparison contains all crisp values. Many researchers applied fuzzy set theory(Zadeh, 1965) for capturing decision makers' opinions to overcome this shortcoming of AHP. Some of the prominent fuzzy AHP concepts are (van Laarhoven & Pedrycz, 1983), (Buckley, 1985) and (Chang, 1996). Although fuzzy AHP has enjoyed a great success nonetheless it fails to capture experts' judgments in a holistic manner. Fuzzy sets are defined by "degree of membership" and "degree of non-membership" but in real world decision problems, there may be a degree of hesitancy in the judgments of experts due to inadequate knowledge, lack of interest or inherent uncertainty in the problem itself. Atanassov(Atanassov, 1986, 1994, 2012) extended the concept of fuzzy set to intuitionistic fuzzy set (IFS), which is defined by "degree of membership", "degree of non-membership" and "degree of hesitancy". Formally, we can define IFS as:

$$A = \{(x, \mu_A(x), \nu_A(x)) | x \in X\} \tag{1}$$

Where x is an element of universal set X, function $\mu_A(x)$ represents degree of membership, function $\nu_A(x)$ represents degree of non-membership and degree of hesitancy is represented by $\pi_A(x) = 1 - \mu_A(x) - \nu_A(x)$.

Owing to its powerfulness in handling fuzzy information, the IFSs have been incorporated with several MCDM methods. (Xu & Liao, 2013) proposed intuitionistic fuzzy extension of the AHP method. They maintain the core principal of the AHP: decomposition, pairwise comparison and synthesis; an intuitionistic fuzzy scale is used to gather experts' opinion (Table 1). They also develop a novel approach to check inconsistency and automatically repair it and priority method to derive priorities of the intuitionistic fuzzy pairwise comparison matrices. Due to the space limitation, only summary of the methodology is given here, for detailed methodology of IFAHP please refer (Xu & Liao, 2013).

Table 1: Original AHP scale & equivalent IFAHP scale (Xu & Liao, 2013)

Original AHP Scale	Linguistic Terms	IFS
1/9	Extremely Not Preferred	0.1
1/7	Very Strongly Not Preferred	0.2
1/5	Strongly Not Preferred	0.3
1/3	Moderately Not Preferred	0.4
1	Equally Preferred	0.5
3	Moderately Preferred	0.6
5	Strongly Preferred	0.7
7	Very Strongly Preferred	0.8
9	Extremely Preferred	0.9

** Use of intermediate values is allowed in both scales to present compromise.

3. Related Work

3.1 Recommender System

Recommender System has been an active research area since years and has been implemented in various applications(Manouselis & Costopoulou, 2007). In realm of e-commerce, recommender system has been an inseparable part of various e-commerce websites (amazon.com, cdnow.com, drugstore.com) and proved itself a significant technique of predicting user's interesting item(Schafer, 2001).

The majority of recommendation techniques are purely based on data mining techniques and co-relation among items and users without considering contextual information and user's need. Preference elicitation is the biggest challenges in the research area. Many researchers have applied different techniques of preference elicitation and user modeling. Francesco Ricci(Ricci et al., n.d.) proposed a critique based mobile recommender system that facilitates acquisition and revision of user preferences. Wang(Wang et al., 2015) proposed an Intelligent Fashion recommender system that recommends clothes according to body shape. Stolze(Stolze & Ströbel, 2003) proposed a need based conversational recommender system called Teaching Salesman (TS). TS help the users to choose items based on their need.

3.2 Application of AHP in Recommender System

Analytic Hierarchy Process (AHP) is a Multi Criteria Decision Making method introduced by T L Saaty in late 1970s. Since then, the simplicity, robustness and group decision making are the features that led the AHP to its widespread popularity in several domain. The AHP is most useful when groups of people are working in complex problems that need human opinion. AHP has been widely used in numerous multifarious application; some are resource allocation, healthcare, forecasting, benchmarking and quality management.

Marlinda *et al.*(Marlinda, Kreshana, & Sensuse, 2012) proposed a multi-criteria recommender system with AHP and Content-based Filtering to support potential students or high school graduates in selecting a field of study. Liang *et al.*(Liang, n.d.) proposed a AHP based recommender system for mobile phone selection. An empirical evaluation system was created by author on 244 individuals for validating the system.

Quan & Cho(Quan & Cho, 2014) proposed a Hybrid TV program recommender system that exploits Bayesian network and AHP. The recommender system consists of 3 parts: 1) Group genre preference inference part that uses a hybrid AHP technique and Bayesian network to predict group preference.2) Candidate Program Integration, in this part candidate program is selected based on group preferences calculated in previous part. 3) Program recommendation, in this part candidate program information is integrated with program preference (elicited by watching history). Proposed system also addressed cold start problem and claimed to solve it using Bayesian network.

4. Application of IFAHP to Life Insurance Recommendation

In this section we explain framework of the proposed system and the results of empirical study made to validate the methodology. The proposed MCRS handles the recommendation problem as MCDM problem. We can summarize that the proposed MCRS collects user specific information and his/her preferences and transform the recommendation problem into MCDM problem. Afterward the best ranked alternatives are suggested as user recommendations.

4.1 System Framework

The internal architecture of the proposed system is threefold: the first phase is building knowledge repository, also called *Domain Modeling*, that contains information about products & insurance regulations which is required by the MCRS before initialization of the actual recommendation process; the second phase is collecting information from users called *User Modeling*; and the third phase is the recommendation phase, in which the proposed MCRS performs policy filtering and combines background information and user inputs in order to make inferences (Fig.1).

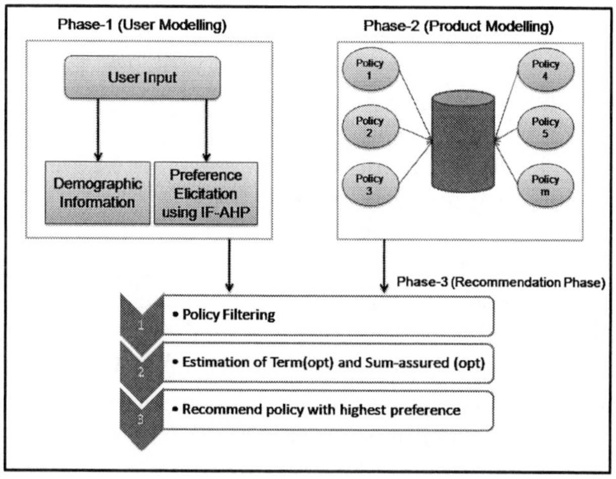

Figure 1 System Framework

4.1.1 Building knowledge repository (Domain Modeling):

In this phase knowledge repository of the MCRS is built that contains information regarding each insurance product exists in policy set and the rules and methods for calculating benefits of the policies. An insurance product contains two subsets: a set of constraints that must be fulfilled and a set of features, which represents the facilities offered by an insurance product to users.

Each insurance product is designed to fulfill specific necessities of different groups of the customer (age group, income group); for instance children's plan is design to secure education and future of children, therefore some constraints are associated with every insurance product. We extracted four implicit requirements of an insurance policy from literature survey and interview sessions with domain experts. In order to purchase an insurance product these constraints, particular to the product, must be matched. These constraints are: *Entry-Age*, *Sum-Assured*, *Term and Maturity-Age.* Entry Age and Maturity-Age define the target age-group, while Sum-Assured defines the "face value" that is payable by insurance company to buyer in case of contingency. *Term* is the time period an insurance contract is valid for.

Feature set of an insurance product defines the benefits and facilities, the product offers to its buyer. We identify nine key features of Life Insurance Products through literature reviews and expert interviews. These features are Premium Amount (C1), Payment Flexibility (C2), Tax benefits (C3), Benefits on death (C4), Benefits on survival (C5), Customer service (C6), Bonus (C7), Special Schemes & Add-ons (C8), Riders plan availability (C9). These features are regarded as evaluating criteria in the proposed system. The proposed MCRS calculates overall priorities of each alternative to a customer by aggregating local priorities of the alternatives over these features.

4.1.2 User modeling:

RS recommend movies, books, songs and other which are likely to be pursued by its user. RSs are expected to make suggestions that match its users' requirements. In order to attain this accuracy, the RS must gain understanding of users' preferences and their decision procedures(Lakiotaki, Matsatsinis, & Tsoukiàs, 2011). In this phase, the proposed MCRS extracts information related to the users in order to accurately suggest products & services targeted to that user. This phase contains two parts: in the first part, the propose MCRS collects user-specific information from the user and in the second part the MCRS models preferences of the user using the AHP. The proposed MCRS requires *Age* and *Income* mandatorily as this information are required to check the eligibility of customer for buying particular insurance products. Also, age and income attributes are used to estimate the maximum worth of insurance a customer can buy; rules to calculate maximum worth can be find in (Hinduja & Pandey, 2017). The proposed MCRS also collect *Time-period* and expected *Receivable-Amount* on the completion of policy term as optional information. If a user hesitates to provide optional information, the MCRS estimate the optimal Time-period and expected receivable amount for the user

Proposed MCRS employs IF-AHP method for extracting users' preferences for attributes of Insurance Policies. These attributes are considered as assessing criteria for an insurance policy. These preferences exhibit users' personalized requirements and expectations from the policy. Pair-wise comparison is key tool for preference modeling in proposed system. All nine features listed in *'features set'* section are compared pair-wise using an HTML form. Users have to choose importance level of one feature over remaining ones and the process is repeated for all features (Fig. 2).

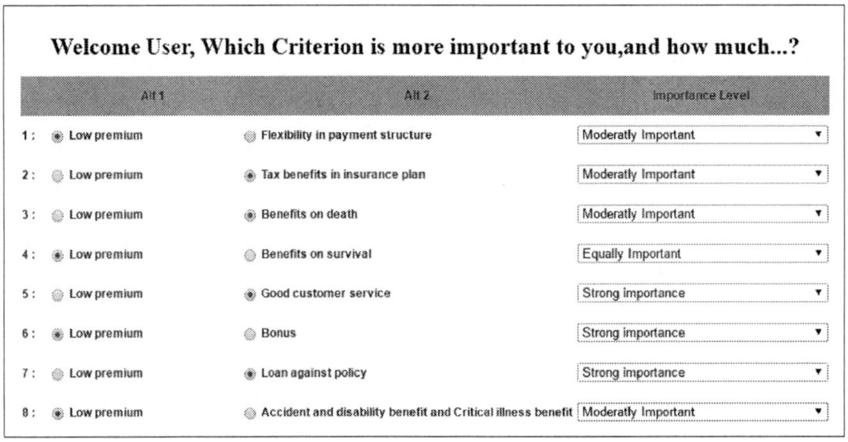

Figure 2: Pair-wise comparison among evaluating criteria of insurance policies

Data collected from pair-wise comparison is transformed into intuitionistic fuzzy pair-wise judgment matrices. The proposed MCRS derives user preferences for each feature from these matrices using priority method of IF-AHP. 'Consistency check and repair' is also performed for preventing users from providing conflicting preferences.

4.1.3 Recommendation Phase:

In order to arrive at the accurate recommendations, the proposed RS combines the information of the knowledge repository and the information collected from users in this phase. This phase consists of three parts: the policy filtering, selection of optimal term and sum-assured and the recommendation.

The proposed RS performs screening of policies by matching information collected from the user with the constraints of insurance policies. The screening process determines the eligibility of users for each policy existing in product set. This process removes the policies the user is not eligible to buy and also mitigates the computation overhead involved in the overall priority calculation.

After screening of policies, the proposed MCRS determines the optimal time-period (term) and expected receivable amount (sum-assured) for the user. For this purpose, the proposed system encompasses complete range of parameters (term & sum-assured) for priority calculation of the policies regarding the users. For a user, the terms and sum-assured are regarded as optimal values for which the policy yields maximum score. In order to calculate the utilities of the policies, the proposed MCRS employs IF-AHP. The user preferences are synthesized with insurance products' partial scores over described nine features. The score of a policy over quantitative criteria is simply estimated by normalizing the quantitative benefits it produces for its customer while the scores for qualitative criteria are obtained by insurance experts and already stored in knowledge repository.

The previous step results in optimal term and optimal sum-assured of each policy, remaining after screening phase, regarding a particular user of the proposed MCRS. Subsequently, the scores of all the remaining policies are calculated with their optimal values for term and sum-assured. The policy with highest scores is regarded as the most suitable policy to user and the proposed MCRS recommends it to the user.

4.2 Results of empirical study

An empirical study has been carried out to validate the performance of proposed MCRS. We obtained list of 230 prospects from an insurance advisor and subsequently collect their demographic information and preferences. From 230 prospects, 195 bought an insurance policy within 6 months of the survey and 178 of them purchased the policy which was recommended by the proposed MCRS. From the results of our empirical study, we can conclude that the accuracy of proposed MCRS is approx 91%. Besides this empirical study, we also validated the proposed MCRS from panel of 5 domain experts. All of the panel members have more than 10 years experience in the area of life insurance either as insurance advisor or as development officer. The panel of domain experts also found the results of proposed MCRS fairly accurate.

5. Conclusion

In this paper, we develop an original perception based MCRS that recommends insurance products. The core of the proposed MCRS is IFAHP method, which derives the best suitable policy for the users of the system using their preference information. Due to today's uncertainty, buying Insurance products is a very crucial decision for contingency management and future financial planning; but understanding multifaceted provisions of each product is a time consuming procedure and always manipulated by insurance advisor's biases. The existing recommender systems mainly focus on relations between products and between customers and for this reason they are not competent to cope with Insurance recommendation problem. The proposed MCRS's recommendations are guided by users' individualized requirements. The MCRS selects insurance policies that are eligible for users by processing their demographic information, determines their suitability to users and recommends policies with highest priority. We have tested our proposed MCRS with different parameters (age-group, user preferences) by distinguish insurance officials and experts. They have validated the results and found them significantly accurate. We also have made an empirical study to validate the proposed system and we the accuracy of proposed MCRS approx 91%.

Our future research work will be focused on simplifying the process of user modeling. Proposed system employs AHP for obtaining user preference. AHP is regarded as one of the best MCDM method when one needs human perception, having said that it has some limitation also. Pair-wise comparisons take significant amount of user's effort and time. We hope to improve our system framework so that it requires less user interactions but have all the advantages of AHP. Also, there is a need of an MCRS that recommends insurance product based on users' demographic information. Insurance is a product that is bought in order to help family in case of unforeseen event and hence the development of a MCRS, that collects demographic information of the users and their families and predicts their current and future needs, will be focus of our future research works.

REFERENCES:

Adomavicius, G., & Kwon, Y. (2007). New recommendation techniques for multicriteria rating systems. *IEEE Intelligent Systems*, *22*(3), 48–55. http://doi.org/10.1109/MIS.2007.58

Adomavicius, G., Manouselis, N., & Kwon, Y. (2011). Multi-criteria recommender systems. *Recommender Systems ...*, (Mcdm), 769–803. http://doi.org/10.1007/978-0-387-85820-3_24

Atanassov, K. T. (1986). Intuitionistic fuzzy sets. *Fuzzy Sets and Systems*, *20*(1), 87–96. http://doi.org/http://dx.doi.org/10.1016/S0165-0114(86)80034-3

Atanassov, K. T. (1994). New operations defined over the intuitionistic fuzzy sets. *Fuzzy Sets and Systems*, *61*(2), 137–142. http://doi.org/http://dx.doi.org/10.1016/0165-0114(94)90229-1

Atanassov, K. T. (2012). *On Intuitionistic Fuzzy Sets Theory* (1st ed.). Springer-Verlag Berlin Heidelberg. http://doi.org/10.1007/978-3-642-29127-2

Buckley, J. J. (1985). Fuzzy hierarchical analysis. *Fuzzy Sets and Systems*, *17*(3), 233–247. http://doi.org/http://dx.doi.org/10.1016/0165-0114(85)90090-9

Burke, R. (2007). Hybrid web recommender systems. *The Adaptive Web*, 377–408. http://doi.org/10.1007/978-3-540-72079-9_12

Chang, D. (1996). Applications of the extent analysis method on fuzzy AHP, *2217*(95).

Hinduja, A., & Pandey, M. (2017). Multicriteria Recommender System for Life Insurance Plans based on Utility Theory. *Indian Journal of Science and Technology*, *10*(14), 1–8. http://doi.org/10.17485/ijst/2017/v10i14/111376

Lakiotaki, K., Matsatsinis, N. F., & Tsoukiàs, A. (2011). Multicriteria user modeling in recommender systems. *IEEE Intelligent Systems*, *26*(2), 64–76. http://doi.org/10.1109/MIS.2011.33

Liang, T. (n.d.). 80 . A Web-Based Recommendation System for Mobile Phone Selection.

Manouselis, N., & Costopoulou, C. (2007). Analysis and classification of multi-criteria recommender systems. *World Wide Web*, *10*(4), 415–441. http://doi.org/10.1007/s11280-007-0019-8

Marlinda, L., Kreshana, P. E., & Sensuse, D. I. (2012). A Multi- Study Program Recommender System Using Content-Based Filtering and Analytical Hierarchy Process (AHP) Methods, *9*(3), 191–196.

Quan, J.-C., & Cho, S.-B. (2014). A Hybrid Recommender System Based on AHP That Awares Contexts with Bayesian Networks for Smart TV. *Hybrid Artificial Intelligence Systems, Hais 2014*, *8480*, 527–536.

Ricci, F., Nguyen, Q. N., & Web-based, F. (n.d.). Acquiring and Revising Preferences in a Critique Based Mobile Recommender System.Pdf.

Saaty, T. L. (1980). The Analytic Hierarchy Process. *Education*, 1–11. Retrieved from http://www.mendeley.com/research/the-analytic-hierarchy-process/

Saaty, T. L. (1988). What is the Analytic Hierarchy Process? In G. Mitra, H. J. Greenberg, F. A. Lootsma, M. J. Rijkaert, & H. J. Zimmermann (Eds.), *Mathematical Models for Decision Support* (pp. 109–121). Berlin, Heidelberg: Springer Berlin Heidelberg. http://doi.org/10.1007/978-3-642-83555-1_5

Saaty, T. L. (2008). Decision making with the analytic hierarchy process. *International Journal Services Sciences*, *1*(1), 83–98.

Schafer, J. B. E. N. (2001). E-Commerce Recommendation Applications. *Most*, 115–153. http://doi.org/10.1007/978-1-4615-1627-9_6

Stolze, M., & Ströbel, M. (2003). Dealing with learning in ecommerce product navigation and decision support: the teaching salesman problem. *Proceedings of the Second Interdisciplinary World* .... Retrieved from http://citeseerx.ist.psu.edu/viewdoc/download?doi=10.1.1.4.2530&rep=rep1&type=pdf

Subramanian, N., & Ramanathan, R. (2012). A review of applications of Analytic Hierarchy Process in operations management. *International Journal of Production Economics*, *138*(2), 215–241. http://doi.org/http://dx.doi.org/10.1016/j.ijpe.2012.03.036

Tang, T. Y., & Mccalla, G. (2009). The pedagogical value of papers: A collaborative-filtering based paper recommender. *Journal of Digital Information*, *10*(2). http://doi.org/10.1109/WKDD.2009.132

van Laarhoven, P. J. M., & Pedrycz, W. (1983). A fuzzy extension of Saaty's priority theory. *Fuzzy Sets and Systems*, *11*(1), 229–241. http://doi.org/http://dx.doi.org/10.1016/S0165-0114(83)80082-7

Wang, L. C., Zeng, X. Y., Koehl, L., & Chen, Y. (2015). Intelligent fashion recommender system: Fuzzy logic in personalized garment design. *IEEE Transactions on Human-Machine Systems*, *45*(1), 95–109. http://doi.org/10.1109/THMS.2014.2364398

Wu, D., Zhang, G., & Lu, J. (2014). A Fuzzy Preference Tree-Based Recommender System for Personalized Business-to-Business E-Services. *IEEE Transactions on Fuzzy Systems*, *PP*(99), 1–1. http://doi.org/10.1109/TFUZZ.2014.2315655

Xu, Z., & Liao, H. (2013). Intuitionistic fuzzy analytic hierarchy process. *Fuzzy Systems, IEEE Transactions on*, *22*(4), 1. http://doi.org/10.1109/TFUZZ.2013.2272585

Zadeh, L. A. (1965). Fuzzy sets. *Information and Control*, *8*(3), 338–353. http://doi.org/http://dx.doi.org/10.1016/S0019-9958(65)90241-X

Ontology development utilizing social network data attributed to drugs

Puja Munjal, Priyank Kumar, Akshay S. Nair
Department of Information Technology
Jagannath International Management School, GGSIPU,
Vasant Kunj, Delhi-110070, India

Abstract—**The role of Social Networking sites are playing a vital role in the awareness of clinical and healthcare Informatics. Nowadays, there's a diversity in different illness, medicines, source, symptoms and prevention methods. So it's difficult to maintain all information regarding healthcare. It's difficult for a doctor to know about each disease and find the cure & proper treatment for a sick person. All information must be structured in a way that we can easily find each disease and their cures according to their category. In this paper, a modular ontology is created which felicitates healthcare for different diseases from both infectious and non-infectious categories. This ontology also includes cures for different diseases with causes of that disease.**

Keywords—Ontology; Knowledge Management; Healthcare Ontology; Diseases Ontology

I. INTRODUCTION

Medical care for each and every individual in a community is important nowadays. So we need to categorize each disease with their symptoms, source, and cure in a structural way so that a doctor, nurse, surgeon or a physician can look for a right cure for a right disease. Healthcare data have been playing a major role in the medical environment. One of the major benefits of using these systems is assisting physicians to collect patient's healthcare information and shorten the process of the medical decision making [1]. Healthcare data is generated from various sources in diverse formats using different terminologies. Due to lack of common vocabulary, the accessibility and utility of the healthcare data are essential for health data analytics and decision-making systems [2].

When a user is looking for healthcare related information on a very particular topic, they might have troubles finding the correct search terms because of the efficient and lay medical dictionaries are not always alike [3]. This problem can be solved by mapping user query to related medical concepts. This type of concept mapping is used in the Semantic Web.

The Semantic Web is an initiative by the W3C in a collaborative effort with a number of scientists with the goal of providing machine-readable Web intelligence that would come from hyperlinked dictionaries, enabling Web authors to explicitly define their words and concepts. The idea allows software agents to analyze the Web on our behalf, making smart inferences that go beyond the simple linguistic analysis performed by today's search engines. Ontology is an indispensable part of the semantic web. Ontologies easily structure and represent domain knowledge in a machine-readable format that humans are capable of understanding; so they can be assimilated into computer-based applications and systems to expedite data annotation, decision support, information retrieval, and common-language processing [4]. For classifying healthcare data in a structure, we use an ontology. In this paper, we describe our general procedure focused on knowledge engineers so as to provide different types of healthcare ontologies based on language eradication from texts [5].

II. ONTOLOGY

Ontology is a term borrowed from philosophy that refers to the science of describing the kinds of entities in the world and how they are related. Ontology is a branch of philosophy concerned with the study of what exists.

As stated by Daniel S. Weld, editor, The American Association for Artificial Intelligence – "An O*ntology* is a theory of a particular domain or sphere of knowledge, describing the kinds of the entity involved in it and the relationships that can hold among different entities. This knowledge is expressed in computer-usable formalisms. The goal of research in ontologies is to create explicit, formal catalogs of knowledge that can be used by intelligent systems."

The ontology allows to formally represent and share knowledge. It congregates the entities (classes) included in a domain and their relationships. Relationships like "is-a" deliver a hierarchical system to the entities [6].

In emergency medical services, doctors, patients, nurse records are stored in the database and it can be retrieved with the help of an ontology in OWL (Web Ontology Language) format [7].

In practical terms, developing an ontology includes:

- defining classes in the ontology,

- arranging the classes in a taxonomic (subclass–superclass) hierarchy,
- defining slots and describing allowed values for these slots,
- Filling in the values for slots for instances.

The figure shown below is the sample human diseases ontology and its four sub-ontologies: categories, symptoms, causes, and treatments – [8]

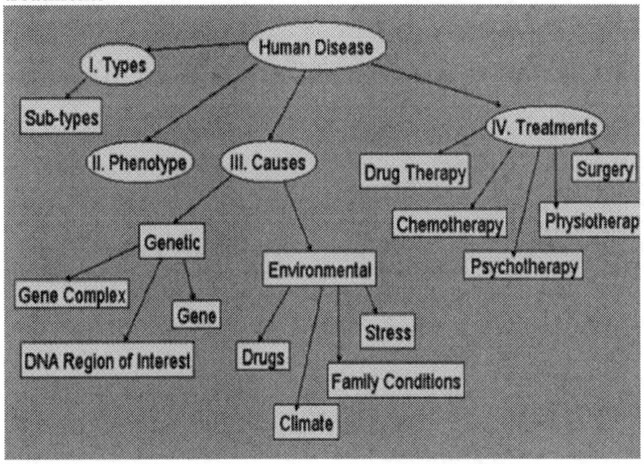

III. TOOLS AND TECHNOLOGIES USED

Here, the software tool we are using to develop the healthcare ontology is protégé. Protégé (http://protege.stanford.edu) is a free, open source ontology development software application that gives a rapidly expanding user community a tool suite to build domain structures and knowledge-based applications. Protégé implements a knowledge-based model compatible with the Open Knowledge Base Connectivity protocol4 which is designed to easily operate between frame-based systems [9].

As a building tool of ontology, Protégé is one of the more uncomplicated and practical development tools. The function of the Software can is divided into one by one in order:

- Build up the document
- Define the entities
- Introduce attributes of the entities
- Establish instances [10]

Protégé also contains OWLVIZ window which generates a graphical visualization of the opened ontology and requires Graphviz software to be already installed on the user's machine. Graphviz basically is open source graph visualization software.

Classes (or we can say entities) and instances are represented as nodes in a graph; different types can be set apart using different color hues. Directed edges (or we can say arcs) are used to show relationships between classes and instances, such as "is-a" relationships between classes in the structure and instance-of relationships which relate instances to their classes [11].

Following are the technologies which are being used to develop an ontology:

- EXtensible Markup Language (XML) -
  i. XML can store and organize any kind of information in a form that is tailored to user's need.
  ii. As an open standard, XML is not tied to a particular company or software.
  iii. XML offers many ways to check the quality of a document, with rules for syntax, internal link checking, comparison to document models and data typing.
  iv. With its clear, simple syntax and unambiguous structure, XML is easy to read and parse by humans and programs alike.
  v. XML is easily combined with style sheets to create formatted documents in any style.

- Resource Description Framework (RDF) –
  i. RDF is an XML-based standard for describing resources that exist on the Web, intranets, and extranets. RDF builds on existing XML and URI (Uniform Resource Identifier) technologies, using a URI to identify every resource, and using URIs to make statements about resources.

  ii. RDF statements describe a resource (identified by a URI), the resource's properties, and the values of those properties. RDF statements are often referred to as "triples" that consist of a subject, predicate, and object, which correspond to a resource (subject) a property (predicate), and a property value (object).

- Web Ontology Language (OWL) –
  i. Building upon RDF and RDFS, OWL defines the types of relationships that can be expressed in RDF using an XML vocabulary to indicate the hierarchies and relationships between different resources.
  ii. In fact, this is the very definition of "ontology" in the context of the Semantic Web: a schema that formally defines the hierarchies and relationships between different resources.
  iii. Semantic Web ontologies consist of a taxonomy and a set of inference rules from which machines can make logical conclusions.

IV. CONSTRUCTION OF AN ONTOLOGY

Basically, when creating an ontology, the first phase starts with the requirements analysis phase where concepts, attributes, relationships, axioms, and hierarchies are identified. In the design phase, a consistent model which is conceptual in nature is defined over a set of tasks which increases the complexity or we can say the classes of the ontology step by step. In the development phase, a suitable ontological language like OWL is used to formally structure the ontology which can help in the modification of the ontology according to the domain concepts in the maintenance phase [12]. The methodology for constructing an ontology is variable which defines what all entities will be taken into existence according to the usefulness and the users of the ontology that is being created. Several ontological researchers have their own summarized explanations and methodologies for constructing an ontology [1-20]. Those methodologies are common in the following aspects: specifying the scope and domain; conceptualizing the concepts and their relationships, including the definition of the class hierarchy; integrating or reusing the existing ontologies; implementing the ontology [13]. Created hierarchy of our work is given below –

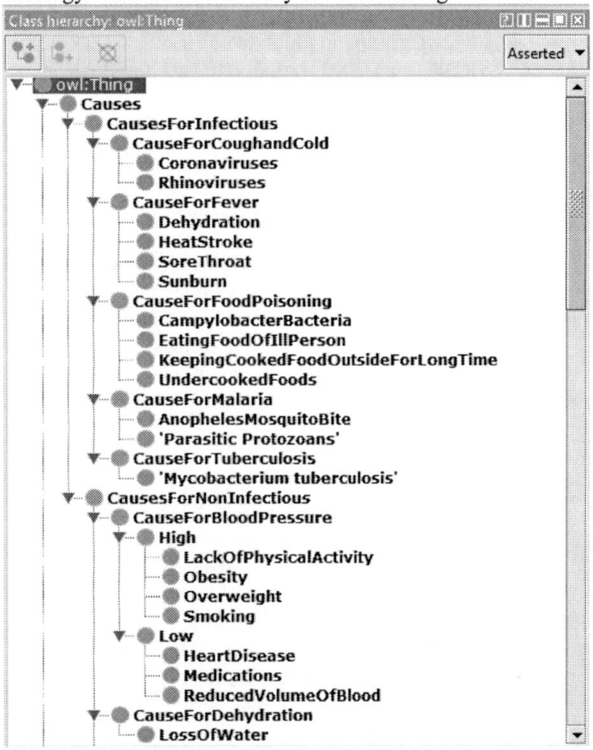

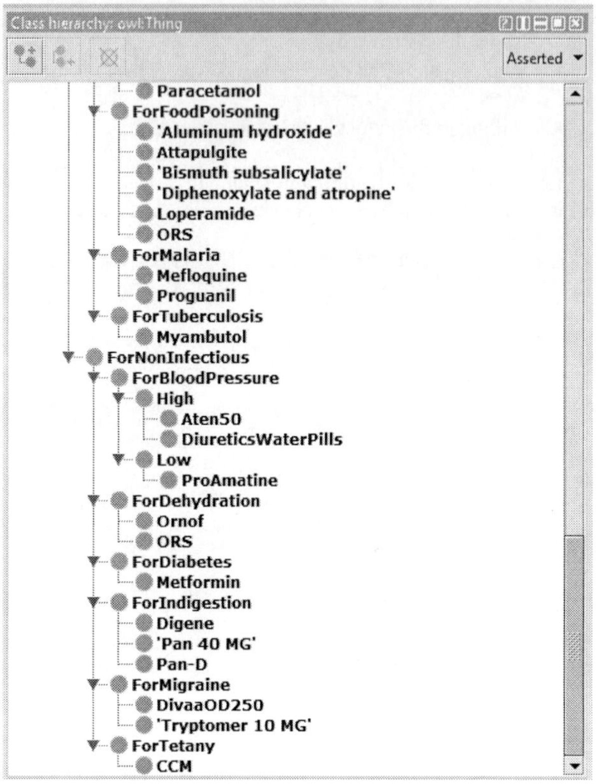

A. Owl: Thing class

This is the default class when working in protégé. This class is by default named as "Thing" [14]. Like in Java Language we have object class which is referred as a superclass of all the classes present in the language. Similarly, "Thing" is defined as the default parent class in ontology hierarchy. In this ontology, our work was focused on three main classes that are –

i. Medicine
ii. Causes
iii. Diseases

Each subclass is having "is a" relationship with owl: Thing and their associated parent class. Following image shows class association of Medicine, Causes, Disease with their subclasses–

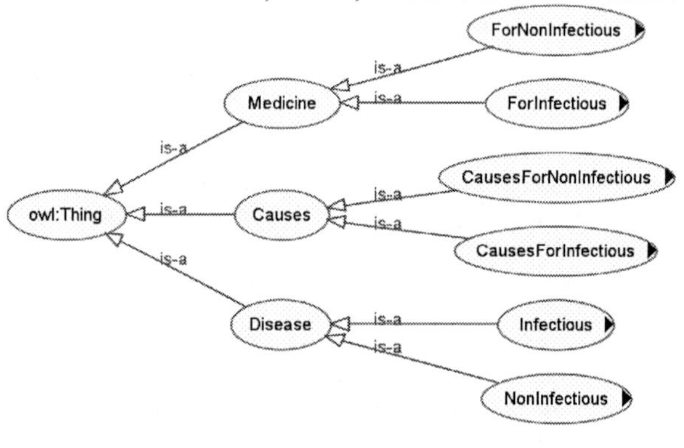

B. Disease class

Disease class is another class taken into existence in our ontology. This class represents some of the sample diseases taken by us that usually occurs in the human body. Disease class consists infectious and non-infectious subclasses which have "is a" relationship with the disease class. Five subclasses are having association with the Infectious class which are –

i. A cough and cold
ii. Food poisoning
iii. Fever
iv. Tuberculosis
v. Malaria

Six subclasses are having association with the Non-Infectious class which are –

i. Migraine
ii. Dehydration
iii. Blood Pressure – high and low
iv. Diabetes
v. Tetany
vi. Indigestion

Following images represent the Disease class and the subclasses residing in it –

C. Causes class

Causes are the second class taken into the existence in our ontology after Disease class. This class shows what all are the causing factors and microbes that becomes a cause of a disease. It has further two subclasses CausesForInfectious and CausesForNonInfectious. Further, both classes have subclasses which are same as diseases class. Each class has "is a" relationship with their superclass. Causes class graphical representation shows what we have explained -

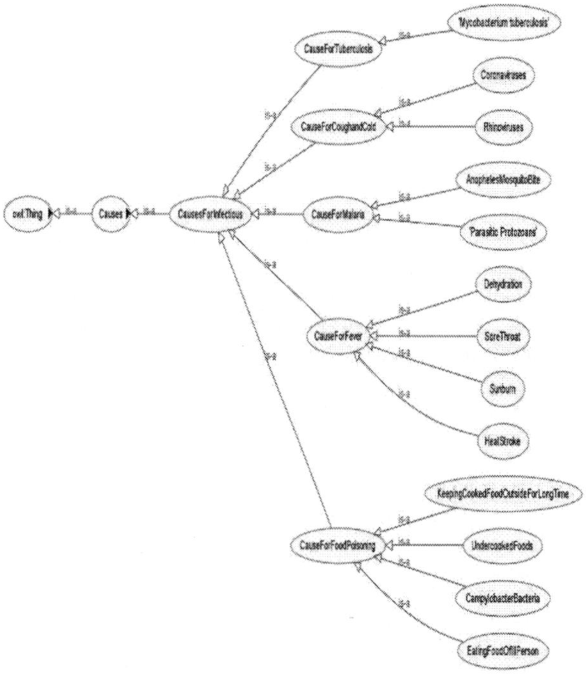

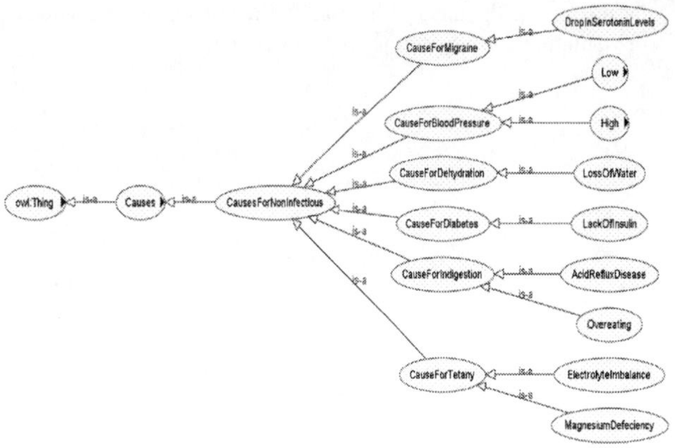

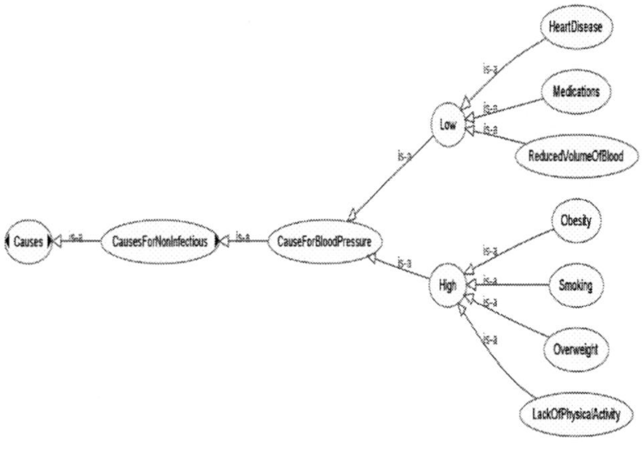

D. Medicine Class

This is the third and the last class taken by us into existence in our ontology. This class specifies some of the medicines and drugs as subclasses for the diseases specified in the disease class in the same hierarchy as disease class which shows some of the medicines and drugs generally prescribed by the pharm specialists and doctors. Images shown below are the hierarchical structure of Medicine Class.

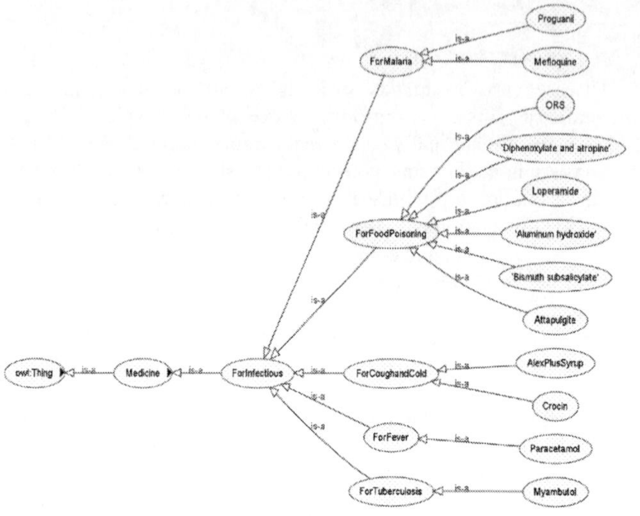

V. Conclusion and Future Work

Ontologies play a significant role in biomedical research over different applications. The ontology was evaluated from the point of view of ontology development, domain knowledge, and administered by domain professionals [15]. They provide the controlled dictionary required for the glossary of biological datasets, the biomedical literature, and patient records, expedite the retrieval of and, more generally, access to information. Such evenness also expedites the exchange of information and supports semantic interoperability among different healthcare systems [16]. With the increasing need for interoperability among different healthcare systems, there is an indispensable need for semantic interoperability among different healthcare systems that share data and knowledge, concept-driven information collection can expedite the creation of modular ontologies that can be used to query diversified systems, gather up patient-related information stored in heterogeneous systems, and potentially automate the workflow associated with diseases common to the participants [17] . We showed that ontology and protégé can play a supporting role in disease classification tasks, provided the standards are logical expressions involving no unpredictability [18]. In future, we can fetch healthcare data for diseases, their source, cures, prevention and symptoms from social media platforms like Facebook, Twitter, etc. We can also fetch datasets related to healthcare from online discussions forums like patient.info, medintu.com, healthboards.com etc.

VI. References

[1] Keke Gai, Meikang Qiu, Li-Chou Chen, Meiqin Liu, "Electronic Health Record Error Prevention Approach Using Ontology in Big Data"; 2015

[2] Dr. Sunita Abburu, Suresh Babu Golla, "Ontology-driven Knowledge-based Health-care Systems An Emerging Area – Challenges and Opportunities – Indian Scenario"; 2014

[3] A. A.Kogilavani, B. Dr.P.Balasubramanie, "Ontology Enhanced Clustering Based Summarization of Medical Documents"; 2009

[4] Tiffani J. Bright, E.Yoko Furuya, Gilad J. Kuperman, James J. Cimino, Suzanne Bakken, "Development and evaluation of an ontology for guiding appropriate antibiotic prescribing"; 2012

[5] Audrey Baneyx (MS), Jean Charlet (Ph.D.), Marie Christine Jaulent (Ph.D.), "Methodology to Build Medical Ontology from Textual Resources"; 2006

[6] Valerie Bertaud-Gounot, Regis Duvauferrier, Anita Burgun, "Ontology and Medical Diagnosis"; 2014

[7] Abinaya, Vinoth Kumar, Swathika, "Ontology-based Public Healthcare System in Internet of Things"; 2015

[8] Maja Hadzic, Elizabeth Chang, "Ontology-based Support for Human Disease Study"; 2005

[9] Monica Crubezy, Martin O'Connor, Zachary Pincus, Mark A. Musen, "Ontology-Centered Syndromic Surveillance for Bioterrorism"; 2005

[10] Xu Binfeng Luo Xiaogang Peng Chenglin, Huang Qian, "Based on Ontology: Construction and application of Medical Knowledge Base"; 2007

[11] Daniel L. Rubin, Suzanna E. Lewis, Chris J. Mungall, Sima Misra, Monte Westerfield, Michael Ashburner, Ida Sim, Christopher G. Chute, Harold, Solbrig, Margaret-Anne Storey, Barry Smith, John Day-Richter, Natalya F. Noy, Mark A. Musen, "National Center for Biomedical Ontology : Advancing Biomedicine through Structured Organization of Scientific Knowledge"; 2006

[12] Furkh Zeshan, Radziah Mohamad, "Medical Ontology in the Dynamic Healthcare Environment"; 2012

[13] Yu Lin, Norihiro Sakamoto, "A Hybrid Approach for Developing An Ontology of Genetic Susceptibility to Common Disease (OGSCD)"; 2008

[14] Alan Jovic, Marin Prcela, Dragan Gamberger, "Ontologies in Medical Knowledge Representation"; 2007

[15] Claire L. Gordon, MBBS, BMedSci; Stephanie Pouch, MD; Lindsay G. Cowell, Ph.D., MS; Mary Regina Boland, MA; Heather L. Platt, MD; Albert Goldfain Ph.D., Chunhua Weng, Ph.D., "Design and Evaluation of a Bacterial Clinical Infectious Diseases Ontology"

[16] O. Bodenreider, "Biomedical Ontologies in Action: Role in Knowledge Management, Data Integration, and Decision Support"; 2008

[17] Hengyi Hu, Larry Kerschberg, "Standardizing the Crowdsourcing of Healthcare Data Using Modular Ontologies"; 2017'

[18] Osama Mohammed, Rachid Benlamri, Simon Fong, "Building a Diseases Symptoms Ontology for Medical Diagnosis: An Integrative Approach"; 2012

A REVIEW ON THE STUDY OF BIG DATA AND BIG DATA ANALYTICS

Neha Garg,
Assistant Professor CSE Department, Manav Rachna International University, Faridabad Sec-43, Aravalli Hills, Faridabad-121006
nehagarg.fet@mriu.edu.in

Dr. Kamlesh Sharma,
Associate Professor CSE Department, Manav Rachna International University, Faridabad Sec-43, Aravalli Hills, Faridabad-121006
kamlesh.fet@mriu.edu.in

Abstract- With the increase use of social media, data is generated with a very rapid speed. Data storing, organizing, and managing have become a very tedious task. Since the handling of data, size of data and the management of data vary from organization to organization. Some organizations may face challenge in storing a data of few terabytes size while other may find it relatively easy. It may be the case that some organizations feel difficult to handle heterogeneous data while others are managing well. With such issues the management of data may vary but the basic concept of big data remains same.

This paper represents a review study that provides insight of importance, challenges, future scope and application area of big data in different areas and various analysis techniques of heterogeneous data. The finding of this review paper gives all relevant information to the researchers about the basics of big data and its analysis in very wide range of domains.

Keywords-Big Data, Big Data Analytics, Digital Media, social Media,

1. **Introduction-** Data which provides information as well as knowledge becomes useful when it is used very carefully and effectively that's how data management comes into play. With the increasing use of social media, the data is generated in such a high pace. The generation rate of the data inceasing daya by day be getting the data of all forms from all kinds of user in a much unpredicted manner. In such a heterogeneous environment, data management is become very difficult using traditional data management systems, analysis system and warehouse. A recent study show that every minute, Google receives around 4 million queries, by using e-mail users send over 200 million messages, YouTube users upload videos of around 72 hours, Facebook users post approximately 2 million pieces of unformatted content, and Twitter users generate 277,000 tweets [5]. With such a growing quantity of data and variety of user queries, it becomes essential to extract information that is best suited to user interest. This challenge shows the rise of BIG DATA applications, which can handle heterogeneous data and perform effective data mining to provide a solution in real time.

2. **Literature Review**- In early years of last the decade integrated database was used extensively not only for intended analytics but also for intra-enterprise consistency and coordination. These structures were also used on organizational portfolio,

organizations chart to define a business to its customers and affiliated. Some IT organizations have also proposed 3 V's to characterize the big data [2]. After the Hace theorem, Tamhane & Sayyad applied the concept of big data on heterogeneous data and heterogeneous user and the era switched from centralized structure to decentralized structures [1]. With the enhanced use of digital media, the definition of big data includes more features and organizations add their own dimensions to its definition according to their organizational structure as *viscosity, virality* [3]. IBM has introduced a fourth V to the already existing V's, *Veracity*. Oracle introduced fifth V as *value* and SAS introduced another V in form of *variability* [8], [20], [22]. In 2013, Phaneendra et. al. demonstrated the difference between big data and other data in terms of its five dimensions such as volume, velocity, variety, value, veracity and complexity [24]. With the increasing capacity of data, analysis has become a tedious task for which various methods of analysis are introduced to handle unstructured data [8], [3], [20]. Sagiroglu & Sinanc described the Big Data component, its issues related to capacity, methods, isolation, security, advantages and challenges. The challenges are identified not only in collecting and managing the data but also in methods of extraction of useful information from collected data [25]. Rubel provides an insight of the history and evolution of big data, what is the cycle of processing big data, what are the various challenges and issues associated with the big data and what are the available techniques and applications of big data[19].

3. **Big Data-**Big data is not only considered as storing and accessing the data; it's a combination of tools that can analyze the data and exploit its values according to user's interest [13].

HACE theorem states that Big Data starts with huge-volume; heterogeneous, independent sources with distributed and decentralized control, and seeks to explore Complex and growing relationships among data [1].
The definition of big data can be change from the perspective of organization as well as. For one organization massive data can be meant as big data, others can specify heterogeneous data as a big data and so on [12].

According to International Data Corporation (IDC) Big Data is defined as: "Big Data technologies describe new generation oftechnologies and architectures designed to economically extract value from very large volumes of a wide varietyof data, by enabling high-velocity capture, discovery and/or analysis"[6][13].
McKinsey Report defines big data as "data sets whose size is beyond the ability of typical database softwaretools to capture, store, manage, and analyze" [7].

4. **Comparison of Big Data from Traditional Data [19]-**

Table 1: Big Data V/S Traditional Data

Characteristics	BIG Data	Traditional Data
Data	Distributed data architecture	Centralized

Architecture		Architecture
Data Types	All types of data	Structured Data
Volume of data	Hundreds of terabytes & petabyte	Gigabyte to terabytes
Data schema	Dynamic Schema	Fixed Schema
Scaling	Flexible	Fixed
Data Integration	Complex	Simple
Data Access	Real time or batch	Integrated

5. **8 V's of Big Data**-Mainly the definition of big data evolve around 3 V's as given by Laney[2], for data management defined as velocity, variety and volume.

- **Velocity-** Velocity states the rate of generating data and the speed at which it move around and it is analyzed or acted upon [8][16]. The rapid increase in the usage of digital devices such as smartphone, laptops etc. has led to an unpredicted rate of generation and results in a requirement of real world analysis and visualization of solutions.
- **Variety**- variety refers to structural heterogeneity of data [8][16].Big data can comprised of data of various types-

Table 2: Various Data Types

Data Types	Source	Format
Structured Data	Business Applications Like financial, student information, employees management system etc.	RDBMS[4], OLAP, Data Warehouse
Semi Structured Data	Web Applications like emails, e-newspapers	XML, HTML
Unstructured Data	Social media, sensors Like comments, Image, Audio, Video	Any type

- **Volume-** Volume refers to the relative size of data to the handling ability.The increasing rate of data is 2.5 quintillion[5].This data is generated from every source e.g. sensors, social media sites, digital pictures videos, organizational records, and so forth to deal with this tremendous amount; The technologies are required that can store enormous amount of information in a versatile way and give distributed methods to locate that data [16].
  With the usage of digital devices the amount of data produced increases in a rapid [3] manner; Two more V *viscosity, virality* dimensions to define Big Data is added recently.
- **Viscosity** -Viscosity refers to the resistance of stream in the amount of data. This resistance may force from various data sources; additional processing needed to transform the data into insight. Technologies manages with viscosity is swift integration bus, enhanced streaming and complex event processing.
- **Virality**- Virality measures how fast the data is spread and shared with every unique node.

IBM has introduced a fourth V, Veracity[8][15], as follows-

- **Veracity** –Veracity characterize the unreliability inherent from some source of data. A billion dollar company can lose million dollars every year because of poor data management. Veracity defines the vulnerability of data, which is caused by data irregularity and deficiency; it prompts another challenge for Big Data. For example- user sentiments and comments are uncertain in nature on Facebook.

  Oracle presented fifth V that many organizations are battling with, finding *value* inside the data[8].
- **Value-** the data received in original form is often has less esteem in respect to its volume. However a high valued data can be acquired by analyzing this data viably and effectively.

  SAS introduced another V *variability* [8][21][22],to tackle the data generation rate and its structure.
- **Variability-** Variability and complexity are the alternate parameters to define big data. Where variability refers to data stream rates. Since data velocity is constant it often contains peaks and troughs. Complexity alludes to the way the data is produced through heterogeneous sources.

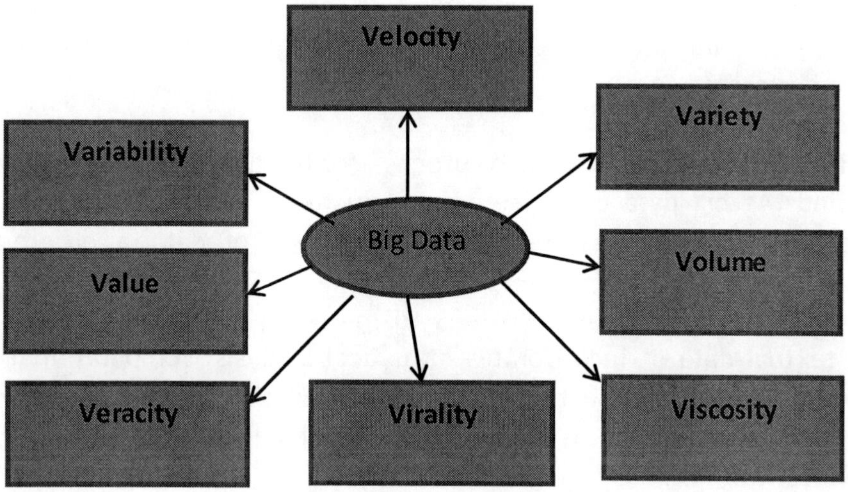

Figure 1: 8V'S of BIG DATA

6. **Cycle of Big Data-** The overall processing of big data comprises of five stages[19]-

- *Captured*
- *Organize*
- *Integrate*
- *Analyze*
- *Act*

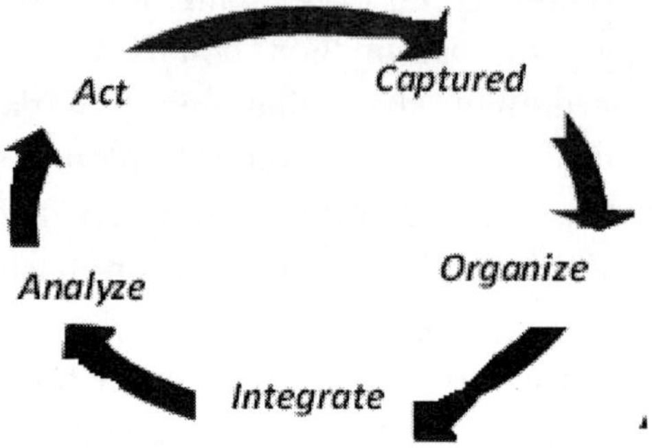

Figure 2: Life Cycle of Big Data

The further categorization them into two processes-

- ***Data Management***-In data management, data Acquisition, Recording (**capture**), Extraction, Cleaning & Annotation (**organize**) Integration, Aggregation & Representation (**integration**) processes are performed.

- ***Data Analytics***- In analytics, Modeling,Analysis (**analyze**) and Interpretation (**act**) processes are performed.

7. **Big data Analytics**- Analysis is the major process for big data using which the effective results can find. As big data comprises of unstructured data of various type, so the analysis becomes a critical part where for each type of data a different analytic technique is required[8].
   I. **Text Analytics-** Text analytics refers to method [10] that extracts information from textual data. It incorporates statistical analysis, computational linguistics and machine learning. Text analytics helps to change huge amount of text data into significant information which in turn help in decision making.
   There are two methods used for text analytics.
   a) Information Extraction to extract structured data from unstructured form [10], based on entity recognition and relation extraction. Entity recognition helps in finding names and categorize them into predefine classes.
   b) Text summarization to generate a summary sheet of multiple documents [10].The two text summarization approaches
   i) Extractive Approach, the resulting summary is a subset of original document.
   ii) Abstractive Approach involves extracting semantic information from text. E.G. NLP techniques
   c) Question Answering Technique will provide answers to the required questions, in natural language. E.G. IBM Watson[15]. The broadly three approaches are used.
   i) Information Retrieval Based- It has three stages-
   - *Question processing used to determine details of question*

- *Documentation processing used to determine semantics of document.*
- *Answer processing to extract answer for candidate question based on previously extracted information.*

ii) Knowledge based QA system provides semantics based description of the question. It can be applied to certain domains like medical area, transportation etc.

iii) Sentimental analytic analyze opinions of people towards entities. It is further divide into sub categories-

- *Document level*
- *Sentence level*
- *Aspect based*

II. **Audio Analytics-** Audio analytics refers to technique that extracts useful information from unstructured data. When comes to the individual verbal language, audio analytics refers to speech analytics. speech analytics follows two common technologies-

a) Large vocabulary continuous speech recognition, employ automatic speech recognition algorithm to match sounds to words from a predefined dictionary.

b) **Phonetic- based system** works on sounds and phonetics.

III. **Video Analytics** involves methodologies that can observe, analyze and extract significant information from video streams [17]. This technique can be used in automated security systems and surveillance system. Depending on system design, there are two approaches for video analytics.

a) **Server based** where all collected data is go to a centralize system for analysis.

b) **Edge based** architecture data analysisis performed locally and on the raw data collected from the camera.

IV. **Social Media Analytics** since social media consist both types of data structured as well as unstructured data captured from various sources[15][17].To analysis that data, the social media analytics can be categorize into two groups

a) Content based analytics focused on data posted by users on social platforms like comments, feedback, reviews, videos and audios.

b) Structured based analytics concerned with structural attributes of data and extract relationships among different entities.

V. **Predictive Analysis**[23] comprises various methods that forecast future outcomes based on historical data. Predictive analysis seeks to uncover patterns and find relationships among them.It can be classified into two ways-

- *Regression technique*
- *Machine learning technique*

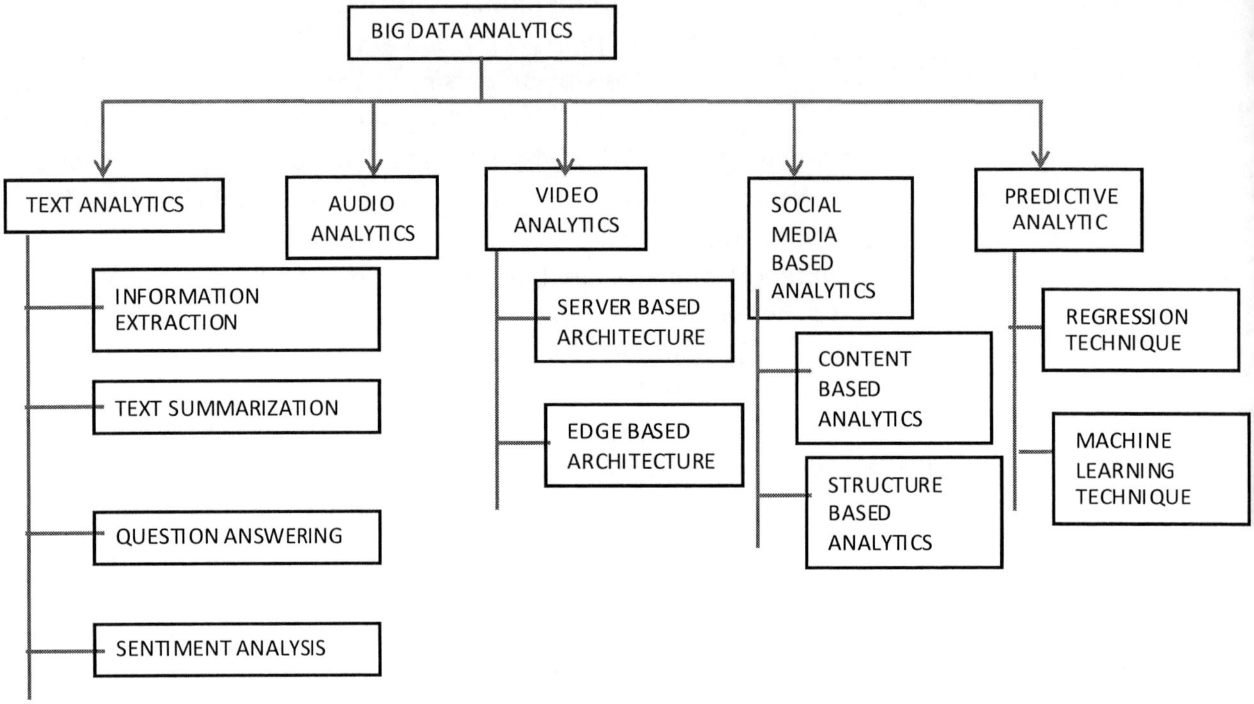

Figure 3: Big Data Analytics Techniques

8. Challenges for BIG Data-

1. **Data storage and quality-** The volume of data created is increasing rapidly. The storage of data is becoming a challenging task [9][11][8][20].Data lakes/ warehouses are designed to capture and store huge amount of unstructured data in original form. The problem, occur when data lakes/ warehouse seek to integrate inconsistent data from different sources, it encounters errors. Inconsistent data, redundant, logically conflict, and omitted data are the major challenge for data management[14].
2. **Good quality analysis-** The organizations utilize big data to find the optimal real time decisions. In turn, the data they are using should be precise; otherwise it may result in ill-advised decision. This high reliance on data quality makes testing of the quality of data a high priority issue, which requires a lot of resources, time and cost to guarantee the accuracy[8][20].
3. **Security and privacy issues of big data-**Once, organizations figure out how to use big data, it provides them a wide range of opportunities. However, it also involves various issues associated with the security [8][20] and the privacy of the data. The variety of range of tools used for analysis, management and utilization of big data. This may leads to a risk of exposure of the data, making it highly vulnerable. Hence, the creation of more data enhances security and privacy issues. Thus making it crucial for analysts and data scientists to think about these issues and handle the data in a way that will not result to the interruption of privacy.

4. **Heterogeneous sources of data-** Handling the volume and the velocity of data at which it is generated is a challenge [8][20]. The data may come from the internal sources of organizations like finance, marketing etc. as well as from external sources like social media, generate very large amount of data. That may result in the extremely diverse and massive data.
5. **Reliable Data-**With the sudden increase in the volume of available data, the challenge is how to distinguish the "signal" of "data" and "valuable information"[8][20]. Unfortunately, a lot of companies have difficulty identifying the accurate data and identify how to best use it. The clash with "spam data" and data quality is a essential problem. Companies must think out of the box and search for beneficial models that are quite different from the existing one.

9. **Conclusion And Open Issues:** -With the rapid growth of digital data, generated from various sources having heterogeneous users, big data has turn into a crucial issue now a days. The main focus of this study is to give an inside of handling, managing and generating user friendly information in real time manner.

The various analytics techniques have investigated, as well as their applications to process the big data efficiently. In this paper various techniques and applications of big data are discussed with respect to following aspects- (i) What are the main technologies and methodologies are presented to collect, store and analyze the big data? (ii) How can one analyze big data to find useful information? (iii) What are the challenges faced in Big Data analytics?

More practically, this survey paper provides an insight of basics of big data, its importance and the methods to analyze it without describing and analyzing the existing and intensively used applications like Facebook, Twitter etc.

Although, it is very difficult to say about the next trendy topic for big data. But there are certain topics on which studies are currently going on-

- **Privacy Issue-** In this digital world, when many users are using digital media and are responsible to generate a huge amount data, the risk of privacy leakage is very high. It becomes a very important issue to protect the privacy of user.
- **Streaming and online algorithms-** In data mining one of the current challenges is to get a well suited algorithm online to analyze massive amount of online data stream. Because traditional methods require the offline labeled data.
- **Data diffusion and visualization Techniques-** Data diffusion and visualization are also the challenges for big data to obtain more consistent methods for fusing multiple features of multimedia, study the dynamics of individual or group behavior, to capture and store new data, capability to analyze these data volumes and to solve spatial-temporal problem[14].

9. References-

[1] Deepak S. Tamhane, Sultana N. Sayyad:BIG DATA ANALYSIS USING HACE THEOREM, International Journal of Advanced Research in Computer Engineering & Technology (IJARCET) Volume 4 Issue 1, January 2015,

[2]Doug Laney: 3d Data management: controlling data volume, velocity and variety, Appl. Delivery Strategies Meta Group (949) (2001).

[3]S.MD.MUJEEB, L.KASI NAIDU: A Relative Study on Big Data Applications and Techniques, India, International Journal of Engineering and Innovative Technology (IJEIT) Volume 4, Issue 10, April 2015, ISSN: 2277-3754 ISO 9001:2008 Certified

[4]R. Elmasri.; S. B. Navathe , Fundamentals of database systems (Third Edition), New Delhi: Addison Wesley, 2000

[5] http://www.domo.com/blog/2014/04/data-never-sleeps-2-0/

[6] Gantz, J., &Reinsel, The 2011 Digital Universe Study: Extracting Value from Chaos.

[7] Internet source, aisel.aisnet.org

[8] Amir Gandomi, MurtazaHaider: Beyond the hype: Big data concepts, methods and analytics, International Journal of Information Management.

[9] https://upxacademy.com/big-data-analysis-top-5-challenges/

[10] Anupama Jha, Dr. Meenu Dave and Dr. Supriya Madan:A Review on the Study and Analysis of Big Data using Data Mining Techniques, ,IJLTET

[11] Puneet Singh Duggal, Sanchita Paul: "Big Data Analysis: Challenges and Solutions", International Conference on Cloud, Big Data and Trust 2013, Nov 13-15, RGPV, pp.269-276.

[12] C.L. Philip Chen, Chun-Yang Zhang: "Data-intensive applications, challenges, techniques and technologies: A survey on Big Data", Information Sciences, www.elsevier.com/locate/ins, January 2014.

[13] James Manyika, Michael Chui, Brad Brown, Jacques Bughin, Richard Dobbs, CharlesRoxburgh, Angela Hung Byers: Big data: The Next Frontier for Innovation, Competition, and Productivity, McKinsey Global Institute, 2012.

[14] Gema Bello-Orgaza, Jason J. Jungb, David Camachoa: Social big data: Recent achievements and new challenge, Information Fusion 000 2015(1-15)

[15]IBM, Big Data Analytics, URL: https://www.ibm.com/analytics/us/en/big-data/

[16]M.A. Beyer, D. Laney: The importance of Big Data: A definition, Gartner, Stamford, CT(2012)

[17]Nada Elgendy and Ahmed Elragal, P. Perner: Big Data Analytics: A Literature Review Paper, (Ed.): ICDM 2014, LNAI 8557, pp. 214–227, 2014. © Springer International Publishing Switzerland 2014

[18] Abhay Kumar Bhadani,India DhanyaJothimani:Big Data: Challenges, Opportunities, and Realities

[19]Rubul Kumar Bania ,JyotishKalita: A COMPREHENSIVE REVIEW STUDY ON BIG DATA, International Journal of Computer Engineering and Applications, Volume IX, Issue XII, Dec. 15 www.ijcea.com ISSN 2321-3469

[20] Jianqing Fan, Fang Han and Han Liu:Challenges of Big Data analysis,National Science Review 1: 293–314, 2014 doi: 10.1093/nsr/nwt032 Advance access publication 6 February 2014

[21](2012, June 26). Small and midsize companies look to make big gains with "big data," according to recent poll conducted on behalf of SAP. Retrieved from http://global.sap.com/corporate-en/news.epx?PressID=19188

[22]Diebold, F. X. (2012). A personal perspective on the origin(s) and development of "big data": The phenomenon, the term, and the discipline (Scholarly Paper No. ID 2202843). Social Science Research Network. Retrieved from http://papers.ssrn.com/sol3/papers.cfm?abstract id=2202843
[23] https://www.analyticsvidhya.com/blog/2015/08/comprehensive-guide-regression/
[24]S.VikramPhaneendra and E.Madhusudhan Reddy, Big Data- solutions for RDBMS problems- A survey, IEEE/IFIP NetworkOperations & Management Symposium (NOMS 2010),Osaka Japan, Apr 19-23 2013.
[25] Sagiroglu, S. and Sinanc, D., Big Data: A Review, International Conference on Collaboration Technologies and Systems (CTS), pp.42-47, 20-24, May 2013.

List Oriented Web-Page By Introducing Logical Structure For Any Browser On Small Screen Terminal.

Neha Garg,
Assistant Professor CSE Department, Manav Rachna International University, Faridabad Sec-43, Aravalli Hills Faridabad-121006
nehagarg.fet@mriu.edu.in

Shefali Singhal,
Assistant Professor CSE Department, Manav Rachna International University, Faridabad Sec-43, Aravalli Hills Faridabad-121006
shefali.fet@mriu.edu.in

Abstract. Now-a-days when everything is going digitalized, internet and web plays a vital role in everyone's life. When one has to ask something or has any online task to perform, one has to use internet to access relevant web-pages throughout. These web-pages are mainly designed for large screen terminals. But due to mobility, handy and economic reasons most of the persons are using small screen terminals (SST) like mobile phone , palmtop, pagers, tablet computers and many more. Reading a web page which is actually designed for large screen terminal on a small screen is time consuming and cumbersome task because there are many irrelevant content parts which are to be scrolled or there are advertisements, etc. To overcome such issues the source code of a web page is organized in tree data-structure. In this paper we are arranging each and every main heading as a root node and all the content of this heading as a child node of the logical structure. Using this structure we regenerate a web-page automatically according to SST size.

Keywords: DOM, Block Extraction, Backtracking, Context structure, Logical structure, web-page regeneration

1 Introduction

A web-page plays a very important role for both the end-users as well as the developers in multiple ways to solve different challenges. But as a developer it is always a matter of concern to make the things simpler and easier to use. There are various techniques, algorithms, designing of user interface and many more things which can be used in this direction.

Independent blocks were created by applying hybrid of DOM (Document Object Model) and VIPS (Vision Based Page Segmentation) techniques on a web page source code [2]. These blocks contain the textual part of a heading in a web page. For an end-user heading and its respective text is the most useful entity of a web page comparatively.

Further, the above discussed blocks along with other information under a heading of a web-page are separately stored using Cube data structures (OLAP Model of Data Mining) and presented on user interface accordingly [1]. Here, we have organized multiple information related to a particular heading in a tree structure and then used this structure to regenerate a user interface to provide an enhanced view which will be easy to use on a small screen terminal (SST).

The paper sections are sequenced as: The background work is explained in the section Literature Review. Then we have discussed certain Rule for Tracing Nodes in Main Heading which we have already discussed [1]. After that Generation of Logical Structure has been discussed with the help of few steps and example. Further, representation on user interface has been discussed which is again divided in few steps and examples as well.

2 Literature Review

This proposed study deals with the problem to enhanced display of webpages on SST. Here mapping of content meant for a large screen to a SST has many problems like choice of appropriate content which will result in a clear view with less time taken task.

Many ideas have been proposed in this field to collect information from a webpage according to the structure of a web-page. Some algorithms are there which are calculating entropy value of each feature [8] and calculating entropy threshold value decide whether this information is informative or redundant.

Vision based extraction [6] is done in VIPS algorithm where webpage is considered as tree and each node of tree as a block. Each block is assigned a value called degree of coherence and based on these values blocks are extracted. Then spatial features (such as position and size) and content features (such as the number of images and links) are extracted to construct a feature vector for each block [4]. Based on these features, learning algorithms are used to train a model to assign importance to different segments in the web page.

DOM and VIPS algorithms are used for block extraction [2] to provide hierarchical structure of the source code i.e., HTML code of a web page. Then there is concept of backtracking [1] for this tree. After backtracking we will get all the main headings containing its other <tags>.

Using these main heading and nodes under <H1> tag, firstly create a context view then logical view. After that map this logical view in form of list of main heading on SST at very first glance. And after selecting a particular heading user can easily choose a tag of his interest.

3 Rules For Tracing Nodes In Main Headings

We have stated Rule-I which helps in backtracking a node to find its respective main heading H1 under <body> tag [1]. Once we have traced main heading, we can track all the nodes under this tag using Rule-II [1], which is mentioned as below-

Rule-II

Following are few rules to be applied when a main heading node is found in a tree:

1. Stop backtracking.
2. Place heading into an array which is to be used for heading collection.
3. Start visiting sibling nodes.
4. Declare a queue for this heading.
5. Place sibling into queue if it is Image, hyper-link or text.
6. If the sibling node contains "div" then make it a reference node and follow Rule-III.
7. Go to another leaf node for finding next main heading in web page.

After execution with Rule-II, we will get a queue containing the various tags like image, text, hyperlink, div, etc. according to their main headings, which will be further used to create a logical structure.

4 Generation of Logical Structure

Once we have retrieved all the tags, we will now arrange them using some logic which results into a certain relationship among UI elements during its display in SST. This relationship will serve in generating a user interface view. Here related tags are arranged vertically. Such type of arrangement is known as a logical structure.

To generate logical structure we have to follow few steps-

Step 1: Mapping Tags into X-Y Axes-

First of all generate a context structure where contents are organized according to category. Here we are mapping them in the 2-dimensional axes [1] to represent them in a context structure, as follows-

X-AXIS

All the main headings of the web page are the unit for x-axis. So, it will show all the array elements of step-2 in Rule-II.

Y-AXIS

All the content part of a heading i.e., text, image, hyper-link and division will be displayed as unit on y-axis. So, if x- and y-axes are mapped at some point, a combination of main heading and its content will be resulting.

Fig. 1. Mapping tags of webpage on x-y axes.

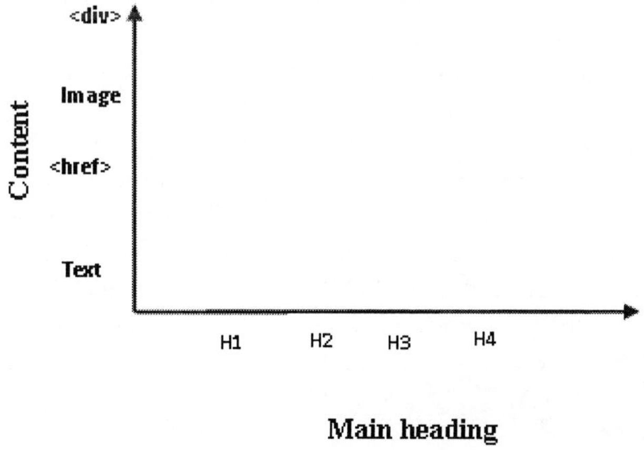

Step 2: Create logical structure-

Once we mapped elements in a context structure we can create a tree structure. For mapping into tree structure, we arrange all headings <H1> at the root of tree and other elements as the internal node of the tree. That's how we are reconstructing a logical structure of webpage where we have arranged each heading <H1> in the form of sub-trees.

Now we are having a logical structure that describes the connection between blocks at layout level.

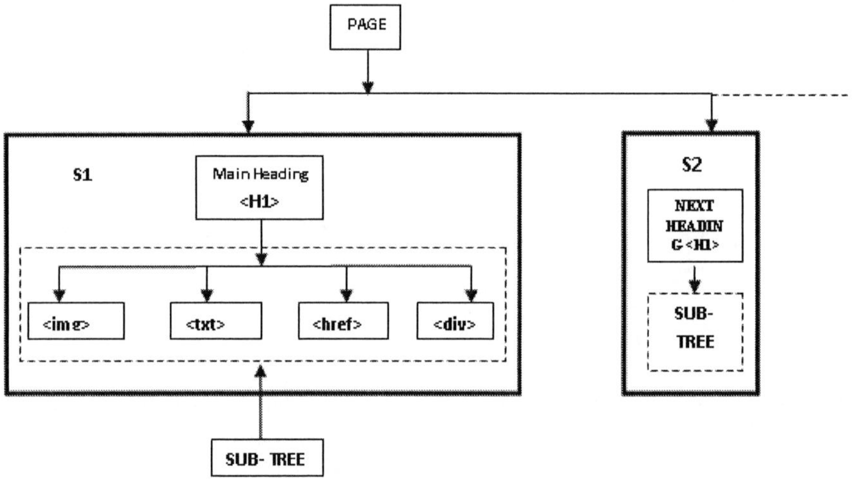

Fig. 2. Logical structure representation for a Webpage

5 Representation on User Interface

After creating logical structure, we can easily map the elements in an enhanced manner so that any GUI on small screen terminal (SST) can be much simpler and easier to access. If a web page is directly accessed on SST then there is a problem of scrolling the page either height-wise or width-wise again and again for each and every heading, due to which the user may loss few of the important details. Also there are lots of additional elements on a webpage like advertisements and pop-ups which may create interruption for a user because of which accessing relevant information is a time-consuming and tough task.

To overcome all these problems a concept is proposed in which we will be using all these aspects collectively. To implement it we have to follow the steps below-

5.1 Mapping to Small Screen Terminal

In this enhanced version on SST, a web page will show only list of all main headings it contains, which is a root node for all sub-trees logically. Such a display will help in decision making in a very short span of time. Once a user has seen all the headings, he may easily choose a heading according to his requirement.

5.2 Arrangement of Headings

As we have already discussed that each heading is a root of the tree, this implies that each heading will contain all the nodes of its respective sub-tree. So when a heading is selected, the user will get consecutively all of its related contents and sub-headings in which he is interested. After selecting that particular node he may get information according to that tag on his SST. This will lead to an enhanced view of whole web page content without navigation problem in SST.

Fig. 3. Mapping of Webpage on SST

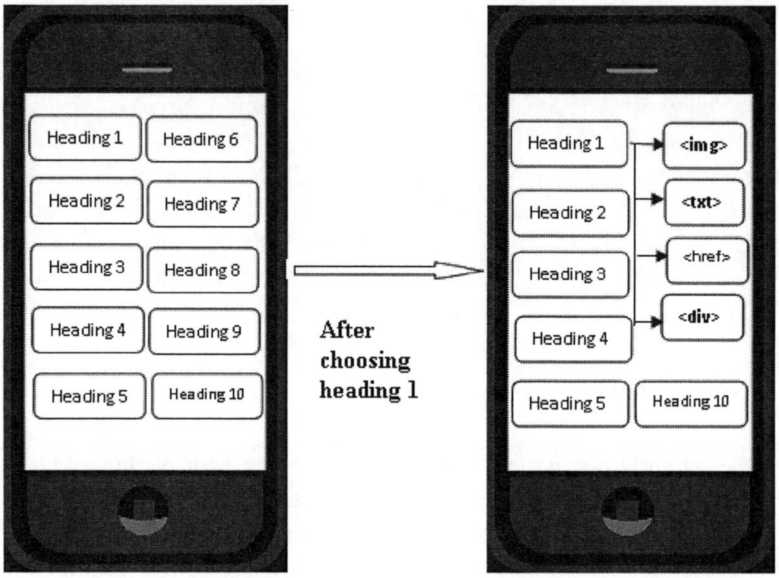

6 Improvements after Rearrangement of Headings

There is a vast difference after applying above techniques. Few of those have been mentioned below:

- User has to go through only heading list at first glance.
- User has a very clear view of content on SST.
- No more vertical and horizontal scrolling is needed.
- As data is arranged according to respective heading, selecting relevant content will take less time comparatively.
- User will get rid of all unwanted contents from screen.

There can be multiple benefits further also!

7 Conclusion and Future scope

This paper is in continuation with our previous work [1] and [2], where starting from the extracted blocks one more concept is followed backtracking on DOM tree and proceeding further by following Rules I, II and III in [1]. Once completed with tree traversal, we are generating here the context structure as well as logical structure. In logical structure we arrange main heading as a root and all other node related to that heading as a sub-node of this root. Once we have organized all the content in the form of tree structure, we can easily regenerate the enhanced user interface for navigation on SST. After comparing the proposed method with the existing methods, one can clearly see that here both the structural and visual aspects of a web page are considered resulting into a better outcome. There can be some betterment in the proposed algorithm if one can add more constraints while the backtracking in Rule-I.

There is a great scope as per future prospect for the above mentioned entities, as this approach can be used for content extraction from a webpage which is very useful for search engines also. Browsers can extract relevant information and create sequential database using proposed method for future reference. Accessing web pages on mobile screen can also become easier by removing unwanted advertisements and widgets. Clustering problems can also get some direct or indirect solutions using this method. For further research, this work can be extended and one can get proven results.

8 References

1. Shefali Singhal, Neha Garg: Web Page Representation Using Backtracking With Multi-Dimensional Database For Small Screen Terminals, in Studies Comp.Intelligence, Vol. 713, Brajendra Panda et al: INNOVATIONS IN COMPUTATIONAL INTELLIGENCE, 978-981-10-4554-7, 429081_1_En (21), July 2017.

2. Shefali Singhal, Neha Garg: Hybrid Web-page Segmentation and Block Extraction for Small Screen Terminals, In IJCA Proceedings on 4th International IT Summit Confluence 2013 - The Next Generation Information Technology Summit Confluence 2013(2):12-15, January 2014.

3. Manuel Álvarez, Alberto Pan , Juan Raposo , Fernando Bellas , Fidel Cacheda : Extracting lists of data records from semi-structured web pages, Department of Information and Communication Technologies, University of A Coruña, Campus de Elviña s/n, 15071 A Coruña, Spain,11 October 2007

4. Ruihua Song, Haifeng Liu, Ji-Rong Wen, Wei-Ying Ma: Learning block importance models for web pages, In Proceedings of the 13th international conference on World Wide Web, ISBN:1-58113-844-X, 2004-05-17

5. Yan Guo, Huifeng Tang; Linhai Song; Yu Wang; Guodong Ding: ECON: An Approach to Extract Content from Web News Page, In Web Conference (APWEB), 2010 12th International Asia-Pacific, 6-8 April 2010.

6. Deng Cai, Shipeng Yu, Ji-Rong Wen, Wei-Ying Ma: Block-based web search, In Proceedings of the 27th annual international ACM SIGIR conference on Research and development in information retrieval, 2004-07-25.

7. Karane Vieira, Altigran S. da Silva, Nick Pinto, Edleno S. de Moura, João M. B. Cavalcanti, Juliana Freire: A fast and robust method for web page template detection and removal, In Proceedings of the 15th ACM international conference on Information and knowledge management, 2006-11-06.

8. Lin, S.-H. and Ho, J.-M., Discovering Informative Content Blocks from Web Documents, In Proceedings of ACM SIGKDD'02, 2002.

9. Shumeet Baluja: Browsing on small screens: recasting web-page segmentation into an efficient machine learning framework, In Proceeding of the 15th international conference on World Wide Web, 2006-05-23.

10. Chakrabarti, S., "Integrating the Document Object Model with Hyperlinks for Enhanced Topic Distillation and Information Extraction," the Tenth International World Wide Web Conference (WWW10), 2001, http://www10.org/cdrom/papers/489/.

A Complete Survey : Load Balancing techniques and Algorithms in Cloud Computing

Abhineet Anand
Faculty, SCSE, Galgotias University,
abhineet.mnnit@gmail.com

Chandra Prakash Tyagi
Student, SCSE, Galgotias University,
chandraprakash.tyagi@galgotiasuniversity.edu.in

Abstract: Every kid coming out of Harvard, Now thinks he can be the next Mark Zuckerberg, and with the new technologies like cloud computing, he actually has a shot. Because with the cloud computing their demand for services and resources are provided at any time, which leads to the tremendous increase in the users, and their demand for different services on the cloud computing platform so fruitful and efficient use of resources in the cloud environment became a critical concern. For this cloud computing requires Load balancing techniques to control and handle overloaded demand and requirements. Load balancing is playing a vital role in maintaining the rhythm of cloud computing. So load balancing in cloud computing becoming a more interested area of research. Many different techniques have been proposed to solve the problems of load balancing. This paper investigates the different algorithms proposed to resolve the issue of load balancing in Cloud Computing.
Keywords: Cloud Computing, Load Balancing, Static Load Balancing algorithms(SLB), Dynamic Load Balancing algorithms(DLB), Virtualization.

Introduction

Cloud computing can be described as the sharing of computing resources-everything from application to datacenters over the internet which can be used by anyone on the pay-for-use basis. It eliminates the need of local servers and personal devices to handle applications with this new technology cloud computing. It is just like rental cars such as

- Rental cars are available when and where client need them.
- When client rent a car, he pay only for the time you use it.
- The rental car company has huge resources that it can rent and can buy more cars to rent if there are consistently many requests.
- Client can rent a different type of car for different situations.
- Client arenâĂŹt responsible for maintaining a rental car.

All these above points satisfy with cloud computing as well. You just have to change rental car with cloud Computing. Cloud computing offers on-demand internet-based services like Saas,Paas,Iaas. With the exponential increase in the cloud users, It becomes very difficult to cope up with overloaded demand and requirements of cloud services, And hence the Load balancing comes into the picture(Nuaimi, Mohamed, Nuaimi, & Al-Jaroodi, 2012).

(3).png

Infrastructure as a Service (Iaas)	Software as a service (SaaS)	Platform as a service (Paas)
In this model third party provider hosts the storage, server and other virtualize computing resources and makes them available to clients at internet.	Saas is a software distribution model in which a third party provider hosted the softwares in the cloud and makes them available over the internet.	Paas is a software distribution model in which a third party provider hosted the application development platform and tools at own infrastructure over the internet.
Ex:GoGrid, Flexiscale Amazon EC2 etc.	Ex:oracle,IBM Google-mail, face book.	Ex:Microsoft Azure,Google app engine

Figure 1. Different services in cloud

LOAD BALANCING:

In the cloud computing environment, Load balancing is a technique which is used to distribute workload evenly on the pool of system nodes to handle all the request at a time.This provides proper resource utilization and better performance during request traffic in cloud system. This also helps to avoid the situation where nodes are underloaded or heavily loaded in the network.

The goals of load balancing in cloud computing are:-

- To maintain system firmness.
- To improve system performance.
- To protect against system failures

(Mishra & Mishra, 2015) Load balancing is done through load balancer which typically comes in two flavor

(1).png

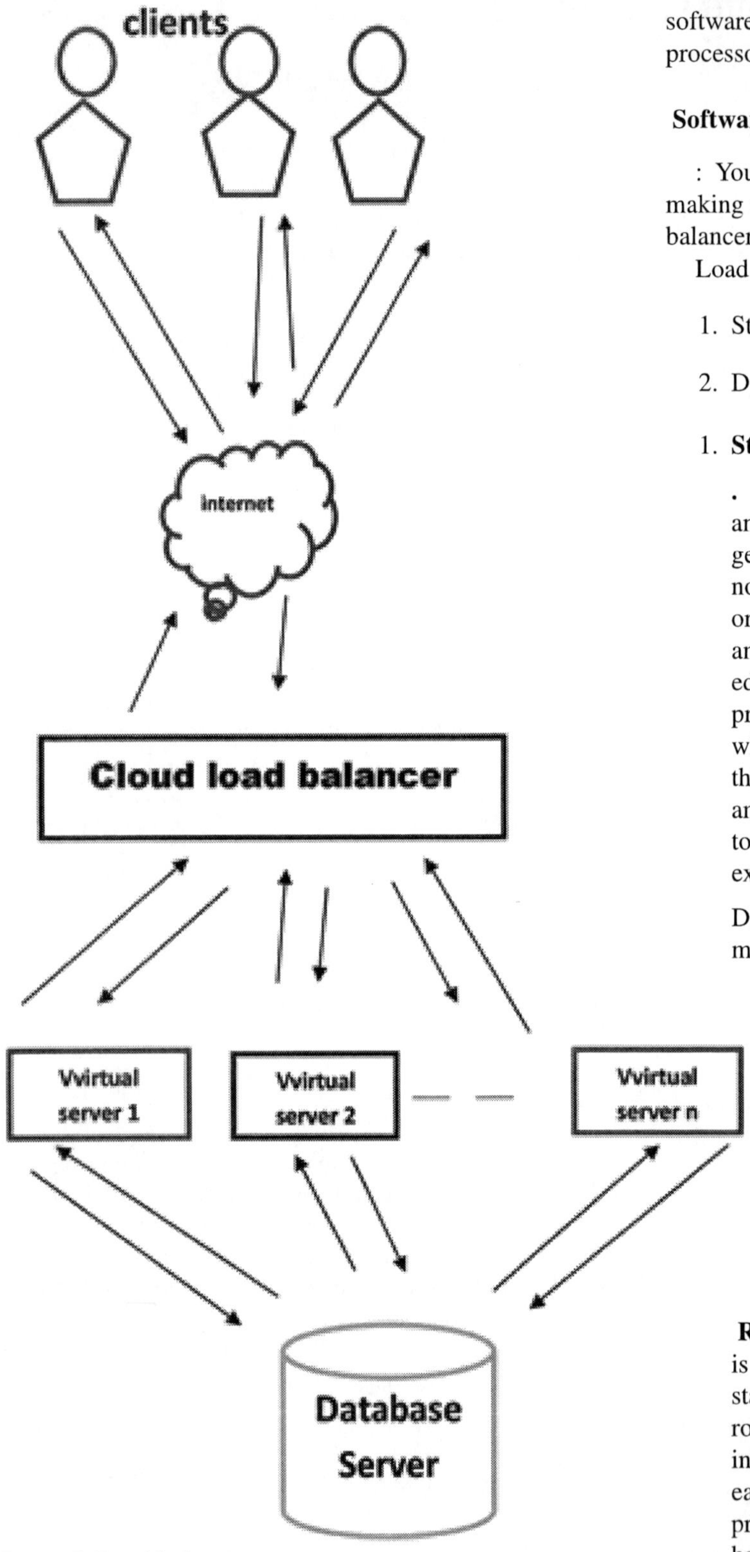

Figure 2. Load balancing

Hardware-based load balancer:

Hardware-based load balancer: Vendors load proprietary software on the machine of their choice with the specialized processor to cope up with web traffic.

Software-based load balancer:

: You can load software on the hardware of your choice making it less expensive and more flexible to use as a load balancer.

Load Balancing Algorithm are of two types:

1. Static load balancing(SLB)

2. Dynamic Load Blancing(DLB)

1. **Static Load Balancing:**

. In static load balancing traffic is evenly divided among the different nodes or servers.it is for homogeneous pool of resources.static load balancing does not depends upon the behaviour of the previous state or behaviour of the node while distributing the load among them.This algorithm requires a prior knowledge of nodes such as user requirement,capacity and processing power.This algorithm is for the systems which has low variation in load.The only drawback of this algorithm is that it can not handle the load balancing at runtime.The goal of static load balancing is to minimizing the communication delays, Reduce the execution time.

Different algorithms best suitable for static environment are:

- Round-Robin
- CLBDM
- Opportunistic load balancing
- Optimization load balancing algorithm
  - Ant-Colony Optimization
- min-min load balancing
- max-min load balancing

Round-Robin Algorithm: Round-Robin technique is introduced by B Sotomayor in 2009.It is well known static load balancing technique, Best for static environment.This algorithm allocates the job to every node in Round Robin fashion i.e Processors are assigned to each process in a circular order without any type of priority and will be back to first node when last node has been reached hence there is no starvation.it works on the principal of time slices.In this algorithm time is divided in to several time slices or time quantum and these time quantum is given to each task or node during operation on the FCFS(first come first serve) basis, But in a circular order.After the expiration of time quantum next request in the queue served for the same time quantum. When operation is not complete with in the given time quantum it has to wait for next turn.

Pros: in the case of equal workload distribution it gives the fast response.

Cons:Different processes have different processing time due to which some node may be heavily loaded and other remain idle, Due to nopriority.

CLBDM(Central Load Balancing Decision Model): CLBDM is introduced by B.Radojevic in 2011.it is an enhancement to the Round Robin technique.The drawback of Round Robin i.e either node may be overloaded or remains idle is overcome by CLBDM.It works on the session switching at application layer.In it claculation of connection time between the client and the node is done and, If it goes above the threshold the coonnection between the client and node is terminated and Task is forwarded to the next node using Round Robin technique.

Opportunistic Load Balancing: OLB(Opportunistic Load Balancing) consider the load request at every node and assigns the unexecuted task randomly to a node, Without considering the expected execution time of the operation that is going on that node.Since OLB does not calculate the execution time of the node, The task to be process processed in a slower manner results in bottlenecks. One advantage of OLB is Simplicity. It is better in terms of load balanced, but gives poor overall performance. The main Aim of OLB is to keep each and every node in working state and maintain load balance.

Ant Colony Optimization Algorithm: Ant colony optimization is introduced by K.Nishant in 2012.This algorithm is based on the techniques that ant uses for searching their food, like ant find the optimal path to reach their food, Load is distributed among nodes in well organized manner using the same technique used by ants.let us assume load balancing node in cloud computing as root head node, In this technique ant starts its movement from root node as the request is initiated and uses the ant behaviour to collect information from cloud node about the node is overload or not, If node is not overloaded it assigns the task to it and start moving forward and if next node is also underloaded it follow same step but, if the next node is overloaded it moves in backward direction.if ant found target it will commit suicide so that it can prevent the unnecessarily movement and all the information are collected and combined together to make a report about load balancing node. (Lagwal & Bhardwaj, 2017)

Min-Min Load balancing algorithm: it is introduced by s.c wang in 2010. It balances the load among the nodes by considering it as a scheduling problem.it works in two phase, In first phase it finds the minimum execution time for all task and then choose the least value from all the minimum value according to this least time task is scheduled on the resource that takes minimum completion time. This process is repeted until all task are scheduled, In the second phase it choose the resources with heavy load and reassigns them with the resources with light load(i.e the algorithm select the node with the highest completion time and corresponding to that node it executes the task with lowest completion time).The process stops when all the jobs are assigned.it works better when no. of small task is more than the no. of large task.

Max-Min Load balancing : max-min algorithm is smilar to min-min load balancing algorithm except that after finding the minimum execution time for all task the maximum value is selected and then this maximum time task is scheduled on corresponding machine.It suffers from starvation when the algorithm having maximum completion time executed first instead of task having minimal completion time.(Priya & Mohanapriya, n.d.)

2. **Dynamic Load balancing:**

. Dynamic load balancing algorithm balances the load at runtime based on the current status of the system.In a pool of systems the master systems collect the information of all the slave processors and use it to assign load based on that information at runtime. Dynamic load balancing can be achieved in two different ways: distributed and non-distributed.

In distributed all nodes of a system pool are participate to make the load balancing. To achieve balanced load Systems also uses two different approaches to interact with each other i.e cooperative and non-cooperative. In cooperative the nodes work in sharing to achieve load balancing, Results in better overall system performance, In non-cooperative each node work independently on a task, Results in better response time of a local task.

In non-distributed either one node or a group of node performe the task of load balancing. Non-distributed can take two different cantrolling forms: centralized and semi-distributed.In centralized form one single node(central node) is responsible for load distribution in the network, While in semi-distributed pool of systems or network is divided in to clusters where each cluster have a central node which follow the centralized form to distribute the load with in the cluster, Hence load balancing of whole pool of systems is achieved through the cooperation of central nodes of all clusters. (Jafarnejad Ghomi, Rahmani, & Qader, 2017) Different Dynamic algorithms are:

- Throttled Load Balancing Algorithm(TLB)
- Honey Bee Foraging Algorithm
- Active Clustering
- Index name server

Throttled Load Balancing Algorithm(TLB):. In this algorithm Load balancer maintains a index table of virtual machine or their state of available and busy. Hence when client requests it first goes to the data center and data centre request to the load balancer to find a suitable virtual machine then load balancer scans the index and check for the availability of virtual machine , Since in cloud computing virtual machine may have multiple instances to handle the different type of task, Hence the the request will be assigned to a lightly loaded instance. If load balancer does not found any virtual machine it will return -1.

Honey Bee Foraging Algorithm: This algorithm follows the bees concept of collectiong the food.The aim of this algorithm is load balancing throughout the virtual machines in a heterogeneous environment.By using this technique the current work load can be determined which tells us about load or unload.Technique follows the ideas of natural foraging behavior of honey bee. The honey bees are corresponding to the removal of tasks from the overloaded VM's, And the food source is corresponding to the low loaded VM's.Low loaded virtual machine can accept the load .

Three group of bees in this concept is followed:

- Scout Bees
- Forager Bees
- Onlooker Bees

Scout bees first goes outside of the honey comb and find the honey sources. After finding the source, they return to the honey comb and do a waggle dance indicating the quality and quantity of honey available . Then, forager bees along with Scout bee go outside and reap the honey from those sources. After collecting they return to beehive and does a waggle dance. This dance indicates how much food is left.

Active Clustering: The concept of clustering is introduced first in cloud computing by the algorithm name Active clustering. Making a cluster based algorithm enhance your algorithmâĂŹs performance.A cluster can be assume as group.The principal behind clustering is to group smilar node together and work on these node as cluster.The technique of making a cluster is based on the technique of match maker node. We have to connect a initial node with the different neighbor node available and that node has to be connect to a smilar neighbor node as first node.

Algorithm / Parameters	Round-Robin	CLBDM	OLB	Ant-colony optimization	Min-Min	Max-Min	TLB	Honey Bee Foraging	Active cluster
Nature	Static	Static	Static	Static or Dynamic	Static	Static	Dynamic	Dynamic	Dynan
overhead	Yes	No	No	NO	Yes	Yes	No	No	Yes
Throughput	Yes	Yes	No	No	Yes	Yes	Yes	No	No
Resource -Utilization	Yes	Yes	No	Yes	Yes	Yes	Yes	Yes	Yes
Fault -Tolerance	No	No	Yes	Yes	No	No	No	No	No
scalibilty	Yes	No	No	No	No	No		No	No
Performance	Yes	Yes	Yes	Yes	Yes	Yes		No	No

Table 1

Comparative Analysis of Static Load Balancing and Dynamic Load Balancing:

Index Name Server: INS is introduced by T.Yu Wu in 2012.The main goal of this algorithm is to minimize the data redundancy and duplication in system. It can handles the load balancing dynamically. INS have defined some parameters which are used to calculating the optimum selection point like the Hash Code of the block of data to be downloaded, the position of the server, the transition quality, the maximum bandwidth.There is also another parameter which determine that weather connection can hold additional node or it is at busy level. Three busy levels are: B(a) B(b) C(c) where B(a) tells us that connection is very busy, B(b) tells us that connections is not busy and can handle additional connections and B(c) denotes connection is limited.

Metrics for load balancing

Nature: It determines whether algorithm is dynamic in behavior or static in behavior.

Overhead: It determines the implementation details of algorithm like inter-process communication, migration of tasks etc.

Throughput: The measure of unit of process that completes its execution in given amount of time is called Throughput, It should be maximised for better performance.

Resource utilisation The proportion of the available time (usually in percentage) that a system or resources is utilising is called Resource utilisation, It should be optimised for better performance.

Fault tolerant: The ability of a system to allow for an unexpected hardware or software failure that is to operating properly even in failure.

Scalability: It is the capability of a system network to handle growing amount of work or its a ability to be enlarged to accommodate that growth.

Performance: The completion of a given task measured against accuracy, completeness cost, speed etc. to check efficiency of any system.

Comparative Analysis of Static Load Balancing and Dynamic Load Balancing: (Beniwal & Garg, 2014)

Conclusion and Future Scope:

In this Paper, we have discussed various algorithm for load balancing in cloud computing, And various issues that must be taken in to account while working on new algorithms in near future. In this paper, we have also compare existing

Static and Dynamic load balancing algorithms on the basis of various parameters called metrics parameters like Nature, Fault tolerance, Resource utilization etc. Further work can be done by exploring new load balancing algorithm in near future.

References

Beniwal, P., & Garg, A. (2014). A comparative study of static and dynamic load balancing algorithms. *Int J Adv Res Comput Sci Manag Stud*, *2*, 12.

Jafarnejad Ghomi, E., Rahmani, A., & Qader, N. (2017, 04). Load-balancing algorithms in cloud computing: A survey. , *88*.

Lagwal, M., & Bhardwaj, N. (2017). A survey on load balancing methods and algorithms in cloud computing.

Mishra, N. K., & Mishra, N. (2015). Load balancing techniques: Need, objectives and major challenges in cloud computing-a systematic review. *Int. J. Comput*, *131*.

Nuaimi, K. A., Mohamed, N., Nuaimi, M. A., & Al-Jaroodi, J. (2012, Dec). A survey of load balancing in cloud computing: Challenges and algorithms. In *2012 second symposium on network cloud computing and applications* (p. 137-142). doi: 10.1109/NCCA.2012.29

Priya, A. A., & Mohanapriya, A. (n.d.). An effective scrutiny of static and dynamic load balancing in cloud.

AUTHOR INDEX

Aarthi, S. 72
Agrawal, Alka 36
Ahuja, Neelu Jyothi 187
Alam, Ashfaue 233
Alkhatib, Ghazi 199
Al-Sarayrah, Khalid 199
Anand, Abhineet 195, 207, 211, 214, 295
Anitha, G. 110, 124
Arockia, Rosaline R. Anto 58, 79
Bafhavathipriya, S. 103
Bagjadab, Amiya Bhusan 180
Banita 160, 251
Barath, M. 79
Bhadana, Amit 7
Bhola, Anoop 1
Chaturvedi, Tanu 240
Chaudhry, Kanika 244
Dash, Dinesh 180
Devi, K. Durga 124
Dhingra, Sanjay 244
Dwivedi, Nitya Nand 23
Ethiraj, M. 72
Garg, Neha 276, 286
Gupta, Govind P. 148
Hashmi, Ahtisham 214
Hinduja, Akshay 170, 261
Jha, Chandra Kumar 1
Joshi, Gaurav 233
Kamboj, Gurpreet Singh 65
Kanika 36
Kaur, AManpreet 148
Kaur, Iqbaldeep 65, 86
Khan, R.A. 36
Kumar, Amit 187
Kumar, Ashish 86
Kumar, Neetish 45
Kumar, Padam 148
Kumar, Priyank 270
Kumari, Geeta 233
Madhan, Kumar P 58
Mehfooza, M. 129
Munjal, Puja 270
Murali, N. G. 72
Nair, Akshay S. 270
Pandey, Brijesh 195
Pandey, Manju 170, 261
Pati, Bibudhendu 116, 139
Pattanayak, Binod Kumar 116, 139
Pavithra, R. 110
Prabha, D. 221
Pradeep, S 58
Pratap, Ram 12
Preethi, S. 58
Priya, S. Baghavathi 72, 93, 124
Priyadarshini, Sushrree Bibhuprada B. 180
Raj, Deepa 45
Ranjan, Aarushi 214
Rath, Mamata 116, 139
Sangamithra, N. 129
Santhankalakshmi, S. 93
Sbha, S. 103
Sharath, Kumar N. 110
Sharma Kamlesh 276
Shivani, S. C. 93
Shree, Raj 19, 29, 52
Siddhartha, P. 110
Singh, Anubhav Raj 207
Singh, Manoj 7, 240
Singh, Ninni 187
Singh, Prabhishek 19, 133
Singh, Shashwat 211
Singh, Shilpi 29
Singh, Sunil Kumar 52
Singhal, Shefali 286
Sishor, Kaushal 133
Tanwar, Poonam 160, 251
Tyagi, Chandra Prakash 295
Vasanthakumar, S. 129
Verma, Amit 65, 86
Vignesh, P. N. 79
Vijay, K. 129
Yadav, Meenakshi 1
Yashwanth, K. Sai 129
Zafeer, K. A. Athar 79
Zaidi, Taskeen 12, 23